D0609501

THE GLADSTONE DIARIES

Gladstone in the early 1870s

THE GLADSTONE DIARIES

WITH
CABINET MINUTES
AND
PRIME-MINISTERIAL
CORRESPONDENCE

VOLUME VIII
JULY 1871 — DECEMBER 1874

Edited by
H. C. G. MATTHEW

CLARENDON PRESS · OXFORD
1982

Oxford University Press, Walton Street, Oxford OX2 6DP
London Glasgow New York Toronto
Delhi Bombay Calcutta Madras Karachi
Kuala Lumpur Singapore Hong Kong Tokyo
Nairobi Dar es Salaam Cape Town
Melbourne Auckland
and associate companies in
Beirut Berlin Ibadan Mexico City

Published in the United States by
Oxford University Press, New York

British Library Cataloguing in Publication Data

Gladstone, W. E.
The Gladstone diaries with cabinet minutes and Prime-Ministerial correspondence
Vol. 8: July 1871–December 1874
1. Gladstone, W. E.
I. Title II. Matthew, H. C. G.
941.081′092′4 DA563.4

ISBN 0-19-822639-X

Library of Congress Cataloging in Publication Data (Revised)

Gladstone, William Ewart, 1809–1898.
The Gladstone diaries.

Vols. 5- edited by H. C. G. Matthew.
CONTENTS.—v. 1. 1825–1832.—v. 2. 1838–1839.—
[etc.]—v. 8. July 1871–December 1874.
1. Gladstone, William Ewart, 1809–1898.
2. Great Britain—Politics and government—1837–1901.
1901. 3. Prime ministers—Great Britain—Biography.
I. Foot, Michael Richard Daniel, ed. II. Title.
DA563.A34 941.081′092′4 [B] 68-59613
ISBN 0-19-822639-X AACR1

Set by Anne Joshua Associates (Oxford)
Printed in Great Britain
at the University Press, Oxford
by Eric Buckley
Printer to the University

CONTENTS

VOLUME VIII

LIST OF ILLUSTRATIONS

All the above photographs, save those otherwise acknowledged, are taken from a family album at Hawarden Castle, by courtesy of Sir William Gladstone.

NOTE ON ABBREVIATIONS &c.

Lists of abbreviations used in this volume and an introduction covering its years will be found at the start of Volume VII.

Sat. July One. 1871. [Chislehurst]

Wrote to Scotts—and minutes. Saw Mr Glyn—Sir W. Tite. Attended festivity on opening of the Cannon Street Terminus: & spoke.[1] Read Lanfrey's Napoleon.[2] Cabinet 2½–5. Then to Chiselhurst.[3]

Cabinet. Jul. 1. 71. 2. 30 PM[4]

√ Lord Mayor's dinner. 29th.
Contagious Diseases Acts. } Postponed[5]
Royal Residence in Ireland. }
√ Tichborne Case. Osborne's Question. A general Bill—& Govt. will arrange to enable Bovill.[6]
√ Committee of Cabinet on Park Accom[modatio]ns [?] with Mr Ayrton: WEG, Chr. of Exr., Ayrton, Kimberley, Ripon, Granville, Cardwell.
√ Lord Granville. May give information to other Govts. respecting proceedings of International—as far as outside the ordinary lines of politics.[7]
√ Emanuel Scheme Address. Advise caution as to any attempt in H. of C. to interfere.[8]
√ Harrow Answer. Disallowance of Statutes in part open to us according to Palmer & Archibald. Chancr. will look to this opinion.[9]
√ Mr. Stansfeld. May bring in a Local Government Bill.
√ Cockburn to be Arbitrator in Alabama Case.

2. 4 S.Trin.

Chiselhurst Ch. mg (H.C.) and aft. Waited on the Emperor Napoleon (as I fell in with him yesterday accidentally at the Station). His conversation was very becoming.[10] Read many Sermons & Tracts. Bp of Winchr came in evg. Much conversation.

[1] Speaking both as prime minister and shareholder; *The Times*, 3 July 1871, 5f.
[2] See 20 Mar. 67.
[3] Visiting Lord Frederick Cavendish and his wife Lucy, Catherine Gladstone's niece.
[4] Add MS 44639, f. 68. [5] See 5, 8, 15 July 71. [6] See 24 June 71n.
[7] On 6 June Favre sent a circular to European govts. requesting suppression of the International; in June *The Times* made several attacks on it; its London conference met in September 1871; see G. Bourgin, 'La lutte du gouvernement français contre la Première Internationale', *International Rev. of Soc. Hist.* iv. 54.
[8] On 30 June, Salisbury carried a motion to withhold the endowed schools commissioners' proposal for Emanuel Hospital: *H* ccvii. 862. The Queen's Address on 3 July withheld assent; ibid. 962.
[9] On 7 July, Lord O. Fitzgerald, comptroller of the household, announced withholding of assent to plea to disallow statute imposing anglicanism as qualification for Harrow governing body; *H* ccvii. 1314.
[10] Napoleon III lived in Chislehurst until his death in 1873.

3. M. [London]

Wrote to Empr Napoleon[1]—The Queen (letter & Mem.)—Ld Spencer—Mr Harvey—Mr Hillyard—Mr Mill[2]—Robn G.—and minutes. Returned to London before 12. Saw Mr Goschen—Mr Lefevre—do *cum* Ld Halifax—Mr Glyn—Mr Forster. Luncheon in G.S. saw Mrs Th. X. H of C. 4¼-8 and 9-2. Spoke on 3° R. Army Reg. Bill.[3] Read Lady Susan.[4]

4. Tu.

Wrote. to Lady Love Parry[5]—Ld Kimberley—Mr Lowe—Ld Brougham—The Queen—D. of Devonshire—Ld Hartington—and minutes. Ten to dinner. Attended the American Minister's *celebration* party.[6] Saw Sir T. Fremantle—Sir T. Biddulph—Mr Glyn—Archdn Harrison—Mr Lambert *cum* Gen. Fytche[7]—Ld Granville—Mr Cardwell—Mr Fowler—Mr Forster. H of C. 2-7 and 10½-2¼.[8] Read Ly Susan—The Watsons.[9]

To LORD KIMBERLEY, colonial secretary, Add MS 44540, f. 65.
4 July 1871.

I decidedly agree with your memorandum or rather your Draft,[10] in ignorance however of what Ripon may have to say against it. Without doubt it should be mentioned to the Cabinet, as our withdrawal from Quebec will be a marked fact in the history of our Colonial relations.

5. Wed.

Wrote to Mr Barry—Ld E. Fitzmaurice—The Queen—Dean of Windsor—Sir H. Rawlinson—and minutes. Cabinet 2¼-5¾. Saw Ld Spencer—Mr Glyn—Ld Granville. Read Miss Austen. Dined with the Ripons. Concert at Stafford House afterwards. Saw two[R].

[1] Sending, as asked, a copy of the Ballot Bill; Add MS 44431, f. 90.
[2] Inviting him to breakfast; Add MS 44540, f. 65.
[3] Army Regulation Bill 3° R then carried in 289 : 231: *H* ccvii. 1064.
[4] See 30 June 71.
[5] Elizabeth, widow of Sir L. P. Jones-Parry, had requested a baronetcy for her son (Sir) Thomas Love Duncombe Jones-Parry, 1832-91, liberal M.P. Carnarvon, 1868-74, 1882-6; cr. bart. 1886. See Add MS 44540, f. 66.
[6] i.e. independence celebrations.
[7] Albert Fytche, 1820-92; just rtd. as commr. of Burma.
[8] Ballot; *H* ccvii. 1097.
[9] Unfinished novel by Jane *Austen in 2nd ed. of J. E. Austen Leigh, *Memoir of Jane Austen* (1871); see 30 June 71.
[10] Of 3 July, at last announcing withdrawal of British troops from Quebec, Add MS 44224, f. 183.

Cabinet Wed. Jul. 5. 71. 2 PM.[1]
√ Quebec Garrison. To be removed.[2]
√ Royal Residence in Ireland—answer to Stacpoole considered.[3]
√ Contagious Diseases. Postponed again.
√ Meeting on Ballot Bill } mentioned
Duration of Bill
√ French Treaty: ask for written statement: examine project.[4]
√ Goschen. Otway & Flogging in the Navy. Particulars to be produced.[5]
√ Stansfeld's Bill—to be introduced.[6]
√ Bruce. Sunday Prosecutions. Sanction of police to be required.
√ Chancellor's Judicial Committee Bill. Amendments approved.

6. Th.

Wrote to Lord Mayor—Ld Sydney—Robn G.—Mr Ayrton—The Queen—Ld Verulam—& minutes. Meeting of the party in D. Street 2.30: most satisfactory.[7] Saw Mr Forster—Mr Layard—Mr Glyn—Prof. Mozley. Fourteen to breakfast. Conclave on Park Communications 3-4. H of C. 4¼-8½ and 9½-1¼.[8] Read The Watsons.

7. Fr.

Wrote to Bp of Worcester—Mr Ouvry—Mrs Th—The Queen (2)—and minutes. Saw W.H.G. (Parishes)—Mr Glyn—Mr Cardwell. H of C. 2¼-7 and at 9.[9] Dined with Mr Glyn. Mrs Th's afterwards: and saw four[R]. Wrote various Mema. Read Life of Miss Austen—Darwin on Descent of Man[10]—Arnold on Free Trade in Law.[11]

8. Sat. [Windsor]

Wrote to Mr Stacpoole[12]—Mr Ayrton—Mr Lister—The Queen—& minutes. Garden party in D. St in the afternoon. Cabinet 12¼-2¾. Saw Bp of Lichfield—Mr Glyn (2)—Mr Cardwell *cum* Ld Granville. Parliamentary dinner party in aftn. Then went to Mad. Bernstorffs to

[1] Add MS 44639, f. 70.
[2] See previous day's letter.
[3] Renewed proposal from William Stacpoole, 1830-79; liberal M.P. Ennis from 1860. Gladstone on 10 July put off the question until next Session: *H* ccvii. 1341.
[4] To pay the German indemnity, France increased tariffs, especially on textiles, against the 1860 Commercial Treaty; Loftus' dispatch of 4 July (*PP* 1872 lxx. 272) announced Ozenne's arrival to renegotiate.
[5] See 28 July 71n.
[6] Local Government Board Bill, 2° R 20 July; *H* ccvii. 78.
[7] On the Ballot Bill, an appeal to liberal M.P.s to facilitate its passage; see *The Times*, 7 July 1871, 5f, 9a.
[8] Elections Bill: *H* ccvii. 1225.
[9] Spoke on French treaty; *H* ccvii. 1289.
[10] By C. *Darwin, 2v. (1871).
[11] Sir R. A. *Arnold, *Free trade in land* (1871).
[12] Asking him to ask a question on Irish royal residence (see 5 July 71n); Add MS 44540, f. 67.

see her guests. Then to Windsor: conversation with Princess Louise on the way. Read Brilliant Prospects.[1]

Cabinet Jul. 8. Sat. 12 o'clock[2]

√ Answer to H. M's letter of yesty. to WEG.[3]
√ Palmer's Address[4] for a Law School or Univ. Two Univv. to give degrees wd. be objectionable.
√ Education Cumulative Vote. Oppose Bill for changing it.[5]
√ Bishops Resignations: Bill to be brought in to make Act permanent.
√ Contagious Diseases Act Report.[6] Report signed by 23. Allowances[?] of dissents. In the Cabinet—for now repealing the later acts & revising the Act of [18]64—no one.

9. 5 S. Trin.

Castle Chapel at 10 & 12. St George's 4.30. Dined with HM: who fired hot shot into Mr Ayrton.[7] Saw H.M. (3½-4¼)—Col. Ponsonby—Ld Lorne—Sir T. Biddulph—Dean of Windsor—Pr. Arthur—Rev. Dr Benson[8]—Ld Camoys—Herbert G. Read Plumptre's Sermon[9]—Bp of Worcester's Charge[10]—Union Review.

10. M. [*London*]

Wrote to Ld Bessborough—Bp of Worcester—Mrs Hope—Mr Cardwell—Robn G.—Mr Ayrton—Ld Spencer—Ld Nelson—The Queen—Ld Hartington—and minutes. Saw Mr Forster—Mr Glyn—Dean of Windsor—Mr Cardwell. Arr. from Windsor 11.15 AM. H of C. 4¼-8½ and 9½-1¾. We made fair progress.[11] Saw The Speaker respecting arrangements for him to enable him to continue in office.[12] Read Miss Austen's Life—Parisiana.[13]

[1] R. L. Johnson, *Brilliant prospects* (1870).
[2] Add MS 44639, f. 74.
[3] On duke of Cambridge and the Army Regulation Bill: *LQV*, 2nd series, ii. 142, 145; see also 10 July 71.
[4] Moved on 11 July; *H* ccvii. 1482.
[5] Apparently not introduced; school boards were elected by cumulative vote.
[6] The royal commission report; all 23 commissioners signed it, but 17 also submitted partial dissentions; *PP* 1871 xix. The main report recommended partial continuation of the Acts, but end to examination of prostitutes. See 15 July 71.
[7] Ayrton infuriated Victoria by insisting on a scheme to feed Windsor Castle sewage into the town conduits; see J. Winter, *Robert Lowe* (1976), 250 and 10 Aug. 71.
[8] Edward White *Benson, 1829-96; prebendary of Lincoln 1869; chancellor of Lincoln 1872; bp. of Truro 1877; made abp. of Canterbury by diarist 1882; died in Hawarden Church. See Add MS 44109.
[9] E. H. *Plumptre, 'The spirits in prison; a sermon' (1871).
[10] By H. Philpott (1871); invited to discuss it; Add MS 44540, f. 68.
[11] Spoke on Elections Bill in cttee.: *H* ccvii. 1351.
[12] He retired in February 1872.
[13] See 24 May 71.

I had a conversation at Windsor on Sunday with Sir Thomas Biddulph respecting the Duke of Cambridge and the Army Bill, from which I gathered that the Duke has been making great efforts and holding rather strong language. He had written that he was quite willing to recommend to the House of Lords that they should 'give full consideration' to the proposal about purchase as one liberal to the officers. I said what was wanted was to substitute for this phrase a recommendation to pass the Bill.

Later in the day, the Queen conversed with me on the same subject and gave me to understand that the Duke was contesting chiefly the claim to his vote, on the ground that he had so rarely voted in the House of Lords. The Queen expressed her wish that we could advance so far as this to meet his wishes. I said that what the Cabinet had mainly discussed and had in view was the Duke's recommendation to the House which would come in a speech: but I observed that the Duke's own position would be most unsatisfactory, and scarcely worthy, if he advised the House of Lords to take a certain course, and then shrank from sharing it himself.

I shall be glad to know how this point strikes my colleagues. I do not think that we could guarantee the defensibility of the Duke's position if he declines to vote; though some weight might be allowed, under favourable circumstances, to the plea that it is his general rule to abstain from voting.[1]

To E. CARDWELL, war secretary, 10 July 1871. Add MS 44540, f. 68.

I send you [a] copy of a letter which I have addressed to the Duke of Cambridge[2] & which will in the main explain itself. It seems that the great hitch is on the vote. But what an unmanly position to advise others not to think but vote & then decline to join them in doing that very thing.

11. Tu.

Wrote to D. of Cambridge—Mr Cardwell—The Queen (2 & Mem.)—Dean of Westmr—Mr Prescott Hewitt—and minutes. Read Memoir of Miss Austen. Saw Mrs Clifton X.—Mr Glyn—Ld Halifax. The Crown Prince & Princess, also P. & Princess Christian came here in the afternoon. Very gracious: the two former keenest about art. H of C. 2½-3¾ and 6-7: also 10¾-1.[3] Dined with the Sydneys.

To E. CARDWELL, war secretary, 11 July 1871. Add MS 44540, f. 68.

[4]I did not fully comprehend at the moment, last night, the purpose of your observation about a Cabinet, but on reflection I suppose it to be of the utmost importance now to consider how far it is right to go in disclosing any intentions as to what would follow on the rejection of the Bill, & in connection with this

[1] Holograph dated 10 July 1871 at Carlton House Terrace; Add MS 44760, f. 53. Replies from the cabinet not found.

[2] Not in RA, but see RA E18/138.

[3] Ballot, Navy: *H* ccvii. 1445.

[4] The previous evening, the duke of Richmond gave notice of an amndt. to 2°R of the Army Regulation Bill in the Lords, to set aside the Bill: *H* ccvii. 1315.

that we should consider among ourselves as to the final *seal* upon these intentions. The Resolution to propose a *Vote* is a stiff one & we ought to adopt it with our eyes open. I would propose 3.30 tomorrow.
[P.S.] I propose to see the Duke of Cambridge at 11-30.

12. *Wed.*

Wrote to Mr Harvey—Lady S.V. Tempest—The Queen—& minutes. Cabinet 3½-6¼ (Army). Saw Mr Glyn—Mr J. Russell—Sir T. Biddulph. The Duke of Cambridge 11½-1: with little apparent result. Epping Forest Deputn at 3.[1] Holland House party. We dined at Richmond with Mr Knowles to meet Tennyson. He appreciates my wife.

Cabinet July 12. 71.[2]
√ Course to be taken by the Duke of Cambridge.[3] Hartington to see him.
√ Language to be held in the Lords Debate on the Army Bill & course to be taken. Alternatives considered—a. To postpone all to next year & commence then anew. b. To ask H. of C. for a Vote *both* for Reg[ulation] & for Over Reg[ulation purchase prices]. c. To ask H. of C. for Reg[ulation prices] and look to next year for a Bill respecting Overreg[ulation]. d. To ask H. of C. as above, & at the same time bring in a Bill for over Reg[ulation] prices. e. To abolish purchase & ask the Vote for Reg[ulation] prices, & then wait to see if Lords go on with Bill. If they do well & good. If they do not, we propose a Bill for over-reg[ulation] Prices.
1. Overregulation prices are a daring violation of the law. 2. This violation is now officially & publicly known. 3. Over regulation prices cannot be put an end to except by the extinction of purchase. 4. Purchase can only be extinguished by the payment at least, of regulation price.

To Rev. W. W. HARVEY, 12 July 1871. Add MS 44540, f. 69.

I am doubtful whether as Southam is a populous & laborious parish it ought not to be given to a man with a longer career of pastoral activity before him than our contemporaries can fairly claim to anticipate.

Ewelme can only be given to a member of the Convocation at Oxford. I am told that if you think fit you might qualify for it. It will not be open till Sept. 29. If you like to act upon this suggestion I am quite ready. Perhaps you will consider & let me know.[4]

[1] *Daily Telegraph*, 13 July 1871, 3.
[2] Add MS 44639, f. 75. See 11 July 71n.
[3] Cambridge gave some support to the Bill: 'I believe their offer to be a very liberal one —more liberal than I could have ever expected', but abstained, despite Gladstone's request that he should explicitly support it, by word if not vote (see Add MS 44431, ff. 106, 131); *H* ccvii. 1695, 1868.
[4] *Harvey (see 2 Oct. 43) accepted Ewelme; Add MS 44431, f. 171; a storm ensued about his eligibility.

13. Th.

Wrote to Lady Brownlow—Ld Ebury—The Queen—and minutes. H of C. 4¼-8¼ and 9½-2¼.[1] Eight (strangers) to breakfast. Saw Ld E. Fitzmaurice—Dr Russell—Mr Monsell—Mr J. Russell—Ld Acton—Ld Granville—Mr Joseph—D. of Devonshire. Read Cont. Dis[eases] Report.

14. Fr.

Wrote to E. Cardwell—D of Cambridge—The Queen—Dean Close—Mr Helps—Scotts—& minutes. Luncheon with the Bernstorffs and an interesting conversation with Crown Princess by whom I sat. Also much pleased with the boys. Dined with G. Glyn. H of C. 3¼-7 and 9-1¾.[2] Saw the Duke of Cambridge. Finished Memoir of Miss Austen.

15. Sat. [*Hatfield*]

Wrote to The Queen—Robn G.—& minutes. Cabinet at 2.30-4.40. Then off to Hatfield. Mem. on Cont. Diseases Bill. Saw Mr Forster—Mr Glyn. We were most kindly received and very happy at Hatfield—Army Bill notwithstanding.[3] Read Acland on Health[4]—Fawcett on Pauperism.[5]

Cabinet. Sat. July 15. 71.2.½ PM[6]

√ Ballot Bill. To persevere as long as the majority holds, without limit of time. WEG to state on Monday the particulars of former years.[7]

√ Course to be taken if D. of Richmond's motion is carried. Sir G. Grey's question as to Overreg[ulation] Prices.[8] Cancel Purchase warrant. Commission—stands over. Ripon, Hart[ingto]n in favour of accepting defeat.

√ Duke of Cambridge's (Speech and) Vote. Not to be pressed unless with prospect of success.

√ Bills.

[*Contagious Diseases Acts*]

1. The present law with regard to brothels, which is of considerable efficacy, ought to be enforced as far as possible, before resorting to such measures as the present contagious diseases Acts. 2. That law, repressive in its principle, might be aided by other repressive enactments. 3. In the Army & Navy, it is not unreasonable to desire that a trial might be made of the system of mulcting in pay for

[1] Spoke on adjournment: *H* ccvii. 1638. Army Bill opened in Lords.

[2] Elections Bill: *H* ccvii. 1744.

[3] Salisbury denounced the Bill on 17 July: *H* ccvii. 1849.

[4] Sir H. W. *Acland, *National health* (1871).

[5] See 10 June 71.

[6] Add MS 44639, f. 77.

[7] See 17 July 71.

[8] Of which he gave public notice on 18 July: *H* ccvii. 1934.

venereal disease. What is the system of foreign armies on this subject? (But a voluntary army, with higher pay, affords more scope for such proceedings than a conscription Army). 4. The Acts do not merely fail to corroborate or enforce the existing law: they operate against it; as they tend to establish a class of approved brothels, subsisting under a kind of *concordat* with public authority, hardly open to any possibility of being put down, and likely to grow, as the French brothels tend to grow, into a vested interest. 5. If we had really reached a state of things in which this disease was fit to be dealt with by authority, we ought in my opinion to go further than the Acts, and to adopt what I understand to be the basis of the French system, namely that the vice shall be self-supporting: that the cost of dealing with those who have ill fortune in its practice shall be borne by the mass of those who practise it. It is not a question of obtaining from a tainted source contributions to the general revenue, but of compelling those who by faulty conduct injure themselves and others to bear the pecuniary charge of remedial measures; instead of the strange and as it seems to me foolish and mischievous proceeding of making indulgence easy, safe, and attractive, at the cost of the general community. All the repressive and all the reformatory results, which are so much pleaded, could be had by this method.[1]

16. 6 S.Trin.

Service in Chapel mg at 11. (with H.C.) & evg at 6. In few Chapels is all so well & heartily done. Walk in aft—& at night on Terrace. Conversation with Ld S. on Dublin Univ. Bill. Read Vance Smith[2]—Miller's Sermon—Fowle's do.—Fletcher's do[3]—Stanley's do on Grote[4]—also on Herschel—Theol. of the Past & Future.[5] Wrote to W.H.G.—Mr Glyn—Mr West.

17. M. [*London*]

Back to town at 12. Wrote to Abp of Canterbury—Ld Chancr—The Speaker—The Queen (2)—Sir F. Grant—Robn G.—and minutes. Saw Commr Andrada[6]—Ld Granville—Mr Glyn—Mr Forster—Sol. Gen.—Mrs Th. X. Dined at Mr Forster's. H of C. 4¼-8¼ and 9¾-2.[7] Read Fawcett—Inside Paris.[8]

[1] Initialled and dated 15 July 1871, Add MS 44760, f. 65. See 8 July 71.
[2] See 4 June 71.
[3] J. C. *Miller, 'Disestablishment; a sermon' (1871); F. W. Fowle, 'Aholah and Aholibah, a sermon' (1871); C. J. H. Fletcher, 'Woman's equality with man in Christ. A sermon' (1871).
[4] By A. P. *Stanley, at Grote's burial in the Abbey.
[5] M. M. Kalisch, *Theology of the past and of the future* (1871).
[6] Unidentified; probably in the Emperor of Brazil's party, see 19 July 71.
[7] Statement on precedents for state of public business: *H* ccvii. 1887. The Lords this night passed Richmond's amndt. to the Army Bill.
[8] See 28 June 71.

18. Tu.

Wrote to Mrs Hope—Ld Chancellor—Dr A. Clark—Ld Granville—Scotts—The Queen (and Tel.)—and minutes. Saw WHG (on Livings)—Mr Levy—Mr Glyn—Ld Powerscourt—Ld Halifax—Mr Bruce. H of C. and Cabinet 2½-7.[1] H of C. again at 9.—10 to dinner.[2] Read Fawcett on Pauperism. Saw two[R].

To LORD HATHERLEY, lord chancellor, 18 July 1871. Add MS 44540, f. 71.

I cannot quite get rid of the difficulty I feel about the Bishops' Resignation Bill. Indeed it now rather takes a two-fold form. 1. The pension of £5000 for the Archbishop of Canterbury is one likely to excite much jealousy should it ever become practical: and perhaps the same consideration applies in *some* degree to two other sees. 2. So large a deduction from the revenues as one third goes materially to fetter the choice of a successor by the Crown in the cases of the Highest Sees. It is certainly possible[?] that an Abp. of York or Bp. of London with £10,000 a year might be willing to take the See of Canterbury with the same income. On the one hand he would have the reversion of the pension whatever it might be worth, on the other hand he must satisfy greater expectations, live at heavier expense & I believe spend *many* thousands in making the change. I speak of money considerations only. I do not of course mean that in either of the Sees named there is a right of succession. But the choice of the Crown ought not to be fettered; & in our life time, three cases have happened in which a Bp. of London & an Abp. of York has been chosen for Canterbury, against one when the selection was made from another quarter. At one time it occurred to me whether the Pension might be put as a sum not exceeding some given maximum. I should like to know what you think of this. I fear it may not be free from objection. Upon the whole, unless some change can be made, my inclination is to leave it to the Archbishop to bring in the perpetuating Bill. We should then see what was the feeling of Parliament, & we might act accordingly. It would not be required, even with my views, to create an obstacle, if it did not spring up elsewhere. I find Ld. Salisbury strongly of opinion that £5000 is too much.

19. Wed.

Wrote to Mr Paget—Abp of Canterbury—Mr Bruce—Sir F. Grant PRA.—The Queen—Provost of Inverness—Mr Glyn—Mr M. Noble—and minutes. Radcliffe Trust Meeting 2½-4¼.[3]

I find the following to be a fair view of my private circumstances. Besides my Salary,[4] and my House, I have an income of say

[1] No agenda found; printed 'Minute of Cabinet' of 19 July 1871, rehearsing events leading to cancellation of the warrant, in Add MS 44617, f. 60; see Guedalla, *Q*, i. 293.

[2] Elections Bill: *H* ccvii. 1936.

[3] See 25 May 55.

[4] £5000.

£ 7400 gross
1400 interest on debts
£ 6000 nett.

The heavy payment of £57000 for the Hawarden reversion has kept this down: but this is in truth investment, though not for me.

Saw Mr Glyn—Dr Acland—Ld Hardinge—Ld Granville—C. Apponyi—the Emperor of Brazil,[1] at Claridge's 10½-11¼: much pleased. Dined at Ld Stratford's. Read Divers Tracts—Parisiana.

To H. A. BRUCE, home secretary, 19 July 1871. Aberdare MSS.

I send herewith a letter from the Provost of Inverness. If, as is not unlikely the Session is destined with or without an adjournment, to a considerable prolongation, how will that bear on the intention of the Cabinet, formed with different expectations, to do nothing during the present year? Please to give directions for the preparation of an answer to Mr. Bright's question, which Glyn will ask him to put off until Monday. I would far rather not answer it, but will do so if it is desired.[2]

20. Th.

Wrote to Brazilian Minr[3]—Dean of Ch Ch—Dr Acland—Sir T. Biddulph—The Queen—and minutes. H of C. 4¼-8¼ and 9½-2¼.[4] Dined at Dean of Westmrs. Breakfast party. Saw Mr Glyn—D. of Argyll—Mr A. de Lisle[5]—Bp of Winchester. Read Fawcett on Pauperism—Cont. Diseases Report.

Cabinet. Jul. 20. 71.—10 AM.[6]
Course to be taken on Army Bill.
Telegram to the Queen read.
Rough d[ra]ft ans[wer] to Sir G. Grey read.

21. Fr.

Wrote to Sir John Stuart[7]—Dr Döllinger—The Queen—Rev. Mr Foxton—Sir Thos G.—Watsons (1. & Tel.)—Mr Forster—and

[1] Pedro II, on a tour of Europe.

[2] On Contagious Diseases; Gladstone answered Jacob Bright's question on 24 July: *H* ccviii. 154. See 3 Dec. 70.

[3] Arranging the Emperor's visit to Oxford; Add MS 44540, f. 73.

[4] Answered *Grey's question on purchase: 'the decisive step of cancelling the Royal Warrant under which purchase is legal' as from 1 November: *H* ccviii. 16.

[5] Ambrose Lisle March Phillipps *de Lisle, 1809-78; Roman catholic convert; promoted union with anglicanism.

[6] Add MS 44639, f. 80.

[7] On minor difference between Sir John Stuart (1793-1876; on judicial cttee. of Privy Council) and *Hatherley; Add MS 44540, f. 73.

minutes. Westmr Chapter House meeting at four.[1] H of C. 2¼-4, 4½-7 and 9-2½.[2] Read Fawcett—Christie's Shaftesbury.[3] Saw Mr Glyn—Mr Forster—Mr Ayrton—Ld Granville—Ld Halifax.

To J. J. I. VON DÖLLINGER, 21 July 1871. Add MS 44140, f. 283.
'Private.'

I learn from Mr. MacColl that it would not be disagreeable to you to hear from me. I therefore write but I stipulate that you shall not be bound to reply. I have refrained heretofore from addressing to you a single word of sympathy during what must have been the most trying crisis of your life. My motive has been the fear that communication with me, coming to be known, would tend to increase your difficulties. If this be not so, it is a pleasure and a relief to me to assure you that you are in my *daily* recollection, and that no pressure of affairs however urgent can for a moment suspend or enfeeble the interest with which I regard all that happens to you. Nor can I charge myself with any exaggeration in the belief I entertain that you are at this moment, by the Providence of God, the foremost in all Europe among the champions of the only union which can save the world: the union of Faith with Reason. It is I believe the union in which historically the Gospel of Christ laid its first foundations, and those foundations cannot be altered, or destroyed. May the same Power which gave to the sling of David the victory over the spear of Goliath, be with you too, and the more abundantly according to the measure of your need.

It is impossible not to wish you were to pay England a visit but I suppress that desire for we should interrupt your labours, weaken your hands for their proper work, and probably 'kill you with kindness too.' There are two persons however whom I have seen within the last two days, much interested in you and your work, whom I cannot refrain from naming. One is the Emperor of Brazil who is going to pass by Munich and who hopes to see you. The Council, he tells me, is a perpetual pain at his heart. The other is Mr. Ambrose De Lisle one of the worthiest and most enlightened among all the members of the Roman Communion in this country. In conclusion let me congratulate Germany on possessing the Crown Prince who has paid us a visit lately and is to-day I believe at Osborne. Prince in name, and Prince in nature.

22. *Sat.* [*Aldworth, Haslemere*]

Up late. Wrote to The Queen—and minutes. Cabinet 2-4¾. Saw Mr Glyn—The Speaker—Mr Forster—Ld Granville. Off at 5 to Tennyson's place in the Surrey & Sussex hills.[4] Long conversations, chiefly of religion & metaphysics. Read Buchanan's Napoleon Fallen.[5]

Cabinet July 22/71/ 2 PM.[6]
√ Army Purchase Warrant.
√ Manipulation of Ballot Bill.[7]

[1] Its restoration by Sir G. *Scott; S. E. Rigold, *The Chapter House* (1976), 9.
[2] Ballot: *H* ccviii. 89.
[3] See 16 May 71.
[4] Aldworth House, recently built by *Tennyson, SE. of Haslemere, Sussex.
[5] R. W. *Buchanan, *Napoleon fallen; a lyrical drama* (1870).
[6] Add MS 44639, f. 82.
[7] See 24 July 71.

√ Parks Regulation Bill: as to public meetings—Bill may be dropped.
√ Point of order on Lords' vote of Censure. Ld Granville will suggest to the Duke of Richmond.[1]
√ Att[orney] Gen's Embankment letter.

23. 7 S.Trin.

Haselmere Ch. mg (3½ miles off.). Mrs T. speaks of a near Church & it seems to be meditated. Read Vance Smith[2]—Perowne's Psalms[3]—Bp Forbes's Sermon.[4] Afternoon walk over the hill. And much conversation morning noon & night.

24. M. [London]

Wrote to Sir C. Locock—T.D. Acland—Sir F. Grant—Mr Gibson—The Queen—& minutes.

Off before eleven. This is a characteristic & delightful abode. In him are singularly mixed true greatness, genuine simplicity, & some eccentricity. But the latter is from habit & circumstance, the former is his nature. His wife is excellent & in her adaptation to him wonderful. His son Hallam[5] is most attractive.

Reached C.H.T. at one. Saw Mr Glyn—Mr Forster. Cabinet 2-3½. Irish Educn Deputn 3½-4¼.[6] H of C. 4¼-8½ and 9½-2¼.[7] Read Buchanan, Fall of Napoleon.

Cabinet Jul. 24. 71. 2 PM.[8]

√ Ballot Bill. Report of Cabinet Committee. 1. To shorten? 2. Postpone parts? 3. Prosecute after an adjournment to October? 4. After a Prorogation? No. Glyn called in. Expression of a desire for (3) in H. of C. to be favoured. Ld. Granville then to consult Duke of Richmond & learn whether his friends had a preference.[9]

To Sir T. D. ACLAND, 11th bart., M.P., 24 July 1871. Add MS 44540, f. 75.

Notwithstanding your kind dispensation, I must thank you for having thought me worthy to be specially informed of your father's release from the burden of the flesh.[10] In him we have lost a pure and manly spirit, & a man whose name

[1] i.e. Richmond's motion deploring govt.'s handling of purchase abolition, moved on 31 July; see *H* ccviii. 454.
[2] See 4 June 71.
[3] See 1 May 70.
[4] A. P. *Forbes, 'The body is for the Lord' (1871).
[5] Hallam Tennyson, 1852-1928; soldier and governor; 2nd baron 1892.
[6] No report found, but see 28 July 71.
[7] Questioned on secret service money; then Elections Bill: *H* ccviii. 169.
[8] Add MS 44639, f. 83.
[9] There was no October session; the Lords voted the bill out on 10 August.
[10] Letter of 22 July 1871, Add MS 44092, f. 116.

will long be held in honour. It is well that his place will be worthily supplied in all respects but one, but there was one of his characters which nowadays sadly lacks representation; & it was that of the eminent & weighty Conservative County Member, a class who were ever available at once to give effective support, & to impose restraint no less effective on the action of party. The absorption of Wilson Patten into the official ranks took away perhaps the last man able & disposed to fulfil this office on the tory side of the House.

I gave the Emperor of Brazil a letter of introduction for Oxford to your brother which I am afraid was rather illtimed. Of course I was not aware of the more solemn & touching call upon his time.

25. Tu. St James.

Our marriage & T.G.s birthday. All anniversaries should bring me gratitude & grief. Wrote to Dean Ramsay[1]—Sir Thos G.—The Queen (2). Saw A. Russell X. Saw Mr Glyn—Ld Granville—Mr Ouvry—Att. General—Mr Goschen—Chancr of Exr. H of C. 2½–7 and 9–1¾.[2] Read Mivart on Darwin.[3]

26. Wed.

Wrote to Ld Lyttelton—Sir T. Biddulph—Mr Burnett—The Queen (Mem.)—Ld Acton—D of Devonshire—& minutes. Read Inside Paris.[4] Saw Mr Forster (2)—Ld Granville—Mr Glyn—Mr Richmond—Mr Thistlethwayte. Luncheon at 15 G. Square. H of C. 3¼–6.[5] Meeting of B. Museum Election Trustees 6–6.30.[6] Having a chill & nausea went to bed at seven.

To LORD LYTTELTON, 26 July 1871. Hawarden MSS.

I thank you very much for your letter[7] & I hope & feel that you & I are on such a footing that these subjects never can create personal differences between us. For this reason especially I should like to assure myself that you really have the points of the case before you. 1. Was it not for us an indispensable duty to extinguish a gross, wide-spread & most mischievous illegality, of which the existence had been certain & notorious? 2. Was it not also our duty to extinguish it in the best manner? 3. Was not the best manner that which (a) made the extinction final, (b) gave the best i.e. a statutory title for Regulation Prices, (c) granted an indemnity to the officers, (d) secured for them compensation in

[1] Regretting his almost certain inability to attend the Scott centenary, as a result of 'the extraordinary obstructions which have been offered to public business'; Add MS 44540, f. 76.

[2] Legal education: *H* ccviii. 239.

[3] S. G. J. *Mivart, *On the genesis of species* (1871).

[4] See 28 June 71.

[5] Metrication Bill: *H* ccviii. 261.

[6] Gladstone proposed *Acton for *Grote's vacancy; he was elected, as was Devonshire; Add MS 44540, f. 77.

[7] Add MS 44240, f. 174 hostile to Royal Warrant method of purchase abolition.

respect of over-regulation prices? 4. Did not the vote of the House of Lords stop us in this best manner of proceeding? 5. Did it absolve us from the duty of putting an end to the illegality? 6. What method of putting an end to it remained to us, except that which we have adopted?[1]

27. Th.

Rose at 11 much better. Wrote to The Queen Mem. &c.—Att. General—and minutes. H. of C. $4\frac{1}{4}$-$9\frac{1}{4}$ and $9\frac{3}{4}$-$2\frac{3}{4}$, ten good hours.[2] Read Inside Paris. Saw Mr Forster—Mr Glyn—Mr Cardwell—Chr of Exchr. Visited Nat. Gallery & inspected the Raphael[3] on view with Sir W. Boxall.

28. Fr.

Wrote to The Queen—Mr L. Ellis[4]—Bps of Chichester, Winchester, Chester, Oxford, Salisbury, B. & Wells[5]—Abp Manning—Ld Bessborough—Ld Granville, and minutes. Saw Ld Granville—Mr Gurdon—Mr Glyn—Ld Bessborough—Att. General—Sir D. Salomons—Mr Otway[6]—Mr Walpole—W.H.G.—Mr Leo Ellis. Read Christie's Shaftesbury. H of C. 3-$6\frac{1}{2}$ and 9-$2\frac{1}{2}$.[7] Dined with Glyn.

To ARCHBISHOP H. E. MANNING, 28 July 1871. Add MS 44249, f. 266.
'Private.'

The question of the higher Education in Ireland was lightly touched in the conversation between the Deputation from Ireland & me,[8] as nothing but mischief could have resulted from an examination of the matter in detail, at this period, so long before we can practically deal with it, & when Mr. Fawcett's Bill is pending. That Bill will probably be met by the previous question & it is not impossible that the debate (as I hear) may occupy the whole of Wednesday. The question, when it comes on, will be a difficult & probably a dangerous one for the Government, as there is no more doubtful point in the composition & tendencies of the Liberal party than its disposition to extremes in the matter of unsectarianism as it is called.

Our course, however, is well marked out by the character of former proceedings & debates which fix the lines of motion for us within narrow limits. In the

[1] Lyttelton agreed to breakfast, as invited in a post-script, 'but I do not think I shall have an inclination to argue'; ibid., f. 178.

[2] Elections, and Local Govt. Bill: *H* ccviii. 323.

[3] See *Art Journal* (1871) x. 294.

[4] Leopold George Frederick Agar-Ellis, 1829-99; liberal-cons. M.P. Kilkenny 1857-73; 5th Viscount Clifden 1895.

[5] Letters to bps. requesting them to support the govt. in the Lords on the Army Bill; Add MS 44540, f. 79. Bath and Wells, Chichester, Oxford obeyed: *H* ccviii. 541.

[6] Who this day elicited govt. intention to end flogging in the navy; *H* ccviii. 392.

[7] Spoke on order of business; ibid. 414.

[8] Manning's letter of 27 July, Add MS 44249, f. 262, on the importance of Irish education.

course of the recess I must endeavour to acquaint myself accurately with the constitution & working of the Dublin University & College. On Wednesday I shall probably do little more than declare Fawcett's Bill to be insufficient. I suspect that its main concoctors have outwitted themselves. I cordially rejoice in the extinction of the Ecclesiastical Titles Act. I gave it malediction in its cradle, & rejoice to have helped to drive the final blow.

29. Sat. [Chislehurst]

Wrote to Watsons—Bp of Lichfield—Ld Lyttelton—The Queen (Mem. and l.)—and minutes. Saw W.H.G.—Mr Glyn—Ld Granville. Cabinet 2¼-5. Dined at the Mansion House and spoke, to the Toast of Ministers.[1] Then went down to Chiselhurst. Read Inside Paris.

Cabinet 2 PM. Ju[ly] 29. 71.[2]

√ Mundella's Bill on Contagious Diseases. Allow him to introduce.
√ Fawcett's Bill.[3] Previous Question.
√ Language to be held as to Adjournment of the House.
√ Dickinson's plan read.[4] May's opinion.
√ Deep Sea Exploration. Goschen agreed.
√ Fiji Islands. Favourable to incorporation with NSW but wait for Colonial initiative.[5]
√ French Treaty. Granville recited proceedings. Questions to be drawn, according to Duc de Broglie's suggestion.[6]
√ Difficulties between Germany and Roumania as to the Railway Bonds. Recommend arbitration. No advice to P[rince] Charles [of Roumania] about vetoing the Bill.[7]
√ Duke of Argyll proposes to protest.[8]

To LORD LYTTELTON, 29 July 1871. Add MS 44540, f. 80.

I had not the least desire to inflict on you an oral discussion, but I hope you will consider the questions I sent you. I fear the House of Lords is going to commit another act of folly: you will remember the consequences of the one which at Ld. Derby's suggestion it performed on the Paper Duty Bill in 1860. The state of public business may make it our duty to refrain from seeking our defence in a heavy counter-blow from the House of Commons: but I am sure you will not think this diminishes our title to equitable consideration.

[1] Ministers were received with 'comparative coolness'; *The Times*, 31 July 1871, 6a, 9a.
[2] Add MS 44639, f. 85.
[3] University Tests (Dublin) Bill; see 2 Aug. 71.
[4] Not found; Dickinson objected to haste in passing Bishops' Resignation Bill; *H* ccviii. 1146.
[5] See 27 Oct. 71.
[6] Negotiations began in August; see 5 July 71n.
[7] See F. Stern, *Gold and Iron* (1977), ch. xiv.
[8] His note of unfulfilled intention on Lords' action, at Add MS 44639, f. 87.

30. 8 S. Trin.

Chiselhurst Ch mg & aft. Read Maret 'Pape & Eveques'[1]—M. Arnold in Macmillan![2]—Piazzi Smyth on Pyramid.[3] Conversation with Dr A. Clark.

31. M. [London]

Wrote to Mr Gilbert—Sir F. Grant—The Queen Mem. & 2 letters—and minutes. Read Ld Southesk on the R. Academy[4]—E. Chatr. Sous Maitre.[5] Saw Ld Halifax—Mr Bruce—Mr West—Mr Glyn—W.H.G.—Mr Burnett. H. of C. 4¼-8¼ and 9¾-2½. Proposed P. Arthur's annuity &c.[6] Dined at Sir A. Clifford's.[7] Saw G. Duke Constantine[8] and [blank] with him. Back from Chiselhurst at 12.

Tues. Aug. One 1871.

Wrote to Dean of Chichester (Tel.)—Canon Gregory—Robn G.—Mr Burnett—Mr Mansel—The Queen—& minutes. Saw Lord Granville—Mr Glyn—Mr M'Coll—H of C. 2½-7 and 9¼-2¼.[9] Dined at Sir E. Buller's.

2. Wed.

Wrote to Dean of Chichr—Ld Essex—Mr Clowes—and minutes. H of C. 12-3¼. Spoke fully on Dublin University Bill.[10] Saw Canon Gregory—Sir R. Phillimore—Mr Glyn—Mr Forster—Mr West—Ld Granville—Mr Fortescue. Dined at the French Ambassador's. Conversation with Earl Russell—Comte de Paris—French Ambassador—and others. Saw Mrs Th. Read Odger on Land.[11]

[1] H. L. C. Maret, *Le Pape et les Evêques, défense du livre sur le Concile Général et la paix religieuse* (1869).

[2] 'On the modern element in literature', *Macmillan's Magazine*, xix. 304; his Oxford inaugural.

[3] C. P. *Smyth, *Life and work at the great pyramid*, 3v. (1867).

[4] J. *Carnegie, Lord Southesk, *Britain's art paradise* (1871).

[5] See 19 June 71.

[6] 51 radicals supported an amndt.; *H* ccviii. 587. Richmond's motion passed in the Lords in 162: 82.

[7] Black Rod; see 29 July 64.

[8] Probably Grand Duke Constantine Nicholayevitch, 1827-92, Russian naval minister 1853-81, rebuilt Black Sea fleet; president of council of state 1865-81.

[9] Answered questions; then Elections Bill: *H* ccviii. 654.

[10] Deb. adjourned, with previous question (see 29 July 71) put; *H* ccviii. 727.

[11] G. *Odger, 'The land question', *Contemporary Review*, xviii. 23 (August 1871).

3. Th.

Wrote to Messrs Eden & Stanistreet—Mr Macfie—Robn G.—Dean Hook (Tel.)[1]—The Queen—Ld Granville—& minutes. H. of C. 4¼-8¼ and 9½-3.[2] Dined with Lady Waldegrave. Saw Mr Russell—Ld Halifax—Mr Glyn—Mr Gurdon—Mr Cadogan—Duke of Argyll—Sir H. Thornton. Read Christie's Shaftesbury.

4. Fr.

Wrote to French Ambassador—Mr Ayrton—The Queen—and minutes. H of C. 2-7 and 9-2. Spoke on Washington Treaty & other matters.[3] Saw Ld Granville—Sir T. Biddulph—Mr Glyn—Mr Ayrton. Troubled with weakness of the head & nausea.

5. Sat. [Stanmore Park]

Wrote to Dean of Windsor—The Queen & Mem.—Duke of Argyll—and minutes. Visited Mr R. Wallace.[4] Saw Mr Glyn. Cabinet 2-4½. Drove down to Stanmore, to spend Sunday with the Wolvertons. Read Alger on Future Life.[5]

Cabinet Au. 5. 71.[6]

√ Bolton Republican Club Letter to WEG. Not to be answered.[7]

√ Ballot Bill. Courses. 1. ask Bill to be postponed & taken up in *H. of L.* next year. *no.* 2. ask them to adjourn it to Autumn: pledge Govt. to ask H. of C. to do the like. 3. Ask them to pass it now. 4. Question of the Percy Wyndham Clause.[8] Discussed. Probable length of Session.[9]

√ Military manoeuvres Bill.

√ Megaera.[10] Correspondence read. Challenge Mr Reed to make good his assertions in today's Times.[11] Not to speak of any independent inquiry—at present.

[1] Failed to persuade *Hook to accept deanery of St. Paul's; Add MS 44540, f. 82.

[2] Defended Prince Arthur's annuity; *H* ccviii. 788.

[3] Irish education, prisons, govt. business: *H* ccviii. 849.

[4] To offer a baronetcy to Richard *Wallace, 1818-90, picture collector, tory M.P. Lisburn 1873-84, for 'eminent munificence & great personal exertion during the siege of Paris'; Add MS 44540, f. 84.

[5] W. R. Alger, *A critical history of the doctrine of a future life* (1864).

[6] Add MS 44639, f. 88.

[7] Called for House of Lords' reform; *Bolton Chronicle*, 5 August 1871, 3.

[8] Apparently never moved.

[9] Comments on business made 7 August: *H* ccviii. 1006.

[10] H.M.S. *Megaera*, an iron screw steamer, sailed for Australia in February 1871, and had to be beached on St. Paul's Island in June, her bottom corroded. The govt. was accused of parsimony.

[11] E. J. Reed claimed to have examined the *Megaera* 'several years ago . . . and reported her fit only for a very brief period of further service'; *The Times*, 5 Aug. 1871, 12f.

√ French Treaty. Board of Trade questions read, and the French answers.[1] Determined to ask for a Draft of the Treaty of 1860 as proposed to be altered.

6. 9 S.Trin.

Ch. mg & evg. Read Alger on Future Life—Pastor of Oppen on Miracles[2]—S.Aug. City of God Transl.—Contemp. Review, divers Articles. Much rest, with these good people.

7. M. [London]

Wrote to Abp of Canterbury—Ld Granville—D. of Argyll—Col Wilson Patten—The Queen—and minutes. Read Christie's Shaftesbury. H of C. 4¼-8 and 9-3.[3] Returned to town at noon. Saw Mr Glyn—Mr Cadogan—Sir J. Gray. Spoke on Megaera case.

8. Tu.

C.G. went at 9.30 [to Hawarden]. Wrote to The Queen (2, & Mem.)[4]—Mr Helps Tel.—Mr Bruce—Dean Ramsay (2)[5]—Sir J. Coleridge—& minutes. Saw Russell X. Saw Ld Granville—Ld Hartington—Mr Dowse—Mr Fortescue—Sir J. Gray—Lord A. Hervey—Mr Henley—Sol. General. H of C: 2¼-7 and 9-2¼.[6] Read Christie's Shaftesbury.

9. Wed.

Wrote to Ld Bessborough—The Queen (2)—Messrs Eden—C.G.—and minutes. Saw Ld Granville—Bp of Winchester[7]—Ld Dufferin—Mr Glyn—Saw Hamilton, Thomas, friend of Wilson X. H of C. 12½-1½.[8] Cabinet 2¼-5. Tea at Mad. Rothschild's. Dined at Russian Embassy to meet G. Duke Constantine[9] who is eminently frank, intelligent, & kind. Conversation with Sir P. Braila—Mr Disraeli—and others. Read Piazzi Smyth.[10]

[1] *PP* 1872 lxx. 283.

[2] Perhaps the author of *Lectures on miracles at Bremen* (1871).

[3] Inquiry into the *Megaera* announced; *H* ccviii. 995.

[4] Guedalla, *Q*, i. 297.

[5] Tribute to Sir Walter Scott; read out by Ramsay at the Scott centenary; Add MS 44540, f. 84 and *The Times*, 10 August 1871, 12d.

[6] Announced 'ample time' for Elections Bill in Lords before prorogation: *H* ccviii. 1092.

[7] *Wilberforce tried to pair for the Lords' division; Add MS 44540, f. 85; see 28 July 71.

[8] Navy; *H* ccviii. 1195.

[9] See 31 July 71.

[10] See 30 July 71.

Cabinet Wedy. Aug. 9. 71. 2 PM.[1]

√ Prorogation and Queen's departure for the North. Largely considered—Chancr. went to Osborne.
√ Mr Torrens. Vote of Censure.[2]
√ Inquiry into Dublin Riot. Sir John Gray.[3]
√ Judicial Committee Bill—Amendments. Stand over for Chancr.
O French Treaty. Wine.
√ Governor Eyre. Supplementary Vote.
√ Friendly Societies Commission Expenses.

10. Th.

Wrote to Sir T. Biddulph—The Queen Mem. 1. & Tel.—Mr Ayrton—C.G.—Chr of Exr—and minutes. H of C. 4¼-8 and 8¾-3. Sad indeed with the Queen.[4] Saw Capt. Galton—Mr Glyn—Mr West—Chr of Exchr—Mr Ayrton—Ld Hartington—Mr Cadogan—Ld Chancellor—Sol. General—Mr Forster cum Mr Stansfeld—Ld Granville. Went to the Agar breakfast at No 15 G.S.[5] Read Christie's Shaftesbury.

To LORD KIMBERLEY, colonial secretary, 10 August 1871. Add MS 44540, f. 86.

On the points in Sir J. Macdonald's letter,[6] I think: 1. That the payment to Canada for the Fenian incursion should remain as Ripon left it. For *what* was it an equivalent? If we have had the equivalent, we should pay: if not, if it was intended to depend on the acceptance of the Treasury by Canada, then the question is a new one for the Cabinet, & I should like to hear the whole case.

2. Though I agree with you that we cannot bind the British Government to denounce [*sic*] on the requisition of Canada at a future date, is it impossible for the Parliament of Canada to limit its assent in such a way as to enable it of its own motion to make the Treaty drop? It seems right that in some way they should keep their free agency if possible.

3. Should not some notice be taken of the very unbecoming language of Sir J. Macdonald? to which I am rather surprised that Ld Lisgar makes no reference.

To R. LOWE, chancellor of the exchequer, 10 August 1871. 'Private.' Add MS 44540, f. 85.

From the inclosed note you will see that Biddulph on the part of the Queen claims the execution of the Bond with reference to Windsor Drainage.[7] This will

[1] Add MS 44639, f. 90.

[2] On 10 August Torrens moved deferment of further consideration of Lords' amndts. to Elections Bill; *H* ccviii. 1400.

[3] Hartington stone-walled on Gray's question next day; *H* ccviii. 1313.

[4] Candlish asked about Victoria's journey to Balmoral before the end of the session; Gladstone announced its delay and that 'I am sure the public convenience will be consulted'; *H* ccviii. 1310. See Guedalla, *Q*, i. 300.

[5] i.e. at Mrs Thistlethwayte's.

[6] See 12 Aug. 71n.

[7] See 9 July 71n.

be a difficult business with Ayrton, but I have written to him in the best manner I could, & I hope he will be conformable under the circumstances.

I imagine he considers himself aggrieved, & I rather gathered from you that you had taken this matter out of his hands, & dealt with it at the T[reasury] without his having had the opportunity of seeing what he could do. I must own that if this is so, I would not know how to defend the proceeding, as I doubt whether the T. has properly an original jurisdiction in the matter, & the subordination of his Department is after all a qualified subordination. But we must try to accommodate the matter with him in point of tone, or scandal will result not only for us but for the Queen. Am I to understand from yours respecting Mr Foster that you have nothing to say as to the Indian C[ouncil?]. I suppose Sir W. Anderson is our old [blank].

11. Fr.

Wrote to Ld Clarendon—Lady Burdett Coutts—C.G.—Ld Lyveden—Mr Mayow—The Queen—& minutes. H of C. 2-5 and 9-2¼.[1] Read Christie's Shaftesbury. Saw Dowager Duchess of Somerset—Lady Beecher[2]—Mr Glyn—Chancr of Exr—Mr Ayrton—Mr Leeman—Mr West—Ld Hartington.

To LORD LYVEDEN, 11 August 1871. Add MS 44540, f. 86.

I value your good opinion & good word too much to let pass what I think is an erroneous statement made by you about me. You say or are said to say I was once not merely a Conservative but an Orange Tory.[3] I am unaware of it. I think you must have spoken not from my words or acts but from an exaggerated assertion of Ld. Macaulay, mixed with kind compliments much beyond my desert, which however does not if I remember right go up to this point. But I would on no account ask you to make any explanation at my request: or unless you are satisfied that there is not adequate ground for the statement. My first Irish Manifesto as far as I know was a speech in March 1835[4] corrected for the *Mirror of Parliament*. I am about further to show my confidence in you by a polemical remark. I always inwardly resent comparisons, or rather an identification, as between the Conservative party of the Duke & Peel & the conservative party of the present day: & I do not think that conservative party to which I belonged would instead of fighting the Ballot Bill like a man as you did, have stooped to reject it on the miserable plea of time. August & Sept. 1835 dispose pretty well of that question.[5]

[1] Spoke on *Eyre: *H* ccviii. 1436.

[2] Elizabeth, widow of Sir William Wrixon-Becher.

[3] Phrase used by Lyveden in the Lords in the Election Bill deb., as reported in *The Times*, 11 August 1871, 5; *H* ccviii, 1277 has 'high Oxford Tory'. See Ramm I, i. 254.

[4] See 31 Mar. 35.

[5] Lyveden replied '. . . what I meant to say and believe I did was an "*ultra Oxford Tory*" '; 11 Aug. 1871, Add MS 44431, f. 197.

12. Sat. [Cassiobury]

Wrote to Mr Adderley—Ld Lyveden—Count Cadorna—and minutes. Saw Mr Glyn. Cabinet 2-4¾. Went to Cassiobury: most kindly received.[1] Drive thro' the beautiful Park. Saw Ld Ebury—Mr Locke—Read [blank]'s Poems—Mrs Butler's Address.[2]

Aug. 12. 71. 2 PM. Cabinet.[3]

√ Attendance in H. of C. of members of the Government.[4]

√ Meeting in Phoenix Park if any to be stopped: in *suite* of the last.

√ Sir J. Macdonald's letter: decline admitting we are bound to pay Fenian claims irrespective of the action of the Dominion Parlt.—but not shut the door agt. any discussion on the ground of expediency. Second point to be examined.[5]

√ Judicial Committee Bill. Amendments.

Ld Ripon & Forster on Education Bill. Shall we sanction ByeLaws wh. remit fees in Rate Schools for children of poor Parents, but not in denom[inationa]l Schools. Decided not to interfere. Much difference, & reluctance of all.[6]

√ Recital of Chancellor's visit to Osborne. Terms of WEG's letter to H.M. considered & approved.[7]

√ East End of London Museum. Establishment to be supplied by Govt. on a limited scale.

13. 10 S.Trin.

Ch in Watford mg & evg. Wrote to C.G. Read Alger on Future Life[8] MP on Dean of Canterbury[9]—Bickersteth's Charge[10]—Denison's Three Policies[11]—and other Tracts. It was sad to see Ld Ebury's sufferings but they were most bravely borne.

14. M. [London]

Wrote to Mr Goschen—Mrs Thistlethwayte—C.G.—Col. Ponsonby 2 Telegr. & letter—The Queen, letter—Mr Baker—Mr Childers Tel. —Abp of York—Ld Granville Tel.—Mr Wingfield Baker—& minutes. Saw W.H.G.—Mr West—Att. General—Mr Goschen—Ld

[1] Lord Ebury's.

[2] J. E. *Butler, *Sursum corda; annual address to the Ladies National Association* (1871).

[3] Add MS 44639, f. 93.

[4] Gone to grouse moors; *Daily Telegraph*, 15 August 1871.

[5] Macdonald to Lisgar, 21 July 1871, PRO CO 880/6/403.

[6] The new Education Code 1871; see G. Sutherland, *Policy-making in elementary education 1870–1895* (1973), 194.

[7] Urging Victoria's remaining until 22 August; Guedalla, *Q*, i. 302.

[8] See 5 Aug. 71.

[9] 'The dean of Canterbury on science and revelation. A letter by M.P.' [J. D. Lewis] (1871).

[10] R. *Bickersteth, 'A charge . . . October 1870' (1870).

[11] G. A. *Denison, 'The three policies' (1871).

Granville—Chr of Exr—Sir E. May—Mr Disraeli. Read Christie's Shaftesbury. H of C. 3-8 and 9-3¾.[1] The H. sat 13 hours.

15. Tu.

Wrote to Ld Spencer—The Queen Mem. and l.—Bp of Tasmania[2] —Bp Claughton—C.G.—Mr Disraeli—Mrs Th.—and minutes. Wrote Draft of Queen's Speech.[3] Saw Mr Glyn—Mr West—Ld Granville. H of C. 3-9 and 9¾-12. Spoke on the Purchase Warrant.[4] Read Piazzi Smyth. Saw Mrs Th. in evg X.

16. Wed.

Wrote to Mr West—Col. Ponsonby—Mr Church[5]—Messrs Eden—Dr Liddon—Mr Fortescue—C.G.—The Queen—and minutes. Read Alger on Future Life.[6] Saw Mr Ouvry—Mr Walpole—Mr Glyn. Finished Queens Speech. 1-6. House & Cabinet. The Speech considered & corrected. Dined with Mrs Th. with whom I then went to see Eilsen Oge at the Princess's Theatre.

Cabinet Au. 16. 71. 2 PM.[7]

Queen's Speech: considered & arranged.
Downing's motion on Dublin Riot. Heads [of reply] agreed on.[8]
○ Castellani Collection. (settled with Lowe).[9]
French Treaty: ask for a draft with the proposed alterations set out.[10]

17. Th.

Wrote to Duke of Argyll—Earl Russell—Ld Ebury—Chr of Exchr —H. Cole—Miss E. Stuart—Mr Childers—Watsons—Ld Fermoy—The Queen—& minutes. Saw Mr MacColl—Mr Glyn—Mr Monsell —A. Kinnaird—Chr of Exchr—Sol. General. H of C. 3-7¾ and 9½-12¼. Spoke on Dublin Riot: an awkward case.[11] Dined (with A.K.)[12]

[1] Questions, then army estimates: *H* ccviii. 1575.
[2] Charles Henry Bromby; business untraced.
[3] Untraced; for prorogation.
[4] Answering *Harcourt; Lords' amndts. then accepted; *H* ccviii. 1683.
[5] Offering him deanery of St. Paul's; Add MS 44540, f. 88.
[6] See 5 Aug. 71.
[7] Add MS 44639, f. 99.
[8] Details in ibid., f. 100; *H* ccviii. 1504.
[9] Obtained for the British Museum.
[10] Granville to Gavard, 21 Aug. 1871, in *PP* 1872 lxx. 289.
[11] *H* ccviii. 1781; the meeting in Phoenix Park had been to call for the release of Fenians.
[12] i.e. A. Kinnaird, his original contact with Mrs. Thistlethwayte; see above v.lxii.

at Mrs Th's. Read The Builders of Babel.[1] Saw Mrs Hampton[2] on her son's case.

18. Fr.

Wrote to Mr Church (Tel)—Ld Hartington—Mr Heron MP—Mr Burnett—C.G.—Mr F. Knowles[3]—The Queen Mem. & l.—Ld Spencer—and minutes. H. of C. 3–5½.[4] Saw Mr Glyn—Mr M'Coll—Ld Hartn and Irish Law Officers[5]—and others. Dined with Mr Glyn. Haymarket Theatre afr.[6] Saw Mrs Th. after. X. Read Alger on Future Life—Arr. with a view to departure. Long conversation with W. Hampton: & with his mother afterwards.

19. Sat.

Wrote to Earl Russell—Sir C. Locock—Dr Guthrie—Mrs Russell—Eden & Co—Mr O'Donoghue—Scotts—Ld Granville—Miss Doyle—Bp of London—C.G.—& minutes. Saw Mr Church—Do *cum* Dr Liddon afr—Mr West *cum* Mr Gurdon—Mr Clack (S. Kensington)[7]—Mr Forster—Mr Glyn—Mr Cardwell *cum* Sir H. Storks. Saw Russell—& others[R]. Read Builders of Babel. Visited S.Kens. Museum—And Internat. Exhibition. A peaceful evening!

To Sir C. LOCOCK, 19 August 1871. Add MS 44540, f. 92.

I have received your letter,[8] & I attach to it all the weight which belongs to your judgment, but I am sorry to say my conclusion is that the grant of two more Baronetcies to the medical profession at this moment, & to one very special branch of it, would be out of proportion with the distribution of honours elsewhere. Your PS causes me concern. I wish we could see our way to any practical measure.

20. 11 S.Trin.

Quebec Chapel[9] 11 AM—Bedfordbury 7 PM. Saw Mr Latham—Mr Twisleton. Wrote to Mrs Thistlethwayte (2)—Col. Ponsonby—Mr

[1] D. *MacCausland, *The builders of Babel* (1871).

[2] i.e. the widow of the deceased butler.

[3] Had sent an urn, accepted 'though I am not sure that I ought to accept it without qualms of conscience'; Add MS 44540, f. 90.

[4] Misc. business: *H* ccviii. 1845.

[5] Meeting to consider 'the course to be taken in Dublin in the event of any immediate or early attempt to hold another meeting'; Add MS 44540, f. 90.

[6] 'My Husband's Ghost'.

[7] T. Clack of the Science and Art Dept.

[8] Untraced.

[9] In Marylebone; F. J. Holland, 1828–1907, its minister 1861–83.

Delisle. Read The Builders of Babel (finished)—Is the Ch. of Engl. the Ch. of God?.[1] Saw Russell: kept late in L.R: but I trust this will go all right. Read the Weekly papers on the conduct of the Govt.[2]

21. M.

Wrote to Mr G. Burnett—Mr Ayrton—The Queen Mem—Mr Barker—Messrs Eden—D. of Argyll—Mr Repington—C.G.—Ld Granard—and minutes. Saw Mrs Scanlan[3]—Mr Glyn. Dined with Harry at Lord Halifax's. Out paying Bills & shopping. Attended the Prorogation[4] 1½-2½—Handshaking all round. Finished Christie's Shaftesbury.[5]

22. Tu. [Whitby]

Wrote to Mr Church[6]—and minutes. Saw Mr West. Off by 10 A M Train to Whitby.[7] Arrived a little before six. Looked into York Minster (observed *dual* arrangements) and executed deed at York. Dr Clark my companion. Met by C. & W., & by numbers at Whitby Station. Read Crabbs Poems[8]—Tennyson's (enlarged) Idylls.[9]

23. Wed.

My first bathe. Wrote to Col. Ponsonby (Tel.)—Ld Granville—Mr Glyn—and minutes. Visited the Scaur, the Parish Church, & the beautiful ruins of the Abbey. Read Tennyson—Crabbes Poems—Saint Beuve on St Priest.[10] Did a scrap of Iliad.

To G. G. GLYN, chief whip, 23 August 1871. Add MS 44540, f. 94.

I am concerned to hear about Surrey[11] particularly because the reports though manifestly bad seem to be in other respects vague. To be beaten by the Licensed Victuallers if disagreeable would not be dishonourable. It would be like the loss of a seat at Coventry after the French Treaty. It is another matter, if our own

[1] A pamphlet of 1870.

[2] Discussed in his Whitby speech, 2 Sept. 71.

[3] Unidentified; household?

[4] By Lords Commissioners; *H* ccviii. 1894.

[5] See 16 May 71.

[6] Prevaricating about accepting St. Paul's; Add MS 44540, f. 93.

[7] He stayed at 1 Crescent Place; W. H. Gladstone had won Whitby from the tories in 1868.

[8] See 17 May 71. Variously spelt by diarist.

[9] Probably 1869 ed.

[10] Start of extensive study of St. Beuve, mostly of his sundry series of *Portraits.*

[11] Glyn to Gladstone, 22 August 1871, Add MS 44348, f. 121: 'I am more than uneasy as to Surrey . . . sad accounts of the state of the party. . . .' The Liberals lost the seat at a by-election on 26 August. Glyn reported, 5 September 1871, ibid., f. 123: ' "Beer" was the thing—but "Income Tax" and a curious revival of the "no popery cry", urged against us, helped.'

bettermost friends are falling away or cooling. But to ascertain extent, I think we may account for these untoward incidents by the reflection that there is something of a tide in politics. At the Election we had an immense impetus & we came back with more than a natural or nominal majority. As that impetus declines, our majority may slowly decline with it. It was so after the Election of 1831. You may remember that Dorsetshire & Dublin were picked up by the Tories & I myself in 1832 came in for Newark on that reaction. Whoever or whatever is to blame, I am sure you are not. I do think there is a spirit of general censure abroad which is usually & suspiciously active at this time: & barring intermediate accidents of an untoward kind I think we shall meet Parliament better than we parted from it. Even the Autumn Sessions the idea of which as you remember wholly sprang up with the party & was repeatedly pressed upon me before I would entertain it, are constantly quoted as one of my threats & as among the numerous proofs of my domineering disposition.

The people here are very warm & hearty.

I hope your trip will do you good. The Queen is still suffering. I do not know when I shall go to Balmoral. Had my first bathe today.

What you said about your house account & young Hampton did not I fear refer to the present but to some time when your London household may be going? G[ranville] seems likely to look in upon us.

24. Th. St Bartholomew

Bathed 2°. Wrote to Col. Ponsonby—Mr Fortescue—Col. French—Messrs Honey & Co[1]—Miss James—Mrs Thistlethwayte—Ld Houghton, & minutes. Saw Mr Samuelson MP—Mr Corner.[2] We went to curiosity shops & did business. Then had tea with old Mrs Turnbull.[3] Read Tennyson—Crabbe's Tales—Saint Beuve's Barante.

To C. S. P. FORTESCUE, president of the board of trade, 24 August 1871. Add MS 44540, f. 94.

I had no idea until I read Sir L. Mallet's Memo this morning that any relic of protection still lurked in our spirit duties. I thought that in 1860 we had weeded it all out. But if this be not so, doubtless the subject is a proper one for investigation. The Board of Inland Revenue will of course have much to say on it.

With respect to the wine duty if the French are to denounce the Treaty, I think it may really be worth considering whether the shilling duty on wine should not be somewhat raised. The 2/6 might perhaps also be diminished with a reduction of the Alcoholic maximum for wine: & without alarming the Ch. of E. the interval might in this way be much diminished. An indication through the Press of a likelihood of our raising the 1/- duty on wine might have a very good effect in France. I do not however presume to speak of it as more than a matter fit to be considered.

The question of the French Treaty, & our duty in regard to it, is, in my view, one of the most nicely balanced questions within my recollection: At least at the

[1] About a bill respecting his Liverpool properties; Add MS 44540, f. 95.
[2] See 2 Sept. 71.
[3] Probably of Thomas Turnbull, Whitby ship builders.

point where we are asked to consent to new protective increments. It is difficult to move backwards in a case where the forward aspect of our measure was the ground reason for adopting it: While on the other hand it may be urged that though we may not be able to retain the whole advantage that is no reason for refusing to retain a part. On the whole in an extended view of the future, I lean to the former course but with much submission[?].[1]

25. Fr.

Bathed 3°. Wrote (draft) to Mayor of Leeds[2]—Ld Kimberley—Mrs Bowers[3]—The Queen (Mem.)—and minutes. We went to Larpool[4] for luncheon: then to Sneaton[5] & had tea: after seeing the waterfall —the views, up & down, very beautiful. Read Remusat on German Philosophy[6]—Saint Beuve's Thiers (a notable portrait, but less searching ethically than Lanfrey)[7]—Tennyson's Vivien[8]—Crabb's Tales. NB. Mr Peter's Pictures.

To EARL SPENCER, Irish lord lieutenant, 25 August 1871. Add MS 44540, f. 95.

1. The points in the case of Macdonnell[9] would I think be that the grant of a second *considerable* honour except upon retirement would be somewhat beyond the usual line of the C.S., though I know it is done in diplomacy which is however more ornate. But in truth there is no description[?] of public business in which I so much feel the want of aid & advice as in the rather nice matter of the distribution of honours: & if you wish it I can consider this further in the Autumn when the Cabinet meet in London.

2. In the matter of the Park meeting, you had an extremely nice & difficult question to deal with in great haste, at the most inconvenient juncture possible; & I think you owe it to your own good judgment & temper that when you have ruled Ireland in most arduous circumstances for nearly three years this should have been the first occasion on which your proceedings have been the subject of serious criticism—you will now I trust be allowed the advantage of a little time for deliberation & I think that if you are threatened with any immediate or early

[1] Fortescue's reply, 27 August 1871, Add MS 44122, f. 234, thought Gladstone's wine proposals 'well worth considering', and thought 'we should make the best of the French proposals'.

[2] Replying to Leeds' resolution on ballot, in *The Tablet*, 2 Sept. 1871, 313.

[3] Wife of G. H. Powers (see 26 Oct. 42) on dispensing power of the crown; see Add MS 44540, ff. 96, 99.

[4] Seat near Whitby of Edmund Henry Turton.

[5] Seat near Whitby of Charles Bagnall.

[6] C. G. M. de Remusat, *De la philosophie allemande* (1845).

[7] P. Lanfrey, *Études et portraits politiques*, ch. 1 (1864); see 19 Sept. 70.

[8] See 22 Aug. 68n; the 1869 ed. included *Coming of Arthur, Geraint and Enid, Merlin and Vivien, etc.*

[9] Sir Alexander Macdonnell, 1794-1875; supervised Irish education 1831-71; cr. bart. Jan. 1872.

meeting, you cannot but derive some advantage from considering with Smyth[1] as M.P. & lawyer should he be a responsible promoter of it: And with others, though in a less degree in proportion as their station may give you less hold over them. I liked, individually, the notion of trying the present state of the law by a course of proceeding taken for the purpose but to this there may be conclusive objection.
3. The reception of the French Deputation[2] seemed to me to be scandalous, & their language as reported, little better. But I hope the reception at least is in some degree to be referred to temporary irritation.
4. I have not been able fully to catch the points of the Kelly trial.[3]
5. You have made in quitting your home & country, as great a sacrifice as could in that form be imposed on any man. But I do not think you will have occasion to repent having renewed the beneficial & honourable connection of your name with Ireland.

If you run across to Germany can you conveniently stop at Hawarden on the way? Where we hope to be about the 4th or 5th.

I should like much to know your views respecting the University question, so far as you have matured them.

If Roundell has ever thought out a plan, I should be very glad to hear of it; the question is critical & I am very anxious that our basis should be sound: & not one chosen *because* it is that of Cullen or of Fawcett, or of neither but for its own sake.

26. Sat.

Wrote to Robn G.—Sir W.C. James—Mrs Hampton—Viceroy of I.—Messrs Eden—Mayor of Leeds (after cons[ideratio]n)—Lord Granville (Tel)—and minutes. 1–6. We went to Mulgrave Castle[4] for luncheon & tea: saw the very beautiful grounds & woods, the interesting bust & picture of Mr Pitt, & Lyte [*sc.* Lythe] Church: guided by Ld M.[5] who is himself well worth seeing. Read Saint Beuve—Tennyson—Crabbe.

27. 11 S.Trin.

Ruswarp Ch mg and St Michael's Evg. Wrote to Sol. General—Lady Beecher—Mr Ayrton—Mr Stansfeld—and minutes. Saw Mrs Trevelyan.[6] Read Thos a Kempis—St George Mivart[7]—Atkins's Reminiscences[8]—Par. Lost B. 1.

[1] Patrick James Smyth, 1823–85; barrister and Home Rule M.P. Westmeath June 1871–80, Tipperary 1880–4.

[2] A French republican deputation to Dublin.

[3] The trial 'showed the Power of the Fenian organisation to intimidate on behalf of one of their emissaries though he was clearly guilty of a murder'.

[4] Seat of Lord Normanby.

[5] Constantine Charles Henry Phipps, 1846–1932; styled Earl Mulgrave; vicar of Worsley 1872–90; 3rd marquis of Normanby 1890.

[6] Of 6 Esplanade, Whitby.

[7] See 25 July 71.

[8] T. Atkins, *Reminiscences of twelve years' residence in Tasmania and New South Wales* (1869).

28. M.

Bathed 4°. Wrote to Mr [G. W. G.] Leveson Gower[1]—J.M. Gaskell—Helen G.—Mr J. Nield—& minutes. We went to luncheon with Mrs [Hannah] Cholmeley[2] at Abbey House: visited the Abbey Church a second time, with undiminished admiration. Then went to Ruswarp & on the river. In the evening we went to the Theatre which was remarkably good. Mr Davis's Company. Read Saint Beuve—Tennyson's (Collected) Idylls. Helen's birthday: God's blessings be upon her.

29. Tu.

Bathed 5°. Wrote to Mr Wright (Hull)[3]—Col. Ponsonby—Col. Stepney[4]—& minutes. Read Saint Beuve—Tennyson's Idylls. Visited the Rector:[5] Bryant's Jet Shops & Magazine: and Turnbull's Ship Yard. We dined at Captain Turton's.[6] Saw Granville in evg.

30. Wed.

Bathed 6°. Wrote to Duke of Argyll—Chr of Exchr—Mr West—J. Breckenridge—Dr Brown[7]—& minutes. Morning's conversation with Granville: who went off at one. Saw Dr Clark in evg. Attended the Agricultural Show. Read Sainte Beuve—Tales of the North Riding.[8]

To R. LOWE, chancellor of the exchequer, 30 August 1871. Add MS 44540, f. 98.

Granville who has been here today tells me he hears you are not well pleased with your revenue. I see your customs are low though improving. This does not surprise me: for I have observed that where trade & industry go down and again where they go up, the effect on revenue only follows with a certain interval of time between. The real question of the future is our expenditure. On this point I should much like to know your anticipations. The question is important to us not only as one of interest, but also at least to me as one of honour & consistency.

I have not yet opened it to Cardwell or to Goschen: but I think of doing so,

[1] Consoling him on losing E. Surrey in the by-election on 26 August; Add MS 44540, f. 96.

[2] *sc.* Cholmley; an important local family.

[3] Unidentified.

[4] Offering him (see 4 July 68) a baronetcy; Add MS 44540, f. 97.

[5] W. Keane; see 12 Sept. 68.

[6] See 25 Aug. 71n.

[7] i.e. J. Baldwin *Brown (see 15 Nov. 64); thanking him for cuttings from unspecified papers; 'they give me further proof of what I have long known—viz. that whatever a portion of the London Press may think or say the mass of the British public continue to applaud[?] liberally, & even indulgently, the efforts of the Govt. to do its duty'. Add MS 44540, f. 98. See 2 Sept. 71n.

[8] By Mary *Linskill (1871); see 16 Sept. 71.

& I should be glad of any lights you can give me. My own impression is that we ought to have 2 millions off the Navy & Army estimates. Against this there will be I suppose a fresh 600000 on account of purchase, but the 1400m to the good would enable you to take off a penny from the Income Tax. We go from hence on Monday to Hawarden. Granville came last night, not looking quite at his best. We could not persuade him to stay over today as he was anxious to rejoin Lady G.[1]

31. Th.

Bathed 7°. Wrote to Col. Ponsonby—Sir F. Rogers—Mr Lambert—The Queen (Mem.)—Watsons—& minutes. Read as yesterday. Saw Duchess Dowager of Argyll: a plain kindly old Scotch-woman.[2] We went off at one to Lyth, Runswick—Port Mulgrave—and Staiths: a mixed expedition of walk, fly, Mr Palmer's[3] four in hand, & Steamer back to Sand's End. Varied & interesting: & Mr and Mrs P. most kind. Home at 8½.

Frid. Sept. One 1871.

Bathed 8°. Wrote to Mr G.K. Richards[4]—Mr Bruce (2)—Ld Fermoy—Sir S. Scott & Co—Mr West—and minutes. Read as yesterday—Also Da Cunha on Portuguese Affairs.[5]—Hayward on purchase.[6] We went with the Clarks to Robin Hood's Bay: Mr Farsyde Cicerone.[7] We had tea at his old Elisabethan House: partly *unawares*. We went to the Play in the evening: the pieces not more than passable. Saw Dean of Peterborough.

To H. A. BRUCE, home secretary, 1 September 1871. Aberdare MSS.

This address of Bradlaugh[8] is a political fact of some significance. I presume it is not within reach of the law.

Please let Granville see it. At some period, the Queen ought to know what is going on; though it has not made much head yet. It would not do to trouble her now.

I should like to have a copy of it (which of course I shall keep secret) if you will kindly send me one.[9]

We mean to go hence on Monday: and I expect to be at Hawarden on Wedy.

[1] No reply in Add MS 44301.

[2] Ann, widow of the 7th duke; she d. 1874.

[3] Charles Mark Palmer, principal landowner at Easington, 15 miles NW. Whitby.

[4] The Speaker's Counsel; business untraced.

[5] J. J. da Cunha de Azeredo Continho, *An essay on the commerce and products of the Portuguese colonies in South America* (1807).

[6] A. Hayward, 'The purchase system' (1871).

[7] George James Watson Farside, J.P., of Thorpe Hall.

[8] Probably a report of Bradlaugh at the London Republican Club, which he inaugurated 12 May 1871; his most notorious speech there was in late Sept. 1871.

[9] Bruce sent a report on political meetings in London since 1867, showing 'while there is evidence of some growth in democratic and revolutionary ideas, they are as yet not very

2. Sat.

A touch of nausea &c. Wrote to York Stat. Master—Chwardens St Thos Seaforth—Mr Gaskell—S.R.G.—Mr Craven—Sir T.G.—and minutes. Finished Sainte Beuve—Finished Tales of N. Riding. Spoke at large political meeting in the Congress Hall.[1] Planted a tree at Mr E[dward] Corner's, Esk Hall.

3. 13 S.Trin.

Parish Church mg (with H.C.) and St Ninian [Baxtergate] evening. Saw Dean of Peterborough—Mrs Trevelyan—& others. Luncheon with the Dowager Duchess of Argyll who was most kind & genial. Wrote to Mr Barry (A.G.I.). Read Hussey's Boyle Lectures[2]—Liddon's Funeral Sermon[3]—Keene's do on his Clerk[4]—Finished Idylls: and read Mr Knowles's notable letter.[5]

To C. R. BARRY, attorney general for Ireland, 3 September 1871. Add MS 44540, f. 100.

In a pretty full speech on the 2d reading of Mr Fawcett's bill at the beginning of last month I expressed strongly my belief that if a spirit of moderation should happily prevail it would be not only possible but easy to settle the question of the higher education in Ireland so as to meet all reasonable expectations. If you share my opinion in this respect, & with what you know of the desire of the Government to consult fairly all Irish opinion & feeling I trust you will not find any impediment in the way of your pressing[?] for such a solution as would be satisfactory to the Irish people. The only reason why it would be difficult for me to use (alone) this formula would be the extreme jealousy with which every word coming from me, on this particular question would be laid hold of. But no one could think the words improper for you to use. I have spoken of the 'higher' Education as that is the crucial branch of the question. With regard to the National System in Ireland, I do not at present see that any very serious difficulty confronts us. I hope that you may find the field safe to enter, & that after entering you may win.[6]

4. M. [Thornes House, Wakefield]

Bathed 9°. Wrote to Baroness Burdett Coutts—Col. Ponsonby—Mr Glyn—Ld Granville—and minutes. Packed my clothes, & china &c.

widely diffused or very seriously entertained by the great majority of the working classes. ... But the time may come ...'; Add MS 44087.

[1] Attacked the London press and London wealth; *The Times*, 4 Sept. 1871, 12a.
[2] See 30 Mar. 51.
[3] H. P. *Liddon, 'The day of work' (1871).
[4] By M. A. Keene (1871).
[5] Apparently James Knowles in print, but untraced.
[6] Barry replied on 6 Sept. 1871, Add MS 44431, f. 233 that he could not contest Limerick 'with any prospect of success'.

After necessary farewells off at one. Saw Ald. Carter—and Dean of Peterborough. A great & warm crowd at the station. I went to Wakefield: where also there was a great crowd waiting.[1] Gaskell received me with much affection. He had a small dinner party. Read Uvelet's Address to Manning[2]—Falkland's Speech on Episcopacy.[3] Long & late conversation.

To G. G. GLYN, chief whip, 4 September 1871. Add MS 44540, f. 102.

We are all rejoiced to receive your prosperous report of your return & Mrs G. All will we hope continue to go well with her. We leave much pleased with Whitby place and people. It ended in a meeting as you will see: & a large & enthusiastic one. The proposal to me was a small deputation: but I thought this would not do particularly as the working men have given us the seat. It is said our coming has done us much good as regards the seat. At any rate I now seem to understand the local politics which I did not before. The Conservatives are a rich minority: & here is the explanation of their ability to fight though without a chance. The reason of the diminished majority last time, I am told, was that as the seat was safe many liberal voters who were under pressure were allowed to abstain from voting.

I fear the Metr[opolita]n Press will not be pleased with what I said of them; but it was time I think to say something for the purpose of reminding people that that press is not the country. Is there any chance of your coming to Hawarden? I think myself safe there till about this day fortnight. Soon after that I may have to move for Balmoral. Of course you will hear anything about Collier. I have written to Barry about Education. Please send me the list of the new Liberal Government.

5. Tu.

Wrote to Mr West—The Queen (Mem.)—C.G.—& minutes. A large deputation came with reporters from Wakefield to present an Address at 5.30: to which I replied.[4] Went with Gaskell to Lupsett,[5] the gardens, & over the place. Read Carlisle's Journal[6]—The Mysterious Mother[7]—Walpole's illness[8]—Trial of Govr Wall[9]—

State Poems }
Hall Stevenson[10] } X

[1] He stayed at J. Milnes Gaskell's house.

[2] Apparently *sic*; untraced.

[3] L. *Cary, Lord Falkland, 'A speech made to the House of Commons concerning episcopacy' (1641).

[4] Spoke on virtues of Sir R. *Peel; *The Times*, 6 Sept. 1871, 3d.

[5] Eighteenth century house on the edge of Wakefield.

[6] Probably A. D. Carlisle, *Round the world in 1870* (1871?).

[7] H. *Walpole, *Mysterious mother; a tragedy* (1791).

[8] Probably in H. Walpole's *Correspondence*, ed. in 7v. (1820-37).

[9] *The trial of Governor Wall* (1867).

[10] Both pornographic, the latter by J. H. *Stevenson.

6. Wed. [*Hawarden*]

Wrote to Mrs Th.—Col. Ponsonby—Telegrams to Mr Mundella, Mr T. Turner.[1] Read divers before starting—. . . on Machiavelli—Statement of Lesseps[2]—recommenced Spectator and Ivanhoe.[3] Visited Wakefield Church—also Thornes School. Off from W. at 1.15—reached Hawarden soon after five. A great crowd at starting: and some salutations on the way. Declined Sheffield & Manchester invitations.

7.

Wrote to Mr Wordsworth—J. M. Gaskell—Mr Bass—Ld Halifax—Mr Glyn—and minutes. Draft to Editor of Echo.[4] A day of unpacking, rummaging, and arranging. Church 8½ AM. Read Waverley—Spectator. Surveying with C., with a view to improvements.

8. Frid.

Church 8½ AM. Wrote to Col. Ponsonby—Gladstone & Co—Mr Lowe—Duke of Argyll. More rummaging and arranging papers. Went with C. to Potter's farm. Read Ivanhoe—Spectator—Picture of Verdun: i.e. account of the Detenus.[5] Saw Mr Burnett respecting the affairs of these Estates. His account is a good one.

9. Sat.

Ch. 8½ AM. Wrote to Mr West—Mr Cardwell—Duke of Argyll—Ed. Lpool Daily Post—Mr Anderson MP.[6]—Mr G. Burnett—and minutes. Cut down a holly by C's orders. Read Smith on Brickyards[7] —What does she do with it[8]—Spectator—Ivanhoe—Picture of Verdun.

[1] Probably on a pension for Sir W. Turner's widow; Add MS 44540, f. 110.
[2] F. M. de Lesseps, 'The history of the Suez Canal. A personal narrative' (1870).
[3] *Scott (1819).
[4] For Catherine Gladstone, on Hampstead Smallpox Hospital, *The Echo*, 9 Sept. 1871, 5.
[5] *A picture of Verdun; or, the English detained in France* [by J. Lawrence], 2v. (1810).
[6] Declining to visit Glasgow; Add MS 44540, f. 104.
[7] G. Smith, *The cry of the children from the brickyards of England: a statement and appeal* (1871).
[8] S. Temple, 'What does she do with it', n. 1 of *Tracts for the Times* (1871), detailed analysis of royal finances sent by West; copies ordered secretly for cabinet, Add MS 44341, f. 73; annotated copy in 44760, f. 143, and 44617, f. 159.

To E. CARDWELL, secretary for war, PRO 30/48/8, f. 122.
9 September 1871.

Your severe labours during the Session and the great ability and courage with which you encountered them give you a strong claim to repose in the recess but the stars are against you and your Department is and must for some time remain, I fear, in *crisis*.

This too, I think is true in more ways than one. The first, in the directness of its bearing upon the position of the country the party and the Government is the routine one of the Estimates. They will be the *key* to our position at the outset of the Session. We may announce Bills, but nobody will believe in them (unreasonable as the unbelief will be), except the Ballot; and that is discounted. On the Estimates will depend our chance of a fair start. Not that this is the consideration which will weigh most with my mind, or yours; but it is I think a truth, & a truth which will tell.

The question now seems to lie thus. The crisis of July 1870, so far as it affected us has gone by; and has left in a state of weakness by land, & yet more by sea, the only country in Europe that has the power of being formidable to us. That crisis brought up, however, demands for reorganisation which do not depart with it & which entail an expenditure such as has raised our estimates for 71–2 to a height which seems to me for a continuance intolerable. I do not suppose we can quite (I mean apart from Purchase) go back to February 1870: but we have to consider how far can we go back, towards the standard of that date?

Of course I do not suppose that even you, and much less that I can form a detailed estimate, or that a precise figure can be pointed out. But I think the country will (things remaining as they are), expect, and I should say justly expect, as a minimum, that of the four million in round numbers (Purchase included) which we have added, two millions at any rate should be taken off. Towards this, reduction of numbers might liberally contribute. And Goschen I hope (but I have had no correspondence with him as yet) would be able to take off, in something like the proportion in which the Admiralty partook of the Vote of Credit.

With this connects itself the question of your reserve; the only further point on which I need trouble you today. How is it coming on? And, more particularly, have you reason to be satisfied with the disposition of the Regimental Officers to assist and encourage entry into it? Have you like reason, with respect to the Horse Guards? Can anything be done, by giving those regiments which supply men to the reserve a prior claim if called into act[ive] service on the men they supply, (or other wise,) to contrive for them an *interest* in promoting the formation of the reserve? If the officers are unduly backward, or if the Horse Guards is [*sic*] shy, have you thought of calling on the Duke of C. to issue a strong circular on the subject?

Probably you are very busy at present with your campaign; and though I was desirous to place these points before you, there is no reason why I should press you for a very early answer.[1]

To the Editor of the *Liverpool Daily Post*, Add MS 44540, f. 105.
9 September 1871.

Mr. Gladstone begs to thank the Editor of the Liverpool Daily Post for an

[1] See 12 Sept. 71n.

interesting article in the paper sent to Hawarden.[1] As the Editor has been led to touch upon the subject, he may perhaps smile when told that when Mr. Gaskell and Mr. Gladstone were at Oxford, Dr. Hampden was regarded as a model of orthodoxy; that Dr. Newman was eyed with suspicion as a Low Churchman (and Dr. Pusey as leaning to Rationalism);[2] and that it was not till three or four [years] after the period named that these Divines respectively acquired any other character before the public. As to politics, both Mr. Gaskell and Mr. Gladstone took Mr. Canning for their great *Exemplar*; and Mr. Gaskell in particular had from the very first strong leanings in matters of religious politics. There is nothing confidential in mere particulars themselves, but it would be inconvenient that Mr. Gladstone should be made in any way responsible for them.

10. 14 S.Trin.

Ch mg & evg. Wrote to Sir Hamilton Seymour—Ld Granville—Mr West—Robn G.—& minutes. Read Union Review—Abp Manning's Four Sermons[3]—Carroll's Tract.[4] Gave an exercise to M., H., & H.

11. M.

Ch. 8½ AM. Wrote to Mr Hammond—Mrs Hampton—Mr Gurdon—Ld Hartington (Telegram)—and minutes. Went with C. and S. to the Aston Works to see the Vases made there. The J.G. Talbots came. Read Lewis on the Influence of Authority in matters of opinion[5]—Picture of Verdun—Spectator—Ivanhoe. The tournament[6] is a truly wonderful description. Wrote Mema on Lewis.[7]

Tu.12.

Ch. 8½ AM. Wrote to Messrs Low & Thomas—Mr Cardwell—Mr Gurdon—Bp of Salisbury—J.W. Patten—Mr Macfie—Mr Glyn—Mr Wm Gladstone—and minutes. Tree cutting with S. Read Low & Thomas on RR. to India—Picture of Verdun—Spectator—Ivanhoe. Read Lewis & made notes.

[1] Its leader of 8 September described diarist's early toryism as 'more fanatical' than Eldon's; this reply not published.

[2] Secretary's copy reads 'Ritualism' but Morley's marginal correction is surely correct; Gladstone later used much the same phrase, see J. Telford, *Life of J. H. Rigg* (1909?), 181.

[3] H. E. *Manning, 'The four great evils of the day' (1871); see 13 Sept. 71.

[4] W. G. Carroll, *The collapse of the Faith* (1871).

[5] By Sir G. C. *Lewis (1849); Gladstone had requested a copy from Sir G. F. Lewis.

[6] i.e. in *Ivanhoe*.

[7] Untraced.

To E. CARDWELL, secretary for war, PRO 30/48/8, f. 132.
12 September 1871.

1. Your reply[1] about Estimates is all I could ask or expect from you; taking into view the season of the year.
2. Should you see cause to desire the authority of the Cabinet for any step to impel the military authorities in the direction of favouring the reserve, my impression is that you might have it by Memorandum sent round without a meeting for the purpose.
3. With respect to your question as to Barracks for the Auxiliary forces. I do not know up to what point we are committed; but I may say that my inclination would be to look a. at the nature of the charge b. at the likelihood of its recurrence c. at its amount d. at its distribution in point of time. If the amount is not very large, the object not clearly marked as extraordinary and unlikely to recur, or the outlay already from the nature of the case self-distributed over a number of years so as to bring the annual charge within reasonable bounds, then I should say the question of providing for it by Terminable Annuity cannot fairly arise. If the reverse of all these be the case, then it may. You will know better than I do how in the particular instance the conditions would be fulfilled.

To Messrs. LOWE & THOMAS of Wrexham, Add MS 44540, f. 106.
12 September 1871.

I have read with much interest the pamphlet in which you have drawn so lucid an outline of the vast undertaking of a Railway from London to Karrachee & Bombay.[2] After what has been accomplished in the present age, it would be neither wise nor equitable to remain indifferent to the proposed undertaking: it is new or strange. It has this presumptive title to favorable attention that its object is alike beneficent & important. But I do not conceive that the Government of this country is the proper judge of the important question, whether that object is at present attainable. This is the business of Capitalists & of Engineers. They are the proper authorities in the case; & it is to consent & concurrence among them that the Government must look in the first instance, before diplomatic or other public action can be entertained. It would be a grave error on our part, were we to assume a responsibility which belongs to those who are to supply the means for the undertaking, & to guarantee its execution. Nor do I see what more can now be stated on our part, than that we should regard with favour, & should wish other Powers to regard in like manner, any well devised plan for extending the intercourse between Europe & India.

13. Wed.

Ch 8½ AM. Wrote to Dean of Ch Ch—Mr Graham—Mr Glyn[3]—Dr Candlish—Mr Bruce—Ld Houghton—Mr Forster—Watsons—&

[1] Of 10 September 1871, Add MS 44119, f. 264. Cardwell's draft scheme took off '(irrespective of Purchase) a million and a half', the half million involving a reduction in numbers. Cardwell argued that payment of barracks should not fall entirely on the annual vote.

[2] Printed in *The Times*, 11 October 1871, 12b.

[3] Asking his advice on accepting the Freedom of Aberdeen; Add MS 44540, f. 107. See 26 Sept. 71.

minutes. Conversation with Herbert[1] on his future profession: also a Latin exercise. No one can be more amiable: & his ideas are sensible. Dinner party. Clearing a plantation with S. Read Spectator—Picture of Verdun (finished)—Lewis on Authority.

To LORD HOUGHTON, 13 September 1871. Houghton MSS.

I cordially reciprocated your regrets for a meeting with you is always both pleasant and instructive.

Your criticisms[2] on my speech at Whitby are marked by a kindly tone which is habitual with you. Though I do not agree in every thing you say about property, I am at a loss to recognise any conflict between it and any part of the Speech: and cannot but think you may have been misled by some abstract or inaccurate report. In *petto* I have a good deal to say about property or rather wealth: but I have never said it. At Whitby I spoke of it only in two views: its domination in the Clubs, and in the army. But I think that in a political view the spirit of ploutocracy requires to be vigilantly watched and checked. It is a bastard aristocracy, & aristocracy shows too much disposition, in Parliament especially, to join hands with this bastard.

In a religious point of view I believe the case to be yet worse, and I groan over the silence and impotence of the pulpit. I almost wish for a Savonarola or part of one. Manning has said some good things about it in the second of Four Sermons just published.

What stupidity to alter the name of the Corso, & other streets in Rome. I would keep the Sow. Can anything be done? Remember Hawarden, if you come this way. I go on 25th to Balmoral.

14. Th.

Ch. 8½ AM. Wrote to The Queen (Mem.)—Dean of Lichfield—Robn G.—Mr Anderson—Scotts—and minutes. Worked in the Plantation. Read Spectator—Ivanhoe—'The Famous Whore'[3]—Mr Parker's Roman Papers.[4] Unpacking & arranging books.

15. Fr.

Ch. 8½ AM. Wrote to Mr E. Freshfield—Ld Halifax—Mr Stuart—Mr Hammond (letter & Telegr.)—Mr S.W. Hill[5]—Ld Mulgrave—Ld Sandhurst—Mr Glyn—and minutes. Saw the forester respecting divers trees to be taken down. Read Spectator—Ivanhoe—Macaulay's Bacon.[6]

[1] Went up to University College, Oxford, 1872, initially to read classical moderations.
[2] Of 10 September 1871, Add MS 44215, f. 74: 'there is a Demon, not of Demogogism but of Demophilism, that is tempting [you]'.
[3] Untraced.
[4] J. H. *Parker, 'Roman exploration fund' (1871).
[5] Librarian and amateur artist in Whitby; Add MS 44540, f. 111.
[6] T. B. *Macaulay, 'Lord Bacon', *Critical and historical Essays*, ii (1843).

16. Sat.

Ch. 8½ AM. Wrote to the Lord Chancellor—Chancr of Exr—Mr Goschen—Ld Lyttelton—Lady Cleveland—Mr E. Griffiths[1]—Lady Loudoun[2]—Mr Hammond—Miss Linskill[3]—& minutes. Mr Glyn came—conversation with him. Read Ivanhoe—Macaulay's Bacon—Parker on Catacombs—Smith on Julian.[4] Employed in clearing a plantation—with S. & H.

To G. J. GOSCHEN, first lord, 16 September 1871. Add MS 44540, f. 112.

I have been writing to Cardwell about the Estimates, to the effect that we ought in the next Session to present them, between Army & Navy, circumstances continuing as they now are, with a diminution of not less than two millions. His reply leads me to believe that he will be able to do his share of that work. That share I have not assumed to be in the same ratio as the increase since the Estimates of 1870, because changes, & consequent charges, have been called for in the Army to which there is nothing similar in the case of the Navy. But I have supposed it to be about $\frac{2}{3}$ as against $\frac{1}{3}$, or in the ratio in which the Vote of Credit, which was the true measure of our war preparations, was divided. I hope it will not be very difficult for you to come up to this standard. From Childers, I used to understand that, when the extended or accelerated building operations, to which the Vote of Credit was applied, should have been cancelled, matters could without violent effort return to their old course. I do not ask you at this very early date for an answer definite as to details: but I have no doubt that even now there must be matters of business coming forward, which will be affected one way or another by the views you may see cause to entertain respecting the Estimates of next year. I will not trouble you with particulars, but I hope you may think my hopes reasonable.[5]

17. 15 S.Trin.

Ch mg (with H.C.) and evg. Wrote to Ld Provost of Aberdeen[6]—Dean of Windsor—Mr J. Watson—Mr Gurdon—and minutes. Stephy preached in evg: excellent matter. Conversation with Mr Webb[7] on Zacchaeus: and research among Commentators. Read L'Abbadie on the Eucharist[8]—Sermons by Thomson.[9]—&c. Conversation with Glyn.

18. M.

Church 8½ AM. Wrote to D. of Argyll—Mr Sotheron Estcourt—Lady Herbert—Mr Hammond—Mr T.B. Potter—and minutes.

[1] Unidentified. [2] Edith Maud Abney-Hastings, 1833-74, countess of Loudoun.
[3] Mary *Linskill, 1840-91, novelist. See 30 Aug. 71.
[4] i.e. *Smith's *Classical Dictionary*; see 10 Oct. 56n.
[5] Printed in Elliot, *Goschen*, i. 115 with Goschen's reply.
[6] Agreeing to go to accept the freedom of the city; see 26 Sept. 71.
[7] i.e. the ecclesiologist; see 4 July 57.
[8] J. Abbadie, 'Chemical change in the Eucharist' (1867).
[9] Perhaps J. Thomson, 'A sermon on the nature of theism' (1870).

Conversation with Mr Webb—Mr Glyn—Mr Parker. Tree cutting: & discussion on the very difficult elm in the Stable yard. Read Spectator—Ivanhoe—Sir G. Lewis on Authority. Large party.

To E. HAMMOND, 18 September 1871. PRO FO 391/24.

If I understand rightly the draft of Treaty proposed by France it is not worth the paper it is written on & indeed that paper ought itself to blush. Instead of a most favoured nation Clause it seems to place the stipulations themselves during the limited term of the Treaty at the mercy of the Assembly. I hope I am wrong. And if there really is anything to discuss I would suggest that that should now be done which the Cabinet asked but which France has not thought proper to do for us: videlicet that a paper should be drawn showing in parallel columns 1. the present Treaty. 2. The conditions, proposed to be substituted (in outline) & adding a brief note of the commercial changes effected or occasioned as part of the present French policy though outside the Treaty.

19. Tu.

Ch. 8½ AM. Wrote to Mr Thornewill—Ld Granville—Mr Bruce[1]—Ld Monck—& minutes. Clearing a plantation with S. & H. in aftn. Large party. Conversation with Mr Glyn. Finished Macaulay's Bacon—Read Ivanhoe—Spectator.

Wed. 20.

Ch. 8½ AM. Wrote to Mr Hamilton—Mr Hammond—Ld Hartington—Padin Woon (Burmese)[2]—Mr E. Robinson[3]—and minutes. Latin translation lesson with Herbert. Saw Mr Burnett. In the forenoon we brought the tree down: large audience, much sensation, a narrow escape for the Stables. Went with Mr B[urnett] to Mold & saw the stock & sheep at the show. Read Sir G. Lewis—Ivanhoe.

21. Th. St Matthew

Ch. 11 AM. Wrote to Mrs Thistlethwayte—Ld Kimberley—Ld Lifford[4]—Dean of Waterford—Robn G.—Sir F. Heygate—H.N.G.—

[1] Requesting an inquiry into working of the 1860 wine licences (see above, v. xxxii); Add MS 44540, f. 115. See 24 Aug. 71.

[2] Sec. to king of Burma; Add MS 44430, ff. 41, 53 etc.; on an interview.

[3] Of Dukinfield, apparently a miner; Gladstone answered his complaint (untraced) of lack of working class legislation: 'If any of the miners are dissatisfied with our conduct, I do not think that feeling wd. be removed by any professions or promises I cd. make; & I wd. rather we shd. be judged by our acts than by our words', pointing to Irish Land, Education and the Ballot as 'mainly concerned with the welfare of the labouring population'; Add MS 44540, f. 116.

[4] James Hewitt, 1811-87; 4th Viscount Lifford 1855; on an application for a post; see Add MS 44540, f. 117.

Ld Chancellor[1]—Mr Jackson—and minutes. Read Spectator—Ivanhoe—what a noble book.—Sir G. Lewis on Authority. Went with S. to cut my own Aston trees in afternoon.

22. Fr.

Ch. 8½ AM. Wrote to Mr Hammond (Tel.)—Ld Provost of Aberdeen—Col. Ponsonby—Duke of Argyll—Mr Lock—Mr Gurdon—Dean of Windsor—Mr McClure MP., and minutes. Cutting with S., about the old castle. Read Lewis—Ivanhoe—Spectator. Party in evg.

23. Sat.

Ch. 8½ AM. Long conversation with Dr Clark respecting the Queen. Wrote to Mrs Wm Gladstone—Ld Granville—Mr Goschen—Ld Dufferin—Mr Gurdon—Count Cadorna—and minutes. Walk with Dr Clark. Read Lewis (finished)—Ivanhoe (finished)—Spectator.

24. 16 S Trin.

Ch. mg & evg. Saw Mr Burnett. Wrote to Abp Manning—Mr Vernon Darbishire—Mr Ffoulkes—Mrs Ross[2]—and minutes. Read Huntington's Work of the Ch. in large towns[3]—Amy Dutton (Miss Wilbraham)—Mr Wilkinson on the Inner Life—Ffoulkes's Sermon—Farrar's do[4] . . . &c.

25. M. [On train]

Ch. 8½ A.M. Wrote to Ld Granville—Mr Cardwell—Mr Glyn—and minutes. Packing and preparing for departure. Began a Mem. on Selection of Officers.[5] Examined some of the old Trees about the castle with C. Off to Chester & Lpool at 3.30. Dined with Robn & his sons at Courthey. Left Edgehill by the 11 P.M. Train for Perth and Aberdeen. Read Marcus Antoninus waiting at Newton.

[1] Sending 'What does she do with it?' (see 9 Sept. 71): 'The writer . . . exaggerates extremely; but on the other hand he omits *much* that wd. be in favour of his case'; Add MS 44540, f. 117.

[2] Wife of J. L. Ross, see 24 Nov. 29.

[3] See 18 Sept. 64.

[4] *The streets and lanes of a city, being the reminiscences of Amy Dutton* (1871); G. H. Wilkinson, *Instructions in the devotional life* (1871); E. S. *Ffoulkes, 'Union at Home first' (1871); F. W. *Farrar, 'The conquest over temptation' (1871).

[5] See 5 Oct. 71.

26. Tu. [*Balmoral Castle*]

Reached Perth at 9 A.M. Saw the Lord Provost.[1] Warmly received there, & at the roadside Stations. Aberdeen at 12.15. Spoke in the Music Hall at 2: afterwards briefly to the Working Men; & at the Lord Provost's luncheon. There was much enthusiasm for the Government. Off at 4.25 with Ld Huntley whom I liked. Also was struck with Mr Barclay. Reached Balmoral at 6.40. Saw Col. Ponsonby. Conversation with Sir W. Jenner on the Queen's health & regime. Playing 'battle' in evg. Read Epictetus.[2] Wrote to The Queen (& copy)—C.G.[3]

27. Wed.

Wrote to Ld Granville—Mr Stansfeld—Mr Gurdon—Mr Whalley—Sir R. Church—Ld Prov. Aberdeen—Mrs Th.—Ld Prov. Perth—Archbp Manning—& minutes. Conversation with Sir W. Jenner on branches of Education—With Col. Ponsonby on the state of feeling about the R. Family—With Princess Louis of Hesse[4] at dinner. Read Epictetus. Fielding's Amelia.[5]

28. Th.

Wrote to Ld Hartington—Count Maffei—Mr Jackson—Dean Ramsay—Ld Halifax—Ld Provost of Aberdeen—C.G.—& minutes. Conversation with Mr Lumley—Sir T. Biddulph (H. Park &c.)—Princess Louis, whose walk I joined, by invitation. Read Amelia—Johnny Gibb,[6] with the help of Jamieson's Dictionary.[7]

To LORD HARTINGTON, Irish secretary, 28 September 1871. 'Secret.' Chatsworth MSS 340. 469.

The Cabinet will meet on the 21 October at latest, sooner if the Foreign Office should require it, but there are several matters which may quite well be considered

[1] Who proposed he return to accept the freedom of the city; Gladstone declined; Add MS 44540, f. 123.

[2] *Works*, tr. T. W. Higginson (1865).

[3] Letters on the visit are in Bassett, 190 ff. Description of Aberdonian ceremonies in *The Times*, 27 Sept. 1871, 6a; the speech was partly on Home Rule, see 25 Nov. 71 and J. R. Vincent, 'Gladstone and Ireland', *Proc. Brit. Acad.*, lxiii, 232.

[4] i.e. Princess Alice; see 2 June 43.

[5] See 6 Sept. 42.

[6] [W. Alexander], *Johnny Gibb of Gushetneuk, in the parish of Pyketillim; with glimpses of the parish politics about A.D. 1843* (1871). Gladstone told William Alexander (d. 1894, ed. *Aberdeen Free Press*) of 'its merits as a vigorous & truthful delineation of local character drawn from a portion of the country where that character is most peculiarly worthy of study & record'; 4 March 1872, Add MS 44541, f. 87.

[7] J. *Jamieson, *An etymological dictionary of the Scottish language*, 2v. (1808).

before we touch upon Irish policy or legislation, so far as I am able to judge of them.

It appears to me that we can hardly reckon on disposing of the question of Irish University Education next year. But with Fawcett's Bill we must deal. And I incline to think we may, if driven to it, do this by accepting the Anti-Test Clause or Clauses, & striking out the reconstruction. The objection to this is, perhaps, that it would weaken the inducements of the Liberal party to support a measure of University reconstruction when afterwards attempted. But there may be very little choice left us in the matter, as the bulk of the Conservatives, will, I think, discreditably enough join hands with Fawcett in the business, to baulk the Roman Catholics, & as they think embarrass the Government. Can you when in Ireland learn, but with the *utmost secrecy* whether the Roman Catholic party would acquiesce in the passing next year of a measure for the abolition of Tests only? I say with the utmost secrecy, for I would far rather remain entirely silent than that the smallest indication should be given to those who might make ill use of it, that we entertained such an idea.

[P.S.] The Queen is now making considerable & satisfactory progress. NB. I have had no information about the Fenian soldiers.

29. Fr. St Michael

Wrote to Ld Hartington—D of Argyll—Mr Angerstein[1]—Ld Granville—Ld Sandhurst—Mr Ayrton—Mr Proctor—Dr Miller—Sir T. Biddulph—Mr Bruce—C.G.—& minutes. Conversation with Dr Robn on Deer Forests—Sir T. Biddulph Hampton Court Park. Read Fraser's Poems—J. Gibb—Fielding's Amelia. Dined with the P. of Wales at Abergeldie.[2] Played whist, against him. He showed great memory.

30. Sat.

Wrote to Mr Gurdon—Dean of Windsor—S.E.G.—Sir J. Bowring—C.G.—and minutes. Wrote on Army Officers.[3] Read Fielding's Amelia. We had a philological discussion after breakfast. Conversation with Pss Louis, & P. Louis, at & after dinner.

17 S.Trin. Oct. One 1871.

Wrote to Ld Granville (2)—Ld Bessborough—Mr Glyn—Sir T. Biddulph—Mr Goschen—Sir F. Rogers—Ld Dufferin—The Queen (Mem)—Mr Parker—Mr Law—and minutes. Attended Crathie Ch in mg. Rain through the whole day. Read Life of Rev R. Davis[4]—Bp

[1] Arranging the Greenwich meeting; see 28 Oct. 71.

[2] His house near Balmoral.

[3] See 5 Oct. 71.

[4] J. N. Coleman, *A memoir of the Rev. R. Davis, for thirty-nine years a missionary in New Zealand* (1865).

of Worcester's Charge[1]—Part of Jackson on Positivism.[2] Well handled.

Audience Balmoral. Oct. 1. 71.[3]
Dublin Address—French Treaty—Honours, Dufferin, Rogers—Political Offices coming—Judicial appointments.

To G. G. GLYN, chief whip, 1 October 1871. Add MS 44540, f. 126.

1. I return Brand after perusing with interest. I do not feel certain whether we are precluded from granting Lopez a Commission should it be pressed. Though kind as ever he is very *landy*?[4] indeed. 2. I retain Coleridge's longer letter.[5] Perhaps it would be a good preparation for other proceedings were I at once to make the offer to Ld Penzance? There seem to me to be two sides to the proposal about Sir R. Palmer, with the land question in our view, on which he is a good deal committed. Our position is a peculiar one in this: each of our sections puts the pistol to our head (one much more rudely than the other) for having done too much for the other. 3. The Queen has greatly & steadily improved after a *severe* illness which was at one time near being dangerous. Disraeli has done much & varied mischief by his speech.[6] I go from here Wednesday morning, unless invited to stay on a little. Address: London. I am to be in Edinburgh a day or two.

2. M.

Wrote to C.G.—Mr Gurdon (l. & Tel.)—Mr Hammond (Tel)—Ld Granville—Ld Huntley & minutes. Wrote Mem. on French Treaty question.[7] Read Tract on Fr. Treaty—Fielding's Amelia (finished) —Johnny Gibb: who cracks me with laughter & for him alas I lay aside Epictetus and Marcus Antoninus. Called on Mrs Taylor (for Dr T.)[8]—Lady Biddulph.[9]

3. Tu.

Wrote to The Queen 2 (& copies)—Ld Granville—Sir Thos G.—Jane Robertson—J. Wortley—Mayor of Sheffield[10]—C.G.—Ld Chancellor—Mr Gurdon—Dean Ramsay—Mrs Th.—Sir T. Biddulph—and minutes. Long interview with H.M. She was very kind:

[1] See 9 July 71.
[2] W. Jackson, 'Positivism. A lecture . . .' (1871).
[3] Add MS 44757, f. 18.
[4] Queried by the copyist.
[5] Letter on J. D. Coleridge's future, suggesting Palmer as Attorney General; Add MS 44348, f. 137.
[6] Disraeli's speech on Victoria, that she was 'physically and morally incapacitated'; Buckle, v. 144.
[7] See 9 Oct. 71.
[8] Rev. Malcolm C. Taylor, minister at Crathie 1867-73.
[9] Mary Frederica, the queen's bedchamber woman, wife of Sir T. M. *Biddulph.
[10] Thanking him for a Resolution of support; Add MS 44540, f. 128.

& much better. Walk with Col. P[onsonby] in Glengairn. Read Johnny Gibb—Epictetus. Wrote Mema.

4. Wed. [Aboyne Castle]

Wrote to Mr Gurdon (Tel)—Lady C. Paget[1]—Ld Advocate—Sir B. Frere—Col. Ponsonby—Dr Hooker[2]—C.G.—and minutes. Saw Princess Louis & conversed about the Queen. Set out at 11 for Glen Muick and Ballater. A delightful walk: but I never love leaving this district. Nothing sets me up in mind & body like a mountain solitude: not even perhaps the sea. Read Epictetus—Johnny Gibb. Reached Aboyne at 5.45. Most kindly received.[3] Conversation with Rev. Mr Stephen:[4] & Col. Farquharson.[5]

5. Th.

Wrote to C.G.—Ld Granville—Mrs Weldon[6]—Mr Cardwell—Mr Walpole—& minutes. Screwed up my courage to finish my Memorandum on officering the Army.[7] Long walk with Ld H[untly] about his Estate. Arranged for my little mountain passage & Walter's journey. Conversation with Mr Stephen. Read Epictetus.

6. Fr. [Glen Clova]

Read Johnny Gibb—Bairn of the Dee (M'Gillivray).[8] After travelling arrangements, & packing my pockets, I went off: reached Ballater at 10.10. & went up the Valley of the Muick to the lake, over the long & broad back of the hills on the South and East, deeply trenched with bog & stream by a path hard to find in parts, but for poles &

[1] Martha, wife of Lord C. E. *Paget, unsuccessfully requested a peerage for him; Add MS 44540, f. 129.

[2] (Sir) Joseph Dalton *Hooker, 1817-1911, directed Kew Gardens 1865; on Ayrton's mismanagements there; Add MS 44540, f. 128.

[3] By the marquis of Huntly; a liberal and lord-in-waiting; see 6 July 70.

[4] Perhaps John Stephen, free church minister in Aberdeen.

[5] Probably George McBain Farquharson of Breda, Aberdeenshire. Version in Morley, ii. 379.

[6] Declining to give Georgina Weldon, litigant, an introduction to Thiers; Add MS 44540, f. 130.

[7] Printed, marked 'confidential'; Add MS 44760, f. 110; on safeguarding the State's ability to retire post-purchase officers without excessive expense; 'the best and most effectual mode of reserving this discretion would, it seems to me, be a notice that the commissions hereafter to be issued would not, until after the lapse of some moderate number of years, say, six or seven, entitle the receiver to the conditions of permanent service.' Copy in PRO 30/48/8, f. 170. The Warrant of 20 July 1871 required a further Warrant by 1 November 1871; see 25 Oct. 71.

[8] W. MacGillivray, perhaps *The natural history of Deeside and Braemar* (1855).

cairns: these are almost the very crown of Mount Capel with two very sharp & deep ravines right and left. The pit of Loch Muick made a fine object on one side surmounted by the Masses of Lochnagar: and the stream of the Glassalt with that from the Dhu Loch streaked the dark mass to the N.W. The first view into the open glen of Clova may be called grand.

Besides rests, it took me 2 h. 35 min, all uphill, from Ballater Station to the point of sighting the Glassalt House before well commencing the ascent from the Loch Valley: and 3.10 to the Inn at Clova, much of it level & more down hill, but with worn road over the back: The first is stated at 9 in Murray[1] I think rightly or nearly so. The latter also called 9 I take to be eleven or not far short of it. The lonely Inn was comfortable. But my heels only in middling condition.

7. Sat. [*Edinburgh*]

Managing protection for my heels as well as I could, I came down to breakfast and started at 8.25 15 miles (not 16 as Murray says) to Kirriemuir arriving with one rest of 10 min at 11.35. A beautiful though unequal walk. Taking the rail went to Forfar, thence to Perth & Edinburgh & reached Dean Ramsay's at 6.45. Found that dear friend well, & as affectionate as ever. He had a most agreeable dinner party with Ld Colonsay, the Ld Advocate,[2] Ld Benholme & others. Late conversation with him & bed at midnight. Read Johnny Gibb. NB. on Wed. I started at 11. Took 1 h. 55 m. to the fork of the road above the Muick: 30 more to the Linn: 45 to Birk Hall: 40 to Ballater. In all 4 h. 5 m. 15 miles. Non sum qualis eram.

8. 18 S.Trin.

St John's mg & aft. The Dean preached on Ruth. It was most striking & moving. A delightful day as usual. Drs Begbie & J. Brown[3] at dinner. Went with the Ld Advocate to see the Fettes College.[4] Much pleased with Mr Potts.[5] Read Guardian—Prayerbook weighed in the Balance[6]—&c. Wrote to Mr MacClure—C.G.—and minutes.

[1] *Murray's Handbook for Scotland*, route 51.
[2] G. Young (see 27 July 68); lord advocate 1869–74.
[3] Physicians; see 18 Oct. 50, 12 Dec. 59.
[4] Anglican boarding school (then in country) E. of Edinburgh.
[5] A. W. Potts, 1834–89, first headmaster of Fettes.
[6] Untraced.

9. M.

Drs Guthrie & Alexander[1] to breakfast: most pleasant. Finished Johnny Gibb. Read Dr L. Alexander on Incarnation.[2] Saw Ld Provost —Lady Burdett Coutts—Mr Morton Crown Agent (my 2d cousin)[3] —Large dinner party at Ld Advocate's—Saw his collection. Shopping in aft. Worked on French Treaty & finished Mem.[4] Wrote to Ld Westminster—Col. Ponsonby—C.G.—Ld Penzance—A.G.—Ld Granville—& minutes.

10. Tu.

Wrote to Ld Spencer—Mr Reverdy Johnson—Ld Dufferin—Ld Monck—Mr J.S. Wortley—Mr Gurdon—Sir S. Adair—Mr Bruce—Mr Gourley[5]—Mr Ellice—Station Mr at Warrington—Mr Capes—C.G.—and minutes. Read Dean Ramsay on Utterance.[6] Drive & shopping with him—Also much conversation. Saw Mr Shand's[7] pictures & China. Saw Dr Christison—Miss Scott—Mr Potts—Sol. General. Packed for departure.

11. Wed. [Hawarden]

Wrote to Mr Hubbard—Mr Cardwell—Mr Glyn—Messrs Farrer—Sir J. Gray—Govr of I. of Man[8]—C.G.—Miss Scott—Mrs Russell (P.C.)[9]—and minutes. A moving farewell at 10. Reached Hawarden soon after 6. Mr Rollo[10] & Miss Cochrane[11] *would* be at the Station. Arranged my matters for work. Read Hugessen's Article[12]—Proctor's Spiritualism[13]—Contemp.Rev. on Sir Geo. Mackenzie.[14]

[1] Divines; see 31 Dec. 49, 16 Apr. 60.

[2] W. L. Alexander, *The incarnation* (1871).

[3] Charles Morton, 1806-92; Edinburgh W.S. and Crown Agent; the relationship, presumably through Morton's mother, unestablished.

[4] See Ramm I, ii. 267 and 24 Oct. 71.

[5] Suggesting (Sir) Edward Temperley Gourley (1828-1902; liberal M.P. Sunderland 1868-1900; kt. 1895) send his proposals for a National Technical University to Forster; Add MS 44540, f. 132.

[6] E. B. *Ramsay, 'The art of reading and preaching distinctly' (1869).

[7] Probably John Shand, W.S., lived in Fettes Row.

[8] (Sir) Henry Brougham *Loch, 1827-1900; governed Man 1863-82, the Cape 1889-95; cr. Baron 1895. On difficulties of creating a bpric. in Liverpool; Add MS 44540, f. 134.

[9] Obscure; a rescue case, see 29 Oct. 71.

[10] H. J. Rollo, see 28 Nov. 55.

[11] Unidentified.

[12] [E. H. Knatchbull-*Hugessen], 'How is the work of the nation done?', *Macmillan's Magazine*, xxiv. 409 (October 1871); Gladstone told him (12 October 1871, Add MS 44540, f. 134): 'it seems to me, as a whole, an able & valuable contribution'.

[13] Perhaps in R. A. *Proctor, *Light science for leisure hours. Essays* (1871).

[14] *Contemporary Review*, xviii. 248 (September 1871).

12. Th.

Ch. 8.30 AM. Saw Mr Chamberlain. Wrote to Mr Hugessen—Mr Walpole—Mr Hamilton—Ld Chancellor (l. & Tel.)—Mr West—C.G.—and minutes. Cutting with Harry. Read Wood on Hamlet[1]—Macchiavelli's [*sic*] Discorsi[2]—Perricone on Macchiavelli[3]—Contagious Diseases Acts—T. Moore's Prefaces.[4]

13. Fr.

Ch. 8½ AM. Wrote to Bp of Winchester—Mr Watson—Mr Ouvry—Mr Butti[5]—C.G. (2)—Robn G.—and minutes. Read Moore, Fudge Family[6]—Macchiavelli, Storia[7]—Hoyle 'Our National Resources'.[8] Woodcutting in afternoon. Saw Mr Burnett—Agnes & Harry made painful communications about household. Spoke to Prisk[9] on them.

14. Sat.

Ch. 8½ AM. Wrote to Ld Granville (l. & Tel.)—Mr Rathbone—Mr Buxton—Sir S.R.G.—Mr Gurdon—Scotts—Robn G.—C.G.—and minutes. Woodcutting in aftn. Read Macchiavelli's Storia. The Spencers came. Two long conversations with him on Irish questions—Univ.—ViceRoy—Atty [General]—Ld Dufferin—Belfast invitn[10] & Home Rule. C. came. Conversation with her late.

15. 19 S.Trin.

Ch. 11 AM. with H.C. and 6½ PM. Wrote to Ld Chancellor—Mr Cardwell—Mr Walpole—Mr Goschen—Mr West—Sir T. Biddulph—Ld Granville—D. of Cambridge—and minutes. Several conversations with Ld Spencer on a long list of Irish matters. Also with C. on the troubles in the House. Read Bp of Brechin on Papal Infallibility.[11] A much invaded Sunday.

16. M.

Ch. 8½ AM. Wrote to Bp of Brechin—Dean Ramsay—Mr M'Gill—Mr Whalley MP—Mr West, Tel.—Att. General—& minutes. Further

[1] See 23 Jan. 71.
[2] First published in 1531.
[3] C. Perricone, *Su Niccolò Machiavelli* (1871).
[4] T. *Moore, *Works*, 2v. (1833).
[5] J. A. Butti, Edinburgh art dealer.
[6] T. *Moore, *The Fudge family in Paris* (1818).
[7] *Istorie Fiorentine*, first published 1532.
[8] W. *Hoyle, *Our national resources and how they are wasted* (1871).
[9] The governess?
[10] See 21 Oct. 71.
[11] A. P. *Forbes, *The Church of England and the doctrine of papal infallibility* (1871).

conversation with Ld S. Much occupied with the House troubles which however softened a good deal in appearance. Read Macchiavelli—Macrae's burlesques[1]—Keary on Nations Round.[2]

To Sir R. COLLIER, attorney general, Add MS 44540, f. 136.
16 October 1871. 'Private & Confidential.'

In consequence of some intimations which led me to suppose you were inclined to exchange your present very laborious office for the Bench, I am desirous to mention the only opening which now exists, & to enquire whether it would be agreeable to you to take one of the appointments to be made to the Judicial Committee under the act of the last Session.

Had Ld. Penzance vacated the Divorce Court, I should have hastened to offer & submit your name to the Queen for it; but he has declined to move.

In making my present offer I hope you will understand it as an offer only: glad as I shall be if it pleases you, I shall also be glad if you continue to give us your able assistance on the Treasury Bench.[3]
I do not refer to the *incidents* of the appointment for they must be more fully & freshly within your knowledge than my own.

To A. P. FORBES, bishop of Brechin, Add MS 44540, f. 137.
16 October 1871.

Accept my best thanks for the tract you have sent me taken from your recent charge. Apart from this or that shade of colour, & point of opinion, it is to me singularly refreshing. As I am bound to say on the other hand it is very rare to read an argument of this kind couched so deeply in the historical as distinguished from the polemical spirit, upon the cardinal questions relating to the Church of Rome & to the Reformation. I earnestly hope it may attract much public attention; & cannot help wishing it had appeared as part of the entire charge, as the public is more accustomed to that kind of document especially in the case of Bishops. The para. which begins in page 29 seems to me 'all gold' & I follow with strong general sympathy what follows to the end.

Pray remember in case of your coming to London after Easter our breakfasts on Thursday at 10. I go Southwards on Friday.
I have been staying with Dean Ramsay who had been greatly struck with the charge.

17. Tu.

Ch. 8½ AM. Wrote to D. of Devonshire—Ld Granville—Ld Lurgan—Col. Ponsonby—Col. Hogg—Warden of A. Souls—Sir J. Gray—Ld Monck—Mr Glyn—and minutes. Reconnoitred trees with C. who returned to London: & cutting with Willy. In the forenoon we

[1] D. Macrae, *Diogenes among the D.D.'s: a book of burlesques* (1883 first traced ed.).
[2] A. Keary, *The nations around* (1870).
[3] Collier accepted; he had to be made a judge *en route* thus provoking a 'noisy scuffle'; Morley, ii. 382.

further examined the house feuds & accusations: & at last thank God reached a fair ending. Read Macchiavelli—Malden on Universities[1] —Scott's Introdn & Notes.[2]

18. Wed. St Luke.

Ch. 11 AM. Wrote to Fletcher & Co.[3]—Ld Houghton—Mr Parker —Mr O. Morgan—Robn G.—Mr Tremenhere[4]—C.G.—Mr . . .[5] (Greenwich)—Mr West (Tel)—Mrs Th.—and minutes. Cut a large beech with Willy. Read Macchiavelli—Scott's Introductions.

19. Th.

Ch. 8½ AM. Wrote to Ld Granville—Mr J. Watson—Miss Scott—D. of Argyll—Mr Glyn—Mr Strahan—C.G.—Bp of Ely—Mr West 2 Tel.—and minutes. Read Macchiavelli—Scott's Introductions—Lucian's Dialogi Deorum. Saw Sir Thos. Frost.[6]

To G. G. GLYN, chief whip, 19 October 1871. Add MS 44540, f. 140.

Thanks for this curious letter.[7] It is desirable to get to the bottom of the matter. The wizard of Hughenden Manor is behind the scenes. I wish you would quickly move Brand to develop his idea about the Ld Lcy. of Ireland. Why he mentions it now, & what he thinks of the feeling of the House.
I think Gray would be a very good man. Will you move him or shall I?

20. Fr. [London]

Ch. 8½ AM. Wrote to Mr Lingen. Willy & I spent 2½ hours in cutting a beech wh made a fine fall. His brave little terrier pup ran barking at it as it fell. Packing & putting away. Read Scott, Introdn. Left Hawarden 4.15. Arr. C.H.T. 10.50. Went to work upon my chaos. Saw Wilton[R].

[1] See 20 May 48.
[2] *The poetical works of . . . Scott . . . with all his introductions, notes . . . ,* ed. J. G. Lockhart (1857).
[3] Wine merchants.
[4] Giving a C.B. to H. Seymour Tremenhere, inspector of mines.
[5] i.e. James Spencer on arrangements for the Blackheath meeting; Add MS 44540, f. 139, 28 Oct. 71.
[6] Sir Thomas Gibbons Frost, 1820-1904; liberal mayor of Chester 1868-9 and in 1880s; kt. 1869; see 9 Sept. 73.
[7] Untraced, and no reply found.

21. Sat.

Cabinet 2½-5¾. Wrote to Justice Willes—Sir J. Colvile[1]—The Queen—& minutes. Saw Ld Chancellor—Lord Granville—Mr Forster—Mr Glyn—Mr Cardwell—and then together—D. of Argyll—Ld Ripon—Mr West & Mr Gurdon. Mr Glyn dined: long conversation. Read the new Q.R.—Tract on Metr.Dist. RR.[2]

Cabinet. Oct. 21. 71. 2.30[3]

√ 1. French Treaty. Circulate papers. Cons[ider at] next Cabinet.[4]
√ 2. Offices of Att. & Sol. General. Next Cabinet.[5]
√ 3. Univ. Commission. WEG to prepare letter.[6]
√ 4. Army Selection.[7]
O 5. WEG: invitation to, from Belfast.[8] (to see Hartington.
√ 6. Abp. [of] Cant[erbury] & Bp. W[ilberforce]. Ch[urch] legislation difficult to undertake new[?] matter likely to create division or take time with uncertain prospects.[9] Bp. of Ely. Suffragans.
O 7. Suffragan for Ely. saw Chancr.
√ 8. Fenians in San Francisco } conversation.
Compensation for Raid }
√ Course of business in the next Session. Considered 1. Ballot. 2. Scotch Ed[ucatio]n. 3. Mines. 4. Cont[agious] Diseases. 5. Corrupt Practices. Subject to what may be decided as to Irish Educ[atio]n.
√ 10. Cutting out of U.S. Vessel from N[ova] Scotia Port.[10] Ask for information.
√ 11. Sale of Saint Pierre[11] by France to U.S. Inquire *informally* as to the facts.

22. 20 S.Trin.

Kept my bed till 1½.—Morning prayers alone. Chapel Royal at 5.30. Wrote to Ld A. Clinton—Mr Lefevre—Mr M'Coll—and minutes. Saw Edith after her confinement: & a charming baby.[12] Long & interesting conversation with Abbé Michaud.[13] Read the Baptistery[14]—

[1] Offering paid membership of judicial cttee. of privy council to Sir James Shaw Willes (see 4 Feb. 52n.), 1814-72; Irish judge from 1855; a suicide. Also to Sir James William Colvile, 1810-80, already on it.

[2] He was a shareholder.

[3] Add MS 44639, f. 101.

[4] Chambers of commerce representations etc., F.O.C.P. 2057.

[5] See 24 Oct. 71.

[6] See 24 Oct. 71.

[7] See 5 Oct. 71.

[8] Declined; Gladstone told his prospective host, Lurgan, 'nothing could be more agreeable to me personally than to accept it'; Add MS 44540, f. 138.

[9] Ritual Commission's proposals, and resignation of cathedral dignitaries; see *Tait to Gladstone, 1 November 1871, Add MS 44330, f. 209, and Add MS 44540, f. 134.

[10] 'Samuel Gilbert' incident: PRO CO 880/6/209.

[11] Report from Lyons on island off Newfoundland; remains French; CAB 41/3/38.

[12] i.e. his great-niece, Agnes Susan Elizabeth Dumaresq.

[13] Eugène Philibert Michaud, 1839-1917, old-catholic theologian and apologist.

[14] By [I. *Williams]; see 31 Dec. 43.

Church Work in Honolulu[1]—Pusey's Essay on Union[2] & other matter.

23. M.

Wrote to Sir G. Pollock—Mr Fortescue—Vice Chancellors of O. & C. *dft*—Lady Willes (Tel.)—and minutes. Saw Duke of Argyll—D. of Cambridge *cum* Mr Cardwell—Mr Murray—Christies—Mrs Th —Mr Glyn—Miss Cooper.[3] Read Capes on the Movement.[4]

24. Tu.

Wrote to The Queen Mem.—Mr Stephenson—Mr Monsell—Sir T.E. May—Mr Bright—Chancr of Exr—Mr Lock—The Queen—Gen. Fytche[5]—and minutes. Cabinet 2½–6½. Saw Ld Hartington—Abp Manning—Mr Glyn—Rev. M. M'Coll—Sir W. James—Ld Halifax. Read Secularist Hymn Book[6]—Reverdy Johnson v. Roundell Palmer.[7] The Jameses dined.

Cabinet Tues. Oct. 24/71. 2½ PM[8]

√ French Treaty. Lengthened discussion.
√ Army Warrant partially considered.
√ Offices of Att. & Sol. General. Salaries to be 6700 & £ 6000 + the fees for contentious business.[9]
√ Letter to Vice Chancellors. Passage read & approved.[10]

French Treaty.[11] Discussion without divisions.
For going on: Fortescue, Forster, Halifax. *Against*: Kimberley, Granville, Lowe, Gladstone, Argyll.
Middle: Goschen, Cardwell, Hartington. *Silent*: Bruce, Chancellor, Ripon, Stansfield [*sic*].

[1] Perhaps W. Ellis, *The American mission in the Sandwich Islands* (1866).
[2] E. B. *Pusey, 'An Eirenicon. Part 3' (1870).
[3] Unidentified.
[4] J. M. Capes, 'Prospects of the new German Reformation', *Contemporary Review* (October 1871).
[5] Albert Fytche, 1820–92; recently back from India after illness.
[6] Sent by J. W. Watson; see next day. He quoted, at Blackheath on 28 Oct., from this 'questionable book, verses which I think contain much good sense'; see Bassett, *Speeches*, 423.
[7] R. Johnson, 'A reply to a recent speech of Sir R. Palmer on the Washington Treaty and the Alabama claims' (1871).
[8] Add MS 44639, f. 103.
[9] *Collier's controversial move to the judicial cttee. of the privy council allowed J. D. *Coleridge's promotion to attorney general, and the appointment as solicitor general of (Sir) George *Jessel, 1824–83, liberal M.P. Dover 1868–73; master of the rolls 1873; the first Jewish judge.
[10] Sent this day, asking their cooperation in a Commission on Oxford and Cambridge property and revenues; if not a statutory commission would be required; printed in *The Times*, 2 Nov. 1871, 5d.
[11] For the French proposals, see *PP* lxx. 323.

To John BRIGHT, M.P., 24 October 1871. Add MS 43385, f. 156.

After the improved accounts I have seen of your health, in various forms, & after our relations in politics & in the Cabinet, which have left behind them on my part indelible recollections, I am sure you will excuse my writing to say how very much I desire an opportunity of seeing you, to converse with you on the state of public affairs. Though in 1869 & 1870 some problems seemed to find a solution, yet more remain behind; & those who have official responsibility must ever feel a natural anxiety to arm themselves with the best assistance & advice.

I am not certain whether I can assume that your health would permit you to come to London. If it does, I am sure you will not grudge the trouble. Before the middle of November, I hope to be at Hawarden, & there I well know my brother in law Sir S. Glynne would be very happy to see you. But the earlier any opportunity you could give me of meeting you, the better. Should you come to town, I hope you would allow me to find you a host, & to insure your not having any personal trouble or risk of discomfort in your visit. I should hope to be that host myself; but am a little uncertain as much of my house is still occupied by a niece who has been here for her first confinement.
[P.S.] On my showing this note to Granville, he expressed a hope that you should visit him in Bruton Street.[1]

25. Wed.

Wrote to Bishop of Worcester—Bishop of Ely[2]—Ld Chancellor—Mr Forster—Mr J. Watson—Sir W. Knollys—The Speaker—The Queen—Mr Murray—& minutes. Saw Bishop of Winchester—Ald. Salomons—Mr Glyn—Ld Granville *cum* Mr Glyn. Cabinet 2¾-6. C. & I dined at our old & valued friend Mrs Barber's.[3] Read O. Barrot on Centralisation.[4]

Cabinet Oct. 25. 71. 2½ PM.[5]
√ Kimberley announced a Telegram respecting the 'cutting out' in Nova Scotia.[6]
√ Army Warrant. Amended & agreed on.[7]
√ Megaera Commission. Agreed on. Names discussed partially.[8]

26. Th.

Wrote to Ld Granville—V.C. Cambridge—Ld Ripon—Ld Kimberley—Arthur Gordon[9]—and minutes. Dined with the Goschens. Saw

[1] Bright replied on 27 October, agreeing to come to Hawarden; Add MS 44112, f. 181. See 13 Nov. 71.
[2] Declining to give him a suffragan bp; Add MS 44540, f. 144.
[3] See 16 Aug. 50; she was housekeeper to the National Debt Office until 1873.
[4] C. H. O. Barrot, *De la centralization et de ses effets* (1861). See 10 Nov. 71.
[5] Add MS 44639, f. 107.
[6] See 21 Oct. 71.
[7] Details of promotion procedures without purchase; *London Gazette*, 31 October 1871.
[8] See 3 Nov. 71.
[9] See T.A.P.S. n.s. li, part 4, 59.

Mrs Beadel: also 3 X. Saw Mr Capes—Mr Glyn—Mr Webb—Ld Granville—Mr Forster *cum* Ld G. & D. of A. Read 'The Goodwife at home'[1]—Mrs Meteyard's Group of Englishmen.[2]

To LORD KIMBERLEY, colonial secretary, 26 October 1871. Add MS 44540, f. 145.

1. At length I reply to yours of the 22nd.[3] I agree to your scheme of a dispatch in reply to Sir H. Barkly; feeling sure that in opening the door to the re-incorporation of the Boer States in the Empire you will (as is your wont) take due precautions against extension of the responsibility of the H[ome] Govt. These States have been formed on the principles of self-defence; their inception was, I think due to our interfering with that policy; & I should see with regret any change which went to relieve them of what may indeed be a burden, but is also a duty & a source of strength & vitality. I also agree that the adoption of responsible government is to be looked [at] as an essential preliminary.
2. Having now heard Lady Gordon's as well as her husband's[4] account of their case as the parents of young children in the Mauritius, I would express an earnest hope that your arrangements may permit you to offer him an early change of government. The grounds of his desire are real: & he has shown, by referring to Trinidad, that he would not be fastidious; though I presume that reference only expressed what in the last resort he would be willing to do.

27. Fr.

Wrote to Ld Granville—The Speaker—The Queen—Mrs Russell—and minutes. 11-1½. Went to Sir R. Murchison's funeral: the last of those who had known me or of me from infancy.[5] And so a step towards the end is made visible. It was a *great* funeral. Cabinet 2¼-5½. Tea at Duchess of Somerset's: much conversation on the Newcastle family.[6] Eight to dinner. Saw Mr Glyn (2)—Mr Cardwell—The Lord Chancellor. Read Fawcett in Fortnightly.[7]

Cabinet Oct. 27. 2 PM.[8]

○ French Treaty. (Draft now prepared to be printed for Cabinet.)
√ Contagious Diseases. Bruce will propose plan. Cabinet nearly all prepared to give up *all* compulsory exam[inatio]n.

[1] Possibly [L. M. Alcott], *Good Wives* (1871).
[2] E. *Meteyard, *A group of Englishmen . . . being records of the younger Wedgwoods* (1871).
[3] Add MS 44224, f. 212: 'a Confederation [in S. Africa] under British rule . . . would be very desirable', predicated on 'responsible government' at the Cape.
[4] i.e. Sir A. Gordon.
[5] *Murchison's and Gladstone's mothers had been close friends; Robbins, 8. See Morley, ii. 380.
[6] Lord A. Clinton faced court martial; see Add MS 44540, f. 141.
[7] H. *Fawcett, 'The House of Lords', *Fortnightly Review*, xvi. 491 (October 1871).
[8] Add MS 44639, f. 111.

√ Irish Education. Ld Hartington: Univ. question. Cabinet disposed not to legislate but meet F[awcett] by accepting Test Clause & by a Resolution.[1]
√ Greenwich Speech. WEG invited contributions, or cautions.
√ Parliamentary business. Sir E. May. WEG to propose an informal conversation.
√ Speaker. to have no pension. WEG to mention the subject.
Speaker's pension.[2] Coleridge. Cardwell respecting Speakership.[3]
√ Feejee Islands. Tell N[ew] S[outh] Wales if they like to frame a plan for annexing, we will entertain it, with proper native consents.[4]

28. Sat. SS.Simon & Jude.

Wrote to Solr General—Mr Glyn—& minutes. 11-12. French Exhibn of pictures. Reviewed subjects & made notes for Greenwich. 1¾-6. My expedition to G. or rather Blackheath: a vast assemblage; I spoke 1 h. 50 min.; too long yet really not long enough for a full development of my points: physically rather an excess of effort. All went well thank God.[5]

6-7. Saw MM Ozanne [*sic*] & Tissot[6] on the French Treaty. Saw one X. Read Gaume[7]—Secular Hymn Book—Finished R. Johnson v. Palmer.

29. 21 S.Trin.

Chapel Royal; and Bedfordbury Chapel evg. Saw Sir H. Holland—Sir W. James—Mrs Th. X.—Mrs Russell: whom I am to see again. Wrote to Ld Granville. Read Gaume—Reid's Past & Present.[8]

[1] Later marginal note reads: 'This Resolution taken out for Cabinet Apr. 20. 72'.

[2] *Denison's resignation reached Gladstone on 25 Oct.; Gladstone, giving him a viscountcy, told him: 'we need entertain no apprehension on the score of means, as to the support of the dignity of the Peerage, & for this reason only I do not make any proposal [of a pension]'; Add MS 44540, f. 146.

[3] Undated holograph at Add MS 44639, f. 116, reads: 'Cardwell asks a day or two to consider about the Speakership. I gave reasons why he shd. not have it—& why Br[and] should. He said *nothing* definite. Except that at the end of the Session the Speaker & Lady Charlotte asked them to luncheon, & showed them over the whole house from top to bottom.' 'Does your consent to his considering the question imply an offer on your part? [Granville]' 'No.'

[4] See 31 Oct. 71. The islands were eventually annexed 1874; see E. Drus, 'The colonial office and the annexation of Fiji', *T.R.H.S.*, 4th series, xxxii. 99.

[5] See *The Times*, 30 Oct. 1871, 3, estimating the crowd 'from 10000 to 12000', and Bassett, *Speeches*, 401.

[6] J. E. Ozenne and C. J. Tissot, negotiating the French treaty; see Ramm I, ii. 278.

[7] J. J. Gaume, *Où en sommes-nous? Étude sur les événements actuels 1870 et 1871* (1871). See 10 Nov. 71.

[8] H. G. Reid, *Past and present; or society and religious life in the north* (1871).

30. M.

Wrote to Baron Bramwell—Sol. General—The Speaker—Sir H. Holland—W.H.G.—Bishop of Ely—M. Ozanne [*sic*]—Mr Murray—Ld Granville Tel.—Mr Newdigate—Captain Harris—Ld Blomfield[1]—and minutes. Saw Messrs Farrer (clerk)—Mr M'Coll—Mr Ayrton—Mr Glyn (3)—Ld Halifax—Baron Beaulieu—Mr Hayward—Mr Stansfeld. Dined at Lady Waldegrave's: much conversation with her. Read Meteyard's Group of Englishmen.[2]

31. Tu.

Wrote to M. de Laveleye—Mr Nolan[3]—Mr Bruce—The Queen (Mem. and l.)—Mr Cardwell—Mr Ayrton—and minutes. Saw Ld Granville—Mr Glyn (3)—Ld Wentworth—Conclave in D. St on the Speakership—Attorney General—Ld Chancellor—Mr Kinnaird. Cabinet 2½-5¾. Attended the Alfred Theatre to see Pennington in King John. Read Meteyard. Received from Mr E. Atherstone his works: some 45000 lines of verse! nearly = Il + Od + Æn. + Paradise Lost, I think.[4]

Cabinet Tues. O. 31. 2.30.[5]

√ London Muncipal Govt. Ayrton's paper read. Decided not to go forward. Bruce to write to Mr Beal.
√ The Speaker's letter. Read & approved.[6]
√ Feejee Islands. Dispatch: allowing NSW to annex it. approved.[7]
√ French Treaty. Dispatch read—& approved.[8]

Wed. Nov One 1871 All S.

St Paul's Kn. 5 P.M. Prayers & the Baptism. Wrote to Ld Chancellor (2)—Justice Willes—A.S. Wilkins[9]—Mr Murchison[10]—Justice M. Smith[11]—Sol.Gen. (Tel.)—Ld Halifax—Mr Bright—W.H.G.—The

[1] *Sc.* Bloomfield.
[2] See 26 Oct. 71.
[3] Had sent a resolution on Fenians; Add MS 44540, f. 149.
[4] Edwin Atherstone published sundry epics, 1828-61.
[5] Add MS 44639, f. 114.
[6] Accepting a peerage without a pension; see 27 Oct. 71n.
[7] New South Wales declined; see W. P. Morrell, *Britain in the Pacific Islands* (1960), 159.
[8] Granville to L. West, 1 November 1871, criticising protectionism and vagueness of French proposals; F.O.C.P. 2057.
[9] Augustus Samuel Wilkins, professor of latin in Manchester, had sent a volume.
[10] Declining Kenneth Robert Murchison's request for a baronetcy claimed on his late uncle's achievements; Add MS 44540, f. 150.
[11] Sir Montagu Edward Smith, 1809-91; justice of Common Pleas 1865; on judicial cttee. of privy council Nov. 1871-81.

Queen (Tel.)—Mrs Beadel—and minutes. Saw Attorney General (3)—Mr Cardwell—Mr Glyn—Ld Halifax—Mr Lambert—Herbert J.G. Read Report Ch. Reform Union—Leonard Morris.[1] Dined with the Wests.

To John BRIGHT, M.P., 1 November 1871. Add MS 43385, f. 158.
'Private.'

I thank you very much for the free expression of your opinions on the difficult question of the French proposals:[2] I only wish they were urged from what was once your accustomed chair in a certain room.

During the prolonged consideration of these proposals, for which we have all had time, my mind I think has moved in a direction opposite to yours. From the first I have thought it a bad business; & I now think it worse than at first. At the same time I own the difficulties of the case: & do not seek unduly to press my opinion upon others.

Having said this, so as to create a distinction between what I think & what I should push to the uttermost, I own my great disappointment at finding that the Treaty of 1860, which I looked to as the great instrument of further & more effectual progress, is to be made by the French Government the starting point of a backward movement, of which the present proposals may be only a first manifestation. And I think we are generally averse to entering into debate with France upon details. On the other side there is a great desire to avoid offence & to exhibit sympathy, even though we are called to do it in the strange form of assisting her to do herself a mischief. We have pointed out to her certain difficulties: but no final step has yet been taken.

I am much pleased to find you think favourably of my speech at Greenwich. [P.S.] I hope to be at Hawarden by the 11th. Would that suit you?

2. Th.

Wrote to Sir W. Stephenson[3]—Mr Tomline—The Queen (Mem)—Commr of Police—and minutes. Dined at Mrs Thistlethwayte's. Read Sir E. May's Evidence on Parl. proceedings.[4] Wrote Mem. on Fr. Treaty.[5] Saw Ld Bloomfield—Ld Granville—Mr Knowles—Mr M'Coll—Mr Glyn—Sir J. Lacaita—M. Wolowski—Ld Lyttelton—Ld Halifax. Book shopping.

[1] J. L. *Lyne, *Leonard Morris; or the Benedictine novice* (1871).

[2] Letter of 31 October 1871, Add MS 44112, f. 183: 'you will commit a great error if you make no attempt to continue it [the French treaty] even with some modifications'.

[3] Arranging for Louis François Michel Raymond Wolowski, French economist, to have research access to Inland Revenue records; Add MS 44540, f. 151.

[4] To the select cttee; see 17 Apr. 71.

[5] PRO 30/29/60; see Ramm I, ii. 278.

3. Fr.

Wrote to the Queen l. & Mem.—Sir W. Heathcote—Mr Jessel—Sol. General—D. of Argyll—Mr Engleheart—Bp of Worcester—Mr W. Williams—and minutes. 12-1¾. Conclave at Sir E. May's on Parl. Procedure.[1] Saw Ld Granville—Mr Cardwell—Mr Goschen—D. of Argyll—Ld Halifax—Mr Glyn. Cabinet 2¾-5¾. Read Meteyard. Nine to dinner.

Cabinet Nov. 3. 71. Friday 2.30 PM[2]

√ Law Officers remuneration. Further considered. WEG writes to Sol. Gen.[3]
√ Megaera Commission. Names of Commissioners. I 1. Heathcote 2. Devon II. Sir M. Seymour III. 1. Harman (?) 2. Bramwell 3. Brewster IV. Arrow V. Chapman.[4]
√ Information to be had as to Militia Storehouses—by Circulars.
√ Contagious Diseases. Provisions to be made if & when Compulsory Examination is given up: proposed & discussed.

4. Sat.

Wrote to Ld Granville—Col. Ponsonby (Tel)—S.R. Glynne—Dr Barry—and minutes. Dined with the Lytteltons. Saw Mr M. Foster—Mr Glyn—Scotts—Ld Penzance—Sir R. Palmer—Ld Lyttelton. Saw one X. Arranged China Cabinet & other parts of my room. Read Leonard Morris—Le Sousmaitre.[5]

5. 22 S.Trin.

Went to St Mark's Ham. Terrace mg & was much pleased.[6] Chap. Roy. 5.30 PM. Wrote to Abp of Canterbury—Dr Hannah—W.H.G. (Telegr.). Read Abp of Dublin's Charge—Bp of Chester's Charge[7]—Plumptre's Sermon[8]—Authority & Conscience[9]—Gaume's Ou en sommes Nous[10]—Sermon by . . .

[1] See 8 Nov. 71.
[2] Add MS 44639, f. 117.
[3] Attendance allowance at the Lords to be given; Add MS 44540, f. 152.
[4] See 8 Nov. 71.
[5] See 19 June 71.
[6] In St. John's Wood; R. Duckworth, vicar there since 1870; see 24 Jan. 69.
[7] Charges by R. C. *Trench and W. Jacobson (1871).
[8] See 9 July 71.
[9] Perhaps W. H. *Lyttelton, *The testimony of Scripture to the authority of conscience and of reason* (1861).
[10] See 28 Oct. 71.

To A. C. TAIT, archbishop of Canterbury, 5 November 1871. Tait MSS, 89, f. 298.[1]

I have to acknowledge your Grace's two letters of the 1st & 2nd,[2] & I return the inclosures after an attentive perusal. I shall be very glad, though not on my own personal account, if Dr. Pusey's letter[3] open the way to any proceeding in relation to the Athanasian Creed which may have the effect of allaying scruples.

When Your Grace's materials are further prepared, I shall be most happy to consult with you further & to take the opinion of the Cabinet if need be on the introduction of any Bill. The difficulty with the Bill of last Session was extreme; & I am very fearful of the breaking down of the dyke which stands between us & confusion as to legislation affecting the Church. Some test of the temper of the House will be afforded by the manner in which it may deal with Mr. Cowper's most indiscreet bill, should it appear, as is probable. It will be most difficult, perhaps impossible, to deal with any of the recommendations of the Commission & shut out the Athanasian Creed: especially with any of those on which the Commission was not unanimous. Your Grace's correspondence with Dr. Pusey may perhaps open a way of meeting this difficulty.

I told the Bishop of Winchester it seemed to me that we ought to have a Resignation Bill for Deans & Canons. It appears to me that it might be framed in analogy to the Episcopal Bill:[4] only requiring perhaps the assent of the Bishop. The pension might perhaps be $\frac{1}{3}$ of the Income: but not less than £400 for a Dean (in England, £300 in Wales) or £250 for a Canon: nor more than £800 for a Dean. I shall be glad to know hereafter your Grace's views. We shall probably separate in the end of this week; & meet again about the 2nd week in December. I have asked Dr. Barry to allow me to submit his name for the vacant Canonry of Worcester. (This is *Private*).

6. M.

Wrote to Mr Cardwell—The Queen (2)—Ld Dudley—Bp of Worcester—& minutes. Conclave in D. St at 2. Cabinet 2$\frac{3}{4}$–6. Finished Leonard Morris. Saw Ld Advocate—Mr M'Coll—Mr Gurdon—Mr Gray—Mr Glyn—Mr Grogan.

Cabinet Mond. Nov. 6. 71. 2.30 PM[5]

√ South African Federation explained by Ld. Kimberley who desired to give it a general encouragement. Agreed. A question as to Natal.[6]

√ Scottish Education. Ld. Advocate attended & explained: especially as to the

[1] Partly printed, undated, in R. T. Davidson and W. Benham, *Life of . . . A. C. Tait* (1891), ii. 134.

[2] Add MS 44330, ff. 209, 211, on ritualism.

[3] On the Athanasian creed, see Liddon, *Life of Pusey*, iv. 237; Liddon and Pusey threatened secession if Tait tampered with the creed, Marsh, *Victorian church*, 49.

[4] i.e. the Bishops Resignation Act, sponsored by Tait in 1869.

[5] Add MS 44639, f. 118.

[6] Kimberley's approach assumed colonial initiative; Natal's constitution differed from the Cape's; see C. F. Goodfellow, *Great Britain and South African Confederation* (1966), 40.

Board. Free religious instruction—conscience Clause—Denom[inationa]l Schools.[1]

√ Commission on Endowed Schools in Scotland. To be by a Clause in the Act.[2]

√ Extinction of right to obtain augmentations of stipend out of unexhausted Teinds. Agreed to.[3]

√ Licensing. Three parts. (Bruce) 1. Licensing authority. 2. Numbers [of licenses] 3. Police Regulations. Discussed. Lean to *3* only.[4]

To E. CARDWELL, war secretary, Add MS 44540, f. 154.
6 November 1871. 'Private.'

We met today to consider the subject of the Speakership, & the result of our considerations was to arrive at a practical conclusion of an important though -ve.[5] character, namely, that we should act unwisely if we were to entertain the idea of supporting the Candidature of any member of the Government itself. We have not proceeded to any further conclusion, but I propose to resume the conversation on Wed. at 2 precisely, when I hope you will give me the advantage of your presence & judgment.[6]

7. Tu.

Wrote to Sir E. Lechmore[7]—Abp of Canterb.—Mr Burnett—Ld Spencer—The Queen (Mem)—& minutes. Read Odilon Barrot.[8] Conclave on Parl. business 2½-5½. Saw Mr Goschen—W.H.G. (on Nuneaton)[9]—Ld Lyttelton—Mr Glyn. Saw Mrs Th. Dined with Mad. Ralli.

8. Wed.

Wrote to Mr Scrivener[10] —Mr Edw. Poste[11]—Ld Acton—Mr Forster (l. & Tel.)—The Queen—Sir H. Holland—Ld Granville—Mr

[1] Decision to rely on the Privy Council, not a General Board in Edinburgh; see *Scottish Educational Studies* (1972), 121.

[2] In the Education (Scotland) Bill 1872; but govt. agreed to a motion for a Commission: *H* ccx. 1747.

[3] Ld. Advocate to introduce a Bill for Scotland (PRO CAB 41/3/44), but this not done.

[4] The first two, especially restriction of licence numbers, had been the most controversial of the 1871 bill; 'numbers' was dropped in the 1872 bill; see Harrison, *Drink and the Victorians*, 264, 271.

[5] *Sic*; copyist probably means 'negative'.

[6] On 7 November Cardwell declined to come; Add MS 44119, f. 283.

[7] Sir Edmund Anthony Harley Lechmere, 1826-94; 2nd bart 1856; banker and tory M.P. Tewkesbury 1866-8; Worcs. 1876-92.

[8] See 25 Oct. 71. Sent by *Manning, see 10 Nov. 71.

[9] Living vacant there; see Add MS 44540, f. 148.

[10] i.e. F. H. A. *Scrivener, see 18 Aug. 45, giving him a civil list pension; Add MS 44540, f. 155.

[11] Putting off a deputation from Oxford; Add MS 44540, f. 155.

Campbell—The Speaker—Mr Cardwell—Mr Brewster—and minutes. Saw Lord Lyons—Mr M'Coll—Mr Glyn (2)—Mr Gurdon —Mr Brand[1]—Mr Stansfeld—Chr of Exr. Cabinet 2½–5¾. Conclave at 2 on Speakership. The Newman Halls to tea at 8.30. A rather severe though kindly discussion on Education Act till near midnight. Read Odilon Barrot.

Cabinet N. 8. 71. 2.30[2]

√ Business of the House. WEG reported the result of discussions in various propositions adopted—others unadopted. To resume before the Session.
√ French Treaty. Ld Granville related.
√ Meeting [of Cabinet] in December. Monday 11th 3 PM.
√ Ld Lisgard's letter. read.[3]
√ Repatriation of Lunatics. Propose all should remain in the country where they are & be treated as the lunatics of the country are.
√ Megaera Commission. Names agreed to: 1. Ld Lawrence or Ld Devon. 2. Brewster, 3. Admiral (M. Seymour). 4. Chapman 5. Arrow.[4]
Mr Bright. WEG will see him. Announced.[5]

Sketch.[6] *Proposals as to business of the House*
We considered several questions on which I have no progress to report. 1. Shall there be a Clôture. 2. Shall factious Adjournment be restrained a) by providing that after (2) motions have been rejected (by ⅔), the main questions shall be put without debate. b)[7] by providing that after (2) motions have been rejected, no motion for adjournment, which is objected to, shall be put for the space of (an hour). 3. Shall an attempt be made to organise Great Committees for certain Bills, or classes of Bills.

To LORD ACTON, 8 November 1871. Cambridge University Library.

I most heartily wish well to your design of obtaining access to the Reports of the Council held at the Vatican, and there could be no impropriety that I see, in your mentioning this to Remusat as a matter within your knowledge if you thought it expedient. I am however doubtful whether at this moment he is in good humour with us or likely to be impelled in the right direction by the knowledge of my wish. The objection [to] any communication, mediate or immediate, from me to him on this matter I think is, that I am really without any proper title to approach him.
[PS] I have consulted Granville on your letter.[8]

[1] Who accepted the Speakership, to be kept secret as long as possible; Add MS 44540, f. 162.
[2] Add MS 44639, f. 119.
[3] Probably that of 15 Aug. listing Canadian reservations to the Treaty of Washington, answered by Kimberley on 23 Nov.; *PP* 1872 xliii. 135.
[4] Lawrence was chairman, with A. Brewster, Sir M. Seymour, Sir F. Arrow, H. C. Rothery, T. Chapman; *PP* 1872 xv. 1.
[5] See 13 Nov. 71.
[6] 'Submitted to the Cabinet Nov. 8', noted in top corner; Add MS 44639, f. 121.
[7] 'Cabinet rather favourable N. 8.' noted in margin.
[8] Of 3 November, from Paris, Add MS 44093, f. 137, on the Council's reports; docketed by Gladstone 'Can this be done? After a short time?', with Granville's suggestion to Gladstone to write as above.

To E. CARDWELL, war secretary, Add MS 44540, f. 156.
8 November 1871.

I am truly sorry that we could not have the advantage of your counsel. We have further considered the matter with our undivided opinion that on the whole the Government would do best to use whatever influence it can legitimately exercise in favour of Brand. And we purpose that not only this, but the Speaker's meditated resignation should be kept secret as long as may be.

9. Th.

Wrote to Mr Holland—Bp Moriarty—Ld Chichester—and minutes. Read 'De La Centralisation'.[1] Saw Mr Thistlethwayte—Mr Bagehot—Mr Fowler—Mr Glyn—D. de Broglie—Sir R. Phillimore—and others. Luncheon at Ld Lorne's & saw Dyce's most lovely picture. Conversation with Princess L[ouise] respecting Sir C. Dyke.[2] Some meditation. Attended Guildhall Feast & spoke in returning thanks for ministers.[3]

10. Fr.

Wrote to Mr Brewster—Chancellor of Exr—Mr Cardwell—Duke of Argyll—Mr Glyn—Ld Granville—Mr Murray—Mr C.A. Wood—The Queen (M 2)—Abp Manning—Sir T.E. May—Ld Chichester—(C.J.) Cockburn—Ld Hartington—& minutes. Saw Mr Campbell—Mr West—Mr Hammond—Sir R. Phillimore—B. Beaulieu—The Ld Chancellor—F. Cavendish—Mr Thistlethwayte. Dined with the Phillimores. 15 G. Square afterwards.[4] Correcting Speech at Blackheath.

To ARCHBISHOP H. E. MANNING, Add MS 44540, f. 160.
10 November 1871.

I return M. Odilon Barrot, whom I have read from end to end & I have nearly done the same with M. Gaume.[5] I cannot tell how it is possible to bring the two

[1] See 25 Oct. 71.

[2] *Sc.* *Dilke, whose speech at Newcastle, 6 Nov., in *The Times*, 9 Nov. 1871, 6d, on costs of monarchy seemed republican; 'if . . . a Republic here will be free from the political corruption that hangs about the Monarchy, I say, for my part—and I believe the middle classes in general will say—let it come (Cheers)'. Cuttings from sundry newspapers on the speech are in Add MS 44760, f. 117ff. A republican 'Alphabet' read: '*L* for Louise and her money making beau, And for the matchless Prince of matches, Old Bob Lowe'; Add MS 44760, f. 114.

[3] Spoke largely on foreign affairs; *The Times*, 10 Nov. 1871, 5d; see also Ramm I, ii. 279.

[4] i.e. the Thistlethwaytes; his letter to Chichester on 9 Nov. (Add MS 44540, f. 157) put Thistlethwayte's case to the ecclesiastical commissioners respecting Paddington.

[5] See 25 and 28 Oct. 71.

into the same category. The one is full, wisely full I think, of the spirit of liberty. The other appears to omit it altogether from his system, & the system consequently has (to my mind) neither base nor balance. It is a great centrifugal force, driving headlong through infinite space. I do not however deny that the Christian religion is, in its relation to society, slipping back to the position which it held before Constantine & I feel difficulty in reconciling this moment with a favourable view of the general movement of society, which I should regard as distinctly a movement towards good, were it satisfactorily related to the present question of belief. Here is a problem reserved for easier days. I noted the speech of Huxley in which his premise did not warrant his conclusion.

11. Sat. [*Hawarden*]

Wrote to Mr Hammond—Mr Brand—Mr Reed MP—Ld Granville —& minutes. Hard work in putting by & arranging for journey. Worked on Corr. Speech. Saw Mr Ouvry—Mr West. Off at 2.20. reached Hawarden 8.20. Unpacking &c. in evg. Read the Sousmaitre.[1]

12. 23 S.Trin.

Ch mg & evg. Wrote (Telegrams) to Mr West—Col. Ponsonby—Ld Granville. Walk & conversation with Sir Geo. Prevost. Read Brother Placidus[2]—Brewer's remarkable Tract on Athanasian Creed[3]—Abp of Syros & Mr Freshfield MS.[4]

13. M.

Church 8½ AM. Wrote to Mr E. Freshfield[5]—Mr Bellairs—Mr West (l. & Tel.)—Mr Gurdon—and minutes. Cut a tree with WHG. Finished correcting Speech. Arranging my room a little. Saw Mr Burnett. Two long conversations with Mr Bright who arrived at one.— [A.] Hayward & [John] Murray in evening: a debate on Bp Philpotts. Read Sargant on Royal Dowries[6]—D. Melville on Relig.Instr. in Rate Schools.[7]

[1] See 19 June 71.

[2] By [J. L. *Lyne] (1870).

[3] J. S. *Brewer, *The Athanasian Creed* (1871); anti-A. P. *Stanley.

[4] See next day.

[5] Edwin Freshfield, of the solicitor's family; had been on a tour of the East; Gladstone forwarded his report on the Bulgarian schism, and abp. Lykourgos' letter also on it, to the foreign office on 21 Nov., and to Acton for Döllinger; Add MSS 44540, f. 173ff, 44432, f. 161.

[6] W. L. *Sargant, 'The Princess and her dowry', ch. ii of *Essays of a Birmingham Manufacturer* (1869–72).

[7] D. Melville, *Religious instruction in School Board Schools* (1871).

To E. FRESHFIELD, 13 November 1871. Add MS 44540, f. 162.

Arriving here on Saturday evening I found awaiting me your letter of the 7th & I have perused it with great interest. The earlier part of it, in relation to the general condition of the Eastern Ch. calls for no remark beyond this, that for very many years I have felt a lively interest in whatever tends to make that Ch. a little known to our countrymen & that the longer [*sic*] I feel the more lively that interest becomes. With regard to the condition of the Turkish Empire I cannot regard the Mussalman rule in Europe as normal or permanent, but I do believe that their administrative system is improved though their finance is not & in Asia I have ever supposed they had a greater chance of duration with a fairer field. I must own that in no case can I desire to see this country taking charge of Constantinople. We have enough, to say the least, on our hands. What you say of the Bulgarian question is important & I have never yet seen it thoroughly explained, in our official papers. I will if you like send to Ld. Granville that portion of your letter. Meanwhile I inclose to you for perusal a long but very interesting letter from the Archbp. of Syra, who, as I understand your letter, is now Metropolitan. I might perhaps send to Ld. G. what he, also, says of the Bulgarian question. Where & what is the Theological School of Halki, which speaks such good sense?

14. Tu.

Overslept Ch. time through a pious fraud of C.s. Wrote to D of Argyll —Tel. & Letter—Mr West Tel—Robn G.—Ld Chancellor—Ld Chichester—Sir R. Collier[1]—Mr Forster—Alderman Dakin[2]—Col. Ponsonby—& minutes. Some five hours in conversation with Mr Bright: Also I opened my proposal to him: wh he took kindly, tho' cautiously.[3] A general walking party in afternoon Sir G. Prevost, Murray, Hayward, all harmonise with Bright. Read the Sous-maître. My conversation of yesterday evening with him kept me awake till four. A most rare event. But my brain assumes in the evening a feminine susceptibility, and resents any unusual strain: tho' strange to say, it will stand a debate in the H. of C.[4]

15. Wed.

Ch. 8½ AM. Wrote to Ld Kimberley—Ld Granville—Mr West Tel. —Ld Halifax—Scotts—and minutes. Forenoon with Bright, who departed, having charmed everybody by gentleness. Began the cutting

[1] Had written offering to withdraw from the judicial cttee. following ferocious attack by *Cockburn; Gladstone wrote: 'it goes against me that there shd. be any retrogression, and change of front, in the face of a highly unwarrantable & improper attack, which I conceive Cockburn's attack to have been'; Add MS 44540, f. 163.

[2] Knighting Thomas Dakin, 1808-99; London druggist; lord mayor 1871.

[3] That he should rejoin the cabinet, without heavy work; see Ramm I, ii. 281.

[4] See Morley, ii. 381.

of a large beech with Willy. Literary conversation freely given by Hayward. Read Sargant on Compar. Morality[1]—Harcourt Amt of the Laws.[2]

To LORD HALIFAX, lord privy seal, Hickleton MSS A4. 88.
15 November 1871. 'Secret.'

Bright came about midday on Monday and went off at the same time today. We passed many hours in most friendly, detailed, and confidential communication. I explained to him *every* thing as far as I could. His appearances, movements, & faculty of discussion plainly enough showed or seemed to show me that though he requires much care & selfrestraint he ought really to be available for the moderate demands we should make upon him. The upshot is that he has not refused, but receives, & entertains, the proposition, while he expresses apprehension about it. He will consider the matter carefully.

16. Th.

Ch. 8½ A.M. Wrote to Mr Goschen Tel.—Mr West l. and Tel.—Mr Murray—Chancr of Exr—Ld Fermoy—Mr Harcourt—D. of Argyll—Lady Loudoun—Rev B. Brown—and minutes. Conversation with Hayward on the affair of the Secularist Hymn Book.[3] I decided to take no further notice of the controversy. The Belpers[4] came. Read Jules Favres (Diplomatic Volume) on Rome & France[5]—Le Sousmaître—Sargant on Comparative Morality.

17. Fr.

Ch. 8½ AM. Wrote to Mrs Thistlethwayte 2—Mr Bright—Mr West Tel.—Mr Bruce[6]—Mr Glyn—and minutes. Saw Mr Burnett. Finished the felling of a large beech with W. Its 3d afternoon. Singing in evg. Read Jules Favre—Sousmaitre &c. (finished)—Curci on Address to the Pope.[7]

18. Sat.

Ch. 8½ AM. Wrote to Ld Hartington—Mr Machin—Abp Manning—

[1] W. L. *Sargant, 'Comparative morality' from *Essays*; see 13 Nov. 71n.
[2] Sir W. *Harcourt, 'Plan for the amendment of the law' (1871).
[3] A storm followed his quotations at Greenwich; see 28 Oct. 71.
[4] Emily, *née* Otter m. 1837 1st Baron Belper (see 30 Mar. 54).
[5] J. G. C. Favre, *Rome et la République Française* (1871).
[6] 'Together with you I can hardly believe in the report about Roundell Palmer and the Dilke speech. It would be madness to prosecute him [i.e. Dilke]'; Add MS 44540, f. 168.
[7] C. M. Curci, perhaps 'Nella inaugurazione della Società romana per gl'interessi cattolici' (1871).

Sir B. Frere—Mr Delane[1]—and minutes. Tree cutting with Willy. Conversation with Mr Balfour[2] about the Secularist's Book. Read Wilkins on Phoenicia and Israel[3]—Jules Favre's Vol—Finished Curci.

19. 24 S.Trin.

Ch 11 AM with H.C. and 6½ P.M. Wrote to Lord Chancellor—Ld Kimberley—Ld Advocate—Ld Chichester—Mr Goschen—Mr Thistlethwayte—and minutes. Read Bp Forbes, Introduction[4]—Wilkins, Phoenic. Religion—Bp of St Asaph's Charge[5]—Churchwork in Hawaii.[6]

20. M.

Ch. 8½ AM. Wrote to Ld Granville—Mr Cardwell—Mr Hick MP[7]—and minutes. Cut a tree with WHG. Wrote part of a Mem. on the Royalty question. Read J. Favre's Roman Vol.—Mackenzie's Grievances of Orkney[8]—Wilkins on Phoen. & Israel. Conversation with Mr Balfour and with Mr Shaw Stewart.[9]

To E. CARDWELL, war secretary, 20 November 1871. 'Most private.' — Add MS 44540, f. 171.

It would greatly be for the advantage of the government as well as the credit of the parties if we could reconcile Lowe & Ayrton. There are *many* questions pending in which their cooperation is indispensable to satisfactory results. It is easy to talk of uprooting Ayrton, but even if it were just it will, as Glyn would tell you be very difficult. But Lowe perhaps proceeds more like Moloch & Ayrton in the manner of Belial. Why cannot they follow the good example of those worthies who cooperated in Pandemonium? If you thought you could manage Lowe I would try to tackle Ayrton. I commend this subject to your meditations. Ayrton is in Paris & it would be best to deal *viva voce.*[10]

[1] Asking Delane to deny on diarist's authority that Favre's claim in his book (see 16 Nov. 71) that the proposal for a conference on the Papacy was Gladstone's idea; Add MS 44540, f. 169; see *The Times*, 20 Nov. 1871, 9f, and Matthew, 'Vaticanism', 432.

[2] Arthur James *Balfour, 1848–1930; not yet an M.P.; first visit to Hawarden, as a friend of Mary Gladstone; see L. Masterman, *Mary Gladstone* (1930), 70; K. Young, *A. J. Balfour* (1963), ch. 2.

[3] A. S. Wilkins, *Phoenicia and Israel* (1871).

[4] A. P. *Forbes, perhaps introduction to *An explanation of the Thirty-nine Articles* (1867).

[5] By T. V. *Short (1865?).

[6] Perhaps G. E. *Biber, *The kingdom and Church of Hawaii; a historical sketch* (1865).

[7] John Hick, 1815–94; tory M.P. Bolton 1868–80.

[8] J. Mackenzie, ed. A. G. Groat and H. Cheyne, *The general grievances . . . of the isles of Orkney and Shetland* (1836).

[9] i.e. J. A. Shaw-Stewart; see 19 Dec. 65.

[10] Cardwell feared 'the evil is inveterate', 22 November 1871, Add MS 44119, f. 285.

21. Tu.

Church 8½ A.M. Wrote to Ld Hartington—Ld Suffield[1]—Mr Cowen—Mr Hammond—Mr Lowe—Ld Sydney—Mr Pim MP—Mr West (l. and Tel.)—The Queen (Mem.)—and minutes. Conversation with Mr. Duckworth[2] respecting Queen & R. Family. Read Jules Favre (finished)—Wilkins Phoen. & Israel (finished)—Renan Langues Semitiques[3]—Pim on Ireland[4]—Croesus.[5] Saw Mr Burnett.

To R. LOWE, chancellor of the exchequer, 21 November 1871. Add MS 44540, f. 173.

I send you a letter from Harcourt and therewith his pamphlet in case you should not have seen it.[6] Pray consider whether you can turn him to account for the purpose of examining and reducing our enormous expenditure in the legal and judicial branch. I think the question of a Commission well worth entertaining, provided we can see our way to manning properly.[7]

To J. PIM, M.P., 21 November 1871. Add MS 44540, f. 173.

I thank you for your tract on the subject of Home Rule, which I have read with much interest. I am obliged to demur altogether to the accuracy of the view which you have presented in it of my speech at Aberdeen, but I should be unwilling to dwell upon anything which would tend to create or exhibit differences of opinion in a matter where I think as to all questions of principle we are really agreed.

22. Wed.

Ch. 8½ A.M. Wrote to The Queen—Ld Granville—Lady Ely—D. of Argyll—Mr West—Viceroy of Ireland—Mr Ouvry—Mr Bright—Bp of Winchester—and minutes. Read Renan—Mrs H. Gray.[8]

[1] Charles Harbord, 1830-1914, 5th Baron Suffield 1853; liberal courtier.

[2] R. Duckworth, governor to Prince Leopold; see 24 Jan. 69n.

[3] J. E. Renan, *Histoire générale et système comparé des langues sémitiques* (1855).

[4] J. Pim, *Ireland and the imperial Parliament* (1871); see 25 Nov. 71.

[5] *Croesus; a new and original historical tragedy* (1871).

[6] See 15 Nov. 71. Gladstone had already drawn Lowe's attention to it on 16 November (Add MS 44540, f. 166): 'I have been reading Harcourt's able tract on Law Reform. My means of passing judgment on it are but slender. But it pleases me a good deal. I have told him however that in my opinion as it stands it would cause a considerable increase of immediate expense....'

[7] Lowe replied, 24 November, Add MS 44301, f. 215: 'As usual I see no need for a Commission—the abuses are gross, open, palpable.'

[8] E. C. Gray, probably *The Empire and the Church, from Constantine to Charlemagne* (1857).

To the DUKE OF ARGYLL, Indian secretary, 22 November 1871. Add MS 44540, f. 174.

As Lowe is not satisfied with our joint opinions, I conclude you will bring the matter before the Cabinet,[1] & if you stand upon the interpretation of the entire Act I cannot but think the general issue will be favourable to yours. I cannot guarantee you any maximum number of Cabinets in Dec. but I think either 4 or perhaps 5, as likely as any other to be the number. We must fix the basis of the Estimates & try to put onwards some of our Bills. The heads of the Scotch Education Bill will have to be carefully reviewed. That question looms larger & darker than heretofore. I hope your weather has not pressed upon the Duchess.

23. Th.

Ch. 8½ AM. Walk to Q[ueen's] F[erry] where C. has housed her junior Orphanage to escape fever. Arranged my Privately Printed, 15th Cent. & Aldine Books &c. Examined the use of ἄγριος.[2] Read Dobbs on Representation[3]—Lady Herbert on Ammergau.[4] Dinner party. We cut a large tree. 1 h. 45 min. hard work. Wrote to Mr Stacpool—Col. [Weld-]Blundell—Mr Bruce—Mr N. Hall—Mr Childers—Italian Minister—& minutes.

To Rev. C. NEWMAN HALL, 23 November 1871. Add MS 44540, f. 176.

I thank you very much for Mr Dale's letter[5] which I shall keep by me as one of the important documents of the Education Question. I see Mr Dale is alarmed about Ireland but I believe in his candour & less of the golden rule, & I think he will not find reason to condemn us in the matter of Irish education. I wish I could see my way as well through the difficulties of the English question. But the materials of judgment have not yet been as copiously collected on this side of the water. At present it is hard to bring together the local indications which reach us. An influential person in the Diocese of Salisbury acquaints me by this post that 185 laymen, sent to represent nearly all the Parishes i.e. the Church of England in them, have unanimously declared against *any* change in the Act. My duty for the present is to watch & reflect.

24. Frid.

Ch. 8½ A.M. Wrote to Mr Henderson—Sir D. Salomons—Mr West

[1] Prolonged dispute about treasury control of Indian finance; Add MS 44102, ff. 57–77. See 19 Jan. 72.

[2] 'living wild'; see next day n.

[3] A. E. Dobbs, *General representation on a complete readjustment and modification of Mr. Hare's plan* (1871).

[4] M. E. Herbert, *The Passion Play at Ammergau* (published 1890).

[5] Letter from R. W. Dale to Hall, 16 November 1871, forwarded by Hall on 21 November; Add MS 44188, f. 107. Dale complained: 'I think he is under the impression that Ireland is to be governed on "Irish principles".'

—Mr Waddell[1]—Mr Lowe[2]—Mr Hammond—Robn G.—Mr Hick MP.—and minutes. Willy & I cut a yew tree, without ascertaining its species: a great mistake. Read Renan—Peregrine Pickle.[3]

25. Sat.[4]

Wrote to Mr Lowe—Ld Granville—The Speaker—The Queen (Mem)—Ld Chichester—Sir W. Knollys—Mr Watson—Mr Bright —Ld Halifax—and minutes. Wrote Mem. on Rate Schools. Inspected the new Railway line. Read Talandiers 'Civilisation'[5]—Peregrine Pickle—Renan's Langues Semitiques—Dale's Manchester Speech.[6]

Memorandum on Education Act.[7]

1. The elective Boards to be allowed to determine the nature of the religious instruction, if any, in Rate Schools. Subject to the one condition of the Time-Table Conscience-Clause. 2. The Board to be allowed as above, with the additional (Second) condition that no Catechism or Formulary distinctive of a particular denomination shall be used. 3. As above, with the additional (third) condition that the exposition of Scripture shall be unsectarian. This word has two meanings, which differ widely. i. Includes all matter on which the bulk or generality of Christians agree e.g. The Divinity of the Saviour—the Command to baptize. ii. As explained in the motion of Mr Jacob Bright,[8] it excludes everything which is in favour of or against the tenets of any particular denomination. This seems the more logical & consistent meaning. 4. The Board to have power to direct the reading of Holy Scripture but no exposition whatever of the same, nor any other form of religious instruction. 5. The application of the Rate to be confined by law to secular teaching only.

NB. But in this and in all the other cases, there need be nothing in the law to forbid the teaching of religion in any manner in which the Board think fit to permit out of School hours, provided the dealings of the Board with the Master of the Schoolhouse, the School, the School Times, and the Rate are strictly confined to Secular purposes.

To John BRIGHT, M.P., 25 November 1871. Add MS 43385, f. 165.
'Private & Confidential.'

I return your inclosures. The subjects will not permit me to act on your considerate and kind suggestion, and refrain from troubling you with an answer.

[1] William Wardlaw Waddell, of Balliol, had written on use of ἄγριος in *Juventus Mundi*; Add MS 44432, f. 194.

[2] Asking him what he intended to say in Halifax about the royal finances; Add MS 44540, f. 176. See 2 Dec. 71.

[3] By *Smollett (1751).

[4] Prince of Wales' typhoid this day became serious.

[5] Untraced.

[6] R. W. *Dale moved resolutions opposing use of school board funds to pay fees in denominational schools; *The Times*, 25 Nov. 1871, 5b.

[7] Holograph, initialled and dated 25 November 1871; Add MS 44760, f. 125.

[8] Of 30 June 1870; *H* ccii. 1270.

1. I agree with your remark on the substance of Mr Pim's pamphlet.[1] His representation of my Speech at Aberdeen[2] is invidious & unfair, and so I have told him. There are few, I think, who would be disposed to go so far as I should in the direction of Home Rule: subject to two conditions, which I am confident you would approve; a) that what is given, be not given or offered at least, to Ireland exclusively. b) that the supreme authority of the Imperial Legislature be both theoretically and practically preserved.

2. The state of things as to the Education Bill is singular, and threatening. The subject lay deep in my mind & motives when I saw you: but I did not dwell on it very largely, as it is hardly ripe for its crisis. At least not ripe in the view of the Government; but there is so much jealousy, suspicion, and irritation, that it may ripen, or explode, without our agency. It seems more likely than any other matter to be the death of this Government, in connection with some one of the three countries.

As to me, I know not whether the Nonconformists & I shall always be able 'to put our heads' together, but they have behaved honourably & handsomely to me, and I desire to reciprocate in fair and straightforward conduct. I should wish to retire from public life, rather than at this advanced hour of my little day go into sharp and vital conflict with them.

I feel also that some reserve in speech, & much careful reflection, are the present duty of the Government with regard to the question of English Education in its present stage.

It may be interesting to you that I should state what took place in the Cabinet to bring the provision as to Rate Schools & the religious instruction in them to its present form.

I enclose a mem. containing five methods of dealing with this point, all of which had advocates. No. 1. was that chosen deliberately by the Government (I rather think before you left it, but as to my present purpose this is immaterial); and I for one think as I believe we generally think that if the country would have taken it this is the *best*. But it was, or was deemed, untenable in Parliament.

This being so, my own view was, and still is, that there was no other solid and stable ground to be taken except that of No. 5. But this was not the view of I. The Cabinet. I may add that I doubt whether anything would have induced Forster to acquiesce in it. II The Church: which without doubt much preferred No 1: but yet the body in general acquiesced in No 2, and a not unimportant portion of the Clergy recommended it. A fraction of this fraction would have taken No 3. III. The Dissenters. This I know well because my own preference of No 5 was too decided to allow me to be blind to any indications in its favour. I satisfied myself by separate and detailed communications with many deputations, and with such men as Miall, Richard, and Winterbotham, that they were, in vast majority, determined on having No 2, if they could not get No 3, which the Church would not have tolerated, and which would only have laid the foundation of fresh controversies. Some went as far as No 4, but a decided minority.

Nonconforming opinion is now altered & altering, & part of the blame they award to Forster is because he was then & now of the opinion which they held then but not now.

I think what I have said will show (of course to you & in great secrecy as to the *Cabinet*) how we were led to our conclusion. I think I can say it was the only form, in which the Bill could have passed, and that it should pass was what all demanded.

[1] See 21 Nov. 71. [2] See 26 Sept. 71.

I hope that a little time will bring the Dissenters to clear & decided views, not only on Clause xxv (for the matter cannot be dealt with piecemeal) but on the whole subject so that we may know with what materials we have to deal. Upon the whole matter, I do not despair; I am rather inclined to despond; but I wish not to hurry.

An Election fought on this battle at the present time would certainly I apprehend throw the Liberal Party into a minority, as the whole party has not adopted, nor indeed has the whole Protestant part of it adopted, the creed of the dissatisfied as it stands. I do not even feel that I yet understand the whole argument. As far as I do understand it, I am not surprised that the Dissenters should run restive.

Finally: I have read with care Mr Dale's most able & striking speech: a speech quite sufficient of itself to mark a man. I only make on this matter this one observation. It contains no answer whatsoever to the question, 'what right have you, on your own principles, to compel the rate-payer to pay for what you are pleased to term unsectarian religious instruction in Rate Schools, when he chooses to object to it?' The more so, as this unsectarian instruction is to a great extent Dissenting instruction; *the* instruction, which a Nonconformist would spontaneously give in a school of his own: being in brief Christian instruction *minus* Catechisms, Church, Clergy, and Sacraments. It seems hardly too much to say that the Speech blinks this question.

26. 25 S. Trin.

Ch. 11 AM & 6½ PM. Wrote to Ld Granville (l. & Tel)—Mr West (Tel.)—Mr Forster—Chancr of Exr—Mr Bruce—Mr Otway—Robn G.—and minutes. Read Christ & the Scriptures[1]—Macduff St Paul in Rome[2]—R. Neville Grenville on Cathedrals[3]—Brother Placidus.[4]

27. M.

Ch. 8½ AM. Wrote to Ld Granville (Tel.)—Archbishop of Syra & Tenos[5]—Mr Hammond—Ld Acton—& minutes. Arranging some papers. Cut part of a big tree with W. Read P. Pickle—Langues Semitiques—Capper's Wanderings in War Time.[6]

To E. HAMMOND, 27 November 1871. PRO FO 391/24.

1. I return the papers about the Bulgarian Church question.[7] It is probable that the original movement was Bulgarian, and was founded on real grievances, but that Russia perceiving how the land lay turned them to account for her own

[1] A. *Saphir, *Christ and the Scriptures* (1867).

[2] J. R. Macduff, *St. Paul in Rome* (1871).

[3] R. N. Grenville, 'Cathedrals' (1871).

[4] See 12 Nov. 71.

[5] On Old Catholics and the Eastern Church; in German and French; Add MS 44540, f. 180.

[6] S. J. Capper, *Wanderings in wartime* (1871).

[7] Sent by Hammond on 26 November, Add MS 44183, f. 459.

purposes exactly as in the case of the civil grievances of the Christians of the Turkish Empire generally. But in the latter case she was watched & stopped by Europe. In the former there has not been the same means of doing this, though all that Sir H. Elliot says seems fair & proper. I never could understand the refusal of the Porte to allow the meeting of a Council which appears to me to have been a foolish as well as a somewhat oppressive act. Please let the papers I sent be considered confidential.

2. Unless there is any point considered to be open, I have no desire to see the case relating to San Juan, which I could not effectually review here, or probably even in London; but I shall be very glad to see that which relates to the Alabama & her class, if it can conveniently be sent.

3. I do not see what could be taken from, or added to, the Chancellor's view of the Confederate Bonds.[1] Nor do I at present understand how the British creditors of the Ex-Confederate States can be entitled to a position, in such a case, different from that of their fellows.

4. There cannot I think be too much friendly pressure in the Spanish Morocco case. But I hope we shall attempt (if need be) to save our traffic with Tangier by friendly means, & not as was done some ten years ago by Ld. Russell.

28. Tu.

Ch. 8½ AM. Wrote to The Queen—Scotts—Mr Hammond (l. & tel.)—Chancr of Exr—Ld Ripon—Bp of Lichfield—Mr West—Mr Childers—Ld Granville—and minutes. Wrote Mem. on question of Confederate Bonds.[2] Cutting with Willy. Saw Mr Burnett *cum* Mr Fisher. Dined at the Rectory. Read Cappers Wanderings—Romeo & Juliet.

29. Wed.

Ch. 8½ AM. Wrote to Duke of Edinburgh—Sir W. Knollys—Mr West—Ld Chancellor—Mrs Th.—Ld Granville—Robn G.—Bss M. Rothschild—Mr Bright—Sir J. Hanmer—Ld Spencer—Lord Ardmillan—Ld Ripon—Messrs Eden—and minutes. Finished cutting the big ash at the Wint. Read Renan—Peregrine Pickle—Capper.

To John BRIGHT, M.P., 29 November 1871. Add MS 43385, f. 173.
'Most Private.'

I do not think that the language held by the Government during the Debates on the Education Bill would be entirely consistent with their holding that the Act in its spirit contemplated and so to speak desired the absorption of denominational Schools. But I doubt whether this is a practical question at the present

[1] Lowe's view was 'that we could not have refused to present the claims; that it is for the Commission itself to decide upon them'; ibid.

[2] Untraced.

time, at any rate as between you & me. For you would assert that those Schools ought to have fair play, and I should assert that they ought to have nothing more. In a word the Education Department ought to be strictly impartial in regard to them. This principle I think cannot be too firmly held; and I cannot for a moment believe that Forster has ever intended to depart from it. A letter just received from him[1] assures me he is confident that on examination of details the impartiality of the Department will come out clear.

I believe reasonable satisfaction was given in a general way to Dissenters present by my Declaration at Greenwich[2] that the Act aims at separation between public rates or Taxes and religious differences.

I hope we may be able to work on this basis; but that a little time will be given us for the collation of the facts before we are peremptorily called upon to act at all.

As to Ireland. Fortescue of course must answer for himself, as I do not know to what words or acts of his any exception is taken. But for my own part I cannot plead guilty to having given just cause for any of the suspicion that prevails. Over and over again I have declared that the State ought not to found, or to support, either a Roman Catholic University, or a Roman Catholic College. There are in truth but two charges against us that cannot be refuted. One is that if in your language we have been endeavouring to drive six omnibuses abreast through Temple Bar we have at least refused to add a seventh. The other is that, being I hope sane & not mad, we have refused to promulgate our measure until we have a reasonable hope of passing it. I feel confident you would find no cause for dissatisfaction in the attitude of the Government with respect to this question.

But there is an indispensable condition, and mainstay, of a Liberal policy in this country with respect to which I feel a great anxiety at the present moment. Now that the pressure of European difficulties has passed, I am most anxious that we should give effective and not merely transient or doubtful indications of our intentions with regard to public economy. It is on this question, even more than any other, that I am desirous of your cooperation, and that in the only place where it can effectively, I had almost said even usefully, be given.

I cannot help adding, though perhaps it is a little presumptuous and beyond my province, that I am impressed by the belief that it could be given there with less of a strain upon and risk to yourself, than in any other form which you could choose for the exercise of public duty.

30. Th. St Andrew.

Ch. 11 AM. Wrote to Mr West l. & Tel.—Ld Lyttelton—Chancr of Exr—V.C. of Cambridge—Mr Melly—Dean of Rochr—Mr Glyn—Robn G.—Count Apponyi—and minutes. Worked on the tree. Put down some notes of Homeric Propositions. Read P. Pickle—Capper. Read also Tennyson's Last Tournament[3]—M. Müller Philos. of Mythol.[4]

[1] Not found.
[2] See 28 Oct. 71.
[3] In the *Contemporary Review*, December 1871.
[4] F. *Max Müller, probably *Chips from a German workshop* (1867), ii.

Frid. Dec. One. 1871.

Church 8½ A.M. Wrote to Ld St Germans—Ld Granville—Mr Glyn—Mr G. Howell—Mr West—and minutes. Homeric notes; but *few*! Read Eliot papers[1]—Peregrine Pickle—Howell on Waste Lands. Saw the Bp of Chester—Mr Chidlow.[2]

To George HOWELL, 1 December 1871. 'Private.' Add MS 44432, f. 210.[3]

I have read with interest the tract you have been good enough to send me.[4] I consider that all plans, which aim at the greatest freedom in the disposal of land, at the profitable use of cooperative associations, and at the increase of the produce of the soil (provided that increase be not sought by uprooting a settled and self-supporting population), to be closely connected with the national welfare. But (whatever I may see hereafter) I have never yet seen a plan for reclamation of waste lands by the agency of the State which did not leave on my mind the belief that it would end in failure as to its immediate object and in a too real addition to the public burdens. Great good however is likely to be done in a country like this where sober ideas and respect for right prevail by the discussion of the subject, for as a rule every landlord and every occupier has it in his power within his own sphere to confer benefit at once on himself and his country by the improved cultivation of the soil.

2. Sat.

Ch. 8½ AM. Wrote to Mr West Tel.—Mr Hammond Tel.—Mr Bouverie—Robn G.—Ld Kimberley—Ld Acton—Ld Denbigh—Mr Rawson—and minutes and minutes. The Lowes came. Long conversation with him in evening on Civil List[5] & other matters. Read Eliot papers (finished)—Per. Pickle.

3. Advent S.

Ch. 11 AM with H.C. and 6½ PM. Wrote minutes. Walk & lengthened conversation with Lowe. Discussion with Mrs Lowe on Xty. Read Ffoulkes on the Creeds[6]—Brother Placidus (finished)—Matrimonial Union[7]—Bp of Lincoln's Two Sermons.[8]

[1] E. G. *Eliot, Lord St Germans, *Papers relating to Lord Eliot's mission to Spain in the spring of 1835* (1871).

[2] Charles Chidlow, unbeneficed priest in Liverpool.

[3] Marked 'Copy out on signed sheet'.

[4] G. Howell, 'Waste lands and surplus labour' (November 1871), n. 2 of 'Papers for the People' issued by the Greenwich Advanced Liberal Association.

[5] Lowe was invited prior to his Halifax speech; see *The Times*, 6 Dec. 1871, 3e and Add MS 44301, f. 221; Gladstone found the speech disappointing; Ramm I, ii. 289.

[6] E. S. *Ffoulkes, *The Athanasian Creed* (1871).

[7] C. Homeford, *Matrimonial union considered* (1871).

[8] C. *Wordsworth, 'The Maccabees and the Church' (1871).

4. M.

Ch. 8½ AM. Wrote to Ld Chancellor—Mr McClure—Mr Bright—Mr Gurdon (Tel.)—Ld Halifax—& minutes. Further conversation with C. of E. who went off at 11 to Halifax. Walk with the gentn guests. Read for 4 or 5 hours the Alabama case[1]—And Capper's book. Dinner party.

To LORD HALIFAX, lord privy seal, 4 December 1871. Add MS 44541, f. 4.

1. It is true as you suppose that the Cowen knighthood virtually preceded the Dilke speech. But what you say[2] upon the subject is beyond my comprehension. I have heard but cannot vouch for it that the *son* is an ultra-politician & perhaps the critics think the distinction immaterial. As to the father he is a radical & as far as I know no more. We have hardly a better or steadier supporter in the H. of C. But it is not for this that he is knighted. It is for an immense local service, which has been indirectly a great national service performed by him as Chairman during many years of the Commission who have had charge of the noble works of improvement on the Tyne. A better case I have never had to do with. 2. I do not know if you read constantly the newspapers of both our wings, but I find we are fired into pretty early from opposite quarters, & we must expect plenty of sharp criticism if not something more. The Dilke campaign is part of a most serious question, but I marvel at those who think that it is in the power of the Government to put down such declarations & movements by holding strong language. I have no doubt much satisfaction might be given, & much popularity acquired, by it but it would tend to establish rather than end the controversy. What is needed is that we should if possible do or cause something to be done of a nature likely to remove the dissatisfaction, of which the absurd republican cry is an external symptom. 3. It seems to me worth considering whether [the] statement about a Federal scheme for Ireland, deserves more contradiction as it appears to proceed from a responsible person. Perhaps the Irish Govt. could inform us what he is as to character & weight. 4. Bright corresponds with me about Educational & other matters, & altogether that affair does not look unhopeful. 5. The Alabama *Case* is now printed. I have asked Lowe to read it. Would it be well if you also could do it. It seems to me well done as far as I have yet seen.

5. Tu.

Wrote to The Queen—Mr Hammond l. & Tel.—Bp of Worcester—Abp of Canterbury—Dean of ChCh (V.C. Oxf)—Ld Lyttelton—Mr Morgan—& minutes. Cut a walnut tree with W. Much pleased with S.s guests, the Cunliffes. Conversation with Mrs Gordon respecting Arthur's affairs. Read P. Pickle. Finished Alabama Case.

[1] Government's presentation of the Alabama case (see 27 Nov. 71), which he found 'admirable', save for one passage; see Add MS 44541, f. 5. Final version in *PP* 1872 lxix. 1.

[2] Halifax's letter untraced; Sir Joseph Cowen and his son; see 22 Aug. 62 and 26 Apr. 70.

6. Wed.

Ch. 8½ AM. & 7 P.M. to hear Mr Williams. Wrote to Mrs Thistlethwayte—Ld Granville—Ld Halifax—Rev. Mr Harvey—Med. Officer of Guy's[1]—D. of Argyll—The Queen—and minutes. Cut a tree with Willy. Read P. Pickle—Renan. Dinner party in evening.

7. Thurs.

Ch. 8½ A.M. Wrote to Dean Ramsay—Mr Cardwell—Mr Bright—Ld Lyttelton—Mr Baxter—Mr Murchison—Mr Gurdon—Mr [E.G.] Salisbury—and minutes. Read Renan—P. Pickle. Cutting with W. We went off to Chester—dined at the Mayor's (Mr R. Frost's) and went to the Volunteer's Ball afterwards. Back at 1¼. Found a Messenger & wrote Mem. for F.O. on Cotton Loan.[2] Late to bed.

8. Fr.

Ch. 8½ AM. Tel to Sir W. Knollys—do. to Ld Granville—Wrote to Attorney Gen.—Ld Lyttelton—Ld Monck—Mr Hammond—and minutes. When W. & I were about to haul down a walnut tree we had cut there came telegrams with the unfavourable tidings of the Prince of Wales. On consideration I decided to go up in the morning, partly with a view to a Council tomorrow—and wrote to Abp of Canterbury—Telegrams to Mr Gurdon—The Queen—Col. Ponsonby—Ld Ripon—Ld Granville. Saw Mr P. Ralli—Bp of St Asaph respecting Welsh Univ. Dinner party. Read Renan—Tylor on Culture.[3]

9. Sat. [London]

Off at 8¼. Reached C.H.T. before 3. Telegr. to The Queen—WHG—Mr Helps—Wrote to Lady Westminster—Dean of Rochr—Mrs Th.—The Speaker[4]—Mr Glyn—Eccl. Commrs—Ld Kimberley—& minutes. Saw Ld Halifax—Ld Chancellor—Mr Forster—Mrs Cooper. Council 3¼-4½. Dined at Mr Thistlethwayte's. Conversation with him & A. K[innaird] respecting Paddn Est. & Eccl. Commn.[5] Read Mr Sargant's Essays[6] and Bisset on Sir W. Scott.[7]

[1] Business obscure; prince of Wales?

[2] Untraced; America pressed that Britain accept cotton bond claims along with indirect claims; Britons claimed for losses on confederate cotton: PRO FO 5/1247; see 14 Dec. 71.

[3] Sir E. B. *Tylor, *Primitive culture*, 2v. (1871).

[4] *Denison had pressed Whitbread as his successor but came to accept *Brand; Add MS 44541, f. 10.

[5] See 10 Nov. 71.

[6] See 13 Nov. 71.

[7] A. Bisset, 'Sir Walter Scott' in *Essays on historical truth* (1871).

10. 2 S.Adv.

Vere St Chapel mg. Ch. Royal aft. Also looked in at St Paul's [Marylebone]: a wilderness! Wrote to Ld Granville—Telegrams to Hawarden. The afternoon brought another sad change, almost shutting the door of hope. Dined with L[yttelto]n: conversation with him on Univ. Commn, & St Paul's; & *warned* him about the 'Church *Reform & Defence* Association'.[1] Read International Resolutions &c.—Life of Andrew Reed[2]—Dale Owen's Debateable Land[3]—and Tracts. Saw Mr West—Harry—about his employments & prospects.

11. M.

Wrote to Mr Cardwell—Ld Shaftesbury—Sir W. Jenner—Ld Kimberley—The Queen—Professor Blackie—C.G.—Duc de Broglie—& minutes. Dined at Mr Thistlethwayte's. Saw Mr Glyn—Abp of Canterbury—Ld Granville. C.G. came in evg. Cabinet 3-6. All the accounts from Sandringham summed up in one word—painful suspense. Read Harness's Life[4]—Buchanan's Drama.[5]

Cabinet Monday D. 11. 71. 3 PM. [16] Bruton St.[6]

√ The Collier appointment. Statement by Ld Chancellor & general conversation. No disapproval. G[ranville?] said corp[oratio]n[?] was responsible.

√ {The Speakership.
WEG's narrative: no obj[ectio]n.

○ Sir C. Dilke's Speech.[7] Civil List. Queen's Income Tax.

√ University Commission. Names disclosed. See list. Mem[oria]l. men[tione]d. forward not withstanding.[8]

Army Estimates. Navy Estimates.

√ In event of the Prince [of Wales]'s Death. Regency & immediate session? Speakership?
General conversation & opinion. Princes shd. be Regent. Meeting of Parlt. to be about middle of January but no decision taken.

√ French Treaty. Conversation on tone to be adopted in reply to Remusat.

[1] i.e. the Church Institution, reformed as the Church Defence Institution 1871, supported by Tait and most bps.; 'almost a tool of the Conservative Party', Marsh, *Victorian Church*, 145-6.

[2] A. and C. Reed, *Memoirs of Andrew Reed* (1863).

[3] R. D. *Owen, *The debatable land between this world and the next* (1871).

[4] A. G. K. L'Estrange, *The literary life of W. Harness* (1871).

[5] R. W. *Buchanan, *The drama of Kings* (1871).

[6] Add MS 44639, f. 124.

[7] On republicanism, at Newcastle, 6 November. See 17 Nov. 71n etc. Gladstone next day requested official details on Queen's income tax; reply, showing tax not deducted on classes iv or vi, in Add MS 44617, f. 140.

[8] Duke of Somerset was asked to chair it, and declined; Add MS 44541, f. 12, see 15 Dec. 71. The duke of Cleveland eventually accepted.

To E. CARDWELL, war secretary, 11 December 1871. Add MS 44119, f. 299.
'Private.'

1. I do not understand the figures in the page of your interesting letter[1] which I have marked in pencil. Will you kindly say whether they are right?
2. You will I daresay remember my opinion, at the close of the War in the beginning of the present year, that we ought to take a million off our Army Estimates, in part, by a reduction of men; the difficulty with which I then gave way to you & others; the part I had to take in the H of C. in assuring our friends (with a pretty clear reference among other things to the number of men) that our Estimates were transition Estimates. This was at a time when the 'million' not only existed on paper but were still in arms. Since that time your Reserve has grown: your short service men have greatly increased: no circumstance of danger or apprehension affecting us has come into view. Under these circumstances I do not say that the Government is not free, but *I* am not free in honour to be a party to the same vote of men as I reluctantly agreed to last year.
3. Will you kindly let the accompanying sheet be filled up for me—it will not I think give trouble.
[P.S.] No other point in your sketch calls I think for remark from me at present.

12. Tu.

Wrote to D. of Somerset—Serj. Armstrong[2]—Mr Ayrton—Mr Bruce—and minutes. Saw Mr Glyn (2)—Mr Cardwell—Ld Granville—Duc de Broglie. Saw Graham X Terry. Read Harness's Life—Buchanan's Drama. Dined at Mad. Ralli's: a delightful harp & p[iano] f[orte] music. A shade better in the news from Sandringham.

Army Estimates
I compare the force deemed sufficient by us at two former periods with that set down in the letter of 11 December 1871. I add together in such case, as alike available for defence, the Army and the Army Reserve. I have not included Militia Reserve. I separate volunteers with Yeomanry from the rest, as they may be taken at the same figure.

	1870–1 (Feb.)	1870–1 (July)	1872–3
1. Army and Army Reserve	116000	136000	142000
2. Militia	98000	98000	139000
3. Pensioners	20000	20000	30000
	234000	254000	311000
4. Volunteers & Yeomanry	184000	184000	184000
	418000	438000	495000

At the beginning of 1870, we contended that we had much improved the position of this country for defence, as compared with previous periods, by withdrawing

[1] Of 9 December 1871; Add MS 44119, f. 287; pencil marks against Cardwell's estimate of £14,851,700, i.e. £811,900 more than 1869–70, £956,700 more than 1870–1, £282,000 less than 1868–9.

[2] Richard Armstrong, 1815–80; former liberal M.P.; failed to obtain requested promotion at the Irish bar; Add MS 44541, f. 12.

soldiers from points where they were not wanted, and placing them where they were wanted. In August of that year, at the outbreak of the War, and with the appearance of grave danger hanging over Belgium, we thought 136000 men a sufficient army force (as above defined). The circumstances of the present period are for us no less grave by a great deal, both in Europe and in America. In the interval, the permanent foundation of Army Reserve has been laid by Short Service, which now begins to be really at work; the force of the Artillery and Engineers has been much increased; 51000 men have been added to the Militia and Pensioners.

All these circumstances, to mention no others, appear to recommend and warrant a diminution and not an increase under my head No. 1, which includes the Regular Army and Reserve.[1]

13. Wed.

Wrote to Mr Bruce—Eccl. Commrs—Mr Wright—Mr Cartwright MP—Ld Blachford—Ld Granville—Mr Morgan—Col. Ponsonby—Sir W. Knollys—and minutes. Saw Rev S.E.G.—D. of Argyll—Mr Glyn—Mr Chaffers—Mr Goschen—Mr Cardwell (with whom I came to an arrangement on the Army Estimates)[2]—Mrs Davidson—Mrs Thistlethwayte. Dined with Lady Lyttelton. Read Life of Harness—Life &c. of Hookham Frere—Haweis on Music.[3]

14. Th.

Wrote to Ld Lisgar—The Queen—and minutes. Cabinet 3-7. For $2\frac{1}{2}$ hours we discussed Army Estimates, mainly on reduction, & the C. of E. did not speak one word! Saw Ld Wentworth(!)—Mr Monsell—Mr Moore—Sir Aug. Paget—Mr Glyn—Mr Goschen—Ld Halifax & the Chancellor on the Paddington Estate &c. Dined with Ld Halifax. Saw Beecher X & one. Read Life of Harness.

Thurs. Dec. 14 71. 2.30. [16] Bruton St.[4]

√ Army Estimates. General statement. Reduction 6000. Saving 1170 + 80 repayment from India = 1250 m[ille]. Less than 68-69 by 433 m[ille]. (in Colonies by $1\frac{1}{2}$m). Total force at home 102,808. & a C[ommander] in C[hief].[5]

○ Scotch Education. (Monday)

○ Navy Estimates—put off.

√ Duke of Devonshire's letter on Univ. Commn. described. Proposals to proceed as intended.

[1] Initialled and dated 12 December 1871; Add MS 44760, f. 126.

[2] See next day's cabinet.

[3] H. R. *Haweis, *Music and morals* (1871).

[4] Add MS 44639, f. 126.

[5] Total announced by Cardwell was 133,649, a saving of 1398 men; *H* ccix. 880, 22 February 1872.

√ Ld. Kimberley announced annexation of the Diamond Fields by the Govr. of Cape's own Act. No objection taken.[1]
√ Ld. Granville mentions his conversation with Broglie on French Treaty. D[itt]o WEG briefly. Draft to be prepared.[2]
d[itt]o [i.e. Granville:] Abolition of Slavery in Puerto Rico & Cuba. Shall the dispatch wh. has been written be presented? Conclusion: to press within limits, as to Puerto Rico, at any rate for more practical measure.[3]
√ Note of joint invitation by U.S. and G.B. to accede to rules of Washington Treaty—Dispatch respecting terms of this note as to the word open read & approved.[4]
√ Cottonhouse Bonds. to be presented as Claims? Not unless inclosure for Cotton was to become property.[5]
√ St. Alban's Raid claims. Ld. G[ranville] to see Gen. Schenk.
Est. stand over to Monday.
√ Army. The Guards. Mr. Cardwell proposed his plan to abolish: Exceptional privileges of army promotion—Distinctions involving discipline—Financial advantage except when cause can be shown—Reports to be had on all these.

15. Fr.

Wrote to Princess Louise—The Queen—Ld Brougham—and minutes. Cabinet 2¼–5½. Dined at Mr Goschen's. Read Life of H. Frere.[6] Conclave on Mr Reeve's Salary.[7] Saw Bp of Winchester—Mr Childers—Mr Ffoulkes—Mr M'Coll—Mr Glyn. Saw one[R].

Frid. Dec. 15. 71. 2 PM. [16] Bruton St[8]
Univ. Commission. D. of Somerset declines.[9]
Licensing Bill. Discussed at great length & main provisions determined.[10]
Next Cabinet Monday.

16. Sat.

Wrote to T.M. Gladstone—The Speaker—Sir R. Phillimore—The Viceroy—Ld Chichester—Mr Dodson (draft)—Col. Ponsonby (Tel.)—Wrote Mem. on Scots Ch.Patr.[11] Saw Mr Glyn—do *cum* Mr Brand—do *cum* Ld E. Clinton—Duchess of Argyll—Mrs Russell. We dined at Stephy's with him & H. A most satisfactory little menage. Read Life of Frere—Life of Harness.

[1] Plans for confederation thus being shelved; see C. F. Goodfellow, *Great Britain and South African Confederation 1870–1881* (1966), 39.
[2] Mineral oils; Lyons to Remusat, 26 December 1871, PRO FO 27/1886.
[3] See *PP* 1872 liv. 750.
[4] See PRO FO 5/1391.
[5] See F.O.C.P. 2061 and 7 Dec. 71.
[6] Probably *The works of J. H. Frere in verse and prose . . . with a prefatory memoir by W. E. and Sir B. Frere*, 2v. (1872).
[7] As registrar of the privy council.
[8] Add MS 44639, f. 129.
[9] See 11 Dec. 71n.
[10] The 1872 Licencing Act; see Harrison, *Drink and the Victorians*, 271.
[11] Untraced.

17. 3 S.Adv.

Chapel Royal mg (Mr Kingsley)—St Peter's E[aton] Square evg (Mr Wilkinson). Saw Ld Granville—Mr Glyn—Mr Ayrton. Wrote to the Queen—Messrs Farrer & Ouvry—Bp of London—Mr A. West—and minutes. Read Life of Bedell: how noble[1]—Bp of London's Charge.[2] Evening meal at Mr Warner's.

18. M.

Wrote to Sir W. Jenner[3]—Mrs Dyce Gardiner[4]—Mr Beet[5]—Chancr of Exr—Mr Brand—The Queen (2)—Sir G. Grey[6]—Ld Kimberley—W.H.G.—& minutes. Saw Mr Glyn. Cabinet 2¼–6¾. Dined with the Phillimores. Saw Mr Glyn—Sir R. Phillimore (Sir R. Collier &c.). Read. . . .

Monday D. 18/71[7]

√ Army Estimates: 1. Scheme of Estimates 2. Guards. 3. Petitioning of officers; on suppression[?]. Not to agree. General scheme agreed to.
Sir J. Burgoyne. No public vote for a monument.
√ Meeting of Parliament. Feb. 6. Tues.
√ Speakership—To be announced.[8]
√ Canada. Fenian losses compensation. Decided by 8 to 7 to authorise Canadian Govt. to announce independently of the acceptance of Treaty by Canadian Parlt.[9]
√ Goschen: Navy Estimates. To consider of changing 8½ hours[?] to 9: & to redress army special wage grievance. Coal & hemp 70,000 increase. Chatham base 70m decrease. Pensions 30m incr[ease]. Troops conveyance 30m decr[ease]. Shipbuilding &c admit a reduction of 300m. Agreed to.
√ Scotch Education Bill. Basis of last year as to religious instruction & denominational schools.
√ Belgian Minister complains of seizure of boat. to go to Law Officers.

19. Tu.

Wrote to the Queen—Ld Kimberley—Ld Chichester—Mr Dodson

[1] *Life of Bishop Bedell*, ed. J. E. B. Mayor (1871).
[2] J. *Jackson, 'The parochial system. A charge . . . 1871' (1871).
[3] Asking how soon *Wales will be fit enough for a thanksgiving service; Add MS 44541, f. 16.
[4] About a picture by W. *Dyce; ibid., f. 17.
[5] Of Conduit Street; business untraced.
[6] Asking him to propose the nomination of *Brand as Speaker; Grey had himself been a possible choice; Add MS 44541, f. 18.
[7] Add MS 44639, f. 133; at Bruton Street.
[8] i.e. in the press.
[9] For: Forster, Hartington, Fortescue, Argyll, Goschen, Kimberley, Ripon, Stansfeld; against: Granville, Lowe, Bruce, Cardwell, Hatherley, Halifax; ibid., f. 134.

(sent dft of D.16)[1]—Messrs Strahan—Sir W. Knollys—Mr Westell—Mr Kinnaird—The Queen—& minutes. Cabinet 2-5¼. Saw Mr Glyn—do *cum* Mr Tufnell[2]—Sir Barnes Peacock. Saw Mrs Th: a painful scene: my fault perhaps. Dined at Sir R. Phillimore's and attended the Westminster [School] Play. The Epilogue very amusing. Read Frere's Life.

Cabinet D. 19. 71. 2 PM 16 Bruton Street[3]

√ Contagious Diseases. Ripon proposed to maintain the Acts. Determined: to repeal the Acts. New provisions considered.

√ Fenian Losses. Dispatch founded on Draft amended—to bind Canadian Govt. to procure acceptance of the Treaty 'by every means in their power'.

√ Sanatory [*sic*] Acts.

√ Act of Thanksgiving.

1. Ballot—& present Corrupt Practices.

2. Scotch Education—Mines Regulation—Licencing—Sanatory Bills—Contagious Diseases.

Judicial Reform Acts—Ministries Bill—Irish Education—Municipal Govt. of London—Local Taxation—Scotch Church Patronage.

20. *Wed.*

Wrote to Mr Bright—D. of Cleveland—Ld Clinton—Mast. of St John's—Prof. Price—Mr K. Hodgson—Mr Strutt[4]—Ld F. Cavendish—Sir G. Grey—Mr Thistlethwayte—Miss Milbank—Ld Chichester—Mrs Russell—Bp of Chester—The Speaker—and minutes. Saw Sir T. Biddulph—Ld Halifax—Mr West—Ld Hartington—Mr Glyn. Long & interesting conversation with the Duke of Cambridge. Saw Berry [R]. Read Life of Harness. Dined at Mad. Ralli's & again enjoyed the music.

21. *Th.* [*Hagley*]

Wrote to Mrs Thistlethwayte—Mrs Bennett—Dean Stanley—Rev Mr Mayow—Mr Cardwell—and minutes. Packing for journey. Off to Windsor before 12. Council there: & long interview with the Queen. Off in evg to Oxford & Hagley. Saw Col. Ponsonby—Dean

[1] Offering him the judge advocateship (as compensation for the Speakership), reminding him of necessity of cooperation with Brand if he continues as chairman of cttees.; Add MS 44541, f. 18. He declined the judgeship, Gladstone told Cardwell, 'in all good humour'; ibid., f. 25.

[2] Perhaps Edward C. Tufnell, school inspector for local govt. board.

[3] i.e. at Granville's house; Add MS 44639, f. 140.

[4] Asking John William *Strutt, 1842-1919, physicist; 3rd Baron Rayleigh 1873, to serve on Oxford and Cambridge commission; Add MS 44541, f. 20.

of Windsor—Ld Ripon—Duke of Argyll—Ld Sydney—Finished Life of Harness.

Windsor Dec. 21. 71.[1]

The Queen received a letter yesterday from Ld Halifax, in which he expressed pleasure at hearing that she had agreed to go in state to St Paul's to return thanks for the recovery (on its being completed or sufficiently advanced) of the Prince of Wales. Of this I heard on reaching Windsor yesterday; and I learned that it had much discomposed the Queen. She had, upon the occasion thus given, written a letter to Col. Ponsonby in which she very clearly & succinctly separated three subjects. First, some communication, by which she should make known to the country her warm sense of the sympathy & loyalty shown during the illness.[2] Secondly, a form of thanksgiving to be used in public worship throughout the country. Thirdly this idea of a procession to St Paul's: on which she did not, in the letter, put an absolute negative, but she treated it as something ulterior & contingent, to be considered separately, if at all, on its own merits.

I told the Queen her view of the case had been communicated to me & I entirely concurred in it—it was then decided by H.M. to write to me a letter, in which she should express her own feelings for herself, about the manifestation of sympathy by the people: this I am to send to Bruce as Home Secretary for publication. As respects the form of thanksgiving, I said Sir W. Jenner had informed me that Dr. Gull and he could not as yet speak of any particular interval, after which convalescence might be reasonably anticipated, and until they had done so, it seemed plain that nothing could be said. I was then proceeding to introduce the other subject, that of going solemnly to St Paul's, when the Queen delivered a very strong declaration against it. She objected to it because she disliked in an extreme degree the Cathedral service. She objected still more because she thought such a display, in point of religion, false & hollow. She considered that no religious act ought ever to be allied with pomp or show. Nothing should induce her to be a party to it. It would be of no use to press her as this was her conviction with regard to the religious part of the subject.

I first tried the point of time, & said that there could be no occasion to press H.M. at present, as it would be premature. But she said it was no question of time with her; that she wished now to deal with it once for all, and that she hoped I would never return to the subject.

[1] Initialled; finished on Christmas Day, 1871; Add MS 44760, f. 129. See *L.Q.V.*, 2nd series, ii. 181 and A. Ponsonby, *H. Ponsonby* (1942), 101.

[2] Guedalla, *Q*, i. 323. Printed, addressed to Bruce, in *The Times*, 30 December 1871, 7 f.

Then I fell back on the Princess of Wales, & said I had understood she was very desirous that there should be a public & solemn act of this kind by which to render thanks: and I could not help thinking that very probably the Prince of Wales would share this feeling. I said it would be very difficult to refuse to them, and to her, the gratification of such a wish. The Queen replied she did not think the Princess of Wales would now press it so much, after what she (the Queen) had said to her.

'Well, madam', I said, 'I grant all that your Majesty had urged with reference to the nature of these ceremonials, if they are to be considered merely as vehicles for the expression of the religious feelings of those who are to be the principal actors in them. But in the first place I feel convinced that there will be a very general desire expressed for something of this character, and if done it will give universal satisfaction—the sympathy of the country has gone beyond precedent—& beyond description: feeling has been wrought up to the highest point, and nothing short of a great public act of this kind can form an adequate answer to it—But besides this, Madam, let it be considered if you please whether Y.M. or those who are to appear as principal personages may not properly cast aside all thought of themselves; and their own feelings, in the matter: it may be most unsatisfactory to them individually, but ought we not to remember the great religious importance of such an act for the people at large: on them it will make a deeper impression—it will be a signal honour done to religion in their view. There are in these times but few occasions on which great national acts of religion can be performed; and this appears to be one of them, for which the opportunity has now been offered.'

These considerations appeared to tell very much with the Queen. I then dwelt upon the extreme solemnity of the occasion: not only for the Prince, as anyone after such an illness must be individually a better or a worse man for it, and not only for the Queen & Royal Family, but for the future of the Monarchy & of the country as connected with it. It had worked in an extraordinary manner to the effect of putting down that disagreeable movement with which the name of Sir C. Dilke had been connected. And what we should look to I thought was not merely meeting that movement by a more powerful display of opposite opinion, but to getting rid of it altogether, for it never could be satisfactory that there should exist even a fraction of the nation republican in its views. To do this it would be requisite to consider every mode in which this great occasion could be turned to account, & if possible to take away the causes which had led to the late manifestations.

The Queen urged that the state of things in France had had much to do with them & that in 1848 the case was worse.

I admitted both but said that since 1848 the foundation of the movement of that date had been broken up & all tendencies of that kind pretty well got rid of: also that it was to be feared that France might continue for a long time to be a source of sympathetic incitement, mischievously disturbing this country. I glanced at the necessity of finding for the Prince of Wales some means of living worthily of his great position & greater prospects: but this brought out no direct response; only there was a hope expressed by the Queen in some part of the conversation that the illness, and the display of feeling, would act directly in a beneficial manner on the Prince's character and conduct.

The latter part of the conversation turned more towards details: the Queen urging in them all the difficulties—the uncertainty whether the Prince's health might allow him to take part, until the season was far advanced, when the ceremony would have lost all meaning. Then she said it would be more convenient & appropriate at Westminster Abbey where they were crowned. I said it was bad to go against the established tradition, as it provoked adverse remark: such for instance would be the case if a Sovereign desired to be crowned at St Paul's. At length the Queen contracted her objection to the length of the service: and here I was able entirely to agree that the whole proceeding would have to be shortened. I referred H.M. to the Annual Register of 1789 (from which it appears that the Commons set out at 8 am; the King & Queen at 10, and their Majesties only returned to the Palace at half past three.)[1]

When the objection was at the highest, I observed to the Queen that there were various modes in which if she were able to take part her participation might be arranged and reminded her of her appearances at Windsor on the occasions of Royal marriages in St George's Chapel.

I also told her in the course of arguing for the proposal that I admitted its religious importance was that of a symbol, but it was not therefore to be accounted slight: Royalty was in one point of view a symbol, and one of great consequence: its character & duties had greatly changed among us in modern times but perhaps in the new forms they were not less important than in the old.

At one time we got upon the topic of the lowered tone of society in the highest rank. This is a question the Queen has repeatedly opened to me: & I took the opportunity today of admitting the fact, and of observing that it was the active influence of the Court on that

[1] On 23 April 1789, George III's supposed recovery.

particular circle which had done so much to elevate & purify its tone during the earlier part of the reign. The Queen replied that they had observed this lowering process at work before the Prince's death and that he was accustomed to attribute it to the augmented intercourse with France.

At one moment she started the idea that a day of Thanksgiving might be appointed to be observed as a general holiday—I considered that this would be viewed by many as an actual hardship, and by many more as involving something like a character of compulsion. Whereas if the procession to St Paul's set the example while the day would be very much kept, I thought, all the observance would have the grace of being entirely voluntary.

The upshot of the whole was that the Queen is in no way committed, & that the whole idea is subject to considerations of health, but it is entertained, & not unfavourably. At one time the Queen said the Prince & Princess might go without her: but she did not dwell on this & I think saw that it would not do very well.

22. Fr.

Wrote to Col. Ponsonby—The Queen (Mem)—The Speaker—Ld Granville—Ld Macduff[1]—Ld Chichester—Mr Bruce—and minutes. We finished the felling of a great beech, begun before I came. Read Short Statement of Powers of Eccl. Commn[2]—Newman's Essays[3]—Guizot's Duc de Broglie.[4]

23. Sat. [*Hawarden*]

Wrote to Mr Roundell—Mr Macdonnell—Mr Bruce—Dean of Westminster—Col. Ponsonby—The Queen (l. & Mem)—Ld Halifax—and minutes. Charles & I felled an oak. Walk with Lyttelton. After a short but pleasant visit, set out at 6. Reached Hawarden after midnight: having for once been betrayed into Xmas travelling. Wrote Mem. of conversation with H.M. on Thursday.

[1] Offering Elgin ld. lieutenancy to Alexander William George Duff, 1849-1912, lord MacDuff, 6th earl of Fife 1879, m. 1889 the Princess Royal, duke of Fife 1889; he accepted.

[2] Respecting the Paddington estate; A. F. Thistlethwayte wished the commissioners' bill stopped; Gladstone asked Bruce if he agreed with him that Thistlethwayte was right; Add MS 44541, f. 22.

[3] J. H. *Newman, *Essays critical and historical*, 2v. (1872).

[4] F. P. G. Guizot, *Le Duc de Broglie* (1872).

24. 4 S.Adv.

Ch mg at 11 and 6.30 P.M. Wrote to Viceroy of Ireland—Ld Granville—Mrs Th.—Mr Dodson—& minutes. Read Humphry on the New Lectionary[1]—Story's Life of Lee.[2]

25. Xmas Day.

C. & I went with five of our children to H.C. at 8.30. Stephy is detained at his Church, Willy waits till later. How little am I worthy of this blessing. Also Ch. 11 AM & 7 P.M. Wrote to Ld Granville—and minutes. Finished Mem. of conversation at Windsor. Read Life of Lee by Story—Macdonald's Love Law and Theology.[3]

26. Tu. St Stephen.

Ch. at 11 A.M. Wrote to Serj. Armstrong—Abp Manning—Ld Spencer—Canon Oakeley—Sir Thos G.—and minutes. Saw Mr Burnett (RR)—Mr [C. S.] Parker (Game, Scotl.)—Walk with J. Warren,[4] & literary conversation. He is very notable. Read Life of Frere—Life of Lee by Story—Heron's Hist.Univ. Dublin[5]—Love Law & Theology.

27. Wed. St John.

Ch 11 AM. Wrote to Duke of Cambridge—Duke of Argyll[6]—The Queen—Mr Cashel Hoey—Mrs Slade—and minutes. Attended the Rector's Annual Supper & proposed his health. We began the cutting down of a great Ash. Read Story's Life of Lee—Australian Debates—Life of Frere.

28. Th. H.Innocents.

Ch. 11 A.M. Telegrams to Mr Gurdon—Mr Hammond—Mr Bruce. Wrote to The Queen—Mr Cardwell—Mr Gurdon—Ld Halifax—Dr Brady—Mr Bruce—& minutes. We continued our work on the

[1] W. G. *Humphry, *The new table of Lessons explained* (1871).

[2] R. H. *Story, *Life and remains of Robert Lee*, 2v. (1870). See 27 Dec. 71n.

[3] By A. Macdonald (1869).

[4] John Byrne Leicester Warren, 1835-95, 3rd Baron de Tabley 1887; author and poet.

[5] D. C. Heron, *The constitutional history of the university of Dublin* (1847).

[6] 'I am reading Lee's *Life* by Story, in wh. you are often mentioned. It is impossible not to sympathise with this too pugnacious & idiosyncratic & not really very strong man, for he was deeply afflicted, & struggled hard to bear his double burden. The Biographer is contemptuous to opponents . . . he must be a different man except in name from the Story whom you so much I believe justly praised'; Add MS 44541, f. 24. For Gladstone's attack on Lee's *Erastus*, see 31 Aug., 3 Sept. 44.

tree. Saw Mr Roundell—on Univ. Commn—Mr C. Parker on Scots Educn. Finished Lee (Vol. II)—Finished Frere—Read Sir J. Hanmer.[1]

29. Fr.

Ch. 8½ A.M. Wrote to The Queen (Mem)—Ld Kimberley—Ld Spencer—D. of Cleveland—Robn G.—Mr Wykeham Martin—Ld Granville—and minutes. Also Tel. to Ld Spencer—Mr Gurdon. Conversation with Mr Roundell on Univ. Commn. We pursued our work upon the great ash: but owing to failure of the tackling it was not brought down. Read Zincke's Egypt[2]—Ld Ormathwaite on Astron. & Geology.[3]

And so ends my three score & second year. And yet my life is but half life while it is oppressed entangled & bent as it now is with the heavy burdens upon me which exhaust in public affairs the moral force of the soul. Not that this is my excuse. But it gives me hope that God in His mercy may soon deliver me into a freer and purer air.

To LORD KIMBERLEY, colonial secretary, 29 December 1871. 'Private.' Add MS 44224, f. 240.

I have received your letter, & the Australia papers.[4] What you write is always pleasant to read: but as to your inclosures I must say that a less agreeable Christmas box I have not received for many a day. I will set down as briefly as I can what occurs to me.

1. This seems to be a subject not for mention only but for full & careful discussion in the Cabinet. With that view should you not cause a very careful précis to be prepared of the whole case, but especially of the precedents & the grounds on which they were adopted & allowed in the several cases.

2. I am at a loss to understand the easy manner in which the question of Treaty seems to have been disposed of. The point to be determined is whether the several colonies, having been invested with an absolute sovereignty over their own Customs Law, are in respect of a matter of Customs Law to be considered as 'other countries' within the meaning of the Zollverein Treaty, & for the purpose of entitling to admission of goods at the low rate to be paid on the produce of those several colonies or some of them. I own it appears to me highly probable that they are to be so considered. But this is merely my opinion, or rather leaning towards an opinion. What I take to be certain & very material is that the interpretation of the Treaty is not for our Law Officers, except provisionally or for us. It is a matter of international law. We might be invited to go to Arbitration upon it, with the alternative even possibly of war: & this by *every* country with which we have a Commercial Treaty, if it contains a favoured Nation Clause, as

[1] Probably Sir J. *Hanmer, 'Notes and Papers . . . [on] the Parish of Hanmer' (1872); see 2 Jan. 72.

[2] F. B. *Zincke, *Egypt of the Pharaohs and of the Khédive* (1871).

[3] J. B. *Walsh, Lord Ormathwaite, *Astronomy and geology compared* (1872).

[4] Replies to Kimberley's circular despatch of 13 July 1871, *PP* 1872 xlii. 744.

is commonly the case: & this as a very cheap method, according to Gov. DuCane,[1] of conciliating the present Colonial Ministers & majorities.

I presume the obligation is terminable at a certain period; but I doubt as at present advised whether we can safely act in the sense desired by the Colonists within that period.

3. It seems to me that we ought to regard the demands of the Colonists as a whole, which they have avoided doing themselves, so that they are in part only to be gathered by implication. But I understand them to be these 3: a. They are to have the same powers of regulating the whole matter of Customs' duties, as independent countries possess. b. They are not to be bound by Treaties concluded by the sole authority of the Imperial Government. c. They are to establish direct relations of business with Foreign countries for themselves; as is set out: as I understand to be set out in the Papers & in the Australian debates, which I have seen, on the subject of this Tariff question, & of their Postal arrangements. d. They are to maintain 'the closest & most affte. relations' with this country. (So does the Boa Constrictor with the rabbit; but they are one-sided.)

4. Now whatever the alleged precedents have done, they have not as yet made fools of the British Nation in the face of the whole world; & this is what I fear we stand in some danger of, in the present case.

If I understand the papers rightly, none of the precedents go to 3[?] points or any of them. I do not understand that British N. America either is or has claimed to be supreme in the matter of Customs' duties. Certain concessions were made, the Imperial Power remaining otherwise intact. What were those concessions? When the Principal B.N.A. Colonies had united themselves in the Dominion we (I believe) both allowed them to be one for Customs purposes, (which we have long ago offered to Australia) & gave them the power or some power of regulating duties as between themselves & the minor members of the same group; in the expectation as it is said (but I will not dwell on this) that these also would come in. A limited power given to the already coalesced principal members of the body with regard to the outstanding fragments is stated to require us to grant a power without limit to be made in perhaps six wholly different modes by six different Colonies with reference not only to one another, but to all other Colonies, & not only to these, but to all Foreign Countries.

Frankly, I do not as yet see my way. I think I am not like you if you are more or less prepared to concede everything except neutrality in war, & then to stop at that point. My present leaning would be to take the demands as a whole & in the most becoming language to say that as a whole, that is the three first along with the fourth, they could not be granted: but I would not arrive at this, or indeed at any conclusion until I was more sure than I am now about a precise definition of the demands, & about the question of Treaties.

The insolence (for such it is) of Mr Duffy[2] & others I should silently pass by as local patriotism & in this I think you would agree.

Pray consider what I have said about the précis. I am very desirous that the Cabinet should not dispose of this matter without information both full & accurate.

I really do not see upon what foundation any duty of military & naval protection on our part is to rest, if the foreign relations of Colonies are to pass

[1] (Sir) Charles Du Cane, 1825–89; tory M.P. N. Essex 1857–68; governed Tasmania 1869–74; kt. 1875; chaired customs board from 1878.

[2] C. Gavan Duffy, chief secretary and premier of Victoria; chaired inter-colonial conference asserting independence of fiscal policy, 18 September 1871, *PP* 1872 xlii. 757, 763.

out of our hands into theirs. Would Mr. Duffy be kind enough to give us a definition of the Colonial relation, as to rights & duties, on the one side & on the other, as he would have it. *What* will be the remaining duties of the Colony towards the mother State?[1]

30. Sat.

Ch. 8½ A.M. Wrote to The Home Secretary—Ld Granville—Dr Elder—Serj. Armstrong—Scotts—and minutes. Saw the fall: but took no further part on account of a touch of rheumatism. Party to dinner: & a round game. Conversation with Messrs Bate, Johnson, & Kelly respecting the Railway question.[2] Read Smollett's Per. Pickle.

31. S.aft Xmas.

Staid in bed till 1½, without profit. Read the mg prayers. Ch in aftn. Wrote to Ld Powerscourt[3]—Ld Granville—Mr Glyn—and minutes. Read W. Lyttelton's Sermon—His Tract on Ch. Establishments[4]—Macdonalds Love Law & Theol.—Life of Lee Vol 1.—Bp Forbes on Art. XXVIII.[5]

Another year passes into the abyss. My mind is divided between the vast interests of life which bind me here and the confession how good (as it seems to one poor sight) it would be if all the mass of sin and sorrow were swept away and the Great Peace of Creation reestablished. So long as this is not God's will, let us each labour hard at the infinitely small fraction of the work which is committed to the hands of each. Farewell O year: and may that which now comes carry with it when it passes away a better record of good done and of sin resisted.

[1] Kimberley's despatch of 19 April 1872, replying to Australian demands, rejected an Imperial Customs Union, and requested further consultation before colonies acted fiscally autonomously; *PP* 1872 xlii. 748.

[2] N. Wales, Chester, Birkenhead railway, finished 1890.

[3] Offering Mervyn Wingfield, 1836–1904, 7th Viscount Powerscourt 1844, a lordship in waiting; he declined; Add MS 44541, f. 26.

[4] W. H. *Lyttelton, 'Church establishments; their advantages, social and religious' (1861).

[5] A. P. *Forbes, *An explanation of the Thirty-Nine Articles* (1867).

Hawarden

Mond. Jan. One. 1872. Circumcision.

Missed Church on account of rheum. and wet. But walked with Mr Thompson[1] to talk Irish affairs in afternoon: & went to tea at Mr Burnett's where we discussed Estate matters. Wrote to my sister Helen—Sir R.P. Collier[2]—Ld Granville—& minutes. Drew up (loosely) my little annual statement of Property.[3] Conversation with Mr Thompson on Irish affairs. Read Senior on M. Berryer &c.[4]—and Hanmer's Book.

2. Tu.

Ch. 8½ A.M. Wrote to Musurus Pacha—Lady Essex—Mrs Th.—W.H. Lyttelton—Ld E. Bruce—Sir Thos G.—Mad . . . (dupl.)—& minutes. Read Senior on M. de Coudray—Peregrine Pickle. Saw Mr Thompson. Cards in evg. Walk with Sir J. Hanmer.

To Constantine MUSURUS, Turkish ambassador, 2 January 1872. Add MS 44541, f. 27.

I have been requested to state to you my opinion of the proceedings & position of a person named Hatherley who it seems has by some means obtained ordination from the Patriarch of Constantinople for the purpose of carrying on a proselytizing operation at Wolverhampton. This request has been made to me by Mr. E. Freshfield, a member of a legal firm highly respected in the City, & one with which my family have long been connected as their confidential advisers. It is from my respect for this gentleman that I presume to trouble you with an opinion which is private & personal, & which relates to a matter in its *direct* aspect & operation perfectly insignificant. I call it so in itself, because his operations must, unless he be a man of astonishing gifts, which I have never heard, be an utter failure. So pure a piece of self-will can strike no root into the soil. The Church of Rome we know, the Church of England we know, Protestant Nonconformists we know: but of an Eastern Church proselytizing in the West we know nothing. I have named the three main religious powers in this country. The simple Protestants & the Roman Catholics unite in abhorrence of the Greek Church. The English Churchman, above all in this country, comprehends & respects the position & the character of the Eastern Church on its own ground: appreciates its merits & makes allowance for its weaker points, dealing out to it the liberal consideration, which he is aware that he much needs for himself & his

[1] H. S. Meysey-*Thompson, see 28 Aug. 61.

[2] Asking for documents useful for the defence of Collier's appointment; Add MS 44541, f. 27.

[3] Hawn P.

[4] N. W. *Senior, 'Berryer' and 'Tronson du Coudray' in *Biographical Sketches* (1863).

own Church. Now it is just this body, the *only* body in this country that has any sympathy with the Eastern Church, which Mr. Hatherley seeks to wound & to estrange. Upon the whole, though in my lifetime I have known many things causeless, foolish, insignificant & yet mischievous, I have never known a proceeding more causeless & more foolish, or which united so much insignificance with as much mischief (to the Eastern Church itself) as this proceeding of Mr. Hatherley. It is sure to bring dissatisfaction & discredit on all who have to do with it & the sooner it dies a natural death the better.[1]

3. Wed.

Ch. 8½ A.M. Wrote to The Queen (Mem.)—D. of St Albans—Sol. Gen.Irel.—D. of Argyll—C. of E. (2)—Ld Granville—Sir A.R. Adair—Viceroy of I. (Tel.)—Col. Ponsonby—& minutes. Read Per. Pickle—Love Law & Theology[2]—Thompson on Vice Royalty of Ireland.[3] Dinner party & Cards in evg. Finished Heron on Dubl. Univ.[4] Took Sir J. Hanmer to see the Aston Hall Works.

4. Th.

Ch. 8½ A.M. Wrote to M. Reitlinger—Sir H. Holland—Mr Glyn—Mr G.G. Scott—and minutes. Worked on arrangement of Library. Singing!! in evg. 'Non più andrai' &c.[5] Read Per. Pickle—L.L. & Theology—Taylor on Dublin Univ.[6]

To F. REITLINGER, 4 January 1872. Add MS 44541, f. 30.

For my family & myself I thankfully accept your good wishes,[7] & not less heartily return them. When we had the pleasure of seeing you,[8] your country was engaged in a struggle which called for & drew forth, portentous efforts. The task now before her, though less appalling is not less arduous. I do not mean the mere payment of her charges. The genius of French industry armed as it is with the resources of toil on the one hand & of thrift on the other, is fully equal to these demands, enormous though they be. I mean the consolidation & stable adjustment of her institutions. Europe must be ill unless France is well. God grant that the extraordinary powers & capacities may be as effectively applied to this, as they have been to nearly every other field of human exertion.

5. Fr.

Wrote to Sir B. Peacock—Dr Acland—Bp of Argyll—Lady Essex[9]

[1] Musurus wrote he would write privately to the Patriarch of Constantinople; Add MS 44433, f. 17. For Hatherley, see P. Anson, *Bishops at Large* (1964), ch. 2 and Matthew, 'Vaticanism', 438.

[2] By A. Macdonald (1869).

[3] See 1 Jan. 72.

[4] See 26 Dec. 71.

[5] From Mozart's *Le Nozze di Figaro*.

[6] Untraced.

[7] Of 31 December; Add MS 44432, f. 337.

[8] 23, 28 Dec. 70.

[9] Louisa, 2nd wife of 6th earl of Essex; see 13 July 46n.

—Robn G.—Chairman LNWRR.[1]—Ld Lyttelton—and minutes. 11-2. Mr Barker *cum* Mr Burnett, & Hawarden Trust Meeting—also on the unsettled claims respecting Aston Estate. Worked on Library. Cut some Alders. Read P. Pickle—L.L. & Theology—Lady G. Fullerton's Poems.[2]

6. Sat. Epiphany

Ch 11 A.M. C.s birthday. Her youth & strength are wonderful. Her gifts & graces ever grow. If mine do not, she adds weight to the responsibility. Wrote to The Queen (Mem.)—Ld Granville—Mr Burnett—Mr Hammond—Ld Chichester—D. of Devonshire—Archdn Sinclair, & minutes. Cut a lime with W. Arranging Library. Finished L.L. & Theology. Read Per. Pickle.

7. 1 S.Epiph.

Ch 11 AM. & H.C. where Herbert again appeared—also 6½ PM. Wrote to The Queen (Mem)—and minutes. Read Life of Lee Vol. 1.[3]—Birch's Sermon[4]—Bp Wordsworth's Charge[5]—Ffoulkes on Ath. Creed.[6] Herbert's 18th birthday. He is very dear & charming: eminently a taking boy, by looks & otherwise: the question of his profession is still depending. God grant him every blessing.

8. M.

Ch. 8½ AM. Wrote to Ld Powerscourt—Mr Bickersteth—Dr Monsell—Mr Cardwell—Mrs Bennett—Ly Londonderry—and minutes. Went over the line of the RR. in progress. Read Peregr. Pickle—Capper's Letters (finished)[7]—Life of Lee—A Gentleman's Letter to his Son become R.C.[8]

9. Tu.

Church 8½ AM. Wrote to Vicar of St Martin's—Sir Wm Jenner—Dr Gull[9]—Bp of Winchester—Ld A. Hervey—Sir A. Panizzi—Mr

[1] (Sir) Richard Moon, 1814-99; chairman of L.N.W.R. 1861-91; cr. bart. 1887; on link of Connah's Quay with Liverpool; Add MS 44541, f. 30.

[2] G. C. *Fullerton, *The gold digger and other verses* (1872).

[3] See 24, 27 Dec. 71.

[4] Probably T. *Birch, 'The wisdom and goodness of God. A sermon' (1749).

[5] C. *Wordsworth, 'A charge . . . 1870' (1870).

[6] E. S. Ffoulkes, *The Athanasian Creed reconsidered* (1872).

[7] See 27 Nov. 71.

[8] Untraced.

[9] Offering baronetcy; see 28 Oct. 69.

Watson—Sir R. Wallace—Sir J. Hogg—and minutes. 2¼-5¾. At the Rent dinner where as usual I made a speech. The company seemed happy and hearty. Read Per. Pickle (finished)—Case of Irish Ch. Curates[1]—Lady Nairne's Life & Songs.[2] A round game in evg.

10. Wed.

Ch. 8½ AM. Telegrams to Queen (3)—Chancellor of Exchequer—Ld Ripon. Wrote to The Queen—Mr Cardwell—Mr Bright—Ld Prov. Watson[3]—Ld Ripon—Lady Lothian—Mr Forster—Dean of Windsor—Duke of Cambridge—and minutes. Read Sir J. Hanmer (finished)[4]—Lady N[airne] Life & Songs—Story's Life of Dr. Lee.

To G. V. WELLESLEY, dean of Windsor, 10 January 1872. Add MS 44541, f. 36.

You have done good service & I have only to say ditto to your note[5]—I never thought we could, given the general conditions of the problem, get or *ask* from the Queen *both* the thanksgiving & the opening, & the first is worth ten of the other. I have told H.M. I think the announcement should be made in good time so as to prevent speculation about the Opening [of Parliament].

The public will be as I expect hugely pleased. I hope no Nonconforming whispers will disturb the harmony. But the dissenters are not at present in their best humour; however they must take their chance.

I see no objection to your writing to the Archbishop about the form of prayer.

11. Th.

Ch. 8½ A.M. Tel. to Queen. Wrote to D. of Newcastle—Ld Granville—Mr Glyn—Ld De Tabley—Mr Lowe—Mr Bullock—Mrs Th.—and minutes. Tree cutting with W. & Herbert. Round game in evening. Conversation with Mr Tollemache.[6] Read Story's Lee—Lady Nairne (finished).

12. Fr.

Wrote to D. of Argyll—Mr Richard MP—Mr Lowe—Mr McClure MP—Dean Ramsay—Rev Mr Molesworth—& minutes. Wrote MS (part) on Ld Derby & his Speech.[7] Church 8½ AM. Read Guizot's

[1] Anon. pamphlet.

[2] *Life and songs of the Baroness Nairne* (1869).

[3] i.e. James Watson, his stockbroker in Glasgow.

[4] See 28 Dec. 71.

[5] Of 8 January 1872, Add MS 44340, f. 1.

[6] J. T. Tollemache was resigning from his W. Cheshire seat.

[7] On *Derby's speech on Collier accusing Gladstone of 'transparent violation' of the Act, *The Times*, 10 Jan. 1872, 10; see 22 Jan. 72.

Duc de Broglie[1]—Brougham's Letters to Forsyth.[2] Felling with W. & H. Round game in evg.

13. Sat.

Ch. 8½ A.M. Wrote to D. of Sutherland—Sir A. Panizzi—Robn G. —General Fox—A. West—Ld Kennington—Mr Forsyth—Ld Ripon (Tel.)—and minutes. Saw Mr Burnett—Mr Tollemache (Household Suffr. in Counties &c.) Cut down a beech with W & H. Read Ld Ormathwaite[3]—Guizot's Duc de Broglie.

14. 2 S.Epiph.

Ch. mg 11 AM and 6½ PM. Wrote to Mrs Wm Gladstone—Ld Granville—Scotts—Ld Hartington—Mr Dodson—Mr Tennyson[4]—Mr T.B. Potter—Bp of London—Ld Stratford de R.—and minutes. Read Barry's Address[5]—Story's Lee (finished Vol. I.)—Ld Ormathwaite's Essays—Gentn's Letter to his Son on R.C. Religion. Conversation with Herbert on his future profession. Also with C. on the same.[6]

15. M. [London]

Ch. 8½ AM. Wrote to Ld Ormathwaite—Ld Granville—Ld Acton —Ld Hartington—H.J.G.—Mr West (Tel.)—M. Guizot—Mr Fairbrother—Mr Jones—and minutes. Finished Guizot's Duc de Broglie—Read Exile of Calauria.[7] Saw Mr [E.] Venables—W.H.G. respecting Herbert—And Herbert, on his own matters. Packing, putting by, &c. Off at 4.15. London at 10½. Saw Mrs Th.X.

To LORD ORMATHWAITE, 15 January 1872. Add MS 44541, f. 43.

I think myself highly favoured in being presented with one of the copies of your recently printed Volume.[8] I have read the two first of the three essays, with much concurrence, pleasure & advantage.

[1] See 22 Dec. 71. Sent by the author; diarist's fulsome thanks at Add MS 44541, f. 44.

[2] H. *Brougham, *Letters from Lord Brougham to William Forsyth* (1872).

[3] See 29 Dec. 71.

[4] *Tennyson had asked Gladstone to obtain employment for his neighbour, Capt. Speedy, Prince Alamayu's guardian; Argyll docketed that there was no Indian post available; Add MS 44433, f. 54-8. See 22 Jan. 72.

[5] Probably A. Barry, 'The Church questions of the day. An address' (1868).

[6] He went up to University college, Oxford, later in 1872.

[7] By S. *Canning, Lord Stratford de Redcliffe (1872); sent by him; Add MS 44433, f. 52.

[8] See 29 Dec. 71.

Though very little acquainted with the works of Darwin, for in simple truth I have not brain force enough for scientific subjects while laden with my present occupations, I have long ago seen there was something truly portentous in the avidity with which the age (as it is called) leapt to ulterior conclusions [at] which his first book was thought scarcely to hint, & which his physiological theory did not even require. You have I think laid down in dealing with him some propositions of great importance & value to which I own I do not see the answers. But I do not believe it is given to Mr. Darwin or Mr. Buckle to sweep away that fabric of belief which has stood the handling of 1800 years & of stronger men perhaps than any now alive. I wish I could see that improvement of the choicest individuals of our race which he seems to promise us. I read with admiration works of yours, which were in all men's hands at a time when you did not know of my existence; & it is a great pleasure to me now again after forty years to derive the same feeling from the same source. May it be given to us all to use as well as you appear to do, the season of ripe years & partial infirmity.

16. Tu.

Wrote to Bp of Winchester—Abp of Canterbury (2)—Ld Granville—Mr Cardwell—The Queen (Mem)—Rev. Dr Rigg—Ld Houghton—and minutes. Saw Ld Powerscourt—Capt. Helbert—Mr West—Chancr of Exr—Ld Ripon *cum* Mr Forster. Conclave on the Cole case.[1] Dined with Panizzi: much conversation *a 4 occhi*:[2] Mrs Th. afterwards. X. Read [J.] Morley's Voltaire.[3]

To J. H. RIGG, methodist minister, 16 January 1872. 'Private.' Add MS 44541, f. 45.

I appreciate highly the spirit of your letter,[4] & I thank you also for the articles which I have read, & shall read with care.

In your mode of approaching the Irish University question I find little indeed to complain of. When you say an Examining or Governing Board shall be colourless, I am sure you do not mean it shall be composed of men without religion or men in whom no religious men will have confidence; but persons on whom the entire community will rely. I am afraid however that when you say we have a glorious opportunity, I am unable to follow you. We should have one if the real difficulties of the case were the measures of the obstacles in our way, or if all men had minds open & fair as yours. But I sorrowfully repeat that I have not in all my life known a case in which wholly gratuitous and unwarranted jealousy and suspicion has done so much, when added to the spirit of religious animosity, to *poison* the whole atmosphere of a great public question & prevent a solution which ought to have been arrived at without difficulty. However I still hope.

I take it to be my chief duty to the moment[5] to avoid inflaming these quarrels within by premature announcements or by controversial remarks.

[1] Henry *Cole, see 21 Mar. 54; often in disputes over development of S. Kensington; details of this one untraced.

[2] 'by four eyes', *tête-à-tête*.

[3] J. *Morley, *Voltaire* (1872).

[4] Not found; *Rigg published widely in Wesleyan periodicals; Gladstone does not record reading these articles.

[5] 'movement' corrected to 'moment'.

17. Wed. [*Osborne*]

Wrote to The Queen Tel.—Sir T. Biddulph—R. Palmer—S. Scott & Co.—Mr [S.] Morley—Mr Forster—Mr West—Abp of Canterbury —& minutes. Off at 10.50 to Osborne. Arr. 4.30 after a wild passage. Saw Col. Ponsonby. Long interview with H.M. Very cheerful, well, & kind. Saw Ld F. Kerr. Read Q.R. on Theatre[1]—Finished Ld Stratford's (at 84?) very remarkable Exile of Calauria. Dined with H.M. & further conversation—I am delighted to see how fond she appears to be of Catherine, whose manners with H.M. I think cannot be surpassed.

Osborne Jan 17-19 [*1872*][2]

1. Sir W. Jenner—thanks. 2. Abp of Syra & Tenos d[itt]o. 3. MacCormick d[itt]o. 4. Ld Powerscourt d[itt]o. 5. ½ hour ¾ & 1 hour service Dean W[ellesley] Dean of Windsor. 6. Announcement of St. Paul's with Thanksgiving. 7. In church of Dissenters on as early a day after the 20th as can be arranged—wh. H.M. hopes to attend. NB. Police to report as to H.M.'s probable reception.

18. Th.

Wrote to The Queen—Ld Granville—Rev. Mr Capes—and minutes. Saw The Queen—1¼ hour, in the evening, before dinner—Sir T. Biddulph—Col. Ponsonby—The two together for a conversation respecting P. of Wales & Ireland: they I think agree with me. Walk with Col. P. & visit to his wife. Saw 3 of the *Wales* children, small but with much charm, & forthcoming as children ought to be.[3] Dined again with H.M. Read Q.R. on Bp Berkeley.[4]

To the Rev. J. M. CAPES, 18 January 1872. Add MS 44541, f. 47.

The strongest of the words used in your painfully interesting letter[5] come from you with a peculiar force because you have shown yourself to be eminently free from the polemical spirit. If I do not echo them it is only because I am determined not to enter into this department of the Educational controversy before the time when I may be obliged to do it with a practical purpose in view. I do not know how far you have weighed a question ulterior to but consistent with what you have written; whether & if at all how far it is the duty of the State to limit the civil privileges of Roman Catholics in the matter of Education on account of a well grounded belief or it may be knowledge that they will themselves lay their freedom as far as they possess it at the feet of their Bishops.

The most deplorable characteristic of these days in my view is first the sacrifice of liberty in the name of Religion, & secondly & to a great extent by way of reaction the sacrifice of religion in the name of liberty.

[1] *Quarterly Review*, cxxxii. 1 (January 1872).
[2] Add MS 44757, f. 19.
[3] The three eldest were: Albert, duke of Clarence, George V and Louise, duchess of Fife.
[4] *Quarterly Review*, cxxxii. 85 (January 1872).
[5] Untraced; see 23 Apr. 71.

19. Fr. [London]

Wrote to Dean of St Pauls—Ld Chamberlain—Sir R. Palmer—The Queen (l. & Mem.)—Ld Cawdor—Mr Cardwell—Ld Hartington—and minutes. Cabinet 3¼–6¾. Saw D of Argyll *cum* C. of E.—Mr Glyn: who also dined with us. Read Morley's Voltaire—Q.R. on Dickens. 8¾ AM to 1: Journey from Osborne by Portsmouth to London & C.H. Terrace.

Cabinet Frid. Ja. 19. 72. 3 PM.[1]

√ Irish Sol. Generalship[2]
√ Address from R.Cs of Dublin Diocese—minute of reply.[3]
Appointment of Indian Auditor—D. of Argyll & Ch. of Exr.
√ Report 1. as to Thanksgiving 2. as to some employment for the P. of Wales, by WEG from Osborne.
√ French Treaty. Ld Lyons in Dispatch of Jan. 16. quoting Thiers. Ld G's Telegram of yesterday approved. Dft. dispatch in reply to Lord L[yons] read and approved.[4]
√ Westbury's letter & advice. Approve the reservation to the Counter Case.[5]

20. Sat.

Wrote to Ch. of Exr—Mr Cardwell—Mr H. Strutt—Dr Paget—Mr J. Colman—Circular l. to Members[6]—The Queen (Mem.)—Mr Barry—Bp of Winchester—and minutes. Saw Ld Sydney—Mr M'Coll—Mr Grogan—Col. Ellis—Mr Glyn. Saw Mrs Graham[R]. Read Q.R. on Sir H. Holland[7]—Houghton on H. of Lords[8]—M'Carthy on Home Rule.[9]

To E. CARDWELL, war secretary, 20 January 1872. PRO 30/48/9, f. 7.
'Private & Early.'

I should be glad to know whether you are a party to the measure which has been taken with regard to the United Service Institution, as described in the inclosed Memorial—and whether you are satisfied with it. I am really incompetent to judge how far this Institution contributes to the great work of exercising and developing Brains in the Army & Navy, but if it is really addressed to the Science & Art of War I should be disposed to look upon it with something of the same favour which we have shown to the other 'learned Societies'.[10]

[1] Add MS 44640, f. 2.
[2] Christopher Palles became Irish solicitor general on 6 Feb., succeeding R. Dowse, promoted to attorney general, replacing C. R. Barry.
[3] Address from Cullen and others on Roman catholic educational disabilities, and draft of reply, at Add MS 44433, f. 67.
[4] See Ramm I, ii. 301.
[5] On Alabama; ibid., ii. 298.
[6] On opening of parliament.
[7] *Quarterly Review*, cxxxii. 157 (January 1872).
[8] R. M. *Milnes, Lord Houghton, on the Lords in *Fortnightly Review*, xvii. 1 (January 1872).
[9] J. G. MacCarthy, *A plea for the home government of Ireland* (1871).
[10] Cardwell replied, 21 January 1872, PRO 30/48/9, f. 8, suggesting rooms at Burlington House.

21. 3 S.Epiph.

Chapel Royal mg. In afternoon went to a mission service of Mr Henderson's in a Lodging House. It was very interesting. Wrote to The Queen—and minutes. Read Report of French Rescue Society[1]—Lyttelton's Ephemera Sacr.[2]—A. Christie's Martyrdom of St Cecilia.[3]

22. M.

Wrote to Ld Chancellor—Mr Cardwell—Ld Sydney—Ld Hartington—Mr Goschen—Lord Derby—The Queen—and minutes. Read Q.R. on Irish Educn.[4] Saw Mr T.M. Gibson—Mr Ayrton—Mr Glyn (2)—Ld Chancellor—Mr West—Sir W. Farquhar. Cabinet 2¼-6. Dined with the Farquhars.

Cabinet Monday Jan. 22. 2 P.M.[5]

Fee Jee Islands Slave Trade. Bill & Mem. to be produced by Ld Kimberley.
East African Slave Trade. a. negotiate with Foreign Powers. b. inquiry as to line of steam communications.
√ Alamayo—exchange for Speedy—named.[6]
√ Sir R. Collier. a. write to Ld Derby.[7] b. approach F.O. to Fawcett.[8]
√ Mr Ayrton's Park Bill—*the Clause as to meetings in the Parks?* disposed to take it. Will bring it in unless inhibited. Yes.
√ Procession to St. Paul's. Sydney's letter considered.[9]
Ballot Bill considered & approve[d].
Corrupt Practices d[itt]o.

To E. CARDWELL, war secretary, 22 January 1872. PRO 30/48/9, f. 9.

Reserving all that is due (& it is much) to the authority of the Chancellor of the Exchequer in the matter,[10] I think there is much to recommend your proposal with respect to the United Service Institution and while I think the initiative lies with you and Goschen I shall as at present advised be a well wisher.

It would be well, if there is to be action in this or any like sense, that it should take place before the newspapers shall have added this fresh count to the long indictment against us.

[1] Untraced. [2] See 27 Mar. 57. [3] By A. J. Christie (1865).
[4] *Quarterly Review*, cxxxii. 228 (January 1872). [5] Add MS 44640, f. 6.
[6] Capt. Speedy had been instructed to bring to Britain Prince Alamayu of Abyssinia (1861-79); he had done so but then failed to hand him over; see mem. at Add MS 44618, f. 26 and 14 Jan. 72n.
[7] Asking *Derby if his speech was correctly reported; Add MS 44541, f. 51. See 10 Jan. 72.
[8] This phrase barely legible.
[9] Gladstone told Sydney this day: 'The Cabt. are sorry that the Q. only goes in half State, but it is well that the Carriage be open, & as to the whole matter we can only acquiesce & be thankful for what has been obtained . . .'; Add MS 44541, f. 51.
[10] See 20 Jan. 72.

To LORD HARTINGTON, Irish secretary, 22 January 1872. Add MS 44541, f. 50.

I return the MS part of the papers as you desire.[1] I certainly think the plan of enabling districts in Ireland to purchase is well worth examining. Lowe seems to me to be right in saying that it would be dangerous for the Government to accept privilege or special responsibility, *if* it is also to be a lender of money. But I should not absolutely & *in limine* bar the idea of moderate loans when the interest is actually covered by free revenue.

23. Tu.

Wrote to The Speaker—Bp of Lichfield—Mr Ayrton—Ld Hartington—Ld Sydney—The Queen (l. & Mem). Saw Ld A. Hervey—Mr Glyn (2)—Bp of Moray (Tel)—Ld Chancellor. Saw Mrs Th. & Mt Ferrand X. Also Mrs Tyler. Cabinet dinner 8-9½ and Cabinet 9½-11¼. Read Lushington's Evidence[2]—M'Carthy on Home Rule[3]—Johnstone's Memoirs.[4]

Cabinet Dinner. 8. PM. Jan. 23. 72.[5]
Mr Cardwell: Guards Minute—approved: subject to communication with the D. of Cambridge.
Mr Palles. Letter of acceptance accepted.[6]
Palmerston & Peel inscriptions [for statues] to follow the Votes.
Queen's letter. WEG's answer considered.[7]

24. Wed.

Wrote to Ld Granville—M.Mich. Chevalier—Mr Colman MP—Mr R. Johnsone—Bp of Moray—Bar.Cav. Campobasso[8]—and minutes. Saw Mr Gurdon—Mr Glyn—Mr Farrer—Bp of Winchester—Sir R. Lush[9] *cum* Dowager Duchess of Somerset—Mrs Russell X. Read Johnstone's Memoirs—M'Carthy on Home Rule.

To M. CHEVALIER, 24 January 1872. Add MS 44541, f. 54.

I have watched as you may suppose with a deep interest the recent proceedings in the French Assembly, & I am truly gratified to you for the luminous

[1] Papers on purchase of Irish railways, sent by Hartington on 15 January; Add MS 44143, f. 137.
[2] Probably in *Tichborne* v. *Lushington*, widely reported.
[3] See 20 Jan. 72.
[4] J. de Johnstone, *Memoirs*, tr. C. Winchester, 3v. (1870, 1871).
[5] Add MS 44640, f. 8.
[6] See 19 Jan. 72n.
[7] On the service at St. Paul's; see Guedalla, *Q*, i. 329.
[8] Not further identified; letter in Italian, on liberty, in Add MS 44541, f. 54.
[9] Sir Robert Lush, 1807-81; judge of court of queen's bench 1865-80.

details you have been kind enough to give me.[1] The position you occupy among the most distinguished of all French Economists & Free Traders, as the friend of Cobden & with the Emperor (from whom this justice must not be withheld) the resolute champion & the intellectual expounder of the Treaty, must have rendered these events to you yet more intensely interesting. Regretting that anything should occur to embarrass the actual Government of France which requires repose, I cannot regret that the Assembly contrary to expectation or at least to announcement should have proved itself to have made a greater progress in sound ideas than the Govt. The expectations we all entertained in 1860 of real advance in these matters have thus been fully sustained. I must not touch on the details of your letter. I will only say for my colleagues & myself that we have done nothing & said nothing to compromise the principles known to guide our legislation; & that we have taken measures to obviate or remove so far as depends upon us any misapprehensions which may exist on your side of the water. The enormous capabilities which French manufacturers have shown especially since 1860 have been such that we might be tempted as rivals in third markets to see with a lurking satisfaction that she was disposed to fetter & diminish (as she will, in spite of drawbacks) her powers of exports; & if our trade in French markets were to be curtailed, it is probable that we should derive from this source an ample or sufficient compensation. But it would be a wretched *mesquine* consolation & one which I should not like to appropriate. I am not disheartened at what you say of your navigation law. On that subject opinion commonly lags a little. It did so, undoubtedly, in this country. But it is a woeful sight when a great nation goes back to unlearning the most elementary lessons of Free Trade by taxing raw materials, & is taught to imagine that *this* is the mode by which public credit is to be supported.

To Reverdy JOHNSON, 24 January 1872. Add MS 44433, f. 104.

I am much obliged by your note of the 12th[2] and particularly by the frank & explicit expression of your opinions on matters of much delicacy. Indeed I should have thought it an added favour had I known what were the expressions, real or imputed, of mine which you had thought open to exception, and which if I understand you rightly, shared in producing irritation on the part of the American Press; especially as this emotion, if it existed, may have extended more or less to the American public.

I can readily believe with you that your countrymen consider their case on the Alabama Claims to be a clear one, but I am not sure that I understand your meaning when you state that unless the arbitrators decide in their favour, excitement will be renewed, and they will believe however unjustly, that the Washington Treaty was but a contrivance to defeat their claims. For I am confident that the American people will never as a body think unjustly of the body which they have selected to be the depository of their confidence. I apprehend that in a case of arbitration, the duty of both parties is the same, and is perfectly clear. I imagine they should responsibly urge no claim on their own behalf except what they believe to be well-founded. That they should state every thing in behalf of their claims which they can state with honour, & nothing which they cannot. That

[1] Not found.

[2] From Baltimore, on Gladstone and Palmer's comments on the Washington treaty; Add MS 44433, f. 49.

arguing honourably they should also argue freely and unreservedly, and that each should pay the other party the compliment of crediting him with so strong a love of justice, and so much self-command, as to feel confident that he will not take offence. Finally that an award against their own side, within the limits of the reference, is to be accepted and obeyed I do not say with the same pleasure, but with the same promptitude and fulness, as one in his favour, opposed as it may be not only to his inclinations but to his convictions. I do not say these duties are always easy; we may not find them so; but they are clear; and if they be clear, the difficulty of clear duties is but a part, and the very best part, of the discipline of life. I trust that, if I have described them truly, we on our part shall be enabled to perform them. And I think much too highly of American character and civilization to believe that you will on your side fail. But above us both there is that high tribunal of the moral judgment of the civilized world, which, besides being disposed to attach great weight to the authority of the Arbitrating body, would never approve of complaint even against a sentence which it deemed to be questionable, if that complaint so much as looked like a tendency I do not say to disobey but to retain a grudge and a feeling of resentment capable of influencing future conduct.

I am so sanguine as to believe that we shall not differ as to the principles which appertain to the right conduct of Arbitration; and that, in our joint acceptance of them, we shall both lay the firmest basis of our own future friendship, and raise to the highest point the value of the boon which by our example on this occasion we are I hope conferring on the world.[1]

25. Th. St Paul Conv[ersion]

Wrote to Abp of Canterbury—The Queen—Bp of Cape Town—Bp of Lichfield—Ld Kimberley (2)—Mr Bright—& minutes. Read Johnstone's Memoirs—Bourdeaux Free Trade Tract—M'Carthy on Home Rule—Mormon Trials.[2] Saw Mr Crittenden[3]—Mr Glyn—Ld Sydney—do *cum* Mr Brand—Abp of Canterbury—do *cum* Ld Chichester. Cabinet 2½–5¾. Conclave on Mr Reeve's case.

Cabinet. Jan. 25. 72/ 2.30[4]
√ Thames Embankment. To refuse to bring in a Bill.
√ The Eyre Vote. No escape.[5]
√ The Abp. of C[anterbury]'s proposal.[6] Reported by WEG. No objection.
√ Ballot Bill. To be as last year's.
√ Brand's application to Bright. WEG to write to B.[7] Done.

[1] Holograph draft, dated 24 Jan., marked 'copy for sign.', sent 26 January.
[2] Perhaps J. Bonwick, *Mormons and the silver mines* (1872).
[3] John Denton Crittendon, 1837–77, sculptor; his bust of diarist (see 28 June 72) not recorded in diarist's list of self-images in Hawn P.
[4] Add MS 44640, f. 10.
[5] Campaign for reinstatement of Gov. Eyre; Gladstone refused a pension for him on 26 Feb.; *H* ccix. 1028.
[6] 'Abp. C. Ld Chic[hester] wish Mr P[alles?] to begin with £1100 on acc. of special respons. & services'; Add MS 44640, f. 11.
[7] See letter following.

Sydney's preparations reported.[1]
√ Dilke's application for information from Treasury respecting Queen's Income Tax—ask him to write.[2]
√ Law Officers to see Chancellor on the question of the mode of preventing detriment thro' bringing illegitimate matter before the Arbitrators [at Geneva].
London Municipal Government—Local Taxation—English Universities—Irish University—Succession to Land—Scotch Church Patronage—Currency—Game Bills?[3]

To J. BRIGHT, M.P., 25 January 1872. 'Private.' Add MS 43385, f. 191.

On conversing with Mr. Brand about the question who shall be asked to propose & second him, I find him desirous to ask you to undertake the former of these offices.[4]

I could not wonder at or disapprove his desire to secure for himself this important advantage.

Considering the very confidential nature of the communications which I have had with you on the subject of a resumption of office, I did not feel justified in interposing them as an objection. I trust however and venture to assume that you will not allow the request which Brand is about to make to you, to interfere in any measure with your decision on the larger question.

To LORD KIMBERLEY, colonial secretary, 25 January 1872. Add MS 44541, f. 56.

I have read the papers newly prepared.[5] I think they show two of the three demands I mentioned. The *third*, that of communicating with Foreign Countries direct as to reciprocal arrangements, I drew from the report in the Victoria Hansard of the Debates on contemplated postal arrangements. If you can throw light on this by Saturday, pray do so. The opinion of the Law Officers on the meaning of the word country seems to me to be a very unsafe ground for us to take in a matter of constitutional right. What should we care for the opinion of French Law Officers on the meaning of the Treaty of 1860 as to 'droits compensateurs'? The case of the Belgian Treaty which I had not before seen is I think still worse. That with Italy does not seem so formidable, but *one* is enough to do all the mischief. I can hardly conceive with what face we can hold that the different colonies are not for the purpose of commerce under the Treaty different countries, when the very thing they are claiming of us involves their being treated as such & made such ground the very point in question.

26. Fr.

Wrote to Mr [J. W.] Strutt (Rayl)—Lt Col. Ellis—Abp of Syra—Ld Kimberley—and minutes. Arranging some papers. Dined with the

[1] The procession to St. Paul's.

[2] 'Dilke wishes to have the facts respecting H.M.'s Income Tax with a view to an expl. understood to be apologetic'; holograph note, ibid., f. 11.

[3] Measures for the session.

[4] Bright declined; R. Palmer and Locke King acted.

[5] See 29 Dec. 71, 27 Jan. 72n.

Wests. Saw Mr G. Burnett (respecting the Prescott Estate &c.)—Mr Goschen—Mr Glyn—Walk with C. Saw Mrs Th. Saw Beecher & another[R]. Read Johnstone's Memoirs—Ld E. Fitzmaurice on Land question.[1] Wrote Mem. on Australian Tariffs—and on French Treaty.[2]

[*Australian Tariffs*]

1. To treat the demands in the Five Resolutions as a whole (with the Postal demand) and to refuse them as a whole.
2. To state that H.M. Govt. are not prepared to affirm that the demands can be conceded conformably with the provisions of existing Treaties. That the risk cannot be run of our finding ourselves involved in the breach of engagement by reason of the Acts of Colonial Governments taken without our consent. That the first step must therefore be to obtain by communication with Foreign Countries power to authorise these Acts. That we shall then be prepared to receive Acts for consideration from time to time and that we will be advised to assent unless special grounds of objection should appear.[3]

27. Sat.

Wrote to Ld Granville—Rev Dr Innes—The Queen—and minutes. Sat to Mayall 12½–1½. Cabinet 2½–6. Saw Ld Chancellor—Ld Granville—Wrote Mem. on Alabama Case. Saw Mrs Th. X who is advised by Sir W. Gull to go to Egypt. Read Voltaire (Morley)—Johnstone's Memoirs.

Cabinet. Jan 27. 72/ 2.30 PM.[4]

√ Cardwell read letter to H.M. disposing of the case as to Rank promotion & discipline in the Household Troops.
√ French Treaty. Date of Denunciation: & expression of views ascribed to H.M. Government.[5]
√ as to giving copies of the 'case' respecting the Alabama. Give freely but not to publish: But Ld G. to see Sir R. P[almer?].
√ Long discussion on Australian Tariffs question.[6] Ld Kimberley to prepare materials for elucidating the bearing of Treaties on the question.
I American precedent: 1. As to local extent, 36 degrees of latitude, 63 degrees of longitude. 2. As to *view* of future union. 3. As to peculiar reason growing out of the proximity of U.S. by land. 4. As to demand made a. limited or unlimited (B.N.A. limited to agricultural produce?) b. involves right of Treaty.
II Zollverein Treaty and consequent d[itt]o. Belgian Treaty and consequent d[itt]o.

[1] E. Petty-Fitzmaurice, 'The English land question', *Contemporary Review*, xix. 419 (March 1872).
[2] See Ramm I, ii. 302n.
[3] Undated holograph; Add MS 44640, f. 15; probably this day's mem.
[4] Add MS 44640, f. 14.
[5] Dispute with the French on the date; Ramm I, ii. 302n.
[6] Précis on Australians' fiscal rights by E. B. P[ennell], 23 Jan. 1872, in PRO 30/29/69.

III Ensemble of demands. 1. Absolute power without reference to Parliament or the Crown for regulation of indirect Taxes (quoad[?][1] with all (Colonies) or States? 2. G.B. not to bind the Colonies by any Treaty with a Foreign Power in these. 3. In the Postal matter direct communication with Foreign States on their Postal arrangements (N.Z. case).

Ld. K. If we refuse, shall we persevere?

Neutrality in War: deny

Negotiation with foreign countries: deny.

28. Septua S.

Chapel Royal mg & aft. Saw Lady Herbert & others. Wrote to Ld Granville (2)—Mr J.R. Hope Scott—and minutes. Read Morley's Voltaire—Ecce Episcopus[2]—E. Denison's Remains[3]—Tracts on Dioc. Synods: and other Tracts.

29. M.

Wrote to The Queen—Chancr of Exr—Mr Ayrton—Sir R. Palmer —Sir B. Frere—Dr John Brown—Mr Lowe (2)—and minutes. Worked on accounts & paid some Bills &c. Read Morley's Voltaire— Johnstone's Memoirs. Saw in R. St at 5 a creature of 18 so pretty & simple yet committed: not without hope. Nine to dinner. Conversation with Mr Hayward on Alabama—Mrs Gurney—&c.

To R. LOWE, chancellor of the exchequer, 29 January 1872. Add MS 44541, f. 60.

Doubtless you have memoranda of the sums agreed by the Cabinet to be reduced on Army & Navy Estimates; you do not state what augmentation there is on account of Purchase.[4] But I am at a loss to conceive how the reduction can be brought down to £400,000 per ann. Again with respect to the Navy. I understood the Cabinet to accept a reduction of 300,000 with reference to men & the First Lord to undertake to consider how he could make a small diminution of men which would have a further saving. You certainly do not as far as my recollection goes—& I have notes to which I can refer in case of need, on which my reports to the Queen were grounded—overstate the Army reduction apart from Purchase at £125,000 or thereabouts. I think you had better see the respective heads on this subject which as the Cabinet has decided it should not be carried there again unless it be necessary. The prospects of the Miscellaneous Estimates as you describe them I think do you much credit.

[1] Word here illegible.

[2] Anon. (1872).

[3] *Letters and writings of the late Edward Denison*, ed. Sir B. Leighton (1872).

[4] Mem. 'which I think should be brought before the Cabinet—we are I fear drifting straight on the rocks as we did last year', sent this day, Add MS 44302, f. 14.

30. Tu.

Wrote to Mr Locke King—Sir T. Biddulph—Mr Bruce—Mr Fortescue—The Queen—Abp of Canterb.—and minutes. Eleven to dinner. Saw B. Benjamin—Mr Crittenden—Mr Lowe—Mr M'Garel—Mr Bryce—Lady L. Tenison[1]—Dr Clark—Ld Granville. Read Johnstone's Memoirs—Hopkins on Alabama Case.[2] At Christie's. Cabinet 2¾–6.

Cabinet. Jan. 30. 2½ P.M.[3]

√ Business of H. of C.: Prop[ositio]n agreed to—Move a Committee.[4]
√ Order of introduction of Bills—And days. Considered & fixed.
√ Leave to Convocation (by a 'Letter of Business') to discuss 4th Report of Ritual Commission: to be given.[5]
√ Alabama Case of the Americans. Proper course to take discussed: adjourned.[6]
√ N[orth] A[merican] Squadron not to be diminished.
√ R. Bonny Oil Trade. Stop war by threats? No. Let the traders refuse to trade with those who make war improperly.[7]
√ tr. of Dutch Gold Coast settlements by Treaty mentioned.
√ Greenwich Hospital: to be made centre of Naval Education.
√ South Sea Kidnapping. Ld Kimberley's proposed Bill approved.

To G. G. GLYN, chief whip, 30 January 1872. Add MS 44541, f. 61.

The Cabinet thinks Bills &c might be introduced as follows.
Friday Feb. 9. Business of the House—Ballot—Corrupt Practices.
Monday Feb. 12. Scotch Edn—Mines.
Tuesday Feb. 13. Sanitary Comn. Bill. Contagious Diseases Bill.
Thursday 15. Estimates—if not too soon.

Stansfeld's father is dead, & he has not been in the Cabinet; this therefore is a decision *quoad* his bill, subject to what he may have to say. Very glad to hear better accounts of Mrs Glyn.

31. Wed.

Wrote to Ld E. Clinton—Mr Hope Scott—Mr W.E. Forster—Sir D. Norreys—Ld Granville—The Queen—Dean of Windsor—and minutes. Read Irish Ballad Poetry[8]—Morley's Voltaire. Saw Ld Halifax—Dean of St Paul's *cum* Dr Liddon—Mr F. Lawley—Mr Strutt

[1] Lady Louisa Tenison, da. of Lord Lichfield, wife of E. K. Tenison.
[2] Untraced pamphlet by J. B. Hopkins.
[3] Add MS 44640, f. 18.
[4] On 8 Feb.; the motion had to be withdrawn; *H* ccix. 153.
[5] Letters arranged for York and Canterbury; Add MS 44541, f. 61.
[6] The American 'Case' revived their 'indirect claims', and argued that the Washington treaty included them in the arbitration.
[7] Ja Ja's bid for power in the Niger delta; see K. O. Diké, *Trade and Politics in the Niger Delta* (1956), ch. 10.
[8] W. Barry, 'The current street ballads of Ireland', *Macmillan's Magazine*, xxv. 190 (January 1872).

—Dean of Westminster—Duke of Argyll—Mr Hayward. Dined at the Dean of Westmrs. Luncheon at 15 G[rosvenor] Square. Mrs Th X.

To W. E. FORSTER, vice president, 31 January 1872. Add MS 44541, f. 62.

Nothing can be more desirable than the thorough sifting among all the members of the Cabinet of this grave point about the Alabama case & therefore than the circulation of the paper drawn by one of those amongst us whose thoughts as well as feelings have been most exercised upon the subject.[1] Please to observe my query in pencil 'when' on which something turns. I presume that under your memorandum, if the other Arbitrators showed a disposition to proceed, the British Arbitrator would withdraw. A decision for us by the majority is better than a diplomatic repudiation; a decision against us worse. And I am afraid, to use Mint[?] language—the worseness is bigger than the betterness, tho' less likely.

Thurs. Feb. One 1872

Wrote to Ld Hartington (Tel.)—Col. Ponsonby (2)—The Queen (Mem.)—and minutes. Read American Case—Memoir (Ital.) of Pius IX.[2] Looked up American Speeches.[3] Law Educn Deputn at 11.[4] Saw Mr Lawley—Mr Glyn—Mr M'Coll—Abp Manning—Sol. General *cum* Mr Lowe—Sir R. Palmer—Mr Gurdon—Ld Granville. Prepared Draft of Queen's Speech & left it with Ld G.

2. Fr.

Wrote to Mr Ryan—The Queen (Tel. and letter)—Dean of Windsor—Col. Ponsonby—Mr Cardwell—Mr Hayward—and minutes. Council at 2.[5] Cabinet 2½–7. Saw Mr Niewenhuys—Mr Crittenden—Mr Glyn—Mr Goschen. Sheriff—Dinner at Ld Ripon's. Saw St Ange & another. Read Life of Pius IX.

Cabinet. Feb. 2. 72. 2½ PM.[6]

√ Queen's Speech—*minus* Alabama and Treaty of Washington.

[1] Untraced; see Ramm I, ii. 304.

[2] 'Le Orgie e Diletti de' Papi', lent him by *Manning, whom he told (7 Feb. 1872, Add MS 44541, f. 66): 'The book has all the appearance of a most wicked and disgraceful libel.' He asked Enfield to protest about it to the Italian government; ibid., f. 67.

[3] He next day asked Ryan to look up his explanation of his 1862 Newcastle speech; Add MS 44541, f. 63. See 6, 17 Oct. 62.

[4] Led by Sir R. Palmer, see *The Times*, 2 February 1872, 5c; Gladstone told Palmer on 17 Jan. 1872 (Add MS 44541, f. 47): 'I am concerned to find that the Dpn. on Legal Edn. is to be of the demonstrative . . . Class, . . . such depns. are among the most painful[?] grievances of official life.'

[5] Printed minute at Add MS 44618, f. 46.

[6] Add MS 44640, f. 18.

√ Communication to Fish discussed generally & outline agreed on.[1]
√ Alabama Paragraph [of Queen's Speech] determined.
√ P. of Wales place in procession—Thought awkward.

3. Sat.

Wrote to The Queen (2)—Abp Manning—Ld Bury—Ld Sydney—Prince of W.—and minutes. Saw Ld Granville—Mr Gurdon—Mr Glyn—Ld Ripon—Ld G. *cum* Ld Tenterden[2]—do *cum* Sir R. Palmer—Mover & Seconder 11-12[3]—Sir W.C. James (Cont.Dis.)[4] Cabinet 2½-5¾. Dined with the Jameses. Read Life of Pius IX.

Cabinet. Feb. 3. 1872. 2.30 PM.[5]

√ Draft of dispatch or note to Gen. Schenck communicating view as to indirect losses.[6]
James to speak about Collier? He may.[7] Also question considered as to H. of L.
√ Contagious Diseases Act—Provision as to detention considered. Disposed of.

4. Sexa S.

Chapel Royal with H.C. mg—(How much at this moment to offer & to plead)—Bedfordbury evg. Saw Ld Granville—Ld Halifax—Mr Glyn. Finished the strange Life of Pius IX in Orgie e Diletti. Read Contemp. on Ward Beecher[8]—Rossetti's Shadow of Dante.[9] Wrote to the Queen & Telegr. to the Queen. Wrote to Mr West. Reviewed MS. of [Queen's] Speech.

5. M.

Wrote to Mr Thring—and minutes. Saw A. St Ange[R]. Saw F. Lawley—Mr Glyn—Ld Halifax—Mr Forster—Ld Granville—Sir R. Collier—do *cum* Mr Forster—Ld Ripon—Baron N. Rothschild—

[1] Informing him that in the U.K.'s opinion 'the claim for indirect damages is not within the intention of the [Washington] Treaty'; see Fish's Diary, 3 February 1872, and Schenck to Fish, 6 February 1872, N. 137, National Archives, Washington.

[2] On Alabama; see Ramm I, ii. 304.

[3] Of the Queen's Speech: H. G. Strutt (1840-1914, liberal M.P. E. Derbyshire 1868-74; 2nd Baron Belper 1880), and J. J. Colman.

[4] i.e. Contagious Diseases.

[5] Add MS 44640, f. 20.

[6] See Cook, *The Alabama Claims*, 218 and Ramm I, ii. 304. General Robert Cumming Schenck, 1809-90, American minister in London 1871-6. The crucial dispatch, denying competence of the tribunal to consider the indirect claims; in *PP* 1872 lxix. 655, draft in Add MS 44618, f. 51. See 13 May 72. 'Schenck' is often spelt 'Schenk' by diarist.

[7] He did not speak in the Collier deb. on 19 February.

[8] *Contemporary Review*, xix. 317 (February 1872).

[9] Miss M. F. *Rossetti, *A Shadow of Dante* (1871).

Duke of Argyll—Mr Hayward—Duke of Cambridge—Ct Brunnow—Musurus Pacha—Bn Beaulieu. Speech dinner (32) and an evening party afterwards. Read The Earl & Doctor[1]—Cairnes on the Slave Power[2]—Westm. Rev. on Ld Stanley (Derby)[3]—Elze on Lord Byron.[4] My rule was *very* hard tried at night.

6. Tu.

Wrote to D. of Newcastle—The Speaker—The Queen—Mr Bright—and minutes. H. of C. 4-8¾. Spoke 1 h. after Disraeli on the Address.[5] Saw Mr Childers—Mr Glyn. Read Lecky Leaders of Opinion[6]—Johnstone's Memoirs. The Alabama & Washington question lay heavy on me—till the evening. Even during the Speech I was disquieted & had to converse with my Colleagues.[7]

7. Wed.

Wrote to Mr Goschen—Lady Clarendon—The Queen—Ld Granville—and minutes. H of C. 12-3½. Spoke again at length on the U.S. question.[8] Saw Mr Otway—Earl Dufferin—Mr Glyn—Ld Granville—Sir E. May—Dined with Mrs Th. X. Read Lecky—and. . . .

8. Th.

Wrote to Ld Granville—The Speaker—Abp Manning—Sir A. Paget—Abp of Canterb.—Ld Enfield—Mr Helps—Mrs Cardwell—The Queen—and minutes. H. of C. 4½-8¼. Spoke on Speaker's retirement &c.[9] Read Lecky—The Earl and the Doctor. Saw Dean of Durham—Mr Ayrton—Ld Granville—Mr West—Mr Glyn—The Speaker. Dined with the Jameses.

9. Fr.

Wrote to Abp of Canterbury—Ld De Tabley—Mr Tennyson—Ld Kimberley—Ld Granville—The Queen l. & mem.—and minutes. Small party to dinner. Saw Mr Kinnaird—Bishop of Chester—Mr F.

[1] *South Sea Bubbles. By the Earl [of Pembroke] and the Doctor [G. H. Kingsley]* (1872).
[2] See 1 Dec. 62.
[3] Perhaps *Westminster Review*, xcvi. 184 (July 1871).
[4] C. F. Elze, *Lord Byron, a biography* (1872).
[5] Denying the Washington treaty included the 'indirect claims'; *H* ccix. 73.
[6] W. E. H. *Lecky, *The leaders of public opinion in Ireland* (1861, new ed. 1871).
[7] See Morley, ii. 409-11.
[8] *H* ccix. 111.
[9] And moved (and withdrew) motion for select cttee. on public business: *H* ccix. 148, 153. Inconsistent reporting of the speech led to controversy; see Ramm I, ii. 305; 15, 22 Feb., 2 Mar. 72. See Add MS 44618, f. 70 for newspapers' various reports.

Lawley—Mr Goschen—Mr Glyn—Robn G. Saw Mrs Th. X. Read Lecky—Morley's Voltaire.

To LORD KIMBERLEY, colonial secretary, Add MS 44541, f. 69.
9 February 1872. 'Private.'

1. In any telegram to Lisgar[1] at this moment I would include a hope of further consideration soon so as not to throw the thing too much abroad.
2. In respect to the Australian case I think a plausible & not unfair argument may be raised against us on the Zollverein Treaty. The point is not touched in the memo you have circulated.[2]

The Grande Bretagne in the Belgian Treaty is a good point unless it can be shewn that the English version is alone of authority?

An extreme scrupulousness as to Treaties is now more than ever incumbent upon us. Suppose we were to put this query or something like it to Foreign Countries affected by the Zollverein Treaty. Will *you* acknowledge the liberty of Colonies (or of neighbouring Colonies) as among themselves, provided you have every advantage enjoyed by the U.K.? Could any friendly country hesitate as to the answer. But in any case I think my preceding remark is strong.

10. Sat.

Wrote to The Queen—Mr Cyrus Field—Mr West (2)—and minutes. 1-2. Conclave at War Office. Cabinet 2¾-7. Saw Ld Bessborough—do *cum* Mr Glyn—then with Ld Granville—Ld Bury—Mr M'Coll—Chancr of Exr. Dined at the Duke of Argyll's. Much interesting conversation on U.S. question with Mr Cyrus Field. At General Schenck's afterwards. Read Lecky.

Feb. 10. 1872.[3]

√ Collier case—Argued.[4] Amendment framed—Ld Romilly in the Lords—whom failing . . . Sir R. Palmer in the H. of C.—whom failing, WEG.
√ Canada. Telegraph to? Private to Lisgar to ask for information.
Australian Tariffs.[5]
√ John Bright: substance of communications mentioned.
√ Production of U.S. and British [Alabama] Cases? British may be moved for as a. not controversial, b. as US Case is widely known. U.S. not until given to Congress.
√ Reduction of the Army Estimates:[6] to be retracted as to men? To be considered on Thursday.

[1] Kimberley sent précis on Canada and the Washington treaty, 9 February, Add MS 44224, f. 256.
[2] See 29 Dec. 71n.
[3] Add MS 44640, f. 21.
[4] Annotated Commons order paper with Cross' question for 19 February, at ibid., f. 22; cabinet papers setting out the facts, at Add MS 44618, f. 73ff.
[5] Mema. in PRO 30/29/69.
[6] 'I suppose the American question makes no difference to the Army Estimates' [Cardwell] 'I think not, without any doubt' [Gladstone]; cabinet note, Add MS 44640, f. 23.

√ As to giving the French time to negotiate and deducting it from the 12 months notice.[1] To be done only if he [*sic*] can show a prospect of admissible proposals.

√ As to a committee on Railway Amalgamations.[2] C[ommittee] of Cabinet appointed.

Ld. Advocate may bring in: Feudal Tenure Bill [Scotland]: not Entails Bill.

11. Quinqua S.

Chapel Royal mg—All Saints Evg. Wrote to Ld Granville (2)—Mr Monsell—The Queen—Mrs Cardwell—& minutes. Saw Ld Cork—Mr West—Ld Granville—Mrs Th. for goodbye. It is well for me that she goes & I hope all blessings will follow her.[3] Read Ramsgate Tracts—Westcott on Cathedrals—Pike's Ancient Meeting Houses—Phillimore's Letter to Archbp.[4]

12. M.

Wrote to Mr J. Watson—Ld Bessborough—The Queen—Ld Sydney—Bps of Winchester, Chichester, Bath & Wells, Oxford, Carlisle, Salisbury[5]—& minutes. H of C. 4½-8 and 9½-11½.[6] Read Earl and Doctor—Palmer on Alabama Case.[7] Saw Mr Glyn—D. of Argyll—Sir W. James—Dss of Argyll—Dss of A *cum* Ld Granville—D. Devonshire *cum* Ld Granville—Ld Granville—Mr Lawley—and others. Saw Vane &c. at Mortlock's.[8]

13. Tu.

Wrote to Ld Chamberlain—Ld Granville—Duke of Argyll—Rev W.W. Harvey—The Queen—& minutes. H of C. 4½-8½ and 9¾-11½.[9] Read The Earl & the Doctor—Saw Ld Halifax—Mr Cyrus Field—Mr Glyn—Mr F. Lawley. Worked on correcting Speech on Address.

[1] i.e. the denunciation of the 1860 Commercial Treaty.

[2] Members: Fortescue, Halifax, Ripon, Hartington, Lowe; ibid., f. 24.

[3] Visit to Egypt for her health; she was back by May 1872; see 27 Jan. 72.

[4] B. F. *Westcott, *Cathedral foundations in relation to religious thought* (1872). G. H. Pike, *Ancient meeting houses; or memorial pictures of nonconformity in old London* (1870). R. J. *Phillimore, 'Clergy discipline. A letter to . . . the Archbishop of Canterbury' (1872).

[5] Asking them to attend for the motion on the Collier affair in the Lords on 15 February; Chester, Chichester, Durham, London, Ripon, Winchester, voted for the govt.; Add MS 44541, f. 71.

[6] Parks, Mines, and Scottish Education Bills 1°R: *H* ccix. 276.

[7] R. *Palmer, 'Speech . . . in the House of Commons on the "Alabama" question' (1863).

[8] William Mortlock, china shippers.

[9] Questions: *H* ccix. 306.

To the DUKE OF ARGYLL, Indian secretary, Add MS 44541, f. 72.
13 February 1872. 'Private.'

I think neither Kimberley nor Spencer are available.[1] I expected to have found in your communication the name of Northbrook—about whom I have received today a letter from Halifax which I send you herewith. He I think, undoubtedly stands no. 1. for the Cabinet among the official Peers. He is a widower & his two children are all but grown up. He is a man whom I always find more highly esteemed in proportion as the man who speaks is near him & has known him well. Independently of other matters, the growing tribe of baby children in the other quarter would be a great impediment. But N. is the stronger-backed man.

There is another N. that would much like it; but I do not think he stands in our first line.[2]

14. Ash Wed.

Chap. Royal at 12. Wrote to M. Forcade de la Roquette—Duke of Argyll—Mr Moffatt—Ld Granville—The Queen—and minutes. Saw Mr Glyn—Mr Gurdon—Mr West—Ld Granville: on Treaty of Washington, & Estimates—Conclave on P. of Wales & Royal Residence in D. [Street]. 3-4¼. Read Elze's Byron—Johnstone's Memoirs finished—The Earl & the Doctor.

To A. DE FORCADE DE LA ROQUETTE,[3] Add MS 44541, f. 72.
14 February 1872.

I received with great pleasure your tract in defence of the Treaty of 1860.[4] We are naturally concerned to find that governmental authorities in France, desirous to find relief from the pecuniary difficulties of the moment, should seek in measures which according to our view tend to retard her commercial expansion and her growth in wealth.

But I am, for one, much comforted by observing what a vigorous growth the principles of Free Trade have made in France, and how their defence is undertaken by men of such a stamp that their abilities and authority cannot fail to produce a further progress.

15. Th.

Wrote to Mr Thistlethwayte—Mr G. W. Smalley—Mrs Th.—Ld R. Grosvenor—Mr Dodson—Mr Smalley—Mr Girard[5]—Mr Burnett

[1] Mayo, the viceroy, had been assassinated. Argyll this day had proposed Dufferin and fought a considerable, ultimately unsuccessful, battle to avoid Northbrook; Add MS 44102, f. 118.

[2] *Northcote?

[3] Bonapartist minister of finance at the time of the 1860 treaty; see 26 Jan. 67.

[4] 'Défense du traité de commerce avec l'Angleterre' (1872).

[5] Pierre Girard, London agent of the *New York World* wrote wishing, as West docketed, 'to interview you, wishing to dispel misconceptions' about British policy; Gladstone declined, but agreed to answer written questions; Add MSS 44433, ff. 157, 160, 168 and 44541, f. 74. This letter to Girard (in *The Times*, 16 February 1872, 10d) defended the Washington Treaty as unambiguous.

—The Queen—and minutes. Saw Ld Rosebery[1]—Mr Glyn (2)—Mr Lowe—Ld Granville—Mr Lawley—do *cum* Mr Cardwell. Cabinet 2½-4. H of C. 4½-8 & 9½-12.[2] Saw Grey.

Cabinet. Thurs. Feb. 15. 2.30 PM.[3]
√ Queen's Route on 27th. Much prefer Oxford Street.[4]
√ Army Estimates. Keep Army + Reserve = those of last year. Reduction 1006 m[ille]. √ Navy d[itt]o. unaltered.
√ French Treaty. Ld G. announced his [blank][5] with Duc de Broglie as to re-opening negotiations.
√ Railway Amalgamation Bills. A joint [Lords/Commons] Committee? (Rule as to the Chair? to be decided by the Committee). To promote, if no obstacle, in the Lords.[6] Terms of the Reference considered.
√ Irish Railways. Answer to Mr. Maguire agreed to.[7]

To G. W. SMALLEY,[8] *journalist*, 15 February 1872. Add MS 44541, f. 73.

Towards the close of a letter signed by you and inserted in the Times of to-day, I find a paragraph which I understand to involve the assertion that I had made an 'insinuation on the part of the U.S. as baseless as it was insulting.'[9] The temper of your letter adds weight to any opinion expressed in it, and I should not quarrel with your description of such an insinuation if it had been made. But I am sure you will allow me to ask, not in the spirit of a controversial challenge, but with a view to accuracy, what are the words used by me, or even imputed by me, which you consider to convey the insinuation you have described.[10]

16. Fr.

Wrote to Ld Lyttelton—The Queen l. and Mem.—Ld Sydney—Ld Kimberley—and minutes. H of C. 4½-8¼ & 9½-12½.[11] Saw Mr Milner Gibson—Mr Glyn—Ld Granville—Mr Dodson—Mr Stansfeld—Mr West—Lady Hatherley. Comm. on Thanksgiving arrangements 1-2. Worked on letter to Gen. Schenk. Finished The Earl & the Doctor: a truly painful book though there are elements of good.

17. Sat.

Wrote to Sir R. Palmer—Col. Ponsonby (Tel.)—The Queen l. & Mem.—Ld Advocate—Mr Watson—and minutes. Cabinet 2¾-6¼.

[1] Seen at Gladstone's request, he voted with the govt. this evening; Add MS 44541, f. 71.
[2] Govt. survived attack on the Collier affair by one vote in the Lords; *H* ccix. 461.
[3] Add MS 44640, f. 26.
[4] Cutting from *The Times* on this; ibid., f. 27.
[5] Heavily deleted.
[6] Joint cttee. appointed; *H* ccix. 945, 1017.
[7] *H* ccix. 645.
[8] George W. Smalley, London agent of the *New York Tribune.*
[9] *The Times*, 15 February 1872, 10e, attacking diarist's speech of 6 February on the Washington Treaty.
[10] Smalley's letter in *The Times*, 19 February 1872, 10e, did not offer an exposition.
[11] Questioned on Ewelme living: *H* ccix. 528.

Saw Ld Lyttelton—D. of Argyll—Mr West—Ld Provost of Glasgow—Do *cum* Mr Graham MP.—Mr Glyn. Conclave in D.St. 2.15 on Gov. Generalship. Read Lecky.[1] Framed my paper of propositions on 'Amicable settlement' under Washn Treaty.[2] 12 to dinner (incl. Schencks) and small evening party.

Cabinet. Sat. Feb. 17.[3]

√ Treaty of Washington. Proceedings in Canada to be put forward? Delay definitive reply[.] Not to discourage, or condemn their views.[4]
Bank Holiday on Tues. 27th to be general? Not to decide yet. But no general Thanksgiving. Postpone Council till Windsor. WEG Telegraphed words read.
Preliminary conversation on the various alterations in Alabama Case.
Ld. Chancellor respecting Mr Erle.[5]
Ld Granville—*ask* about U.S. Case?
Mr. Bruce. Glasgow revenue. [Glasgow Municipal] Bill.[6]

To E. HAMMOND, 17 February 1872. Add MS 44541, f. 74.

I was deeply impressed in or about the year 1843 with the letter of Mr. Everett in the correspondence by which he claimed & obtained the repayment of certain duties levied upon rice contrary to our Treaty with the U.S. I wish you would have those very interesting letters carefully read, for I think they *may* be found to contain some passages on the strict construction of Treaties usefully applicable to the Alabama controversy in its present phase.[7]

18. 1 S.Lent.

Chapel Royal mg & St James evg. Wrote to Col. Ponsonby—Dr Swainson—Ld Ripon. Saw Ld Granville—Mr Glyn—Count Bernstorff—Lady Burrell. Read Rainy's 3 Lectures[8]—Swainson on Ath. Creed[9]—Lightfoot's Preface to 2d Edn[10]—Stanley's Lecture.[11]

[1] See 6 Feb. 72.

[2] Printed for cabinet, Add MS 44618, f. 99, arguing the treaty was grammatically correct and clear, and that the indirect claims were not to be considered except '*in the event of no amicable settlement being made*'.

[3] Add MS 44640, f. 30.

[4] Deleted jottings on the Canadian position at ibid., f. 38 and by ?Hammond at Add MS 44618, f. 86.

[5] Note by Hatherley on retirement of Peter Erle, 1795-1877, as chief charity commissioner; Add MS 44640, f. 32.

[6] Note to and from Bruce, eliciting that he intended to object privately to the Glasgow Municipal Bill sponsored by Provost J. Watson, Gladstone's stockbroker; ibid., f. 35 and Add MS 44541, f. 74.

[7] See 14 Oct. 72.

[8] R. Rainy, 'Three lectures on the Church of Scotland' (1872).

[9] C. A. *Swainson, *Further investigations as to the origin and object of the 'Athanasian Creed'* (1871).

[10] J. B. *Lightfoot, *On a fresh revision of the English New Testament* (2nd ed. 1872).

[11] A. P. *Stanley, 'Lectures on the history of the Church of Scotland delivered in Edinburgh in 1872' (1872).

19. M.

Wrote to Col. Ponsonby—The Queen (2)—Mr Baines—and minutes. Read Clarendon—Lecky. Saw Ld Granville—Duke of Argyll—Scotts—Mr Glyn. H of C. $4\frac{1}{2}$-$8\frac{1}{4}$ & $8\frac{3}{4}$-$2\frac{1}{4}$. Spoke on the Collier case and voted in 268:241.[1] Worked on Collier case.

20. Tu.

Wrote to Ld Granville—Col. Ponsonby (Tel.)—Mr Bruce—The Queen Tel. and 2 letters—Dean of Westminster—Ld Prov. of Glasgow—Abp Manning—& minutes. Saw Ld Ripon *cum* Mr Forster[2]—Ld R. & Mr F. *cum* Mr Lowe—Mr Glyn—Mr Winterbotham—Ld Enfield *cum* Ld Tenterden—Sir T. Fremantle—Mr Bruce—Deputn of Sugar Refiners.[3] H of C. $4\frac{1}{2}$-8.[4] Dined with Mrs Glyn.—Saw Two X. Read Currie's Burns[5]—Graves on Amalgn of Railways[6]—Cotton Bonds Claim.

To ARCHBISHOP H. E. MANNING, 20 February 1872. Add MS 44541, f. 76.

1. I will send the brutal production 'Le Pere Duchèsne'[7] which your letter incloses to Bruce & I should hope the police will be able to dispose of it summarily. A marvellous change has been wrought in London for the better, with regard to filthy books in general. This Pere Duchèsne seems to be a pure example of the θηριωδές[8] as far as these minutes of inspection have shown me. 2. The Milan book[9] you sent me has through our F.O. been made known to the Italian Minister of Foreign Affairs for the first time & we shall learn what he is able to do. I cannot help thinking the copy sent must be an accidental copy. Can you get me any particulars as to the purchase.

21. Wed.

Wrote to Mr Hammond—Rev Mr Harvey—Mr Forster—Dean of ChCh—Mr Bright—W. Goalen (Tel.)—Mr Bruce—The Queen M. and l.—and minutes. H of C. $4\frac{1}{4}$-$5\frac{1}{2}$.[10] Saw Ld Granville—Mr Power *cum* Mr D'Arcy—Mr Lawley—Mr Glyn—Conclave in D St on Washington Treaty $5\frac{1}{2}$-$7\frac{3}{4}$. Saw Att. General—Ld Clanwilliam—Sir R. Phillimore. Read Lecky. Dined at Sir R. Phillimore's. Saw D'Alleyn[R].

[1] *H* ccix. 740. The govt.'s majority was better than expected.
[2] See next day's letter.
[3] No report found.
[4] Spoke on Occasional Sermons Bill: *H* ccix. 794.
[5] J. Currie, *The works of Robert Burns* (1800).
[6] S. R. Graves, 'Railway amalgamations' (1872).
[7] Not found published or in MSS; probably an updated version of Hébert's revolutionary journal (1790-4).
[8] 'full of wild beasts'.
[9] See 1 Feb. 72.
[10] Game Laws Bill: *H* ccix. 818.

22. Th.

Wrote to Sir R. Palmer—Dr A. Clark—Ld Sydney—Col. Ponsonby (Tel. and l.)—The Queen (2)—Mr Mowbray—and minutes. Worked on report of Speech F. 7. Saw Mr Forster—Ld Sydney—Mr Glyn (2)—Att. General—Ld Granville—Sir S. Northcote. Dined with the Farquhars. Read Lecky. H of C. 4½-8 and 9¾-1.[1]

23. Fr.

Wrote to Dean Ramsay—Ld Ripon—Dean of Westmr—Mr Bruce—Queen, l. & Mem.—Ld Poltimore—Sir T. Biddulph—& minutes. Worked on report of Speech F. 7. Saw Sir H. Elliot—Mr West—Mr Glyn—Mr Forster—Mr Bruce—Col. Beresford[2]—Ld Elcho. Dined with the F. Cavendishes. H of C. 4½-8¼ & 9½-1¼.[3] Read Lecky—Denison Correspondence.[4] Correcting Reports of 6 & 7 Feb.

To LORD RIPON, lord president, Add MS 43514, f. 140.
23 February 1872.

It is the business of the Chancellor of the Exchequer to look into questions between Mr Ayrton & Dr. Hooker[5] & to him Dr. Hooker ought to have made his appeal. Nevertheless while declining to take up the matter officially I endeavoured to mediate & obtained from Mr Ayrton what seemed to me something, from Dr. Hooker nothing. I could therefore only remit the matter to its proper channel. There is a plan which would put an end to the relation between them, & the C. of E. was very anxious to put it forward, but it hung upon his scheme for South Kensington or seemed to do so.

I hope you will not think I am evading my duties. But while it is my duty to deal with all difficulties arising between members of the Govt., it is wholly beyond my power & in no way belongs to my province, to examine & settle the controversies which may arise between them & civil servants who are employed under them. Perhaps you will speak to the C. of E.

24. Sat.

Wrote to D. of Argyll—Mr Brassey—Mr Bruce—Sir R. Blennerhassett—Gen. Schenk—The Queen—Ld Enfield—and minutes. Saw Ld Granville—Ld Stanhope—Mr Glyn—Mr Hayward[6]—Worked on draft letter to Gen. Schenk. Cabinet 2¾-7. Dined with Ld

[1] Questioned on Alabama, spoke on royal parks: *H* ccix. 870, 930.

[2] Col. (Francis) Marcus Beresford, 1818-90; tory M.P. Southwark 1870-80.

[3] Ex-Nawab of Tonk: *H* ccix. 962.

[4] See 28 Jan. 72.

[5] Dispute between Ayrton and Joseph *Hooker about lack of resources for Kew Gardens.

[6] *Hayward produced a plan to settle the Alabama affair, forwarded to Enfield; Add MS 44541, f. 80.

& Lady Ashburnham. Lady Cork's afterwards. Conversation with Lady Beaconsfield, who seems old in mind.[1] Read Lecky (finished).

Cabinet. Sat. Feb. 24. 2½ PM.[2]

√ Thanksgiving: Illumination: Route & place for Cabinet: Wives: Col. Henderson[3] sent for; area by Bridge St. & Embankment; Woolwich & Deptford, holiday 27th—yes in the Metropol. Distr. only.

√ Embankment question considered. Question of a lease for life. Life interest involved to be valued.

√ Alabama Claims. Much discussion on presenting our arg. to American Govt: on presentation of the Counter Case & collateral proceedings to cover it: on the various alternatives of [*sic*] a final settlement: on pleading before the Arbitrators a. as to competency b. as to the merits: on taking first the question of neglect, and the direct losses.[4]

√ Dixon's motion on Education. Mr Forster to move amendment.[5] Terms agreed on.

Q[uer]y Thus:[6]

1. We shall put in our Counter Case. 2. We shall frame it upon our view of the scope of the Arbitration. 3. We acquaint you that in this proceeding we convey no pledge to submit to a reference of any matter which we hold not to be included in the Treaty.

25. 2 S.Lent.

Chapel Royal mg and Wells St Evg. Wrote to Ld Blachford—Ld Sydney—Ld Granville (2)—Bp of Bath and Wells[7]—and minutes. Saw Mr Glyn. Tea with the Heywoods. Vast numbers in the streets. Read Nazareth[8]—Michaud's[9]—Irons's Athanasius[10]—Percy Chapel (Gibson).[11]

To LORD BLACHFORD, 25 February 1872. Add MS 44107, f. 320.

You cannot do us a greater favour than by assailing mercilessly, as far as it is in

[1] Mary Anne Disraeli, cr. Viscountess Beaconsfield 1868; she d. December 1872.

[2] Add MS 44640, f. 39.

[3] (Sir) Edmund Yeamans Walcott *Henderson, 1821-96; chief commissioner of metropolitan police 1869-86; established Special Branch to counter Fenianism; K.C.B. 1878.

[4] Schenck had called when Gladstone was out; meeting for Monday arranged; Add MS 44541, 80. America regarded the counter-case as 'equivalent to asking us [U.S.A.] to withdraw our claims'; *F.R.U.S.* 1872, ii. 429.

[5] Moved on 5 March; *H* ccix. 1395, 1421.

[6] Noted on separate sheet, dated 24 February; Add MS 44640, f. 42.

[7] See Lathbury, i. 381.

[8] [G. S. Drew], *Nazareth; its life and lessons* (1872).

[9] E. Michaud, perhaps *Programme de Réforme de l'église d'Occident* (1872).

[10] W. J. *Irons, 'Athanasius contra mundum; being a letter to . . . the archbishops and bishops of both Provinces' (1872).

[11] W. S. *Gibson, 'The renaissance at Alnwick' in *Lectures and essays on various subjects* (1858).

your nature, our argument on the Washington Treaty.[1] I never could feel quite comfortable while your authority is not with me.

I am inclined to think you have hit a flaw in the word 'express' par. 1. Let us suppose it struck out. In truth the whole Paragraph is merely statement & is no part of the argument. I admit in Par. 6 much of what your Mr Fish urges. But I observe that you pass by, & do not deal with, that principal portion of the argument, which lies in Par. 7-14 & especially Pars 9-11. As yet therefore I believe the grammar & logic of the case to be inexpugnable. Your (I admit most able) Mr Fish, while pleading for strict construction proceeds altogether not by interpretation but by paraphrase. He says he will not consent to any amicable settlement abandoning the claims except after adverse decision of an Arbitrator. But this is *not* what he told our Commissioners. He told them (see no. 9) that he would only go for indirect losses in the event of no such settlement, & 'no such settlement' grammatically means no amicable settlement, & does not mean grammatically 'no amicable settlement in the particular shape of a gross sum without arbitration'. In truth your Mr Fish is a very wicked man. I even suspect him of being Jesuit. He converts a general proposition into a particular one by means of a mental reservation. Qu. 'Did you steal my purse?' Ans. 'No—I did not steal it' (this morning) or here. Qu. 'Will you give up indirect losses, unless we can come to no amicable settlement?' Ans. 'Yes I will give them up unless we can come to no amicable settlement (in the shape of a payment of a gross sum without specification).['] Is he not wicked?

26. M.

Wrote to Atty General—D. of Argyll—Chancr of Exr—Ld Petre—Rev Mr Harvey—Mr Bruce—Mr Tupper—The Queen—Ct Bernstorff—and minutes. H of C. 4½-8½ and 9-1½. We got a valuable Resolution.[2] 12½-2 with Gen. Schenck on the U.S. question. Conclave on U.S. communications, 3½-4½. Finished draft l. to Gen. S.[3] Drew part minute of conversation with him. Read Milman's St Paul's.[4]

To Rev. W. W. HARVEY, 26 February 1872. Add MS 44541, f. 82.

I write one line to inform you that I am *advised* that your presentation to Ewelme is valid your having become according to the provisions of the Act a member of the Convocation of Oxford. You will understand this is not a judicial sentence & does not rule the law but it is an opinion such as carries weight & such as the Government constantly proceed on.

27. Tu. The Thanksgiving Day.

Went off at 11.20 in the chariot having previously dispatched 6 chil-

[1] Letter of 25 February 1872, Add MS 44107, f. 320 with notes on diarist's mem. on an 'Amicable Settlement'. See 4 Dec. 71, 17 Feb. 72.

[2] Resolution approved facilitating passing the estimates: *H* ccix. 1099.

[3] See 2 Mar. 72.

[4] See 10 Jan. 69.

dren (18 to 29 years old!) in the large carriage. All the arrangements were admirable: the service short but impressive: the spectacle in & out doors magnificent: the behaviour of the people admirable (to us very kind).[1] The ceremony lasted an hour. We were at home at 2.30. Walked out to see the illuminations in the evening.

Revised my letter to Schenk. Wrote to Mr Richard MP.—and minutes. Saw Dr Lightfoot—Sir R. Palmer—Mr Twisleton—Lord Acton—Ld R. Grosvenor. Dined at the Club. Read Milman's St Paul's—Molesworth's History of Engl.[2]

28. Wed.

Wrote to Ld Granville—Chancr of Exr—Mr Bruce—Gen. Schenk—Mr Cyrus Field—Cardinal Cullen—Ld Sydney—The Queen (l. & two Mema)—Ld Tenterden—Atty General—& minutes. Saw Sir Thos G.—Mr J. Russell—Mr Glyn—Ld Granville. Saw Chantell: an interesting case[R].[3] Wrote Mem. on Washn Treaty.[4] Revised for press Speech of Feb. 6. Read Milman on St Paul's.

To H. A. BRUCE, home secretary, 28 February 1872. Aberdare MSS.

I see in the Morning Post that two addresses are about to be presented to the Queen and Prince of Wales respectively in connection with the celebration of yesterday 'from the Catholic Archbishop and Bishops' of England.

This is I believe a new (as well as an impudent) assumption. At least I wish to call your attention to the point, which I hope as to the question of novelty you will examine. Should not Sir W. Knollys also be warned? Rely upon it this is no accident but a purpose. It is a part of the system of aggression which is not to be put down by law, but from which I conceive that the Government should steadily withhold its countenance. I am the more prompted to notice the matter lest it should pass as matter of routine.[5]

To General R. C. SCHENCK, American minister in London, 28 February 1872. Add MS 44541, f. 83.

We live nowadays in glass beehives, & I cannot do better than send you a minute which after seeing you I sent down to my Priv. Secy, with his reply. 'Preposterous' is as I supposed nowhere. I think it quite probable I may have said it was absurd to suppose that we with our eyes open should have gone into a Treaty under which claims might be made upon us in comparison with which the

[1] Though some saw *Disraeli's favourable reception as significant; see Buckle, v. 182.
[2] W. N. *Molesworth, *The history of England from the year 1830*, 3v. (1871-3).
[3] This phrase concealed in the facsimile in Masterman, 176.
[4] Perhaps the jottings at Add MS 44618, f. 130, marked 'Cancelled F. 72'; notes on it by Blachford at Add MS 44108, f. 322.
[5] No reply from Bruce in Add MS 44087; see 1 Mar. 72.

Franco-German indemnity is insignificant. This is to speak of the claims, as the philosophers say, objectively. I am not willing, though perfectly prepared, to develop the calculation. What the claims may be *subjectively* that is to say in the intention of the American Govt. as yet perhaps we do not know.

29. Th.

Wrote to Mr G. Burnett (2)—Mr S. Ponsonby—Robn G.—Mr Mowbray—Mr Ayrton—The Lord Mayor & Sheriffs (sep[aratel]y)—Mr M'Clure—Watsons—The Queen (2)—& minutes. Saw Bp Moriarty —Mr Forster—Mr Glyn—Mr Stansfeld—Mr West (2). Read Russell-Killough on France and England.[1] Attended the Queen's Court at 3 & noticed closely her receptions of each person at all notable. It is a work of art that she performs. H of C. 4½-8 and 9¼-11¾.[2] Col. Hardinge came to me with the news of the strange attempt on the Queen, wh I stated to the House. Dined with the Wests.

Frid. Mch One 1872.

Wrote to Mr Burnett—Mr Bruce (3)—Mr Caird—Ld Chancellor—The Queen—Mrs Thistlethwayte—and minutes. Saw Mr Glyn—Mr F. Lawley—Ld Granville—Mr Macarthur—Col. Ponsonby. Saw The Queen 1¼-2: in an excellent frame, & quite serene. Corrected Revise of Feb. 7. (part) for press. Dined with Sir W. James. H of C. 4½-8¼ and 9½-12¾. Spoke on Sir R. Palmer's Resolutions.[3]

To H. A. BRUCE, home secretary, 1 March 1872. Aberdare MSS.

I believe the designation of Catholic Bishops assumed by the Romish hierarchy to be an illegal designation; and I suspect that, if it is novel, they have advisedly taken advantage of an opportunity for a step in advance at which they might hope that every body being in a good humour no objection would be taken to their proceedings. Strafford was perhaps not a great legal authority but I think in his time some Recusant made a bequest for a 'Catholic Bishop' & he said he would show the man, & did show him, who was the Catholic Bishop.[4] If I am wrong about illegality, the interpolation of Roman though needful is quite sufficient. If the title they have assumed under the Pope's authority be an illegal one, I am not quite sure that it is.

[1] H. Russell-Killough, *Angleterre et France* (1871).

[2] Questions, then interrupted deb. on the ballot to announce an attack by A. O'Connor with unloaded pistol on the Queen in her carriage, to obtain a pledge for release of Fenians: *H* ccix. 1164.

[3] *Palmer's Resolutions for a London school of law: *H* ccix. 1221.

[4] Wentworth declared the anglican bp. the natural recipient of a legacy to 'the Catholic bishop of Limeric'; see W. Knowles, *Letters of Strafford* (1739) i. 171, H. Trevor-Roper, *Archbishop Laud* (1940), 244.

[P.S.] My objection was wholly to the designation. Of presentation personally I had not heard.

2. *Sat.*

Wrote to Mr G. Burnett—The Queen (2)—Robn G.—Sir W.R. Farquhar—and minutes. Dined with the Speaker. Mrs Sturges's afterwards.[1] Saw Mr Glyn—Chr of Exr—The Speaker—Att. Genl. Cabinet 2½-6½. Read Blackwood on The Ministry[2]—Manning on the Daemon of Socrates.[3]

Cabinet. Mch 2. 72. 2½ PM.[4]

√ Sir E. Thornton's Telegramme of Feb. 29. Gen. Schenck's communication of yesterday & Ld G's refusal. His conversation with Cockburn. Remain silent for the present.[5]
√ Telegramme from Lisgar read. Time for a conclusive rest course.[6]
√ Letter to Schenck. Not to go. Game Committee, Welsh Judges, Macarthur Brixton: see below.
√ Australian Tariff Treaty question argued at great length—meeting to be held with Law Officers.
√ Ld Mayo. Offer a public funeral, found not feasible.
√ Eyre question. We considered we had no alternative.[7]
√ Return of proprietors in Ireland Resident and Absentee. To be given.[8]
√ O[sborne] Morgan—amend by adding words.[9]
√ Convict Prison (of Pentonville class)—look about for another site.
√ Game Laws. A govt. committee.[10]

Draft letter to Gen. Schenck[11]

I think I can give very strong reasons against dealing with my portion of the Chapter of Motives in any one of three modes which have been suggested. 1. By

[1] Unidentified.
[2] [W. G. Hamley], 'Ministers before parliament', *Blackwood's Magazine*, cxi. 368 (March 1872).
[3] H. E. *Manning, 'The daemon of Socrates. A paper' (1872).
[4] Add MS 44640, f. 45.
[5] Thornton wired Fish maintaining indirect and cotton bond claims; Granville replied Britain would not withdraw from arbitration: PRO FO 5/1394.
[6] Lisgar formally resigned as Canadian governor-general in June 1872.
[7] To reimburse 'certain expenses' of Eyre; see answer to McArthur's question, *H* ccix. 1525, 7 March 1872.
[8] See *H* ccix. 1616, 7 March 1872, and *PP* 1872 xlvii. 775.
[9] Draft amendment at Add MS 44640, f. 48, to Morgan's motion on ability of Welsh judges to speak Welsh; Gladstone asked Hatherley after cabinet to improve the amndt., which was never moved; Add MS 44541, f. 87, *H* ccix. 1658.
[10] Ward *Hunt's on Game Laws: *PP* 1872 x.
[11] Initialled and dated 2 March 1872; Add MS 44433, f. 264. Much confusion in America resulted from reports of Gladstone's speeches on 6 Feb.; see 6, 15 Feb. 72n. Schenck responded with cuttings from foreign papers favourable to America; Add MS 44434, f. 1. Vastly extended letter eventually sent 28 Nov. 72.

a speech in the H. of Commons. 2. By anonymous or intermediate writing in the public Journals or in any Periodical. 3. By argument in the Countercase. Again I am not much afraid: Of criticism—as they can hardly say more against me than I have said against myself: Of rejoinder—for nothing can well be produced from the speeches to sustain the first garbled extracts wh. will *now* attract great attention.

I am not sure how far any possible proceeding by Lord Russell should be taken into account: but it will be borne in mind that I shall in any case have to allow some weeks to pass before any public step is taken. I am afraid the alternative lies between this & nothing—so far as I can see.

3. 3 S.L.

Chapel Royal mg & evg. Saw Prince of Wales $1\frac{1}{2}$-$2\frac{1}{2}$. Dean of St Paul's $3\frac{1}{4}$-4. Wrote to Col. Ponsonby—Mr Bruce—Ld Granville—and minutes. Read Oakley[1] & Pye on Educn[2]—Church & Wife[3]—Blackwood on Voltaire[4]—Irons on Athan. Creed (finished)[5]—Union Rev. on Reformation Period, &c.[5]

4. M.

Wrote to Ld Chancellor—Sir G. Pollock—Mr W. Alexander[7]—Mr Harvey—Ld Granville—The Queen Mem. & l.—and minutes. H of C. $4\frac{1}{2}$-$8\frac{1}{4}$ and $9\frac{1}{2}$-$12\frac{1}{2}$.[8] Visited Christie's. Saw Mr Cyrus Field—Mr Lawley—Mr M'Coll—Mr Thring—Mr Glyn—Ld Granville—Mr Moffatt—Mr Gurdon—Sir R. Palmer. Read Christie on Ballot[9]—Milman's St Paul's—Holland's Recollections.[10]

5. Tu.

In bed till 3.30 from a slight attack: wrote by minutes entirely except in evg to The Queen. H of C. $4\frac{1}{2}$-8 and $8\frac{3}{4}$-$12\frac{3}{4}$.[11] Read Milman's St Paul's—V. Hugo's Shakespeare.[12] Saw Mr Glyn.

[1] F. *Oakeley, 'The question of university education for English Catholics' (1864).

[2] G. Pye, *Education* (1872).

[3] R. C. St John, *Church and wife* (1872).

[4] *Blackwood's Magazine*, cxi. 270 (March 1872).

[5] See 25 Feb. 72.

[6] *Union Review*, 312 (January-December 1872).

[7] William Alexander, d. 1894, ed. of *Aberdeen Free Press*, author of *Johnny Gibb*: on the latter see 28 Sept. 71n.

[8] Army estimates: *H* ccix. 1328.

[9] W. D. *Christie, *The ballot, and corruption and expenditure at elections* (1872).

[10] Sir H. *Holland, *Recollections of past life* (1872).

[11] Dixon's Resolutions on education (see 24 Feb. 72): *H* ccix. 1395.

[12] V. M. Hugo, *William Shakespeare [an essay on his works]* (1864).

6. Wed.

Wrote to Mr Layard—Mr Chambers MP—Ld Sydney—The Queen (Mem.)—Robn G.—Dean of Ch.Ch.—and minutes. Levee at 2. Dined with Sir C. Lambson [*sc.* Lampson]. Lady M. Beaumont's afr. Saw Russell X. Saw Gen. Schenk 11-12.—Mr M'Coll—Count Beust —Mr Glyn—Mr Cardwell—Mr Hayward—Duc de Broglie—Sir A. Panizzi—and others. Read U.S. Case on San Juan—British Case on do (finished)[1]—Milman's St Pauls.

7. Th.

Wrote to Ld Chancellor—Mr Samuelson—The Queen (2)—Ld Granville (2)—and minutes. H of C. 4½-8 and 9½-2.[2] 13 to dinner. Saw Ld Granville—Mr Fortescue—Mr F. Lawley—Mr Glyn—Ld Petre—Mr Bruce—Chr of Exr—Mr Cardwell. Read Milman's St Pauls.

8. Fr.

Wrote to Ld Kimberley—Abp of Canterbury—Mr Goss[3]—The Queen (2)—and minutes. Read Milman's St Paul's—Megaera Report.[4] Saw D. and Dss of Argyll—Mr Gurdon—Mr Glyn—Mr B. Price—Mr Mowbray—Ld Granville. H of C. 4½-8¾ & 9¾-2¼. Spoke on Ewelme Case[5]—& other matters.

To A. C. TAIT, archbishop of Canterbury, 8 March 1872. Tait MSS, 90, f. 82.

1. The Cabinet meets tomorrow & I will bring before my colleagues your Grace's proposal as to a Bill for shortened services.[6] I presume that *no* other matter would be brought or allowed to enter, in it, at least if of an important character.
2. I transmit a reprint of the Deans & Canons Bill as amended. I have, the claim being made almost in common, let in Ch. Ch. with the two other Deaneries. This of course is open to reconsideration by your Grace.
3. I see no impediment in the way of your Grace conferring with Mr. Thring as to the best mode of dealing with the Bishops Resignation Bill.[7]
4. As regards the Cathedral Statutes, I would venture to suggest that any formal conference with Mr. Thring would best come after the basis of a plan shall have

[1] Schenck was proposing that the U.S.A. would drop the indirect claims if Britain dropped claims to San Juan; Cook, *The Alabama Claims*, 222.
[2] Scottish education: *H* ccix. 1599.
[3] Knighting John *Goss, 1800-80, for his anthem for the Prince of Wales' recovery.
[4] *PP* 1872 xv.
[5] *H* ccix. 1685; no vote taken, as no motion was moved.
[6] Sent on 5 March 1872, Add MS 44331, f. 46.
[7] To extend the provisions of the 1869 Act.

been agreed upon: but I have no doubt he would gladly answer any specific questions, as to this or that form of legislation, which you might desire to put to him.

9. Sat.

Wrote to Ld Blachford—Col. Ponsonby—Abp of Canterb.—The Queen—and minutes. Dined with the Halifaxes. Saw Mr Glyn—Ld Chancellor—Ld Granville—Gen. Bedeau [*sic*].[1] Saw Blake & another: much hope[R]. Cabinet 2¾-6. Read V. Hugo's Shakespeare.

Cabinet. Mch. 9. 72—2½ PM.[2]

√ Auditor of Indian Accounts—offer to Mr Macaulay.[3] Decision of Cabinet announced: form of announcement to H.M. agreed to.[4]
√ Chancellor's Bill. Resolution to be drawn severing the jurisdiction. Proceed by Resolution.[5] Ex chancellors to serve in Court of Appeal & *earn* pension.
√ Archbishop's letter. Bill for Shortening [services]—his No 1 may be brought in—by him.[6]
√ Wedderburn's motion: act for the best.[7]
√ Fawcett's [University Tests (Dublin)] Bill. Support 2R. Hart[ingto]n to communicate with Ld O'Hagan on behalf of the R.Cs.[8]
√ Newdegate's Bill Feb. 19. Not oppose introduction at any rate unless opposed by Mr Villiers & the committee.[9]
√ Parliamentary Elections Bill—Torrens's Amendment. Oppose strongly.[10]
√ Cabinet Committee on Hours of Polling. Bruce, Halifax, Hart[ingto]n, Stansfeld.
√ Rylands on Treaties. Depreciate any dissention at that moment.[11]
√ Mr Dodson's Resolutions. Considered. Ld Hartington's view for Ireland approved generally.[12]
√ Q[uer]y ask Dilke whether he intends to indicate the nature of the points connected with Civil List which are comprehended within the very general terms of his motion for Tues. 19th? Yes.[13]

Within is an important letter from Col. Ponsonby.[14] It seems nearly to kill the *little* Irish plan; to exhibit fresh difficulties in the way of the large one; and to

[1] Probably Col. Adam Badeau, assistant secretary of the U.S. legation.

[2] Add MS 44640, f. 50.

[3] C. Z. Macaulay, who declined; Sir Charles R. M. Jackson was auditor 1872-4.

[4] Further illegible phrase scribbled in margin.

[5] Resolution for an Imperial Supreme Court of Appeal, moved on 15 April, later withdrawn; *H* ccx. 1246.

[6] See previous day's letter and *H* ccix. 1751.

[7] Wedderburn's motion on Scottish parliamentary business, counted out on 12 March: *H* ccix. 1853.

[8] *H* ccx. 327, 20 March 1872.

[9] Leave to introduce Bill to appoint commissioners to oversee convents etc.: *H* ccx. 1686, 23 April 1872.

[10] Amndt. that candidates should not pay for returning officers' expenses, defeated: *H* ccx. 2001, 14 March 1872.

[11] Rylands and Lawson moved a motion for an address on treaty obligations on 12 April: *H* ccx. 1157.

[12] Private legislation in parliament: *H* ccx. 17, 15 March 1872.

[13] See 11 Mar. 72.

[14] See Ramm I, ii. 316.

project, so to speak, a shadow of some other schemes of public employment, which may or may not have a substance.

It appears to me that there is one duty imperatively demanded by the great and favourable crisis which has been offered us. It is to make a resolute endeavour at improving the relations between the Monarchy and the Nation by framing a worthy and manly mode of life, *quoad* public duties, for the Prince of Wales.

This will I hope be our unanimous opinion.

If it is so we must now endeavour to make our choice between the possible plans.

When so much has been done as shall embody the essential points, I presume it will be right for me to open the subject to the Queen and to take her pleasure on the question whether she will allow me to state what must I suppose in that case be termed simply my views; or whether I shall bring the subject before the Cabinet with a view to offering her their collective advice.

It will be a calamity if we fail, either with the Queen, the Prince, or both. But, even then, the failure need not be final. And in any case the risk of it, which we of course shall do nothing needlessly to increase, seems to me in no degree to dispense with the duty which looks us in the face.[1]

To LORD BLACHFORD, 9 March 1872. Add MS 44107, f. 334.

When shall you be in town, & when you are here, would you come & see me? In some way or other we seem to be unable to make ourselves reciprocally intelligible,[2] but in speech I think I could make it more clear that you (in my view) make a case for the Americans by simply erasing for all practical purposes the second Claim of what I term, & you refuse to term the Waiver.

I am anxious about this for I want to see by probing to the bottom, whether there is a bonâ fide or rather a substantial doubt in the case. It is a very serious question, for disgrace falls upon the Government and the Commissioners, & through them on the Parliament & country which could find no better agents if in this, the only real point which was to be made for us against all we gave, we have really contrived to make an ambiguous Treaty: & if the public mind settle down in the conviction towards which a large part of the Press have (as I think) erroneously & perversely directed it, I should not even wonder if it ended in a constitutional change.

But we cannot get to close quarters, except through *vivâ voce.*

10. 4 S.Lent.

Ch. Royal mg and evg. Wrote to Col. Ponsonby—Mr Taylor Innes and minutes. Saw Ld Salisbury—Mr Taylor Innes—Sir W. Farquhar—& minutes. Read Massey on Spiritualism[3]—Taylor Innes on Stanley's Lectures[4]—Maitland on completing the

[1] Initialled and dated 9 March 1872; Add MS 44760, f. 174; apparently for circulation, but destination not docketed.

[2] See Blachford's letter of 8 March 1872, Add MS 44107, f. 330, and 25 Feb. 72.

[3] G. Massey, *Concerning spiritualism* (1871).

[4] A. T. Innes, 'Dean Stanley at Edinburgh', *Contemporary Review*, xix. 443 (March 1872); letter of appreciation at Add MS 44541, f. 91.

Reformation[1]—Church & Wife[2]—and other Tracts. Luncheon with the Salisburys. Tea with Lady M. Farquhar.

11. M.

Wrote to Bp of Winchester—Sec. M.D. Railway Co.—Ld Ln—Sir T. Biddulph—Ld Carew—Sir C. Dilke—Mr Tupper—Mr Colman MP—Mr Disraeli—Ld Kimberley—The Queen—and minutes. Saw Mr M'Coll—Mr F. Lawley—Mr Glyn—Mr Levy—Mr G. Duff—M. Marciartu.[3] H of C. 4½-8 & 9½-12¾.[4] Dined with the Jameses. Read Milman's St Paul's—Tacitus, Germania—F. Lawley's Art. on Gen. Lee.[5] Saw Blake X. Conclave in D. St on P. of Wales's avenir.[6]

To Sir C. W. DILKE, M.P., 11 March 1872. Add MS 44541, f. 90.

I observe that the notice of motion, which you have given for the 19th with respect to the Civil List, is couched in very general terms, & I take the liberty of inquiring whether with a view to the further elucidation of the case you intend to amend or develop it so as to indicate the heads of topics which you mean to discuss, & on which it is desirable that the Government & the C. of E. in particular, should prepare themselves to afford you & the House full information. On a subject of this sort you will probably agree with me that it would be particularly unfortunate if from a virtual want of notice such information were not to be forthcoming, & important questions to remain unanswered or partial & erroneous views from want of proper answer to prevail.

To S. WILBERFORCE, bishop of Winchester, 11 March 1872. Wilberforce MSS, d. 38.

Alarming rumours reach me about movements against the Athanasian Creed, & their probable consequences. I cannot however as yet get accurate information as to the exact character of these movements. And when you come to town next I should be glad if you could enlighten me. On Saturday I acquainted the Abp. that the Govt. would support any Bill introduced by him for shortening Services agreeably to the Report of the Commissioners & with the assent of Convocation. But if extraneous matter, & especially formidable & explosive matter were to be forced in, the position might be much altered.[7]

[1] S. R. *Maitland, *Essays on subjects connected with the Reformation in England* (1849).

[2] See 3 Mar. 72.

[3] Unidentified.

[4] Army estimates: *H* ccix. 1762.

[5] F. C. *Lawley, 'General Lee', *Blackwood's Magazine*, 111. 348 (March 1872).

[6] Reported to Spencer on 14 March (Add MS 44541, f. 94): '. . . I think there is a feeling that the minor plan, wh. towards the end of last Session appeared to be in almost exclusive possession of the field, has been overshadowed by events wh have since occurred & wh seem to call for a larger treatment of the case.'

[7] Wilberforce replied: 'I believe that I have convinced the Archbishop that he must *for the present* drop the Athanasian creed attempt'; 13 March 1872, Add MS 44345, f. 217.

12. Tu.

Wrote to Bp of B. & Wells[1]—M. Laveleye—Prov. of Oriel—The Queen (Mem.)—Ld Dufferin—& minutes. Visited Christie's. Saw Sir T. Biddulph—Mr Glyn—Chancr of Exr—Mr West—Sir R. Phillimore. H of C. 4½-8¼.[2] Read Fowle on Science &c.[3]

Th[eology][4]

In the great contemporary Poem on Simon de Montfort,[5] the case is supposed of an incurably wrong-minded Prince, & the question asked what is in such cases to be done? 'What authority then remains? None, but that of the community. In the collective memory of the nation alone the truth concerning the laws & customs of the realm can be discovered. Appeal must therefore be made by the community: its opinion be ascertained.'

Now this is the *quod semper quod ubique quod ab omnibus* of theology. It is the community as distinguished from classes, the body as distinguished from its parts. It is not an appeal to mere numbers. Neither is it an appeal to individual authorities. The collective sense is different from numerical preponderance: it is sometimes called moral unanimity. So also is it different from an array of individual authorities. We deal not so much with authorities who make a rule as with witnesses who tell us what it is. They do not rule the body but speak for it. It has many organs, and these[?] are the organ which we call the wise.

It is probable that many who bristle with jealousy against the *doctrine* of Vincentius[6] would admit freely, as a real though an indeterminate law, the sister to that *dictum* which applies the very same sense to problems of political philosophy.

To E. L. V. de LAVELEYE, 12 March 1872. 'Private.' Add MS 44541, f. 91.

I thank you much for your valuable article.[7] I have often cited European opinions against my country. It now greatly pleases & sustains me to find daily increasing proof that it stands on our side. And I think that we are in our argument sustaining the cause of peace & of the world. Who will ever arbitrate if arbitration is to be made a vehicle for giving public recognition to extravagant & incredible caprices? I take the liberty of enclosing a sort of skeleton argument upon the phrase 'amicable settlement' in the Protocols & Preamble, for your perusal, if you are good enough to give it the short time required. It is in substance one of the Branches of our argument.

[1] On purgatory; Lathbury, i. 382.

[2] Spoke on Wedderburn's motion (see 9 Mar. 72): *H* ccix. 1877.

[3] T. W. Fowle, 'Science and immortality', *Contemporary Review*, xix. 461 (March 1872).

[4] Holograph dated 12 March 1872; Add MS 44760, f. 176.

[5] 'Polit. Songs Ed. Wright p. 72. Prothero, p. 181'; diarist's note added later; i.e. T. Wright, *The political songs of England . . . John to Edward II* (1839), and G. W. *Prothero, *Life of . . . de Montfort* (1877).

[6] St. Vincent of Lérins, author of the Vincentian canon (*quod ubique, quod semper, quod ab omnibus . . .*) whose order was frequently misquoted, as here.

[7] On international relations, place of publication untraced, sent on 7 March; Add MS 44433, f. 277.

13. Wed.

Wrote to Mr Dodson—Mr Cardwell—Mr Bruce—Abp of Canterb. —The Queen—Mr Grant Duff—Ld Kimberley—& minutes. Saw Sir J. Lubbock—Mr Farrer—Mr Hine—Sir R. Palmer—Mr Glyn—D. of Argyll—Ld Hartington. Read Milman's St Pauls.

14. Th.

Wrote to Viceroy of Ireland—Abp Manning—Ld Granville—The Queen (l. mem. & Tel.)—and minutes. H of C. 4½-8 and 8.45-1.45.[1] Queen's levee at 3 P.M. Saw Mr Pollen (Dublin Exchr)[2]—Mr Tylden Wright—Mr Glyn—Ld Granville—Read Milman's St Paul's.

Memorandum for R. LOWE, chancellor of the exchequer, 14 March 1872. Add MS 44541, f. 93.

I do not see that the Sugar Refiners have done anything which should expose them to censure or damage their position before us. The Convention of 1863 was I believe made, as far as intention is concerned, in the interest of the Consumers. It was a relief from a great embarrassment & an apparent end to an awkward controversy, which it has laid asleep these last eight years. With respect to an uniform duty I will only at present make these observations. 1. The lowness of the present rate greatly mitigates the difficulty, but our Sugar duty should perhaps be like our Army, one easily capable of that expansion in case of war which it almost certainly [would] receive. 2. I do not know whether you have in view a duty which shall be uniform over *all* descriptions of Sugar, including what is or was called double-refined. I *used* to find that the uniform duty party were not so much disposed to face this difficulty. 3. Small as is comparatively the additional burden now to be imposed by an uniform duty, the sugar trade is perhaps one of those in which the competition is peculiarly close—& there may be a great deal of fighting over any change proposed. 4. I think it would be very difficult to carry a really uniform (duty) without establishing the system of refining in Bond both for the home market & for export with the heavy cost it would entail. These papers should I think be communicated to Mr Fortescue, & I should advise asking the aid also of Cardwell who made himself completely master of the whole case before the Convention.

15. Fr.

Wrote to Abp Manning—D. of Argyll—Bp of Lichfield—Sir W. Dunbar—Sir T. Biddulph—Ld Chancellor—The Queen—and minutes. Read Milman's St Paul's. Visited Christie's. Saw Sir W. Anderson (2)—Mr Lawley—Sir Thos G.—Mr Glyn—Mr Goschen—

[1] Spoke on the ballot: *H* ccix. 1995.

[2] Perhaps John Pollen, emigration and exchange agent in Dublin.

Ld Kimberley *cum* C. of E.—3-4. Conclave in D. St on Australian Tariffs. H of C. 4½-8 and 8¾-1½.[1]

16. Sat.

Wrote to Mrs Barton[R]—Abp of Canterbury—Mr Bruce—Bp of Winchester—Mr Burnett—Mr Poulett Scrope—Sir Thos G.—Marquis of Lorne—The Queen—& minutes. Cabinet 2¾-7: laborious: chiefly on the Washington Treaty. Saw Mr Donaldson[2]—Mr Glyn—Ld Granville—Mr Hayward. Eleven to dinner: small evg party. Saw A. Wilson.

Cabinet. Mch. 16. 2½ PM. D. St.[3]

√ Sir C. Dilke's motion. Oppose returns respecting Civil List.[4]
√ Mr Fawcett's Bill Wedy. Already decided.
√ Motion of Private Business of Law Officers. Cannot accept any present Resolution.
√ Removal of the Jurisdiction of Appeal from the Lords—opposition probable.[5] Composition of Lords Branch of Appeal Court considered.
√ Johnstone's motion. Give up Party processions Act.[6]
√ Ld Granville announced the Denunciation yesterday of the French Treaty. Dispatch setting forth wrongs to be prepared.
√ Washington Treaty. Fish dispatch. No *plans* to be suggested. No further development of instructions to be given. See Separate Mema.[7] Ld G. may submit his two fine suggestions.

17. 5 S.Lent.

Ch. Royal at noon. Wrote to Chancr of Exchr—The Queen—and minutes. Worked on parts of the dispatch for America. Saw Count Bernstorff—Ld Lyttelton—S.E.G.—Read Tyndale's Life[8]—Bp Alexander on the Gospels[9]—Jelf on Mariolatry.[10]

To R. LOWE, chancellor of the exchequer, Add MS 44541, f. 96.
17 March 1872.

I shall be happy to talk over the matter with you,[11] but my inclination as to your surplus would be to convert some more Stocks into terminable Annuities,

[1] Answered Disraeli on treaty of Washington, later on public business: *H* ccx. 49, 94.
[2] Not further identified.
[3] Add MS 44640, f. 53.
[4] See 9 and 19 Mar. 72.
[5] See 9 Mar. 72.
[6] Hartington denied suppression of Derry demonstrations had been under the Party Processions Act, 22 March, *H* ccx. 543.
[7] Jottings, at Add MS 44640, f. 55, mem. at 44760, f. 196; Fish's despatch of 27 Feb., received 14 March: *PP* 1872 lxix. 656.
[8] R. *Demaus, *William Tyndale. A biography* (1871).
[9] W. Alexander, *The leading ideas of the Gospels. Five sermons* (1872).
[10] In R. W. *Jelf's Bampton Lectures for 1844 (1844).
[11] Lowe's letter untraced.

if you have any which are available, so as to absorb say £200,000 to £300,000, & keep the rest as surplus. I think the House would agree. I believe our Treasury Annuities have not yet reached the point at which they stood in 1859, whereas they ought to be raised above it. I forget the exact condition of coffee duty: probably you have considered it. The removal of a tax which mainly touches the classes having property together with the reduction of the I[ncome] T[ax] would, I think, again raise the reproach last year unjustly made, of a capriciously one-sided legislation.

18. M.

Wrote to D. of Cambridge—Mr Engleheart—Mr Synan[1] MP—Mr Disraeli—Dean of Westmr—The Queen—and minutes. H of C. 4½-8¼ and 9½-1.[2] Read Olrig Grange.[3] Saw Mr Gurdon (2)—Ld Tenterden *cum* Mr Bernard—Sir R. Palmer—Att. General—Mr Lawley—Mr Glyn—Chancr of Exr. Dined with the F. Cavendishes. Saw one [R]. In conclaves much heavy work on Alabama.[4]

To B. DISRAELI, M.P., 18 March 1872. Add MS 44541, f. 96.

The D. of Argyll's gout has limited my communication with him & prevented my fulfilling my promise to let you know the proceedings of the Indian Council in the matter of Lady Mayo.[5] I was not made aware of their decision at the moment when it was taken & I have been anticipated in this communication by the newspapers. I propose to reply today to the portion of your question of Friday respecting the American dispatch which was then left unanswered.

19. Tu.

Wrote to D. of Argyll—The Queen l. & 2 Tel.—and minutes. Saw Mr Glyn—Dr Brady—Chancr of Exr. Cabinet 11-2 and 2½-3½. H of C. 4½-10. Spoke against Sir C. Dilke's motion.[6] Dined with the Lytteltons. Read Milman's St Pauls.

Cabinet. Mch. 19. 1872. 11 AM.[7]

√ Ld Granville stated purport of communications with Schenck.

√ Draft of reply to Dispatch of February 27[8] considered & amended. Concluding portion added.[9]

[1] Edmund John Synan, 1820-87; liberal M.P. Limerick 1865-85. On Irish education; Add MS 44541, f. 97.

[2] Answered questions: *H* ccx. 126.

[3] *Olrig Grange*, ed. H. Kunst [W. C. Smith] (1872).

[4] Morley, ii. 410.

[5] Disraeli had written on 11 March suggesting the govt. make provision for the Viceroy's widow who had 'only a thousand per ann:'; Add MS 44433, f. 285.

[6] *H* ccx. 291; see 9, 16 Mar. 72.

[7] Add MS 44640, f. 61.

[8] Schenck gave Granville a copy of Fish's letter of 27 February insisting on indirect claims, *F.R.U.S.* 1872, ii. 429.

[9] Draft at Add MS 44640, f. 62; the British reply proposed a supplemental article to the treaty of Washington; see *PP* 1872 lxix. 659, Cook, *The Alabama Claims*, 223 and *F.R.U.S.* 1872, ii. 436. Printed draft with holograph annotations, at Add MS 44619, f. 29.

To the DUKE OF ARGYLL, Indian secretary, Add MS 44541, f. 97.
19 March 1872.

I have not been successful in finding a man for your accountership.[1] Neate's name was peremptorily set aside by Lowe. I consulted Anderson & found that neither Chisholme nor Ryan would accept. This negative result was only attained yesterday evening. This morning I asked the members of the Cabinet generally to submit *to you* any names which any one of them might think unimpeachable, (as I saw no advantage in my taking the initiative when I had no direct knowledge) but I shall be most happy to confer with you on them if you find occasion.

I am much concerned at your renewed attack, it was doubly kind of the Duchess to come on Saturday without you. I should not wonder if the Mayo pension affair fanned by the Press, were to break out into some further discussion.

We are working on the draft reply to Fish's dispatch & hope it will go to Schenk tomorrow.
2 p.m. The revision has been very long but very useful & harmonious.

20. Wed.

Wrote to Ld Halifax—Sir T. Biddulph—Abp of York—Ld Tenterden—Gen. Schenck[2]—Ld Chancellor—D of Argyll—Sir T. Twiss—The Queen—and minutes. Rose late, having had a slight attack last night. Saw The Speaker—Mr Brady—Sir E. May—Mr Glyn—Ld Northbrook—Ld Penzance—Mr Fortescue & Lady Waldegrave. Dined with the Abercrombies. H of C. 12-2½—and 5-6. Spoke on Herman's question: & on Fawcett's Bill.[3] Read Olrig Grange. Saw one X.

21. Th.

Wrote to Chancr of Exr—Duchess of Argyll—Mr J.J. Lake[4]—Mr Fortescue—The Queen—and minutes. Eight to dinner. H. of C. 4½-8¼ and 9½-1½.[5] Saw Mr F. Lawley—Mr Gurdon—Mr Glyn—Mr West. Read Olrig Grange (finished).

22. Fr.

Severe bronchial attack came out—met by physic & strong perspiration through the whole day. Transacted business through West—W.H.G.—Mr Glyn—Ld Granville—& Cardwell, who went to & fro between the Cabinet below stairs & me. To all these I whispered with

[1] Auditor of Indian Home Accounts; Sir C. R. M. Jackson, see 9 Mar. 72n.
[2] Thanking him for papers; Add MS 44541, f. 98.
[3] On Irish University tests; *H* ccx. 343; see 9 Mar. 72.
[4] Had sent a Homeric geography; probably John W. Lake, *The mythos of the ark* (1872).
[5] Navy estimates: *H* ccx. 408.

some difficulty. Read Milman's St Paul's. Tel. to Col. Ponsonby—Note to G G G[lyn][1]

23. Sat.

In bed all day but greatly better. Read Milman's St Pauls. Business done through Mr Glyn & West. Also saw Ld Granville & Sir R. Phillimore.

24. Palm S.

Rose at 5 P.M. Ch. service alone. Saw Ld R. Cavendish—Dr A. Clark—Mr Glyn—Read Hook's Life of Parker[2]—S. Brooke on Freedom in Ch.[3]—Milman's St Pauls (finished)—Ommaney on Ath. Creed[4]—Account of Miss S. Robinson's work.[5]

25. M.

Rose at one. Wrote to Sir T. Biddulph—Chancr of Exr—Sir S.R. Glynne—Sir J. Hanmer—Ld R. Cavendish—and minutes. H of C. 4½-8.[6] F.C. dined. Saw Earl of Shaftesbury—Mr Gurdon (R.B.)—Mr Glyn—Mr Stacpoole—Chr of Exr—Ld F. Cavendish. Read Caldicott on Religious Education[7]—Account of East African Slave Trade[8]—Dean Hook's Life of Parker.

26. Tu.

Wrote to Ld Spencer—Mr Stacpoole—The Queen—Mr Dodson—Mr Bright—Mr Bonham Carter[9]—Ld Kimberley—and minutes. H of C. 4½-6.[10] Saw Ld Granville—Mrs Cooper[11]—Mr Gurdon—Mr Glyn (3)—Mr M'Laren—Mr Bonham Carter—Conclave on amendments in Parks Bill.—Mr Cardwell. Read Hook's Life of Parker—

[1] See Morley, ii. 410.
[2] W. F. *Hook, *Lives of the Archbishops of Canterbury*, ix (1872).
[3] S. A. *Brooke, *Freedom in the Church of England. Six sermons* (1871); see 1 Apr. 72.
[4] G. D. W. *Ommanney, 'The Athanasian Creed; its use in the services of the Church' (1872).
[5] *Active service or [Miss S. Robinson's] work among our soldiers* [by Miss J. E. Hopkins] (1872).
[6] Lowe's budget: *H* ccx. 603.
[7] J. W. Caldicott, 'Religious education and religious freedom. . . . A letter to W.E.G.' (1872).
[8] E. F. Berlioux, *The slave trade in Africa in 1872* (1872).
[9] Asking him to succeed *Dodson as chairman of Ways & Means; he agreed; Add MS 44541, f. 100.
[10] University Tests (Dublin) Bill 2° R: *H* ccx. 732.
[11] See 24 July 70.

'Resoconto' of the discussion at Rome on St Peter's Pontificate there.[1] Rose before noon.

27. Wed.

Rose as usual. All Saints 5. P.M. Wrote to Ld Granville—Mr Williams Wynn—Mr MacLaren—Mrs Th—Ld Blachford—D. of Argyll—and minutes. Packing books. Saw Col. White[2]—Mrs Macnamara—Ld R. Cavendish—S.E.G. Read Döllinger's Lectures on Church of England[3]—Hook's Life of Parker—Lord Kilgobbin[4]—and much bad poetry: *weeding* a large lot of volumes.

28. Th. [Latimer][5]

Wrote to Dean of ChCh (V.C.)—Author of Olrig Grange[6]—Rev. Mr Clark (U.S.)[7]—Bishop of Derry—Ld Kimberley—& minutes. Read Lord Kilgobbin—Ciriani, Stato d'Europa[8]—Hook's Life of Parker. Arr. papers letters &c. Off at 3.20 for Latimer. arrived too late for Church. Whist in evg.

To H. G. LIDDELL, dean of Christ Church, Oxford, 28 March 1872. Add MS 44541, f. 102.

I think it right to say that on reference to Lord Ripon I am satisfied that the [Privy] Council office has not been disposed to treat the cases of College Statutes as matters of routine, but has taken great pains to inform itself for which credit is really deserved.

Do not suppose that I at least therefore think your letter[9] purposeless as to its substance. The questions arising in conjunction with this affair of College Statutes are of great difficulty. It is idle to suppose that the governing bodies of Colleges, in which youth may sometimes dangerously predominate, are gifted with such an all [seeing?] wisdom, or are so exempted from the human failing of selfishness as to make it safe to rely on their authority. I am sure we shall do our best but I feel that our difficulties are great & our chances of error many.

I shall be very glad if the Colleges themselves suspend operations during the enquiries of the Commission.

[1] Perhaps report in *The Tablet*, 23 March 1872, 365.
[2] Perhaps *sc.* Captain; see 22 June 68.
[3] J. J. I. von Döllinger, *Lectures on the reunion of the Churches* (1872).
[4] C. J. *Lever, *Lord Kilgobbin*, 3v. (1872).
[5] Lord Chesham's; see 25 Feb. 65.
[6] Thanking the anon. author, [W. C. Smith], through Maclehose, the publisher; Add MS 44541, f. 102. See 18 Mar. 72.
[7] Unidentified.
[8] F. Ciriani, *Del presente e futuro stato politico d'Europa* (1871).
[9] Untraced.

29. Good Friday.

Church 11 AM and 6 PM. Wrote to Mr Skeffington[1]—Ld Kimberley—and minutes. Read T.A. Kempis—Skeffington's Sermons (finished)—Life of Tindal[2]—Stopford Brooke's Sermons.[3]—The Rothschild Book.[4]

30. Easter Eve.

Church 6 PM. Wrote to Ld Tenterden—and minutes. Read Counter Case on Alabama—Ld Kilgobbin—Taine Notes sur l'Angleterre[5]—Saul of Tarsus.[6] Drive to Amersham & Chesham. Saw the two Churches. Whist in evg.

31. Easter Day:

for which the weather opportunely cleared. Church 11 AM & 6 P.M. Holy Commn in mg. Wrote to Ld Kimberley—Ld Lyttelton—& minutes. Read T.A. Kempis—Life of Tindal—S. Brooke's Sermons (finished)—with much perturbation of mind. Walk with the party.

Easter Monday Ap. 1. 72.

Chesham Water Ch 7 P.M. Wrote to S.R.G.—W.H.G.—G.G. Glyn—Robn G.—and minutes. Chesham Deputn at 3.30. At 6.15 we went over to the Working Men's Club to whom I made a short address.[7] The service was remarkable: church crowded. Saw Mr Moore—Ld Granville. Read Ld Kilgobbin—Rousseau's Letters to Hume.[8]

To G. G. GLYN, chief whip, 1 April 1872. Add MS 44541, f. 104.

Here is an application for Sir Watkin as Lord Lieutenant of Denbigh. I have said no. What I want to know is whether [Cornwallis-]West[9] can take it, being High Sheriff. Clare waits. I should have thought Macnamara's a name to be considered. He is said to have the largest Lib. property in the county.[10] No answer

[1] Sydney William Skeffington, assistant master at Charterhouse, had sent his *The sinless sufferer. Six sermons* (1872).

[2] See 17 Mar. 72.

[3] See 24 Mar. 72.

[4] Perhaps C. de Rothschild, *The history and literature of the Israelites* (1870).

[5] H. A. Taine, *Notes sur l'Angleterre* (1872).

[6] By W. B. *Mackenzie (1864).

[7] On virtues of working men's clubs, described as 'Retaliation' (to Disraeli's publicity for his Manchester visit) by *The Times*, but only reported on 8 April 1872, 12e.

[8] *A concise and genuine account of the dispute between Mr. Hume and Mr. Rousseau, with the letters that passed between them* (1766).

[9] He took it, see 3 May 72.

[10] Charles W. White was appt. ld. lieut. of Co. Clare.

from Bright yet. As regards the other offices, you know I am waiting for the Judge Advocateship to be settled, as they may be affected by it.

I have read S. Brooke's sermons on Freedom,[1] & am sorely staggered by them: while there is much in them that I like, & that I admire, they seem to me to be characterised by that mental rashness which is so characteristic of the mind, & of the criticism of the present age. They leave me in a great bewilderment. To form an adequate judgment of such subjects, my first step must be to resign, & divest myself of every other thought or care, & spend some undivided years upon them.

To Sir S. R. GLYNNE, 1 April 1872. Add MS 44541, f. 103.

I have received your letter[2] inclosing that of Major Ffoulkes, & I am truly sorry to be obliged to pass by Sir Watkin [Williams-Wynn] considering his position & his connection with your family. But if politics are to be regarded at all as entering into these questions of appointment to Lord Lieutenancies, it would be trying too severely the patience of the Liberal Party in the County & in Wales, were I to select when there are perfectly competent & proper gentlemen of Liberal politics in the County ready to take the office, one of their most powerful & thoroughgoing opponents. It would be an act quite beyond the range of my discretion that in my position I am entitled to exercise, & whatever the local feeling may be I am certain that such a proceeding would excite a feeling of amazement throughout the country. With your candour & information, I think you will be sensible of this, for such matters we all know are governed in this country to a great extent by usage, & what usage requires is too plain to be mistaken. I go back to London on Wednesday.

2. Tu.

Ch. 6 PM. Wrote to Mr Goschen—and minutes. Read Ld Kilgobbin—Crebillon's La Nuit et le Moment.[3] What an exhibition. Saw Ld Granville. Long conversation with Mr Doyle on the Vatican decree & kindred matter. We drove to Moor Park—how beautiful.[4]

3. Wed. [*London*]

Wrote to Mrs Davidson[5]—Duke of Cambridge—Sir Thos G.—Robn G.—C.G.—and minutes. Saw Graham—& two others. X. Read Ld Kilgobbin—Ciriani, Stato Politico d'Europa. 12-2½. Back to London. Dined with Mrs Glyn.

To Sir Thomas GLADSTONE, 3 April 1872. Add MS 44541, f. 104.

I do not think that interest in the Navy, in the old sense of the word, has the power that it once possessed; but that can be no reason why the qualifications

[1] See 24 Mar. 72.
[2] Hawn P.
[3] C. P. Jolyot de Crébillon, *La nuit et le moment* (1762).
[4] Lord Ebury's house.
[5] On a patronage case; Add MS 44541, f. 105.

of a good man should not be made known in the proper quarter, & if you will kindly send me the particulars in the case of our cousin Mr Scott, I will take care that it is done.

4. Th.

Wrote to The Queen l. & Mem.—Ld Kimberley—C.G.—Mr Disraeli—& minutes. Saw Mr Bonham Carter—Mr Wykeham Martin—Sir J. Lacaita—Mr Glyn—Scotts—and Ch of Exr. Dined with Mrs Glyn. H of C. 4½-8 and 9½-1½.[1] Read Lord Kilgobbin Vol. 3—finished Ciriani.

To B. DISRAELI, M.P., 4 April 1872. Add MS 44541, f. 105.

Mr Dodson proposes to retire from his Parliamentary offices, & I intend to propose Mr B[onham] Carter as his successor. I should have made this intimation to you a few days ago but for an accidental delay in Mr C's reply. As this delay has occurred I do not propose to make the Motion before Monday.

5. Fr.

Wrote to Mr Chadwick—Ld Lyttelton—Mr Bright—Ld Granville (2)—The Queen—& minutes. Dined at Pol.Econ. Club for a discussion on 9 hours labour.[2] Saw Dr A. Clark—Att. General—Mr Forster—S.E.G.—Mr Glyn—Ld Chancr—Conclaves on Counter case first with Cardwell & Lowe—then with Tenterden & Sanderson—much confusion.[3] H of C. 4½-6½ and 9¼-12.[4] Cabinet 2-4½. Read Ld Kilgobbin.

Friday. Ap. 5. 1872. 2 PM.[5]

√ Alabama. Countercase. Telegramme to U.S. agreed on to Fish, & recalled. Passage agreed on to eliminate Chapter of Motives & other alterations.[6]
√ Canada. Fisheries instructions approved.
O Fawcett's Bill.[7]
√ Lady Mayo. Views to be declared when motion is brought on.[8]
√ Conversation of P. of Wales with Pope. answer agreed on.[9]
O Elcho's Committee.[10]

[1] *Harcourt's motion to reduce national expenditure: *H* ccx. 735.
[2] Discussion led by E. *Chadwick; *Political Economy Club* (1872), 63.
[3] See Morley, ii. 410.
[4] Public Health Bill: *H* ccx. 850.
[5] Add MS 44640, f. 64.
[6] See Ramm I, ii. 317.
[7] See 9 Mar., 13 Apr. 72.
[8] Question of her pension; *H* ccx. 892.
[9] To a Commons' question; *H* ccx. 813 and Lee, *Edward VII*, i. 326.
[10] Not found; probably departmental, on naval questions.

6. Sat. [Brighton]

Wrote to Chancr of Exr—Ld Granville—The Queen (Mem.)—Mr Hammond—C.G.—and minutes. Off at 11 to Brighton: W. & I went to 'Royal M. Crescent Hotel'. The Theatre in evg.[1] Saw Mr Gurdon—Mr Glyn. Made purchases at Ambrosini's.[2] Read Ld Kilgobbin—Guizot's Tract[3]—Contemp. R. on Fenianism.[4]

7. 1 S.Easter.

Parish Ch. mg: Mr Purchas's Chapel evg: a singular exhibition, not without striking features but awry.[5] Saw Mr Watts & Miss Prinsep.[6] Went on the Piers. Saw R. Clinton. Read Michaud on Ch. of Rome—Bp Chester on Ath. Creed—Bp Lincoln on do.[7]

8. M. [London]

Back by 11 A.M. train: leaving a glorious sea-wind behind me. Saw Dr Clark—Mr Glyn—Mr Rathbone—Mr Forster—Mr Cardwell. Wrote to Ld Annaly—Mr Ayrton—Ld Granville—Mr West (Tel.)—The Queen—and minutes. H of C. 4¼-8 and 9-12¾.[8] Read Hook's Life of Parker—Ld Kilgobbin (finished).

9. Tu.

Wrote to Ld Hartington—Brighton Hotel—Att.Gen. Ireld—The Queen (2)—Mrs Th. (4)—and minutes. Cabinet 2-4½. Saw Mr Burnett—Do *cum* Mr Barker—Ld Granville—Mr Monsell—Mr Glyn—Saw Jacobs & another X. H of C. 4¼-8 and 9-12½. Read Hook's Parker—. . . on Alabama Case.

Cabinet. Tues Ap. 9/72. 2 PM.[9]

√ Mr Fowler. Entail of Land Admissions to be general—Previous question if necessary.[10]

[1] To see Sardou's 'Nos Intimes'; his attendance aroused puritan comment; see Add MS 44434, f. 62.

[2] See 20 Apr. 65.

[3] F. P. G. Guizot, 'Christianity viewed in its relation to the present state of society and opinion' (1871).

[4] *Contemporary Review*, xix. 624 (April 1872).

[5] J. *Purchas, the ritualist; see 18 Apr. 56, 25 Feb. 71.

[6] Mary Emily Prinsep, 1853-1931, friend of *Watts; m. A. Hichens 1874; 2nd Baron Tennyson 1918.

[7] E. Michaud, *Comment l'Église Romaine n'est plus l'Église Catholique* (1872); W. *Jacobson, 'On the Athanasian Creed. A speech' (1872); C. *Wordsworth, 'On the Athanasian Creed. A speech' (1872).

[8] Ballot: *H* ccx. 896.

[9] Add MS 44640, f. 67.

[10] He this day unsuccessfully pressed W. Fowler not to divide on his Resolution on entail, which was defeated: *H* ccx. 1026.

√ Canada demands for further concessions (beyond the 2½m̂ guaranteed)—decline to extend.[1]

√ Communications from M. Gavard. Confirm expression of willingness to [*sic*] entertaining for con[sideratio]n any definite proposition which French Govt. may be disposed to make.[2]

√ Alabama Case. 1. Protestation to cover the Counter Case read & approved. 2. Determination to put it in taken. 3. Ld G's letter approved, which transmits the Protestation to Gen. S[chenck].[3]

10. Wed.

Wrote to Mr Cole—Sir A. Panizzi—Ld Lyttelton—Ld Stratford de R.—Chancr of Exr—and minutes. Saw Jacob, & another X. Read Hook's Parker. Saw Mr Glyn—Mr Bright 12-2½.[4] Greenwich Clergy Deputn—Belfast Festival Deputn, to whom I made a kind of speech.[5] Dined at Mad. Ralli's. Heard Sainton.[6] Baron M. Rothschild's after.

11. Th.

Wrote to Dean of Windsor—Abp of Canterb.—Lady Halifax—Mr Johnson—The Queen (l. & Tel.)—Ld Ripon—and minutes. H of C. 4¼-8¼ and 9¼-12¾.[7] Read Hook's Parker—Lambeth Review.[8] Saw Sir J. Lacaita—& C.C. L[acaita]—Mr Crawford—Mr Glyn—Mr K. Hodgson—Mr Forster—Ld Granville—Mr Bruce—Atty. General—Mr Morley *cum* Sir T. Bazley. Dined with the Wests.

12. Fr.

Wrote to Chancr of Exr—Mr W. Fowler—The Queen—Mr Kinnaird—Ld Hartington—& minutes. H of C. 4¼-8¼ & 9½-12¾. Alabama business & Guarantees.[9] Levee at 2. Saw S. Kensington Agent—Mr

[1] Canadian demands for increase of the fortification guarantee; Gladstone told Kimberley (29 March 1872, Add MS 44541, f. 103): '. . . To the augmentation of the total amount I feel more & more averse.'

[2] Gavard and Ozenne negotiated the commercial treaty with France signed on 5 November 1872.

[3] Comments by Cardwell, at Add MS 44640, f. 68: '. . . it is, we see clearly, the policy of the U.S. government to draw us step by step & to bring us before the Arbitrators. This we regard as the one thing, which on Feb. 3 the Cabinet resolved not to permit. The U.S. practically refuse to negotiate with us about the indirect claims. We think that if things remain in statu quo, the Countercase cannot go in.'

[4] See Walling, *The diaries of John Bright*, 349.

[5] He accepted in principle the invitation of Ulster liberals to visit Belfast; *The Times*, 11 April 1872, 4d, 15 April 1872, 9d.

[6] Prosper Sainton, 1813-90; French violinist.

[7] Ballot in cttee.: *H* ccx. 1090.

[8] *The Lambeth Review*, I (March 1872).

[9] *H* ccx. 1176.

Russell—Mr Glyn—Mr Barker *cum* Mr Burnett—Ld Granville—Ld Kimberley—Count Bernstorff—Italian Min.—A. Cooper—Col. Ponsonby—Mr Forster. Read Hook's Parker—Yorke's Hist.Internat. Society.[1]

13. Sat. [Windsor]

Wrote to Mr Melly—Mr J.H. Scott[2]—Mr Ayrton—The Queen—& minutes. Cabinet 2-5½. Visited Baron Rothschilds pictures &c. Saw Mr Lawley—Sir J. Hanmer—Mr Glyn—Mr Hayward. Saw the T.G.s. Off at 5.50 to Windsor. We dined with H.M.—Conversation with Prince Arthur. Read Howe's Address[3]—and Tracts.

Cabinet. Sat. Ap. 13. 2PM.[4]

√ The Queen & O'Connor.[5] Agree about the sentence & the Judge—Henderson reports there will be no difficulty in sending abroad.
√ Presentation of Countercase to Parliament. Present on Tuesday. Also Ld G.'s dispatch reciting conversation with Schenck.
√ Mr. Fawcett's Bill. Three courses. Hartington to give notice of an Instruction for dividing the Bill into two Bills.
√ Dr. Hooker. Mr Ayrton attended. WEG to write to Mr A. as within.[6]
√ Lady Mayo. If Osborne cannot come on, give way, in deference only to feeling of H. of C.—& promise further cons[ideratio]n generally.[7]
√ Licensing Bill. To be introduced at once in H. of L for Monday: Cardwell, Lowe, Hartington, Stansfeld, Bruce, Kimberley.
√ Mint Site Bill—to stand over.
√ Lopez & Acland Tues. 16th Oppose Lopez and stand on things already agreed.[8]
√ Committee on Life & Property—Cave. admit his motion—if it comes on.[9]
√ Albert & European [Life Assurance Companies (Inquiry)] Bill. To decline assenting to the clause for Commission unless in connection with a plan for Govt. assurance.[10]
√ Kimberley's dispatch on Austr. Tariffs approved.[11]

[1] O. Yorke [i.e. W. H. Dixon], *The secret history of 'The International'* (1872); hostile to Marx, the 'Caesar of their cause'.

[2] Of Brighton; had sent Homeric comments; Add MS 44541, f. 108.

[3] Perhaps T. Howe, 'A farewell address [on 2 Cor. vi. 11-13] delivered at Walpole' (1767).

[4] Add MS 44640, f. 70.

[5] i.e. the attempted assassin; see 29 Feb. 72.

[6] On Kew Gardens; Add MSS 44640, f. 72 and 44541, f. 108.

[7] Her pension; see 5 Apr. 72. After Gladstone's statement on 18 April, Osborne withdrew his motion; *H* ccx. 1479.

[8] On local taxation; *H* ccx. 1399; see 16 Apr. 72. In 1871, the govt. moved the previous question; *H* cciv. 1037.

[9] Not moved; on 28 June, Cave moved and withdrew, a resolution for a govt. inquiry into recent insurance failures; *H* ccxii. 380.

[10] Cave's bill for a govt. paid commissioner for life assurance company inspection; *H* ccx. 1407, 17 April 1872.

[11] Sent on 20 April; see Knaplund, *Imperial policy*, 117; draft in Add MS 44619, f. 46.

√ **Irish Land Bill. Indulgences to Waterford Tenants given retrospectively, to be prospective up to 2/3 valuation.**

14. 2 S.E.

Castle Chapel at 10 and 12—St George's 4.30. The boy Cooke sang with wonderful power. Walk with the Two Deans.[1] The lilacs bursting into flower: & the trees (in Ln) give much shade. Saw Prince Leopold's China. Saw Sir T. Biddulph. Migrated in afternoon to the Deanery: after seeing the Queen. Much conversation with the Dean. Read Tyndale's Life[2]—Michaud on the Church[3]—Bp Thirlwall's Sermon[4]—Reichel on the Ordinal[5]—&c.

15. M. [London]

Wrote to Ld Hartington—Dean of Windsor—Mr Bruce—Mr S. Crompton[6]—Sir Thos. G.—and minutes. H. of C. 4¼-8 and 9-1½.[7] Dined with the Jameses. Returned from W. by 10.20. Saw Dean of Windsor—Mr Glyn—Mr Ayrton—Scotts—and others. Read Amn Countercase—Hook's Life of Parker.

16. Tu.

Wrote to Sir Thos G.—Ld Granville—The Queen—and minutes. Saw Sir H. Elliot—Mr F. Lawley—Mr Glyn—Ld Enfield—J. Hope Scott—Visited Christie's. H of C. 4¼-8¼ & 9½-1.[8] Read Hook's Parker. Attended Ld Bute's marriage breakfast.[9]

17. Wed.[10]

Wrote to The Queen—Ld Granville—Chancr of Exr—Ld Hartington—Mr Ambrosini—& minutes. Dined with the Ripons. Took books to Jacob—Graham[R]. Saw Mr Taylor Innes—Ld Granville

[1] i.e. G. V. *Wellesley and another. [2] See 17 Mar. 72. [3] See 6 Apr. 72.

[4] C. *Thirlwall, 'Missionary duties, difficulties and prospects. A sermon' (1872).

[5] C. P. *Reichel, 'Shall we alter the Ordinal? A paper . . .' (1872).

[6] Samuel Crompton had sent Machiavelli's *Istorie*, signed in 1692 by two of diarist's Gledstanes ancestors; Hawn P and Add MS 44541, f. 109.

[7] Questioned on Alabama; *H* ccx. 1267.

[8] Lopes' motion on local taxation carried agst. govt. in 259:159; *H* ccx. 1331; see 13 Apr. 72.

[9] John Patrick Crichton-Stuart, 1847-1900, 3rd marquis of Bute, m. Gwendolen, da. of 1st Baron Howard of Glossop; she d. 1932.

[10] The *New York Herald* this day published the Alabama documents, and Grant's message to the Senate's secret session; *PP* 1872 lxix. 732.

—Mr Glyn—Mr Forster—Sir R. Palmer—Lady Llanover—Ld Ripon—Mr Cardwell. Read Hook's Parker—and Tracts. H of C. $4\frac{1}{2}$-$5\frac{3}{4}$.[1]

18. Th.

Wrote to D. of Argyll—Mr Bernal Osborne—The Queen—Bp of London—M. Marcoartu—& minutes. H. of C. $4\frac{1}{4}$-$8\frac{1}{2}$ and $9\frac{1}{2}$-$1\frac{1}{4}$. Ballot Bill—rough water.[2] Saw Ld Granville—Mr F. Lawley—Mr Glyn. Read Q.R. on Parliament[3]—Giffen on Cost of Fr.G. War.[4] Visited Messrs Agnews.

19. Fr.

Wrote to D. of Windsor—Mr Morley—Mr Fawcett—Mr Chadwick—The Queen—and minutes. Visited Christie's. Meeting of Nat. Portrait Trustees at 3.30. Saw Mr Glyn—Mr Ayrton. Read U.S. Tract on Indirect Claims—Holland's Recollections[5]—Q.R. on Jackson's Journal.[6] H of C. $4\frac{1}{4}$-8 and $9\frac{3}{4}$-$12\frac{1}{4}$.[6] Dined with the Wests.

To H. FAWCETT, M.P., 19 April 1872. Add MS 44541, f. 111.

Although as you say we have differed more frequently than either of us could wish, I have the pleasure of concurring not only in your opinions on the subject of which Sir M. Lopez presented to us the other night a little tag or tail, but in your estimate of its enormous magnitude, & the very serious danger it threatens to thc country.[8]

I also lean to the opinion that this danger cannot be encountered except by a measure so large as to be a Congress[?] of measures: & such as to require the whole strength of a vigorous Government & the united party to work it, or them, through Parlt.

The basis of the whole should be an endeavour to strengthen the principles & practice of local Government: & if this result can be obtained much good will have been extracted out of a menacing evil.

Notwithstanding the encouragement you give me, much beyond my deserts, I am not sanguine: yet I do not despair.

[1] Selwyn-Ibbetson's drink bill: *H* ccx. 1409.

[2] Caused by *Harcourt; Cardwell did not support the bill, offered resignation, which was refused; Add MS 44120, f. 23: *H* ccx. 1502. Also statement on Lady Mayo; ibid., 1479.

[3] *Quarterly Review*, cxxxii. 450 (April 1872).

[4] Sir R. *Giffen, 'The cost of the Franco-German war of 1870-1', privately printed March 1872, reprinted in *Essays in Finance* (1880).

[5] See 4 Mar. 72.

[6] *Quarterly Review*, cxxxii. 494.

[7] Misc. resolutions; supply: *H* ccx. 1550.

[8] Fawcett to Gladstone, 18 April 1872, Add MS 44156, f. 18: 'Lopes' motion indicates a very grave danger for the future of this country. It plainly shows that demands will be put forth with increasing urgency to throw local charges upon the Consolidated Fund.'

I shall read the Vol. you sent me[1] with much interest; especially where I may find it touches the subject which your letter handles in a manner to me at least so satisfactory.

20. Sat.

Wrote to Mr Warburton—Chancr of Exr—The Queen—Sir C. O Loghlen—The Ld Advocate—& minutes. Visited Agnew's—& the Water Colour Exhibition. Saw Mr Crittenden—Mr Hayward—Ld Lytton—Sir W. Boxall—Ct Beust—Count Bernstorff—Mr Glyn. Cabinet 2-6¼. 12 to dinner: and evening party afterwards. I went to bed unwell. Read Quart. Rev.

Cabinet. Sat. Ap. 20. 72.[2]

√ Denbighshire Lieutenancy. Take opinion of L[aw] O[fficers] & proceed for event[?] if it is clear on the point of law.[3]
√ Stacpoole's question. Remind him it is not a merely administrative matter.[4]
√ Duff's question. Ask Young to see Chancellor. 'decline to commit Govt.' to bring in a bill.[5]
√ Ld. Hartington's motion. How far develop policy? No Resolution to be moved. Offer Fawcett a day?—not before Tuesday.[6]
√ Sir C. O'Loghlen's Bill. Remind him of former Bill; question prudence of pressing his Bill at this time. If he perseveres we shall not vote agt. 2d R. Will explain *vivâ voce* if he likes.[7]
√ Sir J. Colebrooke's motion on Commission for Endowments in Scotland. Agree to a small Commission.[8]
√ Ld Granville to explain that we did not *condition* putting in our Counter Case on the assent of the Americans.[9]
√ Ld Ripon—open Kensington Museum on Sundays? No.
√ Bill about exemptions from rating—proceed with it, after Lopez's victory? Wait.[10]
√ Conventions Act—repeal. Not to be admitted.[11]

To R. LOWE, chancellor of the exchequer, 20 April 1872. Add MS 44541, f. 112.

I received last night from Mr Cave the enclosed application from the West India Body in support of the Sugar Refiners. They are a body who will certainly

[1] Ibid.; H. and M. G. Fawcett, *Essays . . . on social and political subjects* (1872).
[2] Add MS 44640, f. 73.
[3] Whether it could be offered to Cornwallis-West, who was already High Sheriff; Add MS 44541, f. 122; see 3 May 72.
[4] On royal residence in Ireland; *H* ccx. 1678.
[5] On entail law; *H* ccx. 1630.
[6] Hartington proposed to divide Fawcett's University Tests (Dublin) Bill into two; for Gladstone's comment, see 24 Apr. 72.
[7] Religious Disabilities Abolition Bill, withdrawn after 2° R: *H* ccx. 1760, ccxi. 288.
[8] *H* ccx. 1747.
[9] *H* ccx. 1620.
[10] The bill was dropped.
[11] See 2 May 72.

not acquiesce in a pure negative from the Government, & in clear anticipation of a Party struggle (of course with the opposition against us) as the consequence I think we should well consider our ground. I would recommend calling in Cardwell (& Fortescue if he likes, but I do not suppose he has actually made himself master of the question as yet); & having a conference with Fremantle & Ogilvy[1] for the Customs on any day after Wednesday next.

To Sir C. M. O'LOGHLEN, M.P., 20 April 1872. Add MS 44541, f. 112.

I have consulted my Colleagues on the subject of your Bill. On a former occasion I warmly supported your proposal as to the Lord Lieutenancy of Ireland: but it failed. I fear that the times are now greatly more unfavourable.

In truth we doubt the expediency of your going forward with the measure at present, as little success is to be hoped for with reference to the particular proposals, while damage may be done in other quarters. On the merits I think as I did; & I by no means wish to convey that the Government will if you proceed vote against the second reading of the Bill.

To G. YOUNG, lord advocate, 20 April 1872. Add MS 44541, f. 112.

The view of the Cabinet is very unfavourable to your introducing the proposed measure [with] reference to Scotch Entails.

If you will speak to the Lord Chancellor he will explain to you better than I could the general strain of observation of the subject. Generally I may say that the proposed relief to the older proprietors was considered to be too sharp an interference with the vested rights of persons in being.

21. 3 S.E.

Kept my bed. Morning prayers alone. Read Q.R. on D of Somerset[2]—Tyndale's Life[3]—Brewer on Athn Creed[4]—Abp Manning on Education[5]—Baldwin Brown's Address[6]—& other Tracts. Conversation with Herbert on Oxford & his future career. He was very satisfactory.[7]

22. M.

Wrote to Mrs Cunynghame—Chancr of Exr—Mr Robn G.—Dean of St Paul's—Miss Marsh—Mr Cardwell—Ld Granville—The Queen—Mr West—and minutes. H of C. 4¼-8 and 8¾-1½.[8] Read Hook's

[1] Robert Ogilvie, surveyor general of Customs; see 21 July 64.
[2] *Quarterly Review*, cxxxii. 423 (April 1872). [3] See 17 Mar. 72.
[4] J. S. *Brewer, *The Athanasian origin of the Athanasian Creed* (1872).
[5] H. E. *Manning, *National education and parental rights* (1872).
[6] J. B. Brown, 'Religious equality in the light of history. A lecture' (1872).
[7] He successfully matriculated at University college, Oxford, in May 1872.
[8] Ballot: *H* ccx. 1564.

Parker—Don Juan[1]—U.S. Tract. Saw Mr F. Lawley—Mr Glyn—Ld Advocate—Mr Kinnaird—Mr Bright—Dr L. Playfair—Mr Ayrton—Messrs Miall, Dixon, Richard[2]—Ld Granville—Sir F. Goldsmid[3]—Visited Christie's.

To R. LOWE, chancellor of the exchequer, 22 April 1872. Add MS 44541, f. 113.

Monsell has applied to me[4] to urge a further consideration of the difficult question you have had to deal with about the Letter Carriers of the three great towns of L[iverpool] M[anchester] and B[irmingham]. While the case as the Postmaster General represents it is very urgent, on the other hand there is great force in your objection that we cannot accurately follow the rise or fall of wages, & that the public will be much injured if we follow the rise only. In this difficulty it occurs to me to suggest for consideration whether it might be possible to meet the case by a temporary measure having reference to the present state of the labour market & so framed as practically to give the men for the year what they want. In the course of that time, the Government might see its way further into the future; & might also consider whether anything can be made of one at least of Mr Lingen's suggestions, that about the soldiers to be used by way of reserve. Please let me talk to you about this.

23. Tu.

Wrote to Sir T.E. Moss—Abp of Canterb.—Ld Granville—Mr Burnett—The Queen—& minutes. Read Hook's Parker—Alabama Tract. H. of C. 4¼-8 and 8¾-1.[5] Saw Ld Lansdowne—Mr Goschen—Mr West—Mr Glyn—Ld Granville—Bp of Brechin—The Speaker—Deputn on Ld Lieutenancy Bill. Wrote dft on communication to be made to Gen. Schenk.[6]

To Sir T. EDWARDS-MOSS,[7] 23 April 1872. Add MS 44541, f. 114.

I cannot decline your most kind present & if you will order the cask[8] to come here I shall much prize the opportunity it will give me of appreciating the results of your skill. Events & convictions have divided us, but I hope that for me the time is approaching & almost in view when after forty years of fighting I may cease to have political differences with anybody by ceasing to have any active politics at all. To come to a more terrestrial matter, I presume that a 1d duty on

[1] Presumably *Byron's (1819-24).

[2] The nonconformists next day failed to get leave to introduce a bill to repeal Clause 25 of the 1870 Education Act; *H* ccx. 1718.

[3] Who had raised the question of Rumanian Jews in the Commons on 19 April.

[4] Letter not in Add MS 44152.

[5] Questions, then education deb.: *H* ccx. 1744.

[6] Secretary's draft at Add MS 44434, f. 82 on publication of information on the Washington Treaty.

[7] See 29 Sept. 25.

[8] Of demerara sugar; Add MS 44434, f. 78.

all classes [of sugar] might work but how should we stand if a great necessity should unhappily arise for raising it materially in the event of a War.

24. Wed.

Wrote to Mr Watkins[1]—Ld Granville—Robn G. (2)—General Schenk—The Queen (Mem)—Dr Bradley—Mrs Th.—& minutes. Visited Christie's. H. of C. 12-12¾ to reply to Prof. Fawcett.[2] Saw Ld Lansdowne—Baroness B. Coutts—Mr Glyn—Mr Monsell—Ld Granville—Dean of Windsor. B. Palace party 5-6¾. Inquiries: & saw Lewis X. Dined with the Civil Engineers, and returned thanks for ministers.[3] Read Letters on Scottish Patronage.[4]

To General R. C. SCHENCK, 24 April 1872. Add MS 44541, f. 115.

I return with many thanks the papers which you sent me some time ago. And I fear I may have conveyed to your mind some degree of my misapprehension as to my estimate of the state of foreign opinion. But my intention was to limit myself to foreign opinion on the indirect claims in themselves & as subjects for arbitration, not to assume that foreign writers generally had studied our arguments or expressed approval of them with reference to the interpretation of the Treaty; arguments which in truth have not been before them.

25. Th.

Wrote to The Speaker—Mrs Berry—Col. White—Baroness Burdett Coutts—Sir T.D. Lloyd—The Queen—and minutes. Breakfast party at 10. (1st). Saw Mr Crawford M.P.—Ld Granville—Mr Glyn—Mr Gurdon—Mr Cardwell—Chancr of Exchr—Conclave on Sugar Convention.[5] H of C. 4¼-9 and 9¾-1½. Spoke in answer to Fawcett and Co.[6] Read Q.R. on Masson's Milton.[7]

26. Fr.

Wrote to The Queen—Mrs Berry—& minutes. H of C. 4¼-8.[8] Dined

[1] Affairs of Helen Gladstone; see 10 June 51 and Add MS 44541, f. 114.

[2] Gladstone stated that support for Hartington's motion to divide Fawcett's University Tests (Dublin) Bill into two, was essential, but not a vote of confidence as a report in *The Daily News* had stated; *H* ccx. 1754.

[3] In *The Times*, 25 April 1872, 12e.

[4] Not found.

[5] See 20 Apr. 72.

[6] Declining to give priority to Fawcett's bill; govt. defeated in 169:261, *H* ccx. 1839 and *The Times*, 27 April 1872, 7d.

[7] *Quarterly Review*, cxxxii. 393 (April 1872).

[8] Requested rejection, on grounds of lack of time, of Trevelyan's motion for extending the county franchise; motion defeated; *H* ccx. 1907.

with Mr C. Foster. Read Freeman on Constitn.[1] Saw Lewis (2): who will go home[R]. Saw Mr M'Coll—Ld Granville—Mr Glyn—Ld Kildare—Mr Levy—Mr Burnett—Scotts.

27. Sat. [St. George's Hill, Weybridge][2]

Wrote to The Queen—Mr B. Osborne—Mr West—Master of University Coll.—Mr W. Johnson—and minutes. Cabinet 2-5. Read Claudian[3]—and [blank]. Saw Mr E. Freshfield—Ld Granville—Mr Glyn—Mr M'Coll—Mr Goschen—Ld Chancellor—Mrs Cooper—Ld Ripon.

Cabinet. Sat. Ap. 27. 2 PM. 1872.[4]

√ Lady Mayo's further pension. £1000 (Consol. Fund).
O Irish Railways.[5]
√ Irish National School Teachers.[6]
√ B.N.A. Fisheries. Omission in Art. 23. Substance of reply for Ld Kimberley agreed to. He will minimise the difficulty. Telegram from Thornton. Propositions agreed on. Inquiry (3) to be made from Gen. Schenck.[7] And Tel. to Thornton agt. double channel.
√ Irish Church Bill. Hartington to get rid of possible amnts.
√ Week's work gone through.
√ Present to Parliament correspondence on Indirect Claims? Committed[?] to Ld G. & WEG. Avoid as long as possible.
O Stansfeld Mem.[8]
√ Ld Russell's motion—to be dealt with at the time by the Peer ministers.[9]
√ Mr. Cardwell's points under the Purchase Act. His mem. approved.[10]
√ Shortened Services Bill. Abp. of Cant's letter. Shall Govt. introduce? Yes. Uncertainty as to time of carrying to be mentioned.[11]
√ Glyn's statement of the voting last night noticed.[12] (the guilty abashed).

28. 4 S.E.

Ch. mg. (1½ m off). Wrote to Abp of Canterbury—Ld Granville—Ld Cowper. Walk with the party. Saw Capt. E[gerton] on Ldship

[1] E. A. *Freeman, *The growth of the English constitution from the earliest times* (1872).
[2] Capt. F. Egerton's; see 6 Aug. 70.
[3] Fourth century Greek poet.
[4] Add MS 44640, f. 76.
[5] Papers by F. H. Rich supporting state purchase and R. *Lowe opposing, had been circulated to the cabinet; Add MS 44619, ff. 4, 52.
[6] Hartington's printed mem. circulated; Add MS 44640, f. 79.
[7] Draft for it; ibid., f. 82.
[8] Not found.
[9] Interdicting arbitration without U.S. abandonment of indirect claims; postponed on 29 April to 6 May; *H* ccx. 1927.
[10] Not found.
[11] Letter to Tait offering govt. support subject to time-tabling problems, at Add MS 44541, f. 117.
[12] Probably the poor govt. turnout to vote down the county franchise, and the prominent liberals voting for it; *The Times*, 29 April 1872, 7f.

Admty.[1] Read Gallus—Life of Tyndale—Irish Revision Proceedings[2]—Griffiths's Sermon.[3]

29. M. [London]

Walk to the Station through the woods; London at 11.40. Wrote to Ld Hartington—Mr Otway—Dr Dollinger—Mrs Th.—Sir S. Robinson—Mr Gurdon—Mr Hadfield MP.—The Queen—Ld Granville—and minutes. Went down to Kennington to see M. Berry who will I hope go home tomorrow[R]. Saw Ld Granville—Sir G. Grey—Mr Goschen—Mr Glyn—Chancr of Exr—Mr Levy. Quasi-Cabinet 5.20-6.45.[4] H of C. 4¼-8¼ and 9½-1½.[5] Read Hook's Parker.

To J. J. I. von DÖLLINGER, 29 April 1872. Add MS 44140, f. 286.

I cannot help availing myself of the kindness of the Bishop of Brechin [A. P. Forbes] for the purpose of sending you amidst your many anxieties and labours a word of greeting, and of good wishes for you and for the great cause you have in hand.

Many here have read with the greatest interest those lectures[6] in which you touch the case of the Church of England. There was a general surprise not at the interest but at the knowledge and appreciation which they displayed. I need not say this surprise did not extend to me; but I shared the pleasure which they gave.

I venture to send you herewith a tract which I wrote in 1850 on the historical idea of the Royal Supremacy,[7] according to the Sixteenth Century view of it and the constitutional settlement then arrived at. I have never seen cause to recede from it. The condition of the English Church has since that time been much worsened by the spread of rationalising unbelief. On the other hand, besides that its activity and spiritual life have continued to open out with growing vigour, it has gained one corporate advantage of immense value, namely its collective voice in its two representative Convocations for the two Provinces of Canterbury and York. These bodies now meet regularly, may give *utterance* to their judgments on any matter they choose and though they have no binding legislative power have been to a certain extent recognised in the previous examination of measures affecting the Church which have been afterwards submitted to Parliament.

At *no period* in or since the sixteenth century has Parliament touched the detail of the authoritative Books of the Church of England; and the Prayerbook has been ratified, as the Calendar of Lessons was altered last year, only on the joint initiative of the Crown and the Church in Convocation.

On this account what I have said in the Tract respecting the helpless condition of the Church under the Judicial Committee of the Privy Council has become inapplicable. Indeed the Judgments of that Committee seem to lose weight, and one which it passed last year has not been generally accepted or obeyed.

[1] Rear-adm. F. B. P. Seymour appt. on 4 May.

[2] Untraced.

[3] T. Griffith, from *Farewell sermons* (1872).

[4] No record kept by diarist. Probably to consider the American reply on the indirect claims, reported verbally by Schenck; see Ramm I, ii. 323 and *H* ccx. 2019.

[5] Questioned on Canadian guarantee; *H* ccx. 1934.

[6] See 27 Mar. 72.

[7] See 28 Apr. 50, 18 Dec. 64.

30. Tu.

Wrote to Chancr of Exr—The Queen (2)—and minutes. Also to Sir W.S. Maxwell—Ld Ossington—Mr Macfie—Ld Enfield. Visited Christie's. Saw Graham—& two more[R]. Saw Dean of St Paul's—Mr M'Coll—Mr Glyn—Abp Manning[1]—Ld [blank]—Ld Chancellor. Meeting of Trustees of Museum 3¼ to Elect Ld O[ssington] & Sir W.S. Maxwell.[2] H of C. 4–8.[3] Read Hook's Parker. Early bed & quinine for my aching face.

To R. A. MACFIE, M.P., 30 April 1872. **Add MS 44541, f. 119.**

I sympathise with your generous disposition towards the colonies but I have not yet, as I must own, seen any method by which they could be united with the people of the United Kingdom in a system of joint imperial representation. Mr Hugessen's speech of last year on this subject must I am sure have been interpreted by you as a token of at least good will.

Wed. May 1.1872.

Wrote to Ld Hartington—D. of Argyll—Lady Cowper—and minutes. Read Hook's Parker. Saw Mr Glyn—D. de Broglie—Sir R. Phillimore—Mr Moffat—Ld Ossington—Mrs Th. X—Ld Granville (2)—Sol.Genl.—Abp of Canterbury. Dined at Lambeth: service in Chapel preceding. Evening party at home followed.

To LORD HARTINGTON, Irish secretary, 1 May 1872. **Add MS 44541, f. 120.**

Individually I should have thought we might do well to postpone the question of Rating for Education in Ireland until we should have obtained a little more English & Scotch experience. For the abandonment of the idea of rating is the abandonment of giving Ireland a chance of advance in self-government & local government both of which I prize very highly in her behalf while I admit the difficulty of determining in favour of rating at the present time. If the Cabinet sees no sufficient force in the reason I have advanced, I am aware of no other objection to the course you propose.[4]

2. Th.

Wrote to Ld Granville—Ld Halifax—Sir F. Grant—Abp of Canterb.

[1] Who was concerned at possible appropriation of the English College in Rome by the Italian govt.; Gladstone asked Enfield to inquire; Add MS 44541, f. 119. The Italian govt. 'somewhat indignantly denied' it, and complained of Britain's reliance on rumour; ibid., f. 123.

[2] The two names suggested by Gladstone to *Tait on 23 April; Add MS 44541, f. 114.

[3] Short statement on the American reply; *H* ccx. 2019.

[4] Hartington's letter untraced.

—The Queen—and minutes. Read Hook's Parker. Breakfast party. Saw Ld Blachford—Ld Dufferin *cum* Ld Hartington—Mr Forster —Mr Glyn—Dean of St Pauls—Mr Ayrton—Ld Beaumont—Ld Granville. Visited Mr E. Sanders.[1] Dined with Mrs Glyn. H of C. $4\frac{1}{4}$-$8\frac{1}{2}$ and $9\frac{1}{2}$-1. Spoke on Convention Act.[2] Cabinet $2\frac{1}{2}$-$4\frac{1}{4}$.

May 2. 72. Thurs 2.30 PM. D. St.[3]

√ Alabama Claims. 'Preface' to our proposed note to Gen Schenck considered, amended & approved.[4] Terms of announcements for this evening considered & agreed on.[5]
Irish Education.
√ Scotch Educn. Bill. A Scotch temporary commission for distributing the country into districts may be conceded if needful.[6]
√ Epping Forest Bill. Has not been adopted by the Cabinet.[7]
√ Fish supply. Mr Bruce to inquire into lady B.C.'s statements.[8]
√ Amts. to Licensing Bill. Committee to consider.[9]

To VISCOUNT HALIFAX, lord privy seal, Add MS 44541, f. 120.
2 May 1872. 'Secret.'

Your words[10] are most acceptable tho' I still miss your handwriting. The Alabama matter looks thoroughly healthy at present, tho' as there is hope where there is life, so is there fear. But it is difficult to see now how it can break down. We are however delayed by difficulties & delays of bad rendering of the cipher by Gen. Schenck. There is a reasonable expectation that everything material may be settled by Monday or even by Saturday. Our course seems very clear & I imagine you need feel no anxiety as to what is likely to happen between this time & Whitsuntide. You will now I hope make steady & rapid progress.

3. Fr.

Wrote to Ld A. Compton—Abp of Canterb.—Robn G.—Mr West (Ruthin)[11]—Mr Knowles—The Queen—& minutes. Read Hook's Parker. Saw Mr Farrer—Mr Glyn—Sir Thos G.—Mr Wm G.—Mr T.S.G.—Mr Dickinson—Mrs Brand—Att. General. H of C. $4\frac{1}{4}$-8 and $8\frac{3}{4}$-$1\frac{1}{4}$.[12]

[1] The dentist.
[2] Declining to repeal it: *H* ccxi. 160. See 20 Apr. 72.
[3] Add MS 44640, f. 87.
[4] Printed in *PP* 1872 lxix. 717.
[5] Notes at Add MS 44640, f. 88.
[6] It was; *H* ccxi. 2026.
[7] See L. Stephen, *Life of Henry Fawcett* (1886), ch. vii.
[8] i.e. Lady Burdett *Coutts, who wanted a commission; Add MS 44541, f. 115.
[9] Bruce's bill was incompetently drafted; see Kimberley, *Journal*, 29.
[10] Not found; a telegramme?
[11] Offering ld. lieut. of Denbighshire to William Cornwallis Cornwallis-West of Ruthin, 1835-1917; liberal (unionist) M.P. Denbighshire 1885-92; see 20 Apr. 72.
[12] Misc. business: *H* ccxi. 247.

4. Sat.

Wrote to Viceroy of I.—Ld Kimberley—Ld Hartington—Ld Granville—The Queen l. & Mem.—and minutes. Breakfasted at Grillion's. Finished Hook's Parker. Saw Ld Granville (2)—Mr Glyn—Ld Ripon—Ld Chancellor—Abp of Canterbury. Royal Academy 2¼–5¼ to see the pictures. Attended the dinner & returned thanks for Ministers.[1] Evening party afterwards: to meet the King of the Belgians.

To LORD KIMBERLEY, colonial secretary, 4 May 1872. Add MS 44541, f. 122.

In the matter of the new charter for Natal, if there is no reason for a recourse to Parliament but the general one is of a certain gravity & no precedent binding or leading us to adopt such a proceeding, I think that upon the facts shown in your letter you would be warranted in acting by Order in Council:[2] & that possibly you might obtain sufficiently the assent of the Cabinet by circulating your letter, together with this note if you think fit.

5. 5 S.E.

Chap. Royal mg. St Anne's evg. Saw Ly Brownlow. Wrote to Ld Shaftesbury—Abp Manning. Saw Ld Granville. Read Tyndale's Life (finished)—Bp of Oxford's Charge[3]—Union Review—Michaud on Western Ch—Jesus the Messiah.[4]

To LORD SHAFTESBURY, 5 May 1872. Add MS 44541, f. 123.

When you spoke to me yesterday about Sir E. Ryan painted[5] as in the midst of dessert dishes & decanters of wine I had not seen the picture nor therefore observed the costume. When I came to it I could hardly believe my eyes. The exhibition of this work is in my opinion, a disgrace to the Academy (the only one I can recollect during the Exhibitions of forty years) & I hope that the public displeasure may cause its removal from the walls. I spoke of it to several Academicians & found but one opinion. I trouble you with this note because I am unwilling to treat lightly a matter which seems to me a grave one.

6. M.

Wrote to Ld Granville—The Queen (2 l. & Mem.)—Mr Childers—Mr Gibson—Ld Kimberley—Mr West—and minutes. King of the Belgians came to breakfast. Party of 17. Saw Ld Hartington—Ld

[1] *The Times*, 6 May 1872, 9c.

[2] None issued; the Natal Charter of 1856 was modified with respect to electoral divisions, see G. W. Eybers, *Select Constitutional Documents* (1918), 188–98.

[3] By J. F. *Mackarness (1872).

[4] By [C. T. Beke] (1872).

[5] As secretary of the Dilettanti Society, by *Leighton.

Granville—Mr Glyn. Cabinet 1-3. Read Ingelow's Poems.[1] Saw Greenwich Depn on Permissive Bill.[2] H of C. 4¼-8¼ & 9½-1½.[3] Dined at Mr Fortescue's to meet the King [of the Belgians]. Saw one X.

Mond. May 6. 72. 1 PM.[4]

√ Washington Treaty. The draft agreed to by the Cabinet on the basis of Schenck's proposal with our amts. having now been referred to Am[eric]a & Mr Fish's answer received, it was further considered & amended. a. 'Have regard' retained. b. Words in 'Preface' omitted if answer is not put into American reply. c. omit recital of our holding as to scope of Arbitration. d. omit 'similar circ.' &c. e. submission to judgment of the Arbitrators understood to be waived except as contained in presentn. of notes & records as to wh. Gen. S[chenck]'s words were adopted. f. Decl[aratio]n of an abstract principle declined.[5]
Ld Granville to ask Schenck whether the engagt. wd. be complete (Senate). And to promise *either* progress or a statement *before the recess.*[6]

There are limits to the reason & forbearance wh. we can ask from Parliament. It cannot be expected to separate for Whits. without either the presentation of papers or an account from the mouths of min[ister]s themselves of the state and prospects of the negotiation.[7]

7. Tu.

Wrote to Mr Potter—Ld Shaftesbury—Mr Guildford Onslow—Col. Ponsonby—Mr Burnett—The Queen (l. & Mem)—and minutes. Saw Mr Russell—The Turkish Ambassador—Mr Levy—Mr Glyn—Mr Dodson—Ld Granville—Mr Leeman—Ld Advocate. Visited Christie's. Mr Pennington's[8] Recitations in the Park D. room came off at 3. The impression was good: & I hope C. has given him a new starting point. Read Sir H. Holland.[9] H of C. 4¼-8 and 8¾-2½.[10]

[1] J. *Ingelow, *Off the Skelligs*, 4v. (1872).

[2] Supporting the Bill with 10,000 signatures; *Greenwich and Deptford Chronicle*, 11 May 1872.

[3] In the Lords, Russell again agreed to put off his Alabama motion, for a week; in the Commons, govt. defeat by 7 on Scottish education: *H* ccxi. 289.

[4] Add MS 44640, f. 89. Separate note, dated this day, proposing to offer the Chancellorship of the Duchy (Dufferin resigning) to Childers, circulated to Granville, Lowe, Argyll, Cardwell, Ripon; ibid., f. 91. Childers declined *pro tem.*

[5] Draft statement of agreement given to Schenck, that if U.S. dropped indirect claims, Britain would not urge them in any future analagous situation; Fish immediately replied that Senate ratification would be needed; drafts of 2, 5, 6 May and replies in *F.R.U.S.* 1872, ii, 486.

[6] i.e. to counter Russell's motion; *H* ccxi. 632; see Cook, *The Alabama claims*, 225.

[7] Holograph note, docketed 6 May 1872, apparently written in cabinet; Add MS 44619, f. 70.

[8] Shakespearean-actor; the gathering, which Princess Louise attended, was to encourage Pennington's career and highlight neglect of Shakespeare; *The Times*, 8 May 1872, 9d.

[9] See 4 Mar. 72.

[10] Clare lord lieutenancy: *H* ccxi. 422.

8. Wed.

Wrote to Mr Childers—The Queen 2 Mema & letter—and minutes. Dined at Sir R. Phillimore's. Bridgwater House afterwards. Saw Ld De Tabley—Rev Mr Molesworth—Mr Forster *cum* Mr Glyn—D. of Argyll—Mr Stansfeld. Conclave of Cabinet on Irish Educn with Mr Keenan[1]—Deputn on Irish Railways—Cabinet 4½-7¼. (U.S.). Luncheon at 15 G[rosvenor] S.—Saw Mr Thistlethwayte. Read Laveleye[2]—Formes de Gouvernement.[3]

Cabinet. 4½ AM [sic] May 8. 72.[4]
Last communication from Gen. Schenck. Agreed: not to frame an article:[5] to fall back on exchange of notes. Explanation of Sir R.P.[6] of 'the principle' approved. Mr Adams—proposed overtures to Arbitrators. Within limits, not disapproved.

9. Th. Ascension Day.

Chapel Royal (in haste) at 12. Small breakf. party. Saw Mr Childers—Mr Ayrton—Mr Glyn—The Queen—and minutes. H of C. 4¼-8¾ and 9-2½.[7] Quasi Cabinet 1-2½.[8] Wrote to D. of Devonshire—Mr Cardwell—Mr Harcourt—Abp of Canterbury—Ld Granville—Mr Cross. Read Laveleye.

10. Frid.

Wrote to The Queen—Col. Elphinstone—Ld Kinnaird—Watson & Smith—and minutes. H. of C. 4¼-7½.[9] Attended Maskelyne's Lecture on Meteorites.[10] Sir H. Holland's afr. Cabinet 11-2¼. Saw Mr Glyn—Ld Monck—Ld Blachford *cum* Dean of St P.—and others. Read Sir H. Holland—Jean Ingelow. Saw Denison—& another Lloyd X.

[1] (Sir) Patrick Joseph Keenan, 1826-94; commissioner of education for Ireland from 1871; K.C.M.G. 1881.
[2] Sent by the author.
[3] E. L. V. de Laveleye, *Essai sur les Formes de Gouvernement* (1872).
[4] Add MS 44640, f. 93. The cabinet was postponed a few hours in the afternoon on Schenck's request; *PP* 1872 lxix. 721.
[5] i.e. no new Article to Treaty of Washington (see 6, 10 May 72).
[6] View of Palmer (or just possibly Phillimore, see this evg.), noted in diarist's hand: 'If negligence is suspected through which ships escape & damage is sustained no claims shall be made under the three heads of indirect loss stated in the American case on account of any mere want of due diligence on the part of the neutral Powers'; Add MS 44640, f. 94.
[7] Commented on Commons sittings on Ascension Day; *H* ccxi. 507.
[8] No record found, but see *H* ccxi. 659.
[9] Questioned on Alabama; *H* ccxi. 607.
[10] By M. H. N. S. Maskelyne.

Cabinet. 10 D. St. May 10. 72. 11 AM.[1]
Alabama Claims. In continuation of informal meeting of last night. Draft of a possible article with a covering letter considered & agreed on.[2]

11. Sat.

Wrote to Ld Granville—M. Musurus—and minutes. Missed Denison: saw Rivers X. Saw Ld Granville—Mr Glyn—Capt. Helbert—Col. Ponsonby. Visited Christie's.—do French Pictures Bond St. Saw Mrs Thistlethwayte. Off at 6.35 to Windsor. Back after midnight. Dined at the Castle. Conversation afterwards with the Queen—And with the Empress [of Germany]. Read . . . on Austr. Colonies—Brown on Poseidon.[3]

12. S.aft Asc.

Chapel Royal mg. St Paul's aft. Tea with Mrs Barker: & walk with C. Dined with the F.C.s. Wrote to The Queen—Ld Granville—Mrs Th. —Lady Salisbury. Saw Ld Granville: who brought good news from America. Read Saul of Tarsus[4]—Ramsgate Tract—Jesus the Messiah. Conversation with F. C[avendish].

13. M.

Wrote to Watson & Smith—Rev Dr Irons—Ld Portman—The Queen (3 or 1)—and minutes. Dined with the Jameses. Read B. Powell on Colonies.[5] Saw Ld Portman—Mr Glyn—Ld Hartington—Sir S.R.G. (respecting Webb.)[6]—Ld Granville—Cabinet 2¼-4¼. H of C. 4¼-8½ and 9½-12¾. Made statement on the Washington Treaty.[7]

Cabinet. May 13. 72. 2 PM.[8]
√ Washington Treaty. Present Papers tonight? No.
√ Explanatory reply to Mr Fish's last of Ap. [blank]. To be sent to Thornton.[9]
√ Field of the respective statements for today considered.
√ Review[?] the position adopted on Feb. 3. All our proceedings have been taken with reference to it—and the opinion formed on Jan. 18.

[1] Add MS 44640, f. 95.
[2] Ibid., f. 96; new draft Article to Treaty of Washington given to Schenck: *F.R.U.S.* 1872, ii. 500 and *PP* 1872 lxix. 707, 729.
[3] R. Brown, *Poseidon; a link between Semite, Hamite and Aryan* (1872).
[4] See 30 Mar. 72.
[5] G. S. *Baden-Powell, *New homes for the old country* (1872).
[6] Perhaps Benjamin *Webb; see 4 July 57.
[7] *H* ccxi. 654.
[8] Add MS 44640, f. 98.
[9] *PP* 1872 lxix. 694.

14. Tu.

Wrote to Ld Granville—Abp of Canterb.—The Queen—and minutes. Dined with Sir W.C. James. Mrs Loyd Lindsay's after. Attended the Lawley marriage at St George's:[1] & then breakfast at Harewood House. To think that I knew the grandmother of the bride before marriage![2] 3-5. Attended meeting for King's College & spoke at some length.[3] Saw Lady Clarendon—Scotts—Mr Glyn—Sir W.C. James—Mr West. Visited Christie's—Sotheby's. Arranging letters & papers.

15. Wed.

Wrote to Sir Thos G.—Rev. Mr Eardley Wilmot—Rev. Dr Irons—and minutes. Packing books for Hawarden. Visited Christie's—Caponetto.[4] Saw Bp of Winchester—Ld Granville—Ct Brunnow—Mr M'Coll—Mr Delane—Mr Moran.[5] Visited Christie's. Dined at 15 G.S. Baron Rothschild's afr. Conversation with K. of the Belgians. Saw Perry—White. Read R. Montagu[6]—M. Laveleye—what a contrast.

16. Th.

Wrote to S.E.G.—Sir S. Northcote—The Queen—Miss Syfret—Mr Freeland—Mr M'Coll—& minutes. Saw Sig. Caponetto and purchased the non-Elisabethan Hern &c. Visited Christie's. Saw Mr Cox—Sir F. Grant. Attended meeting of N.P. Gallery Trustees. Saw Sir W. Maxwell—S.E.G.—Dined with the Farquhars. Read R. Montagu(!!)—Laveleye—Manning on Authority[7]—& other Tracts. Went to Mr Richmond's with C. and saw Lewis, not yet gone. Saw Sir A. Panizzi.

17. Fr. [*Hawarden*]

Wrote to Herbert J.G.—J. Watson & Smith—Ld Granville—Sir W. Maxwell—and minutes. 1-2½. Attended Sale at Christie's. Saw Mr

[1] Beilby Lawley, later 3rd Baron Wenlock, m. Lady Constance Mary Lascelles, da. of 4th earl of Harewood.

[2] i.e. Harriet Canning, who m. 1st marquis of Clanricarde 1825; see 29 Sept. 31n.

[3] Meeting in Willis's Rooms to open an appeal; King's College Minutes and *The Times*, 15 May 1872, 10f. Bp. Moriarty protested about his comments on papal infallibility; Add MS 44434, f. 134.

[4] A dealer; see next day.

[5] Probably Benjamin Moran, secretary of the American legation.

[6] R. Montagu, *Arbitration instead of war, and a defence of the Commune* (1872).

[7] H. E. *Manning, 'That legitimate authority is an evidence of truth. A paper' (1872).

Cox—Rev. Mr Perry. Read Brown on Poseidon—Laveleye on Govt. Off at 4.30. Reached Hn soon after eleven. Unpacked my importation of books.

18. Sat.

Ch. 8½ AM. Wrote to Sir S. Scott & Co—Saw Mr Burnett on Estate & money affairs, & on the Prescott Sale. Went with him & H. to view the Railway: wh will not I think be open before July. Read Voltaire on Ninon de l'Enclos[1]—Letters of do (supposititious)—Voltaire on Louis XIV[2]—Ampère's Rome[3]—Gray's Poems—Hist. of France. Handling books &c.

19. Whits.

Hawarden Ch 11 AM (with H.C.) and evg. Wrote to Abp Manning—Rev Mr Ffoulkes—Mr West—Sir S. Northcote—and minutes. Read Saul of Tarsus[4]—Life of St Chrysostom.[5]

20. M.

Wrote to Mrs Th.—Mr West—& minutes. We cut down the remains of the great poplar. Church 11 AM. Read Ampere's Rome—V. Hugo's Shakespeare[6]—Martial . . . & [blank]. Saw Mr Selby.[7]

21. Whit Tu.

Ch 11 AM. Wrote to The Queen l. & Mem.—Mr Hammond—Ld Ripon—Sir A. Panizzi—Abp of Canterbury—& minutes. Saw Mr Burnett. Woodcutting with my sons. Read Pliny—Rcport on Temple of Ephesus[8]—Don Juan—Finlay's Mediaeval Greece[9]—Ampere's Rome—Victor Hugo's Shakespeare.

To LORD RIPON, lord president of the council, 21 May 1872. Add MS 43514, f. 156.

I have written to the Queen about the Council & have told her you will be ready to receive the expression of her pleasure.

[1] *Lettres de Mlle de Ninon de Lenclos au marquis de Sévigné . . . augmentée de notes et de remarques philosophiques trouvées dans les papiers de M. de Voltaire*, 2v. (1782).

[2] See 8 Oct. 70.

[3] J. J. Ampère, *L'Empire romain à Rome*, 2v. (1867).

[4] See 30 Mar. 72.

[5] W. R. W. Stephens, *St Chrysostom* (1872).

[6] See 5 Mar. 72.

[7] Henry Selby, diarist's tenant at Queensferry.

[8] Probably E. Falkener, *Ephesus and the temple of Diana* (1863).

[9] G. *Finlay, *The history of Greece, 1204-1461* (1851).

Hammond has sent me what are supposed to be the amendments in our draft suggested by the Foreign Affairs Committee of the Senate. They seem to carry their purpose on their face; & I see no harm in them. The change in the last paragraph due apparently to a momentary forgetfulness on the part of Argyll in the final reduction, is certainly unfortunate because it has given rise to cavil as it imparts a theoretical ambiguity.[1]

22. Wed.

Ch. 8½ AM. Wrote to Rev Mr M'Coll—Ld Portman—and minutes. Woodcutting in aft. Read Finlay—Ampère's Rome—Fêtes et Courtisanes de la Grèce[2]—Don Juan.

23. Th.

Ch. 8½ AM. Wrote to Chancr of Exr (Tel.)—Do letter—Dr Acland—Viceroy of Ireland—V.C. of Oxford—Archbp Manning—and minutes. Woodcutting with W. & S. Read Finlay—Ninon de L'Enclos—Ampere—Don Juan.

To ARCHBISHOP H. E. MANNING, 23 May 1872. Add MS 44250, f. 40.

You always I know endeavour to temper with personal kindness & friendship the rigour of official propositions, & you could not give a more conspicuous instance of it than in your letter of yesterday.[3] The propositions it contains will lie by me until a day of liberty of which I hope for an early dawn. I do not require to set aside 'the intervention of the Church', for nothing is more clear to me than its place in the Divine Revelation. But my 'Pope' so to speak is Bp. Butler & his lessons as to modes of thought lead me to view & handle these matters in a way which I am afraid would give no satisfaction in Rome.

24. Fr.

Ch. 8½ AM. Wrote to Bp Moriarty—Mrs Thistlethwayte—and minutes. Woodcutting with S. & W. Read Finlay—Boccaccio Dec. II.7.[4]—Tylor's Primitive Culture[5]—Ampère's Rome—Don Juan (C.II.)

25. Sat.

Ch. 8½ A.M. Wrote to Ld Hartington—Mr Glyn—Mr Hammond—

[1] Granville had left it to Argyll to note the cabinet wording in the supplemental article; see Kimberley, *Journal*, 31.

[2] By P. J. B. Chaussard, 4v. (1801).

[3] Add MS 44250, f. 36, with nine propositions on infallibility.

[4] On the amorous adventures of the Sultan of Babylon's daughter.

[5] See 8 Dec. 71.

Mr Hammond Tel.—Mr Gurdon Tel.—& minutes. Saw Mr Burnett. W., S., and I, finished off the Oak on 'Breakneck Brow' before Luncheon. Visited the Potters. And the work in the Old Castle. Read Don Juan—Ampere—Finlay.

26. Trin.S.

Kept my bed (agt returned cold) till 1½—Ch. in aftn. Wrote to Ld Granville—Dean Ramsay—Mr Airy—Earl Brownlow—Mr Gurdon —& minutes. Read Pelage's Letter[1]—Saul of Tarsus—Memoir of Bp Terrot[2]—Divers Tracts.

27. M. [London]

Off at 8.15. In C.H.T. at 3. Cabinet 3.15.—H of C. 4.15-8 and 11-1½.[3] U.S. question bristles with difficulty.[4] Dined with the Duke of Edinburgh. Saw Adm. H. Stewart—Mr Cardwell—Mr Glyn—Ld Granville. Wrote to the Queen—C.G.[5]—& minutes. Read Essay of a Working Man[6]—Confessions of a French R.C. Priest[7]—Mackay on Sculpture[8]—Blackie on Modern Greek.[9]

Cabinet May 27. 72. 3.15 PM.[10]

O Duchy of Lancaster: Chancellorship of.[11]

√ Amendments to Article as Amended by Senate of U.S. considered & agreed on.[12]

√ Ld Granville not to *advise* deviation from rule of F.O. respecting Foreign Orders in the case of . . . [*sic*][13]

28. Tu.

Wrote to The Queen (l. & Mem.)—and minutes. Luncheon at No. 15 G.S. Saw Ld Granville (2)—Mr Gurdon—Mr Glyn—Ld Chancellor

[1] Abbé Pélage, *L'Abbé Junqua et l'archevêque de Bordeaux* (1872).
[2] E. B. *Ramsay, *Memoir of the late Bishop Terrot* (1872).
[3] Closely questioned on Alabama; *H* ccxi. 714.
[4] See Morley, ii. 410.
[5] Bassett, 194.
[6] Probably *Autobiography of a working man* (1862).
[7] C. L. Trivier, *How I came out from Rome: an autobiography* (1872).
[8] Not found.
[9] J. S. Blackie, 'On the living language of the Greeks. . . . An introductory lecture' (1853).
[10] Add MS 44640, f. 99.
[11] Vacant on Dufferin's move to Canada; Childers declined to fill it (see 6 May 72n.). Gladstone used the vacancy to suggest reforms in the Duchy, wishing to join it with the other crown lands; the court wanted an independent chancellor; to Portman, 22 May 1872, Add MS 44541, f. 130. Childers accepted it in its old form in August 1872.
[12] Sent to Schenck this day; *PP* 1872 lxix. 737.
[13] See Ramm I, ii. 328.

—Mr Fauchon[1]—Chancr of Exr. Cabinet 3–4¼ on U.S. H of C. 4¼–8.[2] Lay up in evening, for a slight attack. Read Confessions (finished)—Dean of Wells's Statement[3]—and other Tracts.

Cabinet. May 28. 3PM. 10 D. St.[4]
√ Washington Treaty. Thornton's Telegram reporting Fish's conversation read —explanatory statements of our Amendment on the Amn. Amendment agreed to.[5]

29. Wed.

Rose at 11. Wrote to Ld Hartington—Sir T. Bateson—Ly Brownlow—The Queen (Mem)—and minutes. Twelve to dinner. Visited Christie's. Saw Dr A. Clark—Mr Gurdon—Mr West—Mr Glyn—Ld Stratford de Redcliffe. Saw Mrs Th: tea X. Read Laveleye—Molesworth's Hist. Vol. II.[6] Arranging room.

30. Th.

Wrote to The Queen Tel. Mem. & 2 l.—and minutes. Visited Christie's. Read Sir H. Holland's Reminiscences[7]—Laveleye. Breakfast party. Conversation with Mr Tom Taylor[8]—Mr Blunt[9]—Mr Knowlys [*sic*]—Mr Pennington who afterwards recited Ld Macaulay's Virginius.[10] Saw Ld Granville—Mr Stansfeld—Mr Glyn—Sir Gilbert Lewis—Mr Holt. H of C. 4¼–8 and 8¾–1¼. During the evg 2 long conferences on Washn Treaty with Ld G. & the Lawyers—and a Cabinet 10–1. Worked Uniformity Bill through Committee at intervals.[11]

Cabinet May 30. 10 PM in Mr G's room at H. of C.[12]
√ American reply to communications of 27th & 8th considered. New draft agreed to be framed. terms discussed.[13]

[1] Unidentified.
[2] Questioned on Alabama, then defended Derby day adjournment; *H* ccxi. 783, 793.
[3] G. H. S. Johnson, 'Statement . . . in reference to his acceptance of the living of St Cuthbert' (1872).
[4] Add MS 44640, f. 100.
[5] *PP* 1872 lxix. 739.
[6] See 27 Feb. 72.
[7] See 4 Mar. 72.
[8] Tom *Taylor, 1817–80, dramatist and journalist; ed. *Punch* 1874–80.
[9] Unclear which; too early for W. S. *Blunt.
[10] In *Lays of Ancient Rome* (1842).
[11] Bill amending Act of Uniformity to allow shorter services; *H* ccxi. 891.
[12] Add MS 44640, f. 101.
[13] New proposal remedying Senate's ambiguities; Cook, *The Alabama Claims*, 232. New draft in *PP* 1872 lxix. 745. Granville next day told Schenck the British would ask for an adjournment at Geneva without presenting the British case; ibid.

31. Fr.

Wrote to Sir T. Bateson—The Queen—and minutes. H of C. 4¼-8 and 8¾-1.[1] Saw Mr Russell—Mr Thring—Mr Glyn—Ld Granville —Mr Ayrton. Read Humphrey's Hist. Printing[2]—Holland's Reminiscences—Finished Laveleye.

Sat June One. 1872.

Wrote to The Queen—Archdeacon Bickersteth—Ld Shaftesbury—Att. General—. . . Ber. . [*sic*]—and minutes. Cabinet 11-4.[3] Saw Ld Granville—Ld Dufferin—Gen. Schenk. Visited Lady Inglis: now very infirm. Saw Lloyd X. Birthday Dinner—Prince Arthur dined. Large evening party followed. Read B. Powell on Australia.[4]

2. S 1.Trin.

Chapel Royal mg & H.C.—Mr Tufnell's Chapel aft. Saw Ld Ripon—Mr Glyn—Tea with Dowager Duchess of Somerset. Wrote to Ld Granville. Read Plea for Free Inquiry[5]—Bp Moriarty's Pastoral Letter[6]—Kennedy, Inaug. Address[7]—Warleigh on Endless Torments[8] —Miracles of Healing[9]—Gospel in the B. of Joshua.[10]

3. M.

Willy's birthday—God bless him. Wrote to Sir B. Peacock—The Queen (2)—Ld Hartington—Att. General—Viceroy of Ireland—Sir M. Lopez—and minutes. Wrote Mem. on Irish Tithe Rent Charge[11] —Luncheon at No 15 G.S. Made an appearance at the Musurus marriage.[12] Saw Count Bernstorff—Ld Granville—Mr Glyn—Gen. Schenk—Sir G. Grey—Sir Geo. [blank]. Abn Bust Commee meeting

[1] Questioned on Alabama; *H* ccxi. 911.

[2] H. N. Humphreys, *A history of the art of printing* (1867).

[3] No minutes found; Gladstone to Victoria this day (CAB 41/4/25): 'The Cabinet declines to sign the Article as amended by the Senate but notes the approximation of opinion between the two Governments'; French communists in Britain also discussed.

[4] See 13 May 72.

[5] Sent by Thomas *Scott of Ramsgate (see 16 May 55), dealt in part with bp. *Butler; diarist requested his other publications, known as 'The Ramsgate Tracts'; Add MS 44541, f. 139; see 14 July 72.

[6] D. Moriarty, perhaps his sermon 'On Christian Brothers' Schools' (1866).

[7] J. *Kennedy, 'Our place in Christendom and in the Catholic Church; the inaugural address' (1872).

[8] H. Smith, afterwards Smith-Warleigh, *Hear the Church of England which is proved to have expelled from her Articles the dogma of endless torments* (1872).

[9] T. W. Belcher, *Our Lord's miracles of healing* (1872).

[10] Anon. (1872).

[11] Add MS 44541, f. 135.

[12] Warner Heriot m. the Turkish ambassador's da.; *The Times*, 4 June 1872, 7f.

at noon. Cabinet 3-4¼.[1] H of C. 4¼-8½ and 9½-1½. Made a statement on the Treaty of Washington. The House behaved *well*. Also got the Act of Uniformity Bill read 3°.[2] Its Preamble is really a notable fact in 1872.[3] Read Holland.

4. Tu.

Wrote to The Queen—Ld Granville—and minutes. 9¾-4¼. To Eton. Speeches: *wretched* R.R. conveyance. Herbert gave very good promise.[4] Saw Ld Granville—Mr B. Johnstone—Mr Dickinson. H of C. 4¼-7 and 9-1¼. Much conference with our Peer colleagues.[5] Read Powell.

5. Wed.

Wrote to Dean of Windsor—Abp of Canterbury—The Queen—Sir P. Braila—and minutes. Cabinet 2¼-5¼. Saw Mr Lawley—Mr Gurdon—Mr Glyn—Ld Granville. Visited Sothebys. Dined with the Goschens. Saw Davison X. Queen's Concert in Evg. Saw P. of Wales —D. of Cambridge—Gen. Schenk—Mr C. Howard. Read B. Powell, & Tracts.

Cabinet. Wed. June 5. 2¼.[6]

√ Thornton Telegram June 4-5. Schenck's communication to Ld G. & respecting Art. V Threefold offer as in Mem.[7]

√ Guard's Band to go—satisfactory assurance from Gen S. & from Boston. Percy Wyndham's question.[8]

[9]The Cabinet agreed to offer the Govt. of U.S. either

1. To agree in an application to the Arbitrators on the 15th to adjourn at once without presentation of either argument.
2. To conclude a new arrangement with the Treaty-making Powers for the enlargement of the time.

[1] No minute found; apparently the meeting described to Victoria on 4 June (CAB 41/4/26): preparation of govt. case for statements; Scottish education; shorter church services. Schenck gave Fish's tel. on draft Article to Granville: *F.R.U.S.* 1872, ii. 558.

[2] And answered question on Keogh's judgment; *H* ccxi. 1032, 1089.

[3] On Convocation; see letters to Tait, 5 June 72, and Döllinger, 6 Sept. 72.

[4] His son gave a speech from G. *Eliot's 'The Spanish Gipsy'; *The Times*, 5 June 1872, 14f.

[5] The Lords the previous day voted agst. the govt. for a select cttee. on the 1870 Irish Land Act, and this day Russell moved his often postponed motion on Alabama; *H* ccxi. 1021, 1095.

[6] Add MS 44640, f. 103.

[7] See PRO FO 362/1, ff. 41-4.

[8] On Alabama, next day.

[9] Undated holograph; Add MS 44640, f. 104; these points put to Schenck next day, *F.R.U.S.* 1872, ii. 558.

3. To conclude the Supplementary Treaty with two additions agreed on today.

A & B & the American A (see MS) either in the body of this Instrument—or, if preferred by U.S., through a supplemental Declaration having the authority of the Senate as to B.

[1]1. To sign Article (with the enlarged explanation as to indirect claims).

2. With that explanation to put in 'Argument' & then ask Arbitrators to adjourn.

3. Without the explanation to state to Arbitrators that we cannot plead to the indirect claims or take any part in the Arbitration if they are entertained—& then put in the Argument.

To A. C. TAIT, archbishop of Canterbury, 5 June 1872. Tait MSS, 90, f. 129.

We read the Act of Uniformity Bill 3° on Monday night, after a Second Division on the reference to Convocation in the Preamble. In this Division our majority was larger than before. Still, it cannot be concealed that the difficulties of Church legislation are extreme, and are increasing. The good side is, an indisposition to meddle: the bad, an increase of difficulties in the way of practical improvements.

The point was taken that the Reports of Convocation had not been presented to Parliament. This in point of form was a decided flaw. It was condoned, so to speak, by the majority. But it hence became necessary that I should consent to strike out the *latter* of the two Clauses referring to the Reports as the basis of the Bill: which was done accordingly *nem con.*

No amendment was made in the body of the Bill except one or two which were strictly verbal and in furtherance of the evident purpose.

6. Th.

Wrote to The Queen—Ld Granville (3)—Mr Bruce—Abp of Canterbury—and minutes. Attended Sotheby's Sale and had lessons from Lady C. Schreiber.[2] Saw Bp of Manchester—Col. Higginson—Mr Glyn—Ld Granville. U.P. Deputn on Educn.[3] Dined at C. Forster's. H of C. 4¼–8 and 9½–1¼. Spoke on Washn Treaty & Scots Educn. The H. *too* well pleased as to the former.[4] Read Powell. Attended Sir J. Lacaita's Lecture on Vesuvius.

7. Fr.

Wrote to Archbp of York—Sir R. Blennerhassett (dft)[5]—Ld Granville—The Queen—& minutes. Dined at Mr Glyns. Saw Mr Grindley[6]

[1] Add MS 44640, f. 105. [2] See 1 May 55. [3] No record found.

[4] *H* ccxi. 1276, answering P. Wyndham, and on the adjournment.

[5] Refusing request of Blennerhassett and 29 Irish M.P.s for release of remaining Fenians; Add MS 44434, f. 160.

[6] Unidentified; perhaps of the banking family.

—D. of Argyll—Mr Ouvry—Mrs Chetwynd—Mr Glyn—Mr Stansfeld—Sir R. Palmer—Mr Macmillan—Mr Bass—Mr Stansfeld. Visited Sotheby's—Christie's. Finished Sir H. Holland—Read Martin,[1] & divers Tracts. H. of C. 3¾-7 and 9-12½.[2] Saw Graham[R].

8. Sat. [Chislehurst]

Wrote to Ld Dufferin—Sir S. Scott & Co.—The Queen—& minutes. Cabinet 2-4¾. Off at 4¾ to Chiselhurst. Saw Mr Glyn—Mr West—Ld Granville—Sir R. Palmer cum do. Read Barr's Poems[3]—Account of Palestine.[4]

Cabinet. Jun. 8. 72. 2PM.[5]

√ Washington Treaty. Telegrams of today. Offer to adjourn agreed on, with notice we shall withdraw one Arbitrator: argument to be put in.[6]

√ Adderley's request for a day for Health Bill declined.[7]

9. 2 S.Trin.

Chiselhurst Ch. 11 & 3.30. Much conversation with J. Grey.[8] Read Plea for Free Inquiry[9]—Pryce on Ch. in Wales[10]—Whittle's Cathm & the Vatican[11]—Mr Peyrat on French Synod & Vatican Schism.[12]

10. M. [London]

Wrote to The Queen—and minutes. Off at 10.30—Saw the Prince Imperial. Saw Sir H. Moncreiff—Sir R. Palmer—Mr Bass—Mr Glyn—Mr J. Talbot *cum* Mr Hope—Ld[13] Granville—Mr Forster—Ld Ripon—and others. Cabinet 2½-4¼. Meeting late in evg. In truth we are now hardly ever out of Alabama. H of C. 4¼-8 and 9-2¼. Spoke on divers matters.[14] Read 'Thrown Together'.[15]

[1] Probably Sir T. *Martin, *Notes on the present system of private bill legislation* (1872).

[2] Scottish education: *H* ccxi. 1352.

[3] M. Barr, *Poems* (1872).

[4] Perhaps *Our work in Palestine. Exploration Fund Report* (1872).

[5] Add MS 44640, f. 109.

[6] Jottings at ibid., f. 110; see Granville's letters to Schenck, *F.R.U.S.* 1872, ii. 562.

[7] Letter explaining this to Adderley, in Add MS 44541, f. 137.

[8] Perhaps John Grey, 1829–95, s. of 2nd Earl Grey and vicar of Houghton-le-Spring.

[9] See 2 June 72.

[10] J. Pryce, *Lay agency as an auxiliary to the Christian ministry in Wales* (1864).

[11] J. L. Whittle, *Catholicism and the Vatican with a narrative of the Old Catholic Congress at Munich* (1872).

[12] E. Peyrat, *Le Synode Protestant et le Schisme Catholique* (1872).

[13] Start of facsimile in Masterman, 160–1.

[14] Questions, estimates: *H* ccxi. 1509, 1524.

[15] By F. Montgomery (1872).

Cabinet. Mond. Jun. 10. 72. 2½ PM.[1]
√ Washington Treaty. Telegrams recd. today. Sir R. P[almer] attended, d[itt]o A[ttorney] G[eneral]. Communication to Amn. Minister agreed on.
At night in quasi-Cabinet agreed to urge Sir R. P[almer] to go to Geneva.[2]

11. Tu.

Wrote to The Queen and minutes. Wrote on Treaty of Washn. The Cabinet met at 2 & sat intermittently with the House to 5¾. Again 9½-1. Wrote afterwards. Saw Ld Granville—do *cum* Ld C. Justice[3]—Ld C. Justice—Ld Tenterden. House 3-5 and 5¾-7.[4] Read Thrown Together. A day of great pressure, after yesterday.

Cabinet. Tues. Jun. 11. 2 PM. H. of C.[5]
Met at 2: Sir R. P[almer]—Law Officers—Ld Tenterden—attended. Broken meeting until 5¾.[6]
Presentation of Argument, or Summary, discussed. Ld T[enterden] to see C[hief] J[ustice] Cockburn. Instructions to Agent some points approved.
Reassembled 9½ Ld Chancellor's Room, & F.O. Further discussion on Presentation of Argument.

12. Wed.

Wrote to The Queen—Ld Chancellor—Ld Lyttelton—and minutes. Dined at Mr Ellice's. Lady Herbert's afterwards. Saw Mr V. Stuart[7]—Mr Lawley—Mr Glyn—Ld Granville—Mrs T. X[8]—Mr Fortescue—Ld Dudley. Saw Gibbons[R]. Read Tabaraud.[9] Cabinet 12-2. An Impasse. Drive with C.

Cabinet Jun. 12. 72. 12 noon.[10]
√ Washington Treaty. After long debate it was settled that the Agent shd. make

[1] Add MS 44640, f. 113.
[2] Holograph dated 10 June 1872, draft, probably for Palmer to take to the Arbitrators, denying their competence to consider indirect claims, offering to lodge the Argument if the Arbitrators deny intending to consider indirect claims; ibid., f. 114.
[3] *Cockburn was the British arbitrator; he assumed the arbitration would fail, and had not read the arguments; see Cook, *The Alabama Claims*, 238.
[4] Scottish education: *H* ccxi. 1615.
[5] Add MS 44640, f. 117.
[6] Note passed between Gladstone and Halifax led to 'R.P.s' withdrawal for a time; ibid., f. 118.
[7] Possibly lt.-col. Villiers Stuart; business untraced.
[8] Obscured in facsimile in Masterman, 160.
[9] M. M. Tabaraud, *Histoire critique des projets . . . pour la réunion des Communions chrétiennes* (1824).
[10] Add MS 44640, f. 119. Diarist's holograph note to Hatherley, dated 12 June, ibid., f. 120, reads: 'You cannot put in the Argument while it is uncertain whether the result of putting in the case will be to obtain an adjournment.'

his[1] efforts to obtain an Adjournment without lodging the Summary. If he fail, to telegraph for instructions.[2]

[3]Previous assurance from the Americans that if we present the Summary, they the same, & we then forthwith ask for an adjournment, they will agree—without any other proceeding.

Put in the Summaries—(under reservation such as that of Ap. 15). Ask for the adjournment. If it is refused, & the claims are not put aside, withdraw the Arbitrator. If the matter is not settled during the term of the Adjournment, do the same.

13. Th.

Wrote to Bp of Lincoln—Ld Granville—Ld J. Manners—The Queen (2)—Archdn Harrison—Ld Chancellor—Mr Ellice—Sir S.R. Glynne—and minutes. Saw Mr Glyn—Col. Amcotts[4] with Mr Martin—Ld Granville—Ld Chancr—Ld Ripon (2). Saw the Doré Pictures.[5] H of C. 4¼–8 and 9–1¾. We have now a little Alabama daily.[6] Read Thrown Together.

Since Tuesday morning I have constantly revolved or discussed this proposition: that we should not be justified in breaking off the proceedings at Geneva, if an Adjournment can be had after presentation of the Summary, upon a refusal to present it. My determination upon it is now firmly rooted & tested by all the mental effort I can apply: & the time I thought had come today for looking forward as well as backward. I therefore wrote to the Queen[7] in terms which might a little prepare her for difficulties in the Cabinet: saw Granville first, who had not reached my point but seemed to come up to it; then arranged for him to see Halifax, Ripon to see Kimberley, & the Chancellor to see Cardwell; as the *knot* of the probable difficulty is in these three. On the whole, I hope we shall in one way or another work through: at any rate if anything like a Government can be held together, I will not shrink.[8]

14. Fr.

Wrote to The Queen—Dr Lightfoot—Ld Granville—Sir C. O'Logh-

[1] Instead of 'every', deleted.

[2] Summary of diarist's views if this happened, at Add MS 44640, f. 127. This decision went against Gladstone's wish; see 13 June 72 and Kimberley, *Journal*, 32. Granville's draft note for presentation by Tenterden to the arbitrators requesting adjournment pending conclusion of a supplementary convention, the Argument being withheld, in *PP* 1872 lxix. 765.

[3] Undated holograph of unpursued alternatives; Add MS 44640, f. 122.

[4] Weston Cracroft Amcotts of Hackthorn, 1815–83; deputy lord lieutenant of Lincolnshire.

[5] 'Christ leaving the Praetorium', at the Doré Gallery; *Art Journal* (1872), 193.

[6] *H* ccxi. 1693.

[7] CAB 41/4/31.

[8] This para. in Morley, ii. 411.

len—Mr Thos. Scott—& minutes. H of C. 2-7 and 9-1¼. Spoke on U.S. & on French Treaty.[1] Dined with Mr Glyn. Saw Mr Glyn—Ld Granville. Read Thrown Together.

15. Sat.[2]

Wrote to Ld Halifax—The Queen l. & Tel. & Mem.—Abp of Canterbury—Mr Goschen—Ld Sydney—and minutes. Read Forsythe on manuscripts &c.[3] Cabinet 12-2¼ & with brief intervals *to* 7½. Dined with Princess Louise. Saw Ld Granville—Bp of Winchester—Mr Glyn.

After dinner Granville & I went to see Mr Hammond (whose state of health I did not like) then on to F.O. where we got (before midnight) the Protocol of today from Geneva. Thank God that up to a certain point the indications on this great controversy are decidedly favourable.[4]

Cabinet. Jun. 15. 72. Noon.[5]

√ Inclosure Bill this year—the Lords? To be introduced by Ld Morley.
√ Corrupt Practices Bill. To be postponed.
√ Public Health Bill—in Lords? No. To follow Mines Bill.
√ Govr. Eyre. Make no argument. Cabinet vote for it. We do not deal with the merits. Leave of absence may be given.[6]
√ Contribution to Exhibition at Vienna. Expenses of Commissioners to be paid. C. of E. & Ld R[ipon] to consider.
√ Telegram to Tenterden (12. 30)—not to press to extremes the term of 8 months if U.S. prefer a shorter one.[7]
√ Middlesex Registry—question as to Fees—arranged.
√ (on the route through Burmah to China—) Mahomedan de facto inland Power have sent envoys who have come here (Indian Govt. paying their charges) with presents. Are they to be received? And returned? Ask Sir R. Alcock for his opinion. Queen's name not to be used.[8]
√ Bernstorff—has read Circular to Ld Granville respecting Election of next Pope, & interference of Govts. Ld G. to say British feeling is very much opposed to Ultramontanism, but we have no *locus standi* for interference.[9]

[1] *H* ccxi. 1739, 1792.

[2] By the treaty, the arbitrators were this day to meet and arguments be handed in. The Americans deposited their Argument, Tenterden asked for eight months' adjournment without submitting the British Argument; the conference adjourned until 17 June; *PP* 1872 lxix. 761.

[3] W. *Forsyth, 'History of ancient manuscripts. A lecture' (1872).

[4] See Morley, ii. 411.

[5] Add MS 44640, f. 123.

[6] *Eyre was voted £4133 (to defray his defence expenses) after much deb. on 8 July; *H* ccxii. 798.

[7] PRO FO 5/1418.

[8] A Burmese mission was in London from 6 June.

[9] See Russell's despatch enclosing extract from *Deutsche Allegemeiner Zeitung*: PRO FO 64/745.

√ Jews in Roumania. There can be no joint intervention. British Govt. will use efforts with circumspection—recommending others to act in the same sense.[1]
√ Treasury to pay part of the expenses of the Agency at Zanzibar.
√ Indian return of £2700 cost—not to be charged on Indian Revenues.
√ Irish National Schoolmasters. Hartington's proposal discussed; to be further explained between him and the C. of E[xchequer].

[The back inside cover has at top and bottom wax seals to which at some time some kind of strip seems to have been affixed. At the top, partly covered by the top seal, the following, in pencil:—]

P.C.
Vere St 15 Oct Russell
Kinloch Lodge Ballach

[1] See F. Stern, *Gold and Iron* (1977), 371.

[VOLUME XXIX][1]

[The inside front cover has:—]

Private. No 29.

JUNE 16. 72–FEB. 12. 74.

ἀλλὰ κἀκ τῶν λειψάνων
δει τῶν δὲ ρωμὴν νεανικὴν ἔχειν. ἐγὼ
τοὐμον νομίζω γῆρας εἶναι κρειττον ἢ πολ-
λῶν κικίννους νεανιῶν
καὶ σχῆμα

. . . Sphekes 1070.[2]

He spake no word, he thought no thought
Save by the stedfast rule of Ought.

'I am a feeble, wavering, feverish being, who requires support & consolation, which his energies are too (much?) exhausted to return.'

Relics of Shelley 1862[3] p. 151.

'Rationalism tried at the bar of Reason'

[And in pencil:—]

Oriens tibi victus, ad usque
Decolor extremâ quà tinguitur India Gange.

Ov. Met. IV. 20.[4]

D.G.Ben + £150

[1] Lambeth MS 1443.

[2] Aristophanes, *Wasps*, 1070, chorus of Old Men: '[Our hair is white]. But even of these relics (of our former selves) one must make youthful strength. For my part I think that my old age is better than the curls and posturing [and effeminacy] of many young men.' Gladstone omits the bracketed word in the second sentence, *κεὐρυπρωκτίαν*, literally 'wide-arsedness'.

[3] Shelley to Hogg, in R. Garnett, ed., *Relics of Shelley* (1862), 151; '(much?)' is Gladstone's addition.

[4] 'The East has fallen conquest to you, even as far as where swarthy India is bathed in the far waters of Ganges.'

Sunday 3 Trin. June 16 1872.

(Bunker's Hill Anniv.?)[1] Chapel R. mg & evg. Wrote to The Queen l. & Tel. Saw Ld Granville—Mr Glyn—Cabinet here 1½–3¼. We sent off a Tel. wh. I hope may finish the good work at Geneva. Read Curteis B. Lecture[2]—Presb. Angl. on Eternal Punishment[3]—Tabaraud Projets de Reunion. Dined with the Argylls at C[ampden] Hill.

Sunday June 16. 72. 1½ PM.[4]

√ Washington Treaty. Communications from Geneva considered. Telegram agreed on authorising acceptance of Decl. by Arbitrators if spontaneous.[5]

17. M.[6]

Wrote to Mr Goschen—Abp of Canterbury—Dr Lightfoot—Earl of Cork—Baron Beaulieu—The Queen—and minutes. H of C. 4¼–8 and 9¾–1¾.[7] Saw Ld Granville—Mr Goschen—Ld Portman—Mr Glyn—Ld Prov. of Aberdeen—Chancr of Exr—Mr Bass—Atty General—Chauvine. . . . Dined at Mr C. Foster's. Read 'Thrown together'—Tollemache on H of C.[8]

To G. J. GOSCHEN, first lord of the admiralty, 17 June 1872. Add MS 44541, f. 140.

So far as I am concerned I answer your question without hesitation.[9] Under no circumstances that I am aware of, could or can the indirect claims become the subjects of negotiation between the two countries on their merits. Had the Treaty never been made, or, after it had been made, had the Case not contained them or thirdly, the Case having in one sense brought them into the Arbitration & we having (*ex hypothesi*) got them kicked out again; if under any of these conditions (& no others occur to me) the U.S. bring or had brought forward the indirect claims I know of no way of meeting the overture except a firm & unconditional refusal. At the same time I doubt whether the Cabinet can legitimately be asked as a Cabinet to make these affirmations, inasmuch as, according to my view, they are not within the purview of its present undertaking—that undertaking has reference exclusively to the scope of the Arbitration. We have con-

[1] No: 17 June 1775.

[2] G. H. Curteis, 'Dissent in its relation to the Church of England', Bampton Lectures (1871).

[3] By Presbyter Anglicanus (1864).

[4] Add MS 44640, f. 142.

[5] Declaration made on 19 June, *F.R.U.S.* 1872, ii. 577.

[6] The Geneva conference again adjourned, until 19 June.

[7] Questioned on Keogh's judgment on Galway election petition, & Alabama: *H* ccxi. 1860.

[8] Perhaps untraced pamphlet by J. T. Tollemache.

[9] Goschen's letter of 15 June reiterated his views expressed in Cabinet, that the indirect claims must not be allowed to remain an unsettled question; both letters in Elliot, *Goschen*, i. 134–6.

tended all along that the claims could not legitimately come before the Arbitrators. One of our reasons, in itself conclusive, has been that by the language of the Treaty & the Protocols, they had been extinguished. But we have never demanded the assent of the Americans to our reasoning, only to our conclusion, that the claims were not within the scope of the Arbitration. If indeed their exclusion left them in a better condition than they would have stood in if never included, there would be a ground for our touching them further. This case would have arisen, had we taken what we suppose to have been Adams' words. But, those words once withdrawn, there is no such case. It is my view (but this is quite another matter) that they lie cast aside, a dishonoured carcass, which no amount of force, fraud or folly can again galvanize into life. You will see then, in sum that (if I rightly understand you) I accept for myself broadly & freely what may be called the extreme doctrine against the Indirect Claims, but I think the Cabinet cannot fairly be challenged for an official judgment on a matter not really before it. I hope you may be inclined to take the same view. But everyone must appreciate & none can misapprehend your honourable scrupulous anxiety.

18. Tu.

Wrote to Sol. General—Bp of Manchester—and minutes. Ten to dinner. H of C 3-7.[1] Saw Lord Granville—Rev N. Hall *cum* Dr Cuyler[2]—Lord Spencer—Mr Glyn—Mr Gurdon. Conclave on Ballot amt.[3] Read Marsden's Lect.[4]—'Thrown Together'. Saw Mrs Jeffries & 2 more X.

19. Wed.[5]

Wrote to The Queen—Mrs Munro[6]—and minutes. Heat, headach (for some time) & exhaustion led me to make an idle day as far as I could. Saw Ld Granville—Mr Glyn (2)—Mrs Th. Dined at Baron M. Rothschilds—Duke of Norfolk's afr. Read Thrown Together—Hist. of Printing[7]—Memoir of Baron Maule.[8]

20. Th.

Wrote to Canon Blakesley—The Queen (mem. and l.)—and minutes.

[1] Scottish education: *H* ccxi. 1934.

[2] Theodore Cuyler, American evangelist; apparently not the meeting described in Hall's *Autobiography*, 279.

[3] Carried on previous day by tories in the Lords: *H* ccxi. 1842.

[4] J. H. *Marsden, *Two introductory lectures upon archaeology* (1852).

[5] This day the arbitrators themselves cut the knot by ruling out the indirect claims, a ruling accepted by the Americans on 25 June. The solution was engineered by C. F. Adams; *PP* 1872 lxix. 769-80.

[6] The sculptor's wife; see 18 July 51 and Add MS 44541, f. 141.

[7] See 31 May 72.

[8] *Memoir of the early life of... Sir W. H. Maule*, ed. E. Leathley (1872).

Read Keogh's Judgment[1]—Memoir of Maule. Dined with the Wests. Breakfast party. Saw Mr Stephenson—Duke of Argyll—Mr Glyn—Ld Granville—Sol.Gen.—Ld R. Grosvenor. H. of C. 4¼-8¼ and 9¼-1½.[2]

21. Fr.

Wrote to Mr Foljambe[3]—Earl Spencer—Ld Gr. (mem)—The Queen—and minutes. Attended Q. Bench at 10 but was not examined. Saw Mr Glyn—Conclave on Ballot Bill—Mr. . . . H of C. 2-7 and 9-1½.[4] Dined with the Glyns. Read Thrown Together—Keogh's Judgment (finished).

To EARL SPENCER, Irish lord lieutenant, 21 June 1872. 'Private.' Add MS 44541, f. 142.

Many thanks for this correspondence.[5] I read your excellent letter to the Queen with much pleasure. There is a manifest *twist* in the Queen's mind with respect to Ireland, which you do your best to correct. Bad laws & policy make bad men; & men bad by habit & inveteracy are not converted but provoked by the removal of the bad laws & change of the bad policy: & this blowing up of statues is their plot to sow dissension between England & Ireland—a plot which the Queen unwittingly is apt to fall in with.

22. Sat. [*Windsor*]

Wrote to Ld Chancellor—The Queen—and minutes. Attended the Levee. Cabinet 2½-4½. Queen's Bench 10½-11½. Saw Mr Glyn. Then we went to Windsor. We dined with the Queen. Attended Q. Bench in mg to give evidence in the case of L. Edmunds. We were all sorry for him, be he what he may.[6] Read Forsythe's Lecture.[7]

Cabinet Sat. June 22. 72. 2½ PM.[8]

√ Tichborne Claimant. Chancellor to obtain further information.

√ Ballot Bill Amts. What. By whom. To be considered in a Cabinet on Wedy. or Thursday.[9]

[1] On the Galway election petn., on which he had already spoken; see 3, 17 June 72.

[2] Scottish education: *H* ccxi. 2017.

[3] Francis John Savile Foljambe, 1830-1917; liberal M.P. E. Retford 1857-85.

[4] Misc. business: *H* ccxii. 47.

[5] Spencer to the Queen, 15 June 1872, R.A. D27/111.

[6] Edmunds v. Gladstone, Lowe and Stansfeld, for alleged libel in treasury minute of 14 Dec. 1871; Edmunds conducted his own case and was nonsuited; the affair originated with the Westbury scandal in 1864; *The Times*, 24 June 1872, 13b; 7 Aug. 72.

[7] See 15 June 72.

[8] Add MS 44640, f. 143.

[9] Gladstone had passed a note to Granville at the previous cabinet suggesting this course; Granville urged delay, as Kimberley and Halifax 'rather object', until this day's meeting. Ibid., f. 144.

√ Telegram to Geneva, empowering our agent to withdraw appln. for adjournment: agreed on.
√ Business of the week considered on various heads. Stansfeld.
√ Bill this Session to suspend Imperial Fishery [?] Act.[1]
√ Answer to Ld Abinger. Address agreed on.[2]
√ Oppose Fiji Island Protectorate. Continue in plan of recognising De Facto Govt.[3]

23. 5 S.Trin.

Castle Chapel at 10 & 12: St George's at 4.30. Wrote to Mr Cardwell—Duke of Argyll. Audience of H.M. at 3.30. Saw Sir T. Biddulph—Col. Ponsonby. Walk & conversation with the Dean. Read Scott's Life of Jesus[4]—Irons on Holy Orders[5]—Do on Tyndale[6]—Barton on Future State.[7] Migrated to the Deanery.

24. M. St J.Bapt. [*London*]

Off by 10.20 train. Wrote Mr Ayrton—Rev Dr Lowe—Mrs Leech[8]—Ld Kimberley—Mr G.G. Scott—Lady Burdett Coutts—The Queen—and minutes. Saw Mr Glyn—Mr Cardwell—do *cum* Ld Granville—Mr Kinnaird—Mr Lowe—C.J. of New York.[9] H of C. 4¼-8 and 9-1¼.[10] Saw Mad. D'Alice X. Read Ellis on Birds[11]—Thrown Together.

25. Tu.

Wrote to Bp of Lincoln—The Queen (2)—and minutes. H of C. 2-6¾ and 9-1¾. Spoke on Fiji motion.[12] Finished Maule's Life—Thrown together. Nine to dinner. Saw Ld Granville—Mr Forster—Mr Glyn—Mr Stansfeld *cum* Mr Lambert—Mr Cardwell—Mr Crittenden. Attended the Herbert marriage.[13]

[1] As last year, not introduced; see 10 June 71.
[2] On purchase and the science corps; see *H* ccxi. 1906 (18 June) and *H* ccxii. 272.
[3] He spoke strongly to this effect on McArthur's motion 25 June; *H* ccxii. 215 and W. P. Morrell, *Britain in the Pacific Islands* (1960), 159.
[4] T. *Scott, freethinker, *The English life of Jesus* (1872).
[5] W. J. *Irons, *Considerations on taking Holy Orders in the Church of England* (1872).
[6] *Professor Tyndall's 'Fragments of science for unscientific people' in relation with theology and religion* (1872).
[7] J. Barton, *The reality, but not the duration of future punishment, is revealed* (1865).
[8] Declining request of Ann, the artist's widow (see 21 Apr. 65), to buy his 'outlines' for the nation; Add MS 44541, f. 144.
[9] Sanford Elias Church, 1815-80, chief justice of New York State from 1870.
[10] Questioned on govt. timetable for bills; *H* ccxii. 106.
[11] Untraced.
[12] *H* ccxii. 215; see 22 June 72.
[13] Of Elizabeth, S. *Herbert's da., to Sir C. H. H. *Parry; see 30 Aug. 66.

26. Wed.

Wrote to Ch. of Exr—The Queen—Ld Granville—and minutes. Cabinet 3-5¼. Luncheon at 15 G.S. Saw Mr Crittenden—Ld Granville—Mr Glyn—Mr Moffatt—Mrs Leech—Lady Stanley—Gen. Schenck—Abp of Canterbury. Dined at Mr D. Robertson's. B. Palace Concert afterwards. Saw Pr. & Princess of Wales: also D. of Cambridge, to whom I explained my silence up to this date.[1] Visited Christie's.

Cabinet. June 26. 72. 3 PM.[2]

√ Treaty of Washington. With Verbal insertion of [']ask leave' before 'to deliver the printed argument'—accept Palmer's proposed statement.[3]

√ Ballot Amendments. Amend scrutiny—reject optional ballot—deal with polling places—remove decl. of illiterate voters—give a general notice.[4]

√ Public Health Bill. Settled as over:[5] reduce Bill to organisation clauses. If afterwards it is found necessary: pay half the salaries of medical officers of health & inspectors of nuisances—provisionally, & without prejudice. Loan clause 3½ more [?]. Repeal exemptn. clause.[6]

√ Order of business. Ballot Friday at 2. Supply on Monday Civil.

√ Tichborne Witnesses. Chancellor reported, no progress. To see Att. Gen[eral].

To R. LOWE, chancellor of the exchequer, 26 June 1872. Add MS 44541, f. 145.

With reference to your Mem. on Refining in Bond,[7] I would suggest that you might advantageously confer through the Customs with the applicants in this country on the first of the two points which you have raised, or rather mentioned. If the objections of Holland & Belgium are peremptory & final, & if the concurrence of all the Governments in a common system of refining in bond is essential to its adoption here—the difficulty seems to be very great & it would be well to know before taking any further step what our refiners have to suggest upon the second point. I agree with you that it would not be politic, hardly indeed seemly, to invite Germany & Austria to join the Conference at a moment when we are so near a dead lock, *even* if it might be suitable at another time.

27. Th.

Breakfast Party. Wrote to The Queen—Mr Bruce—and minutes. Saw Mr Blakesley—Ld Russell—Ld Granville—Professor Price—Mr C. Fortescue—Mr Forster—Mr Glyn. Holland House breakfast

[1] Obscure; on the American negotiations?

[2] Add MS 44640, f. 146.

[3] Next day Tenterden asked leave to withdraw the application for adjournment, and to present the British Argument; *PP* 1872 lxix. 771.

[4] See next day's statement; *H* ccxii. 290.

[5] MS continues on next page.

[6] Bill given royal assent 10 August.

[7] Untraced.

party. H of C. 4¼-8½ and 9½-2. Made explanations on the Ballot Bill —& the Washington Treaty (Thanks be to God.)[1]

28. Fr.

Helen's birthday. Wrote a few words to her. Wrote also to Ld Chancellor—Chancr of Exchr—Mr Keble—Prof. Rawlinson—Mr West —Mr G. Burnett—H.J.G.—The Queen—& minutes. Mr Crittenden had his last sitting (or rather flying).[2] Saw Dean of St Pauls—Rev Mr Childers—Mr Glyn—Mr Gurdon—Ld Dalhousie. H of C. 2¼-7. Spoke on Ballot Bill and 10½-1.[3] Dined at Lansdowne House. Saw Mrs Brand. Saw Hastings & 2[R]. Read Marsden's Lectures.[4]

To R. LOWE, chancellor of the exchequer, 28 June 1872. Add MS 44541, f. 146.

Viewing Ayrton's position both as Commissioner of Works & as Member for the Tower Hamlets would it not be well to give him an opportunity of stating his views to you or to the Government upon the Mint Bill before taking any decision to introduce it? I doubt its being carried without its [*sc.* his] cooperation, & it would be well not to be beaten upon it a second time.[5] This suggestion is altogether independent of the special point I mentioned to you about the removal of the Building from the labour, which so far as I know was not noticed in the House. I have had no conversations with Ayrton on the Bill this year but last year I remember that he thought himself aggrieved, as he considered that he had been required to bring in the Bill without having been consulted on it.

29. Sat.

Wrote to Dean Ramsay—Rev. W. Rawson—Sir S.R. Glynne—The Queen (2)—Ld Lyveden—and minutes. Saw Mr Glyn—Mr West—Dowager Lady Westmoreland—Mrs Heywood. Cabinet 2½-4¼. Worked on papers & otherwise to get my room tidy. Prince & Princess of Wales & Princess Louise, with a party dined: all very gracious. Some conversation on Rome & Italy with the Princess. Read Marsden on Archaeol.[6] Saw Sir R. Palmer in evg.[7] Saw 2 X.

Cabinet. June 29. 72. 2.30. PM.[8]

√ Eyre Vote. Notice to be given but not to be given *first.*[9]
Lifford Committee on [1870 Irish] Land Act.[10]

[1] *H* ccxii. 293; the Americans had effectively dropped the indirect claims from the arbitration.
[2] See 25 Jan. 72.
[3] *H* ccxii. 355.
[4] See 18 June 72.
[5] No bill was introduced.
[6] See 18 June 72.
[7] Back from Geneva.
[8] Add MS 44640, f. 148.
[9] See 15 June 72.
[10] *PP* 1872 xi. 1; Lifford co-drafted its report, though not its chairman.

Treaty of Washington.
√ Tichborne Witnesses. Decision. Chili [*sic*] & Australia not to be scoured. Chancellor to communicate (Cabinet much divided).[1]
√ Dropping Bills: Masters & Servants: Contagious Diseases: Land Transfers Scotl: Jury Bill Ireland? (not *yet*.).
√ Business of the week.
√ Charge for the Vienna Exhibition.

30. 5 S.Trin.

Ch. Royal mg & evg. Saw Mr Glyn—Mr G. Richmond. Read many Sermons & pamphlets. Dined at Argyll Lodge.

Mond. Jul. One 1872.

Wrote to The Queen (Mem. & l.)—Ld Granville—Ld Devon—Ld Ossington—Bp of Winchester—Bp of Salisbury—& minutes. Saw Col. Ponsonby—Mr L. King—Sir R. Palmer—Ld Granville—Ld Halifax—Ch. of Exchr—Rev. S.E.G.—Conclave on Ballot & offices. Inq. for Hastings—Lewis—Russell. Saw R. Dined at Ralph Neville's. House of C. 4¼-8¼ & 10-1.[2] Read Memoir of Julian Fane.[3]

To G. MOBERLY, bishop of Salisbury, 1 July 1872. Add MS 44541, f. 147.

The Ballot Bill will I believe return tonight to the House of Lords & will (it is said) be considered there on Monday next. The Lords have unfortunately adopted the very strong measure of inserting in the Bill an amendment which by making secrecy optional in the act of *giving* the vote destroys all security for any secrecy in the Bill. It is very dangerous to mistake the general sentiments of the people on this subject, & though most unwilling to press upon your Lordship with respect to any political matter, I cannot help representing the great importance of your aid, should you be able to give it, in preventing the very serious evil of a collision between the two Houses with the consequences it might entail.[4]

2. Tu.

Wrote to Sir W. Stephenson—Mr Burnett—The Queen—& minutes. H of C. 2½-7 and 9-2. Spoke on Mr Miall's dreary motion.[5] Saw Rev. Mr Molesworth—Dr Liddon—Mr Glyn—7 to dinner. Read Life of

[1] The Crown decided to prosecute the claimant, following a grand jury indictment.
[2] Supply: *H* ccxii. 434.
[3] E. R. B. *Lytton, *Julian Fane, a memoir* (1871).
[4] He sent a shorter, similar appeal to S. Wilberforce; Add MS 44541, f. 147.
[5] *Miall's motion for a royal commission on Anglican property, defeated in 94:295; he accused Miall of making the Commons 'discharge the functions of a debating society'; *H* ccxii. 572.

J. Fane. Began *the* formidable letter to H.M.: by wh I am willing to live or die.[1]

3. Wed.

Wrote to Ld Granville—Ld Napier—Col. Ponsonby—Bp of Winchester—Ld Bessborough—and minutes. Saw Mr Glyn—Dr Hooker—Ld Bathurst. Mr Tollemache drove our party to Kew where we spent 2 h. under the able guidance of Dr Hooker & returned to a late dinner in St J. Square. Luncheon at 15 G.S.—Visited Ld Bathurst's house after. Read Memoir of J. Fane. Worked on letter to H.M. Saw A.[R].

To the EARL OF BESSBOROUGH, 3 July 1872. Add MS 44541, f. 149.

Bp of Winchester will be on the ground. I have no answer from Sarum. The evidence of ill intention on the part of the [tory] leaders is, I fear, complete.

To G. G. GLYN, chief whip, 3 July 1872. Add MS 44541, f. 148.
'Most private.'

Since you were here, I have *seen* a very alarming indication for Monday next in the Lords: not an ordinary note from the [tory] Whip, but a lithographed letter from the Leader, couched in strong terms. Granville is away & I shall have no opportunity of seeing him today. But I cannot doubt that under the circumstances you should let the trumpet blow that the Lords may know before the time comes what the country thinks. Doubtless the London press[?] will make it an appeal to their wisdom not their fears, but they cannot do wrong in pointing to the extreme gravity of the consequences.

4. Thu.

Wrote to Bp of Salisbury—Bp of Bath & Wells—The Queen—& minutes. Breakfast party. Saw Ld F. Cavendish—Dr Monro—Mr Glyn—Mr Forster *cum* Mr Glyn—Ld Bessborough—Ld Granville. Saw A. Hamilton—Murray. H of C. 4¼-8½ and 9½-1½.[2] Finished my very difficult letter to H.M. respecting Prince of Wales & the kindred matter. Gave it to Ld G. to read. Read Memoir of J. Fane.

5. Fr.

Wrote to Ld Bessborough—Sec. Free Museum Lpool[3]—Ld Lisgar—The Queen—Robn G. Also further revised & sent off (after C.

[1] See 5 July 72. [2] Questioned on Keogh's judgment; *H* ccxii. 635.
[3] Items from his collection were loaned to it.

had perused it) my letter to H.M. on the great subject.[1] Saw Mrs Th. (who is to make up a *dinner* on Monday)—Ld Granville (2)—Mr West—Mr Glyn—Mr Levy—Mr Dowse—Mr Forster *cum* Mr Glyn. Dined at Mr Glyn's. H of C. 3½-7 and 9-1¼.[2] Read Memoir of Fane.

6. Sat. [*Chislehurst*]

Wrote to Ld Bessborough—Ld Spencer—Mr Maguire—T.S. Gladstone—The Queen—Mr Ouvry—and minutes. Cabinet 2½-6. Dined at Stafford House: the rooms are the seat of many memories. Saw Mrs Murray. Breakf. at Grillion's. Saw Ld Stanhope—Col. W. Patten—Mr Forster—Ld Chancellor—Mr Glyn—Mr Fowler—Mr Welby. Off by 11.40 PM. train to Chislehurst. Read Fane's Memoir.

Cabinet. Sat. Jul. 6. 1872. 2 PM.[3]

√ Ballot. Lords Amendments. If beaten on optional Ballot, adjourn Debate. If Bill lost, autumn session & another trial before Dissolving to be in November.[4]

Six alternatives.

1. Resignation.
2. Making Peers.
3. Acceptance of Bill.
4. Resuming Bill next year.

} Rejected

5. Immediate Dissolution.
6. Autumn Session—further trial—& dissolve upon trial.

√ Keogh. Galway Election motions. General conversation on Charge and on protection of Judge agt. looting[?]: give him cavalry.[5]

√ Order of business. Licensing 2R? Cabinet Committee reappointed. Public Health Monday: Supply—Cardwell's Bill. Tues: Mine Report &c. Thurs: Licensing 2R—Irish Bills—Cardwell's Bill. Frid: Public Health—Mines 3r.

√ Prison Ministers Bill—Memorial. Regret we cannot give time.[6]

√ Admiralty Bill—drop for the year.

√ Reduce the ½ Sovereign to a token 9/- of gold. C. of E[xchequer] to confer with the Bank.

√ Intercolonial Tariffs. Previous question if necessary.[7]

√ Foreign Bondholders Charter. To follow general rule: not to have the Charter. Sick and wounded ass[ociatio]n—d[itt]o.

√ Vienna Exhibition. P of W[ales] inclined to resign but will not.

[1] Prince of Wales' residence in Ireland, linked with reform of the Irish lord lieutenancy; Guedalla, *Q*, i. 351.

[2] Misc. business: *H* ccxii. 704.

[3] Add MS 44640, f. 151.

[4] See 8 July 72n.

[5] Burning of Keogh's effigy: *H* ccxii. 787.

[6] Memorial by J. F. Maguire and others; Add MS 44434, f. 249; see 13 July 72.

[7] No motion put, but a question: *H* ccxii. 1145 (15 July).

Jul. 6. 72. Glyn's Report[1]

Present majority	86
Loss of seats, in a Dissolution 'without a cry' 32 Votes[2]	64
Probable majority	22

Possible gain by new Register 10 seats—by Ballot question. . . ? By Licensing Bill. . . ?

7. 6 S.Trin.

Chislehurst Ch 11 AM (with H.C.) & 3.30 PM. Conversation with R. C[avendish] & Mr Williams. Saw the 'Imperatrice'[3] at Camden Park. Read Union Review—Hyacinthe's Réforme Catholique.[4]

8. M. [London]

Wrote to Attorney General—Ld Lyttelton—Robn G.—Mr Edw. Rice—H.J.G.—The Queen—& minutes. Returned from Chislehurst at 12. H of C. 4¼-8¼ and 9-12¾.[5] Saw Mr Lawley—Ld Beaumont—Mr Glyn—Mr Forster—Mr Dowse—Att. General—Mr Lefevre. Read Memoir of Fane.

9. Tu.

Wrote to Abp of Canterbury—Mrs Helbert—Mr Ouvry (2)—Mr Goschen—The Queen (2)—& minutes. H. of C. 3½-7.[6] Luncheon at 15 G.S. Saw Ld Lisgar—Sir W. Stephenson—Mr Glyn—Mr Forster—Mr Ayrton—Ld Bathurst—Ld Spencer—Mr Fortescue—Sol. General. Dined with the Wests.[7] Read O'Keeffe Papers[8]—Shipping do—Memoir of J. Fane—Planché's Memoirs.[9]

[1] Add MS 44640, f. 154.

[2] i.e. the loss of 32 seats counts 64 on a division.

[3] i.e. Eugénie.

[4] C. J. M. Loyson [Père Hyacinthe], *De la réforme Catholique*, i (1872).

[5] Spoke on Keogh. The Lords unexpectedly ceased demanding amendments to make the secret ballot optional; *H* ccxii. 778, 786.

[6] Mines Bill: *H* ccxii. 874.

[7] He told West of his appt. as I.R. Commissioner; Add MS 44541, f. 153; West continued as private sec. until the end of the Session, West, *Recollections*, ii. 48.

[8] The Irish National Education Commissioners had upheld the dismissal by *Cullen of O'Keeffe for taking action in a civil court; a series of court actions resulted; O'Keeffe lost his first agst. Cullen in June 1872; see Norman, *The Catholic Church and Ireland*, 431 ff. Papers etc. at Add MS 44434, f. 54 ff.

[9] *The recollections and reflections of J. R. Planché*, 2v. (1872).

To G. J. GOSCHEN, first lord of the admiralty, 9 July 1872. Add MS 44541, f. 152.

Your facts[1] in relation to the rise in prices are very strong. But I greatly doubt whether on general principles you ought to take a Supplemental Estimate to meet this rise during the present Session. If you do, you may ask more than you may ultimately find you want; but you may also ask less, & may require a second Supplemental Estimate before the close of the year. It is a great & sound rule of financial administration to make a great & serious matter of these Suppl. Estimates, which disturb the *annual* reckoning with the H. of C. It is most important to keep that annual reckoning definite & fixed. This cannot always be done; but in the cases of exception it is important that the disturbance itself should as far as possible be definite & substantive, & not itself liable to the chances of further correction. To mention the state of facts, & to indicate the likelihood of a rectifying estimate before the close of the year would I think be open to no objection.[2]

To A. C. TAIT, archbishop of Canterbury, 9 July 1872. Tait MSS, 90, f. 166.

There is no longer any reason that I am aware of for delaying the Bishops Resignation Bill in the Lords. I am told the Act of Uniformity Bill[3] is also dormant, & to prevent any possibility of mistake I may as well say that I made no request that its progress might be delayed. Indeed I was under the impression that it was desirable to get it out of the way but perhaps you are waiting to settle with those who desired to make amendments in the Bill beyond the scope of the Commons amendments.

10. Wed.

Wrote to Chr of Exr—Ld Chancellor—Ld Devon—Rev Mr Branston—J.S. Wortley—Sir W. Stephenson—Mr Glyn—The Queen (Mem:) mem & l.)—Ld Hartington—Capt. Cole—Dowr Ly Westmoreland—Col. Ponsonby—& minutes. Saw Mr Glyn—Count Bernstorff—Count d'Harcourt—Ld Bathurst—Mrs Th. Cabinet 3-4¾. Garden party in D.St. Attended the Albert Hall Gounod Concert. I was astonished at the progress in musical execution exhibited by the singing of a Chorus of some 800, without any accompaniment or other guide than Gounod's admirable conducting.[4] Read Planché's Memoirs—Creasy on the Constitution.[5]

Cabinet. Wed. Jul. 10. 72. 3 PM.[6]

Ballot. Lords Amendments. Schools: Ld R[ipon] to Communicate with Ld Salisbury: reckon the time agt. the 400 openings. Clause for striking off *a*

[1] Accompanying letter of 8 July, Add MS 44161, f. 206, requesting 'a Supplemental Vote now while the rise in prices is notorious . . .'.

[2] Part in Elliot, *Goschen*, i. 120.

[3] See Marsh, *Victorian church*, 50.

[4] Gounod conducted his setting of Byron's 'Maid of Athens'.

[5] Sir E. S. *Creasy, *The imperial and colonial Constitutions of the Britannic Empire including Indian institutions* (1872).

[6] Add MS 44640, f. 156.

vote: Retain. The time: give in. Illiterate voters declaration: to be made before a registered Elector as witness; preliminary settlement with D. of Richmond.[1]

○ Incl[osu]res.[2] Stand over.

√ O'Keeffe. Talked over.

√ No more College Statute questions to be dealt with by P.C. until report of D. of Cleveland's Commission unless in [ ][3] circumstances.[4]

√ Rumours as to St. Pierre & Miquelon. Best to be silent.[5]

√ Corrupt Practices Bill. Move Speaker out of the Chair after Licensing & Public Health. But cannot undertake to deal with all the Amnts.[6]

√ Order of business. Thurs. 1 Licensing 2R. 2 & 3. Mines Report & Met. mines.[7] Friday: 1: Ballot 2. Public Health.[8]

√ Licensing Bill. Question of closing hours discussed & language agreed on.[9]

11. Th.

Wrote to Dr Newman[10]—Duke of Cambridge—The Queen—and minutes. A large & interesting breakfast party. Radcliffe Trust Annual Meeting 2–4. Saw Count Strzelecki—Lady F. Cavendish respecting Mrs Helbert—Sir W. Heathcote—Mr Forster. Read Planché. H of C. 4¼–8¼ & 10–1½.[11] Mr Balfour dined.

12. Fr.

Wrote to The Queen (2)—Ld Granville (2)—Mr Helps—Ld Chancellor[12]—and minutes. H of C. 2–7 and 9–1½. Spoke on Persian Mission.[13] Saw Mr Carnegie—Mr Ayrton—Mr Glyn—Mr Goschen. Saw Russell—Stansfield X. Read Acland on Health—O'Keeffe's case.

[1] Forster announced on 12 July: the Education Code to be altered so that polling days counted towards the 400 school meetings required; declaration of illiteracy before registered elector sufficient; Act only to work until 1880; *H* ccxii. 1043.

[2] Reading uncertain; see 15 July 72.

[3] Word illegible; possibly 'essential'.

[4] Cleveland commission on university and college property: *PP* 1873 xxxvii.

[5] French islands off Newfoundland; see 21 Oct. 71.

[6] See *H* ccxii. 1124.

[7] Conflation of Metropolitan Tramways and Mines Regulation.

[8] Note passed by Stansfeld reads: 'I can arrange with Lopez not to oppose the Health Bill on the terms of paying half salaries of Medical Officers of Health & Nuisance Inspectors. Shall I do so?' Gladstone replied: 'We understand this to be a temporary arrangement, *without prejudice on either side*?' Add MS 44640, f. 159. See Lopes' speech on Stansfeld's concession: *H* ccxii. 1244.

[9] Clause 24; see Bruce on 27 July; *H* ccxii. 1987.

[10] Unsuccessfully inviting him to breakfast to meet *Argyll; Newman, *Letters and Diaries*, xxvi. 134.

[11] Spoke on corrupt practices; *H* ccxii. 950.

[12] Who had written of his intended retirement; Gladstone requested 'that we shall at least have the benefit of your aid until the Cabinet shall proceed to consider the provision of Bills which it may be expedient to introduce in the coming Session'; Add MS 44541, f. 155.

[13] Opposing placing relations with Persia under the India office; *H* ccxii. 1114.

13. Sat. [Cassiobury Park][1]

Wrote to Mr West—Ld Kimberley—Ld Spencer—Ld Halifax—Abp Manning—Sir T. Biddulph—Scotts—Lady F. Cavendish—Mrs Th. —Ld Hartington—Mr West Tel.—& minutes. Saw Ld Granville—Mr Glyn—Mr West. Luncheon at 15 G.S. Saw Mrs Th. Off to Cassiobury at 4. Began letter to the Queen. Most kindly received as always: & a pleasant evening. Read Planché. Saw Woolidge's Antique Gems.

To ARCHBISHOP H. E. MANNING, 13 July 1872. Add MS 44541, f. 156.
'Private.'

I am afraid the end of the Session is not yet close at hand. We think we have 4 weeks work remaining[?]. As respects the Prison Ministers Bill,[2] I send you a copy of a reply which I recently addressed to a letter from Mr Maguire. In writing to you I may add the expression of my full belief that the adoption or virtual adoption of this measure by the Government at the present juncture would greatly thicken the fight, as well as enlarge its field, & would not improve the chances, such as they may be, of its passing. The causes of this state of things are, as far as they are special, to be found in what has happened abroad, & in Ireland also. You will find me most ready to see you—at 11 any morning except Tuesday, or on Thursday at 10 if you would then kindly join that open institution our open breakfast table.

14. 7 S.Trin.

Watford Ch. mg & evg. Wrote to Mr West Tel.—Sir W. James[3]—Robn G.—& minutes. Read Pere Hyacinthe—Sermon by Ignatius[4] —Womans (Scott) Tract on Prayer &c.—Scott Tract on Pantheism.[5] Dairy in aftn. Made the acquaintance of Mr R. Capel,[6] with pleasure.

15. M. [London]

Wrote to Chancr of Exr—Ld Halifax—Mr Ayrton—Messrs Freshfield—Mrs Th.—Mr Burnett—Robn G.—The Queen (L. and Mem) —and minutes. Back at 12.15: left poor Lord E[bury] suffering

[1] Lord Ebury's.

[2] Manning's letter of 12 July, Add MS 44250, f. 42. See 6 July 72.

[3] Stating J. A. Godley is too inexperienced to fill West's place; Add MS 44541, f. 156; see 9 July, 26 Aug. 72.

[4] J. L. *Lyne [Father Ignatius], probably *Modern infidelity. A sermon* (1870).

[5] A. J., *Conversations*, ed. 'by a woman for women'; F. H. J., 'Spiritual pantheism', published by T. Scott of Ramsgate (1872).

[6] Reginald Algernon Capel, 1830–1906; s. of 6th earl of Essex; G.N.R. director; lived at Little Cassiobury.

much. Saw Ld Granville—Mr Ayrton (2)—Mr Glyn—Mr Grogan—Mr West—Sir T.E. May. H of C. 4¼-8 and 11-2¼.[1] Read Planché.

Mem. Jul. 15. 72.[2]
1. Public Health: tomorrow. 2. Licensing: go on. 3. Corrupt Practices: endeavour to find a day. 4. Local Govt. Ireland. 5. Inclosure Bill: hope to carry. 6. Merchant Shipping. 7. Thames Embankment Bill: for agreeing aft. Supply on Monday. 8. Forster's Education Bill Lords. 9. Army Bill.

1. Keogh—week *after 25th.*[3]
2. Chance of closing in a reasonable time depends upon the concession by Indept. Members of more time on Tuesdays or Weds.

16. Tu.

Wrote to Mr Ayrton—Town Clerk of Liverpool—Mr Gilpin—Mr Fowler—Lord Granville—Dean St Paul's—Sir R. Palmer—The Queen (Parl.)—Ld Hartn—and minutes. Also completed my letter to the Queen & accomp. Mem. on the great question.[4] Saw S. Kensn Officer—Mr Engleheart—Mr West—Mr Burnett—Mr Glyn—Mr Gurdon—Mr W. Hunt. Saw two. H of C. 2½-7 and 9-11.[5] Eight to dinner. Read Planché.

17. Wed.

Wrote to H.N.G.—Sir T. Biddulph—The Queen—Mem: also l. and Mem. to accompany it. It cost me much pain as well as labour. Granville recommended curtailing it & abandoning what relates to herself. C[atherine] reviewed it & suggested some useful softening changes. It is at any rate an act of duty; done upon much reflection. God prosper it.[6] Cabinet 2¾-5½: and wrote to H.M. upon it. Saw Mr Gurdon—S.Kens. Packers[7]—Mr Glyn—Mr West—Ld Ripon—Major Worsley.[8] Drove at 6 to Wimbledon where we dined with Ld & Lady Ducie in their tent & he took me over the whole camp: most pleasant hospitality.[9] Went to Marlborough House Ball after. Read Planché.

[1] Spoke on the govt.'s timetable: *H* ccxii. 1138.
[2] Add MS 44640, f. 162.
[3] i.e. a day for deb.; *Butt's motion moved on 25 July.
[4] See next day.
[5] Public Health Bill: *H* ccxii. 1244.
[6] Victoria had not responded favourably to that of 5 July; Guedalla, *Q*, i. 361.
[7] No account found.
[8] Business untraced.
[9] Preparing for the annual inspection; *The Times*, 22 July 1872, 12a.

Wed. Jul. 17. 72. 2.30.[1]

1. Galway Election. a. A[ttorney] G[eneral] for I[reland] to declare his instructions as to certain parties on Tuesday. b. to move as within in case of need for setting aside James.[2]
2. Order of business: Public Health Tomorrow; Army next; Licensing third; Corr[upt] Pract[ices] to be given up.
3. Case of O'Keeffe in H of L. tomorrow (to come before the courts in Novr.). Govt. not to go further towards identifying itself with the act of the [board of] Commissioners.[3]

√ Hartington's plan for the *tenure* of Irish National Schoolmasters as to notice adopted.

√ Scotch Education Bill. As to the Board—be considered outside & Cabinet summoned if nec[essar]y.[4]

Subjects for 1873[5]

1. Public Health (residue). 2. Appellate Jurisdiction & Courts of Judicature. 3. 'Local Taxation': in how many branches. 4. Irish University Education. (5. Ireland. Ld Lieutenancy). 6. London—municipal reform. 7. Land Transfer Inheritance & Settlement. 8. Corrupt Practices. 9. Currency &c. &c.

18. Th.

Wrote to Mr Engleheart—The Queen—& minutes. Breakfast party. Ten to dinner. Saw Ld F. Cavendish[6]—Ld Hartington—Mr West—Att.Gen. Ireland—Mr Glyn—Ld Granville—Ld Halifax—Mr Burnett *cum* Mr Fowler[7]—Mr Monsell—Mr Gilpin—Lord Spencer. H of C. 4¼-8¼ and 9½-2¾.[8] Read Planché. Saw Graham: with hope [R].

19. Fr.

Wrote to Ld Spencer (2)—Mr Fortescue—The Queen—& minutes. Dined with Mr Glyn. Saw Mr Gurdon—Mr Stansfeld—Mr Glyn—Ld Hartington—Col. W. Patten. Read Planché—Life of Keogh.[9] H of C. 2-6 and 9-2½.[10] Garden party in D. St.

[1] Add MS 44640, f. 160.

[2] Draft motion at Add MS 44760, f. 181. H. James defended Keogh on 25 July: *H* ccxii. 1819.

[3] See 9 July 72n.

[4] See 24 July 72.

[5] Initialled and dated 17 July 1872; Add MS 44640, f. 164.

[6] Who succeeded West as private sec., see 23 July 72.

[7] Case of Gladstone's agent's son, dismissed from the Metropolitan Railway for incompetence; see Add MS 44541, f. 159.

[8] Questioned on Canadian defence; *H* ccxii. 1365.

[9] Perhaps *A record of traitorism; or the political life and adventures of Mr Justice Keogh*, the *Nation*, June 1872.

[10] Statement on Commons business, claiming Tuesdays for the govt.; *H* ccxii. 1417.

To EARL SPENCER, Irish lord lieutenant, Add MS 44541, f. 159.
19 July 1872.

I found Hartington leaning & more decidedly than you did, to the dismissal of Granard. Dowse disposed to encourage his resignation. I consulted 6 or 8 colleagues in both houses after seeing Hartington & found every one clear & distinct against dismissal. All would I think be glad if Ld. G. disappeared by a voluntary act & by himself.[1] Some wished he could be encouraged to go though feeling that a Government can only suggest resignation out of kindness to the individual i.e. when if he does not resign he will be dismissed. This is I think the substance to which I will only add on my own account that I shall be glad if you are rid of an indiscreet Ld. Lieutenant, though sorry that his disappearance should change to give a sort of triumph to a man who is far from deserving one. I also think that any official suggestion to him at this moment would be specially dangerous if it could be used to support the change. But we were endeavouring by this means to shelter our own supposed delinquency *in re* Keogh.
I gave Bateman a dilatory reply. Stands for Monday.

20. Sat. [Hatfield House]

Wrote to Ld Granville—Duke of Cambridge—Mr A Peel—The Queen (Mema)—and minutes. Off to Hatfield at 5. Saw Mr B. Benjamin—Mr Bowman—Mr Glyn—Ld F. Cavendish—Mr West—Mr Gurdon—Ld Greville. Luncheon & conversation with Mr & Mrs Th. at 15 G.S. Most kindly received—as always. Read Planché.

21. 9 S.Trin.

Hatfield Ch. & H.C. mg. Then looked at the Church & Monuments, Chapel service evg. Walk in aft. Read M'Coll on Ath. Creed[2]—Ramsgate Tracts.[3]

21. [sc. 22] M. [London]

Lady S. drove me up to town: in thunder and rain following the extreme heat & brilliancy of the morning. Wrote to The Lord Mayor—The Spanish Minister[4]—The Queen (2)—Mr B. Benjamin—and minutes. Saw Mr Glyn—Mr Ayrton—Sir S. Northcote—do *cum* Ld

[1] On 22 July 1872, *H* ccxii. 1498, Granard announced his resignation as ld. lieut. of Leitrim rather than embarrass the government over his comments on the Keogh affair, 'without the slightest pressure having been put on me' by the government.

[2] M. *MacColl, 'The "Damnatory Clauses" of the Athanasian Creed . . . in a letter to Gladstone' (1872).

[3] i.e. sent by T. *Scott; see 2 June 72n.

[4] Regretting attempted assassination of the king of Spain; Add MS 44541, f. 161.

Halifax—Mr Forster—Sir J. Lubbock. Much trouble respecting the Ayrton controversies.[1] H. of C. 4¼–8 and 9¼–1¼.[2] Read Planché.

23. Tu.

Wrote to Ld Lurgan—Circular to official members—Miss Berry[R]—The Queen—and minutes. Read Planché. Saw Mr Gurdon—Ld F. Cavendish: for the first time as Priv.Sec.[3]—Mr Glyn—Mr Forster—Mr Ayrton—Mr Bruce—Sothebys.[4] H of C. 2¼–7 and 9–2¼.[5] Eight to dinner. Went to Sir T.G.s with C. A great afflictive trial, with rays of hope.[6]

Circular to Members of Government not in the Cabinet.[7]
The state of public business renders it necessary that I should call your attention to the inconveniences, which will arise if the members of the Government are absent from the House of Commons during the remaining discussion on the Estimates & on Government Bills. And I must express my hope that you will be able to make your arrangements for a continuous attendance in the House during the remainder of the Session.

To BARON LURGAN, lord lieutenant of Armagh, 23 July 1872. Add MS 44541, f. 161.

I have communicated with the Ld. Lieutenant on the subject of your very kind letter[8] & he will give me his advice after his return to Ireland which is to take place almost immediately. There was no authority for the announcement in the Morning Post. On every ground both of gratitude & of policy, I look for the time when my engagement of such long standing may be fulfilled. But the Galway Election, followed by the Keogh Judgment, has imparted a new element of distraction into the case, for it will I find be the duty of the Attorney General under the Statute to institute rather extended prosecutions & these may cause much excitement in a large part of Ireland. If however the result of our further reflections should be that the visit is to take place I shall take the liberty of writing to you further. In the mean time I will only ask you to accept my sincere thanks.

24. Wed.

Wrote to The Queen—Mr Ayrton—Scotts—and minutes. Cabinet

[1] This time, about Kew Gardens and Hyde Park; Gladstone had asked Ayrton to have his statement checked by a 'Minister who has looked into the papers' before presenting it; 14 July 1872, Add MS 44541, f. 157; see 24 July 72.
[2] Questioned on Granard's 'spontaneous' resignation; *H* ccxii. 1518; see 19 July 72.
[3] Succeeding *West.
[4] The auctioneers.
[5] Questioned on political deportations to France, declining to expel the Jesuits, and spoke on the army; *H* ccxii. 1623, 1644.
[6] Apparently his brother's toryism; extant letters suggest no family crisis.
[7] Copy dated 23 July 1872, Add MS 44541, f. 161.
[8] Untraced; Lurgan was an active liberal and a Lord in Waiting; see 15 Dec. 68.

2¾-6. Went to Mansion House dinner & returned thanks for Ministers.[1] Saw Ld Chancellor—Mr Stansfeld—Mr Glyn—Scotts. Read Q.R. on Stuarts[2]—Planché Vol. II.

Cabinet. Wed. July 24. 72. 2½ PM.[3]

√ Local Taxation. The County Members. WEG to endeavour to frame a[nswer] consulting C of E[xchequer], Goschen, & Stansfeld.[4]
√ Irish Railways. No present Declaration required.
O Irish Visit.
√ Galway Debate, Course of it considered.
√ Cape. Responsible Govt. Bill to be assented to. Carried by maj[ority] of one.[5]
√ Park Rules. Mr Ayrton heard. WEG instructed to write. Comm[ittee] of Cabinet appointed.[6]
√ Scotch Educn. Bill. Preamble. A new form to be adopted. Other parts settled: except initiative in framing the code: Ld Adv[ocate] to propose in H. of C. to secure it for P.C., not Scottish Board.[7]
√ Mr Benjamin—to have a Patent of Precedence.
Mr Stansfeld respecting R. Confed[?] (to be in D. St).
Ld Granville—Duchy—12.45 tomorrow.[8]

25. Th.

Wrote to Mr Scudamore—Chancr of Exr—Mr Ayrton—Mr Bruce—The Queen—Mr Bright (Tel.)—and minutes. Saw P.M. General—Ch of Exr—Ld Granville—do *cum* Mr Glyn—Abp Manning—Mr Bowman—Mr M'Coll—Mr Boodle—Lord F.C. H of C. 4¼-8¼ & 9½-3¼.[9] Dined with the J. Talbots. Read Planché.—Q.R. on Taine.[10]

To R. LOWE, chancellor of the exchequer, 25 July 1872. Add MS 44541, f. 162.

Monsell has been to me in great distress about the Telegraphic Establishment & I have received the recent letter in the case. I promised him that I would ask you to be so good as to meet him in *my* room behind the Chair tomorrow when the House goes into Committee on the Licensing Bill which will probably be soon after two.
Ayrton has agreed to make the statement required.

[1] *The Times*, 25 July 1872, 12a, which noticed Gladstone 'was welcomed with the heartiest applause'.
[2] *Quarterly Review*, cxxxiii. 167 (July 1872).
[3] Add MS 44640, f. 165.
[4] Given on 1 August; review in the recess, with hope of proposals; *H* ccxiii. 245; see 11, 14 Oct. 72n.
[5] Assenting to Molteno's Responsible Government Bill passed at the Cape 15 June 1872; C. F. Goodfellow, *Great Britain and South African Confederation* (1966), 43.
[6] Notes for new rules at Add MS 44640, f. 167.
[7] Thus effectively controlling Scottish education from Whitehall; see G. Sutherland, *Policy-making in elementary education 1870-1895* (1973), 14 and 31 July 72. A board of education was established in Edinburgh, subordinate to the P.C.
[8] See 26 July 72.
[9] Spoke on Keogh's judgment; *H* ccxii. 1847.
[10] *Quarterly Review*, cxxxiii. 199 (July 1872).

To F. I. SCUDAMORE, second secretary at Post Office, 25 July 1872. Add MS 44541, f. 162.

I have received your letter[1] with much interest & have seen Mr Monsell. I have invited the C. of E. to see me tomorrow with the P.M.G. & I hope the result will be satisfactory. You may be assured that my opinion of you & my disposition to attach weight to your judgment are the same as when I had ample opportunities of forming them on the sure basis of personal experience, the same in substance only corroborated by the constant ripening of the results of your labours. In '68 as far as my memory goes, on hearing the statement with which the Bill of that year was introduced, I thought there were several points which presented difficulty & required explanation. For this explanation I sincerely hoped as I had from the first been favourable in principle to the plan & had moved Ld Stanley to set you upon the execution of it. One thing only appeared in '68 to be vital, it was the monopoly, & this in '69 we obtained. I still look constantly at the Post Office Savings Bank figures & am delighted to see the steady fattening of the account.

26. Fr.

Wrote to Ld Spencer—Ld Aylesbury—The Queen—& minutes. H of C. 2¼-7 and 10½-1¾.[2] Read Planché. Saw Lord F.C.—Mr Glyn—Mr M'Clure—Mr Monsell *cum* Mr Lowe. Dined with Mr Glyn: & then had a long & promising conversation with Mr Bright about his taking the Duchy.[3] Saw Ld Halifax—Attorney General.

27. Sat. [Ashridge]

Wrote to Mr Burnett—The Queen Mem.—and minutes. H of C. 2¼-3¾.[4] Off at 4¼ to Ashridge.[5] Saw Lord F.C.—Mrs Th.—and various calls. We had a charming evening at Ashridge. Lady Marion, Mr Browning, Ld & Lady B. & Lady G. were the attractions. The trees seemed more wonderful than ever.

28. 9 S.Trin.

Ch mg & Chapel at 3½ P.M.—Organ for an hour or more in evg; very delightful—Mary played some. Wrote to Sir R. Wallace. Walk in the endless glades and conversation with Lady B[rownlow] about the Queen & Princess, & high matters. Read M'Coll on Ath. Creed[6]—Arg. for the Extinction of the Lost[7]—Père Hyacinthe Ref. Catholique.[8]

[1] Of 24 July, on the funds of the telegraphic dept.; Add MS 44434, f. 289.

[2] Licensing Bill: *H* ccxii. 1890.

[3] And on his attitude to Keogh; Walling, *Diaries of John Bright*, 349. Bright had a further hour with Gladstone, on Keogh, next day. He declined the duchy by letter on 30 July; ibid., 350.

[4] Licensing Bill: *H* ccxii. 1954.

[5] Lord Brownlow's; see 25 June 70.

[6] See 21 July 72.

[7] Untraced tract.

[8] See 7 July 72.

29. M. [London]

Returned to C.H.T. at 12.20. Wrote to The Queen (2)—Mr Burnett—Ld Huntley—& minutes. Saw Mr Engleheart—Ld Hartington—Ld F.C.—Att. General—Mr Glyn—Ld Granville—Mr Capel—Mr Stansfeld—Mr Lowe—Mr Leeman. H. of C. 4¼-8¼ and 10-2¼.[1] Read Planché—Abel on Gun Cotton.[2] Dined with Sir W. James.

30. Tu.

Wrote to Watson & Smith—Mr M'C. Torrens—Mr Leeman—Bp of Moray—Ld Mayor—The Queen (2)—and minutes. Saw Sir R. Phillimore (2)—Lord F.C.—Mr & Mrs Th.—Mr Glyn—Sol. General. Dined with the F. Cavendishes. H of C. 9¾-2½.[3] But kept off the bench. Read Planché—Galveston[4]—Hebrera [*sic*]—Q.R.

In the morning we learned by Tel. the very sudden death of my brother in law Henry Glynne in his peaceful house a little after 5 A.M.[5] What a breach & wrench of all our calmly settled life. Much there will be to weigh. Much there is to feel: most for Stephen; & for Mary Glynne—even more than Gertrude. In 33 years of close relationship I have not had from or with him an unkind word. Peace & rest be his in his Saviour Christ.

31. Wed.

Wrote to The Queen (l., Tel, & Mem.)—Ld Spencer (Tel)—Ld Huntley—Ld Advocate—Mr Bright—Mr Rathbone—Bp of Rochester—& minutes. Family dinner: (F.C.s & L[yttelto]n:). Saw Sir John Lubbock—Sir S. Northcote—Sir W.C. James—Mr Burke—Sir Thos Gladstone—Mr Glyn—Mr Rathbone—Ld F.C.—Ld Granville—Ld Halifax—Read Planché. H of C. 12¼-2. Spoke on Eccl. Courts Bill.[6] Cabinet 2¾-5¾. Calls. Saw Griffiths X.

Cabinet. Wed. Jul. 31. 72. 2½ PM.[7]

√ Irish Nat. School Teachers. Notice on dismissal. Ld Hart[ingto]n's proposal agreed to. (Increase of Sal[ary] on condition of accepting the term of notice).

√ O'Keeffe. Take an opinion of the L[aw] O[fficers] as to the best effect any

[1] Navy estimates; *H* ccxiii. 50.

[2] Sir F. A. Abel, 'On explosive agents applicable to naval and military uses, as substitutes for gunpowder' (1872); see 1 Aug. 72!

[3] Jervoise (see next day) and Scottish education: *H* ccxiii. 160.

[4] *Galveston . . . By the author of 'Milly Clifford'* (1868).

[5] He told Sir W. Farquhar on 29 August 1872, Add MS 44542, f. 3, 'He owed his death to lightning, & to perseverance in the work of his calling after he had been touched by it.'

[6] *H* ccxiii. 193.

[7] Add MS 44640, f. 171.

decision in the suit against Card[inal] Cullen may have on O'Keeffe's position.

√ Writers. Discussed. Given 1/-.[1]

√ Agent at Rome. Refer to L.O. whether there is anything illegal.[2]

√ Scotch Educn. Amendment as to prep[aratio]n of code considered & words agreed on for amending in case of need. D[itt]o Scotch Education Department: Ld Pres[ident], Duke of A[rgyll], Mr Gladstone, Chancr. of Exr., Mr Bruce, Mr. Forster, Ld Advocate. Edinburgh Board of Education. *2 Unpaid*: Ld. Adv[ocate], Sir W. Stirling Maxwell. *3 Paid*: [blank].[3]

√ French expedition.[4] Grin & bear for the present.

Thurs Aug. One 1872.

Wrote to C.G. (l. & Tel.)—S.R.G. (Tel.)—The Queen (2 l.)—Mr Burnett—Ld Granard—Mr Engleheart—Mr Monsell—& minutes. Saw Mr Childers (who resumes Office—The Duchy)[5]—Sir E. Landseer—most touching—and (respecting him) The Lord Chancellor—Ld Essex—Sir R. Phillimore—Chr of Exr—Sir S. Northcote—Mr Stansfeld—Mr Goschen—Saw Russell X no progress.

Gun Cotton experiments in D. St Garden 2½-3½. A good hundred panes shattered, contrary to assurances: but the operation was most remarkable.[6] The Phillimores dined, with the F.C.s & C. L[yttelton]. H. of C. 4¼-8 and 9¼-4.[7]

To EARL SPENCER, Irish lord lieutenant, 1 August 1872. Add MS 44541, f. 166.

1. Your appointment to the Ld. Lieutenancy of Northamptonshire will now go forward—and Granville has written a very good letter to the Duke of Grafton who would have been the proper man had you not been on the ground.
2. I am afraid the case for the Leitrim Lieutenancy hardly admits of our appointing Tenison.[8] I agree with you that Southwell is the proper man all things considered. Let me know when you wish me to act.
3. I hope to hear from you on the question of my visiting Ireland.[9] Mr McClure whom I should think rather a good judge agrees with me that the matter is still unripe. The Galway prosecutions are a material element in the case, as it appears to me.

[1] Temporary writers in civil service; see *H* ccxiii. 251.

[2] C. J. Monk on 30 July questioned the legality of Jervoise's position as agent to the Roman states, the Pope having lost his sovereignty; *H* ccxiii. 153. Gladstone was 'sorely puzzled' about Jervoise; see Ramm I, ii. 337, 341.

[3] See 24 July 72n.

[4] Phrase in brackets here illegible.

[5] After his illness, and Bright having refused it; see 26 July 72.

[6] Demonstration of effectiveness of gun-cotton in felling trees, organised by Sir Frederick *Abel, 1827-1902, chemist. See West, *Recollections*, ii. 58.

[7] Public Health Bill: *H* ccxiii. 260.

[8] Edward King Tenison, already lord lieut. of Roscommon; 4th Viscount Southwell was appt. *vice* Granard; see 19 July 72 and Add MS 44307, f. 127.

[9] Reply untraced.

2. Fr.

Wrote to The Queen—Robn G.—C.G.—Sir R. Phillimore—and minutes. Wrote part Draft of Speech from the Throne. Saw Mr Farrer —S.E.G.—Mr West—Ld F.C.—Mr Engleheart—Sol Genl—Sir J. Hanmer—Chr of Exr—Ld Hartington—Mr Ayrton—Att.Gen. Ireland.—Mr Cardwell. H of C. 2¾-7 and 9-2½.[1] Saw Mr & Mrs Th. (at luncheon). Read Planché.

3. Sat. [*Hawarden*]

Wrote to J. Watson & S.—The Queen Mem & 2 l—Lord Huntley—Ld Granville—Mr G.O. Morgan—and minutes. H. of C. 12¾-7½. We closed supply.[2] Saw Sir J. Lubbock—Mr Pringle—Mr Branston(?) —Mr Glyn—Sir A. Panizzi—Mr Goschen—Mr Pringle [*sic*]—& others. Off with W. at 8.40 by Mail. Reached Hawarden between 3½ and 4.

4. 10 S.Trin.

Ch. mg & evg. We sat near the door. The Church crowded: the people in mourning. Mr Chamberlain preached well. Wrote to Mr Glyn—and minutes. Read Ramsgate Tracts—C. Elisabeth's Memoirs.[3] Much conversation with Stephen who bears up well. Also with Phillimore —and Catherine.

5. M. [*London*]

At 8.30 we all went to Holy Communion. Our seven children all knelt there. The funeral was before 12. We walked from the Rectory round to the great gate of the Church Yard: & from thence to the open grave. The Church was crowded & there were crowds without: many (Phillimore said) were in tears. And so he went to his last home. Peace be with him in Christ our Lord.

Saw Sir R. Phillimore—Dr Moffat—Dr Waters[4]—Mr Barker—Mr Burnett—Mr Brewster—Archdn Ffoulkes. At 3.40 off to London—Much conversation with Stephy on the great question of the living, offered him by his uncle.[5]—Reached H of C. at 11.10—Spoke on the O'Keeffe Case.[6]—Home at 3.45 A.M.

[1] Licensing Bill: *H* ccxiii. 314.
[2] With further deb. on Jervoise; *H* ccxiii. 425.
[3] Perhaps E. Hervey, Countess of Bristol, *Life and memoirs* (1788).
[4] Edward Waters, physician in Chester.
[5] i.e. Sir Stephen Glynne; he accepted it.
[6] Defending the Irish education board; *H* ccxiii. 535; see 9 July 72n.

6. Tu.

Wrote to Ld Sefton—Mr Maguire—Mr West—Mr Levy—C.G.—The Queen (2)—S.R.G.—Lady Clarendon—and minutes. Saw Mrs Th X. House of C. 2-6 & 9-10½.[1] Dined with Mr Glyn. Saw Sir J. Lubbock—Mr Ayrton—Lord F.C.—Att. General—Mr Glyn—Lord Hartington—D. of Argyll—and others.

To E. LEVY[-LAWSON], 6 August 1872. Add MS 44541, f. 167.

As I am (I believe) summoned to Guildford tomorrow to give evidence for the defendants in the Action brought by Leonard Edmunds,[2] I think it but fair to tell you that if the Counsel for the Plaintiff does his duty, my evidence can be of no manner of use to the side for which I am called. The question is did I sign a certain minute.

I am told I did and I can see no reasons why I should or might; but I have no recollection on the subject and can neither, as matter of fact, affirm or deny it. You will therefore I hope hold me acquitted if your (I believe very just) cause does not derive from me the expected profit but the reverse and I should be glad that the other defendants should through your kindness know as much.

7. Wed.

Wrote to C.G.[3]—Ld Northbrook—Mr Levy—Col. Kingscote—and minutes. At 11.20 off to Guildford. Back at 3.10—unexamined! with L. & S.[4] Saw Chr of Exr—Mr Glyn—Mr Stansfeld—Ld F.C.—Att. General—S.E.G.—Baron L. Rothschild—Baroness do—Gen. Sherman[5]—Duke of Argyll—Sir W. James—High Constable of Sussex. Gurdon & F.C. dined. Lady Ripon's afterwards. Consulted various Colleagues on the Paragraphs of the Speech in draft wh touch their Bills respectively. H. of C. 3.10-6.[6] Saw Mrs Murray—and [blank] [R].

To E. LEVY[-LAWSON], 7 August 1872. Add MS 44541, f. 169.

In spite of all remonstrations we were taken down to Guildford this forenoon: & then sent back unexamined. According to all appearances, this has been a very wanton & flagrant use of power & directions will be given to get the whole of the facts clearly before us. Do not suppose that in saying this I am less sensible than I was yesterday of the kindness of your letter;[7] but I thought it right to mention our intentions to trace[?] the matter home.

[1] Indian budget; *H* ccxiii. 562.

[2] See next day's n.

[3] See Bassett, 194.

[4] Series of unsuccessful libel actions against London newspapers by Edmunds (see 21 July 57) for printing the treasury minute (see 22 June 72); *The Times*, 8 August 1872, 11a.

[5] William Tecumseh Sherman, 1820-91; United States general, on leave in Europe 1871-2.

[6] Licensing Bill; *H* ccxiii. 650.

[7] Untraced.

8. Th.

Wrote to Ld Chancellor—Gen. Sherman[1]—Mrs Th.—Dr L. Playfair—C.G.—Sir W.S. Maxwell—M.A. Berry[2]—The Queen (2)—& minutes. Dined with Mr Foster. H of C. $3\frac{3}{4}$-$8\frac{3}{4}$ and $10\frac{1}{2}$-4.[3] Saw Mr Clark Jervoise[4]—Mr Warwick Brooks—Sir J. Lubbock—Mr Glyn—Sir W. James—Mr Locke King—Mr Fawcett. Cabinet 2-$3\frac{3}{4}$ for the Speech. Finished & sent it off. Read Powell—on Australia.[5]

Cabinet. Aug. 8. 2½ PM.[6]
Queen's Speech.
Att. Gen. for I[reland]—is it important that *he* should prosecute?[7]
Order in Council to relieve Officers (nearly =), who did not do it before 1868, from taking their Oaths before the *Queen in Council.*[8]

9. Fr.

Wrote to Ld Chancellor—The Queen (Mem.)—C.G.—Mr Fleming—& minutes. Went around to Mrs Th (luncheon)—Sir E. Landseer (saw Miss L.)[9]—Lady Beaconsfield (to inquire)[10]—Mrs Tyler—the T.G.s—the Wortleys—and business. Packing, and preparations for departure. Dined with A. Panizzi. Saw Mrs Th. in evg. That has been a mysterious destiny. God prosper it.

10. Sat. [*Hawarden*]

Wrote to Mr R. Allen—Mr Williamson—Mr Caird—Archbp Manning—Sir W. James—Lord Dalhousie—Sir R. Palmer—Ld Prov. of Perth[11]—Sir A. Helps—and minutes. Packing & putting away. Luncheon with Mrs Th. on my way to the Train 2.45-$8\frac{1}{4}$ when I reached Hawarden. Saw Sir A. Helps—Mr Capel—Rev S.E.G.—Mr Glyn—Mr Gurdon—Mr Westell. Unpacking books &c. at Hawarden in the Temple of Peace. Read Echoes of a famous Year.[12]

[1] Regretting mourning for H. Glynne prevents his being invited to Hawarden; Add MS 44541, f. 170.
[2] Apparently the rescue case; see 20 Dec. 71.
[3] Spoke on Hooker and Kew gardens: *H* ccxiii. 752.
[4] (Sir) Harry Samuel Cumming Clarke Jervoise, 1832-1911; diplomat; British representative in Rome 1870-4; in F.O. 1878-94. See 31 July 72n.
[5] See 13 May 72.
[6] Add MS 44640, f. 177.
[7] i.e. should prosecute 'the bishop of Clonfert and some 20 priests' in the Keogh case, deb. this day: *H* ccxiii. 782; the case was not heard till Feb. 1873, and most of the prosecutions were abandoned.
[8] But apparently not done in 1872.
[9] On Landseer's mental instability.
[10] Her poor health became much worse on 17 July; she left London in September and died on 15 December; Buckle, v. 223.
[11] Unable to visit Perth to receive its freedom; Add MS 44541, f. 172.
[12] By H. *Parr (1872).

11. 11 S.Trin.

Ch mg & evg. Mr Brewster & Mr Cooper[1] preached, each extremely well. Wrote to Chancr of Exr—and minutes. Conversation with Mr B. respecting Stephy & his Parish[2]—Also with C. on this & much beside. Read Wedgwood on J. Wesley.[3]

12. M.

Ch. 8½ AM. Wrote to Mr Browning—Dean Ramsay—S.E.G.—Ld Granville—and minutes. Spent the morning chiefly in ransacking & arranging letters and papers. Read Brassey's Life[4]—Tylor's Early Culture.[5]

13. Tu.

Ch. 8½ AM. Wrote to Dean Ramsay—Chancr of Exr—Mr Capel—Mrs Th.—& minutes. Long conversation with Mr Burnett. Then we walked up to Aston Hall Works to survey the Rail there: & home over part of the Prescott Estate, seeing a few of the new Tenants. The whole body now pass a hundred. Read Jas Smith's Remains[6]—Brassey's Life. Spent the morning in writing a paper on the meaning of the word *ἀμύμων*.[7] I have not done such a thing since taking office in Decr 1868.

To R. LOWE, chancellor of the exchequer, 13 August 1872. **Add MS 44541, f. 173.**

Having now had time to read the letter of the Associated Railway Companies respecting the duty on Third Class Passenger Receipts, I send it for any remarks which you may be inclined to make. I understand the Companies to contend first, that it is the duty of the Board of Trade, not of any Revenue Department, to construe & apply the Law which grants an exemption on certain conditions in respect of such Passengers, & second, that the trains on which it is proposed to levy the duty for their third class passengers do the work of that large part of the community with greater advantage to them than did the trains to which Parliament granted the exemption, & thus are within the spirit no less than (as they think) the letter of them. But I only know their case from this communication.

[1] See 22 Sept. 42 and James Hughes Cooper, d. 1909, rector of Tarporley 1865–88; Hawarden Visitors Book.

[2] See 5 Aug. 72.

[3] J. *Wedgwood, *John Wesley* (1870).

[4] Sir A. *Helps, *Life and labours of Mr Brassey, 1805–70* (1872).

[5] See 24 May 72.

[6] G. *Pritchard, *Remains of... James Smith ... being extracts from letters and sketches of sermons* (1840).

[7] 'blameless' or 'excellent'. He sent his notes next day to R. *Scott for comment, observing 'with the common rendering of which as "blameless" I have never been satisfied'; Add MS 44541, f. 174.

14. Wed.

Ch 8½ A.M. Wrote to Duke of Bedford[1]—Mr Bouverie—Sir Thos G. —Sir H. Elliot—Mr Barnes—Ld Brougham—S.E.G.—Provost of Dundee[2]—Mr Gurdon—The Queen (Mem.)—Dean of Rochester—Mr Gurdon (2 Tel.)—& minutes. Inspected the Railway with Mr Burnett from the River up to Aston Bank. Saw Mr Burnett. Read Brassey's Life—Tylor on Early Culture.

To E. P. BOUVERIE, M.P., 14 August 1872. Add MS 44541, f. 174.

You have probably been in communication with the priest O'Keeffe: at any rate you take a deep & friendly interest in his case. And I know of no one whom I can so properly address on the subject that I now have in view. Let me call your attention (1) to his letter of Aug. 8.[3] But it is very long—the material part is only from p. 7: though it is curious, in the preceding part, that he seems to accept the recent Dogma as an innocuous thing—(2) to my minute of Aug. 10 written just before I left my house for the Railway. (3) to his short reply dated Aug. 12. It appears to me that he is making a great mistake, injuriously to himself: but that some one, who like you has distinctly befriended him, can more easily convince him of it than I can. In the first letter, he complains of my language—in the second, only of the inaction of the Government; but he sticks to his charge, which as it seems to me it is for his interest to abandon. He takes no notice of the fact that both Hartington & I have expressed our dissent from the proceeding of the Education Board, while that of the Poor Law Commissioners has never (to my knowledge) been brought under discussion. Why should he treat our inaction as hostility? The error of the Education Board consisted in not recognizing the *status quo*. We should repeat that error were we now to reverse their act. It *may* be that the civil court will give a judgment sustaining Cardinal Cullen. I do not know this, but as the case is defended it is my duty to presume so much. How absurd would be the position if we were to restore Father O'Keeffe against the National Board and the Poor Law Commissioners (I am not aware of any distinction in principle between the 2 cases) & then, as a legitimate consequence of failure in his suit, he were a second time to be put out. I put the argument thus, not as against you, for I hope you agree that finding the thing done, and not having been accessories before the fact, we are right in letting it stand till the suit is settled, as we understand that suit will virtually carry the judgment of the court on O'Keeffe's position. But, let him take the cases as he will, & even if we are governed by a hostile *animus* (of which I do not think the H. of C. saw any proof) it is surely most impolitic in him to withdraw at this juncture & thereby shut out (as far as I can see) the possibility of any legitimate proceeding in his favour. With this view of the facts, I shall make no answer to his letter of Aug. 12 until I hear from you. And I hope you may induce him either to withdraw it, or at least to relinquish the *attitude* in which he wrote it, so that things may go regularly forward. You will perceive that I am

[1] Offering him the Garter; he declined on account of age; Granville docketed 'very queer ... it must be the £1000 [fee]'; Add MSS 44541, f. 175, 44434, f. 97.

[2] Cannot attend to accept freedom of the city; Add MS 44541, f. 175.

[3] Add MS 44435, f. 35.

not writing in the interest of mere party convenience. The course which he seems to announce would save us from trouble. Neither do I in the least blame him: on the contrary, I respect the courage he has shewn, & I do not doubt he has been hard driven & worried beyond endurance—ever since I became first acquainted with some of the facts of the case—which was on the printing of the papers—I have felt its deep importance. It is the sense of this importance which now induces me to trouble you at so much length, & which will, I hope, induce you to forgive the intrusion.[1]

15. Th.

Ch. 8½ A.M. Wrote to Sec.Met.Dist. Railway[2]—Messrs Freshfield—Mr Bruce—Mr Etwall[3]—Mr Glyn—Mr R. Burnett (Tel)—Scotts—The Queen (2)—Robn G.—Ld Provost of Glasgow—and minutes. Saw Mr Burnett. Conversation with C. on family matters and plans. Today we hear of Stephy's acceptance of the Parish: an event in his history, & ours.[4] May God guide him in this & all his ways. Read Brassey's Life (finished)—Tylor on Early Culture.

16. Fr.

Ch. 8½ AM. Wrote to Messrs Watson & Smith—Dean Ramsay—Mrs Th.—Chancr of Exr—Mr Capel—Sir H. Elliot—Abp of Syra—& minutes. Tried some lines of Sh[ield] of Achilles. Saw Mr Elliot from Massachusetts on the subject of transmitting Art Collections to America.[5] Cut part of a dead beech. Read Tylor—Art. on Paulicians[6]—Aubrey de Vere's St Patrick.[7]

To C. W. ELLIOT, of Boston, U.S.A., 16 August 1872. Add MS 44541, f. 176.

With reference to our conversation of this day, I may as well put on paper the promise which I made to this effect that if (as is probable) the idea with which you came to me should prove unavailable, I shall be happy to place at the service of the Boston Society which you described to me, from the summer of 1873 to Easter 1874, a collection which I possess of Italian Cinque Cento Jewels (as they are termed) & other works in metal, should there be a desire to make use of it.

[1] Secretary making the copy adds: '(Papers enclosed)'.
[2] The railway in which Gladstone continued to hold shares had just made agreements with the G.W.R.; see A. Edmonds, *History of the Metropolitan District Railway* (1973), 72.
[3] Had applied unsuccessfully for a job; Add MS 44541, f. 176.
[4] He was rector of Hawarden until 1904.
[5] Charles Wemyss Elliot of the Boston Household Arts Society, staying at Colwyn Bay. Elliot's first suggestion appears to have been an exhibition of Gladstone's china, already on view in Liverpool.
[6] Untraced.
[7] A. T. de *Vere, *The legends of St Patrick* (1872).

Part of this collection, though it is small, is of a more rare & costly character than the collection of porcelain at Liverpool. As respects the porcelain (which is of the English, German, & Italian fabrics only) I have felt myself precluded from anything which might appear like an indirect attempt to withdraw from Liverpool a part of what I had freely tendered & given it for a seven years loan. It might happen that you should find that the authority of the Museum there do not desire to retain it, from finding it less appreciated than had been expected, or otherwise. In that case I certainly would not interpose any bar to its going to America for a time. Whatever may be the upshot of this particular portion of your quest, I must again assure you of the lively interest & satisfaction with which I heard from you that the idea of obtaining from Europe works of art executed by former generations has now taken hold of root in America. I believe that the energetic prosecution of this idea will afford the best means of fostering & developing among your countrymen the love of Beauty, a passion which no country has ever yet indulged in to excess, unless possibly the Athenians of some 2,200 years ago, & the Italians of the 15th Century: & that you will thus supply your civilisation with an element altogether indispensable to its perfection.

17. Sat.

Ch. 8½ AM. Wrote to Lord Granville—Dean Ramsay—Mr Erle Q.C.—& minutes. Cutting wood with W. & H. Wrote on Homer. Read Tylor—A. de Vere's St Patrick—Ilgen's Prolog. to the Hymns[1]—Hermann do[2]—Hymn to Delian Apollo.

18. 12 S.Trin.

Ch mg (with H.C.) and Evg. (Albert Lyttn preached). Wrote to Sir H. Holland—Mr Childers—Dean Hook—Bp Jenner—Mr Mayow—and minutes. Conversation with A. L[yttelton]. Read Bp of Lincoln on Congress[3]—D. of Westmr on Ath. Creed[4]—and other tracts.

To Sir H. G. ELLIOT, ambassador to Turkey, 18 August 1872. Add MS 44541, f. 179.

The Archbishop of Syra has addressed to me a long & very interesting letter on the Bulgarian Schism in which he sets forth his views with much clearness & ability. With the nature of them you are familiar. I have at his request addressed to him my reply through the Embassy, & I trouble you with a copy of it as I am desirous you should know exactly (& I hope you may approve) what I have said to him.[5] From the first I have deeply regretted the Bulgarian quarrel, without

[1] Untraced introduction by C. D. Ilgen on Homer.
[2] J. G. J. Hermann, *Homeri hymni et epigrammata* (1806).
[3] C. *Wordsworth, 'Old Catholic Congress. A letter on . . . the Congress at Cologne' (1872).
[4] A. P. *Stanley, *The Athanasian Creed* (1871).
[5] Copy also sent to Musurus, the Turkish ambassador; Add MS 44541, f. 181.

knowing the rights of it, & I still continue to regard it as a quarrel dangerous to the East.[1]

To A. LYKOURGOS, archbishop of Syra and Tenos, 18 August 1872. Add MS 44541, f. 179.

I have read with much interest the letter which your Grace did me the honour to address to me on the 27th of July.[2] The labyrinth of affairs into which it enters, is I fear too complex to allow one so ill informed as myself to enter it with advantage, in the way of forming any definite conclusions. From my recollections of your Grace's mission to England, I am very sensible of the large & conciliatory view which you take of ecclesiastical questions, & I feel confident that you would not, without strong cause, recommend a course to be hastily adopted which might end in a formal schism between the Russian & Bulgarian Churches on the one hand, & the Ancient & venerable communions which look to Constantinople as their centre of unity, on the other. Your Grace will however understand that it is difficult for me, at this distance, at once to recognise a necessity for running such fearful risks, especially as, according to all I learn, the violent partisans on the Bulgarian side are themselves disposed to precipitate the sharpest issue to the controversy. I enter very much into your Grace's views as to the aggression of the Panslavist against the Hellenic element, either in religion or otherwise. But while, as a Christian, I must cordially desire the union of all your churches, I find myself led to a similar form of feeling by my duty as a Minister. We in this country are anxious for the peace of the Levant. To this end it is material that there should be harmony between the Ottoman Porte & the Christian Churches within its dominions. But for this purpose it seems to me also much to be wished that more churches should be in harmony with one another. Since, if they are at variance, Foreign Powers may be tempted to step in, and under cover of religion, to promote political aims, of a nature adverse to peace, by taking up some one of the rival interests & working against another. This has been known to happen in other days, through differences between the Greek & Latin communions, differences which far more, I suppose, than any other cause, brought about the downfall of the Byzantine Empire. The evil will, I fear, be greatly aggravated if permanent discord spring up among the Orthodox Churches themselves, & it would be especially sad, in these days of so many perils to religion, that a schism should be established among those who agree together in matters of faith. Had I therefore (which I have not) any power in this deeply interesting question, my aim would be first to procure the intervention of a little time, which, by allaying heats, cures so many disorders: and then to see whether it was quite hopeless to procure from the Bulgarian Church a due observance of the rights of the Patriarch and the Eastern Church, before proceeding to extremities. I must now crave pardon of your Grace for the great frankness with which I have written, while avowing my incapacity on all accounts to deal fitly with the subject. I am sure that I shall have credit for meaning well, & I can ask nothing more. But I do not think that in what I have said, whether my particular conclusions be right or not, your Grace will see any indication of hostility or indifference. I shall transmit this letter, as you have suggested through the British Embassy at Constantinople, & I shall also send a copy of it to our Ambassador

[1] Secretary making the copy adds: '(enclosing copy as follows).'
[2] Add MS 44434, in German, on the Bulgarian schism.

Sir H. Elliot, who I am sure enters with a sincere & intelligent interest into these matters. I have taken the liberty of writing in my own tongue, & thereby I fear causing your Grace some trouble, because I was desirous of giving accurate expression to my thoughts, & fearful that if I made use of a foreign language when writing of necessity in haste, I might fail in point of precision, of freedom, or of both.

It only remains for me again to crave indulgence, & express my earnest good wishes, for the welfare both of Turkey & of Greece, & to subscribe myself with much respect your Grace's dutiful & faithful servant.[1]

19. M.

Church 8½ AM. Wrote to Mr Ogilvy—Mr Aubrey de Vere—M. Musurus—Mr Bouverie—Father O'Keeffe—Mr Brassey—Mr Gurdon—Lord Lyttelton—& minutes. We began on a great dead beech. Saw Mr Barker—Mr Burnett. Read Tylor—West on Indian Adminn[2] —Piozzi's Johnson.[3]

To FATHER R. O'KEEFFE, 19 August 1872. Add MS 44541, f. 181.

I have postponed for some days my reply to your letter of the 12th.[4] It did not appear to me to convey adequate information in reply to the query I had put to you, & I sought for light from others as to the position you had taken up & appeared to maintain as I am still however entirely at a loss to conceive how you can justly attach to the language held by me in the House of Commons on Mr Bouverie's motion, or to the attitude of the Irish Government the construction you appear to give to them: & I seriously regret the publication of your letter of the 8th of Aug.[5] I think it calculated to convey false impressions. Indeed I am led to suppose that you may yourself have been mislead by some abridged & imperfect report of a debate which took place at a very late hour. Desirous that, standing as you do in a position of difficulty, you should not be misinformed, I will add a few words of recital. Lord Hartington & I both gave our opinions on the vote of the Education Board, which alone was under discussion. He then referred, & I followed him, in the reference to the action which, as we understood, was in progress, & which we were advised might throw light upon your present position in the eye of the law. Such being the case we added it was intended to await the issue of that action before giving further consideration to the matter. This is a position which, relatively to the facts as they stand will, I am confident, be generally recognised as conformable to justice & good sense.[6]

[1] Partly printed in Lathbury, ii. 304.

[2] A. E. *West, *Sir C. Wood's Administration of Indian affairs from 1859 to 1866* (1867). See his letter to West, 21 August 1872, West, *Recollections*, ii. 19.

[3] See 23 July 52.

[4] To Gurdon; Add MS 44435, f. 52.

[5] Add MS 44435, f. 35.

[6] Copy sent to E. P. Bouverie; Add MS 44541, f. 182; see 14 Aug. 72.

20. Tu.

Ch 8½ AM. Wrote to Principal Tulloch[1]—Mr Hammond—Robn G.—Dr Hooker—Scotts—Mr Ayrton—and minutes. We brought down the big dead beech. Saw Mr Burnett. Conversation respecting plans for Mary Glynne.[2] Read West on India—Piozzi's Johnson—Poston on the Parsees.[3]

To E. HAMMOND, 20 August 1872. PRO FO 391/24.

I rather feel inclined to wish we could spur on the Emperor of Germany. I say this in the belief that his decision will be against us.[4] Give & take enters into Arbitration, though it ought not to do so: & Geneva would be more lenient if Berlin had already taken the other side.

In this disagreeable Chinese business,[5] I suppose you have purposely left vague the expression as to the official persons who are to be punished—& quite properly I think. We do not seem to have a case against the Governor; but the two Magistrates behaved abominably.

I hope you have both kept & gained ground since I last saw you on an anxious Washington Treaty night.

21. Wed.

Ch. 8½ AM. Wrote to Lady E.M. Pringle[6]—Ld Granville—Mr West—Mr Cardwell—Abp Manning—Ld Hartington—Mrs Th.—Sir E. Landseer—& minutes. Conversation with Dr Woodford.[7] Walked to Buckley to see Mr Stephenson. Mary was charming on the way back. Read West on India (finished)—Tylor's Prim. Culture—Piozzi's Johnson.

To E. CARDWELL, war secretary, 21 August 1872. PRO 30/48/9, f. 65.

1. I return Thring's memorandum.[8] Probably my best course will be to mention in the Cabinet without blaming & indeed without referring to any one in particular the manner in which our Bills have of late been drawn, & to lay stress upon the great necessity (1) of their being personally settled in all material points with the Draftsman before introduction. (2) If any necessity for extensive change after the printing for Parliament should be found to exist, then to put them according to the old practice through committee *pro formâ*.

[1] John *Tulloch, 1823-86; principal of St. Mary's college, St. Andrews; liberal anti-disestablishmentarian.

[2] See 26 Aug. 72.

[3] C. D. Poston, 'The Parsees; a lecture' (1870?).

[4] In the San Juan arbitration.

[5] Attack on a British citizen; see Hammond's docket on this letter.

[6] Lady Elizabeth Maitland Campbell Pringle, d. 1878, widow of Sir J. Pringle, 5th bart.

[7] J. R. *Woodford; see 28 Sept. 62.

[8] On drafting of Licensing Bill; sent by Cardwell on 19 August 1872, Add MS 44120, f. 42.

I am surprised at the account of Stansfeld, who in the House has certainly succeeded in shewing conciliation as well as firmness.
2. Your letter *taps* me on a subject on which I had thought of writing to you. You have accomplished a large, & I hope a permanent and salutary work; & have introduced into the British Army changes of greater extent than (I apprehend) it had undergone between the peace of 1815 & your accession to office. It seems to me well worthy of your consideration whether it would not be desirable to publish in a Pamphlet a full but *popular* account of our army system as it now is. This tract might or might not be *ex professo* an account of your administration of the War Office. You would I am sure desire that it should bear as little as possible the character of a panegyric. I mean it should eschew epithets & studied setting of the facts. In substance, happily, it must be a panegyric, but that is not your fault. It would be an act of justice to yourself. With this perhaps you can dispense, for you are beginning to get justice. But it would help to stereotype a state of opinion you have well earned. And it would be extremely useful & interesting to the public, if rightly handled by a right man, as information on a subject about which now-a-days every man wishes to be informed more or less. I think that in this view taken alone there may be a sufficient case for it. Pray think over the matter.
3. I have no doubt of the great interest & beauty of the spectacles you are about to witness, any more than of the genial hospitality you are enjoying.[1] But I am at present absolutely governed by a clamorous demand for rest, in which I suppose as well as in other things the approach of old age displays itself. When that has been in some degree satisfied, I know not as yet which way my face will turn.

To LORD HARTINGTON, Irish secretary, Add MS 44541, f. 184.
21 August 1872.

1. It seems to me that one of the most important parts of our preparation[2] for handling the Dublin University question consists in ascertaining the feelings & desires of the central governing body of Trinity College. Are we to suppose that Fawcett & his bill represented the whole of them? As this can hardly be, what measures are you to take to ascertain the views & feelings of others who are otherwise minded? This part of the work should be performed as thoroughly as possible. It has sometimes occurred to me as worth consideration whether such a man as Roundell should be employed in getting up for us the whole material of this question. I do not know in what condition you stand as to the statistics of the case. I will assume that you are simply informed as to the present & prospective values of the property of the College. One part of its organisation which should be very closely examined is that which relates to the resident students. This cannot be thoroughly or completely marked out. It is on this that the adversary will rely, to shew that the R.C. has no practical grievance. How far is this system rooted in the constitution & practice of the College? To what extent does it work? An increasing or diminishing extent? And is it found to give satisfaction? I think we ought also to have careful accounts drawn up of the present working both of the Queen's colleges & of the Catholic University: the state of the competition between them: which gains upon the other: what their

[1] Cardwell was at Ranston, Blandford.
[2] Hartington requested general guidance on Irish universities, 19 August; Add MS 44143, f. 176.

chances would be if neither had any state support. In truth, the Cabinet will expect that all the information necessary for forming a right judgment on this difficult & critical question should be collected & got into the best shape to assist in the formation of their judgment. Much of it, from your letter, I have no doubt you have already well in hand. A commission would I am afraid be regarded as a subterfuge.
2. You must indeed have been appalled at the Belfast rioting, if it is truly represented in the morning papers. It is horrible. Of course you will spare no effort, and delay none, in the supply and use of means for putting it down. I am glad to see the Times has already recanted its first announcement, which laid the mischief to the account of the repeal of the Party Procession Act.

22. Th.

Ch. 8½ AM. Wrote to Dr [W. B.] Carpenter—Rev. Mr Mayow—H.N.G.—Mr Pease MP.—Ld Acton—and minutes. Walk with Dr Woodford and Stephen. Saw Mr Burnett. Read Goschen's Address—Piozzi's Johnson (finished)—Life of Johnson (1785) began[1]—Tylor on Culture.

To LORD ACTON, 22 August 1872. Add MS 44093, f. 140.

Granville sent me yesterday your interesting letter about the Papal Election,[2] and I made the brief answer which suggested itself at the moment. But on thinking the matter over I am struck with what seems to me something like an essentially false position in the case of the Italian Government. From the formation of the Italian Kingdom, or at any rate for a great many years, the Italian Government has refused to take any cognizance of the state of parties in the Roman Church. *Tros Tyriusve mihi nullo discrimine habetur.*[3] There is a party there which is at war with liberty and civilisation. There is another party which holds principles favourable to both. The first party is strong, the other weak. The Italian Government has done nothing to uphold the weak and nothing to discountenance the strong. And now with the Papal Election in view it desires to find means of averting the mischiefs which are too likely to follow from an election conducted by the dominant or Papal party. Its arguments criticisms and wishes seem to me to be in hopeless contradiction with its own conduct. Were it indeed possible to treat the question as purely religious, their attitude might be justified by logic. They might say governments do not interfere in theological questions: we want our Ultramontanes to be good citizens, and such they may be, however extravagant their merely ecclesiastical or theological opinions. Do they then hope to convert and pacify Ultramontanism in the civil sphere by letting it alone in the religious sphere? That may be possible, although I do not think it free from doubt, in England. But it is utterly and evidently impossible in Italy until the idea of restoring the temporal power shall have been utterly abandoned. Meanwhile temporal means, the powerful engine of starvation, are

[1] Probably by Sir J. *Hawkins, though first published 1787; see 23, 24 Aug. 72.
[2] Not found.
[3] 'I shall treat Trojan and Tyrian without discrimination'; Virgil, *Aeneid*, I 574.

freely used by the ecclesiastical power against any priest who makes peace with the Kingdom of Italy. And nothing (as I believe) is done to sustain such priests in their unequal conflict. If this is so, how can the Italian Government wonder that its deadly and irreconcilable enemies should act towards it in conformity with the policy which it allows them to enforce against its own loyal subjects? The German Governments (I do not speak of the law against the Jesuits, on which I am ill able to give an opinion) are surely far nearer the mark, for they give some kind of support and countenance to what may be called the rational party in the Church. I feel deeply the reasonableness of the views of the Italian Government about the new election, but I also feel that it lies with itself to take the first step towards causing such views to prevail by giving countenance within its own sphere to loyal and right-minded priests.

These are the impressions which your letter leaves upon me.

I have sometimes had an idea of serving three or four purposes at once by running to the Continent for a fortnight or three weeks, perhaps as far as Munich, altogether unseen. But I know not whether it can come to anything.[1]

23. Fr.

Ch. 8½ AM. Wrote to Mr Burnett—The Queen (Mem)—and minutes. Worked on Homer: the word Νύμφη.[2] Read Tylor—Report on N. York Taxation—Life of Dr Johnson (finished). Walk with Dr Woodford.

24. Sat.

St.Barth.Ch. 11 AM. Wrote to The Queen (Mem.)—Mr Hammond—Mr Ayrton—Agnes G.—Ld Hartington (Tel.)—Mr Gurdon (Tel.)—Sir R. Palmer—and minutes. Worked on Homer: ἀμβροσιος.[3] Read Tylor—N.Y. Report—Hawkins's Johnson. Kibbling the big tree.

To E. HAMMOND, 24 August 1872. Add MS 44541, f. 187.

I thank you for your note & I hope you may, at the time you name, be able to secure that rare prize a real holiday. On reviewing the Mem.[4] you have sent me on the last commercial proposals from France, I make the following remarks, partly in their *favour*. In the cases of wool, flax, hemp, jute, & silk, no drawbacks are to be allowed. If this is so, the import duties cannot be very serious. On the other hand the compensation duties are not placed on the right basis. We are told for instance that the compensatory duty on yarns & tissues of flax is scarcely 1½ to 2 per cent of the *value*. But the value is not the true test. A compensatory duty ought to impose on the flax or hemp contained in the yarn or tissue a duty equal to that laid on the raw material, *plus* an addition representing

[1] In Figgis and Laurence, *Lord Acton's correspondence*, 40, and Lathbury, ii. 55.
[2] Homerically, 'a Nymph'. [3] 'immortal'.
[4] Mem. by Hammond circulated to Gladstone, Granville, Lowe, and Fortescue; no other ministers replied, see Hammond to Gladstone, 8 September 1872, Add MS 44183, f. 474.

the quantity of the raw material which the French manufacturer must waste in making this yarn or tissue. But it is only a person minutely acquainted with the particular trades who can inform us whether the burdens will be serious. If they are not serious in amount, I think we might waive the abstract principle. If we are to consider the matter in the interest of our own exporters, it ought to be borne in mind that these import duties on the raw material without drawbacks will damage the French exporter in neutral markets. It is obvious to observe that the 'advantages' offered us are those of equality, for which it is extremely dangerous to pay a price. If I agreed, I should agree not on account of the advantages but on account of the special circumstances of France, and the claims growing out of them.

25. 13 S. Trin.

Ch. mg & evg. Wrote to Mr Thompson—and minutes. Read Life in the Spheres[1]—Bp of Carlisle's Charge[2]—De Vere's St Patrick—Margoliouth's Serm. & Tracts.[3]

26. M.

Ch. 8½ AM. Wrote to Brazilian Minister—Abp Manning—Rev A. King[4]—Dr Carpenter—Mr Godley (Tel.)[5]—& minutes. Worked on Homer (ἱερός).[6] In the afternoon, we went to choose a site for a new house for Gertrude & Mary between the Village, the Park and the Wint.[7] Read Hawkins's Johnson—Tylor's Early Culture—Smith's Hist. of the East.[8]

To ARCHBISHOP H. E. MANNING, 26 August 1872. Add MS 44250, f. 59.

This short note will be written within the lines laid down.[9] 1. As to Rome we must both rather desire to ascertain the real facts, than be set upon holding to our respective impressions of them. And I think I have pointed out a method, by which if they are as you suppose, the truth may be brought to light. But I do not understand your judgment to depend on them. 2. Your argument from Ireland

[1] H. Tuttle, *Scenes in the spirit world* (1855).

[2] H. *Goodwin, 'A charge . . . July 1872' (1872).

[3] M. *Margoliouth, 'The bane of a parasite ritual' (1872).

[4] Probably Alexander King, rector of Sherrington.

[5] John Arthur *Godley, 1847–1932, s. of J.R.* and s. in law of Sir W. James; private secretary 1872–4, 1880–2; I.R.B. commissioner 1882–3; Indian under-secretary 1883–1909; cr. Baron Kilbracken 1909. He began as 'third man' in the private secretary's office on 10 Aug. 1872.

[6] 'relating to the gods'.

[7] *Sc.* Wynt; 'The Cottage', also known as 'Glynne Cottage', lies NW. of the old castle.

[8] P. *Smith, *A smaller ancient history of the East* (1871).

[9] Manning's letter, 23 August, Add MS 44250, f. 55, on condition of Rome, and Ireland: 'I am also unable to maintain the justice of our holding Ireland if the Pope had not a just sovereignty over Rome.'

does not hit me—for I have not maintained the doctrine that Italy was entitled to absorb the Roman States, against the will of their inhabitants. But over & above this I cannot accept your belief as to the people of Ireland. I know of no proof that they desire separation from this country. We shall know more on this subject perhaps after an election under the Ballot Act. The largest demand ever made in Ireland, so far as I know, except the Fenian demand, has acknowledged the Sovereignty of the Crown & has aimed at no more than is now enjoyed by states of the Austrian Empire. Even this I do not know to be the desire of the people of Ireland generally.

Nor have I ever cast on America the responsibility connected with Fenianism. I believe the American influence, as it was (for it is now nearly dead) to be the contre-coup of an influence having its root & seat in Ireland itself. The bayonets in Ireland are Irish as well as English & Scotch, but I know of no influence which they do or can exercise on the free expression of opinion. I am glad to suppose you have had a quasi-holiday.
[P.S.] I am sorry to say that in one matter, which lies at the root of all, I am hardly less a follower of Cassandra than you; for I think there is a more powerful combination of influences now at work in the world, which have atheism for their legitimate upshot, than at any former period known to me. They are alike hostile to God the Creator, God the Ruler, & God the Judge; & the only deities they have are the Gods of Epicurus.

27. Tu.

Ch. 8½ AM. Wrote to Lord Spencer—Mr Falkner Lloyd[1]—Mr Ayrton—and minutes. Wrote on Αἰόλος.[2] Saw Mrs Thom: as new Tenant.[3] Read Tylor—Hawkins—Smith on the East.

To EARL SPENCER, Irish lord lieutenant, 27 August 1872. Add MS 44542, f. 2.

I will run as succinctly as I can over the points contained in your interesting letters,[4] beginning with assuring you how much I appreciate and sympathize with all your cares in the sad business of the Belfast riots. 1. I take it to be clear that we can do nothing from the Public Funds for a R.I. Residence in Ireland without a previous vote of Parliament, so that I think Ld Portarlington cannot be too soon informed as you propose. (I have no progress to report in the other & greater branch of that important question). 2. With regard to the riots at Belfast, I have not seen in either the friendly or the independent Press a disposition to cast blame on the Irish executive, any more than I can see that much blame would have been deserved. Fault has been found with the administration for the repeal of the Party Processions Act, but the Times, which committed itself in this sense, I think speedily recanted. It is indeed grievous to read of such strange

[1] Had written about the 1873 Eisteddfodd; Gladstone agreed to attend if possible; Add MS 44541, f. 190. See 19 Aug. 73.

[2] 'quick-moving', or, of armour, 'easily-welded'.

[3] Sarah, wife of William Thom of Springfield, Hawarden, though she was strongly hostile to diarist.

[4] Of 26 August 1872, Add MS 44307, f. 129.

folly & crime mixed together: but if the R.C.'s gave a semi-Fenian character to their demonstration, the blame must be shared between the parties though even then the large share will rest with the assailants. Your argument as to special Proclamation is of the clearest; & I conceive you were indisputably right as to the Cork celebration, although it had ugly features, in which I am loath to include the green flag; for after all it is the national flag of Ireland, & has therefore I think a footing distinct from & higher than the orange one. 3. Your tour appeared to be eminently satisfactory: it is well that mine was not attempted. 4. As to the University question, I hope you will endeavour to sift, as far as possible, the important enquiry whether we can work in harmony either with Trinity College (its governing body) or with any important part of it. 5. I trust you saw Dr Hooker's letter about Potatoes in the Times.[1] Would it not be worth while to make sure that the contents of it are made generally known in Ireland. Dr. Hooker assured me that even in badly diseased potatoes *one third* of the bulk of matter might be saved. 6. We talked over the matter of Dowse & of the judgeship in the Cabinet. I have a strong suspicion that your judgeships ought to be reduced. But if this cannot be done then comes the question as to the holder. Hartington, I have no doubt, has fully apprehended the view of the Cabinet. I think there was a great wish that Dowse should conduct the prosecution which he had instituted under statute, & therefore that every effort should be used to get rid of the business next term, which indeed is most desirable on other grounds. But I think also the feeling was that if these efforts being made should from any cause prove ineffectual, it would be hard to overlook Dowse's claim to the Judgeship, & that therefore when the time came beyond which it could not properly be left vacant, he should be appointed to it, and the prosecutions handed to his successor. 7. I am likely to see O'Keeffe, at his request, within the next few days.

28. Wed.

Helen's birthday. She is as granite. May all blessings go with her. Wrote to Ld Chancellor—Mr Bouverie—Sir A. Helps—Mr Burnett—Mr Sturt—Sir J. Coleridge—Ld Halifax—The Queen (long l. & long M[emorandum])[2]—Mr Gurdon (3 Telegr.)—and minutes. Saw Mr Burnett—S.E.G. (who arrived)—Mr Shaw (Architect).[3] We began to cut trees & clear a site for the orphan nieces. Read Smith's Hist.—Life of Lord J. Manners.[4]

To LORD HALIFAX, lord privy seal, 28 August 1872. Hickelton MSS A4. 88.

With regard to the conversation which you report to me,[5] I feel that you had

[1] Stating Gladstone's support for publicity for means of using diseased tubers; *The Times*, 24 August 1872, 7 f.

[2] On Prince of Wales; Guedalla, *Q*, i. 374.

[3] George Shaw, Yorkshire architect; built 'Temple of Peace' 1866 and some later additions; perhaps mentioned at 6 Aug. 64.

[4] [Non-elector], *Lord John Manners. A political and literary sketch* (1872).

[5] Halifax to Gladstone, 25 August 1872, Add MS 44185, f. 298, reporting Victoria's objections to the plan, and his tacit acceptance of them.

a difficult task imposed upon you, but I am rather sorry that you fell back, without more ado, upon a silence which I am afraid is little better than a shadow & which might be regarded as an imposture. For I feel that my position is weakened accordingly; and I am not prepared to abandon it except in the last resort, that is after having tried every available means, and I am also conscious that the office I hold imposes upon me a responsibility from which no one can relieve me.

What is wanted for the Prince of Wales is not a driblet of business coming up now & then but a plan of life. The Irish scheme is of course surrounded with difficulties but combined with other things it makes a plan of life. It is no plan of life to be put 'into communication' with the Indian Office. And as to the particular Office my fear is (though I am not a judge, [as] you are) that only a very limited portion of its business would be otherwise than highly repulsive to a man who has yet to acquire the taste. There is certainly no great department of business which is so little popular with the public or with Parliament.

I quite grant that even if the Queen's repugnance can be overcome, the plan cannot take effect against the will of the Prince. But it is rather much that this plan should go to the ground because of his repugnance when he has never heard of it except from the Queen who is herself as one sided in her hostility as she can be, and when I have never yet been permitted to state it to him: a point which I shall certainly bring forward before any final abandonment. And when that stage arrives there is much to be considered as to the manner and terms of the retreat. The whole subject is one which it is easy to deal with on hand to mouth principles. There is no political inconvenience to be expected from this source today or tomorrow, this year or next. But the bitter fruit will be reaped hereafter and the retrospective judgment passed upon any neglect of mine, at a golden period such as the illnesses of last year have offered, would justly be most severe.

I will not now any longer delay writing further to the Queen. I do not know whether you could, if you have an opportunity, at all cover my ground by *dropping* an observation to the Queen that I am rather obstinate or tenacious —& have dwelt long upon this matter.

29. Th.

Ch. 8½ A.M. Wrote to The Lord Chancellor—Dowager Duchess Argyll—Mr Bright—Ld R. Grosvenor—Sir J. Hanmer—Mr Tollemache—Mrs Th.—Duke of Cambridge—Sir W. Farquhar—& minutes. Clearing the plantation in afternoon—family party. Saw Mr Chamberlain. Read Ld J. Manners (finished)—Hawkins's Johnson—Smith's Hist. of the East.

To LORD R. GROSVENOR, 29 August 1872. Add MS 44542, f. 3.

Let me give you an idea of the state of the Flintshire Register from an individual case—my own. I was on the Register in 1840 with a mere[?] qualification: from about 20 years ago for my own property; much the greater part of what I have is here. The day before yesterday I chanced to see the Register of 71, & look for my own name. I had been struck off: at least I am omitted. No notice of objection was ever served on me. It seems a trick, & the multiplication of such tricks might produce incon[venien]t consequences. Unfortunately my discovery is a month & more too late to come on again this year.

30. Fr.

Ch. 8½ AM. Wrote to Sec.Metr.Distr.R.R.—and minutes. Woodcutting. Saw Mr Burnett—S.E.G. Read Hawkins—Smith—Tylor.

31. Sat.

Ch 8½ A.M. Wrote to Mr Glyn—and minutes. Woodcutting. Read as yesterday & Rawlinson's Ancient Empires.[1]

14 S.Trin Sept One 1872.

Ch mg (with H.C.) & evg. Stephen by advice officiated at Seeland Ch. not here. Mr Chidlow preached a remarkable Sermon in evg. Long conversation with him on the development Theory & like matters. Read Tuttle—Horbery on Future Punishment.[2] Wrote to Ld Granville—& minutes.

2. M.

Ch. 8½ A.M. Wrote to Mr Hammond—Ld Granville—& minutes. Worked on Homer (Hellespontos). Saw Mr Barker. Explained to C.G. the state of my affairs: why & how more pinched. Read Smith—Hawkins. Saw Mr Chidlow—Bp of Winchester. Woodcutting.

To LORD HALIFAX, lord privy seal, Hickleton MSS, A4.88.
2 September 1872.

I thank you very much for your letter[3] and I am both sorry & glad that I misunderstood you.

My *suggestion* was on the supposition of your being still at Balmoral. My letter to the Queen is gone & must be in her hands. I never like to *ask* her to speak on a matter of this kind because I think it causes her much suffering. I think my two chief practical points are 1. to press for a development of the scheme of successive attaching to the public Departments 2. to suggest that before my plan is abandoned I ought to have an opportunity of seeing the P. [of Wales] on it if he wishes.

[1] See 30 Nov. 62.
[2] M. *Horbery, *An enquiry into the scripture doctrine . . . of future punishment* (1744).
[3] Of 31 August, Add MS 44185, f. 304; Halifax used 'the words "if possible" . . . in order not to set H.M.'s back up'.

Can he be put on the I[ndian] C[ouncil] without an Act or a vacancy? Do you feel quite sure as to the safety of asking for an Act?[1]

3. Tu.

Ch. 8½ AM. Wrote to Mr Cardwell (2)—Mr Hammond (Tel.)—Ld Halifax—Att.Gen.Irel.—Mr Gurdon—Ld Spencer—& minutes. We drove to Eaton: vast works are in progress. Cela donne a penser.[2] Conversation with the Bp on Athn Creed—Winchr Deanery. Read Hawkins—Smith's Hist.

To E. CARDWELL, war secretary, 3 September 1872. PRO 30/48/9, f. 73 and Add MS 44542, f. 4.

[First letter:] When I referred to you about the memorial from Woodstock on Soldiers' labour,[3] I was not aware that the subject was dealt with by the Queen's Regulations & was therefore strictly within the ordinary business of your Department. But as it is so I think I had better reply (not adversely to the spirit of your suggestion) that I am not aware of any cases such as they describe, & if they will indicate to me the place & time, I will refer them to you for inquiry, as I am certain that no departure from the letter or spirit of the Queen's Regulations will ever be permitted by you.

The Memorial refers to Lockouts only. I think, however, it is difficult to justify the use of soldiers' labour in the case of strike, unless the circumstances of the strike be extraordinary. [P.S.] I have replied as above, not including the last paragraph.[4]

[Second letter:] I am glad you are going to have the Statement[5] prepared on the ground alike of justice to yourself, & of public utility. I agree with you about the authorship or at least the inspiration of the Article in the Gdn. I am sensible of the importance of the question you mention with regard to the Army. For myself I own I have never understood how you could work together on the same tables[6] Indian & British recruiting, & this drove me to suggest, perhaps rashly, a severance of the two armies as to the men & n.c.o. I daresay you have found a mode of attaining the object. But if the upshot is to be a rise in the rate of general pay on account of liability to Indian service, I do not see how such an augmentation can justly be charged on the British Taxpayer. Perhaps a reaction in the winter from the present state of things may relieve you from your difficulty.

To R. DOWSE, Irish attorney general, 3 September 1872. Add MS 44542, f. 5.

I have had Fr. O'Keeffe with me for 2 or 3 hours today, & have obtained a good deal more light upon his contentions. The Viceroy has I believe left Ireland &

[1] See 8 Sept. 72.
[2] 'That gives grounds for thought'; *Waterhouse's reconstruction began 1870.
[3] Protest meeting against employment of troops; *Oxford Chronicle*, 24 August 1872.
[4] No reply from Cardwell found.
[5] Statement of achievements in army reform; Add MS 44120, ff. 47, 56; see 21 Aug. 72.
[6] Reading unclear, word smudged by copyist.

I therefore write to you but[?] I shall send him a copy of this letter. *He* returns to Dublin meaning to stay 2 or 3 days on his way home. He seems to meditate an endeavour to see the Lord Chancellor. I should be glad if you were to see him; for my opinion is that unless unforeseen circumstances should occur to prevent it, we shall hear much more of his matter in Parliament. As regards Cardinal Cullen, he contends 1. That the Bull Apostolica Sedis, under which alone he could be suspended has not been received, & is not current in Ireland. 2. That if it were it could only be applied by a competent judge, which the Cardinal was not. 3. That if he were he could only apply it according to the rules of the Canon Law, which Cardinal Cullen did not. As regards the Education Board, he contends not only that they ought to have taken measures to learn whether they ought to treat him as Parish Priest of Callan or not: but that even if he is not P.P. of Callan they have no right or power to remove him from the managership of the Schools; & that in fact he is not removed, & still continues to manage the Schools, with the incident of having to pay the Salaries. He says this action against Cardinal Cullen is one for libel, but part of the libel charged is the Cardinal's proclaiming & pretending that he is not P.P. of Callan; so that he expects the court in passing judgment on this part of his case be called upon to give its opinion upon the three points to which I have above referred as lying between him & the Cardinal. He signified to me by way of parenthesis that he had no means of proceeding except by money borrowed for the purpose. I told him that if he had any statement of that kind to submit to the Government it could only be received with propriety in writing. Of course I was careful to let him understand that I saw him with a view only to information; & that the question what the Government might or might not have to say to his case would only arise when we had obtained the best aid for our judgments accessible to us, namely through the coming judgment of the Court of Law. In my own mind I cannot but think he has been wrongly used, & this (to all appearances) by the Poor Law Commissioners, as well as by the Board of Education. He says the bulk of his people stick to him; but no priest dare lift a finger for him or (I understood) be seen speaking to him.

4. Wed.

Ch. 8½ AM. Wrote to Sir H. Elliot—Mr Moffatt—Mr Gurdon—Mr Burnett—& minutes. Visited Aston Hall with S.R.G. & Sir C.A.[1]—Saw its antiquities. Read Hawkins—Smith—Lenormant.[2] Saw Bp of Winchester. Worked on Homer.

To Sir H. G. ELLIOT, ambassador to Turkey, 4 September 1872. Add MS 44542, f. 5.

I am very glad to find that I had been led to much the same views of the Bulgarian question as had commended themselves to you with your greatly superior means of judgment.[3] If there is a point in which I should incline to vary a little from

[1] Sir C. H. J. Anderson (see 19 Oct. 54), staying at Hawarden; Hawn Visitors' Book.

[2] F. Lenormant, *Essai sur la propagation de l'Alphabet Phénicien dans l'ancien monde* (1872-3).

[3] Elliot to Gladstone, 26 August 1872, Add MS 44435, f. 146.

you, it is in this, that the Turks seem to me to have a very strong interest in composing the Bulgarian quarrel, on the ground that when the Christian subjects of the Porte are at odds among themselves, it is an open point in the armour at which Russia can find entrance, & the Austrians seem to be little less biased by narrow & selfish considerations, if less aggressive in their for[eign] views. I read with disgust a telegram in which (Sept. 2) Sir A. Buchanan announces that the Austrian minister for Foreign Affairs considers the evil of a reconciliation between the Churches 'under Russian mediation' 'more serious than any danger arising from the excommunication of the Russian Church' (should it occur which he thinks improbable). How is it possible to give greater real strength to Russia with the Christians of the Ottoman empire, than by objecting to her being allowed to do them (& Turkey) good. It is paltry to the last degree. I wish with all my heart I could see Russia seriously engaged in such an enterprise, if she is to mix at all in the matter. I am quite at loss to understand Archbishop Lycurgus.

5. Th.

Ch. 8½ AM. Wrote to Ld Ossington—Ld Advocate—Ld Dufferin—and minutes. Worked on Homer: respecting Memnon. Read Hawkins—Lenormant, Phoenicians. Saw Mr Burnett. We fixed the spot for the new House.[1]

6. Fr.

Ch. 8½ AM. Wrote to Ld Granville (l. & Tel.)—Mr Hammond—Mrs Th.—Mr Maguire[2]—Ld Leigh—Dr Döllinger—The Queen—Mr Tollemache—& minutes. Saw Mr Burnett. Read Hawkins's Johnson—Tylor's Culture: finished Vol. I. Worked on Homer 'Memnon'.

To J. J. I. von DÖLLINGER, 6 September 1872. Add MS 44140, f. 289.
'Most Private.'

Your official letter, conveying the Diploma which your University has done me the honour to confer, has just reached me, and I will send an official reply to acknowledge it as well as I can though not as well as it deserves.

I have had a vision of a short trip to the Continent and of knocking at your door as I did in 1845. I am sure of one thing; you could not receive me now more kindly than you did then. This vision has I fear melted into thin air; and I am very sorry for it. I should much have liked half an hour's conversation with you before your coming Congress.

A question has arisen in Ireland, the first within my recollection, which involves considerations and principles in a great degree corresponding with those which (as I understand the matter) the Bavarian Government has had to consider

[1] See 26 Aug. 72.

[2] Agreeing to ask Bruce to look into alleged ill-treatment of Fenian prisoners Michael Davitt and Wilson; Bruce's vindication, sent on by diarist to Maguire; both published in *The Times*, 18 October 1872, 3c.

in the case of those Priests who have refused to adopt the recent decrees of the Vatican Council. Mr. O'Keeffe, Parish Priest of Callan, has been suspended by Cardinal Cullen in the name of the Pope, and has prosecuted the Cardinal for libel, part of the libel consisting in the allegation that he is suspended. Two subordinate Departments of the Government have accepted the suspension as valid in their relations with the Priest, although he continued to discharge the duties of his office and was supported by the bulk of his people. But the *Government* itself has as yet taken no part, and will take none, until they see the issue of the action now in progress, which may lead to a judicial declaration on his legal status.

In your luminous, and dispassionate or friendly, review of the position and state of the Anglican Church, you referred to its weak as well as to its stronger points, and among others to Erastianism. I should like to have given you the results of my own careful observation during forty years on that subject. Speaking generally, Erastianism belongs to a period of close and intimate relations between the Church and the State, in which the State is much stronger than the Church. These relations with us are less tightly laced than they were; and the Church, losing some of its legal privileges and preferences, has been thrown back on its own moral strength, notwithstanding that it is torn with fiercer divisions, is still both morally and politically very powerful. Meanwhile Erastianism, which was the general creed of the political world when I entered Parliament in 1832, has greatly lost ground; it has entirely departed from many minds, and is weakened in almost all. The Convocations of the Church are allowed to sit and speak freely, after a virtual suspension of much over a century; and this year their concurrence has been recited in the Preamble of an Act of Parliament which dealt with ecclesiastical matter.

I see that the Bishop of Lincoln, Dr. Wordsworth, is about to attend the Congress and you may perhaps fall in with him. He is greatly respected; a man of very high character, much ability, and immense industry. His piety would perhaps best be judged of from some very good Hymns which he has written. He partakes rather too much perhaps of John Bull for the function he is about to engage in: at least I should say there is a certain rigidity of intellect about him though I believe he is full of charity in feeling. In this he is the opposite of our very remarkable Bishop of Winchester [Wilberforce] whose intellect is so subtle as almost to want a little *gluten*.

I sometimes hear from Lord Acton, and among the pleasures of correspondence with him is this that it always brings you into my mind. May you be sustained consoled and guided, in all you have to say and do.

7. Sat.

Ch. 8½ A.M. Wrote to Ld Granville (Tel. D.)—Bp of Winchester—and minutes. Saw Mr Thorn—Mr Shaw (Architect). Read Lenormant—Hawkins's Dr J. (finished)—Renan on Semitic Races[1]—Lucian περι πένθους—and ἔρωτες (part).[2]

[1] J. E. Renan, *De la part des peuples Sémitiques dans l'histoire de la civilization* (1862).

[2] Short essays by Lucian, the second on the relative merits of homo- and heterosexual love; see 16 Sept. 72.

8. S.15 Trin.

Hn Ch. 11 AM and Buckley Evg. Wrote to Dean of St Paul's—Ld Halifax—Mr Gurdon—Dean Ramsay—and minutes. Walk with S.E.G. Read Horbery on Eternal Punishment:[1] and several of the Ramsgate[2] and other Tracts.

To LORD HALIFAX, lord privy seal, 8 September 1872. Hickleton MSS A 4.88.

The Queen's answer to my last letter precludes any further effort on my part. I have told her I will inform the Cabinet—will speak to the P. if he speaks to me—& will consult the Cabinet about the Indian Council, as to which I did not clearly see my way.

But your letter of the 6th which I received this morning,[3] & for which & the enclosure I thank you, completely disposes (I think) of this matter. The objection of *responsibility* is conclusive. On the other hand you point out most clearly what (at some permanent sacrifice on the part of the Indian Secretary of State who is pretty well be-Councilled already,) might be done: though obviously it will be far more difficult to work the Prince into a corner of business already complicated by multiplicity of agents than it would have been with a Minister acting alone in Ireland.

9. M.

Ch. 8½ AM. Wrote to Lord Lyttelton—W.B. Gurdon—M.A. Berry—and minutes. Indulged myself in an inquest respecting the horse of Homer and wrote on it.[4] Saw Mr Hubbard. Viewed H. G[lynne']s Library. Read Picard La Vieille Tante[5]—Pennant's Scotland[6]—Lenormant—Bryant[7]—&c.

10. Tu.

Ch. 8½ AM. Wrote to Bp of Peterborough—Ld Spencer—Mr Goschen—Mr Forster—Robn G.—Mr Hammond—M. Gavard—& minutes. Finished my paper on the Homeric Horse. Read La Vieille Tante—Le Normant—Il. 23.

To EARL SPENCER, Irish lord lieutenant, 10 September 1872. Add MS 44542, f. 8.

My motive for wishing Dowse to see O'Keeffe was that he might at once be put in full possession of the case. At least for myself I must confess that while

[1] See 1 Sept. 72.
[2] See 2 June 72n.
[3] Add MS 44185, f. 310 and Hickleton MSS A 4.88, enclosing letter to Ponsonby; Halifax opposed putting Wales on the Council, suggesting instead a room at the Indian Office.
[4] Iliad 6. 506 ff.
[5] Untraced.
[6] See 19 Sept. 53.
[7] Probably W. C. Bryant, *Picturesque America*, 2v. (1872-5).

in London I did not get it adequately before my own mind. I have no doubt that a mistake has been made by both Departments which have acted in this case: & although my impression of his character when I saw him was very much in accordance with views of it which you had kindly stated to me, I think the case is very strong & enough to float him, & that we shall hear a good deal more before we have done with him. Yesterday morning I received from him the inclosed note, & you will see on it the purport of my reply.

11. Wed.

Ch. 8½ A.M. Wrote to Mr Cardwell—M. Wolowski—The Speaker—Mr Hammond—Mr Ellice (tel)—& minutes. Saw Mr Cotgrave.[1] Worked on Rectory Library—and my own. Read Lenormant—Mrs H. Gray's Etruria[2]—La Vieille Tante (finished).

12. Th.

Ch. 8½ A.M. Wrote to Mr Hammond Tel. & l.—Ld Granville Tel.—Mr Goschen—Mr Gurdon Tel.—Mrs H. Gray[3]—Bp of Manchester—Mr Ramsay[4]—Ld Hartington—Mr Fortescue—& minutes. Worked on Homer. Saw Mr Burnett. Read Grote (His ultra sceptical spirit has made utter havock of all the early ground in Greece)—Le Normant.

13. Fr.

Ch. 8½ A.M. Wrote to Mr Hammond—Messrs Agnew—and minutes. Worked on Homer. Read Le Normant—Lucian ἔρωτες—Irvingism.[5] Conversation with Herbert [Gladstone].

14. Sat.

Ch. 8½ AM. Wrote to Ld Prov. Glasgow—Mrs Ellice—Robn G.—Mr Cardwell—Scotts—and minutes. Worked on Homer. Read Nabathaean Agriculture (Renan on)[6]—Lucian's ἔρωτες. We felled a good elm. Round game in evg.

[1] Not further identified.

[2] E. C. Gray, *History of Etruria*, 3v. (1843-68).

[3] Elizabeth Caroline Gray, 1800-87; archaeologist; wife of J. H. (see 10 May 38).

[4] Offering John Ramsay (1814-92; liberal M.P. Stirling 1868-74; Falkirk 1874-86) seat on Scottish education board; he accepted; Add MS 44542, f. 9.

[5] [J. Harrison], *The Catholic Apostolic Church—Irvingism—its pretensions and claims considered* (1872).

[6] J. E. Renan, *An essay on the age and antiquity of the Book of Nabathaean Agriculture* (1862).

15. 16 S.Trin.

Ch. 11 AM. and H.C.—6½. Wrote to Mr Hammond (Tel.)—Ld Granville l. and tel.—Mrs Th.—Bp of Winchester—and minutes. Advising Stephy on the theological part of the Rectory Library. Read Horbery on future Punisht[1]—'Cath.Apost.Ch' (finished)—Bp Moberly's Sermon & Appx[2]—Erasmus's Prayers.[3]

16. M.

Ch. 8½ A.M. Wrote to Dean of Chichester—Sir R. Palmer[4]—Mr Glyn—Dr Döllinger (official)[5]—Ld Granville—& minutes. Saw Mr Burnett. Further work on Library at the Rectory. Cutting & Kibbling at the new site. Read N. York Report on Taxation[6]—Athenaeus B. XIII—Lucian ἔρωτες finished: a singular and painfully instructive work—Sheridan's (trumpery) Trip to Scarborough.[7] The Prologue on fashions is interesting. Worked a little on Homer. I now bid him goodbye. It has been my first course of this medicine since 1868: and a very short & slight one.

To G. G. GLYN, chief whip, 16 September 1872. Add MS 44542, f. 10.
'Private.'

Unhappily we start for Scotland on Wednesday, I expect to be back by or before Oct. 10. It is very tantalising to have your offer:[8] but as it has not been factiously rejected, I trust you will renew it. I agree with you about Preston.[9] The special circumstances, which in other cases had been against us, were here as I take it in our favour. If so, the election confirms my impressions that our hold over the Constituencies is weakened, & that the Conservatives may begin soon to think of another advent to power, although unless they do much more than they have yet done in laying f[urther] grounds for confidence, it will only be for a short lease. I have plenty to say to you which must keep: but may now mention that I expect the Chancellor will retire in the middle of next month, & that I have today written to Palmer. Your account of your father is most acceptable & on your silence about Mrs Glyn I put the best construction.

[1] See 1 Sept. 72.
[2] G. *Moberly, 'He that believeth and is baptised shall be saved' (1872), with app. on Athanasian creed.
[3] Tr. C. S. Coldwell (1872).
[4] Offering him the Lord Chancellorship on Hatherley's retirement through ill-health; he accepted; Selborne II, i. 280.
[5] Official thanks for doctorate; see 6 Sept. 72.
[6] See 23 Aug. 72.
[7] R. B. B. *Sheridan, *A trip to Scarborough; a comedy* (1781).
[8] Of 14 September, to stay; Add MS 44348, f. 184.
[9] Ibid.; 'I hardly hoped to win, but did hope to make a closer fight'; liberal organisation was superior but 'jealousy amid our local leaders' counteracted; seat lost at by-election this day.

17. Tu.

Ch. 8½ A.M. Wrote to Mr Hammond—Mr Woodgate—Robn G.—Mr Gurdon (and 2 Telegr.)—Mr Fortescue—Sir T.G.—and minutes. Woodcutting: we rather mauled a chestnut by a bad fall. Read 2d New York Report—Goschen's Report on Local Taxation.[1] Saw Mr Burnett. Conversation with Herbert about study. Some preparations for departure.

To E. HAMMOND, 17 September 1872. Add MS 44542, f. 10.

I sent you this morning early a Telegram through Gurdon which contained my opinion on the Draft reply[2] to Gavard as far as I have one to give. I think we should make no glorification of the Instrument, which taken in itself, is a sorry compromise, though one which we may act wisely in accepting. I must heartily confess that though willing to see either form adopted, as the experts may think best, I like the best the notion of an amending Treaty (*assuming* that it need not be complex). 1. As the simplest. 2. As the furthest from the notion that we are making a new start in matters of commercial Treaty & Free Trade. 3. The most favoured nation Clause without limit of duration, in matters of Commerce & Navigation, will of itself provide best for the second of the 3 preliminaries we have required; but as Ld. Lyons has shown it ought to be in very explicit terms. 4. I send instructions to Gurdon about Telegrams. I do not quite understand when Ld. G. returns to town, after which you will, I hope, experience great relief. Pray understand that although I am going into the hills (a good way beyond Inverness next week) I shall be ready at once to come up if Ld G. sees reason to desire a Cabinet on the Treaty, & Gurdon will summon one accordingly; *or* if he desires my presence individually. I think, however, I have pretty well given my own ideas & the limits of my intervention. 5. I take my Decipher with me, hoping not to use it.

18. Wed. [*Courthey, Liverpool*]

Church 8½ AM. Wrote to Mr Hammond—Duke of Argyll—Mr Gurdon—Mrs M'Donald—Mr Bright—Glasg. Coach Office—Ld Provost of Glasgow—The Attorney General—The Queen—Mr Goschen—Principal Tulloch—Dr Taylor—Sir J. Wauchope—and minutes. Packing & putting away. Off at 3.30 for Chute & Courthey. Conversation with Robn G. respecting Harry—Seaforth—Mr Thornewill—Mr Robt Gladstone. Read Mr Goschen's Report.

To G. J. GOSCHEN, first lord of the admiralty, 18 September 1872. Add MS 44542, f. 11.

I have reperused your speech, & have read for the first time the very able &

[1] *PP* 1870 lv. 177, reprinted in *Goschen's *Reports and speeches on local taxation* (1872).

[2] Sent by Hammond on 14 September, Add MS 44183, f. 480.

elaborate Report which accompanies it: also the curious Reports from the State of New York.
1. Could you not get some one to bring down your report[1] to the present time? There are a few points, too, where the statistics, usually so lucid, might be a little further cleared. 2. But the grave question is this—What case, or rag or shred of a case, have you left to the *Land* to claim relief out of the Exchequer.[2] Pray put yourself in the position of an advocate endeavouring to make a good argument for some such change as is now sought: & tell me how you would set about it? There is but one point that occurs to me, on the side of the Land, that you have not brought out fully. It is the effect of Villiers' Rating Act. That, I daresay, is better known now than it was at the date of your report. 3. There is another question of considerable moment. Take the case of new taxes in towns. They have been paid principally by the occupiers. It is very material to know (a) in what proportion they are mere taxes & in what proportion they represent value received. (b) in what proportion they tend to produce an increase of the rents. What will be the position of an occupier who (1) has paid in the main for certain improvements (2) finds the rent raised upon him in consequence of these improvements (3) and, also in consequence of these is called upon to pay an increase (or, what is the same thing, forego a diminution) of Imperial burdens? The upshot of the enquiries and reflections I have made is that I am at present rather uncomfortable. Not but that I am perfectly ready for martyrdom; but, until I hear what you can say against your own report, I seem but very little to see my way towards doing the thing that the H. of C. wants us to do. I should like to see the whole substance of your Report, with the latest information, put out in the best form, as a great document upon the subject. I have not yet written anything to Stansfeld: for all this is in truth preliminary. We are just off to Scotland for 3 weeks.
I doubt if the Cabinet generally have yet read your Report; it is very needful they should.

19. Th. [*Hillfoot House, Glasgow*]

Off at 8.30. Reached Glasgow at 5.30—Most hospitably received by the Lord Provost[4]—6 miles away. Conversation with the Ld Provost—Mr Irville[4]—Dr Cumming[5]—Wrote to J. Watson & S. Read Schiller's 30 Years War.[6]

20. Fr. [*Banavie, Inverness-shire*]

Off at 7.30 by Rail Steamer Coach & posting to Banavie[7] a journey

[1] On local taxation; letter agreeing, 19 September, finished 6 October, Add MS 44161, f. 210.

[2] 'I confess that while I see considerable arguments for relieving occupiers of houses, & some arguments for relieving occupiers of land, I have scarcely any argument for relieving owners of land'; ibid.

[3] Sir James Watson, Gladstone's stockbroker; there was a large crowd; *The Times*, 21 September 1872, 12a.

[4] Word smudged.

[5] Probably James Simpson Cumming, society doctor.

[6] First published in two parts 1791-2.

[7] At the s. end of the Caledonian Canal.

of near fifteen hours, with much cold but very interesting. At Banavie Inn we found fair accommodation & high charges. The Glencoe descent was grand: rather a nervous business. Read Schiller.

21. Sat. [*Invergarry House, Inverness-shire*][1]

St Matt: & memorable. 7¾-10½. To Invergarry: we breakfasted at our kind hosts. Walk with him & Halifax. Wrote to J. Watson & Smith—Professor Weir[2]—Sir T.G.—J.A. Godley—Mr Read—Maj. Blundell—Mr Fraser—Mr Macmillan—Sir Thos G.—Mr Ogilvy—Mr Burnett—& minutes. Conversation with Mr Malcolm[3]—Ld Halifax. Read Schiller.

22. 17 S. Trin.

Mg prayers & address upstairs. Prayers & hymns in evg. Wrote to Ld Granville—Mr Tallents—and minutes. Read Thos a Kempis—Hine on the Ten Tribes[4]—Jardine on Sacerdotalism[5]—Worked on G.s Note Fr. Treaty[6]—Hervey on Samarin[7]—Dodd's Addresses.[8]

23. M.

Wrote to Mrs Th.—Ld Chancellor—Mr Gurdon—Ld Northbrook—Ld Ln—Hugh W. Gladstone—Ld Camperdown—Mr Temple[9]—Bp of Winchester—The Queen—& minutes. Read Birt [*sic*] on Scotland[10]—Schiller—30 Y. War. We went a beautiful drive: saw falls, & the 'big tree' of Laddie' a [blank]. Conversation with Mr Brewster.

24. Tu.

Wrote to Chancr of Exr—Ld Hartington—and minutes. Read Burton & Tytler's Hist.[11]—Birt on the Highlands—Fergusson on Stone

[1] Seat of Edward Ellice, near Fort William.
[2] Reading uncertain; if Weir, then D. H. Weir, professor of oriental languages at Glasgow.
[3] Probably John Wingfield Malcolm of Poltalloch; M.P. Boston 1860.
[4] E. Hine, *The English nation identified with the lost ten tribes of Israel* (1872).
[5] J. *Jardine, *Christian sacerdotalism* (1871).
[6] See Ramm I, ii. 347.
[7] Not found.
[8] P. H. Dodd, perhaps 'No change for the worse a mistaken notion' (1803).
[9] Robert Temple, 1829-1902, school inspector and priest; on preferment? Add MS 44542, f. 12.
[10] E. Burt, *Letters from a gentleman in the North of Scotland*, 2v. (1754); notes in Add MS 44760, f. 187.
[11] P. F. *Tytler, *Elements of history*, ed. J. H. Burton (1855).

Monuments[1]—Schiller Geschichte des Dreyzigjährigen Kreiges. Hill drive, & walk with Halifax. We had a long conversation on the Govt —Irish Education—& Local Taxation. Whist in evg.

To R. LOWE, chancellor of the exchequer, Add MS 44542, f. 13.
24 September 1872.

We shall probably meet in Cabinet soon after the middle of October, & I hope you will before that time be able to fix your mind upon the heavy questions which are impending with respect to Local Taxation. First & foremost, I recommend the study, if you have not yet read it, of Goschen's Report.[2] It seems to me at first view that he cuts the ground from under the feet of those who contend that new charges ought to be laid upon the Exchequer in relief of the burdens upon landed property. At least I do not yet see what sufficient case they can make. He seems to shew that instead of paying more for rates than they used to do, they are paying (in the pound) less; & if they are not paying more, what just plea have they, or rather can they have, for relief? Other very grave questions arise upon the second great department of the subject—relief to towns; the occupiers in towns have borne heavy charges, the benefit will after a season alight on the owners whose property will be improved & will bring them more rent. This is an odd ground for giving them aid out of the taxes? All this I find very indigestible, & I seek the aid of wiser heads & stronger stomachs. Wishing you a good time at Glasgow.

25. Wed.

Wrote to Col. Ponsonby—Mr Lowe—Sir R. Palmer—Mr Ogilvy—and minutes. Read Schiller—Birt on Highlands. Went to Ardillie—& the Garry falls. Measured some fine birches: 7 f. 6 in to 7.10 in. Whist in evg.

26. Th.

Wrote to Chancr of Exr—Drumnadrochit Hotel—Messrs Watson & S.—Mr D. Robertson—Mr Monsell—Ld Spencer—and minutes. Read Schiller—Birt on the Highland—Drove to see the vitrified forts: & a round homewards. Whist in evg.

To EARL SPENCER, Irish lord lieutenant, Add MS 44542, f. 14.
26 September 1872.

The longer of the two papers[3] which you have sent me contains a number of very important heads on which it will be very useful to the Cabinet to have the

[1] J. *Fergusson, *Rude stone monuments in all countries* (1872).

[2] Lowe replied, 29 September 1872, Add MS 44302, f. 65, that he had read and would reread Goschen: 'I can't agree with him that the occupier pays the rate'; see Lowe's mem. of 8 November 1872, PRO T 168/82 and 18 Sept. 72.

[3] On Irish universities.

existing information well & succinctly put together. Of the heads suggested by Mr. Roundell I think nos. 3-5 are less urgent in point of time than the others. In a former letter, written at or since the end of the Session, I pointed out matters on which we must look for the special aid of the Irish Government, & I do not know that, being without my papers here, I can so well repeat them. There is one [matter] of much importance & delicacy on which I think no one can inform us except you, Hartington, or some person having already considerable acquaintance with *persons* in Ireland, & particularly with the resident governing body of Trinity College. It is the question how far is it practicable & politic for us to attempt to work in concert with Trinity College or with any part of it? I doubt if Brodrick, going to the country as a stranger (if he be such) could perform this part of the duty to be done. I think the person who is to enquire should be put in possession generally of the views of the Government. We are pledged to redress the R.C. grievance; which is held to consist in this, that an R.C. educated in a college or place where his religion is taught cannot by virtue of that education obtain a degree in Ireland. Beyond this, I think we desire that a portion of the public endowments should be thrown open, under the auspices of a neutral University, to the whole of the Irish people. In the Cabinet I think none of us have seen how this part of the design could be fulfilled except by funds drawn from Trinity College, or how the general question could be settled except upon the basis of a severance between Dublin University & Dublin College. Besides the delicate questions I have named, there is another point of difficulty with which a man like Mr. Roundell or Mr Brodrick would be most competent to deal. Our plan seems likely to take the shape of a proposal for establishing an examining University like that of London. Such an University will be vehemently opposed by Playfair, who leads others, on academic grounds. It is most important that we should be in a condition to hold whatever position we take up in reference to this part of the question. These two I think are the portions of the subject on which we shall most want aid. We must know how the principle of an examining University has actually worked, in England Ireland France Belgium or elsewhere. Playfair, in the argument he will probably make in this subject, will be fighting the battle of the college universities of Scotland against an independent examining body. I have now said all that occurs to me in the way of suggestion towards the examination about to be held. For how long a time do you remain in England? I think there will be a Cabinet about the 3d week in October, & if you were in England there might be a great advantage in your attending it. I am going to Guisachan, Beauly, for several days, but my surest address is 10 Downing Street. I return your enclosures. Any report obtained through F.O. should I think, have reference to specific points definitely stated so as to prevent delay.

27. Fr. [*Guisachan, Inverness-shire*]

Wrote to Mr Layard—Sig. Errera[1]—Mr Bruce—Mr Hammond (Tel.)—and minutes. Goodbye after breakf. to this pleasant house. Walk

[1] Complimenting Alberto Errera, Italian economist, for his *La vita e i tempi di Daniele Manin* (1872) (sent by Layard), telling him '. . . it was from him [Manin] that . . . I had my first lessons upon Italian unity as the indispensable basis of all effectual reform under the peculiar circumstances of that country'; Add MS 44542, f. 15. But see 1 July 54.

to Fort Augustus. Mr Rufford's[1] Yacht to Drumnadrochit Pier. Conversation with Mr Wells of the Hotel.[2] Drove to Corrimony:[3] where we surveyed the House and Library and had tea. He is marvellously young at (nearly) 77. Saw his Library. On at 5¼. Reached Guisachan[4] by a grand steep descent at 7½. A large party & warm welcome. Conversation with Mr [blank]—also with the Duke of M.[5] and Ld Manvers[6] respecting the Labourers. Read Schiller.

28. Sat.

Wrote to Mrs Th.—The Queen (l. & Mem.)—Ld Granville—Mr Hammond—Col. Ponsonby (Tel.)—and P. Master of Beauly—and minutes. Rode & walk to see Falls. Plagued with my head wh makes me a plague to others. Sir D. M[arjoribanks] took me over many of his beautiful works of Art. Read Schiller—Birt.

29. 18 S.Trin.

Read aloud prayers & a Sermon (part) by Horsley.[7] Walk with a party to more Falls. My head again a plague. Conversation with Lady M.—It would be hard not to like this family. Read Bp Horsley's Sermon—Abp (Archdn) Manning's Sermons[8]—Wedgwood's J. Wesley[9]—Hugh Miller's Testimony of the Rocks[10]—Thomas a Kempis—Woodgate on Athan. Creed: very able.[11]

30. M.

Wrote to Col. Ponsonby l.—Mr Cardwell—Mr W. Cowper—Col. Ponsonby Tel.—Beauly Postmaster—The Queen (Mem.)—and minutes. Read Birt's Highlands—Schiller (finished Vol. I.) Rode to Loch Affrick: drive back: feast there. The Lodge is only too luxurious: the view from it wonderfully fine: Chisholm Pass resembles Finstermünze[12]—what more can be said?

[1] F. T. Rufford of Cullachy.
[2] Drumnadrochit hotel, on Loch Ness, at the foot of Glen Urquhart.
[3] At the head of Glen Urquhart, seat of Thomas Ogilvy.
[4] On the head waters of the Glass, 22 m. S.W. of Beauly; seat of Sir D. C. Marjoribanks; see 5 Apr. 62.
[5] Marlborough; see 3 Oct. 72.
[6] Sydney William Herbert Pierrepont, 1825-1900; 3rd Earl Manvers 1860; a tory.
[7] See 24 Apr. 59. [8] See 12 Mar. 43. [9] See 11 Aug. 72.
[10] H. *Miller, *The testimony of the rocks* (1857).
[11] H. A. Woodgate, *A common sense view of the Athanasian Creed question* (1872).
[12] Pass between Austria and Switzerland.

Tues. Oct. One. 1872.

Wrote to Mr Ogilvy—Mr Macrae—and minutes. Read Birt—Göthe's Werter[1]—The Old & Remarkable Trees of Scotland. Drive to Cogie through the Burnt Forest. Walk with Lady M[arjoribanks] & conversation chiefly on religion.

2. Wed.

Wrote to Mr Ayrton—Ld Granville—Mr Goschen—Sir R. Palmer—Mrs Th.—and minutes. Read Birt Vol. II—Göthe's Werter—NAR on Dante[2]—Fordown's Chronicle.[3] Walk with Sir D.M. Saw the King Fir—and fresh beautiful objects of which there is no end.

3. Th. [*Strathconan*]

Preparations for going. Read Göthe's Werter. Off at midday: 42 miles to Strathconan.[4] Staid ½ hour at Beauly for Post and Tel. Music in evg. We were in a very Conservative party at Guisachan—Marlboroughs, Darnleys,[5] Manverses, Mr Hughes,[6] and others: but all was genial & cordial as it *could* be. Wrote to Ld Granville Tel.—Mr Maguire—Mr Bass—Lord M.—and minutes.

4. Fr.

Wrote to Mrs Heywood—Dowager Lady Waterford—Agnes G.—Ld Granville—Mr Glyn Tel.—Mr Gurdon Tel.—Ld Granville—Chr of Exr—Miss Barry—Col. Foley—Postmaster at Beauly—and minutes. Long walk, & pleasant tho' in rain & snow, with Mr Balfour. Conversation with Mr Smith his Agent. Read Göthe—Dr Willis's Spinoza.[7]

5. Sat.

Wrote to Mr Gurdon—Sec. LNW Railway—Mr [R. N.] Philips MP—and minutes. Walked to wood & falls with the Balfour brothers.[8] Read Werther—Göthe's Spinoza [*sic*]. Much conversation.

[1] *Sic.* First published 1774.
[2] *North American Review*, cxv. 139 (July 1872).
[3] Joannes de Fordun, *Scoti-Chronicon, sive Scotorum historia* (1684).
[4] A. J. *Balfour's shooting lodge, w. of Dingwall.
[5] John Stuart Bligh, 1827–96, 6th earl of Darnley 1835.
[6] Probably W. B. Hughes, see 16 Oct. 47, by now a tory.
[7] R. Willis, *Benedict de Spinoza, his life, correspondence and ethics* (1870).
[8] A. J. had four brothers: Cecil Charles, 1849–81; Francis Maitland, 1851–82, professor of animal morphology; Gerald William, 1853–1945, politician and 2nd earl; Eustace James Anthony, 1854–1911, scientist.

6. 19 S.Trin.

Mg prayers & a discourse in our rooms at 11—Prayers & Hymns in evg.—Went to the Kirk at 12. A dismal business. The parochial congregation three persons. Wrote to Ld Hartington. Read Wedgwood's Wesley[1]—Willis's Spinoza—Row's Moral Teaching of N.T.—a good book.[2]

To LORD HARTINGTON, Irish secretary, Add MS 44542, f. 18.
6 October 1872.

I have received a letter from Brodrick stating reasons why he cannot comply with our request. I do not suppose he can be further pressed. As we are to meet so soon I need not now enter in the subject: probably you will be prepared with further suggestions. I will only say that, so far as I can see, an Irish University measure ought to be the *first* measure of the Session & ought to be introduced within the first few days of it.[3]

7. M.

Wrote to Queen (Mem)—Postmaster of Beauly—Ld Granville (Tel.)—H.N.G.—Mr Gurdon (do.)—H.J.G.—The Ld Chancellor—Mr Ayrton—Mrs Th.—and minutes. Also wrote a paper of Suggestions, or advice, for our dear son Herbert on his going to Oxford. We went 9 or 10 miles up the Valley: a grand view into the head mountains near the close. More conversation with Mr B[alfour] who is a person of great charm. Read Göthe's Werter—Miss Austen's Emma.

8. Tu.

Wrote to Ld Granville—Mr Baillie Cochrane—Postmaster of Beauly—and minutes. Read Werther—Emma—Curci Pensione Universitaria.[4] Arr[angements] for departure.

9. Wed. [*On train*]

Wrote to C.G. Off before 8 over the hill to Achnanalt with Mr B. & nearly all the party: The lake nearly caused my missing the Train but by effort we gained it.[5] I had a journey of 650 miles without break.

[1] See 11 August 72.
[2] C. A. Row, *The moral teaching of the new testament, viewed as evidential to the historical truth* (1872).
[3] Hartington wrote on 10 October that Spencer said Brodrick would help, if Gladstone asked him.
[4] By C. M. Curci.
[5] See the amusing account in A. J. Balfour, *Chapters of autobiography* (1930), 70, and Bassett, 195.

Bruce got in at Grantown & we discussed various things.[1] Read Werther & Curci. A good night. The Loch Luichart rapid very fine: & the Highland line very fine from Aviemore to Dunkeld.

10. Th. [London]

Reached C.H.T. (1¼ h. late) at 11¼. Worked sharply till after 7½. Wrote to The Queen (l. & Mem.)—Col. Ponsonby—Rev Mr Cowie[2]—Spanish Minr—Mr Pollock[3]—Dean Saunders—Herbert J.G.—Ld Chancellor—Mr Stansfeld—Bp of Bangor—and minutes. Saw Ld F. Cavendish—Ld Lyons—Ld Granville—Mr Bruce—Mr Stansfeld—Mr Glyn—Dean of St Paul's—S.E.G.—and divers Colleagues. Read Werther—Dined at No 15 [Grosvenor Square] & staid late X. Cabinet 3 [*sic*]-7¼.

Cabinet Thurs. Oct. 10. 72. 2 PM.[4]

√ French Treaty. Question between a. a Tariff Treaty. b. a m[ost] f[avoured] n[ation] Treaty—with certain exceptions. General sentiment of the Cabinet in favour of b. M.F.N. Clause to be without limit of time. To include Colonies in the Treaty.[5]

11. Fr.

Wrote to Ld Penzance—Mr T.B. Potter—The Queen—Chancr of Exr—Scotts—& minutes. Wrote to C.G.—Mr Burnett—Agnes G. Saw Ld Lyttelton—Ld Chancellor—Mr Glyn—Mr Stansfeld[6] *cum* Mr Goschen—Ld Hartington—Ld Halifax—Ld Granville. Cabinet 12½-5¼. Finished Werther. Dined with the Godleys:[7] & much conversation. He is notable. Saw Fitzroy[R].

Cabinet. Oct. 11. 1872. Noon.[8]

√ Cons[ideration] of French Treaty resumed. Decision on the Colonial question

[1] Bruce told his wife (*Letters of Lord Aberdare* (1902), i. 351): 'He was very friendly and communicative, and I saw more of him than ever I did before. Like me, he was very much disgusted at being thus summoned to a Cabinet, which is required for the purpose of discussing commercial relations with France.'

[2] Offering deanery of Manchester to Benjamin Morgan Cowie, 1816-1900; dean of Manchester 1872-83, of Exeter from 1883; defended ritualists.

[3] Sir Frederick Montagu-Pollock, 1815-74, 2nd bart.; on his fa.'s recent d.; Add MS 44542, f. 20.

[4] Add MS 44640, f. 179; draft for amended version of the 1860 treaty, marked 'cancelled', at ibid., f. 182.

[5] Most-favoured-nation treaty signed with France on 5 November 1872.

[6] Summoned in anticipation that this day's cabinet would 'take our first bite at the uninviting subject of local taxation'; to Stansfeld, 10 October 1872, Add MS 44542, f. 19.

[7] i.e. his secretary and his wife, Sarah, *née* James.

[8] Add MS 44640, f. 184.

which was begun yesterday. Abstract for submission to the French agreed to in substance.[1]
Irish Education (university). Preliminary conversation.

12. Sat.

Wrote to The Queen—Mr Goulburn—Herbert J.G.—Mrs Heywood—and minutes. Cabinet 1¼–5¼. Saw Freshfields—Ld F.C.—S.E.G. (respecting Herbert &c.)—Ld Halifax—Mr Glyn—The Spanish Minister[2]—Mr Goschen *cum* Mr Stansfeld—Rev. D. Robertson. Read Brief aus dem Schweitz[3]—Menken's Remains[4]—Scott's Life of Dryden.[5] Dined at No 15 G.S. & staid late X: a notable conversation.[6]

*Cabinet. Oct. 12. 72. 1. AM. [*sic*].*[7]
√ Draft of French Treaty—approved for subm[issio]n of substance to M. Gavard and Osanne [*sic*].
√ Appl[icatio]n from Commissioner of Customs. WEG. to reply as within.[8]
√ Ld Granville & WEG not to accept Brazilian Order.
√ Sir B. Frere to go to Zanzibar accredited.[9] Instructions discussed & agreed on.
√ Sir R. Palmer's remuneration. 10m[ille] offered. He himself proposes 6m[ille]. We agree to 6m.
√ Mr Fenwick. Not to be restored at present: case cannot be considered within 7 years. No pledge.[10]
√ WEG stated the upshot of the correspondence with H.M. respecting the P. of W[ales], Ireland, and the Throne.

13. 20 S.Trin.

Chapel Royal mg & St Peter's Lambeth evg. Saw Duke of Cambridge—Ld Granville—H.N.G.—Mr Glyn—S.E.G. Wrote to Mr Fortescue—Mr Forster—Mr Bruce (l. & Tel.)—Mrs Burnett—C.G.—Sir W. Gomm—W.H.G.—Bp of Rochester. Read 'Homo'[11]—The Babel of the Sects[12]—Leading ideas of the Gospels.[13]

[1] Colonies on both sides included in the treaty.
[2] Note passed to Granville in cabinet reads: 'I saw Spanish Minister today; found he had not seen you; spoke to him as we had agreed'; Add MS 44640, f. 189.
[3] Perhaps *Briefe einer reisenden Dame aus der Schweitz 1786* (1787).
[4] G. Menken, probably *Selections from the discourses* (1834).
[5] See 24 July 46.
[6] i.e. with Mrs Thistlethwayte.
[7] Add MS 44640, f. 187.
[8] Draft untraced.
[9] As commissioner to negotiate a slave trade treaty; for disagreements about his instructions, see Ramm I, ii. 357.
[10] Obscure.
[11] Probably W. P. Lyon, *Homo versus Darwin* (1872).
[12] H. T. *Edwards, *The Babel of the sects and the unity of Pentecost* (1872).
[13] *Leading doctrines of the Gospels* (1870).

14. M.

Wrote to Mrs Heywood—M. Chevalier—Herbert J.G.—Ld Kimberley—Agnes G.—The Queen—C.G.—and minutes. Cabinet 1¼-6¼. Saw Ld Ripon—D of Argyll—Chancr of Exr—Mr Glyn—Lord F.C.—Ld Spencer. Dined with Panizzi, & much conversation. Some on religion. Then to No 15 G.S.

Cabinet. Oct. 14. 72. 1 PM.[1]

a.

√ French Treaty. Ld Gr. reported that France objects to giving the Comm[issio]n power to give compensatory duties. Clause II &c. See inf.

√ Lord Mayor's Dinner. WEG. proposes not to go this year. Acquiesced in. Ld G. will attend.[2]

b.

√ Treaty again considered. Art II (the great one) settled.[3] Question of the signature of the powers of the Comm[issio]n. Modifications suggested.

√ General conversation introduced by WEG. on the question of Local Taxation —much prolonged.

[4]Review of present grants & award. Representative. to be applied universally. Division of Rate. Exemptions. Consolidation of Rate. Uniformity of Assessment. 1. Analyse to the last point the division between urban & rural. 2. Also the question how far the rates are remunerative & to whom.

1. To proceed by Resolution. 2. To come *after* Irish Education. 3. To keep the cases of urban & rural entirely distinct in the argument.

As to *rural*. Query take first the secondary points—or the main one. Is relief to be given to the Landowners of the country at the expence of the Exchequer a. without proof that they have suffered an aggravation of their burdens? b. without any augmentation of the Imperial taxes affecting the land?

To M. CHEVALIER, 14 October 1872. Add MS 44542, f. 21.

A few days ago I wrote to Mr Potter,[5] who had sent me a letter of yours, to the effect that he might assure you of my unchanged adherence to the principles & objects of 1860 whatever force there may be in the consideration that the application of such principles must be subject to considerations of time, place, & circumstance. Of this assurance, with respect to my colleagues as well as myself, a practical proof was given when we declined the proposals made to us in 1871 by the Government of France. Since that time, two changes have taken place; the Legislature, that is to say the Nation by its highest organ, has spoken; & the proposals have been materially changed. Whether an arrangement can or will be made I am not yet in a condition to say: but the apparent basis is one much more conformable than I had expected to our declarations of last year, & to what I think you would consider to be sound principle. Although my position, with reference to the Treaty of 1860, was in the second rank & not in the first,

[1] Add MS 44640, f. 190.

[2] Granville fell ill, and the City felt neglected; see Add MS 44542, f. 31.

[3] Timing and nature of tariffs.

[4] Gladstone's notes for local taxation discussion; Add MS 44640, f. 191.

[5] T. B. Potter, on 11 October; Add MS 44542, f. 20.

no one has felt a more lively interest in all that belonged to it. I am glad to see that, in the interesting letter you have sent me, Prince Bismarck does justice to the Imperial Government with reference to its commercial policy, for which your country owes you individually much, in the creation of that strong sentiment in France on behalf of Free Trade which has materially, I think, & beneficially modified the policy of the Government.

To LORD KIMBERLEY, colonial secretary, Add MS 44542, f. 22.
14 October 1872.

I incline to agree with you[1] that under the difficult circumstances of the case the best course will be to leave the Canadian Act 'to its operation' with care taken that it should not operate, in consequence of the non-issue of any order in council for giving it effect. At the same time the understanding from the Canadian side should be a clear one, & I conclude that before definitely deciding on this course you would mention the matter to the Cabinet. On this footing we should be well out of it: at least if I am right in believing that when the great Colonies advisedly determine on adopting any differential system, they will sooner or later, & rather soon than late, carry their point, & we shall not be able to make it an articulus of separation unless they insist on our committing a breach of faith with Treaty Powers. If we have no most favoured nation Clause with America for produce, how was it that Mr Everett in 1843–4 made us pay down a large sum for having admitted W. Coast of Africa Rice at a lower duty than S. Carolina?[2] The answer occurs to me while I write; Ld. Palmerston got it done *I think* on Negrophilistic principles in violation of our own law. It might however be as well to refer back.

15. Tu.

Wrote to D. of Cambridge—Mr Cardwell—The Queen—Robn G.—Sir A. Panizzi—Ld Kimberley—Sir T.D. Lloyd—B. Benjamin—Ld Northbrook—Chr of Exchr—Mr Reverdy Johnson. Saw Mr F. Lawley—Mr Godley—Scotts—Mr & Mrs Stuart Wortley—Baroness Burdett Coutts. Shopping. Dined at No 15 G.S. Saw Russell X. Finished Curci.

To LORD KIMBERLEY, colonial secretary, Add MS 44542, f. 23.
15 October 1872.

I agree with every word in your succinct & able statement on the Montreal guarantee,[3] subject to the slightest reservation. If we part with the secret

[1] Kimberley to Gladstone, 14 October 1872, Add MS 44224, f. 300, on a mem. on 'the Canadn. Act empowering the Gov. Genl. by Order in Council to impose a differential duty on tea & coffee imported via the U.S.'; Lisgar had irregularly accepted the Bill. See 3 Dec. 72.

[2] See 17 Feb. 72.

[3] Kimberley to Gladstone, 14 October 1872, Add MS 44224, f. 303, suggesting acceptance of Canadian proposal for British guarantee of £4 million for 'peaceful works' on determination of fortification guarantees; but secret correspondence with MacDonald should not be referred to. See 28 Nov. 72.

correspondence as you suggest, I think it should still be left to appear upon the papers that it is Canada which proposes the commutation of the Guarantee. It should also, I suppose, be left very clear that we have & give no opinion upon the pecuniary success of the Railroad, & incur no moral or other responsibility with regard to it. In addition to the reasons which you give for giving up the fortification of Montreal, or for no longer pressing it, it appears worthy of being remembered that it would be a direct challenge to the Americans, if they chose to regard it so, & would warrant retaliatory works of theirs. Of the two scowling [*sic*] foundations probably theirs would be the most effective. The fortifying plan was a got-up thing; the breakdown of the estimates I regard as a matter of course; & relief from the whole business will be to me welcome—while on the other hand the gradual education of Canada into something like a real nation, which began with Cardwell in 1864-6 & is now proceeding under your care, is one of the most interesting political processes in the present administration of the Empire.

To LORD NORTHBROOK, viceroy of India, 15 October 1872. Add MS 44542, f. 22.

I need only say a very few words in answer to your interesting letter of Sept. 9.[1] Although I believe no word has dropped from me in public to increase any difficulties con[cerned] with the Indian Income Tax, I confess that the original proposal of it, I think by Mr Wilson, greatly startled me, for with the knowledge I have of the difficulty of working our Income Tax in England, I have never been able to understand how such an Impost could be rendered tolerable under the conditions of Indian Society & administration; & while I have little direct knowledge on the subject I always had impressions of opinion such as yours [as] indication of a desire to get rid of it, if & when possible without incurring greater evils. I have spoken to the D. of Argyll about the financial appointment to be made for next spring, & I am sure that his views and desires correspond with your own. Into the spirit of your remarks on our tenure of India I entirely enter. My own desires are chiefly these, that nothing may bring about a sudden, violent, or discreditable severance; that we may labour steadily to promote the political training of our fellow-subjects; & that when we go, if we are to go, we may leave a clean bill of accounts behind us.

16. Wed. [*Cloverley*][2]

Packed & off at 8.30. Met Mr Sturt MP.[3] in train. Then Robn G. at Crewe. Reached Cloverley at 2.30. Wrote to C.G. Read Q.R. on St Paul's (pt)[4]—Herdmans Lpool[5]—D. of Wellington as Statesman.[6] Much conversation: & seeing the place.

[1] Add MS 44266, f. 26 reporting 'considerable discontent' in India from income and local taxation.

[2] Near Market Drayton, seat of Arthur Pemberton Heywood-Lonsdale of Cloverley and Shavington; also Flintshire J.P.

[3] One of the brothers, both tories: C. N. Sturt, see 20 Apr. 61, or Henry Gerard Sturt, 1825-1904; M.P. Dorset 1856-76; cr. Baron Alington 1876.

[4] *Quarterly Review*, cxxxiii. 342 (October 1872).

[5] W. G. *Herdman, *Pictorial relics of ancient Liverpool* (1843).

[6] [By G. R. *Gleig], *Quarterly Review*, cxxxiii. 293 (October 1872).

17. Th.

Wrote to Bp of Winchester—Sir A. Panizzi—Agnes G.—Archdn Harrison—Ly E.M. Pringle—Sir R. Palmer—& minutes. Further survey of this notable house, & appurtenances. Drove to Shavington (& elsewhere); a sad & saddening sight. Walk about the lake: measured two fine trees. Read Q.R. on the Position of Parties[1]—and Memoirs of Harriette Wilson: a book more immoral than many others which are more indelicate.[2]

18. Fr. [Hawarden]

Agnes's birthday. May every blessing crown her. Wrote to Mrs Thistlethwayte—J. Watson & Smith—Rev R.F. Smith[3]—Ld Granville (2)—The Queen (Mem)—Ld Spencer—Ld Penzance—and minutes. Read Q.R. on Stockmar—Gil Blas.[4] Saw Robn G. on Police case.[5] Planted a tree on the lawn: & left amidst kindly demonstrations soon after noon. Reached Hn at 3.—Found I had to lie up in evg for a cold.

19. Sat.

My chest tight: kept my bed all day. Read Schiller's 30 Years War—Gilblas [*sic*].

20. S.

Mg prayers alone. Came down in evg. Saw Mr Parker on his Roman Labours.[6] Wrote to Mr Bruce—Mrs J. Stuart Wortley—Col. Ponsonby (Tel.)—and minutes. Read Life of Patteson[7]—Sermons on the Prodigal Son[8]—Rawlinson on Sacred & Profane History.[9]

21. M.

Came down in aftn. Wrote to Mr Fortescue—Mr Monsell—& minutes. Read Gilblas—Began V. 2.—Schiller Dreyzigjahr. Kreig—Biogr. Dict. on Le Sage.

[1] By [*Salisbury], *Quarterly Review*, cxxxiii. 558 (October 1872).

[2] 4v. (1825); a noted courtesan, her memoirs written to spite the duke of Beaufort.

[3] Robert Frederick Smith, priest in Southwell, had written on *Juventus Mundi*; Add MS 44542, f. 24.

[4] By A.-R. Lesage, 4v. (1715-35).

[5] Unmentioned in family correspondence; rescue?

[6] i.e. J. H. *Parker.

[7] C. M. Yonge, *Life of J. C. Patteson, missionary bishop of the Melanesian Islands*, 2v. (1872); reviewed by Gladstone in 1874, see above, vol. vii, section X.

[8] Perhaps R. G. Swayne, 'The voice of the Good Shepherd . . . exposition on the parable of the Prodigal Son' (1868).

[9] See 18 June 71.

22. Tu.

Wrote to Ld R. Grosvenor—The Queen (Mem)—Mr Hayward—Ld Granville—Sir B. Frere—Chancr of Exr (2)—Mr W. Evans—Ld Mayor Elect[1]—Herbert J.G.—& minutes. Down before noon: *viewing* at the Rectory in afternoon, & cut two small trees. Read Schiller—Gil Blas.

23. Wed.

Ch. 8½ AM. Wrote to Mr M. Gladstone—Mr Godley—Mrs Th.—and minutes. The F.C.s came. Read Schiller—Gil Blas. Walk with S. Superintending the placing of new bookcases.

24. Th.

Ch. 8½ A.M. Wrote to Ld Granville—L. & Tel.—Bp of Manchester—Ld Ripon—Bp of Peterborough—Mr Cowie—Mrs Heywood—Sir T.G.—The Queen—Mr Godley (2 Tell.)—and minutes. Read Schiller—Gilblas finished Vol. 2. Conversation with Lucy C[avendish] on Future State & Punishment. Went to Aston Hall works with F.C.

25. Fr.

Wrote to Ld Ripon—and minutes. Ch. 8½ A.M. Read Schiller—Gilblas—Playfair on Examining Universities[2]—Tennyson's Gareth and Lynette.[3] Surveying Field & Hedge Trees.

26. Sat.

Ch. 8½ AM. Wrote to Ld Granville Tells[4] 2—Mr Godley Tel.—Mr Hayward—Chr of Exr (2)—Ld Hartington—M. Chevalier—& minutes. Saw F.C. on Surinam case.[5] Read Schiller—Gilblas—Lowe's Speech at Glasgow.[6] Conversation with Canon Blomfield.

[1] See 12 July 66; Sir Sydney Hedley Waterlow, 1822-1906, stationer; liberal M.P. Dumfries 1868-9; Maidstone 1874-80, Gravesend 1880-5; lord mayor 1872; cr. bart. 1873. Gladstone regretted he could not attend the dinner (see 14 Oct. 72); Add MS 44542, f. 29.

[2] L. *Playfair, 'On teaching universities and examining boards' (1872).

[3] From 'The last Tournament' in *Idylls of the King* (1872).

[4] i.e. Telegrams.

[5] Papers not found.

[6] On receiving its freedom; see *The Times*, 27 September 1872, 6a.

To LORD HARTINGTON, Irish secretary, Add MS 44542, f. 32.
26 October 1872.

I do not know whether you have read Lyon Playfair's pamphlet on Examining Universities.[1] Plausible throughout, it is I think really strong in its argument on the exclusive power of directing & cramping thought, through uniformity, which may result from giving over to one body the entire controul of the higher examinations in a country. I am disposed to agree with P. in holding that it is examination which determines study & that a single Board, Senate, or be what it may, ought not to be allowed to determine the studies of a country. If you have not read P., wait till you receive a copy which will be sent to you & postpone till after reading it the consideration of this letter. The problem is, how to maintain variety & independence of study, together with the exclusive possession of it by a single University (if the Queen's University were left out it would make little difference relatively to the present argument) of the right of granting degrees upon examination. It seems to me that probably we might meet this problem by reserving certain rights to the colleges which may furnish candidates to the University. Let Trinity College for example be enabled to lay down a scheme of examination in subjects, textbooks, or both, for its own students; & let the University have a *Veto* upon this scheme or any portion of it for insufficiency until it is brought up to what it may consider the proper mark. Then let the University appoint the Examiners, but with a power to the college to appoint an assessor in each branch who is to take part in the examination. As regards unattached or Private Students they might elect to be examined on any of the reorganised or permitted schemes of examination. Care would be required in adjusting the provisions of such a plan, but I do not see why it might not be practicable. It is sound in principle, for it preserves central controul, & controul is what there ought to be at the centre, not impulsion or imitation which ought to be left open & various. Under such a system, honestly worked, the different metaphysical, ethical, & perhaps historical schools might each find its place. The question is very important. I have *mentioned* it to Lowe. I should like it to be submitted at the proper time to men of the stamp of Roundell. It is also a matter for consideration whether we should or should not beforehand offer to communicate with Playfair himself.
Your brother F[rederick Cavendish] suggests that any deviation from uniformity would perplex the giving of honours & prizes. Would not the numerical standard, to which everything is reduced in answer to questions, furnish the requisite common measure?

To R. LOWE, chancellor of the exchequer, Add MS 44542, f. 28.
26 October 1872.

I have been reading Playfair's pamphlet on Examining Universities, with which you are acquainted; & it has made an impression on me with reference to two questions which it seems to raise. 1. Should it not be answered, by some competent person, more in harmony than Playfair himself is with the views of the Government on the Irish Question? 2. What can we *do*, in framing our plan, to meet the substantial part of his argument, which I take to be that having reference to the excessive & injurious power which may pass into the hands of

[1] Hartington replied, 30 October, Add MS 44143, f. 196, that he had read Playfair, that it was hard to answer him, and enclosing papers by Thompson; see 31 Oct. 72.

an examining body? In other parts of his argument I do not concur: he is fighting for the present system of the Scotch Universities; but it is to be remembered that he has a very strong position in the House with regard to questions of education, that his great ability in speaking will, upon this question, exactly play into the hands of the opposition & induce their warm sympathy, & that whatever really has force in his pamphlet should be met by suitable provisions, but if it be not so met it should carry the whole with a rush. I commend all this to your careful consideration,[1] & I will cause copies of this pamphlet to be sent to all members of the Cabinet & to the Viceroy.

27. 22 S. Trin.

Ch mg & evg. Wrote to The Queen (2 Mema)—Sir T. Western—Mr Bramston — Mr Cardwell — S.E.G. — Secy S.P.G. — Scotts — Mr Chamberlain—Chancr of Exr—G.G. Glyn—Ld Enfield (Tel.)—and minutes. Saw A. Lyttelton *cum* C.G.—Mr Chamberlain *cum* do—Also Stephen, on the murmurs in the Parish respecting changes in Divine Service. Read Bp of Bangor's Charge[2]—Bligh on Revision of the Prayerbook[3]—Life of Bp Patteson.

To E. CARDWELL, war secretary, 27 October 1972. Add MS 44542, f. 29.

It is perhaps because you have seen the full papers, & I only the précis,[4] that I am not quite able to concur with your views of the report on the cases in which the employment of soldiers to get in the harvest has been complained of. The third case seems to be satisfactory. But, in the first, what was the cause of the departure of the men? If it was the refusal of the 14/- wages, I can hardly think it was right to employ soldiers to fill their place, consistently with the doctrine of non-interference. Especially if—which I do not know—the soldiers came from a distance, & with any release from military duties. In the second case, there is no specification of the demands called exorbitant. The allegation of the complainants is not distinctly denied, viz. that the dismissals were for belonging to the Union. The annoyance given by women & children was surely no cause for allowing soldiers to come in, though if they appeared to break the law it may have been a good reason for prosecuting them. Such are my first impressions. Perhaps the matter may be more easily handled in conversation between us. Let me notice that, having F. Cavendish here, I gave him your letter & inclosure, without any intimation of my own opinions: & he, after considering, took objection on the 1st two cases—indeed his argument influenced my mind as to no. 1. Many thanks for your kindness in sending me the mem. as to Mr Foxton;[5] it will be most acceptable in my brother's family.

[1] Reply untraced.
[2] J. C. Campbell, 'A charge . . . 1872' (1872).
[3] E. V. Bligh, *Letters on Church reform* (1871).
[4] Sent by Cardwell on 25 October 1872, PRO 30/48/9 f. 78.
[5] Obscure.

28. SS.Simon & Jude.

Ch. 11. AM. Wrote to Ld Selborne (Chancr)—Bp of Bangor—Mr J. Wilson—Mr [W.] O. Stanley—Dean Ramsay—Ld Lyttelton—and minutes. Read Schiller—Gilblas—Gareth & Lynette: finished. We are not now on the level of Guinevere or the Passing of Arthur: though still on a high level. We felled a beech.

29. Tu.

Ch. 8½ AM. Wrote to Lord Enfield (Tel.)—Mr Cardwell—Mr Goschen—Ld Mayor Elect—Chr of Exr—& minutes. Read Gilblas—Schiller—and Cairnes on Irish Educn.[1] Kibbled the felled beech.

30. Wed.

Ch. 8½ A.M. Wrote to Ld Chancellor—Ld Granville—S.E.G.—Mr Monsell—Mr Glyn—Dr Moffatt—and minutes. Worked on another Beech. Saw Mr Burnett—Mr Agnew respecting the Rectory Prints, & his *métier* generally. Read Schiller—Gil Blas.

31. Th.

Ch. 8½ AM. Wrote to Ld Hartington—Ld Chancellor—Mr Forster—Sir R.W. Bulkeley—Ld Granville (Tel.)—J. Watson & Smith—and minutes. Finished Schiller 30jahr. Krieg. Read Gil Blas—Bp of Lincoln's Acct of A.C. Congress—But what a John Bull exhibn he made[2]—Thompsons papers on Irish Univ. Educn.[3]

To LORD HARTINGTON, Irish secretary, 31 October 1872. **Add MS 44542, f. 33.**

I have read Thompson's pamphlet with much interest—it helps to bring out the difficulties of the question. I suppose it is only with reference to degrees & honours in Arts that there is anything to fear from centralization in the Examining Power. I have perhaps rather overstated what could be safely allowed to the Colleges, but I think the difficulties are not quite so great as you suppose. At Oxford we were by no means limited to a set of books, but the same examination acted for us all; & again, when we wrote an essay on some ethical or historical subject, the point of view for treatment of it might be as different as possible, but the numerical standard brought all the papers into one common measure for

[1] J. E. *Cairnes, 'University education in Ireland; a letter to J. S. Mill' (1866).

[2] Wordsworth told Congress that the English Reformers 'were, in truth, Old Catholics', and warned it against perverting the episcopacy; surprise was expressed that he was allowed to finish his speech; C. *Wordsworth, *Miscellanies* (1879), i. 467.

[3] Apparently unpublished; see 26 Oct. 72n.

comparison. The questions put on paper were the same for all. I cannot however help hoping, & thinking, that some liberty of instruction might be reconciled with a supreme final controul in the hands of the examining University, by allowing the colleges a certain latitude in subject or at any rate in text books. I see no insurmountable difficulty in the idea (within certain limits) of alternative papers. The truth is, all our examns. more or less involve this idea—for no one (as a rule) answers all the questions well or all the subjects with uniform merit. A mixed Board of Examiners would not work I daresay: but some means would have to be taken to maintain confidence if not to insure fair play, so far as variety, or alternatives rather, might be admitted into the examination, & though there would be difficulties of detail I do not see that they need prove insurmountable. If we cannot contrive *some* means of relaxing the Procrustean uniformity as to lines of thought, we shall have much difficulty in encountering Playfair's argument. I enclose for yours & Viceroy's perusal a letter from Forster on Royal Residence in Ireland.

Frid. Novr One 1872. All S.

Church 7 P.M. Wrote to Rev. SEG. L. and Tel.—Ld Granville (2)—Mr Godley—Mr T.S. Baynes[1]—Mr Mason[2]—Chancr of Exr—Mr Bruce—Bp of Bangor—and minutes. Saw Mr Chamberlain on Stephy's matters—Also conclave on do. Read Gilblas—Tract on Ch in N.W.[3]—The Last Tournament.[4]

2. Sat.

Ch. 8½ AM. Wrote to Mr Kennedy Tel.—Mr Godley Tel.—Mr Bruce—D. of Argyll—Ld Selborne—Sir J. Pakington—Sir Thos G.—Mr Galton—Mr T.B. Potter—and minutes. The root-felling of the Beech completed today. Read Gil Blas—Blackie on Modern Greek[5]—Thring on Local Taxn[6]—Dubl.Rev. on Galway Clergy.[7]

To H. A. BRUCE, home secretary, 2 November 1872. Aberdare MSS.

I venture to hope the law may permit & your disposition lead you to allow of the interment, as requested by Canon Liddon in a modest letter herewith, of the Founder of St. Barnabas's Church at Oxford[8] within its walls. Apart from other good works and claims, that one character would seem to constitute a safe ground for an exception? However I write ignorantly & at a venture.

[1] Thomas Spencer Baynes, 1823-87; professor of philosophy at Aberdeen from 1864; had sent an article; Add MS 44435, f. 289.

[2] Offering knighthood to (Sir) Josiah *Mason, 1795-1881, Birmingham manufacturer and benefactor.

[3] Untraced. [4] See 25 Oct. 72n. [5] See 27 May 72.

[6] Mem. and draft bill by Thring in PRO 30/29/69.

[7] *Dublin Review*, xix. 257 (October 1872).

[8] Tractarian church in Jericho, Oxford, built by Thomas *Combe; exception was not made.

To LORD SELBORNE, lord chancellor, Add MS 44542, f. 35.
2 November 1872.

You give me credit for a capacity of choice which I really do not possess. My uniform practice has been to consult & to defer to Ld. Hatherley with respect to such judicial appointments as it fell to me to submit to the Queen. Of course if I had seen anything wrong in them it would have been my duty to decline to act upon his judgment in the selection of persons: but it never happened to me to find myself in this position. And I should wish in like manner to avail myself of your advice & recommendation. In practice I have repeatedly, I think, asked whether it was necessary to fill up the appointment at all; & I likewise advised (on the Attorney General's suggestion I rather think) that Collier should go forward at once instead of remaining for a full time in the common Pleas. It was originally Collier's desire to succeed Lord Penzance, & on hearing that Ld. P. was to retire it occurred to me as worth considering whether Collier should now be sounded on the subject.[1] Lord Hatherley thought this would be dangerous as tending to revive the controversy; I need not say this was not my view or intention. But if the step is really so much as a doubtful one, I at once say it ought not to be taken. The only feeling that remains to me on the subject of this vacancy is that I should like first to try to fill it from the Bench, if you will kindly aid me with it from this point of view.

There is a *most* able parochial clergyman named Greer[2] in the Diocese of Lichfield. He *might* be worth your enquiring about for All Souls—a *candidate* he has never been for anything.

3. 23 S. Trin.

Ch. 11 AM & Holy Commn: & 6½ P.M. Wrote to Ld Enfield (Tel)—Archdn Utterton[3]—Robn G.—& minutes. Read the scandalous letter of the Irreverend Job Lea to the Bp of Chester.[4] Read Sadler's Arg. on Ath Creed[5]—Archdn Utterton's Charge—Dublin Review on Anglican position[6]—Bp Patteson's Life (finished)—and Tracts.

4. M.

Ch. 8½ A.M. Wrote to The Queen (l. & Mem.)—Ld Sydney—Mr Stanley—Mrs Davenport—Mrs Th.—Ld Howard of Glossop—and minutes. Worked on Book Catalogues and the like. We cut a lime. Read Stockmar[7]—Gil Blas.

[1] See 16 Oct. 71.
[2] Richard Macgregor Grier, remained vicar of Rugeley.
[3] John Sutton Utterton, 1814–79; archdeacon of Surrey from 1859, had sent his 'Charge'.
[4] Not found in Hawn P or Chester Cathedral archive. Perhaps on St. Thomas, Seaforth; scc 17 July 67.
[5] M. F. *Sadler, *An argument for the Athanasian Creed* (1872).
[6] *Dublin Review*, xix. 476 (October 1872).
[7] C. F. von Stockmar, *Denkwürdigkeiten aus den Papieren* (1872).

5. Tu.

Ch. 8½ A.M. Wrote to Ld Granville 2 Tell.—Ld Enfield Tel.—Mr Glyn—Mr Kennedy Tel.—Chr of Exr—Mr Cardwell—Mr Gurdon—Mr Bruce—Dr [W. G.] Ward—The Queen (Mem.)—and minutes. Saw Mr Burnett—Miss Syfret—Mr Bayn[1]—Sir Geo. Prevost. Read Stockmar—Gilblas—Dublin Rev. on Rio.[2]

To E. CARDWELL, war secretary, 5 November 1872. PRO 30/48/9, f. 81.

I think we are agreed as to the thing to be done in the matter of the soldiers employed for Harvest.[3] But I am anxious we should consider well the terms of the official announcement, for the matter is of importance. I do not doubt that the papers will have to be produced in Parliament for the subject has taken some hold in the popular mind.[4] I would suggest that there are three points for notice (1) The security to be taken for the future. I am quite satisfied with what you propose. (2) Reference to the past. I incline to think that we cannot wholly pass it by, though we might touch it lightly. Nothing, I think, can be more clear than that, for example, in the case of Farmer Wilsden there was a distinct error on the part of the person, whoever he may be, that permitted the labour of soldiers to be used so as to enable the Farmer to dismiss men for belonging to the Union. Might we say by way of recital that in one or more cases of a more or less novel character permission had been granted, through inadvertence probably due to the apparent urgency of the matter, which were in themselves open to objection & were likely to create or foster irritation? On the necessity of preventing such inconveniences for the future I would found your no. 1. But also (3) I am on the other hand most desirous that we should not even by omission seem to regard with jealousy or to throw discredit upon the employment of the spare time of soldiers in useful civil occupations, since I look upon this practice as one important prop to your great military reforms. Therefore I would throw in either a sentence, or a few words, by way of saving clause, in order that it may not be imagined, even colourably that you or the Government look askance at such employment.

I think there is always a risk, lest the labouring classes should like other classes be led to exaggerate their own rights in such a matter, so deep does the principle of monopoly lie in human nature. Only a few days ago I had a letter from 'Waiters' who contend that we ought to prevent messengers in Government offices from engaging themselves to wait at dinners & parties in the evenings, or in their holidays!

To G. G. GLYN, chief whip, 5 November 1872. Add MS 44542, f. 37.

There has been a rush of Liberal Members in the case of Aberffraw (I must say they have been uniformly considerate in such matters) in which after consulting the Bishop I have recommended Mr. Richards[5] of Amlwch strongly pressed by Mr Owen Stanley & also supported by Lord Sydney. But what I wish you to know is that the 'best Welsh Liberal Members' have, to use the vulgar

[1] Smudged; see 1 Nov. 72?
[2] *Dublin Review*, xix. 448 (October 1872).
[3] Papers sent this day; Add MS 44120, f. 70.
[4] Not published in *PP.*
[5] John Richards, appt. rector of Aberffraw.

phrase put their foot in it! For, though I do not know their favourite, I am told upon high authority from more than one quarter that he is a man whose personal conduct is such as to unfit him for any preferment or favourable notice whatever. 2. I propose to be in London on the 14th & call a Cabinet on the 15th. 3. What do you say to Ripon as the successor to Lord Zetland who gives up the Ld. Lieutenancy of the N. Riding? I hope you are getting on, & I can make a very good report of my wife who means to accompany me to town next week.

6. Wed.

Ch. 8½ A.M. Wrote to Mr Gurdon Tel.—Att. General—Ld Zetland[1] —Sol. General—Mr Kinnaird—Justice Keating—Mr Bulkeley Hughes—and minutes. W. & I cut down an elm. Saw Sir G. Prevost. Read Gilblas—Stockmar, Denkwürdigkeiten—Dubl.Rev. on Catholicity(!) in Germany.[2]

7. Th.

Ch. 8½ AM. Wrote to Chancr of Exr—Ld Granville—Mr Goschen—Mr Stansfeld—Mr Godley—The Queen (Mem.)—and minutes. Cutting with W. & Kibbling. Saw Bp of Chester. Read Gil Blas (finished) —Stockmar Denkwürd.

To R. LOWE, chancellor of the exchequer, 7 November 1872. Add MS 44542, f. 40.

I have read with much interest your letter & Goschen's on rating the owner.[3] They are valuable aids towards opening up a subject on which I hope we shall spare no time & pains to arrive at a right & especially at what we may call an honest conclusion. For myself I must own that I am not far advanced towards a solution of the difficulties which beset the subject. The difficulty of getting rid of Election Boards & Authorities where they arc already established, unless by consent, would I think be insurmountable: but in the rural districts generally they do not exist. Might we not on this subject get valuable information from Scotland, where the general law is on the basis you propose?

8. Fr.

Ch. 8½ AM. Wrote to M. of the Rolls (Irel.)[4]—Bp of Chester—Mr Ellice—Dr Burrows—Mr C. Parker—Bp of Lincoln—Rev W. Smith

[1] Asking him if he wished to exchange 'the ribbon of the Thistle . . . for that of the Garter' (Add MS 44542, f. 38); he took the Garter, resigning the Thistle, the last to be required so to do.

[2] Strong attack on Döllinger, *Dublin Review*, xix. 335 (October 1872).

[3] Correspondence sent by Lowe on 27 October 1872, Add MS 44302, f. 78, on disagreement on whether incidence of rates fell on owners or occupiers; see 24 Sept. 72n.

[4] E. *Sullivan.

—Lord Vane—Mr Justice Hanmer—Ld Granville—Mr Godley (Tel.)—& minutes. Saw Sir G. Prevost (& offered him Beverstone). Saw Mr Burnett. Read Stockmar—Wright's Hist of Women &c.[1]—Q.R. on Stockmar (finished).[2] Viewing & assisting with a dangerous tree near the stable. Lady G. Talbot[3] came out very much in a conversation with me.

9. Sat.

Ch. 8½ A.M. Sir G. Prevost declined. Wrote to Rev Mr Richards—Mr Childers—Robn G.—Mr Goschen—& minutes. I felled a tree: tea at Mrs Potter's. Read Stockmar Denkw.—Ed.Rev. on Stockmar—Henry Vaughan[4]—Wright on Woman.

To G. J. GOSCHEN, first lord of the admiralty, 9 November 1872. Add MS 44542, f. 41.

A line to say I think you were right in proceeding without delay, about Admiral Milne.[5] And, as I have taken up the pen, another line on the more difficult subject of your longer note.[6] It is to a considerable extent a Chancellor of Exchequer question, & I daresay you will speak to Lowe about it before we meet. I will without waiting mention a presumption of mine which may be wrong, viz. that the high prices, so far as they prevail, will tend to slacken work in the next as well as in this financial year, & thus far to limit the inconvenience which you must sorely feel. The question of finance is rather a sore & critical one with reference to the coming year—much more certainly with reference to the Army than to the Navy but the aggregate also is important. For two years I have given in considerably to the wish of the Cabinet; but I must own we do not at present stand foursquare with the (very reasonable) election pledges of 1868. The circumstances of the Continent & of America are now favourable in a degree & with a clearness impossible for alarmism itself to overlook or misapprehend.

10. 24 S.Trin.

Ch. 11 AM and 6½ P.M. Wrote to Mr E. Freshfield—Robn G.—Mr Job Lea—Mrs Maguire—Mr Godley—Ld Hartington—and minutes. Read Rawlinson's Testimony of Ancient Hist. to Scripture[7]—Union Review—Report E. Church Assocn[8]—and other Tracts.

[1] T. *Wright, *Womankind in Western Europe from the earliest times to the seventeenth century* (1869).

[2] *Quarterly Review*, cxxxiii. 386 (October 1872).

[3] See 16 June 56.

[4] *The works in verse and prose complete of Henry Vaughan* (1871 ed.).

[5] Yelverton refusing, Milne to be first Sea Lord; Add MS 44161, f. 219.

[6] Of 7 November, ibid., f. 220, prices driving up costs.

[7] See 27 Nov. 59.

[8] 'Report of the Eastern Church Association' on the Old Catholic congress in Cologne; sent by E. Freshfield; Add MS 44542, f. 42.

11. M.

Ch. 8½ AM. Wrote to Lord Zetland—The Queen—Mr Godley—and minutes. Saw Mr Burnett. We felled an elm: a difficult & successful *fall*. Read Stockmar—Antipapal League Report[1]—Dasents Norse Tales.[2]

12. Tu.

Ch. 8½ AM. Wrote to Ld Chancellor—Ld Granville—Mr Glyn—Principal of Lpool College—Bp of Chester—Mrs Th.—Mr Gurdon (Tel.)—and minutes. Saw Dr Moffatt & Mr Griffiths. Worked on my Library, arranging books. Read Stockmar: finished all the (for us) material parts. Arranging for departure.

To LORD SELBORNE, lord chancellor, Add MS 44542, f. 43.
12 November 1872.

I am afraid I can render you no real aid in the choice of a judge,[3] though all I have heard of Archibald tends to confirm your judgment. You will not be sorry to hear that Ld. Penzance's selection of a successor to himself from the Bench was the same as that which you recommended (& I followed) as to your no. 1. Glyn has sent me the enclosed with many modest expressions: I am only to forward it. Will you kindly prepare yourself to give the Cabinet the benefit of your views as early as possible on the degree of urgency which you may consider to attach to the question of judicial reconstruction as a question for the next session. For any remarks of this kind there would probably be an opening on Friday. To a certain extent they may involve a reference to your views on the nature & scope of the measure itself, but this, I presume, at the present early stage, would only be in the way of general indication. Our first task is to sketch out the order of business; with reference to those questions which are cardinal: & the only conclusion at which we have absolutely arrived, I think, is that the measure relating to University Education in Ireland must be first prepared, & first introduced & carried forward in the H. of C.

13. Wed. [*Keble College, Oxford*]

Ch. 8½ A.M. and 10.15 P.M. at Keble College. Wrote to the Queen (Stockmar)—Ld Granville—Mr Burnett—and minutes. Off at 11¾. Reached Oxford at five, & drove to the Talbots[4] at Keble College.

[1] Report of the Anti-Papal League based in Edinburgh.

[2] G. W. *Dasent, *Popular tales from the Norse* (1859).

[3] As successor to Lord Penzance, Selborne asking for the second time, 1 and 11 November 1872, Add MS 44296, f. 217.

[4] E. S. *Talbot, first warden of Keble; see 3 Feb. 49n. Lavinia Talbot's diary reads: 'Uncle W. in great form willing to see and be seen'.

Dined in Hall—saw the 'staff' who appeared most worthy of their office. Saw Mr Bradley[1] after. Read Döllinger's Lectures.[2]

14. Th. [*London*]

Chapel at 8. Breakfast party followed. Saw Dr Pusey: who behaved with all his old kindness and seemed to have forgotten the Temple business, or rather as if it had never been.[3] Saw Dr Liddon—Mr Robinson of New Coll.[4]—Sir T. Chambers[5]—Sir L. Peel[6]—Mr Gurdon—Mr James—Mrs Th. X—Dr Vaughan. Saw Wright X. and others. Dined at the Middle Temple—it proved to be a great banquet, & we had to speak.[7] Read Compère Mathieu[8]—From Old to New.[9] Wrote to Sir H. Elliot—Musurus Pacha—and minutes.

15. Fr.

Wrote to The Queen (2)—Ld Kimberley—Robn G.—Ld Enfield—Scotts—and minutes. Saw Sir A. Panizzi—Ld F. Cavendish—Chr of Exr—Mr Cardwell—Ld Ripon—Ld Kimberley—Mr Childers—Cabinet 2½–5½. Saw Wright X Some hopes. Harry dined: he is most satisfactory. Read Elgins Papers & Memoir.[10] Saw the very curious collection in Gt Russell Street of remains from Cyprus.[11] Mounted to the roof with Mr Grogan and Kearsley & authorised the necessary outlays following the late accident: wh might have been very grave.[12]

Cabinet. N. 15. 72. 2.30 PM.[13]

√ Order of business. WEG mentioned 6 Subjects of primary. Ld. Selborne desires to introduce Judicature Bill & Land Transfer Bill early, in H. of L.
General conversation on currency, Railways, Health.

√ Granville asked Cabinet for a reply to Spanish Minister who proposes a Tariff Treaty. Shall we have a M[ost] F[avoured] N[ation] Treaty? Yes (But not a Tariff Treaty).[14]

[1] Probably George Granville Bradley, master of University college 1870.
[2] See 27 Mar. 72.
[3] i.e. the appointment of *Temple as bp. of Exeter; this sentence in Morley, ii. 437.
[4] Arthur Edward Robinson.
[5] Sir Thomas Chambers, 1814–91, liberal M.P. Hertford 1852–7, Marylebone 1865–85; barrister.
[6] Sir Lawrence Peel, 1799–1884; judge in Calcutta 1842–55; paid member of judicial cttee. of privy council 1856.
[7] *The Times*, 15 November 1872, 12a.
[8] Untraced.
[9] F. R. Statham, *From old to new. A sketch of the present religious position* (1872).
[10] *Letters and journals of James, 8th Earl of Elgin*, ed. T. Walrond. Preface by A. P. *Stanley (1872).
[11] Count Luigi Palma di Cesnola's collection on display; see 19 Nov. 72.
[12] i.e. of Downing Street; see 1 Aug. 72.
[13] Add MS 44640, f. 194.
[14] Tariff treaty signed 17 July 1877; *PP* 1877 lxxxix. 513.

√ Ld Hartington stated his views on the question of Irish Education. General discussion. Return on Wedy.

√ Goschen. Clerk in Admty has £500 p. ann. from Civil Service Cooperative Socy. Shall he be promoted to be a Chief Clerk? No: on the merits of the particular case. Mr. Lowe to look up precedents & report.

√ Stansfeld. Inquiry respecting hours of Factory Labour. Proposed letter from Mr Bruce, directing it. Allowed.[1]

16. Sat.

Wrote to Robn G.—Italian Minister—Mrs Th.—The Queen (Mem.)—Col. Ponsonby. Saw Russell—A.M.—& a third. Some little good? Terry gone back[R]. Saw Ld F. Cavendish—Mr Forster—Mr Glyn (2)—Mr Gurdon—Mr Eykyn—Mr West—Rev S.E.G. Dined at Lady Herbert's: and had much conversation with Strzelecki on the *two* Stockmars.[2] Tea with Dowager Duchess of Somerset.

17. 25 S.Trin.

Chapel Royal mg and All Saints aft. Wrote to Mr Douglas Gordon—Ld Advocate—Ld Granville—and minutes. Saw Mrs Th. It was distressing: & left me much to ruminate upon: but it was good. Saw Mr Glyn—S.E.G. conversation on the Parish. Read 'From Old to New'—Döllinger's Lectures (finished).

18. M.

Wrote to Ld Advocate—Mr Murphy MP.—Gen. Knollys—Ld Zetland—Mr Erle—Mr Martin—Mrs Th. (& copy)—The Queen (l. & Mem)—& minutes. Cabinet 2½-6½. Dined with Panizzi (and D. of Argyll). Much conversation on Döllinger—Genesis X—Phoenicians—and like topics. Saw Graham: good prospect[R]. Saw Ld Hartington—Ld Granville—Mr Glyn—Mr G. *cum* Mr Lowe & Mr Forster—Mr Cardwell. Read papers on Irish Educn—Brassey on Wages of Labour.[3]

Cabinet. Nov. 18. 73. [sc. 72][4]

√ Thames Embankment. Notice to be given.

√ Railways. Safety. Amalgamation. Council of B[oard of] T[rade] Inspectors to meet Mr. F[ortescue].

√ Prince of Wales' note & intention to converse announced. Discussion on plans: & transition stage as proposed by Cardwell with Lords[?] Justices.[5]

[1] See 18 Nov. 72.
[2] See 4 Nov. 72 and Ramm I, ii. 362.
[3] T. *Brassey, *Work and wages* (1872).
[4] Add MS 44640, f. 200.
[5] See 30 Nov. 72 and Magnus, *Edward VII*, 123.

√ Arms not to be given to the Livingstone expedition—as gift in kind, on the objection *in limine.*[1]

√ Thornton's Telegram respecting San Juan: shall it be given over at once. Circulate Hydrographer's papers. Granville to prepare a reply.[2]

√ Bill for further shortening labour of women & children in Factories. Proposed by Mundella & others. Opposed by many. Both parties recommend a formal inquiry.
Shall there be one? A. Officers of Govt. may give evidence before a Committee of H. of C. & may prepare themselves.[3]

19. Tu.

Wrote to Ld Granville—The Queen (l. & Mem)—Robn G.—Bp of Winchester—Messrs Rivington—Sir R. Blennerhassett—and minutes. Saw Ld F. Cavendish—Messrs Newton & Birch (on the Cesnola Collection)[4]—Mr H. Merritt—Scotts—Mr Glyn. Read Brassey—Irish Edn Papers. Dined at Madam Ralli's. Breakfasted with Mr Cyrus Field to meet an American party. Much information from Mr Smalley.

To Sir R. BLENNERHASSETT, M.P., Add MS 44542, f. 46.
19 November 1872.

I have received your very interesting letter of the 11th.[5] Its matter causes pain but no surprise. There is, in my mind, a character nothing less than awful in the proceedings & intentions of the party now dominant in the Roman Church. But I will not enter upon any part of this subject. It is too large for letter-writing, at least for any letter-writing that I can manage. So also with respect to the position of those who are *not* the dominant party in the Roman Church, & of whom it is difficult to know how their precise standing ground in relation to the Pope & court of Rome should be defined. I certainly agree with you that these matters deeply concern the Anglican Church. They have also a wider interest, for all Christendom. The position of those who resist the Vatican Council completes what may be called a chain of forts reaching from end to end of the great Christian family. For myself, I do not think I have ever read a book on the divisions of Christians which commands from me so nearly an unbroken sympathy as the lectures of Dr. Döllinger. They form a small book indeed; but also how large they are. That is their commanding characteristic. But I hope we may touch these subjects in conversation. If you come to London, or pass through Chester, where Hawarden is close at hand, I hope you will give me notice.

[1] The second R.G.S. expedition; R. Coupland, *Livingstone's last journey* (1945), 217.

[2] Thornton's telegram, asking govt.'s position, at Add MS 44640, f. 201.

[3] For the movement, see W. H. G. Armytage, *A. J. Mundella* (1951) ch. 8; Mundella introduced a bill in February 1873; see 26 Nov. 72.

[4] Count Luigi Palma di Cesnola had offered his photographs of Cypriot antiquities to the Museum; Add MS 44542, f. 47.

[5] Report of 'in France a mysterious society, a sort of Catholic international which has its centre at and receives its direction from Rome'; Add MS 44436, f. 15.

20. Wed.

Wrote to The Queen—Mr W. Alexander (Tel. & l.)[1]—The Ld Advocate—Mrs Th.—A. Kinnaird—Sir Thos G.—and minutes. Saw Mr Glyn (2)—Gen. Cesnola—Ld Hartington—Ld Kimberley—Ld F. Cavendish. Cabinet 2¾-6½. Wrote heads of a measure on Irish University Education.[2] Dined at Dean of Westmrs. Saw Lady Baillie[3]—Mr Motley—Much conversation on Mythology, Art and Popular Assemblies.

Cabinet. Nov. 20. 72. 2½ PM.[4]

√ Granville mentioned the case of the Austrian Treaty[5] which includes by reference the French stipulations. An inquiry is to be made into the strength of wines grown on the Continent. No communication is to be made to Austria at this moment.

√ D[itt]o. French Treaty. French Govt. agree that compensatory duties cannot be improved until the duties on raw materials are imposed.

√ Who is to be the umpire? Propose for cons[ideratio]n: Moran, Moret, Hochschild, Bulow.[6]

√ Irish University Education. WEG's MS read—to be Printed. Hartington's Notes read.[7] Discussion on the Divinity School.

To W. ALEXANDER, 20 November 1872. Add MS 44542, f. 47.

I was much gratified by your Telegram of today[8] & by the proof it afforded that the farmers of Kincardineshire do not even now regard me as a stranger to the county where, during the earlier part of my Parliamentary career, I spent so many long & happy vacations. Nevertheless I was obliged at once to decline an overture of which the form was as considerate as the substance was kind. Having no property or residence in the county, I question whether I should be warranted in exposing my present constituents, who have treated me with such generous favour, to the inconvenience of a new choice, which could not by law be made until after a lengthened period. But I am also much moved by the consideration that, in asking for the suffrages of the county, I should at once bring into action differences of political opinion in the family to which I belong; differences, which are a real misfortune when they exist among persons otherwise united by blood and affection & which should never be subjected to needless aggravation.

[1] W. Alexander (see 4 Mar. 72) had telegrammed an offer of Kincardineshire, vacant on the d. of J. D. Nicol, liberal; Sir G. *Balfour was unopposed at the by-election, and held the seat in 1874.

[2] Untraced, but final draft dated this day printed in PRO 30/29/69.

[3] Lady Georgina Baillie, wife of Evan Baillie of Dochfour.

[4] Add MS 44640, f. 202.

[5] See 13 Feb., 13 Nov. 65 and K. F. Helleiner, *Free trade and frustration: Anglo-Austrian negotiations 1860-70* (1973), ch. 7.

[6] The 1872 French treaty; art. X, avoided naming an Umpire.

[7] PRO 30/29/69.

[8] See *Stonehaven Journal*, 28 November 1872, 3; Alexander, ed. *Aberdeen Free Press*, see 4 Mar. 72.

Such aggravation would be a needless one in this case; for I am entirely convinced of the disposition & ability of the constituency to send to Parlt. a representative who will efficiently defend its interests, & uphold the political principles so consistently supported by your late respected & lamented member.[1]

To Sir Thomas GLADSTONE, 20 November 1872. Add MS 44542, f. 47.

I received this morning, unexpectedly, a Telegram containing what I may describe as a conditional invitation to stand for Kincardineshire. I sent a simple negative by Telegraph, adding that I would write by post. Since that time, I have written the letter of which the inclosed was a copy. I felt it not free from difficulty. Either of the two reasons I have named would have sufficed with me. I could not, however, name Greenwich alone, without leading to the inference that but for Greenwich I should have agreed, whereas the family reason is in my view imperative, & the stronger of the two. I lose no time in sending you this intimation, because the letter addressed to Mr. Alexander will of course be made known to his coadjutors, & may get out—which I cannot properly inhibit.[2]

21. Th.

Wrote to Mr Ouvry—Gen. de Cesnola—The Queen—& minutes. Revised in part my letter to General Schenck. Saw Ld F. Cavendish —Sir J. Lacaita—Mr Glyn (2)—Sir W. Boxall—Mr Kearsley. Read Brassey—Herbert Spencer's First Principles.[3] Dined with the Godleys. Visited the remainder of General de Cesnola's Collection in New Finchley Road.

22. Fr.

Wrote to Mrs Heywood—The Queen (2 l. and Mema)—Mr J. Dundas—Mr Forster—Sir J. Lubbock—Mrs Th.—and minutes. Cabinet 2½-6¼. Saw Ld F. Cavendish—Ld Lyttelton—Mr Goschen—Professor Huxley. Read Brassey.

Cabinet. Nov. 22. 72. 2½ PM.[4]

√ Diamond fields proposed to be a separate Govt. under a Lieut. Governor. Yes. A Council: Governor a casting vote: 3 officials & 4 elected members. This on account of the native element.[5]
√ Prorogation of Parlt.—to Feb. 6.
√ Mr Goschen stated that the Managing Director of Cooperative Soc. has resigned.
√ Subjects for Tuesday's Cabinet considered.
√ Park Rules discussed. Simply to be enforced.

[1] J. D. Nicol, unopposed in 1868; d. 1872.
[2] See introduction above, vol. vii, section VII.
[3] H. *Spencer, *First principles* (1862).
[4] Add MS 44640, f. 203.
[5] i.e. Grinqualand West, thus establishing a third British colony in S. Africa; see C. F. Goodfellow, *Great Britain and South African Confederation* (1966), 44.

√ Arms for defence for the Livingstone expedition. Not to be given in kind—but paid.[1]

√ Irish University Reform. Ld. Hartington read the printed paper (A) of yesterday: & another paper of today. Further discussion. Cabinet generally averse to repres[entatio]n of Colleges.[2]

23. Sat.

Wrote to Col. French—Mr Cogan—& minutes. Six to dinner: conversation with Duke of A[rgyll] & Ld Lyttelton. Saw Metrop. Board Depn on Bridges.[3] Saw Mr Roundell on I.Univ. question—Ld F. Cavendish—Chancr of Exr. Saw Fitzroy X. Read Brassey (finished)—Autobiogr. Cornish Rector[4]—& made some comparison of the Stockmar translation with the original.

24. Preadv.Sunday.

St James's Marylebone mg & St Mary's Lambeth evg for Stephy's farewell Sermon. I was struck & pleased with Mr Haweis.[5] Also there was some vivid chanting and hymn singing. Stephy's Sermon was all earnestness like himself, without egotism, on a tempting occasion.

Wrote to Abp Manning—Mr Burnett—Professor Laveleye—and minutes. Saw Ld Halifax—Mrs Brand—Mrs Hope, & Miss Hope Scott.[6] Read Union Review—Layman's Reasons agt Ath. Creed[7]—Dalgairns Is God unknowable?[8]—Stathams From Old to New[9]—Cazenove on D. of Somerset.[10]

25. M.

Wrote to G. Burnett—Mr Max Muller—Mr Childers—J. Watson & Smith—and minutes. Luncheon in G.S.—Saw Mrs Th. Saw Ld F. Cavendish—The Speaker—Dined at Sir H. Hollands: & had

[1] See 18 Nov. 72n.

[2] Hartington and Acton's mem. and letter in PRO 30/29/69.

[3] See *The Times*, 30 November 1872, 7a and diarist's letter of 29 Nov. to chairman of metropolitan bd. of works, ibid., 7 December 1872, 6e.

[4] J. H. Tregenna [R. B. Paul], *The autobiography of a Cornish rector*, 2v. (1872).

[5] Hugh Reginald Haweis, 1838-1901, fought with Garibaldi; curate of St. James', Marylebone, from 1866; held 'evenings for the people'.

[6] Mary Monica Hope-Scott, da. of J. R.* of Abbotsford, m. 1874 Joseph Constable Maxwell and took name Maxwell-Scott.

[7] J. W. Flower, *A layman's reasons for discontinuing the use of the Athanasian Creed* (1872).

[8] J. B. *Dalgairns in *Contemporary Review*, xx. 615 (October 1872).

[9] See 14 Nov. 72.

[10] J. G. *Cazenove, *Modern theism* (1872), on Somerset's *Christian theology*.

conversation with Mr Leckie,[1] Mrs Leckie, Mr Holland. Read Cornish Rector—Froude's English in Ireland. Paying some shop-accounts.

26. Tu.

Wrote to The Queen, & minutes. Cabinet 2¾-7. Dined at Ld Selborne's. Saw Sir T. Fremantle—Sir Geo. Balfour—Ld F. Cavendish—Mr Clay[2]—Mr Stansfeld—Mr Gibson—Ld Halifax *cum* Mr Goschen. Unwell in evg.

Cabinet. Nov. 26. 1872.[3]

Currency.
√ Railways. Mr Fortescue explained heads of his Bill. Reviewed. Nothing yet as to safety.[4]
√ Metrop. Bridge Tolls.[5] Not to accept proposition. Draft reply sketched.
√ Contagious Diseases. Shall Bill be reintroduced?[6]
Com[missio]n. Subj[ect] postponed—we are not ready to decide the matter yet—Mr Bruce to give a dilatory answer to his deputation on Thursday.[7]

27. Wed.

Wrote to Sir G. Balfour—Ld Zetland—Scotts—Sir J. Lubbock—Mr Bruce—Mr Cyrus Field—Sir S.R. Glynne—and minutes. Saw Ld Granville—Duke of Argyll—Scotts.

Went to Windsor to attend the Council: & had an audience of the Queen. It was rather long: she talked of France, of the R. Family allowances, of Sir C. Dilke, of the railway accidents, of the harvest, of changes in the lower ranks of her household, of Sandringham: & her manner was as usual, kind and pleasing: nevertheless the whole helped to show me yet more that the occurrences & correspondence of this year have led & will lead her to 'shut up' (so to speak) towards me.

Read The Cornish Rector—Le Prince de Bismarck.[8] Gave up Guy's,[9] not being quite sound.

[1] William Edward Hartpole *Lecky, 1838-1903, historian and anti-home-ruler, and his wife Elizabeth; see 3 June 65. His history of Ireland was written partly to refute J. A. *Froude's *The English in Ireland* (1872-4), read by Gladstone this day.

[2] F. Clay, apparently a journalist; permitting moderate quotation of his letter on Kincardineshire; see 20 Nov. 72 and Add MS 44542, f. 48.

[3] Add MS 44640, f. 206.

[4] Railway and Canal Traffic Bill, introduced 10 February; *Victoria was excited about railway safety; Guedalla, *Q*, i. 382.

[5] Notes on them at Add MS 44640, f. 209.

[6] No govt. bill, but Fowler's 1°R, 7 February 1873.

[7] See 18 Nov. 72.

[8] A. Deschamps, *Le Prince de Bismarck et l'entrevue des trois empereurs* (1872).

[9] i.e. proposed visit to Guy's hospital.

28. Th.

Wrote to The Queen—Colonel Ponsonby—and minutes. Finally revised & sent off my letter to General Schenk. Saw Ld Hartington—Ld Granville—Mr Glyn—Ld F. Cavendish—Ld Ripon. Cabinet 2½-6¼. Scots Educ. Commee at 2. Dined at Mr Cyrus Fields banquet: and spoke on friendship with America.[1] Conversation with Mr F.—& with General de Cesnola. Finished Le Prince de Bismarck. Read Statham.[2] Saw two[R].

Cabinet. Nov. 28. 72. 2.30 PM.[3]

√ Currency. Chancellor of Exchequer gave figures in explanation. On the 36m̃ minimum. Min[imum] Circ[ulation] 38300 in 1847, 41800 in 1857, 43200 in 1866. Saving stated as minimum: for U.K. minimum 567m: for England 300m—besides saving from £1 notes, min[imum] £30000 per m̃.[4]

√ Ld. Kimberley. Canadian Fortification Guarantee: shall it be commuted into one for Civil Works? Proposed (4m̃) from Canadian[?] Council. Agree to 3600m. but no increase of aggregate guarantees.[5]

√ Mexico. To remonstrate agt. the Indians invasions of Honduras: (with an ultimate view to reprisals if necessary:) remonstrance to go through the British Admiral.[6]

√ Ld Granville mentioned the clear understanding with the French Government that no compensatory duties should be levied on British goods till the duties on raw materials should have come into force.

√ Irish University Education. Ld Spencer's letter read. D[itt]o Ld H[arting-to]n's new paper in MS.

N[ovember] 28.[7] For the present agreed that we sever[?] Dublin Univ. & Trin. Coll.—that we do not base the Governing Body on repres[entatio]n of the Colleges.

[8][C. S.] Roundell: reported by WEG: a. objects to founding the Governing Body on the principle of represent[atio]n of Colleges. b. wishes Professors to be appointed, & generally much to be done by the Crown. c. wishes that the Univ. should teach in all branches.

WEG's proposals: 1. that thc *Univ. Laws & Statutes* of Trin. Coll. shd. continue until altered. 2. a limited repr[esentatio]n of Colleges if there can be no controul *ab extra* 3. varied principle of Election of Governing Body.

To General R. C. SCHENCK, American minister in London, 28 November 1872.[9]

In the volume entitled the *Case of the United States, to be laid before the Tribunal of Arbitration at Geneva*, with respect to the claims commonly known as

[1] See *The Times*' leader, 30 November 1872, 9c.

[2] See 14 Nov. 72.

[3] Add MS 44640, f. 211.

[4] Apparently a further attempt by Lowe at a Currency Bill; but none introduced.

[5] The final figure, see *PP* 1873 xlix and D. M. L. Farr, *The colonial office and Canada 1867-1887* (1955), 90.

[6] By Yucatan Indians over whom Mexico claimed authority: PRO FO 50/432, f. 18.

[7] Note on separate sheet, Add MS 44640, f. 213.

[8] Ibid., f. 214.

[9] No copy found in Add MSS; printed in *Harper's New Monthly Magazine*, December 1876, from which this copy is taken.

the *Alabama* claims, the second chapter purports to set forth 'the unfriendly course pursued by Great Britain toward the United States from the outbreak to the close of the insurrection of 1861–65.'

Pages 87 to 100 are devoted to the exhibition of 'proof of the unfriendly feeling of members of the British cabinet and Parliament.'

The members of the cabinet referred to are Lord Palmerston, Lord Russell, Lord Campbell, with his successor, Lord Westbury (though there is no citation from either of these two high legal authorities), and myself.

It may seem an impertinence on my part to do otherwise than assume that my own name is overshadowed and eclipsed by the names of these distinguished men. The circumstance, however, that I alone among them am now in office, and that at the moment of the publication of the American Case I chanced to be in office as first minister of the crown, gives a character to my personal share in what I shall for convenience call the Chapter of Motives such as it would not otherwise possess.

But although it is the accident of office which alone gives the subject an aspect such as to acquit me of egotism in troubling you, I address you in a personal capacity, and I make my appeal to you as between gentleman and gentleman, or rather, since there is something invidious in that form of expression, as between man and man. Further, it is not only in a personal capacity, but it is in a non-controversial and a friendly attitude that I present myself before you. For reasons which appeared more than sufficient, the British government declined to treat as part of the argument or controversy the charges against individuals in the Chapter of Motives. Now, when all contention is happily at an end, it is far indeed from my mind to use so much as a single word that could revive it. But it is open to me to do that which as a government we could not do—to adopt the tone of simple explanation. My desire at all periods of my public life has been to promote and not to impede good understanding and warm attachment between our two countries. I feel that the isolated and fragmentary citation which has been made from speeches of mine does not really represent the sentiments of those speeches. I take up this case not as matter of wrong done or suffered, but simply to show to you and to your government, if you think fit to use my letter for the purpose, that I did not at the delivery of those speeches, more than at any other time, deviate from the path of a sincere good-will toward the entire people of America. If I am felt to have given reasonable evidence that my words as they are employed in the Case are misinterpreted when taken to prove hostility, my object will have been gained. But if I do not thus far succeed with you or with your government, I shall not appeal to any other tribunal or take any other step, nor shall I regret having made an effort which I know is well intended, and which I am confident will not be misunderstood.

Let me, then, describe, by a reference to particulars, the position in which I am exhibited by the chapter to the view of the two nations and the world. After the greater part of the chapter has been occupied in argument and denunciation on the 'insincere neutrality' and the 'tortuous courses' of the British government during the war, 'proof of the unfriendly feeling of members of the British cabinet' is adduced in the form of various quotations. So far as I am concerned, there seem to be two. First, a passage is cited from a report in the *Times* of a speech at Newcastle on the 7th October, 1862. This passage declares:

1. 'That the leaders of the South had made a nation;' and,

2. That the separation of the Southern States was, in my belief, 'as certain as any event yet future and contingent could be.'

The second passage is quoted from a speech in which, on the part of the government of Lord Palmerston (who was himself absent from the House, probably on account of illness), I resisted a motion in favour of the recognition of the South. This was on the 30th June, 1863. The material points of this quotation are:

1. That the cessation of the war was to be desired, inasmuch as to warrant its continuance, it must have an object 'attainable,' as well as otherwise just and adequate.

2. That in my opinion, and, as I believed, in the general opinion, the re-incorporation of the Southern States was not an attainable object.

3. That it was a fatal error, even for sincere and philanthropic men, to pursue the emancipation of the negro race through the bloodshed of the war.

A further citation without a reference, which I have not, therefore, verified, repeats the opinion No. 2 last cited, with the substitution of 'we,' the plural, as if on behalf of the ministry, for the singular. And lastly, I am quoted as having stated, when the House was engaged on the Budget of the year, that I should pass by the question of danger as 'between British merchant ships and American or other privateers,' which appears to have been mentioned by 'an opposition member,' not as thinking it insignificant, but from the necessity of discussing the matter then in hand, namely, the financial statement of the year.

I presume that I need not treat these two last-named references, under the circumstances, as adding any thing to the evidence in support of the charge against me. But, as I am about to exhibit the effects of omission, I have thought it a less evil to run the risk of tediousness, and of introducing irrelevant or unnecessary matter, rather than to fail in making a full and fair representation of that portion of the Case in which I am individually brought upon the stage.

Such, then, is the evidence. Next I have to point out the use made of it. That is a very simple task. The Case propounds that the declarations now cited are evidence of 'insincere neutrality,' of 'unfriendly feeling of members of the British cabinet;' there was a 'conscious unfriendly purpose toward the United States;' there was 'unfriendliness and insincere neutrality;' and finally the matter is brought to a head in a perfectly distinct statement that 'various members of the British cabinet,' including myself, 'are seen to comment upon the efforts of the government of the United States to suppress the rebellion, in terms that indicate a strong desire that those efforts should not succeed.'

Upon this distinct allegation I desire to offer the following explanations:

The question, then, is not whether the opinion of what was to happen, expressed by me on more than one occasion, was too hastily and lightly formed; nor is it whether to the error of thus forming it I added a graver error in declaring it at a time when I held public office as a minister of a friendly power. I neither conceal these errors nor will I attempt elaborately to extenuate them by a reference to various motives which do not appear to have been taken into account, or to those unexampled circumstances which misled me, and, in a great degree, misled the world. These errors were confessed in a letter addressed by me some years ago to one of your countrymen, and published, with my full assent, both in American and in English newspapers. That there may be no stint in the measure of this avowal, I have procured, and I forward herewith, a copy of that letter.[1] I am sure you will not believe that the wishes with the expression of which it concludes were got up for the occasion.

But the holding of this opinion and the expression of this opinion do not

[1] To C. E. Lester, 8 August 1867, printed in *Harper's* as appendix A; see 8 Aug. 67n.

form the matter of the complaint prepared by the American government to go before the arbitrators at Geneva. The complaint is that the language held by me, as well as by others, indicated a strong desire that the efforts of the government of the United States should not succeed. And on this complaint an argument is founded that men governed by this desire could not but be adversely biased administrators of British law for the performance of international duty, and that accordingly we did allow sinister motives, whether in the shape of abstract hostility or of selfish regard to British interests, to lead us into a guilty neglect of the public obligations of the country. I might, as will be seen from words quoted above, have stated the charge more strongly, but I wish to keep within the truth.

What I seek to show is that this charge against me is not true and not just.

I seek to show it by evidence to which no fair exception can be taken. I will cite nothing that has been said by me since the triumph of the Union, or after the date at which it may be said that that triumph was distinctly or generally foreseen to be approaching.

I shall show:

1. That my opinion always was that England had a special interest in the quarrel raised by the insurrection of the Southern States.

2. That this interest was that the North and South, far from being severed, should remain united.

3. That at the outset and at various periods of the war I had spoken of the American people, and of the trial they were called on to undergo, in terms of strong sympathy.

4. That these declarations were not less public or less authenticated than the two declarations cited in the American Case as made by me in October, 1862, and June, 1863. And finally,

5. That on the same days, and in the same speeches which are quoted to show my desire as an Englishman that the Union should be broken up, were delivered unequivocal expressions of my belief that English interests would be best served by its continuance.

I shall also direct attention to the time when I delivered the speech at Newcastle, as that contained the passage to which, I believe, attention has been principally directed. At that time—there is nothing paradoxical in saying it—motives of sheer humanity and hatred of the effusion of blood might well lead a man to desire, upon the terms either of reunion or of severance, the termination of the war. But whether this be paradoxical or not, I shall also show that men who had most vehemently supported in this country the cause of the North, and denounced the Southern Confederation as an inhuman and antisocial conspiracy, were admitting the efforts and struggles of the North, wonderful as they were, to be practically hopeless, and were recommending the cessation of the war by the acknowledgment, within a wide extent of territory, of Southern independence. I proceed to deal with these several points.

At the outbreak of the insurrection, in 1861, a member of the British Parliament was unfortunately betrayed into describing what had taken place in America as the bursting of the 'great republican bubble' of that country.[1]

The American Case notices this declaration, and pays Earl Russell the well-deserved compliment of adding that the member who spoke, and whom the American government considerately forbear to name, received from him a merited rebuke.

But I am here busied only with the picture of my own performances; and I

[1] Sir J. Ramsden on 27 May 1861, *H* clxiii. 134.

may therefore be permitted to remark that when it came to my turn to speak, also in the same debate in which the 'bubble' had been introduced, I am reported to have expressed myself as follows:[1] 'I heard with deep regret last night the speech of the Hon. A B, though not, indeed, with the same regret as I heard some other remarks made by the Hon. C D. [The "bubble" speech.] I hope that the Hon. C D will express his regret, before the conclusion of the debate, for having, with or without premeditation, spoken of the American government as a great republican bubble. [A cry of "Hear."] I am sorry to hear that phrase cheered by a single member; and had hoped that was the first and last time we should hear any member allude in a jeering way to the tremendous calamity which threatens to fall upon a great country. But I do not believe that the Hon. C D had any intention to speak in such a spirit.'

There could hardly be from a minister, consistently with the usages of Parliament, a more marked animadversion and appeal. And it was made although the honourable member concerned is reported as having already declared (which the Case omits to notice) 'that no one word ever fell from his lips of exultation over the most unfortunate events which are now taking place in America,' that his allusion was simply to the form of government, and that 'he had referred to the events now taking place there as calamitous events, which we must all most deeply deplore.'

In passing, I remark that neither this nor any one of the speeches quoted in the Case, or referred to in this letter, is reported with any corrections by myself. But I believe the main purport, apart from incidental allusions, to be truly represented, and I will not attempt by the aid of memory, at this distance of time, to modify the forms of expression.

This was the evidence of my share in the alleged conscious hostility, in May, 1861. Several months after, and just when the country had been excited by the affair of the *Trent*, I had occasion to speak at Leith. This speech was on an occasion equally public with that subsequently delivered at Newcastle, and it was reported with not less fullness by the indefatigable activity of the press, though it has escaped the notice of the American government in drawing the Case. What would have been most satisfactory to me in the present circumstances would have been the republication of the whole of these and other speeches *in extenso*. But this proceeding would defeat its own object, as I at once admit that neither you nor any one either in England or America could fairly be expected to face the task of reading them.

I have no choice, therefore, but to resort to extracts, which must, however, be longer than I could wish.

Extract from Mr. Gladstone's Speech at Leith, January 10, 1862. (*Times, January 13.*)

'Mr. Provost, I heartily wish that it was in our power to exhibit to the country of the United States the precise and exact state of feeling that has subsisted in this country ever since the beginning of the tremendous convulsion which now agitates that continent, and threatens its peace and prosperity. I do not believe that, at the time when the convulsion commenced, there was one man in a thousand in this country who had any sentiment whatever toward the United States of America except a sentiment of affectionate and sympathizing goodwill, or who felt any thing but a desire that they might continue to go on and prosper, and to finish the work, whatever it may have been, which Providence

[1] On 30 May 1861, *H* clxiii. 332.

had appointed them to do. I have not the least scruple in saying for myself that my opinion is that not only had England nothing to fear from the growth of the United States in America, but that, so far as we had a selfish interest at all in the matter, our interest was that the American Union should continue undisturbed. . . . Let us look, gentlemen, upon the bright side of that which the Americans have done, and surely a bright side it has. Let us look back to the moment when the Prince of Wales appeared in the United States of America, and when men by the thousand, by tens of thousands, and by hundreds of thousands trooped together from all parts to give him a welcome as enthusiastic, and as obviously proceeding from the depths of the heart, as if those vast dominions had still been a portion of the dominions of our Queen. Let us look to the fact that they are of necessity a people subject to quick and violent action of opinion, and liable to great public excitement, intensely agreed on the subject of the war in which they were engaged, and aroused to a high pitch of expectation by hearing that one of their vessels of war had laid hold of the Commissioners of the Southern States, whom they regarded simply as rebels. Let us look to the fact that in the midst of this exultation, and in a country where the principles of popular government and democracy are carried to extremes, that even in this struggle of life and death, as they think it to be, that even while ebullitions were taking place all over the country of joy and exultation at this capture—that even then this popular and democratic government has, under the demand of a foreign power, written these words—for they are the closing words in the dispatch of Mr. Seward—"The four Commissioners will be cheerfully liberated." Let us take these words, I say, without minute criticisms upon any thing that may have passed at former times, and may have been open to differences of view. Let us accept them with thankfulness to the Almighty for having removed any apparent cause of deadly collision, in which the hearts of the people of this country were united as the heart of one man to vindicate, under all circumstances and to all extremities, the honour of the British flag, and to discharge the duty of protection to those who had placed themselves under its shelter. Let us form good auguries for the future from that which now stands among the records of the past, and let us hope that whatever remains, or whatever may yet arise, to be adjusted in those relations between the two countries which afford a thousand points of contact every day, and must necessarily likewise afford opportunities for collision—let us hope that in whatever may arise or remain to be adjusted, a spirit of brotherly concord may prevail, and, together with a disposition to assert our rights, we may be permitted to cherish a disposition to interpret handsomely and liberally the acts and intentions of others, and to avoid, if we can, aggravating the frightful evils of the civil war in America by perhaps even greater evils—at any rate, enormous evils—by what, though not a civil war, would be next to a civil war—any conflict between England and America.'

And here I stop for a moment to call attention to dates. The escape of the *Alabama*, in July, 1862, forms, in the American view, the greatest offense committed by the British government. It is, therefore, at that time that they find the insincere neutrality and the strong desire for the severance of the Union ripe, and it must be in the preceding period that we are to find it ripening. I wish, therefore, to call your attention to the language employed by me during this very period, and I leave it to you to judge how far it paves the way for the imputation of hostility and insincerity which is applied to me.

I now come to the speeches at Newcastle and in the House of Commons. From these I shall make extracts to show that both the documents which are quoted in the Case to show inferentially my hostility to the continuance of the Union contain distinct and explicit declarations on each occasion of my never-varying opinion that it was for the interest of England that the Union should continue. And, if this be so, I hope that the charge of an adverse bias and an insincere purpose, affecting me as a minister in the maintenance of neutrality, will be felt to have disappeared.

The first document is the report given in the *Times* newspaper (October 9) of the speech at Newcastle, on the 7th October, 1862. From that report I now make the following extract; and I add further passages, by way of appendix,[1] as being calculated, when read with the passages in the Case, to give no untrue picture of my real disposition in the matter:

'I, for one, exercising my own poor faculties as I best could, have never felt that England had any reason connected with her own special interests for desiring the disruption of the American Union. I can understand those who say it is for the general interest of nations that no state should swell to the dimensions of a continent. I can understand those who say—and I confess it to be my own opinion—that it is greatly for the interest of the negro race that they should have to do with their own masters alone, and not, as has hitherto been the case, with their masters backed by the whole power of the Federal government of the United States. . . . I can, therefore, very well understand the arguments of those who think that it is not particularly to be desired in the interests of the negro that the American Union should be reconstituted. But I confess that, for reasons which I need not now explain, I do not think that England has had an interest in the disruption of the Union; and my own private opinion has been that it would be rather for the interest of England if that Union had continued.'

The second document is to be found in Hansard's Parliamentary Debates for June 30, 1863:

'I have always been of opinion that, involved as England is, not so much as a matter of mere interest, but on considerations of duty and honour, with respect to the British North American colonies, the balanced state of the old American Union, which caused the whole of American politics to turn upon the relative strength of the slavery and Northern interests, was more favourable to us, more likely to insure the continuance of peaceful relations in America, as well as the avoidance of all political complications arising from the connection between this country and its colonies, than the state of things which would exist if the old American Union were to be divided into a cluster of Northern and a cluster of Southern States.'

I have only further to sustain my closing proposition. It is that, at the time in question, anticipations of the severance of the Southern from the Northern States —nay, that recommendations that the Northern States should at once come to terms with the insurrectionary confederacy—would not, even had they been unaccompanied by the declarations I constantly made as to British interest in the matter, have justly borne the construction of unfriendly purpose and of insincere neutrality which is put upon them in the Case. For this end I refer to the work of that distinguished and very able writer, Professor Cairnes, who, perhaps more than any other person, became conspicuous in this country during the war for his advocacy of the Northern cause.

In the year 1862, and some time, I think, before I spoke at Newcastle, he published the work entitled *The Slave Power.*[2] This book in its whole staple,

[1] Further extracts in appendix, omitted.

[2] See 1 Dec. 62; i.e. apparently read after the Newcastle speech.

almost in every page, indicated a mind which I may term more Northern than the Northerners. I will endeavor to state fairly the summing up of his argument. He points out with the utmost clearness and force the great military disadvantages of the South. He then proceeds:

'I am far from intending to say that the considerations which have been adduced prove the possibility of accomplishing the object which the North has now in view.' And again:

'For these reasons, I can not think that the North is well advised in its attempt to reconstruct the Union in its original proportions.'

I need not refer to the reasons in detail; they embraced matter of the greatest moment connected with the interests of the negro race, and with the hazard which seemed to threaten the free institutions of America from the continuance of the war.

Professor Cairnes then proceeds to point out 'that settlement of the controversy . . . which on the whole is most to be desired.' It is that the region from the Atlantic to the Mississippi should be acknowledged independent, Louisiana being reserved for the North and for freedom. Professor Cairnes ends by saying, 'This is to be desired as best in the interest of the slave.'

I have cited Professor Cairnes as a witness *instar omnium*, and one whose testimony, as I remember, greatly weighed with me. The ably written periodical which beyond any other studied the interests of the North during the war echoed his words, and in reviewing his work wrote as follows:

'No treaty of separation can be regarded with any satisfaction but one which should convert the whole territory west of the Mississippi into free soil;'[1] and, conversely, the writer plainly conveys his opinion that a separation recognizing the independence of the Southern States to the east of the Mississippi was an object, under the circumstances, to be desired by the friends of America.

I now submit with some confidence that conscious hostility to the United States can not be demonstrated (whatever else may be so) by having entertained, or even by having pronounced, an opinion which was entertained and pronounced at the time by their warmest partisans on this side the water. I conclude with an expression of sincere regret for the trouble I am giving you in addressing to you so long a letter.

29. Fr.

Wrote to Ld Kimberley—Lady Clarendon—Mr Richmond MP.—Mr Billson—Helen G.—Col. Hogg MP[2]—General Cunynghame[3]—Sir Geo. Balfour—Mrs Th.—and minutes. Saw Lord F.C.—Mr Bramwell—Mr Glyn—Lord Mayor—Greenwich Deputn—Ld Mayor & City Deputation[4]—Sir D. Salomons—Lady Ripon. Revised Sketch of Irish Univ. Measure. Dined at Mrs Ralli's: music.

[1] *Westminster Review*, October 1862, 510.

[2] See 23 Nov. 72n.

[3] Sir Arthur Augustus Thurlow *Cunynghame, 1812-84; col. of 36 foot; commanded at the Cape 1873-8; lieut. gov. there 1877-8; had sent his book, see next day.

[4] No reports found.

30. Sat. [Sandringham]

Wrote to Lord Hill—Ld Granville—Ld Russell—The Queen (Mem)—Sir G. Prevost—and minutes. Read Biblical Archaeology[1]—Gen Cunynghame's Travels.[2] Saw W.H.G. (Beverstone)[3]—Ld F. Cavendish—Mr Glyn—Mr Forster—Sir W. Gull—Ld Sydney—Bp of Ely. Off at 11.20 to Sandringham.[4] A large & easy party. Conversation with P. of Wales in evg: on the Indian Fair, but nothing else personal. I sat by the Princess who was most kind & simple as usual. Conversation with Prince Christian on the German duelling laws. Whist in evg: the Prince and I were partners.

Sandringham
Advent Sunday Dec 1.72.

Wrote to Ld Hartington—Ld Granville—& minutes. Ch. mg—none in aftn. The Prince conducted us over his garden & numerous & well-ordered establishments: also we went to the Schoolchildren's tea. Conversation with Princess Christian—Sir W. Knollys—Mr Birch[5]—Col. Ellis. Read Liddon's Sermon[6]—Statham, Social Growths[7]—Strauss, die alte Glaube und das Neue.[8] Much conversation at dinner. This is a pleasant interior: the chief personages carry themselves becomingly, but there is none of the stiffness of a Court. I like the house too, the place, & the air.

To LORD HARTINGTON, Irish secretary, 1 December 1872. 'Secret.' Chatsworth MSS 340.575.

I have received your letter[9] & I think there can be no reason why the subject of it should be mentioned among our colleagues generally. Nothing can be more fair or kind than the way in which you state the question. I earnestly hope that as we proceed to manipulate our Bill, your difficulties will disappear or much diminish. And I am quite certain that there is nothing to compromise your honour or consistency in your continuing to take part in the preparation of this arduous measure; the most difficult, on account of the state of feeling that

[1] *Biblical archaeology*, vol. i. Parts 1 and 2 (1872-3).

[2] Sir A. A. T. *Cunynghame, *Travels in the Eastern Caucasus* (1872).

[3] On its vacant living; John Henry Blunt was appointed.

[4] Visit arranged to discuss the employment of *Wales, who had completely rejected the Irish plan; but alternatives not canvassed by diarist; see Magnus, *Edward VII*, 123.

[5] Perhaps the Prince's former tutor, see 8 Nov. 52.

[6] H. P.*Liddon, 'Noah [a sermon on Heb. xi. 7]' (1872).

[7] F. R. Statham, *The social growths of the nineteenth century. An essay in the science of sociology* (1872).

[8] D. F. Strauss, *Der alte und der neue Glaube. Ein Bekenntniss* (1872); denounced in his Liverpool speech, 21 Dec. 72.

[9] Of 30 November, suggesting his resignation on Irish universities, in Holland, *Devonshire*, i. 109.

prevails, of all our measures relating to Ireland. You will have observed that I have explicitly said in the Cabinet that I have understood none of the resolutions we have taken to be absolute & final; & I noticed that the remark was received with general concurrence. It is plainly I think broad enough to give a complete cover to your position. Deeply should I be grieved if after further reflections & conference with Spencer you found we were moving on lines absolutely opposite to yours; but for the present I can say for myself, & I think it must be the feeling of others that it has been a great advantage to us to hear the question so ably & resolutely argued from your point of view. You have done, I am sure, quite enough to maintain your liberty intact should you unhappily find occasion to use it, & you will I hope for the present let the subject drop & see how we are to dispose of some other grave matters that are before us for immediate consideration.

2. M. [*London*]

Wrote to Mr T.B. Potter—Ld Chancellor—Earl Devon—Mrs Th.—Mr Moran—and minutes. Walked with Forster to the Station: off before 11 & got to London between 3 & 4. Conversation with F. & with Ld Sydney. Saw Mr Glyn—Dean Stanley—Sir T. Fremantle. Dined at Sir T. Fremantle's. Read Strauss—Picton's Hist. of Liverpool[1]—M'Donnell on Irish Univ. Education.

3. Tu.

Wrote to The Queen—Mr Eykyn MP.—Scotts—Mr Locke King—and minutes. Cabinet 2¾-6½. Bss B. Coutts's in evg. Saw Ld Granville—Ld F. Cavendish—Mr Glyn—Mr Locke King—Mr Gurdon—Mr Stansfeld—W.H.G.—Bp of Winchester. Saw Armstrong—Norman [R]. Attended Meeting to hear Mr Smith's Paper read on the Babylonian account of the Deluge.[2] They obliged me to speak a little.

Cabinet. Dec. 3. 72. 2.30 PM.[3]

√ Civil Service Conspiracy. Govt. if it expresses displeasure must be prepared under certain circs. for dismissal. Chancr. of Exr. to get more information.[4]
√ Locke King Succession to Land of Intestates. We cannot deal with the subject at large. we will give him such aid as we can if he proceed promptly.[5]
√ Irish Univ. Education. Draft of Nov. 30 revised in part.
Local Taxation.
√ Park Rules: summons & appeal. Take names & addresses. Att. Gen[eral] attended—will use every effort to get an immediate decision on the appeal.

[1] Sir J. A. *Picton, *The architectural history of Liverpool* (1858).
[2] By George Smith of the British Museum at the Society of Biblical Archaeology; Gladstone added half a column on Homer; *The Times*, 4 December 1872 7c. Diarist's letter of 7 December, protesting at misreporting in *The Spectator*, 14 December 1872.
[3] Add MS 44640, f. 217.
[4] See 9 Dec. 72.
[5] Letter to King explaining this, Add MS 44542, f. 51.

√ Canada Tea Bill. Not to disallow. Leave to operate—a mild arg[ument] for free trade.[1]
√ Mr Beal's note.[2] Govt. of Metropolis. There will be no Bill.
Case of O'Connor. No Avowedly official action, but Mr Bruce to arrange for his going to a distant healthy climate.[3]

4. Wed.

Wrote to Mr Locke King—Lord Russell (2)—Mr Bruce—Ld Granville—Mrs Th.—and minutes. Read Winwood Reade.[4] Saw Ld F. Cavendish—Mr Gurdon—Mr C. [A.] Gore—Mr Glyn—Mr Helmore—Sir J. Grant—Sir H. Maine—Dowager Lady Westmoreland (Baron S.)[5]—Dr Bence Jones—Ld R. Cavendish. Saw Armstrong—Norman X. Dined at Sir J. Colvile's.

5. Th.

Wrote to Ld Hartington—Mr Goschen—The Queen—and minutes. Cabinet 2½-7¼. Saw Chancr of Exr—Ld F. Cavendish. Wrote further Mem. on Irish Univ. question.[6] Dined with the F. Cavendishes. Read Topogr. of Liverpool.[7]

Cabinet. Dec. 5. 1872. 2½ PM.[8]
√ Irish Univ. plan. Memm. reviewed. Further mem: submitted & read in MS. To be printed. Bill to be drawn by Mr Thring with Mr O'Hara. Irish Chanr. & Law Officers to be acquainted. Engl. Att. Gen. to be seen.
√ Movement in Civil Service.
√ Ld Granville. [British] Troops in Japan. To be friendly but circumspect as to the indemnity; liberal: if they show a disp[ositio]n favourable to intercourse.[9]
√ Ld Granville to obtain an implicit assurance or ackn[owledgemen]t from French Govt. that the compensatory duties cannot be levied without the duties on raw materials: by sending to Ld L. a statement in reply to Bradford to that effect.[10]

[1] In fact already an Act and a *coup* for differential duties; D. M. L. Farr, *The colonial office and Canada 1867-1887* (1955), 179.
[2] James Beal, 1829-91; liberal agent in London and proponent of municipal reform (as well as estate agent, see 22 Sept. 68); from 1870 advocated a single London municipality.
[3] See 13 Apr. 72.
[4] W. W. *Reade, *The martyrdom of man* (1872).
[5] Perhaps about her d.-in-law, duchess of Santo Teodoro, who was divorced 1876.
[6] Untraced.
[7] Probably Sir J. A. *Picton, *Memorials of Liverpool, historical and topographical*, 2v. (1873) and see 2 Dec. 72.
[8] Add MS 44640, f. 219.
[9] Japanese mission had raised renegotiation of treaties and withdrawal of British shore troops; I. Nish, *Japanese foreign policy 1869-1942* (1977), 21; CAB 41/4/52.
[10] PRO FO 27/1935; the treaty of 5 November 1872, appendix i, allowed new taxes on raw materials with compensatory duties.

6. Fr.

Wrote to Miss Cochrane—Mr Cardwell (2)—Sir A. Grant—Sir P. Braila—Dr Butler—Robn G.—& minutes. Saw Mrs Th., who was satisfied and as usual. Saw Attorney General—Mr Hignett—Mr Gurdon—Ld F. Cavendish—Mr Hayward—Mr Thring *cum* Ld Hartington: 2 hours conversation to start the drafting Irish Univ. Bill [*sic*]. Read Martyrdom of Man[1]—Conington's Remains[2]—Ld Stowell's Speech on Residence.[3] Dined at Mr Fortescues. Much conversation with Lady W[aldegrave] on unbelief and like topics.

To E. CARDWELL, war secretary, 6 December 1872. Add MS 44542, f. 52.
'Private.'

If you could see me tomorrow forenoon either in C.H.T. or at the W.O. & at such time as might suit you I should like to know, now that the Irish University Bill is in some degree started, what you think you can do for us about Army Estimates. On the one hand I see that, apart from purchase & also apart from any notification of account with the Navy, we have upon the last Estimates taken back all but some 300,000 of the 2,200,000 saving or thereabouts which in Feb. 71 we had made upon the Estimates of our predecessors; while we have a state of foreign relations singularly favourable to us as a defensive Power. On the other side, I do not doubt that you feel in some degree what the Navy will feel more in the high prices of certain commodities. Please to name your own time.

7. Sat. [Hatfield]

Wrote to Mr Dalgairns[4]—Mr Burnett—Miss Doyle—Sir F.H. Doyle—The Queen (l. & Mem)—& minutes. Cabinet 2¼–6¼. Read Haweis[5]—Conington. Saw Ld F. Cavendish—Mr Cardwell: a long and not satisfactory conversation on the Estimates. Dined with the Japanese Ambassadress. I had (as P.M.) to propose the health of the Mikado. The Ambassador proposed H.M. It was an occasion of much interest.[6] Saw Ld Halifax—Ld Granville—Count Brunnow. Off by midnight train to Hatfield.[7]

[1] See 4 Dec. 72.
[2] J. *Conington, *Miscellaneous writings*, ed. J. A. Symonds, 2v. (1872).
[3] 'Substance of the speech . . . of Sir W. *Scott [Baron Stowell] . . . 1802, upon a motion for leave to bring in a bill, relative to the non-residence of the clergy' (1802).
[4] Thanking John Dobree Dalgairns (1818–76, joined Rome with *Newman) for his sermon; Add MS 44542, f. 53 and 24 Nov. 72.
[5] H. R. *Haweis, 'Old violins', *Contemporary Review*, xxi. 85 (December 1872).
[6] A group of Japanese statesmen were touring Europe; see *The Times*, 10 December 1872, 9e.
[7] Lord Salisbury's.

Dec. 7. 1872. 2 PM.[1]

√ Mr Forster's Educ. Mem. & Bill on 25th Clause.[2] Guardians to pay. Compulsion to be universal: but children at work to be partially relieved from attendance. Bill to be drawn for *further cons[ideratio]n.*

√ Local Taxation Bill. Agreed to legislate on: a. consolidated rate b. uniformity of assessment & valuation c. exemptions, abolition of.[3]

Currency Bill—postponed.

√ Lord Granville. French Treaty—difficulties in carrying it into operation. Take opinion of L[aw] O[fficers] on M[ost] F[avoured] N[ation] clause—is it operative forthwith? Get an interchange of notes respecting the levying of compensatory duties unless d. on raw materials are also levied.[4]

Civil Service appl[icatio]n to be received. Intermediate answer to be given by Heads of Depts. sketched[5]—general terms approved.

8. 2 S.Adv.

H.C. at 9 in the Chapel. Ch. at 11—Chapel at 6. Much conversation with Lady S[alisbury]—Mr Brewer—Lord S. Read Pusey's Adv. Sermon[6]—Bp Thirlwall's Charge.[7]

9. M. [Windsor]

Off to London at 10.20—There are no kinder hosts than here. Off again to Windsor at 4.30. Saw Ld F. Cavendish—Mr Glyn—Mr Thring—Mr Cardwell: conversation as long & not more satisfactory. —Mr Stansfeld—Dean of Windsor—Sir T. Biddulph. Wrote to Japanese Ambassador—Rev. Mr Scudamore—Mr Lowe—Mr Cardwell—Mr Gurdon—Sir W.R. . . . and minutes. Read Strauss A. Glaube[8]—Cunynghame's Travels.

10. Tu. [London]

Chapel at 8. Wrote to The Queen—The Speaker—& minutes. Off to London at 10.20. Cabinet 2¾-6¼. Saw Col. Ponsonby—Ld F. Cavendish—Scotts—Mr Goschen—Mrs G. Hope—Mr Locke King—Mr

[1] Add MS 44640, f. 222. A note from Granville reads: 'What about future Cabinets.' Gladstone replied: 'I think we cd. probably finish at our Cabinet on *Wednesday*. I might by that time be able to report progress from Thring with whom I had 2 hours yesterday—rather satisfactory.' Ibid., f. 224.

[2] Jottings at ibid., f. 223.

[3] Legislation was not introduced; instead a select cttee. on boundaries for local taxation was elected; *H* ccxv. 1819.

[4] See 5 Dec. 72n.

[5] Demands for salary increases by civil servants not to be granted while cabinet dispersed for recess; CAB 41/4/52-3.

[6] E. B. *Pusey, 'Eve [a sermon on Gen. iii. 415]' (1872).

[7] C. *Thirlwall, 'A charge . . . 1872' (1872).

[8] See 1 Dec. 72.

E. Talbot—Mr Stansfeld—Sir R. Phillimore. Dined at Ld Lyttel-tons. Read the Cornish Rector.[1]

Cabinet. Tues. D. 10. 72. 2. 30 PM.[2]

√ Ld Hartington Irish R.R. Buying involves working & making new lines.
√ Ld Ripon. Endowed Schools Commission. Opinion of L[aw] O[fficers] as to Ex officio Comm[issioner]s. Chancellor thinks that ecclesiastics may be so appointed—refer to the Comm[ittee] of Council: judicial.
√ Irish Univ. Bill—WEG reported.
√ P. of Wales's. Conversation with P. of W—reported.[3]
The little Irish Residence plan—Ld Hn. will prepare a proposal.
√ Ld Granville—Viceroy of Egypt and Abyssinia—to recommend a friendly reference.[4]
√ Ld Granville reported that Brunnow had spoken in alarm about his dispatch on the Oxus boundary—yesterday reported that there wd. be a conciliatory letter from Gortchakoff.[5]
√ Local Taxation—further discussion on exemptions: esp[eciall]y Country Houses. Also on uniformity of valuation and assessment.

11. Wed.

Wrote to Mr Cardwell (2)—Rev. O. Shipley—& minutes. Saw Ld F. Cavendish—Mr Hutton—Mr Levy—Mr G. Glyn—Ld De Tabley—Chancr of Exr. Educn Deputn in aft.[6] Saw Ld Ripon *cum* Mr F. Saw Lilly. X.[7] Dined at Mr Th's. Struck with Miss Cartwright's[8] conversa-tion. Read Picton's Liverpool. Saw Mr Thring on I.U. Bill.

12. Th.

Wrote to Mr O. Morgan—The Queen l. & M.—C.G.—Mr Cardwell (2)—Mr Thring—& minutes. Cabinet 12½-3. During the whole Cabi-net there was a perpetual under-fire of Mema on the wretched subject of the Army Estimates.[9] Saw Ld F. Cavendish (2)—Mr Gurdon—Mr Glyn—Mr Stansfeld—Mr Goschen—Mr S. *cum* Chancr of Exr —Mr Cardwell. Dined at Mr Grays. Read Mahaffy's Prolegomena[10] —'Off the Skelligs'.[11]

[1] See 23 Nov. 72. [2] Add MS 44640, f. 227. [3] See 30 Nov. 72.
[4] To settle Egyptian-Abyssinian differences; CAB 41/4/54.
[5] See mem. on the Afghan border in PRO 30/29/69.
[6] No report found.
[7] Not Lillie Langtry, still Le Breton and in Jersey; E. Dudley, *The Gilded Lily* (1958), 34.
[8] Perhaps Roma Adelaide Frances, da. of W. C. Cartwright, see 30 Sept. 66.
[9] See n. to following cabinet.
[10] Sir J. P. *Mahaffy, *Prolegomena to ancient history*, 2v. (1871).
[11] See 5 May 72.

Cabinet. D. 12. 72. 12½ PM.[1]

√ Local Taxation. Discussion on Consolidated Rate.

√ 25th Clause Education Act. WEG reported from Deputation of yesterday. Discussion on the Clause.

√ O. Morgan Burials Bill. Cannot undertake.[2]

√ Irish Univ. Bill. Report from WEG as to the progress of Mr Thring in drawing the Bill.

√ Granville explained Moret's[3] request to us to request the Americans to intervene, on terms, with influence to put down the Cuban Insurrection.[4] Agreed subject to proper understanding.

√ Cardwell mentioned having circulated his military paper on wh no objection had been taken. It did not refer to establishments for the year.[5]

13. Fr.

Wrote to Ld Hartington—Mr Cardwell—The Queen—Mr Glyn Tel. —Ld Romilly—Mrs Th.—C.G.—and minutes. Saw Ld F. Cavendish—Mr M'Coll—Mr Ayrton—Mr Stansfeld—Mr Thring—Mr Glyn. We afterwards dined & spent the evening together. He brought an improved account from Cardwell. Read Winwood Reade[6]—Mahaffy's Prolegomena.

14. Sat. [Hawarden]

Wrote to Scotts—Ld Hartington—Mr Hugessen—Lady F. Cavendish—Archbishop of Chios[7]—Ld Ossington—& minutes. Saw Mr Glyn—also Mr G. *cum* Mr Cardwell. The sky clears.[8] Saw Mr Thring on I.U. Bill. Saw Scotts. Left London by 2.45: at Hawarden by 8½. Read Strauss[9]—Crabbe. Packing & unpacking.

To LORD HARTINGTON, Irish secretary, Add MS 44542, f. 54.
14 December 1872.

I have had several long interviews with Thring & he is fully seized of the Memn; & I do not think the points of difficulty that have emerged are more

[1] Add MS 44640, f. 230.

[2] Brought in by Morgan, and lost in cttee.: *H* ccxii. 128; letter informing Morgan of cabinet's decision, at Add MS 44542, f. 54.

[3] Don Sigismondo Moret y Prendergast, Spanish minister in London 1872-3.

[4] See *Hispanic American Historical Review*, xxxvii. 304 (1957).

[5] Cardwell's note of estimates at Add MS 44640, f. 231. Gladstone's holograph comment on it reads: 'In my opinion the case of the Navy with increase of 480m. was a better one than that of the Army with a reduction of 250m. The figures you have given (I think quite correctly) could imply that we have taken 200m. off the better case, & 73m. off the worse (i.e. the worse & better in my eyes.)'

[6] See 4 Dec. 72.

[7] Thanking him for his book on the Armenian church; Add MS 44542, f. 55.

[8] On the estimates.

[9] See 9 Dec. 72.

formidable than might have been expected. But there are several questions that will stand for special consideration in Ireland, besides the general business of reviewing the whole work as it will issue from Thring's hands. One of them is the mode of dealing with prospective vested interests. This I suppose mainly means those of the junior fellows. And the great difficulty their right or tradition of necessaries[?] is as I understand it a right or tradition of succession to what for the most part are merely sinecures. If it were only to offices with duty there would be no great difficulty in dealing with the case. How it should be dealt with as matters actually stand I do not yet know. Perhaps you have a solution ready. If not what I would ask is that you would bring all your available force in Ireland to bear upon it & then be prepared to lay the case before the Government & advise upon it. It will not very seriously affect the *corpus* of the Bill or the draftsman's work upon it. 2. The next matter relates to Galway College. You will be in command of all the facts which bear upon the question (1) whether it should be abolished & (2) whether Cork as well as Belfast should be saved. Upon both these questions I hope you will without very great difficulty be able to get out the material facts & to arrive at clear views which may serve to guide the Cabinet. 3. Another subject of great importance is this. We do not seem to be strong in special knowledge of our ground as far as we have to deal with Trinity College. We want very much some individual who looking at the matter from a Trinity College point of view & thoroughly well acquainted with the laws & working of that institution would form a perfectly dry impartial judgment on the various points of the plan, so that his criticisms might reveal to us the weak places. Some one in short who would do for us, not as a friend but judicially, what Stopford did with me in the matter of the Irish Church. If there cannot be a better man I do not know whether Stopford himself would do, as he may not have the special knowledge. Can such a man be found? If he can I should like to see him. In Stopford's case I told him nothing absolutely but talked over all the points of the subject hypothetically & after seeing him I felt ready on all main points secure.
Cardwell thinks Lawson would be all I want. Has he all the requisite knowledge? Could he & would he come to Hawarden?[1]

15. 3 S.Adv.

Ch mg with H.C. and evg. Wrote to E. Cardwell—Mr Gurdon—Rev R. Smith—and minutes. Read Strauss—H.J. Rose, Xty Always progressive.[2]

16. M.

Wrote to Robn G.—Ld Hartington—and minutes. Conversation with Mrs Hilyard[3] respecting Mayow. Ch. 8½ AM. Read Strauss—Comte's Catechism of Positive Religion.[4] Unpacking books.

[1] Hartington promised, 15 December, Add MS 44143, f. 221, to gather the facts, and recommended John Kells Ingram, 1823-1907, economist and professor of Greek at Trinity College, Dublin.
[2] H. J. *Rose, *Christianity always progressive* (1829).
[3] E. A., wife of E. Hillyard of Chester, Castle guests; Hawn P.
[4] See 7 July 67.

17. Tu.

Ch. 8½ A.M. Saw W.H.G. (livings)—Mr Burnett—Wrote to Bp of Oxford—Sec. Lpool Coll. Institn[1]—Lady Ashburton—Mr Gurdon l. & tel.—Dr Smyth[2]—Earl Russell—and minutes. Read Comte's Catechism—Swinburnes Queen Mother[3]—Dr Smyth's Address—Haweis on Violins.[4]

18. Wed.

Ch. 8½ AM & 7 PM. Wrote to Mr Gurdon (2 tel.)—Robn G.—and minutes. Saw Mr Brewster (who preached; ably, but high.). Woodcutting with Willy. Read Grant Duff's Address[5]—Panizzi on Nicolas's Nelson[6]—Swinburne's Queen Mother: I am much struck by his power. We dined for the first time under Stephy's roof at the Rectory. Began to write an Address for Saturday: with much flinching from the effort.

19. Th.

Ch. 8½ AM. Wrote to Mr Gurdon (tel.)—Chancr of Exr—H.N.G.—Ld Granville—Mr Dalgleish—Mr P. Rathbone—Mr Murray[7]—Ld Provost of Glasgow—Principal Lpool Coll. Inst.[8]—and minutes. Worked much on my 'Address'. Read The Queen Mother. Cut an alder with W. Saw Mr Burnett.

To R. LOWE, chancellor of the exchequer, 19 December 1872. Add MS 44542, f. 57.

1. A letter from Granville will shortly show you that Hammond's objections are nought for any practical purposes. 2. Do not [*sc.* we?] know how you can determine the question of charging the U.S. payment on one year or the other until you get their answer: but prima facie I think it worth considering whether you should brake it, paying one part in Feb. or March & the other in April. Not that the braking is desirable in itself, but if you leave the whole to the year 73–74 may you not be in a deficiency? Again before answering I should like to know your expectations on that head. 3. It cannot be possible for you, I presume, to move in the Malt & Income Tax. The former I cannot think desirable & there are

[1] J. G. Jones.
[2] See 22 Dec. 72.
[3] A. C. *Swinburne, *The Queen Mother. Rosamund* (1860).
[4] See 7 Dec. 72.
[5] Sir M. E. G. *Duff, probably his 'Inaugural address . . . to the University of Aberdeen . . . as Rector' (1867).
[6] A. *Panizzi, in *North British Review*, iv. 413 (February 1846).
[7] Arranging for publication of his address on 21 December 'which is to me rather a serious affair, because I mean to touch upon the noxious abundance at this moment of unbelieving works'; Add MS 44542, f. 57.
[8] i.e. G. Butler.

very serious considerations besides that of revenue now connected with the latter. As to Railways I feel much difficulty in giving any opinion on the merits of the case, for I am considerably interested in it (from what was said as I imagine, though I have never examined) since I have the misfortune to be a shareholder in the Metro-District Line. But speaking of it simply as a Parliamentary question, I very much doubt whether you will be able to hold your ground against the Companies in the H. of C. considering the great impolicy of taxing the locomotion of the working community. 4. I do not know if you have ever considered the feasibility of taking some measure to equalise your March & Sept. Balances which are so unequal under the present otherwise excellent arrangements. You might I suppose make loans of 2 or 3 millions for 6 months in February & March in the open market. 5. I send you a letter from the Ld. Provost of Glasgow & a statement from Mr [R.] Dalglish. I have promised full consideration. I have no reason to suppose the Customhouse folk ignorant of the extraordinary progress of Glasgow, which may make that city more exacting than formerly in its expectations.[1]

20. Fr.

Ch. 11 AM. Wrote to Mrs Thistlethwayte—Chancr of Exr—Mr Gurdon—Mrs Hampton—and minutes. Worked long and late on preparing my address. Cut another alder with Willy.

To R. LOWE, chancellor of the exchequer, 20 December 1872. Add MS 44542, f. 57.

[1]There is another thing I would commend to you—it is to set some competent person to work to make a careful examination of the prices of the necessaries & comforts of life as commonly enjoyed by one or more classes above the labouring class in condition[?] at different periods say 72-52-32. In the Poor Law Department something of this kind was done for me in 53 & I proved in my Budget Speech a material reduction in the charge of living upon which Parliament consented to change Income Tax on Incomes from £100 to £150. But the person who is set to work must set about it with a right *animus*. I imagine it to be the very high price of coal which more than anything has prompted these movements. But I doubt whether best coal is higher in London at this moment than it was in 32—say 32/ per ton. The comparison should be a very careful one & should include lodging, fuel, clothing, food animal & vegetable with all Southern & tropical products, locomotion, books & newspapers. Should you not also inquire into the state of the supply of candidates for public employments at the different periods when Navy & Army Pay were raised—was it not to meet a positive want of men. These & other thoughts of mine upon the subject are very crude. Query whether we could take this ground—that we would accede to none of these recommendations except on the footing of inquiries to ascertain the possibility of readjusting whatever may be superfluous *or* defective, either in numbers or emoluments.

[1] Lowe's reply untraced.
[2] Passage on civil service salaries omitted. No survey found.

21. Sat. [*Courthey, Liverpool*]

Wrote to Earl Russell—and minutes. Off at 9.15 to Lpool: arr at Instn at 11½. Saw Dean Howson—Mr Butler—Mrs Butler.[1] At 12.15 I delivered my Address which lasted an hour as I meant.[2] The Prizes, divers speeches, & the luncheon afterwards. 2700 persons present. Evening at Courthey. Music. Read Villemain's Cromwell.[3]

22. 4 S.Adv.

Drove to Seaforth mg. Congr. 300 or something more: service & music decorous not hearty. Visited the Parsonage before & after. Saw Dr Smith,[4] and 3 daughters of Mr Rawson. After service I saw him:[5] declining gently; very near his end: in perfectly established calm. Requiescat! In evg drove with Robertson to St Thomas's Toxteth. A dismal spectacle. 40 in the Ch. below where there should be 600: Mr Yonge[6] unsatisfactory. Wrote to Ld Granville—Mr Bruce—Agnes G.—Bp of St Asaph—& minutes. Read Strode's Fonseca on Divine Love.[7] Messenger from London at 11 P.M. brought me with wh [*sic*] lasted till one. Music at Courthey in evg. See below [*sc.* above] the account of Mr Yonge: a 'bareback': a sad incubus I fear, & with this a hot Orangeman.

23. M. [*Hawarden*]

Off at 9.15. Visited the Oriental Art Exhibition. Then the Mayor. Off at 11.20. Home 1.30. Wrote to Ld Hartington—Mr Murray—Rev Mr Blunt—Chancr of Exchr—Watsons—and minutes. Set to work on my post: & prepared my Address for the Press: sent it off. Saw S.E.G. on his Buckley difficulty. He had just been forcing down a madman. I was struck with his calm. Finished the Queen Mother. Read Villemain's Cromwell.

[1] i.e. George and Josephine *Butler; he told *Stansfeld on 24 December: 'I had a good deal of conversation with Mrs Butler & was greatly struck & pleased with her. Knowing her feelings about *the* topic [i.e. the Contagious Diseases Acts] I appreciated her perfect absention. Also, I was struck with the force of her mind & I thought her perfectly & rather remarkably feminine, notwithstanding the said material wh. under a strong impulse of conscience she has had to handle'; Add MS 44542, f. 59.

[2] To Liverpool College; Add MS 44693, f. 132, with appendix; published as a pamphlet. See introduction above, vol. vii, section VIII.

[3] A. F. Villemain, *Histoire de Cromwell*, 2v. (1819).

[4] Charles Swaby Smith, Seaforth physician.

[5] i.e. W. Rawson, his schoolmaster, who d. next day; see 4 Aug. 25.

[6] Reginald Yonge, d. 1889; curate of St. Thomas's 1867-82; correct note for 3 Sept. 67.

[7] See 9 Aug. 68.

24. Tu.

Ch. 8½ AM. Wrote to Abp Manning—Mr Stansfeld—The Queen—Ld Granville—Mr Dodson—Mr Max Müller—Mr J.G. Jones—Mr Falkner Lloyd—Mr Gurdon Tel.—and minutes. Cutting with W. & H. Saw H. on his matters. Worked on Appendix to my Address. French Treaty business: F.O. mema from Ld G.[1] Read Rosamond[2]—Noel's Poems.[3]

To F. Max MÜLLER, 24 December 1872. Max Müller MSS, d. 170.

I performed my duty at Liverpool[4] in considerable trouble of mind, but under a *drang*[5] which I really could not resist. Your kind letter cheers me.[6] I took Strauss's Book as a Manifesto: I suppose Bekenntniss[7] might be so translated. Unhappily I do not possess the physical knowledge necessary to deal with the Darwinian question: nor do I know how far he & his immediate allies have carried their statement of propositions. I feel less unable to deal with the non-physical part of the subject. Here, according to my ever strengthening conviction, the strength of belief lies in—Butler:[8] I do not mean (principally) his particular arguments or propositions, but his *method of handling*, which is truly his own, & is the only one known to me that is fitted to guide life, and thought bearing upon life, in the face of the nineteenth century. I can therefore like you feel that there are many arguments I cannot answer: but first have I from the Analogy of my nature a title to expect to be able to answer all arguments; and secondly do they offer me any standing ground which is more of a rock, or less of a quagmire, than that which I now hold? Here is a text: but the Sermon? I am afraid that will not come off, until you are so good & so free as to come here, or until I abandon politics, which God in His mercy grant before long.

25. Wed. Xmas Day.

Ch. at 11 & H.C. Also at 7. Wrote to Archdeacon Jones—Mr Braithwaite—Robn G.—Bp of Chester—Mr Ayrton—Duke of Bedford—Mr Murray—Rev. Mr Mayow—and minutes. Read Mayow's Reply[9]—Memoir of Sachs[10]—Smith, Credibility of Xtn Religion[11]—Colenso, Worship of Baal in Israel.[12] We were all together as a happy family, at the Altar.

[1] Ramm I, i. 367.
[2] See 17 Dec. 72.
[3] R. B. W. *Noel, *The red flag and other poems* (1872).
[4] See 21 Dec. 72.
[5] 'pressure'.
[6] Of 23 December 1872, Add MS 44251, f. 337.
[7] More usually, 'confession'. For Strauss, see 1 Dec. 72.
[8] i.e. Joseph *Butler and his *Analogy of religion* (1736).
[9] M. W. Mayow, 'A reply to a memorial on the subject of ritual' (1872).
[10] Untraced.
[11] S. Smith, *The credibility of the Christian religion* (1872).
[12] J. W. *Colenso, *The Pentateuch and Book of Joshua critically examined*, Part vi (1871).

26. Th.

Ch. 8¾ AM. Wrote to Ld Tenterden (Tel.)—Mr Goschen—Mr Murray—and minutes. Corrected proofs of Address & worked on Appendix. Worked on books. Read Denman's Version from Pope.[1] A round game.

27. Fr.

Ch. 8¾ AM. Wrote to Justice Denman—Ld Clanricarde—Mr Bruce—Mrs Hampton—Archd. Jones—Sir T. Biddulph—Mrs Thistlethwayte—& minutes. Worked on books. Treecutting with my sons. Read Bagehot on Physics and Politics.[2] Conversation with Mr Temple.[3]

28. Sat.

Ch. 8.45 A.M. Wrote to Ld Tenterden (Tel.)—Mr Hugessen—Mr Gurdon—Bp of Bath & Wells—Mr Newton—Ld Hartington—D. of Argyll—The Queen (Mem.)—Bp of Chester—and minutes. Rain: ever rain. Walk in it. Conversation with S.E.G.—Mr Burnett—Mr Temple (Theol. Philos.). Read Compton Reade[4]—M. Müller's Vorlesung.[5] Worked on books.

To LORD HARTINGTON, Irish secretary, 28 December 1872. Add MS 44542, f. 61.

It seems to me that it would be quite worth while to get leave to show Manning's letter to the Cabinet. It sums up the case very clearly & most favourably.[6] Also could not we put to O'Hagan the three points—as a basis & through him let them become known to his Ecclesiastical Chiefs. The light in which I hope you may ultimately see the University question is this: that our path is full of difficulties & many objections may be taken to our plan; but there is no other, essentially different, which we are in a condition to launch with even a ray of hope. Where shall I find an account of the gross numbers & charge of each Queen's College from the foundation onwards in each year? Has the proportion of R.C.'s increased or diminished?

From what the Ld. Lt. writes Ingram[7] seems to be quite the proper man, but I am not quite ready.

[1] G. *Denman, *The First Book of Pope's Homer's Iliad* (1873), dedicated to Gladstone.

[2] W. *Bagehot, *Physics and politics* (1872). [3] See 23 Sept. 72.

[4] C. *Reade, *The 'Golden Crowns' series* (1872).

[5] F. M. *Müller, *Über die Resultate der Sprachwissenschaft. Vorlesung* (1872).

[6] Letter of Manning apparently accepting the plan; see Hartington to Gladstone, 27 December 1872, Add MS 44143, f. 221.

[7] See 14 Dec. 72n.

To E. H. KNATCHBULL-HUGESSEN, colonial under-secretary, 28 December 1872. Kent Record Office.

I sincerely ask your pardon for having allowed two posts to pass without answering your letter.[1] It has been the consequence of a trip to Liverpool & the work it entailed.

You will I am sure understand that I speak in reply to your inquiry only & not as if on the part of the Government I had a title to interfere. From this point of view I should were I in your place decline to join the Church Defence Association:[2] 1. The Liberation Society is a poor affair & out of heart & likely so to continue for the causes which are working in its favour are remote and for the present feeble. 2. The Church has really got an organization for self-defence already in its very frame work & is well able to take up any question that offers itself. 3. & principally—I believe the Church Defence Association if it has not assumed already is sure to assume a political character. Though many Liberals may agree with Tories as to Establishment, when it comes to a question of means this concord can hardly continue & private freedom would I think be much hampered.

29. S.

Ch. 8 A.M. (H.S.)—11 AM.—& 6½ P.M. Wrote to Mr Murray (2)—Mr Mayow—and minutes. Read Gaskell on Unitm[3]—Mr J. Stuart's notable Lecture[4]—Griffiths on the Congress[5]—Oakeley on Ath. Creed[6]—& other tracts.

My 63 birthday comes round as ever with profound associations of thankfulness (or cause for it) & of shame. 'Truth, justice, order, peace, honour, duty, liberty, piety' these are the objects before me in my daily prayers with reference to my public function, which for the present commands (& I fear damages) every other: but this is the best part of me. All the rest is summed up in 'miserere'.

30. M.

Ch. 8½ A.M. Wrote to Mr Hammond (Tel.)—Mr Murray (finished corrections)—Ld Kimberley—Mr Glyn—Viceroy of I. (Tel.)—Sir Thos G.—Rev Mr Sandford—and minutes. Working with W., H., & H. Worked on books. Read Baring Gould's Iceland[7]—Watkiss Lloyd on Sicily.[8]

[1] Not found.

[2] The Church Defence Institution, see 10 Dec. 71n.

[3] W. *Gaskell, 'Strong points of Unitarian Christianity' (1873).

[4] Perhaps J. S. Stuart, 'America and the Americans versus the Papacy and the Catholics: a lecture' (1853).

[5] Not found.

[6] F. *Oakeley, *The Athanasian Creed: four lectures suggested by the present controversy* (1873).

[7] S. B. *Gould, *Iceland; its scenes and sagas* (1863).

[8] W. W. *Lloyd, *The history of Sicily to the Athenian War* (1872).

31. Tu.

Ch. 8½ AM. Wrote to Mr Gurdon Tel.—Professor Abdy[1]—Mrs H.G. —Mr Macfie MP.—Mr Gobat[2]—Mr Sandford—Mr Laird MP—Rev. Mr Temple—Mr Cross MP.—Chancr of Exr—Mrs Malcolm—Sir R. Phillimore—Count A.L. Dusmani—and minutes. Worked on books. Cut a beech with W. & Herbert. Harry went off: with all good omens —I am more than hopeful of his future character and career. Read Nine Fortunes[3]—Dusmani's cleverly written but dishonest Narrative.[4]

And so falls the curtain on another anxious and eventful year: probably the last one of the present cares, and coming near the last of all: How I feel myself bound to earth: but whenever the command comes, with whatever awe misgiving and remorse, I hope to yield it a prompt obedience. May I in the meantime be allowed to do something for my fellow-creatures, in whose welfare lies the glory of God Most High.

[1] John Thomas Abdy, 1822-99; regius professor of civil law at Cambridge 1854-73; recorder of Bedford 1870-93.

[2] Successfully offering St. Thomas', Seaforth, to Samuel Benoni Gobat, vicar of Is-y-Coed; he d. August 1873.

[3] A. S. Leech, *Nine fortunes; an autobiography* (1872).

[4] A. L. Dusmani, 'La Missione di . . . W. E. Gladstone nelle Isole Ionie' (1869-71); given much publicity for its descriptions of Gladstone allegedly attending mass in 1858 in tracts by James Johnstone, sec. of the Anti-Papal League of Edinburgh (see Add MS 44434, ff. 107, 238-47).

Wed. Jan. One 1873. Circumcision. [*Hawarden*]

Ch. 8¾ AM. Wrote to The Queen (Mem)—Sir T. Biddulph—Mr S. Amos—Mr Hammond—Mr E.C. Clark[1]—M. Van de Weyer—Duke of Argyll—Ld Houghton—Ld Provost of Edinburgh[2]—Sir W.R. Farquhar—& minutes. Worked at the Waterfall. Further Corr. of Address for Press. Finished work on books. Read Lpool Dock Extension[3]—Villemain's Cromwell.[4]

2. Th.

Ch. 8½ A.M. Wrote to Mr Hammond—Ld Granville—l. & Tel.—Rev. Mr Gobat—Mr Mayow—Mr J. Palmer—Rev Dr Russell[5]—& minutes. Made out my annual Statement of Property & Income: rather hastily. Farm calls with C. Saw Griffiths—Roberts: our best men. A round game in evg. Read Villemain's Cromwell—Swinburne's Ballads.[6]

To E. HAMMOND, 2 January 1873. PRO FO 391/24.

Loftus' despatch (N. 370)[7] which states the question between us & Russia about the Affghan frontier very well suggests to me whether we might not agree with Russia upon some such footing as this. That she should recognise the *status quo* as to the frontier, including Badakshan & Vakkan.[8] That we reciprocally should recognise it as to the internal government of those provinces. So it would be a condition of the arrangement that the Suzerainty indicated by Tribute should continue, & the *dominium directum* which Russia apprehends could not come into existence without destroying the arrangement.[9]

3. Fr.

Painful state of the gums kept me at home. Wrote to Ld Tenterden Tel.—Ld Hartington Tel.—Ld Granville (2)—Ld E. Cecil[10]—Abp.

[1] Declined to offer to Sheldon Amos (1835–86), but did offer to Edwin Charles Clark (1835–1917), the chair of civil law at Cambridge, which he accepted; Add MS 44542, f. 64.

[2] James Cowan, 1816–95, provost 1872–4; liberal M.P. there 1874–82; unable to subscribe to John Knox memorial; ibid.; see 4 Jan. 73.

[3] 36 & 37 Vict. cxliv expanded Liverpool's docks.

[4] See 21 Dec. 72.

[5] See Lathbury, ii. 144.

[6] A. C. *Swinburne, *Poems and ballads* (1866).

[7] Of 25 December 1872, PRO FO 65/875.

[8] Both north of Chitral.

[9] Docketed by Hammond, disagreeing, as Russia would have pretext for 'interfering to check encroachments'.

[10] Lord Eustace Brownlow Henry Cecil, 1834–1921; tory M.P. Essex 1865–85; on rating of tithe commutation; Add MS 44542, f. 65.

Manning—Ld Sydney—Miss Marsh—Ld J. Thynne—Editor of the Examiner[1]—and minutes. Mr Gobat came: & I stated to him at great length the case of Seaforth Church to assist his cons[ideratio]n of it. Read. Worked on the divesture of the lawn.

4. Sat.

Ch. 8½ AM. Wrote to Ld Tenterden (Tel.)—Mr Hammond (Tel.)—Ld Hartington—Mr Bruce—Prof. Blackie—Mrs Hillyard—Ld Kinnaird—and minutes. Corrected my yearly Statement of Property. Further conversation with Rev. Mr Gobat who will again visit Seaforth. Walk with C. Read London Quart.Rev. on Education.[2] Queen's Univ.Cal. Much Homeric & archaic conversation with Mr Parker.

To Professor J. S. BLACKIE, 4 January 1873. Add MS 44542, f. 66.

Your very kind letter[3] gives me more credit for liberality than I deserve. But the truth is I am obliged to consider all questions of public subscriptions rather narrowly inasmuch as all my proceedings are closely observed. In a case like that of [Thomas] Chalmers, though he was a far sounder Presbyterian than John Knox, I had no difficulty in following my dear friend Dean Ramsay who actively promoted the scheme for a public memorial to that noble & simple man. I do not feel quite the same facility with respect to John Knox. My inclination, & my official position, render it inexpedient for me to enter into controversies, or into commemoration of controversies. For example, I cordially wish well to Dr. Döllinger & his coadjutors, but if a public subscription were founded for them I am not sure that I should while Prime Minister do well to join it. It is perfectly natural & proper, perhaps, for the ninety per cent or more of Scotsmen who are Presbyterians to found even at this late day a memorial to Knox: is it equally in keeping for the other ten per cent who might perfectly well do it for Chalmers? This nut is a little hard to crack: but when you come to London we may, I hope, have an opportunity of talking about it. I was obliged for reasons more than one to decline the honour the Lord Provost proposed for me. I am extremely glad you are pleased with the address at Liverpool.

5. 2 S Xm.

Ch. 11 A.M. (and H.C.)—6½ P.M. Wrote minutes. Walk with R. Cavendish. Read Lond Quart on Strauss—Br. Quart on Curtis's B.L.[4] —Bree on Darwinism[5]—Serm. on Real Presence.[6]

[1] H. Fox *Bourne; commenting, privately, on its article this day on his Liverpool address; ibid.
[2] *London Quarterly Review*, xxix. 429 (January 1873).
[3] Of 23 December 1872, requesting a subscription to a national monument to John Knox; Add MS 44095, f. 397.
[4] *British Quarterly Review*, lvii. 1 (January 1873).
[5] C. R. Bree, *An exposition of the fallacies in the hypothesis of Mr Darwin* (1872).
[6] J. Harrison, *The Fathers versus Dr. Pusey* (1873).

6. M. Epiph[any]

Ch. 8¾ AM. C.s birthday: she is indeed singularly blessed in the richness of the fruits of love she bears.
Wrote to Viceroy of Ireland—Chwardens of Seaforth—Archdn Jones—Rev Mr Gobat—Sir W.S. Maxwell—Robn G.—& minutes. Read Dusmani's Narrative[1]—Sterne Sentimental Journey[2]—Whitelaw & Walsh Hist. Dublin.[3] Cut down a Sycamore with W.H.G.

7. Tu.

Ch. 8½ AM. Wrote to Mr G. Glyn (tel & l.)—Ld Hartington—H.N.G. —Mr Godley—Mr Dodson—Mr Hammond—The Queen—& minutes. Walk with Ld R.C. Conversation with Mr Parker. Read Warren's Rehearsals[4]—München Stiftungsfeier[5]—The Coming K.[6]—Whitelaw & Walsh—Sentimental Journey (finished).

8. Wed.

Ch. 8½ AM. Wrote to Simpkin & Marshall[7]—The Queen (Mem.)—D of Argyll—Mr Gurdon—M. Thierrat[8]—Ld Granville (Tel)—Mr Thring—M. Reitlinger—& minutes. Saw Mr Barker. Worked on Pamphlets. Read Doman's Poems[9]—Wood on Conservatism—Irish Univ. Tracts—Knight on Prayer[10]—Frere's 'Birds'.[11] Worked on accounts of Income.

9. Th.

Ch. 8½ AM. Wrote to Ld Tenterden (Tel.)—Ld Hartington—Mr Cubley[12]—Ed. Examiner[13]—Mr T. Scott—Ld Chancellor—Gertrude G.—Sir R. Phillimore—Dr Hooker—Bp of Winchester—Mrs Th.—Chester Postmaster (Tel.)—and minutes. Saw Mr Burnett. Read ὄρνιθες[14]—Frere's Birds—M. Müllers Vorlesung at Strasburg.[15]

[1] See 31 Dec. 72.
[2] L. *Sterne, *Sentimental Journey* (1768).
[3] J. Warburton, J. Whitelaw, R. Walsh, *A history of the city of Dublin* (1818).
[4] J. B. L. Warren, *Rehearsals, a book of verses* (1870).
[5] Untraced.
[6] *The coming K. By the author of The Siliad, Don Juan* [perhaps E. C. G. Murray] (1860).
[7] London publishers; on poems by Doman; Add MS 44542, f. 68.
[8] Ph. Thierrat of Lyons, had written on Homer; ibid. and 44436, f. 206.
[9] H. Doman, *'The Cathedral' and other poems* (1864).
[10] W. Knight, 'The function of prayer', *Contemporary Review*, xxi. 183 (January 1873).
[11] J. H. *Frere, *Aristophanes. A metrical version of the Acharnians, the Knights and the Birds* (1840).
[12] Of Newark (see 26 Jan. 41) regretting he could not accept nomination there for the next election; Add MS 44542, f. 70.
[13] Declining to allow publication of his letter; Add MS 44542, f. 68, 3 Jan. 73.
[14] By Aristophanes; see 8 Jan. 73n.
[15] See 28 Dec. 72.

To S. WILBERFORCE, bishop of Winchester, 9 January 1873. Wilberforce MSS d. 38.

I am truly sorry that I feel myself disabled from complying with your request.[1] I have considered it carefully, & I have received the personal application of which you speak. It is not that I have any doubt of the expediency or the urgency of your plan, or any slackness (I hope) of good will towards it. But I have taken a very marked step by the recent Address at Liverpool; & were I rapidly to *cumulate* similar manifestations I should assume too much, should go beyond my line, & should weaken my general means of doing good. A good deal of gall seems to have been stirred already, & any fresh manifestation of the 'clerical' mind with which I understand the P[all] M[all] Gazette credits me must I think be postponed. There is a considerate article in the Times of today[2] on this great question of belief. But I think the writer underrates the mischief, & I do not allow that the 'inductive method' has anything to do with it.

10. Fr.

Ch. 8½ A.M. Wrote to Mr Max Müller—Ld Granville—Mr Macfie—Mr Dodson—Mr Gobat—Dean of Winchester—Mr Murray—Mr Burnett—and minutes. After cutting a tree with Herbert, I went to the Rent dinner at Q[ueens] ferry with Stephy, or rather the dessert: where we both spoke.[3] Read Grote on Socrates[4]—M. Müllers discourse at Strasburg on Oxford—Michaelis Prot.Univ. Deutschlands.[5]

To Professor F. Max MÜLLER, 10 January 1873. Max Müller MSS d. 170.

I have now read through the lecture[6] at Strasburg & the Speech relating to the Oxford gift; & I cannot refrain from saying how very much I admire, & with what entire sympathy I follow, in particular the concluding portions of those able productions. I want to know where I can get a general & rough idea of the amount of endowments & state-payments—i.e. of income other than from voluntary services—enjoyed by the German Universities. You would oblige me much if you could direct me to a proper source. Perhaps our statistical bodies ought to have the information at hand. I am also very curious to know in what way these Universities avoid the difficulty which we imagine to subsist where as in the Scottish Universities the same persons teach the Students & examine them for degrees. It is *prima facie* like the case of a contractor for Army or Navy Stores appointed to test the goods which he has manufactured.

I have been reading to-day that queer old book of Michaelis (1768-76) on the German *Protestant* Universities, but have lost myself in it without finding what I immediately want. He says they were too numerous. Is that so now?

[1] To participate in a meeting 'to Evangelize South London'; 6 January 1873, Add MS 44345, f. 240.

[2] Second leader: Gladstone's Liverpool address was 'an exaggerated alarm'.

[3] No report found.

[4] See 8 Feb. 68.

[5] J. D. Michaelis, *Raisonnement über die protestantischen Universitäten in Deutschland*, 4v. (1768-76).

[6] Sent on 23 December 1872, Add MS 44251, f. 337.

We have an important business to transact for Ireland in this line, & it finds & will find me much work.

What an admirable description of Materialismus by Döllinger in his Festrede! 'that dungeon without air or space or light.'

11. Sat.

Ch. 8½ A.M. Wrote to Ld Granville—D. of Argyll—Mr Godley Tel.—C. Lyttelton—Mr Stone—Ld Sydney—Robn G.—Mr Newman Hall—H.N.G.—Ld Provost of Glasgow—Mr Burnett—& minutes. Cut a tree with Herbert. Tea (aftr) at Mr Johnson's. Conversation with Bp of Chester—Mr Johnson. Corrected Directions Suppl. to my Will.[1] Read Smith on Skye[2]—Croll on Molecular Motion.[3]

12. 1 S.Epiph.

Church 11 AM and 6½ P.M. Wrote to Ld Granville—The Queen—Mr Goschen—Mr Bickersteth—Mr Bruce—& minutes. Read Bp of Manchester's Charge[4]—Contemp.Rev. on Creeds[5]—Bickersteth's Home Call[6]—Miss Marsh's Tract[7]—Wilkinson on Prayer[8]—Smith on Credibil. of Religion[9]—Spiritual Phenomena.[10]

13. M.

Ch. 8½ AM. Wrote to Ld Hartington—Dr Carpenter—Mr Bickers—Mr Godley l. & Tel.—Mr Croll[11]—Mr [G. H.] Wilkinson—Chancr of Exr—Mr E. Chambres—and minutes. Worked on Irish Bill. My upper jaw became more painful during the day & sent me to bed early. I took to reading [Scott's] 'Old Mortality'. Saw Archdeacon Ffoulkes. Read also Carpenter on Inland Seas[12]—Wood on Conservatism—Wilkinson on Prayer (finished)—Croll on Motion (d[itt]o).

[1] Increasing amounts left to his children, 'Paper of Memoranda and Directions, Supplemental to my Will', Hawn P; see 29 Aug. 60.

[2] A. *Smith, *Summer in Skye* (1866).

[3] J. *Croll, *What determined molecular motion?* (1872).

[4] J. *Fraser, 'A charge . . . 1872' (1872).

[5] *Contemporary Review*, xxi. 283 (January 1873).

[6] E. H. *Bickersteth, *The master's home-call* (1872).

[7] C. M. Marsh, perhaps *From dark to dawn, or the story of W. Roland* (1873).

[8] J. B. Wilkinson, *Aids to mental prayer* (1871).

[9] See 25 Dec. 72.

[10] *Spiritual Phenomena, or invisibles* (1867).

[11] James *Croll, 1821-90, geologist; see 11 Jan. 73n.

[12] By W. B. *Carpenter, published in *Contemporary Review*, xxii. 372 (August 1873).

14. Tu.

Kept my bed all day after a night of much pain. Wrote to Mr Godley—Ld Granville Tel.—and minutes. Further work on Irish Bill. Read Old Mortality. In the evening I was relieved by discharge, earlier than Dr M. expected.

15. Wed.

Wrote to Mr Murray—The Queen (Mem.)—Scotts—Ld Granville—T.B. Potter—J. Watson & Smith—Sir A. Panizzi—& minutes. Read Old Mortality. Walked out with C. & S: Face well covered, weather like April.

To T. B. POTTER, M.P., 15 January 1873. 'Private.' Add MS 44542, f. 73.

I dare say you may be aware that the prerogative of pardon & mitigation is never politically dealt with: it remains as a departmental subject exclusively in the hands of the Home Secretary, & I have never known an instance of interference on the part of his colleagues. For your own *personal* information however I may state it is within my knowledge that the sentence passed upon the Gas Stokers is under Mr Bruce's careful consideration.[1]

16. Th.

Down to breakfast. Wrote to Ld Hartington—Mr Godley (l. & Tel.)—Bp Moriarty—Abp Manning—Mr Ouvry—Sir H. Holland. Saw Dr Moffatt—Mr Burnett. Dr Ingram[2] came in aft. & I was able to spend several hours with him on the Univ. question. Read Grote's Socrates—Old Mortality.

17. Fr.

Church 8½ AM. Wrote to Ld Halifax—Mr Godley—and minutes. Many hours with Dr I. on the Bill & scheme: in truth, almost from breakf. to dinner. Conversation with him in evg on Homer & ancient questions. Read Old Mortality. Conversation with Dr [H. W.] Acland.

18. Sat.

Ch. 8½ AM. Wrote to Ld Hartington—Mr Godley 2 Tell.—Sir A. Panizzi—Ld Selborne—Mr Thring—Rev. Mr West—and minutes.

[1] Bruce and the cabinet reduced their sentences from 12 to 4 months hard labour. No relevant letter from Potter in Add MS 44282. For the strike, see 22 Jan. 73.

[2] See 14 Dec. 72n.

Also Mema on Irish Univ. Read Q.R. on Irish Univ.[1]—Dr Miller on do—Fottrell on do[2]—Univ. Calendars—Old Mortality. Walk with the party. Conversation with Ld Houghton—Dr Acland—Dr Ingram—Mr E. Talbot.

Secret *Memorandum.*[3]

a. *To found new Colleges in the University*. b. *To establish the non-Collegiate element*. c. To substitute a Council for the Provost & Seven Fellows so far as the Univ. is concerned. d. alter the title to the Univ. of Dublin simply. e. allocate the property. f. grant further endowment. g. absorb the Queen's Univ. (having taken in the Colleges).

Under this rearrangement all the material Clauses would fall in to their places but in a different order & form of presentation.

19. 2 S.Epiph.

Ch. 11 AM (with Holy C.) & 7 P.M. SEG preached well in mg, E. Talbot still better in evg. Wrote to Mr Godley (Tel.)—The Queen—Dr Alexander—& minutes. Read Voysey's Sermon[4]—Griffith on Fundamentals[5]—Dr Alexander's Sermon[6]—Travers Smith's (able) Sermon &c.[7] Walk with Ld Houghton.—Saw Dr Acland—E. Talbot.

To B. DISRAELI, 19 January 1873. Add MS 44437, f. 41.

My reluctance to intrude on the sacredness and freshness of your sorrow may now, I think, properly give way to a yet stronger reluctance to forego adding our small but very sincere tribute of sympathy to those abundant manifestations of it which have been yielded in so many forms. You and I were, as I believe, married in the same year. It has been permitted to both of us to enjoy a priceless boon through a third of a century. Spared myself the blow which has fallen on you, I can form some conception of what it must have been and must be. I do not presume to offer you the consolation, which you will seek from another and higher quarter. I offer only the assurance which all who know you, & all who knew Lady Beaconsfield, & especially those among them who like myself enjoyed for a length of time her marked though unmerited regard, may perhaps tender without impropriety; the assurance that in this trying hour they feel deeply for you and with you.

[P.S.] I have said in my note 'our' tribute; I hope you will allow me to speak for

[1] *Quarterly Review*, cxxxiv. 255 (January 1873).
[2] G. Fottrell, 'Letter containing a scheme of Irish University Reform' (1873).
[3] Initialled and dated 18 January 1873, Add MS 44761, f. 7; on the *verso* are listed other 'Modes of Proceeding'.
[4] C. *Voysey, 'Orthodoxy and pantheism. A sermon' (1872).
[5] T. Griffith, *Fundamentals; or, bases of belief* (1871).
[6] W. L. Alexander, 'The good man' (1873); on E. B. *Ramsay.
[7] R. T. Smith, 'Doctrinal revision; a sermon' (1872).

my wife and daughters as well as myself. And I must beg that you will on no account take the trouble of replying to this note.[1]

20. M.

Ch. 8½ AM. Wrote to The Queen (Mem)—Mr Thring—Mr Glyn—Mr Godley Tel.—Mr W. Fowler—Ld Ormathwaite—H.N.G.—Sir H. Storks—Mr Knollys—and minutes. Felled a tree with W. Went to see old Mrs Huntington, passed 90, who has lately had a paralytic stroke. Read Old Mortality—Newman Office & Work of Edn[2]—Ogilvy Memoir on Defence of France.[3] Drew an abstract of historical facts respecting Dublin Univ. and College.[4]

21. Tu. [London]

Ch. 8½ AM. Wrote to Sir T. Biddulph—Bp of Edinburgh[5]—and minutes. Packing & prepn. Off at 11 & at 11 C.H.T. at 6 PM. Saw Mr Thring—Chancr of Exr—Mrs Th. X. Dined at Sir A. Panizzi's. Read Huber on Strauss[6]—Howley on T.C. Dublin.[7] Arranging papers &c in L[ondo]n.

22. Wed.

Wrote Parliamentary Circular—Mrs Begbie—Mr Glyn—The Queen l. and Mem.—The Lord Mayor—W.H.G.—C.G.—and minutes. Saw Mr Glyn (2)—Mr Gurdon—Ld Granville—Scotts—Mr Cardwell—Mr Childers—Dined with the Lytteltons; as did Harry. Read Dubl.Univ.Cal. of 1833—Ld Ormathwaite on French Rev.[8] Cabinet 2½-6½.

Cabinet. Wed. Jan. 22. 73. 2.30.[9]

√ Irish Univ. Bill. Cabinet agree to the form of drafting as proposed by Mr Gladstone.

√ Gas Stokers Sentence.[10]

[1] Lady Beaconsfield d. 15 December 1872. Partly printed in Morley, ii. 546; original not in Hughenden MSS. Disraeli replied on 24 January 1873, Add MS 44437, f. 65: '... I trust, I earnestly trust, that you may be spared a similar affliction. Marriage is the greatest earthly happiness when founded on complete sympathy....'

[2] J. H. *Newman, *The office and work of the universities* (1856).

[3] Not found. [4] Ibid. [5] H. Cotterill.

[6] J. N. Huber, *Der Alte und der Neue Glaube. Ein Bekenntniss von D. F. Strauss* (1873).

[7] E. Howley, *Competitive endowment and Trinity College Dublin* (1872).

[8] J. B. *Walsh, Lord Ormathwaite, *Lessons of the French Revolution 1789-1872* (1873).

[9] Add MS 44641, f. 2.

[10] London gas stokers struck on 2 December; several were tried and imprisoned for a year; the cabinet agreed to recommend reduction of sentences to four months (CAB 41/5/1); this was done. See 15 Jan. 73.

○ Army Estimates.
○ Navy Estimates
✓ Ld Mayor's dinner. 26 Mch.
✓ Ld Granville. Central Asia. Narrative of proceedings & draft amended & approved.[1]
✓ Ld Granville. French Treaty—agreed to insist that uniform duties shall only be leviable when *all* raw materials are taxed.

To G. G. GLYN, chief whip, 22 January 1873. Add MS 44542, f. 75.
'Secret.'

I think it would be very well if you could be here over business hours tomorrow unless it is very inconvenient to you.[2] As far as I have gathered from Cardwell, the case of the Estimates would stand thus.

His reduction including £80,000 autumn manoeuvres	£413 000
Navy increase not to exceed	£300 000
	113 000
If these A[utumn] M[anoeuvres] continue	80 000
	33 000

This you will see is much too fine. Estimates to be settled on Friday.

23. Th.

Wrote to Ld Hartington—Ld Granard—Dr Hayman—D. of Newcastle—C.G.—Bp of Edinburgh—& minutes. Luncheon at 15 G.S. Worked on books. Saw Mr Glyn. Conversation with Harry: we dined at home together. Read Q.R. on Froude—Do on Princess Charlotte[3]—V. Fitzgerald on India &c.[4]

24. Fr.

Wrote to The Queen—Mr Billson Tel.—W.H.G.—Mr Robn G. Tel.—C.G.—Mr Glyn Tel.—and minutes. Saw Hon. F. Lawley—Ld F. Cavendish—Mr Glyn—Mr Childers—Mr Cardwell. Educn Depn 2–2¾.[5] Cabinet 2¾–6½. Dined with the Lytteltons. Saw Mrs Th. X in evg. Saw A. Hamilton.

[1] See Hertslet's mem. on Russian encroachments, 21 Jan. 1873, F.O.C.P. 2150.
[2] Glyn was acting as negotiator over the estimates; Add MS 44348, f. 217.
[3] *Quarterly Review*, cxxxiv. 169, 1 (January 1873).
[4] W. F. V. Fitzgerald, *Egypt, India and the Colonies* (1870).
[5] From the National Education Union on the 25th clause; *The Times*, 25 Jan. 1873, 9c, 10e.

Cabinet. D. St. Ja. 24. 2½ pm.[1]

√ 1. What Bills? See list herewith.[2] Irish Univ. Bill—Education Bill—Railway Bill—Public Proclamation Bill—Jury Bill—Amalgamation of Municipal & Parl. Roll—Drainage Acts Ireland & other Irish Bills—Amend end[owed] Schools Acts—Colonial copyright Bill. Lords, Ld Chancellor: Land Transfers—Judicature.

O 2. Education. Partially explained: but cabinet found to be of only ten.[3]

√ 3. French Treaty. Discussed at much length. Determined to press the case of silk against levy of duty on our raw materials.[4] proposed but not to break on it: to demand absolutely the applications of the Tax to all but Treaty Powers.

√ 4. Queen's wish that the Ministers shd. go down to Chiselhurst mentioned by Ld Granville.[5]

√ Bruce asked whether we shd. proceed against the remaining summoned persons in the Park business. No further proceedings to be taken.

25. Sat. St Paul.

Wrote to Dr Ingram—C.G.[6]—Mr Thring—and minutes. Saw Ld F. Cavendish—Mr Forster—Mr Palgrave—Mr Carlo Gaskell—Mr Thring 3-5½ on Irish Bill. Attended Ld Lytton's funeral in the Abbey. The Church lighted in a frost fog was sublime.[7] Read V. Fitzgerald, Suez Canal—Grant on Domestic Question[9]—Hoyle on National Resources[10]—Dawburn on Conduct[11]—Hayman's Odyssey Part II.[12] Dined with Ld Ripon to draw the List of Sheriffs. Much conversation with Lowe & Goschen (who are very sound) as well as others on Local Taxation.

26. 3 S Epiph.

Quebec Chapel mg with H. where Mr Holland preached a very weighty Sermon: and Chapel Royal aft. Wrote to the Ld Chancellor—The Queen—Mr Glyn—Miss Marsh—Sir T. Biddulph—& minutes. H. & I dined with the Farquhars. Read Row on Inspiration[13]—Huber on

[1] Add MS 44641, f. 3. Note asking Goschen if he is ready with his estimates, with Goschen's reply, '. . . not quite ready . . .', at ibid., f. 7.

[2] Following bills listed in column, ibid., f. 6. Selborne's mem. printed on 23 January 1873, on the Judicature Bill, at Add MS 44620, f. 33.

[3] Forster noted: 'I just began to open my case, when it turned out that the Cabinet had dwindled'; Reid, *F*, i. 548. See 27 Jan. 73.

[4] F.O.C.P. 2346.

[5] Where Napoleon III d. 9 January; the Prince of Wales had been dissuaded from attending the funeral; see Ramm I, ii. 375.

[6] See Bassett, 196.

[7] See Morley ii. 437 and Add MS 44437, f. 67.

[8] See 26 Oct. 70.

[9] Perhaps B. Grant, 'Mr Gladstone's Missing Link. Lecture' (1868?).

[10] See 13 Oct. 71.

[11] W. Dawburn, *Government, conduct and example* (1867).

[12] H. *Hayman, *The Odyssey of Homer* (ed. 1866).

[13] C. A. Row, *The nature and extent of divine inspiration* (1864).

Strauss—Canon Seymour on Reservation[1]—Voysey agt Atheism[2]—Bastard on Scepticism.[3]

To LORD SELBORNE, lord chancellor, Add MS 44542, f. 76.
26 January 1873.

I have no doubt you have looked carefully into the subject of your note just received,[4] but the question is one which the Queen will justly view with some jealousy, & it is new to me to have it put as a general proposition that judges retiring after a full term of eminent service (unless eminent means special which I do not gather) are usually made Privy Councillors. Perhaps you have collected the facts, & I should like to see a list of the Judges who (not being Privy Councillors) have retired during the last 20 years, and have been made Privy Councillors on retirement. Willis was made P.C. on a special pledge to attend the judicial committee, combined with what was thought a considerable need at the time. I do not doubt your facts, only I do not know them.

27. M.

Worked on books. Wrote to Ld Chancellor (2)—Mod.Gen. Assembly (Ireland)[5]—Chancr of Exr—S.E.G.—The Queen—C.G.—and minutes. Saw Ld Granville—D. of Argyll—Ld F. Cavendish—Mr Acton Adams [*sic*].[6] Cabinet 2½-6½. Evg at home with Harry. Read Nine Fortunes[7]—and other works. Saw Mr Ouvry. He and I had an interview singular enough with the Duke of Newcastle and Mr Arrowsmith.[8]

Cabinet Jan. 27. 2½ p.m.[9]

√ WEG (Ld Granville not having entered) reported the communications from Paris.[10]

√ Forster proposed the schism of his Education Bill. See papers.[11]

√ Fortescue—proposed to stop an *overloaded* German Emigrant ship—at the request of the German Govt. Resolved to decline: but to get legal information for the possible case of the vessel's returning within our jurisdiction.

√ Ld Granville asked how to caution Mr Wade agt. any strong manner without further authority in regard to the Audience question in China.[12]

[1] Untraced tract by M. H. Seymour. [2] See 19 Jan. 73.

[3] T. H. Bastard, *Scepticism and social justice* (1872).

[4] That it is 'usual of late years' for retiring judges to become privy councillors, 25 January 1873, Add MS 44296, f. 231; consequent lists at ibid., f. 233.

[5] William Johnston, had sent its resolutions on Irish universities; Gladstone requested details on Magee college; Add MSS 44437, ff. 71, 103, 44542, f. 77, 44437, f. 71.

[6] i.e. J. Adams-*Acton, the sculptor; see 7 Nov. 64. [7] See 31 Dec. 72.

[8] Meeting with 6th duke of Newcastle on his son's progress; see Add MS 44542, f. 76.

[9] Add MS 44641, f. 8.

[10] Possibly the report on the Assembly in PRO FO 27/1978.

[11] See following memorandum.

[12] France pressed for better audience on the Emperor's majority; F.O.C.P. 2157–8.

Jan. 27. 73. Education Bill.[1]
WEG's preferences: 1. meet the objections to the 25th Clause by requiring $\frac{1}{6}$ to be privately borne. 2. Take indirect compulsion as the next step: or compulsion below a *low* age. 3. The standard of 'sufficiency' not to be pushed so high.

Cabinet agreed to: 1. Compulsion[2] a. direct up to 10. b. indirect above: or elastic dissession[?]. 2. the one sixth plan. A suggestion of Mr Stansfeld's herewith to be am[ende]d by Mr Forster. Negatived.[3]

Clause 25 to be altered by throwing the charge upon the Poor Law & make it relief.

Clause 17—Power of remitting to be repealed.

To LORD SELBORNE, lord chancellor, Lambeth MS 1865, f. 198.
27 January 1873. 'Immediate.'

It may be convenient if I state to you beforehand the points which occur to me upon your able and interesting paper respecting our Higher Courts:[4] apart from the question of the judicial power of the House of Lords, with respect to which I will only say that I do not suppose that the Irish & Scotch Appeals would long survive the withdrawal of English appeals from the tribunal. 1. As the suitor will have a large choice in determining his Court, I presume you intend to make Judges, or some Judges, transferable from time to time so as to prevent a glut of business in one Division with possibly empty benches in another. 2. I am afraid I shall shock you when I give it as my individual opinion that the present Salaries of Puisne Judges and their rates of pension are extravagantly high: and indeed that the present rates of pension are too high altogether. As to the Puisne Judges, the sum of £5000 with a pension of £3500 must be taken as equivalent to a larger sum without pension—perhaps £6000 though no figure can be stated with precision. This appears to me not only a needless but almost an absurd rate of remuneration for our Puisne Judges, whether it be estimated by the stamp and quality of man commonly obtained; or by the relation between their precarious receipts at the Bar and the certainty which is offered by the Bench; or by comparing them with the gentlemen whose services we obtain in the Government Departments as Solicitors e.g. to the Treasury and Board of Inland Revenue for half the money or even less. On the first head I would say that to an external and a Parliamentary eye they are *generally* second rate men: on the second, that a smaller certainty is commonly held the equivalent of a larger uncertainty, but that in this case, unless the Puisne Judges are much wronged they *commonly* obtain a larger income as Judges than they got as Barristers. One case, probably a stronger one than usual, I knew, where the Judge's practice at its best never brought him over £1500 per annum. And on the third point can it be said that, either in weight of duties, or weight of capacity to perform them, Puisne Judges are for the most part superior to such persons as Mr Gray, Mr Greenwood, Mr Melvill, Mr Firman, or Mr Trevor. I will not quote the Solicitor to the Customs because that was an appointment which though made by Sir R. Peel no one ever could understand.

I do not know the views of the Cabinet and my own would certainly not be

[1] Add MS 44641, f. 11. Forster's mem. of 22 January 1873 on Section 25, is at Add MS 44620, f. 29.

[2] 'Chancr. Cardwell. Goschen. WEG'. linked to this word by a bracket.

[3] This word written obliquely over point 2.

[4] Printed for cabinet, Add MS 44620, f. 33.

pushed to an extreme: indeed I admit that if the Salaries of the Ordinary Judges of the Court are to be nought[?] there should be an intermediate Salary for one Judge (query as Vice President?) in each division, between the Puisne Judges and the Chiefs.

From Pensions I should be inclined to dock a certain sum all round in respect of future holders.

And it seems to me well worthy of consideration, after some recent cases, whether there should not be a right, exercisable in case of need, to *require* the retirement of Judges incapacitated by infirmity, or by age beyond a certain limit. The Lord Chancellor as a person responsible to Parliament might be intrusted with the initiative, and the conclusive report on the case when referred by him might perhaps be made by three of the four chiefs acting together. As this letter touches Lowe's province I will send him a copy of it before the Cabinet today when I hope your very important proposal may be put forward.

28. Tu.

Worked a good deal on books. Wrote to Ld Chancellor—Chancr of Exr—Robn G.—Sir R. Phillimore—and minutes. Saw Mr Ramsay—Mr F. Lawley—Ld F. Cavendish—Wesleyan Deputn on Education Act—Mr Thring cum Ld Hartington on Irish Univ. Bill 3-5½. Saw Mrs Th. Dined at Ld Granville's: conversation on Eccl. Judgments &c. Conclave on the German Emigrant ship. Read Ouranogaia[1]—and other works.

To LORD SELBORNE, lord chancellor, 28 January 1873. Lambeth MS 1865, f. 204.

I am sorry to say my conviction as to the over pay of the Puisne Judges is too clear, and my opinion that this is the precise time for the consideration of the question too strong, to allow me to be silent on it. I know no clearer case.

If any other class of public officers can be pointed out, where the relation of emolument to the need for it is the same, I shall be at least equally desirous to hear of it. The legal class is far too powerful to encourage any man, or any Ministers, to say a word wantonly against it.

From the Judges, in my opinion, a strict review ought to be carried downwards through the whole of our judicial and legal expenditure; the only branch of administration as far as I know which admits of & calls for *such* a review.

On the economical question whether there has been a sensible fall in the value of money, my opinion is opposed to yours. I admit no such fall: and if it had been recognised, our united proceeding the other day in reply to the Civil Servants was hardly a fair one.

You speak however all along of Judges: I spoke of Puisne Judges. As far as I can see, there is only rare cause to make a like observation among the Equity Judges, or in the class of Chiefs.

That you are in a majority in doors out of doors & in every sphere I think highly probable. Economy, or what I call economy, has been out of fashion for

[1] K. H. Digby, *Ouranogaia: heaven on earth* (1872).

the last 20 years of my political life, as it was in fashion for the first 20. But that you may see my own views not to be absolutely revolutionary, I send herewith a rough sketch I put down yesterday.[1]

You will perhaps bear in mind that with regard to these subjects it happened to be my duty individually to sound the keynote in 1868, and I am the person on whose shoulders will chiefly rest the blame of unfulfilled expectations.

29. Wed.

Wrote to Ld Chancellor (2)—Count Dusmani—Mr Bruce—The Queen l. and Mem.—and minutes. Finished work on books. Saw M. Van de Weyer—Mr Ouvry—Mr Westell—Mr Cardwell—Ld F. Cavendish—Ld Chanr. Cabinet dinner at home. Cabinet 2½–7¼. Also Conclave in evg on Alabama question. Read Life of Sieur.[2]

Cabinet. Jan. 29. 1873. 2½ P.M.[3]

(Prelim. conversation on drafting Bills & errors in them)

√ German Emigrant Ship. a[nswer] to Count Bernstorff framed and Tel. to Ports to be informed if Ship puts in.

Chancellor's Bill. Adopted as to New Courts of Justice & Appeal—as to no. of Lords—as to Salaries. Pensions to be reduced to one half all round with a max. of £4000: but retired Ld. C[hancellor] shall have £5000 if & while a member of the Court of Appeal.[4] (All seemed to be against moving respecting Salaries except WEG, Lowe, Childers & Stansfeld)[5]

√ Transfer of Land Bill. Agreed that Ld. C. should introduce.

√ Officers' *petition* respecting damage to pecuniary interests. Opinion of L[aw] O[fficers] read. Cabinet cannot interfere to forbid but H.R.H. [the duke of Cambridge] to express formally the disapproval wh. he feels.[6]

√ Cardwell submitted Army Estimates. Men reduced 8-9000 of the 20,000 of 1870 to remain. Reduction on gross sum £400 000. To the bad by prices £285,000.

Goschen Navy Estimates. Reduces men 1000. Increase Estimate 340,000£. To the bad by prices 250m[ille]. Increase of wages in the Dockyard 4/6 to 5/- shipwrights.

30. Th.

Wrote to Mr Bruce—Spanish Minister[7]—Sir H. Elliot—Helen G.—and minutes. Twelve to dinner. Mrs Goschen's Ball. Saw Ld F.

[1] Jottings of proposed salaries, ordinary judges £4000, and '£1000 off the Pensions all round', attached.

[2] Incomplete title; untraced.

[3] Add MS 44641, f. 12.

[4] Notes passed in cabinet on this, in ibid., f. 15; new scale, in diarist's hand dated 27 Jan. 1873 at Lambeth MS 1865, f. 207.

[5] Selborne's Supreme Court of Judicature Bill, reforming the English court structure; part I, clause 12, dealt with pensions, apparently the only aspect of the complex bill discussed in detail in cabinet.

[6] See Cambridge's speech on 10 March; *H* ccxlv. 1606.

[7] See 12 Dec. 72.

Cavendish—Mr Lyttelton—Mr Gurdon—Atty General—Rev. S.E.G.—Mr Godley (Hom)—Dr Birch—Sir P. Braila—Sig. Moret—Count Cadorna—Sir E. May. Saw Charrington [R]. Read Elisée Reclus[1]—Sir J. Napier on Univ. Dublin[2]—Robert Bruce & John Knox.[3]

31. Fr.

Wrote to Sir A. Cockburn—Miss [*sic*] Kortright—D. of Argyll—Chr of Exr—Ld Kimberley—Ld Huntley—The Queen (2)—and minutes. Worked on Queen's Speech. Saw Ld F. Cavendish—Rev Mr M'Coll—Ld Lyttelton—Ld Granville—Mr Cardwell. Dined with the Jameses. Cabinet 2¾–7½. Read Dubl.Univ. Report—Contemp. Review.

Cabinet. Jan. 31. 73. 2½ P.M.[4]
√ What Bills for the [Queen's] Speech? also Canada.
√ Irish Univ. Bill. Provisions much discussed & generally settled down to Cl. 21.
√ Telegram to Ld. A. L[oftus] respecting the Khiva Expn. agreed on.[5]

To R. LOWE, chancellor of the exchequer, 31 January 1873. Add MS 44542, f. 79.

1. Have you taken any step with a view to verifying or correcting the results of the inquiry of (I think) 1861 or 2, with respect to the natural strengths of wine, on which the present scale of duties was founded? 2. Have you made or proposed any arrangements for paying to the American Government the sum awarded at Geneva?[6] 3. I am told there is a question about a vote of Parliament for the Shah of Persia i.e. for entertaining him. This is a very awkward subject. Pray look back to Hansard on the vote for the Sultan—I believe I objected to it; Ayrton if I remember right made a most able speech.

Sat. Feb. One. 1873.

Wrote to Ld Chancellor—Mr Thring—Dr Ingram—Mr W. Fraser—The Queen—and minutes. Dined at Ld Essex's. Saw Abp Manning—Mr F. Lawley—Ld F. Cavendish—Rev. S.E.G.—Sir H. Rawlin-

[1] E. Reclus, *The ocean, atmosphere and life*, 2v. (1873).
[2] Sir J. *Napier, *The college and the university* (1871).
[3] *Robert Bruce and John Knox. By a parish minister* (1873).
[4] Add MS 44641, f. 18; written at top left corner: 'Hessel, Knowles. See Delane?'
[5] Protesting against scale of Russian punitive expedition to Khiva: PRO FO 65/849, F.O.C.P. 2150.
[6] Lowe replied, 1 February 1873, Add MS 44302, f. 92: 'we shall find it better to execute the Treaty literally and call for tenders for doing the business'. See 19 Dec. 72.

son. Read Dr Todd on Univ. Dublin Commrs Report[1]—Buckle[2]—Contemp. Review.

2. Purif. 3 S.Epiph.

Chapel Royal mg (with H.C.) & aft. Wrote to Sir F. Doyle—Chancr of Exr—and minutes. Saw Mr Glyn (Dr Hessel)[3]—Ld F. Cavendish—The Farquhars. Paid a mournful visit to the deathbed of my old friend Milnes Gaskell. He was very affectionate: quite clear: near his end.[4] May the Almighty be with him. Saw Sir R. Phillimore.[5] Death has been very busy around me. Read Pusey's Sermons[6]—Row on Inspiration—Sydow's Actenstücke.[7]

3. M.

Wrote to Abp Manning—Ld Hartington—Watsons—Chr of Exr—Ld Chancr—and minutes. Dined at Sir H. Holland's. Saw Ld F. Cavendish—Ld Granville—Mr Glyn—Dowager Duchess of Somerset. Shopping. Finished Todd's Introduction. Read Life of Manin.[8] Finished draft of Q. Speech: & saw Ld Granville on it.

To LORD HARTINGTON, Irish secretary, 3 February 1873. Add MS 44542, f. 80.

Thanks for your inclosures. We might I should think take the Irish teachers on Saturday when there will be a few points respecting the University Bill to mention. Railways perhaps a little later. I think you have reduced the question of Royal Residence to as good & hopeful a form as it is capable of assuming. Please to consider whether there is any Irish Bill *necessary* to be mentioned in the Speech besides the University Bill. I say necessary because if we have too much Irish flavour Scotland will be jealous.[9]

4. Tu.

Wrote to Ld Bessborough—Sir S. Northcote—The Queen—and minutes. Cabinet 2¾–7. Dined at Ld Abercromby's. Saw Ld F. Cavendish—C. Lyttelton *cum* Mr [W. H.] Stone[10]—Mr Glyn—Ld

[1] See 21 Dec. 44.

[2] H. T. *Buckle, 'Common Place Books', *Miscellaneous and posthumous works* (1872) ii.

[3] Unidentified.

[4] He d. 5 February.

[5] See Morley, ii. 437.

[6] E. B. *Pusey, 'The responsibility of intellect in matters of faith' (1873) and *Sermons preached before the University of Oxford, 1859–1872* (1872).

[7] C. L. A. Sydow, *Aktenstücke betreffend das vom Königlichen Consistorium der Provinz Brandenburg* (1873).

[8] See 9 Dec. 62.

[9] No reply traced.

[10] Coaching for the address; see 6 Feb. 73.

Chancellor—W.H.G. respecting Herbert. Read Dr Potters Pamphlet[1] —Dubl. Comm Report (finished).

Cabinet. Tues. F. 4. 73. 2½ P.M.[2]

√ Queen's Speech—considered & agreed to.
√ Motion respecting days of supply. Mr Lowe to give notice.[3]
O Notice respecting Educn. Bill: withold?[4]
⟨Public Health?⟩
O Irish R.R.
√ Ayrton's Rules. Discussed & settled. See over.[5]
√ Wages in docklands. Shipwright's at 4/6: First L[ord] recommends to be raised to 5/-. Goschen will examine further.

5. Wed.

Wrote to The Queen Mem.—Ld F. Cavendish (Tel)—Mrs Th.—Ld Granville—Mr Gaskell[6]—and minutes. Off at 8.45 to Osborne. Audience of the Queen. Council. Conversation with Childers: with Sir [G.] Burrows: with Sir [blank]. Archbold: with Major . . . : and the Burmese.[7] Back at 6. Read Ld Tenterden's Mem.[8] Official dinner: followed by evening party. Saw Ld Chancr of Ireland—Mr Lyttelton —The Speaker.

6. Th.

Wrote to Ld Tenterden—J. Watson & Smith—The Queen—& minutes. Visited Christie's. Read Memoir of Manin. Saw Ld Granville —Ld F. Cavendish—Mr Glyn—Mr Thring. Worked on bills. H of C. 4¼–11½. Spoke upon the Address. Charles performed his part admirably.[9]

7. Fr.

Wrote to Sol.Gen. for Ireland—Chancr of Exr—Ld Granville—Dean Wellesley—Mr Ryan—The Queen—& minutes. Read Green on

[1] S. G. Potter, 'Of what religion is Mr. Gladstone? Important revelations of a conspiracy to unprotestantize the English Church and Nation' (1873).

[2] Add MS 44641, f. 25.

[3] Implementing the select cttee.'s recommendations; *H* ccxiv. 244.

[4] The bill was mentioned in the Queen's speech, but never introduced.

[5] Notes 'to support Ayrton agt. the charge of breach of faith' at Add MS 44641, f. 26.

[6] Charles George Milnes-Gaskell, 1842–1919; liberal M.P. Morley 1885–92; on his fa.'s d.; Add MS 44542, f. 81.

[7] Burmese mission visiting the Queen; *The Times*, 6 Feb. 1873, 9f. Justice Thomas Dickson Archibald in attendance.

[8] On arbitrations under the treaty of Washington, printed for the cabinet 4 February 1873, Add MS 44620, f. 48.

[9] C. Lyttelton, moved, W. H. Stone seconded, the motion for an address: *H* ccxiv. 57.

Central Asia[1]—Westm.Rev. on the Ministry[2]—The Important Case Statement & Opinion on Trin Coll. Dubl.[3] Saw Ld Granville—Ld F. Cavendish—Mr Glyn—Col. Neville—Mr Burnett. H of C. 4½-8.[4] Dined at Ld Lyttelton's. Saw Wallace X.

8. Sat.

Wrote to The Queen (2)—Mr Thring—Mr Whale[5]—Robn G.—and minutes. Cabinet 2½-6½. *Passed* the Irish Univ. Bill. Scotch Edn Comm. 2 PM. Saw Ld F. Cavendish—Dean of Windsor—Mr Thring *cum* Irish Sol. General—Mr Glyn (2). Ten to dinner. Read Dr Lyon on Irish Univ.[6]

Cabinet. Feb. 8. 73. 2½ P.M.[7]

√ Irish University. Remaining[?][8] points of Bill submitted by WEG—and settled.
Send to Mr Thring.
√ Navy Estimates. Wages in dockyards—Mr Goschen adhered—much argument.
Agreed to.[9]
√ Business of the week. Considered & agreed on.
√ Purchase of Irish Railways—not to be undertaken—door to be left open to proposals from parties for amalgamation &c.[10]
√ Ld Granville. Turkey asks for a combined guarantee of railway to Turkish frontier—declined.
√ Park Rules read & approved.

To Robertson GLADSTONE, 8 February 1873. Add MS 44542, f. 82.

In your letter[11] you take a very rational view I think of the state of things in Liverpool before the fact. The result announced in to-day's papers causes me more dissatisfaction than surprise. The Liberal Licensed Victuallers supporting actively the Tory candidate have I suppose aggravated the majority against us. But there is no cause for crowing. The Session has opened favourably. No real

[1] Perhaps S. Green, *The life of Mahomet . . . and of the empire of the Saracens* (1840).
[2] *Westminster Review*, xliii. 208 (January 1873).
[3] Probably G. Johnstone Stoney, 'Four memoranda on university reform in Ireland' (privately published, 1872); copy in Add MS 44519, f. 22.
[4] Questions: *H* ccxiv. 151.
[5] Regretting he must decline George Whale's invitation to address the Liberal Electoral Association; Add MS 44542, f. 82.
[6] L. *Playfair, *On teaching universities and examining bodies* (1873).
[7] Add MS 44641, f. 27.
[8] Word smudged. Jottings on the bill at ibid., f. 30.
[9] 'The Cabinet reluctantly agreed to an augmentation of wages in the Dockyards, which involves an alteration of a life-contract between the State and its servants'; CAB 41/5/1.
[10] Cabinet paper of 6 February 1873 (Add MS 44620, f. 55) by Hartington recommended government purchase.
[11] On the Liverpool by-election; the tories increased their majority.

damage I think has been done to the Three Rules employed in the Arbitration; & even as to Irish University Education I am not without hope of obtaining fair play, which I trust is all we want.

9. Septa S.

Chapel Royal mg. and aftn. Wrote to Ld Hartington—Rev Dr Russell—Mr Delane—and minutes. Saw Bp of Winchester—Ld R. Cavendish—Mr Glyn—Mr MacColl. Read Row on Inspiration—Via Catholica[1]—Dr Lyon on Univ. Education.

10. M.

Wrote to Ld Hartington—Mr Burnett—Mr Thorn—Lady Ossington—The Queen—Lady Aberdeen—and minutes. Saw Mr Prescott Hewett—Ld F. Cavendish—Mr Glyn—D. of Argyll—Mr Childers—Ld Granville—Rev. Mr West—Mr Delane.[2] H of C. 4½-8 and 8¾-11¾.[3] Read Manin—Lyon Playfair[4]—Finished Lyon.

To LORD HARTINGTON, Irish secretary, 10 February 1873. 'Secret.' Chatsworth MSS 340.524.

I have read your letter[5] with extreme concern, for I had no conception that the subject of Irish Railways involved you in anything like personal embarrassment. Indeed my belief was that you & I were both implicated to about the same extent by favourable expressions not fairly yet plausibly to be construed as pledges, though mine happened to be of the older date & therefore less in view. I presume we shall act as we did last year about the introduction of Sir R. Blennerhassett's Bill, & if so this will give us time to consider how the difficulty is to be met. I am writing under the impression that last year we allowed the Bill to come in. If there is to be debate on the question he had better be blocked out on Thursday.[6]

11. Tu.

Wrote to Dr Ingram—Sir R. Phillimore—Mr Thring—Dr Hayman—The Queen—Mrs Th.—& minutes. Conclave on Irish Univ. Bill 11-3. Saw Mr Burnett—Mr Glyn—Sir T.E. May—Ld Granville—

[1] *Via Catholica; or, passages from the autobiography of a country parson* (1873), ii.

[2] Interview arranged the previous day; Add MS 44542, f. 82.

[3] Govt. resolution to expedite business: *H* ccxiv. 244.

[4] See 8 Feb. 73n.

[5] Of 10 February, Add MS 44144, f. 35, asking that Irish railways be made an open question, otherwise his resignation possible, as he supported state purchase.

[6] Gladstone had personally, though reluctantly, allowed introduction of Blennerhassett's bill on Irish railways in 1872 (*H* ccix. 1485); there was no discussion of the measure on 13 February 1873. See 15 Feb. 73.

Sir R. Phillimore—Ld F. Cavendish—Mrs Th. H of C. 4½-6¾.[1] Read Seyd on Currency[2]—Strauss's Nachwort[3]—Barr's Poems.[4] Dined at Sir R. Phillimore's.

12. Wed.

Wrote to Mr Fortescue—Dr Ingram—Mr Thring—and minutes. Worked much & late on facts & figures of Irish case. Saw Dean of Winchester—Ld F. Cavendish—Mr Glyn—Ld Granville—Dr A. Clark—Mrs Graham—Mr Trevelyan. Dined with the Phillimores. Read Fraser on Cambus-Kenneth Abbey.[5] Saw Mrs Monk[R?].

13. Th.

Wrote to Mrs Agar[6]—and minutes. Worked until 3 upon my materials. Then drove & walked. H of C. 4¼-8½. Spoke 3 hours on introducing the Irish University Bill with much detailed explanation.[7] Dined with the Jameses. Read Buckle's Commonplace Book Vol. II. Saw one hopeful case.

14. Fr.

Wrote to Mad. Novikoff[8]—Mr Knollys (2)—Mr Gourley—Rev Mr Wilson—Ld Acton—The Queen (2)—and minutes. Saw the Bond St & the Mason Pictures.[9] Saw Mr Glyn—Dr Ingram—do cum Mr M'Coll—Mr Gurdon—Mr Roundell—Ld Granville—Mr Cross MP —Mr Burnett. H of C. 4½-8¼. Spoke on proposal agt Treaty-making power.[10] Read Col. Kiréeff on O.C. Congress—Strauss's Nachwort.

To Olga NOVIKOFF, 14 February 1873. Add MS 44542, f. 84.

I shall read with very great interest on the earliest opportunity the tract you have been kind enough to send me,[11] & I shall not scruple, if I find occasion, to avail myself of your kind permission again to trespass upon you with respect to it.

[1] Spoke on business; *H* ccxiv. 286.

[2] E. Seyd, *Reform of the Bank of England Note Issue*, 2v. (1873).

[3] See 1 Dec. 72.

[4] See 8 June 72.

[5] Sir W. *Fraser, ed., *Registrum Monasterii S. Marie de Cambuskenneth* (1872).

[6] Perhaps Helen M. Agar, of the Thistlethwayte household; Hawn P.

[7] *H* ccxiv. 378 and Bassett, *Speeches*, 426. See Morley, ii. 437.

[8] The notorious Olga Novikoff, *née* Kiryeev, widow of General A. Novikoff of the Russian general staff; partly educated by a Scotsman; came to London 1873; politically active ('the member for Russia') from 1876; see Seton-Watson, 115.

[9] George Mason's pictures at Burlington Fine Arts Club; *Art Journal* (1873), 68.

[10] i.e. against Commons' debs. on treaties before ratification; *H* ccxiv. 469.

[11] Sent article by her br., A. A. Kiryeev, 'A Russian view of the Old Catholic Congress', *Union Review* (1873); Add MS 44268, f. 1.

15. Sat.

Wrote to Viceroy of Ireland—Abp Manning—The Queen—Dr Ingram—Ld Kildare[1]—Mr Cardwell—and minutes. Read Nachwort (finished)—Life of Montchretien.[2] Saw Mr MacColl—Ld Hartington—Mr Glyn—Sir R. Phillimore—Chr of Exr—Mr Cardwell. Cabinet 2½–6½. Dined at Lyttelton's. Saw Lewis X.

Cabinet. Feb. 15. 73. 2½ P.M. D. St.[3]

√ Harcourt's motion. To be met by motion for a Committee on Civil Expenditure of which Mr Childers will be [blank][4]
O American Indemnity.
√ Shah of Persia. Vote? Discussed *provisionally*—Lowe to circulate Civil List. Improve.[5]
√ Irish Railways. ?ask Sir R. Blennerhassett to ballot.[6] Circulate Spencer's letter.
√ Week's business cons[idere]d. To vote for Macmahon[7]—Horses Committee.[8] Agree.
√ Ld Buckhurst's Bill in the Lords—to Committee.[9]
√ WEG stated some changes in the text of the I.U. Bill.
Seistan Arbitration. Shall we press[?] our award.[10]
√ Fishery Magistrates in Newfoundland: shall we appoint? Communicate first with France but represent the case & the appt. of magistrates as urgent.[11]
√ Spanish Republic—recognise as soon as regularly accepted.[12]
√ Possible Spanish attempt on Portugal. Lord G. understands—Layard will watch: rather eschew joint action of a forward kind with France.[13]
√ Supply of horses. 'No Comm[ission]—Comm[itt]ee of Lords if they like.'
√ Decline Sir W. Alexander's suggestion to accept an offer to bring Cleopatra's needle here for £15,000.[14]

[1] Charles William Fitzgerald, 1819–87; Baron Kildare 1870; 4th duke of Leinster 1874; Gladstone regretted the university plan 'struck a blow at your office as the Chanc[ellor] of the Q[ueen's] Univ.'; Add MS 44542, f. 85.

[2] A. Joly, *A. de Montchrétien, poète* (1865).

[3] Add MS 44641, f. 37.

[4] Harcourt's motion on excessive expenditure, successfully met by cttee.: *H* ccxiv. 665; Childers chaired 14; *PP* 1873 vii. 387.

[5] Shah Nasr-ul-Deen was planning his European tour, see June 73. £15,000 was found from 'reserve funds'; see note by Gurdon, Add MS 44641, f. 59.

[6] Blennerhassett either did not ballot, or was unsuccessful.

[7] Macmahon's Union Rating (Ireland Bill). 2° R with govt. help; *H* cciv. 771.

[8] Rosebery's motion for royal commission on supply of horses, replaced by select cttee. of Lords; *H* ccxiv. 721, 782.

[9] Railway Accident Bill; *H* ccxiv. 582.

[10] 'The Government think they ought to make an award and urge its acceptance [on Persia and Afghanistan]'; CAB 41/5/9; see 1 Mar. 73.

[11] France opposed appt. of magistrates; Law Officers supported C.O.'s position: PRO CO 194/188.

[12] Amadeo I abdicated 11 February 1873, thus inaugurating the first republic; on 12 February Britain gave him naval help, subsequently delaying recognition; see *H* ccix. 730, 1185; F.O.C.P. 2175.

[13] The Spanish court fled to Lisbon. France informed of H.M.G.'s opposition to her plan for 'a United Peninsula': PRO FO 27/1974.

[14] Sir William John Alexander, 1797–March 1873; attorney general to Prince of Wales. The Needle was erected on the Embankment 1878 by private gift.

√ The Chancellor mentioned a letter he had received respecting a magistrate of Birmingham (Mr Althay) who says he will sign a warrant agt. himself but will not pay a rate under clause 25 [of the 1870 Education Act]. Cabinet thought it could not be overlooked.[1]

√ Committee of Cabinet appointed to consider Exemptions Bill, & so forth.[2]

To EARL SPENCER, Irish lord lieutenant, 15 February 1873. Add MS 44542, f. 85.

1. I send you herewith copy of a letter I have addressed to Dr. Ingram, who will now I presume return to Dublin. 2. I am extremely obliged by your letter[3] about the reception of the Irish University plan, on which I remember that from the first you cast a favourable eye. Manning is perfectly satisfied & as he is personally loyal will I have no doubt do what he can. I suppose that now there can be no objection to your holding conversations either through the Lord Chancellor or Attorney General or otherwise with the R.C. authorities as well as other persons. The measure may look rather bald on the R.C. side but if they take to it kindly they may extract immense advantage from it for educational rather than denominational purposes. 3. I have just opened your letter on Irish Railways & I will read it with care before the Cabinet meets today; I am also to see Hartington at two.

16. Sexa S.

Chapel Royal mg and aft. Saw Ld Granville—Mr Glyn—The T.G.s—Mr West—Count Bernstorff. Wrote to Ld Granville—Abp Manning. Read Row on Inspiration[4]—Via Catholica—Wharton's Life of Bedell[5]—Huber on Strauss[6]—Report to Cardinal Prefect.[7]

To ARCHBISHOP H. E. MANNING, 16 February 1873. Add MS 44250, f. 93.

I shall read the whole tract carefully.[8] I do not know whether I am to return it: if so, please to tell me. I am ill up in these deep questions about the Final School in Oxford, seeming to myself to see but little more than this that German Philosophy[9] has added but little to the stock of our knowledge of the mind & nature of men, if indeed it has added anything. As to the University question in Ireland, I thank you for what you have said & done, & if any suggestion occurs to you I shall hope to hear of it. I am reading a really remarkable book called

[1] Gladstone told Victoria 'certain gentlemen, being magistrates' refused rates under Clause 25, CAB 41/5/9; no action discovered against Henry Wells Allfrey, J.P. in Warwick.

[2] Local taxation exemptions; Kimberley, Halifax, Stansfeld, Goschen, Childers, Bruce; Add MS 44641, f. 39.

[3] Of 14 February 1873, Add MS 44307, f. 157.

[4] See 26 Jan. 73.

[5] T. Wharton Jones, *A true relation of the life and death of . . . William Bedell* (1872).

[6] See 21 Jan. 73. Sent by R. *Morier, Add MS 44437, f. 86.

[7] Untraced.

[8] On 'Mental Philosophy'; author and title untraced; sent on 15 February, Add MS 44250, f. 83.

[9] Manning drew Gladstone's attention to the extent of Hegelianism at Oxford; ibid.

'Inspiration, its nature & extent' by a clergyman named Row. I incline to call it the most Butlerian book of the age; though it is not in every respect satisfactory to me.

17. M.

Wrote to Ld Granville—Chancr of Exr—Mr Thorn—Lady Egerton—Ld Kimberley—Mr Wharton [Jones]—Mrs Th.—Ld Hartington—Scotts—Sir W. Dunbar—The Queen and minutes. Saw Sir W. Dunbar—Mr Glyn—Chancr of Exr—Do cum Mr Rivers Wilson[1]—Mr Childers—Mr Forster—Scotts—Mr Gurdon—Sir H. Verney. H of C. 4½-7¾.[2] Dined with the Jameses. Read Hoskyns on Land[3]—Mrs Th.s MS. I. on Eastern Tour.[4]

18. Tu.

Wrote to Ld O. Fitzgerald—Lord Bowmont—Rev. Dr Smyth—Dean of ChCh—Dr Liddon—Baroness Burdett Coutts—Mr Wren Hoskyns[5]—Rev S.E.G. Tel.—The Queen—& minutes. Saw Ld F. Cavendish—Sir J. Stepney—Sir W. Dunbar—Mr Sherwood[6]—Mr Glyn—do *cum* Mr Childers—Col. Collier[7]—D. of Argyll—Chancr of Exr. Conclave on the Dunbar business.[8] H of C. 4½-8¾ and 9¾-10¾. Spoke on Harcourt's motion respecting economy.[9] Saw [blank]. Read Wren Hoskyns.

19. Wed.

Wrote to Rev. J. Rogers—The Queen (mem)—Ld Granville—Reeves & Turner[10]—Mrs Bennett—Lady E.M. Pringle[11]—Dean of Ch.Ch.—& minutes. Dined at Marlborough House. Conversation with P. of

[1] (Sir) Charles Rivers *Wilson, 1831-1916; in treasury; controlled national debt 1874-94; much involved in Egyptian fiscal reform.

[2] Questions; bills brought in; *H* ccxiv. 545.

[3] C. W. *Hoskyns, *Land in England, land in Ireland, and land in other lands* (1869).

[4] Not found.

[5] Chandos Wren-Hoskyns, 1812-76, liberal M.P. Hereford 1869-74, barrister, had sent his book, see 17 Feb. 73n.

[6] Possibly Stephen Sherwood, inland revenue messenger.

[7] Perhaps James Alphonse Collier, served in India.

[8] Sir W. Dunbar argued that some members of the audit office had been irregularly appointed; Gladstone warned Lowe: 'Dunbar is an awkward customer when he gets a vantage ground'; Add MS 44542, f. 89.

[9] Successfully suggesting select cttee. on civil service expenditure, rather than Harcourt's 'abstract resolution'; *H* ccxiv. 627; see 15 Feb. 73.

[10] Law booksellers.

[11] Asking Lady Elizabeth Pringle if she thought Breadalbane suitable for court office; Add MS 44437, f. 185.

W. on his own case. Saw Bp of Winchester—Ld F. Cavendish—Mr Glyn—Mr MacColl—Mr Knowles—Ld Hartington. Read Hoskyns (finished)—Andrew on Euphrates Line[1]—Mrs Th.s MS. Vol. II—Religion & the School Boards.[2] Went to Mr Balfour's after the dinner.

20. Th.

Wrote to Chancr of Exr—Principal of Brasenose[3]—The Queen (Mem. and l.)—Dean of Windsor—Mrs Th—Dean of Ch.Ch.—& minutes. H of C. $4\frac{1}{4}$-$7\frac{1}{2}$.[4] Saw Fitzroy X. Saw Ld F. Cavendish—Mr Glyn—Do *cum* the Law Officers—Att.Gen. respecting Mr King[5]—Ld Granville. Read [blank]. Dined at Sir J. Stepney's.

21. Fr.

Wrote to Bp of Manchester—President of Queen's Coll. Galway—The Queen—and minutes. H of C. $4\frac{1}{2}$-$7\frac{1}{2}$.[6] Saw Mrs Th. Seymour 37 Gran 38 X. Saw Ld F. Cavendish—Mr Gurdon—Mr Glyn—Ld H. Lennox—Col. Roden[7]—Mr Delahunty[8]—Mr F.L. Gower. Saw Watercolour Soc. Deputation.[9] Dined at Ld Granville's: placed by the Prince of Wales. Began correction of Speech.

22. Sat.

Wrote to Ld Chief Baron—Mr C. Foster—Prof. E. Palmer—Ld Prov. Glasgow—Ld Kimberley—Archbp of Canterbury—Rev. Mr King—The Queen (2)—Archbishop Manning—and minutes. Saw Ld F. Cavendish—Mr Glyn—Chancr of Exr—The Speaker—Mr Cardwell. Cabinet $2\frac{3}{4}$-$6\frac{1}{2}$. Correcting proofs: slowly: such is my aversion. Read Tale of Carisbrook.[10]

[1] W. P. Andrew, 'The Euphrates Valley route to India. A paper' (1873).

[2] Perhaps 'Religion as a subject of national education', *Westminster Review*, xliii (January 1873).

[3] Edward Hartopp Cradock; answering his complaints at govt. rejection of a B.N.C. scheme; Add MS 44542, f. 88.

[4] Spoke on *Plimsoll: *H* ccxiv. 742.

[5] Gladstone was arranging controversially to appt. the ritualist, Edward *King (see 21 Mar. 54), principal of Cuddesdon, as professor of pastoral theology at Oxford; he told G. V. *Wellesley this day, Add MS 44542, f. 88: 'I have no doubt that Mr King is the man in a very special sense for that particular chair.'

[6] Spoke on departmental expenditure: *H* ccxiv. 809.

[7] William Sargent Roden, 1829-1882; liberal M.P. Stoke 1868-74.

[8] James Delahunty, d. 1885; liberal M.P. Waterford 1868-74, Co. Waterford 1877-80; had, with Roden, argued on 20 Feb. for equality of Irish-English laws; *H* ccxiv. 769.

[9] No report found.

[10] Author untraced.

Cabinet. Feb. 22. 2½ P.M.[1]

√ Weeks business considered & arranged.[2]
Contract with Union Co., Cape, cons[idere]d.[3]
√ Recognition of Spanish Republic. Ld Granville stated the case of the Constituent Cortes to be convoked by the Constitution.
√ Irish Univ. Bill—amendments. matric. student College to promise—we shall go forward to meet[?] following examn. After . . . both matric. & next following examn. to be required.[4]
√ Sandwich Islands. American intentions suspected. H.M. ships to be recalled 'unless danger to British life or property is apprehended'.[5]
√ Hardy's motion. WEG drew & read propositions. Determined on the whole to await the coming on of the motion without hindrance.[6]
√ Galway Prosecutions. No more to be carried forward.

To Robertson GLADSTONE, 22 February 1873. Add MS 44542, f. 90.

. . . This coal famine is a great public calamity: how much greater than the cattle plague which made ten times as much noise. It is against the whole people, & in favour of two narrow classes, the coal owners, & those who have land with coal under it not yet rightly opened. It is bringing forward bidders at Hawarden. They have not yet touched most of my land, but may possibly get there. We have great reason to be pleased with the favourable reception in almost all quarters of the Irish University Bill. It seems likely to pass, so far as judgment can be formed thus early.

To J. S. WATSON, lord provost of Glasgow, 22 February 1873. Add MS 44542, f. 89.

I am extremely concerned to read your account[7] of the state of matters in Glasgow. The attention of Parliament is now fairly fixed on the question of the coal supply: & this is all that I can say, for I do not see my way to specific remedies by the action of the Government. A more powerful though a slow remedy is coming into action by the preparation for the opening of new collieries & coalfields. But one of the first things to desire is free working on the part of the men.

23. Quinqua S.

Chapel Royal mg—St James's evg. Wrote to Mad. Novikoff—Rev Mr King. Read Row on Inspiration—Pusey's Sermons[8]—'Scott'

[1] Add MS 44641, f. 44.

[2] Listed on separate sheet, f. 45: 'Plimsoll, Commission. Hardy, address. Weeks business. I.U. Bill—reprint—with Amts? Royal Res[idence] in Ireland'.

[3] Start of the row about the Zanzibar contract; copy of it in *PP* 1873 xxxix. 469.

[4] Words much scrawled; on 3 March Gladstone proposed addition to the bill to clarify 'in statu pupillari', and altered the clause on examinations; *H* ccxiv. 1187.

[5] Instability there during brief reign of William C. Lunalilo.

[6] On 21 March, Gathorne *Hardy moved a motion opposing the principles on which the Geneva tribunal had based its award; *H* ccxiv. 1984. Gladstone's propositions in Add MS 44641, f. 47.

[7] Not found.

[8] See 2 Feb. 73.

Tracts[1]—Speaker's Commentary.[2] Saw Count Bernstorff—Madam Novikoff—Ld Houghton.

24. M.

Wrote to Abp of Canterbury—Mad. Novikoff[3]—The Queen (2)—Mrs Thistlethwayte—Dr Liddon—Mr Burnett—Dean of Christ Church—Mr Curteis—Ld Kildare Tel . . . & minutes. Saw Ld F. Cavendish—The Att.Gen. for Ireland—Mr Glyn (2)—Mr Bright—Mr Gurdon—Dr Acland & Pres. O. Union.[4] Read Bp Cotterill's Sermon[5]—Playfair on Universities.[6] H. of C. 4½-8½. Correcting speech.

25. Tu.

Wrote to Ld Kimberley—Bp of Manchester—Rev Dr Barry—Dr Lyon Playfair—Rev E. King—Dr Ingram—Robn G.—Mr Curteis—The Queen (2). Correcting Speech. Saw Ld F. Cavendish—Chancr of Exr—Mr Glyn—Bp of Moray *cum* Bp of Edinburgh. H of C. 4½-8¼ and 9-11½.[8] Read Tale of Carisbrook.

To LORD KIMBERLEY, colonial secretary, 25 February 1873. Add MS 44542, f. 92.

The question of Fiji[9] & its annexation will I fear grow into a formidable one. It is however well not to force it forward. By the time it is ripe, we may all be more free than we are now. Should we not for the present convey or rather cause to be conveyed to Mr Thurston[10] an answer expressing the hope that in transmitting this important offer he has along with it dispatched all the information which may be necessary to serve as a basis either for consideration or for further inquiry on the subject? These are not good words but will serve for the meaning. You will doubtless communicate with Granville.[11]

[1] See 6 July 73. [2] On the Bible.

[3] '. . . I shall distribute with care the copies of the "Russian view" wh you presented to me yesterday. . . . I know how well it deserves the attention of all who are wisely interested in the religious questions of the day'; Add MS 44542, f. 92.

[4] William Macdonald Sinclair, 1850-1917, schoolmaster and divine; the Oxford Union was organising a fiftieth anniversary dinner which Gladstone did not attend.

[5] H. Cotterill, 'A funeral sermon' (1873); on E. B. *Ramsay.

[6] See 8 Feb. 73. [7] Questions; army estimates; *H* ccxiv. 834.

[8] Spoke on public business; *H* ccxiv. 912.

[9] Kimberley to Gladstone, 24 February 1873, Add MS 44225, f. 10, proposed annexation by Britain, and enclosed Robinson to Kimberley, telegram, 23 February 1873, conveying Fijian request for annexation by the Crown.

[10] (Sir) John Bates Thurston, 1836-97; British representative in Fiji, governed it in 1880s.

[11] Kimberley agreed, suggesting a cabinet discussion prior to the Commons motion; Add MS 44225, f. 15.

26. Ash Wed.

Chapel Royal noon. Wrote to Ld Kimberley (2)—Dr Lyon Playfair—Mr Ouvry—Mr Fortescue—Robn G.—Chancr of Exchr—Mr Glyn—Mr Burnett—Mr Thorn—and minutes. Finished correcting Speech. We went in the evening to the Messiah at the Albert Hall: some grand music; solos weak. *But*. Saw Ld F. Cavendish—Archbp of York—Mr Gurdon—Pr. of Wales (evg)—Mr Glyn—Sir A. Helps—Saw the Wortleys. Midnight conversation on Music—Art—Poetry—greatness. Read Tale of Carisbrook—Brentano on Guilds.[1]

To C. S. P. FORTESCUE, president of the board of trade, 26 February 1873. Carlingford MSS CP 1/179.

I have always heard Mr Bode very highly spoken of but I regret to say the chair is *full*.[2]

As to the R.C. Bishops. It is too much to expect, perhaps too much to desire, that they should wholly quit their old ground. It would suffice for the purpose in view that they should do what the Pope, I think Gregory XVI, did in the case of the Irish National Education, namely leave each Bishop free to take his own course on his own responsibility. Do you think you could write *today* to any one in Dublin who would be able to take care that at least this method of proceeding shall not be *forgotten* to-morrow? I have already spoken to our Attorney General in this sense.

To LORD KIMBERLEY, colonial secretary, 26 February 1873. Add MS 44542, f. 93.

It would be easy to begin a discussion upon the whole question of Fiji, but hard to end it; I fear it will develop great differences of opinion. Why should we go beyond the necessities of the case, i.e. considering what the Telegram requires, which cannot be much? As respects the motion, I think that the offer on its way ought to be an assistance, for the House can hardly require us to anticipate its arrival by a decision. For myself I can give no promise to be a party to any arrangement for adding Fiji & all that lies beyond it to the cares of this overdone & overburdened Government & Empire. Is there any good map of the Polynesian region?, showing what Islands are already protected by or placed in special relations to any Power?

27. Th.

Wrote to Abp Manning—Ld Breadalbane—Robn G.—Lady E.M. Pringle—The Queen—Lady Russell—& minutes. H. of C. 4½-8 and 9-12¼.[3] Attended the Queen's Court. Saw Ld F. Cavendish: (whom

[1] L. Brentano, *On the history and development of Gilds and the origin of Trade-Unions* (1870).

[2] Fortescue wrote this day recommending J. E. Bode for the Oxford chair of pastoral theology, Add MS 44123, f. 33. Irish bps. unmentioned.

[3] Questions; *H* ccxiv. 1038.

I dispatched to Abp M.)[1]—Mr Fortescue—Mr Cardwell—Ld Kimberley—Mr Glyn—Ld Granville—Chr of Exr—Ld Chancr I. *cum* Att.Gen.I.—Ld Hartington—Col. Hogg. Read Stanhope's Conv.[2]—Tale of Carisbrook finished.

28. Fr.

Wrote to Mad. de Novikoff—Abp Manning—Mr Bruce—The Queen—and minutes. H of C. 4½-8 and 9-12¼.[3] Saw Seymour X. Saw Ld F. Cavendish—Ld Bessborough—Mr Thring *cum* do—Mr Glyn—Abp Manning. Read Owen on India[4]—Qu.Univ. Report on the Colleges[5]—Dublin Review on Qu. Colleges.[6]

Sat. Mch One. 1873.

Wrote to Archbp Manning—Viceroy of I.—Mr C. Villiers—Ld Chancr of I.—Mr Monsell—Mr Tupper—The Queen—Mr Thring—Robn G.—and minutes. Cabinet 2¾-5½. Dined at Argyll Lodge: so pleasant. Saw Ld F. Cavendish—Mr Levy—Mr Glyn—Ld F.C. *cum* Mr Thring—Mr Evans (Flint impl. &c.)[7]—Saw Mrs Th. Read Macdonnell on the Queen's Colleges.[8] Mrs Glyn's in evg.

Cabinet. Mch. 1.73. 2.30.[9]

√ Plimsoll's Commission—agreed: with proper limitations of definition.[10] Norwood's motion for a Statutory Commission—with oath: *no*—because of the trials.[11]

√ Univ. Bill. Arr[angements] for debate—WEG to point out certain changes (for an immediate reprint after 2 r[eading]) & the objection to giving names of Council.[12]

√ Week's business on the heads cons[idere]d.

[1] On the University Bill.

[2] P. H. *Stanhope, *Notes of conversation with King Louis-Philippe at Claremont, March 30, 1848* (1873).

[3] Army estimates; *H* ccxiv. 1123.

[4] S. Owen, *India on the eve of the British Conquest. An historical sketch* (1872).

[5] Printed letter to Hartington; annotated copy in Add MS 44620, f. 76.

[6] [J. C. Hoey?], on their failure, *Dublin Review*, xx. 77 (January 1873).

[7] (Sir) John *Evans, 1823-1908, archaeologist, published on flints.

[8] Probably F. H. O'Donnell (see 4 Mar. 73), *Public education* (1867).

[9] Add MS 44641, f. 51.

[10] Commission on merchant navy set up on *Plimsoll's motion on 4 March; *H* ccxiv. 1334.

[11] Never moved.

[12] See 22 Feb. 73. Gladstone told Victoria this day: 'The various interests touched by the Bill are in motion with more or less of hostile demonstrations, the Roman Catholic Bishops in particular are loud and angry, though under a suspicion of not being wholly in earnest as respects at least a part of them. The Government propose to persevere steadily with the measure: at present no serious danger appears to menace it on the second reading'; CAB 41/5/11.

√ Fishery Canada arr. Laws having now been passed, umpire Commr. to be appointed.[1]
√ *Enfreindre motifs*[2] reference to us. remonstrate? No.
√ Suez Canal. Conference shd. be in London.[3] Title thought clear as to repayment of tolls improperly exacted.
√ Persia asks for the establ[ishmen]t of a boundary with Russia. Ask him[4] for information as to the locale, & the Persian view. He said they cannot accept the Seistan arbitration. G[ranville] said it was very serious.
√ Australian Tariffs. Agreed: the obligations of Treaty being saved.[5]
√ Committee on County harmonising areas with Parish & [Poor Law] Union.[6]
√ Scotch Bank Agency in London. Extend privilege to Royal Bank? In quasi Cabinet.
Give no new privilege to a Bank of Issue.[7]

To ARCHBISHOP H. E. MANNING, 1 March 1873. Add MS 44250, f. 102.
'Private.'

I think it right to point out that the Paragraph in the Resolutions which repudiates on behalf of the R.C. Coll. introduction into the University of Dublin, however intended, is really War to the knife, & that a petition against the Bill would have been far less mischievous. How is it possible that this should not have been perceived?

To EARL SPENCER, Irish lord lieutenant, Add MS 44542, f. 94.
1 March 1873.

I at once circulated among my colleagues your report of Cardinal Cullen's conversation.[8] Overhead it is dark, & underfoot a chaos, but our course is perfectly clear & straight & as far as real criticism is concerned the Bill has stood it well. The most serious danger & difficulty I see ahead is mutilation in the Lords, as I do not see how the Government could resign on it.

2. 1 S.Lent.

Chapel Royal mg (with H.C.) & evg. Wrote to Rev. Dr Smyth. Saw Ld Chancr of Ireland—Sir R. Blennerhassett—Mr Glyn. Saw Gerard [R].

[1] Law officer's report in PRO CO 880/6/514.
[2] Reasons for infraction [of the French treaty?].
[3] Britain demanded a conference (held in Constantinople), on exorbitant increases in canal dues; it reported in December 1873.
[4] i.e. Persian minister in London; CAB 41/5/1. F. J. Goldsmid's arbitration accepted by H.M.G.: PRO FO 60/393.
[5] Telegram of 11 February from Sir H. Robinson in Add MS 44641, f. 55. Australian Colonies (Customs Duties) Bill introduced 27 March, royal assent 26 May. See Kimberley, *Journal*, 38.
[6] Reported under Stansfeld, 17 July 1873; *PP* 1873 viii.
[7] But see 5 July 73.
[8] Mem. sent by Spencer on 25 February 1873, Add MS 44307, f. 159: 'I feel pretty sure he will go against the Bill'.

Read Union Review—Row on Inspiration—Pusey's Sermons—Scott (of Ramsgate) Tracts, divers.

3. M.

Wrote to Col. Ponsonby—Mr C. Villiers—Dr Pusey—Abp Manning—The Queen—and minutes. Dined with the Godleys: ½ hour. Saw Ld F. Cavendish—Mr Glyn—Chancr of Exr—Mr Stansfeld *cum* Chr of Exchr. Visited Sotheby's. H of C. 4½-8½ and 9¼-12½.[1] Read Howley on Univ. Competn[2]—Macdonnell on Queen's Univ.

Mr. Mitchell Henry[3] has informed Mr Glyn this morning that he will today announce his intention to move, if the forms will allow him, as an amendment on the second reading of the Irish University Bill, that the *entire subject of Irish Education* (so it was understood) be referred to a Royal Commission.

I presume we should take this as equivalent to a condemnation and rejection of the Bill.[4]

To ARCHBISHOP H. E. MANNING, 3 March 1873. Add MS 44250, f. 105.

I do not see my way to acting upon your suggestion of Saturday[5] if I understand right, nor have I the means of knowing whether it would produce a soothing effect; but there is much which may come up out of the present confusion, as the public & the classes grope their way through chaos to firm land. What I understand from you & from your brethren in Ireland is this, that two great items, which it might have been hoped would have been boons, are grievances, viz. the provision of a teaching body & the introduction of the R.C. college as such into the University.

4. Tu.

Wrote to Chancr of Exr—Ld Chancellor—Ld Ripon—The Queen—& minutes. Read O'Donnell on Q.Univ.—Pattison on Acad. Organisation.[6] Saw Duke of Argyll (2)—Ld Granville—Mr Glyn—Ld F. Cavendish—Mr Gurdon—Mr Monsell. Saw Gerald: some good I hope[R]. H. of C. 4½-8¼ and 9½-12¾.[7]

[1] Spoke on Irish universities; *H* ccxiv. 1186.
[2] See 21 Jan. 73.
[3] Mitchell Henry 1826-1910; liberal (later home rule) M.P. Galway 1871-85, Blackfriars 1885-6.
[4] Initialled and dated 3 March 1873, Add MS 44761, f. 87; circulated to the cabinet, all of whom agreed, Lowe adding: 'as more—as a direct vote of want of confidence—we are not to be trusted with the subject.'
[5] 'Why not make two centres & two groups, under one Chancellor'; Add MS 44250, f. 103.
[6] See 10 Apr. 73.
[7] Questions; *Plimsoll; *H* ccxiv. 1340.

To LORD RIPON, lord president, 4 March 1873. Add MS 43514, f. 179.

I received yesterday morning your note of Sunday,[1] & read it, I need hardly say, with extreme concern. I did not write to you by the same post, in the hope, which was happily fulfilled, that we might soon hear an account giving less cause for anxiety than that which caused your abrupt departure. If I am right in understanding that the original fear had reference to inflammation, then the second account, which reported a good & quiet night, goes very far I trust towards disarming any ulterior apprehension. God grant it may so prove.

As to the moment of your absence, it seems to be critical. On our side, much coldness has taken the place of cheerful acquiescence & support; on the other side of the question, loud though discordant noises are frightening us all from our propriety. Glyn is downcast. But with all this, it is not quite easy to see where or how the fatal blow is to be planted. There is nothing like misgiving or dissension in the Government itself.

I hope Lady Ripon's health & strength have proved sufficient for this trying time. Since I began, I have read with much pleasure this morning's Telegram.

5. Wed.

Wrote to Chancr of Exr—Mr Fortescue (2)—The Queen—and minutes. Attended the Hawtrey Memorial Meeting[2] and C's tea party. Saw Ld F. Cavendish—Mr Glyn—Ld Clanwilliam—Mr Tennyson *cum* Mr Lockyer[3]—Mrs Graham & her mother—Chancr of Exr *cum* Mr Cardwell. Off at 5.30 to Croydon, to attend the dinner to Mr Locke King. Spoke over ½ hour in returning thanks for Ministers.[4] Read the Eustace Diamonds.[5]

Mr Dodson has given notice that after the 2d reading of the University (Ireland) Bill he will move to refer it to a Select Committee.

The Six Ministers marked *a*[6] have been seen & agree with me in thinking we can on no terms accept this motion.

Will the rest of my Colleagues kindly say whether they concur. If not it will be necessary to meet in Cabinet, as I understand it is necessary with reference to the current debate that our view of the motion should be definitely known.[7]

6. Th.

Wrote to Mr Fortescue—Mr T.S. Gladstone—The Queen—Mr R.S. Gladstone—Ld Chancr of Ireland—and minutes. H of C. 4½–8¼ and

[1] Add MS 44286, f. 178; his son injured in France.
[2] *The Times*, 6 March 1873, 10d.
[3] Possibly Norman Lockyer, friend of *Tennyson; *Alfred, Lord Tennyson*, ii. 381.
[4] *The Times*, 6 March 1873, 5d.
[5] By *Trollope, 3v. (1873).
[6] Presumably Hartington, Fortescue, Childers, Lowe, Stansfeld, Forster, on the printed list usually attached to round-robin notes. Granville, Bruce, Lowe, Argyll initialled agreement on this note.
[7] Initialled and dated 5 March 1873, Add MS 44761, f. 89.

$9\frac{1}{4}$-$12\frac{3}{4}$.[1] Read Atalanta.[2] Saw Dr Carpenter 11-$12\frac{1}{4}$—Ld F. Cavendish—Mr Glyn—Mr Murphy MP *cum* Sir J. Gray, Mr Richmond, & Mr Shaw. Dined at Mrs Talbot's.

7. Fr.

Wrote to Lady A. Russell[3]—The Queen Mem. & letter—Dr Candlish—Mr Monsell—T.S. Gladstone—& minutes. Saw Ld Lyttelton—Mr Glyn—do *cum* Ld Halifax—Ld F. Cavendish—Chr of Exr—Mr Gurdon—Mr Cardwell—Mr C. *cum* C. of E. & Mr Goschen—Att. Gen.—Mr Forster—& others. Calls. Mr Haywood—Mrs Hope. Read Macaulay on Ireland.[4]

8. Sat.

Wrote to Sir T. Biddulph—Mr Cardwell—Sir W. Dunbar—Abp Manning—Mrs Th.—R.C. Bp of Raphoe[5]—The Queen—and minutes. Cabinet $2\frac{3}{4}$-$5\frac{1}{2}$. Most harmonious, at this critical time. Saw Ld F. Cavendish—Sir T.G.—Mr Glyn—Ld Chancr Ireland—Missed Ld Granville. Dined with Mr Fortescue and Lady W. Read the Eustace Diamonds.

Cabinet. Sat. Mch. 8. 73. 2½ PM.[6]

√ Irish Univ. Bill. See Report to H.M.[7] WEG recd. instructions as to the essence of the Bill.
√ Emanuel Scheme. Arr[anged] for debate on Thursday.[8]
√ Notice the death of Ld Ossington on Monday? Not unless there cd. be some vote or message wh. we do not see our way to.[9]
1. Tone on Tuesday. High as to our course—keep to the essential of Bill.[10]

To ARCHBISHOP H. E. MANNING, 8 March 1873. Add MS 44250, f. 115.
'Private.'

The violent outburst (as I think it) from the Irish R.C. bishops has been exaggerated, but strange to say the exaggeration marks the views taken by those who follow as much as by those who repudiate them. They as lords & masters (which I suppose them to be) of the R.C. College refuse the place offered it in the Bill. This is a blow to the Bill but it could be borne. They have expressed a desire that

[1] Irish universities; *H* ccxiv. 1398.
[2] A. C. *Swinburne, *Atalanta in Calydon. A tragedy* (1865).
[3] Lady Mary Agatha, da. of Earl Russell; she d. 1933.
[4] J. Macaulay, *Ireland in 1872* (1873).
[5] James M'Devitt.
[6] Add MS 44641, f. 57.
[7] Announcing anticipated defeat of the bill; mostly in Morley, ii. 441.
[8] On Emanuel Hospital; deb. lost in the crisis; *H* ccxiv. 1909.
[9] His death went officially unnoticed.
[10] This sentence, evidently Gladstone's 'instructions', on Add MS 44641, f. 58.

the Bill should not pass in its present form, and the consequence is that I am saluted by their followers with an announcement that they must vote against the 2d reading & so prevent the House of Commons from modifying or altering the form of the Bill in Committee. This is a grave matter: for it comes to a question of votes.

Your (*my*) demands are easily dealt with: I should be ashamed to offer a measure that did not concede them. I shall fight to the last against all comers, but much against my inclination which is marvellously attracted by the vision of my liberty dawning like a sunrise from beyond the hills. For when this offer has been made, and every effort of patience employed to render it a reality, my contract with the country is fulfilled, and I am free to take my own course.[1]

9. 2 S.Lent.

Chapel Royal mg and evg. Wrote to Archbishop Leahy[2]—Sir T. Biddulph—Sir Thos G.—The Queen—and minutes. Dined at Ld Lyttelton's. Saw Willis[R]. Saw Ld Granville *cum* Mr Glyn—Mr Neville Grenville—Mr Glyn. Read Row on Inspiration—Bp Bedell's Life[3]—Introdn to Evangelical Common Prayer—A World at War &c.[4]—Contemp. Review.

10. M.

Wrote to Prof. Robertson—Mr Cardwell—The Queen—Ld Stanhope—& minutes. H of C. 4½–8½ & 9½–12¾. Cardwell's Speech was the event of the evening.[5] Saw Ld F. Cavendish—Mr Glyn—Ld Granville—Sir Thos G. 9½–1. I went to attend the funeral of my cousin & schoolfellow William Gladstone[6] who closed last week his sorely afflicted life. We went from Queen's Gate to Highgate. Read Eustace Diamonds.

11. Tu.

Wrote to the Queen—Dr A. Clark—& minutes. Worked much on the Univ. question. Read Eustace Diamonds. H of C. 4½–8¼ and 9½–2¾. Spoke 12–2 and voted in a division of 284:287, wh was believed to cause more surprise to the opposite side than it did to me.[7]

[1] Manning replied on 12 March, Add MS 44250, f. 115: 'Put yourself like Pitt in his second government, without his reaction, at the head of the Christian culture of England.'
[2] Patrick *Leahy, 1806–75, archbishop of Cashel from 1857, had sent a book; Add MS 44542, f. 97.
[3] See 16 Feb. 73.
[4] Untraced.
[5] *H* ccxiv. 1701.
[6] See 31 July 32.
[7] *H* ccxiv. 1863.

Mch. 11. 73. Childers's Analysis.[1]
L[iberals] against Govt. 45—of these Irish R.C. + 2 Tory, 25, [Irish] Prot., 10.
English & Scotch:[2] Akroyd, Aytoun, Foster W. H., Fawcett, Horsman, McCullagh Torrens, Bouverie, Sir R. Peel, A. Herbert, Whalley.
Majority of Protestants, 20.
R.C.s for us: Monsell, [Sir R.] Blennerhassett, Corrigan, Gavin: 4.
L[iberal] Maj[ority] of Engl. & Scotch: 54.
Irishmen for Govt, 12; against, 69. Irish Abstainers, 22.
Tory Absentees willingly: Collins, E. Cecil, B[eresford] Hope, Liddell, Scourfield.[3]

12.

Wrote to Dean of Westmr—Mr Gurdon—Dr Clark—and minutes. Saw Mr Glyn—Ld F. Cavendish. To Dr Clark at 11.30. The Queen at 12.15. Failed to find Granville. Cabinet 1-2¾. Confab. on my own position with Granville & Glyn: then joined by Bright. To the Queen again at 6. Large dinner party for the Duke of Edinburgh, and an evening party afterwards to hear Joachim. Saw Mr Hayward—and others.

Cabinet Mch. 12.73. 2½ P.M.[4]
√ Division of last night. WEG recommended conversation only *today*. Glyn called in: reported conversation with Sir G. Grey who recommended resignation & thought the other side wd. fail to form a Govt.
Courses: Ignore the vote—*no.*
Revise the Bill—*no.*
O Vote of confidence.
Resignation
Dissolution (Imm[ediat]e or postponed.) } Discussed for some time
Hartington reported Irish opinions (for Diss[olutio]n if *not on* Edn. Bill)
√ Childers to postpone his Expenditure Committee now Standing Committee.
√ Emmanuel [*sic*] College. Postponing Bill to be prepared—to keep alive Crawford's (& Corrance's) right.

[5]Divisions in the Liberal party are to be seriously apprehended: from a factious spirit—on questions of economy—on questions of education in its relation to religion—on questions of further Parliamentary change—on the Land Laws. On these questions generally my sympathies are with what may be termed the advanced party, whom, on other & general grounds, I certainly will never head or lead.
[6]There is now no *cause*. No great public object on wh. the Liberal party are agreed & combined.

[1] Add MS 44641, f. 66, in Gladstone's hand.
[2] These names in column; the first three and last two have a dash by them, the others a plus sign.
[3] Spaces for two more names indicated by dots.
[4] Add MS 44641, f. 64.
[5] Undated holograph; ibid., f. 63.
[6] Remainder in pencil.

The constitutional argument is for Dissolution. Quite willing to resign.
The inequality as to me personally not so great as it may at first seem.
The time is come for me at least to *prepare.*
(always subject to a reserve).
This wd. be done either now, or (in all likelihood) shortly after *our* Dissolution.

13. Th.

Wrote to Mr Glyn—The Queen 3 Mema—Sir R. Shafto Adair—Mr D. Robertson—Ld Normanby—Ld Portman[1]—Mr Chamberlain—Mrs Th.—Abp Manning—The Speaker—and minutes. After seeing Mr Glyn and Lord F. Cavendish I set out at 10.40 to see Dr Clark. He completed his examination & gave me his careful judgment.[2] I went to Ld Granville: sketched out to him and Glyn my views, & went to the Cabinet at 12.15. After Cabinet saw Hartington and others respecting honours. At 2.45 saw the Queen and resigned. At 4.15 saw Granville respecting the announcements: Announcement in H of C. at 4.30.[3] More business in Downing St: home at 6. Saw Sir John Lubbock. At 6.50 came Col. Ponsonby. Made Memorandum of interview with him: & saw Glyn who reported forthwith to Granville. At 8 went to dine with the Jameses. At night wrote Memm on Ministerial Crises. Saw Mr Bright. Visited Mr Millais[4] Studio—Christies. Read the Eustace Diamonds.

Cabinet. Thurs. Mch. 13. 73.[5]

√ The situation. WEG stated the case between the two alternatives of Dissolution & Resignation,[6] (assuming that no other alternatives could be entertained,) so far as regarded himself.

On the side of resignation it wd. not be necessary to make any final announcement: I am strongly advised a temporary rest.

On the other hand if we now dissolve, I anticipate that *afterwards* before any long time difficulties will arise & our mission will terminate.

So that the alternatives are not so unequally weighted.

Information reported.

Cabinet, without any marked difference, or at least any positive assertion to the contrary, determined on tendering their resignations.

√ What is WEG to say to Qu. if Queen desires *time*. To ask the House for it—Friday.

[1] Peerages offered to Adair, Robertson, Normanby, Portman; Add MS 44542, f. 98.

[2] Gladstone recalled, somewhat obscurely, in 1894: 'Clark . . . would give me on medical grounds no encouragement whatever'; *Autobiographica*, i. 112.

[3] That ministers' resignations had been accepted; *H* ccxiv. 1909. Disraeli then told Victoria that he was prepared to form a ministry, but not with the present Commons, and that he did not advise a dissolution; Guedalla, *Q*, i. 396.

[4] (Sir) John Everett *Millais, 1829-96; cr. bart. 1885; first painted Gladstone 1879.

[5] Add MS 44641, f. 74; some in Morley, ii. 446, conflated with diary.

[6] Gladstone's list of precedents since 1832, at Add MS 44761, f. 93.

If she asks *advice*. To observe the natural course is to look to the person who led the assault agt. the Govt. & who was the last Prime Minister.
√ Tell the House: either, has received the tender & is considering, or, has accepted, & we hold office provisionally until other arrangements are made.
√ Mr Forster gives notice of a Bill to meet Crawford's case.
√ Houghton's [Deceased] Wife's Sister Bill; dissent from his going on.

This afternoon at halfpast three I left the Palace having placed at the feet of the Sovereign the ministerial resignations, which were graciously accepted. The Queen informed me that she would send for Mr Disraeli: suggested for consideration whether I would include the mention of this fact in my announcement to Parliament: and added as I was leaving the room, without looking (apparently) for an answer, that she would inform me of what might take place.

At a quarter to seven, or a little later, Colonel Ponsonby called with a communication from Her Majesty. Any news? I said. 'A great deal' he replied: and informed me as follows. Mr Disraeli had been with the Queen: did not see the means of carrying on the Government by the agency of his party under present circumstances; did not ask for the dissolution of the Parliament (this was understood to mean did not offer to become Minister on condition of being permitted to dissolve); did not say that his renunciation of the task was final: recommended that the Queen should call for my advice. Upon this the Queen sent Col. Ponsonby, and 'She considers this as sending for you anew.'

I replied

That I did not regard the Queen's reference of this intelligence to me as Her calling upon me anew to undertake the work of Government: that none of my obligations to the Sovereign were cancelled or impaired by the resignation tendered and accepted: that I was still Her Minister for the purpose of rendering any service She might be pleased to call for in the matter on which She is engaged, exactly as before, until She has a new Minister, when my official obligations will come to an end.

That I felt there was great inconvenience, & danger of misapprehension out of doors, in proceeding over rapidly with a matter of such gravity, & that each step in it required to be well measured & ascertained before proceeding to consider of the next following step.

That I had great difficulty in gathering any precise idea of Mr Disraeli's account of what he could not do, and what he either could or did not say that he could not. That as this account was to present to me the state of facts on which I was commanded to advise, it was quite necessary for me to have an accurate idea of it, in order that I might do justice to H.M.s commands. I would therefore humbly suggest that Mr Disraeli might with great propriety be requested to put his reply into writing. That I presumed I might receive this reply if it were H.M's pleasure to make it known to me at some not late hour tomorrow, when I would at once place myself in a condition to tender my humble advice.

This is an account of what Col. P. might fairly consider as my answer to H.M's communication. I enlarged the conversation however by observing that the division which overthrew us was a party division: it bore the express authentic symbol of its character in having party tellers on the Opposition as well as the Government side: that we were aware of the great, even more than ordinary efforts of Col. Taylor,[1] with Mr Disraeli's countenance, to bring members to London (the £85 story) and to the House; that all this seemed to impose great obligations on the Opposition; and if so that it would be the duty of the leader of Opposition to use every exertion of consultation with his friends and otherwise before declining the task or in any manner advising the Queen to look elsewhere. To Col. P. indeed I observed that I thought Mr D. was endeavouring by at once throwing back on me an offer which it was impossible for me at the time & under the circumstances to accept, to get up a case of absolute necessity founded upon this refusal of mine and thus becoming the indispensable man and party to have in his hands a lever wherewith to overcome the reluctance & resistance of his friends who would not be able to deny that the Queen must have a Government.[2]

To ARCHBISHOP H. E. MANNING, 13 March 1873. Add MS 44542, f. 98.
'Private.'

You give[3] no heed to the wailings & pleas of my old age: but I do, & the future in politics hardly exists for me, unless some new phase arise and, as in 1868, a special call may appear: to such call, please God I will answer; if there be breath in my body. Your Irish Brethren have received in the late vote of Parliament the most extravagant compliment ever paid them. *They* have destroyed the measure; which otherwise was safe enough.

14. Fr.

Wrote Memm for the Queen and Letter[4]—Mr Power—Mr Thring—Mr Hayward—Mr Lefevre—Col. Ponsonby—and minutes. Luncheon at 15 G.S. Saw Col. Ponsonby (10 A.M. and 7 P.M.)—Mr

[1] T. E. *Taylor, tory whip; see 5 Mar. 57.
[2] Initialled and dated 13 March 1873, Add MS 44761, f. 102; part in Morley, ii. 447.
[3] Manning's letter of 12 March on the Bill: Add MS 44250, f. 118.
[4] Expressing incomprehension at Disraeli's position; Guedalla, *Q*, i. 397.

Knatchbull Hugessen—Mr Baxter—Ld Halifax—Ld F. Cavendish—Mr Glyn—Ld Granville (2)—Attorney General. At night prepared a lengthened statement for H.M.[1] Visited No 15 G.S. in evg at Mrs Th.s request. X. Dined at Ld F. Cavendish's. Read Eustace Diamonds.

15. Sat. [Cliveden]

Wrote to The Queen (prepared last night & discussed with G. this morning[)][2]—Col. Ponsonby (2)—Ld Spencer—Ld Granville—and minutes. Saw Ld Granville—D. of Argyll—Mr Glyn—Ld F. Cavendish—The Queen—Col. Ponsonby—Scotts—Mrs Tyler. Off at 5 to Cliveden: most hospitably received in a pleasant party. Read Eustace Diamonds.

16. 3 S.Lent.

Burnham Ch mg—Hedsor beautiful even in the storm of rain, afternoon. Wrote to Mr Gurdon—The Queen[3]—in evg.—Mem. of the Crisis. Read Jerningham's MS.[4]—Row on Inspiration (finished). The party have had the first news of my having again taken to the harness. Conversation with D. of Argyll—Dr Ratcliffe.

The landmarks of the present crisis are as follows. On Wed. morning 2.45 A.M. I apprise the Queen of our defeat. In Cabinet at 1 we discuss the matter with a general tendency to resignation rather than dissolving. Before & after I see H.M. to keep her informed. Thursday at noon the Cabinet determines to resign. At 2.45 I apprise the Queen who accepts (and forthwith sends for Mr Disraeli). Leave H.M. at 3.30. At 4.30 I apprise the H. of C. which adjourns until Monday. Between 6 & 7 Col Ponsonby calls upon me to tell me from H.M. that Mr Disraeli has been seen & has declined: & to ask advice. I advise that Mr Disraeli's answer be asked for in writing. On Friday at 9 Col. Ponsonby sends me Mr Disraeli's answer in writing & calls at ten. Upon examination afterwards I find the paper somewhat ambiguous, and write to H.M. hoping it will be cleared up. Between 6 & 7 I learn from H.M. (and Col. Ponsonby again calls) that Mr Disraeli's answer is an unconditional refusal: and asks for my advice. I reply that the Opposition could not acquit itself of its duty in the matter either by a previous determination to refuse or by a summary refusal

[1] See next day.

[2] Sent, dated this day, outlining lack of precedent for Disraeli's rapid refusal; Guedalla, *Q*, i. 399.

[3] Agreeing to attempt next day to reform his ministry; Guedalla, *Q*, i. 406.

[4] Perhaps H. E. H. Jerningham, *To and from Constantinople* (1873).

without consultation upon the facts: and undertake to state fully my views in writing. I take my Statement (prepared after dinner) to Lord Granville's that night. On Sat. morning I see Ld Granville & Col. Ponsonby: copy out & send off the statement: I see H.M. at 2.45 when I learn that Mr Disraeli did at his interview state that if I decline to resume he would then be at H.M's command. I said to H.M. 'But that fact is not before me' (i.e. not in writing[)]. 'But he said it to me', she replied. My statement or part of it was sent by H.M. to Mr Disraeli; no doubt before she started for Windsor at 4.30. We went off to Cliveden. On Sunday at 10 PM a messenger reaches Cliveden with a fresh summons to me from the Queen to say whether I will resume office. She incloses Mr Disraeli's letter which shows nothing more is to be expected in that quarter.

I send off the messenger at 11 with my answer in the affirmative.[1]

17. M. [*London*]

Adieu to our *most* kind hosts at 10¼. Wrote to Ld St German's—Ld Granville—The Queen—& minutes. Saw Ld Granville—do with conclave on the situation—Ld Halifax—Sir G. Grey—Ld Kimberley—Mr Levy—Ld Chancr Irel.—Col. Ponsonby. H of C. 4½-5½ (& H. of L.) We considered Disraeli's strange statement: foisted in.[2] 11 to dinner. Read The Quaker's Opera[3]—The Eustace Diamonds.

Conclave. 11 C.H.T. Mch 17. 2¼ P.M.[4]

D. of Argyll, Ld Granville, WEG., Mr Cardwell, (Ld Halifax came after)

[5]Dissolution—Bruce, Hartington, √ Baxter.

Education Act, Local Taxation, Budget, before Easter Thurs. 3.
Irish Univ. question, Trevelyan's Franchise Bill.[6]

√ Hardy, 3 Rules. √ Easter Holidays.

18. Tu.

Wrote to The Queen—Dean of Durham—Mr Glyn—Mrs Kennedy—Miss Doyle—Sir H. Verney—& minutes. Saw Ld F. Cavendish—Mr Glyn[7]—Sir A. Panizzi—Ld Hartington—Ld Granville. Dined

[1] Holograph, dated 'Cliveden, Mch. 16. midnight'; Add MS 44761, f. 100.

[2] Disraeli repeated his comments to Victoria (see 13 Mar. 73), though with no reference to a dissolution; *H* ccxiv. 1917.

[3] *The Quaker's Opera* (1728).

[4] Add MS 44641, f. 76.

[5] Apparently topics for discussion at this meeting, ibid., f. 80, with list of names repeated.

[6] Perhaps topics for manifesto in event of a dissolution.

[7] Declining through Glyn an offer of the Brighton seat then held by Fawcett; Add MS 44542, f. 99.

with the Wortleys. Read Quaker's Opera—The Eustace Diamonds. Arranged papers for Circulation & sent them out. The Cabinet met informally at this house at 2 PM. and sat till 5½.

(Informal) Cabinet. Tues. March 18. 1873. 2 P.M.[1]

√ Notice of Cabinet—wrongly published.

√ Shall we resume [office]. Discussed. Yes. See over.[2]

Decided: To resume: with a view if possible of keeping the Parlt. alive to next year. 1. Offer if Playfair brings in a Bill agt. tests to support him: through Cardwell. 2. Fawcett's Univ. plan inadmissable. Budget on a day before Easter. Education & Local Taxation—declare before Easter or soon after Easter.

Report to be sent in soon from the Committee of Cabinet on exemptions.

Educ. on Saty.

√ Statement on Thursday.

√ Hardy's motion—discussed—not to interfere.

19. Wed.

Wrote to The Dean of Windsor—and minutes. Saw Dean of Windsor—Ld F. Cavendish—Ld Granville—Mr Glyn *cum* Mr Winterbotham on the Education Act. Saw Mrs Cooper 138 Kensn Park Road.[3] Went to Windsor at midday: ¾ hour with the Queen. On the resumption: the statement tomorrow: the D. of Edinburgh's marriage: Royal precedence: Tennyson's honour: also she mentioned Railway accidents and an assault on a soldier: & specy luxury in dress & food. Dined with the Duke of Cambridge: conversation with him: with Beust, D'Harcourt & others. At Speaker's Levee: saw Mr Fawcett & other members. Then Mrs Glyn's party. Read The Eustace Diamonds.

20. Th.

Wrote to Mr Fortescue—Col. Ponsonby—Mr Bruce—Mr Forster (2)—Mrs Th.—The Queen 2 l. & Mem.—Dean of Windsor (Tel.)—Ld Fermoy—Mr Gilpin—and minutes. Read Eustace Diamonds—Health of Oarsmen.[4] Visited Christie's; & Lady Charlotte Schreiber's remarkable collections.[5] Saw Ld F. Cavendish—Chancr of Exr—Mr Glyn (2)—Mr Forster—Saw one[R]. H of C. 4½-7¼. Made my explanation. Advisedly let pass Mr Disraeli's speech without notice.[6]

[1] Add MS 44641, f. 81.

[2] Next para. on next page.

[3] Rescue; *London Post Office Directory* (1873) gives this as Mrs. Peacock's house; see 14 June 73.

[4] Untraced.

[5] At the height of her 'china mania'; see 1 May 55, Lord Bessborough, *Lady Charlotte Schreiber* (1952), 127.

[6] Gladstone read from his letter to Victoria of 15 March; Disraeli explained lengthily why a tory ministry could not have dissolved promptly; *H* ccxiv. 1929.

To W. E. FORSTER, vice president, 20 March 1873. Add MS 44542, f. 100.

I had a long conversation with Winterbotham in Glyn's presence yesterday on the question of the Education Act Amendment which has recently assumed such inconvenient proportions. I condensed the result into the enclosed mem. & I should be very glad to see you tomorrow about 11.30 on the subject of it, if not inconvenient.

Interview with Mr Winterbotham. Mch 19. 73.

1. Compulsion, considered apart from all other topics of legislation, would not be regarded as a boon by the Nonconfts. generally. Added to the present Act, it would be a new source of irritation.
2. Repeal of Cl. 17, if leaving Bd. free as Mr F. thinks, would be a boon to the N.C. but would much irritate the supporters of the Voluntary Schools.
3. On Cl. 25. Though a practical improvement excites jealousy from transfer to a Bd. less elective & irritates Dixon and his friends by treating free schooling as Pauper relief.
4. If voluntary Schools were required to find, say $\frac{1}{5}$ or $\frac{1}{6}$ from subscription & the like (in which might be included a fair allowance on the voluntary funds laid out upon the building) it would be a concession to 2 classes of persons in the N.C. quarter.
   a. Those who would regard the 6th as practically corresponding with the charge required to provide religious instruction.
   b. Those who would regard it as weighting the voluntary schools. But it would be opposed by the friends of voluntary schools generally, or at any rate where they are in competition with Bd. Schools.

The question is how far this would be a fair counterpoise to the settlement of the point raised on the 25th Clause.

Mr W's query: Whenever there is a percentage of children certified to be unable to pay where the Voluntary Schools will not receive without payment, a Bd. School shall be established (under compulsion).

21. Fr.

Wrote to The Queen—Miss Doyle—Robn G.—Viscsse de Brimont Brissac—Ld Ripon—Chr of Exr—and minutes. H of C. 4½-8 and 8¾-1¾. Spoke on Mr Hardy's motion & the Three Rules.[1] Saw Mr Milner Gibson—Ld F. Cavendish—Mr Glyn. Read The Eustace Diamonds.

To Robertson GLADSTONE, 21 March 1873. Hawarden MSS.

[2]Well, we have gone through our crisis; and I fear nobody is much the better for it. For us it was absolutely necessary to show that we did not consider return, as we had not considered resignation, a light matter. As to the opposition, the speech of Disraeli last night leaves it to be asked why did he not come in, wind

[1] Of international arbitration; *H* ccxiv. 2050. M. *Bernard's mem. for the cabinet of 7 March 1873 is at Add MS 44620, f. 94.

[2] Passage on Miss Doyle omitted.

up the business of the Session, & dissolve? There is no reason to be given, except that a portion of his party were determined not to be 'educated' again, & were certain that if he got in he would again commence this educating process. The Conservative Party will never assume its natural position until Disraeli retires; & I sometimes think he & I might with advantage pair off together.

To LORD RIPON, lord president, 21 March 1873. Add MS 43514, f. 181.

I am deeply sensible how trying it must be to you to be pestered with any political inquiries at a time when you have not yet emerged, though I trust you are steadily emerging, from a most acute domestic anxiety. Of the latter I will only say that having known of such cases, one *worse*, among my own relatives, I am not disheartened at the slow progress, provided, which God grant, that there be no absolute check.

(*March 21*)[1] Thus far only I got & was not able to finish my letter. However I am now in a condition to refer more distinctly to our position. I cannot say it is reassuring. The University question may very probably be re-adjusted for the year with Fawcett. But over & above the general difficulty of loss of *vital power*, the question of Education looms large and awkwardly. You will remember how it was left by the Cabinet in the winter under a sort of provisional settlement, the circumstances of which were far from normal. We then hoped to approach it with some *way on*: & Forster considered that if the proposal of compulsion proved unacceptable it might be withdrawn. *Now*, we are hardly in a condition to propose with a view to withdrawing: & I fear that F. *greatly* overestimates the favour with which the meditated proposals as to Clause 25 would be received. In circumstances like these we should only approach the view of the question at a great disadvantage to you & to ourselves if we attempted to discuss it in your absence. You will doubtless have had letter or Telegraph from F. to a like effect.

22. Sat.

Wrote to Ld Hatherley—Mr Goschen—Mr T.M. Gibson—Dean of St Paul's—the Queen—and minutes. Cabinet $2\frac{3}{4}$–$5\frac{1}{2}$: again in regular form and place. Tea with Miss Talbot & long conversation. Saw Mr Forster (on Educn)—Chancr of Exr (Budget &c.)—Ld F. Cavendish —Mr Glyn. Dinner party: evg party afterwards. Saw Sir T. Fremantle —Irish Att. General—and [blank]. Read the Eustace Diamonds.

Cabinet. Sat. Mch. 22. 73. 2.30.[2]

√ Fawcett's Bill. WEG stated the bearing, & the transactions.
√ Education Act. Dixon's question for Monday: Forster to say: cannot before Easter: *hopes* to give a definite reply in evening[?] before Easter.[3]
√ WEG to state course of business up to Easter on Monday.
√ Australian Tariffs Bill. Draft agreed to.[4]
√ (Ld Ch[ancello]r) Bill on Scotch Conveyancing—he approves—agreed to. D. of Argyll to review Bill.

[1] Docketed 'Begun 18 March'.
[2] Add MS 44641, f. 84.
[3] See *H* ccxv. 14, 634.
[4] Gladstone's amendments at Add MS 44620, f. 117.

√ Aden & W.O. Bill. Not to be prosecuted.
√ Week's business. St Aubyn.[1] A measure is in preparation of wh this will be a part.
√ Ld Hartington to refer to H.M. as to the power of informing Parlt. that some members of the R[oyal] F[amily] will reside annually for some weeks.[2]

23. S.4 Lent.

Chapel Royal mg and aft. Wrote to Mr Tennyson—Sir C. Biddulph —& minutes. Saw Mr M'Garel[3]—Ld Granville—Mr Glyn. Dined with the Glyns. Read St Anselm's Meditations—M'Garel Sunday Refl.—Life of Davis[4]—Gifts for Men[5]—Lightfoot's Serm.[6]—Rickards' Lecture[7]—Latin Hymns &c.

24. M.

Wrote to The Lord Mayor—Chancr of Exchr—Mr Kingsley—Ld Chancellor—The Queen—and minutes. Ten to dinner. H of C. 4½-8¼ and 9¾-1¼.[8] Luncheon at No 15 G[rosvenor] S[quare]. Saw Sir Thos Biddulph—Ld F. Cavendish—Mr Glyn—Prime Warden Fishmongers Co.[9]—Mr Fortescue—Sir H. Verney. Read The Eustace Diamonds.

25. Tu. Annunciation.

Wrote to Ld Chancellor—Chancr of Exr—Ld Hartington—The Queen—J. Watson & Smith—and minutes. Saw Ld F. Cavendish—Mr M'Coll—Mr Glyn—Mr Cardwell (respecting C. of E.)—Mr Forster (respecting Educn). Saw Stanley. H. of C. 4½-9.[10] Correcting Speech on 2d Reading I.U. Bill. Finished 'the Eustace Diamonds'.

To R. LOWE, chancellor of the exchequer, 25 March 1873. Add MS 44542, f. 102.

On Friday night Mr Rathbone told me he wished to speak to me about the Cape Contract, of which he spoke as a probable source of Parliamentary difficulty.

[1] Question by St. Aubyn on local taxation measure; *H* ccxv. 18.
[2] i.e. in Ireland; no statement by Hartington on this found this session.
[3] Unidentified religious writer.
[4] Perhaps E. A. Pollard, *Life of Jefferson Davis* (1869).
[5] Possibly J. M. Campbell, *Responsibility for the gift of eternal life* (1873).
[6] J. B. *Lightfoot, 'Strength made perfect in weakness' (1873).
[7] G. K. *Rickards, 'The House of Commons; its struggles and triumphs. A lecture' (1856).
[8] Statement on govt. business: *H* ccxv. 7.
[9] James Spicer, 1807-88, nonconformist and treasurer of City Liberal Association.
[10] Spoke on currency and the 1844 Act; *H* ccxv. 155.

I requested him to write, & this morning the inclosed letter reached me.[1] I find Glyn has heard a good deal on the same subject. It was one day mentioned, as I remember, in the Cabinet; but I do not recollect that the facts referred to by Mr Rathbone as to the rules in force were brought out. You will judge better than I can whether the Company can be brought to surrender their contract—could there be a Memorandum prepared in the Treasury setting out the whole case? I shall be glad either to hear from or to speak to you as may be most convenient.[2]

26. Wed.

Wrote to Rev S.E.G.—Chancr of Exr—Atty General—Ld Shaftesbury—The Queen—and minutes. Saw Ld F. Cavendish—Attorney General—Mr Glyn. Read Picton Xtn Pantheism[3]—Reclus on the Ocean.[4] H. of C. 12½-2½ and 3¾-5½. Voted in 280:217 for 2 R of Mr O. Morgan's Bill.[5] Dined at the Egyptian Hall to meet the Mayors: returned thanks for Ministers.[6]

27. Th.

Wrote to Mr de Krausse[7]—Bp of Winchester—Ld Hatherley—Ld Chancellor—The Queen—and minutes. Dined with the Farquhars. Saw Sir Shafto Adair—Ld F. Cavendish—Mr Glyn—Mr Forster—Mr Pugin—Ld Hatherley—Mr Bruce—Chancr of Exchr. Visited the Bernstorff family, & saw the Ambassador dead, in his deep and holy peace. H. of C. 4¼-8¼ and 9¾-1¾.[8] Read O'Keeffe Papers—Fitzgibbons Banded Ministry[9]—Kenelm Chillingly.[10]

28. Fr.

Wrote to Sir A. Panizzi—Capt.(?) Cole[11]—Ld Lytton—Sir T. Biddulph—The Queen—and minutes. Saw Ld F. Cavendish—Lord

[1] Early disquiet about the Cape mail contract, later a major scandal; see July 73 *passim.*
[2] Lowe sent relevant papers, 26 March 1873, Add MS 44302, f. 119.
[3] J. A. *Picton, 'Christian pantheism', *The mystery of matter and other essays* (1873).
[4] See 30 Jan. 73.
[5] Burials Bill: *H* ccxv. 213; an important nonconformist demand.
[6] *The Times*, 27 March 1873, 12b.
[7] First secretary of the German embassy; had written about Bernstorff's d. this day; Hawn P.
[8] Opposed Newdegate's motion for a select cttee. on business; *H* ccxv. 239.
[9] G. *Fitzgibbon, *A banded ministry and the Upas Tree* (1873).
[10] By Lord Lytton (1873), sent by his s. Edward Robert, 1st earl of Lytton 1880; Add MS 44438, f. 131.
[11] Unable to help Capt. Francis Burton Owen Cole, 1838-1912, s. of O.B., get a job in India; Add MS 44542, f. 103.

Chancellor—Mr Myles[1] *cum* Genr. Schenck—Ld Ripon—Mr Glyn (2)—Ld Granville—Att. General—Mr Leeman. H of C. 4½-8.[2] Read J.B. Smith on Currency[3]—Kenelm Chillingly. 15 G.S. in evg. X.

29. Sat.

Wrote to Ld Halifax—Chancr of Exr (2)—Ld Hatherley—Mr Ellice—The Queen—Mr Rathbone—& minutes. Cabinet 2½-6¼. Dined with Sir A. Panizzi: Mrs Glyn's party afterwards. Saw Ld F. Cavendish—Mr Glyn (2)—Mr Leeman. Read Plea for Ch. Defence—Kenelm Chillingly. Visited French Gallery—Maclean's Gallery.[4]

Cabinet. March 29. 73. 2½ P.M.[5]

√ Fawcett's Bill. Memorandum (herewith)[6] adopted. Cardwell to make known to Mr F.

√ Fortescue's Clause—G. G. G[lyn]. Clause considered—to be postponed if possible? I was to arrange with Cross.[7]

Shah of Persia. While Queen's guest, expences must be left to the Civil List. For the other expences a vote: see WEG's letter to Ld Sydney[8]—read before sending[,] to Granville & Lowe.

√ Easter Adjournment. to 21st. 1. Budget, 2. Educn., 3. Local Taxn.

√ App[ointmen]t to the Rolls. Chancellor cannot discharge the duties without a Bill. Halifax to try (with Belper) for the *postponement* of Romilly's resignation with a promise of Chancellor to take the bulk of the business.[9]

√ Dover Harbour Bill. Mr F[ortescue] to put Huwlishaw in communication with Col. Clark as to a plan providing for objects of both.[10]

√ Alderney. Duke of S[omerset] to be asked to postpone.[11] Committee of Cabinet—De Grey, Halifax (Convenor), Cardwell, Lowe, Goschen, Childers, Fortescue.

Ld Chancellor mentioned that a magistrate presided at a Dilke meeting & acted as fugleman to, or otherwise encouraged, for the coming Republic. To stand over to next Cabinet.[12]

30. 5 S.Lent.

Chapel Royal mg & evg: after a severe face ache in part of the night. Wrote minutes. Read Puseys Sermons[13]—The Mystery of

[1] Unidentified.

[2] Misc. business: *H* ccxv. 305.

[3] J. B. Smith, 'An enquiry into the causes of money panics' (1866).

[4] Thomas Maclean, see *Art Journal* (1873), 148.

[5] Add MS 44641, f. 85.

[6] Add MS 44761, f. 116.

[7] Clause 5, on powers of fixing rates, of Railway and Canal Traffic Bill; Cross's amndt., making clear the commission had no power to revise railway rates, accepted by the govt.; *H* ccxv. 361. Diarist's notes, perhaps for meeting with Cross, at Add MS 44641, f. 87.

[8] See *LQV*, 2nd series, ii. 250.

[9] See 22 Apr. 73n.

[10] See Fortescue's answers, *H* ccxv. 1027, 1788.

[11] Alderney Harbour Fortifications; see *H* ccxv. 331.

[12] Apparently not further discussed.

[13] See 2 Feb. 73.

Matter[1]—The Pentateuch—Sacerdotalism—Greg on Christian Life.[2]

31. M.

Wrote to Chancr of Exr (2)—The Queen—and minutes. Luncheon with Mrs Th. Read Kenelm Chillingly. Dined with the Jameses. Saw Ld F. Cavendish—Mr Knowles—Mr Glyn—Duke of Argyll—Mr Sullivan—Lord A. Hervey—Mr Forster—Depn of County Members at H of C.[3] Visited Mr Noble's Studio. Visited Christie's. H of C. 4½-8¼ and 9½-1¼.[4] Wrote Mem. on Currency.

Mem. by WEG on Bank Charter Act of 1844. 29 [sc. 31] Mch. 73.[5]
1. Bank Rates of discount since the year 1844 (passing of the Act) & hereafter, to be recorded at Somerset House.
2. Whenever that rate shall read the highest point theretofore recorded the Bank shall deliver Notes from the Issue Department to all persons applying for them in sums of not less than £ [blank], upon a deposit of Public Securities to an Extent of not less than 30 per cent (acc[ordin]g to the prices ruling) in excess of the issue.
3. A corresponding amount of notes shall be returned by the person receiving the Issue in three months: & the securities held against them shall be sold if they are not so returned. The nett Balance to belong to the receiver of the Issue: subject to a fine of ten pounds per Centum.[6]
4. The interest upon such notes to be deducted at the time of Issue, & to be carried to the public account; & to be at the said highest rate of discount, or such higher rate as the First Lord of the Treasury & the Chancr. of the Exchr. acting together may direct.
5. If the Notes be returned within the three months, allowance shall be made to the receiver of them for the unexpired portion of the term, according to the then last recorded rate of discount at the Bank.

Tues. Ap. One 1873.

Wrote to Mrs Wm Gladstone—The Queen Mem. and l.—Rev. J.B. Miles[7]—Ld Lytton—Ld Chancellor—Ld Romilly—Mr Tennyson —& minutes. H of C. 4½-8½ and 9¼-12¾.[8] Read Kenelm Chillingly. Saw Ld F. Cavendish—Ld Halifax—Mr Bright—Mr Glyn. Corrected

[1] J. A. *Picton, *The mystery of matter and other essays* (1873).
[2] W. R. *Greg, *The creed of Christendom* (1851).
[3] No report found.
[4] Railways: *H* ccxv. 349.
[5] Copied by the secretary, but initialled and dated by Gladstone, Add MS 44761, f. 121. See 17 May 73.
[6] This phrase added in Gladstone's hand.
[7] Had sent details of his work for international arbitration; Add MS 44542, f. 104.
[8] Questioned on his appt. of *King at Oxford; *H* ccxv. 401.

Irish Univ. Bill: a labour of hope![1] Also correcting speech on 2 R. of the Bill.

2. Wed.

Wrote to Mr Childers—Mrs Thistlethwayte—Mr Lake—Robn G.—and minutes. Visited Mr Woolner's Studio. Inquiries respecting Russell & others: saw two[R]. Saw Ld Lyttelton—Ld F. Cavendish—Mr Glyn—Ld Sydney—Persian Envoy[2]—Chr of Exr with Sir W. Stephenson.[3] Dined with Austrian Ambassador.[4] Read Kenelm Chillingly—Ld Russell on Religion.[5]

To H. C. E. CHILDERS, chancellor of duchy of Lancaster, 2 April 1873. Add MS 44542, f. 105.

I am bound to say that I see in clearer & still clearer light the objections towards disturbing the relation fixed by law between the outgoing & the incoming year. Any plan which provides prospectively for meeting the Alabama charge would, it seems to me, be better than this. The idea of abolishing Income Tax is to me highly attractive, both on other grounds & because it tends to public economy, a matter on which you & I are I trust well agreed. But I think your bold plan is open to these remarks. 1. You cannot estimate your prospective surplus higher than the Revenue Departments will let you. 2. You cannot provide the means for abolishing the Income Tax, either in whole or in part, out of new indirect Taxation. 3. Would it not be requisite to go a little beyond this & say that when the Income Tax is abolished *some part* of the means must be got out of some new impost touching property. I have never heard 12/- on spirits mentioned before: but if it can be levied it would be an excellent measure. I hope Lowe may be able to make proposals which will not be unacceptable to you.[6]

3. Th.

Wrote to Earl Russell—Rev Mr Drummond—Chr of Exr—Rev Mr Molesworth—D. of Argyll—The Queen—& minutes. Eight to dinner. H of C. 4½-8¼ and 9¾-2¾.[7] Saw Sir Thos Biddulph—Ld F. Cavendish—Mr Glyn—Mr Lawley—Mr Ouvry—Ld Ripon. Saw Stanley X. Read K. Chillingly—De Claris Oratoribus.[8]

[1] Add MS 44620, f. 131.
[2] See 5 Apr. 73.
[3] To meet a dpn. on brewers' licenses; he could not see how the chancellor 'is to get rid of this tax [the malt duty]'; *Daily Telegraph*, 3 April 1873, 9.
[4] Count Beust.
[5] Earl Russell, *Essays on the rise and progress of the Christian religion in the west of Europe* (1873).
[6] No letter from Childers on this traced, but see his mem. of 22 September 1873 on spirit duties, Add MS 44128, f. 247.
[7] Spoke on *Pall Mall Gazette*'s attack on ultramontanists: *H* ccxv. 540.
[8] By Cicero, on famous authors.

The Picture Gallery at 11, Carlton House Terrace

Sir Stephen Glynne

Lucy and Frederick Cavendish

George Lyttelton and Gladstone

Helen

Herbert

Mary

Agnes

Helen, William, and Catherine Gladstone at Penmaenmawr, with others.
See 27 August 1874.

Catherine and William Gladstone

Gladstone in Privy Councillor's uniform, *c.* 1873

4. Fr.

Confined to bed through the day by a bronchial attack. Wrote to Ld Adv.—& minutes. Saw Mr Glyn. Read K. Chillingly—Ld Russell on Religion.

5. Sat.

Rose at 11.30 for Cabinet 12-3½. Wrote to Ld Hartington—The Queen. 1. & 2 Mema—Chancellor of Exchequer—and minutes. Saw Chancellor of Exchequer—Ld Granville—Mr Glyn—Ld F. Cavendish. Dinner party, with evening party afterwards, for the Prince & Princess of Wales. They were both charming, as usual. All ended a few minutes before 12. Read K. Chillingly—Lord Russell on Religion.

Cabinet. Ap. 5. 73. 12 o'clock. 11 C.H.T.[1]

√ Budget—agreed to.[2]
√ Local Taxation (double reply to L[opes])
√ Education—compulsion given up, for the present—Clause 25 to have a substitute—a Bill.
√ Answer Dixon. Budget first business. Motion of Lopez may attach that subject to the Budget. May make it proper for us to announce our intentions on a very early day. We may therefore probably be obliged to postpone the introduction of the Education Bill until after we have decided our intentions respecting Local Govt. & Local Taxation.[3]
√ Stansfeld's notices of Committee and Bill or Bills to be given. For May?
√ Elcho question. Ld Kimberley will address a meeting in the recess & express general favour to security for improvements. Landlords consent a question of detail.[4]
√ Candlish's question.[5] look to discussion on Fowler's Bill as of more advantage.
√ Ld Granville. Persian min[iste]r suggests asking an engagement from Russia to respect integrity of Persian Empire. The old engagement [of 1834] remains: no new step necessary.[6]
√ Telegram to Penang: tel. arrived saying he[7] has prohibited the export of Arms to Acheen.[8] Ask for reasons: gain time without simple acquiescence. There may be local reasons. (ev[enin]g[?] Dutch it has been done prob[abl]y on special grounds[)].[9]

[1] Add MS 44641, f. 93.

[2] Jottings on it at ibid., f. 96.

[3] Substance of answer to Dixon on 7 April; *H* ccxv. 634.

[4] Elcho's question on a private member's bill on 7 April; ibid. 644; for Kimberley's speech at Ipswich, see *The Times*, 18 April 1873, 6a.

[5] Never asked.

[6] 'It would be highly inexpedient to make any observations to Russia which might imply a doubt as to the continued validity of the 1834 agreement'; to Thomson, 24 April, PRO FO 60/348.

[7] i.e. Sir Archibald Edward Harbord Anson, 1826-1925; governed Straits 1871-3, 1877, 1879.

[8] War had broken out in Sumatra between the Dutch and the Achinese.

[9] This phrase apparently added later. See Granville to Sir E. Harris, 3 April, PRO CO 273/73; note by Kimberley, 4 Apr., CO 273/73: 'It was agreed between Ld. Granville & me last night that we would *not* forbid the export of arms'. See 10 May 73.

6. Palm Sunday.

Kept my bed again, till 7 P.M. Then much better. Read my service. Wrote to Rev Mr Bickersteth—Madam Novikoff—Canon Selwyn —& minutes. Read Pusey's Sermons—Ld Russell (finished)—Canon Selwyn on the Creeds[1]—Armstrong's Trag. Israel.[2]

7. M.

Wrote to Lord Huntley—Archdn Stopford—The Queen—Master of Lovat—Ld Rosebery[3]—Lady C. Schreiber—Ld Stair—J. Watson & Smith—Mrs Wortley—Mayor of Bradford—Mr Baxter—Sir A. Spearman—& minutes. Saw Ld F. Cavendish—Mr Stansfeld —Mr Glyn. Read Atalanta.[4] H. of C. 4¼-8 and 9-2. The Budget & its reception make a real onward step in the Session.[5] Luncheon at 15 G.S. Finished correcting Speech on 2 R. Univ. Bill.

8. Tu. [Windsor]

Wrote to Mr [A.] M'Lelland[6]—Prov. of Dumbarton[7]—Mr Macmahon—Mr Eastwick—B. Benjamin—Ld Granville—Sir T. Biddulph (Tel.)—and minutes. Read Kenelm Chillingly. Saw Ld F. Cavendish—Mr Glyn—Mr Stansfeld—Sir T. Biddulph. Packing books &c for departure. Off to Windsor at 5. Long audience of H.M. who was extremely well & very gracious. Dined with H.M. Whist with Prince Leopold.

To P. MacMAHON, M.P., 8 April 1873. Add MS 44542, f. 109.

I have the honour to acknowledge your letter of the 3d.[8] in which you transmit a representation signed by a large number of Irish members & expressing the desire that a Bill may be passed for the purpose of placing the representation of the Irish people on the same footing as that of the people of England. My own views of the last Irish Reform Bill are sufficiently upon record, but I am not convinced that it would be possible to comply (so far as the Government are concerned) with the Representation now before me unless when Parliament was prepared to enter upon the question more at large. At least I fear I cannot give any promise at this period of the Session to deal with the subject during the present year.

[1] W. *Selwyn, *The creeds of Nicaea, Constantinople, Athanasius, with extracts* (1873).
[2] G. F. Armstrong, *The tragedy of Israel*, 3 pt. (1872-76).
[3] Offering him the lord lieutenancy of Linlithgow, eventually accepted; Add MS 44542 and Crewe, *Rosebery*, i. 85.
[4] See 6 Mar. 73.
[5] *H* ccxv. 669.
[6] Thanking him for support of a public meeting at Kilmarnock; Add MS 44542, f. 109.
[7] Enclosing copy of letter of thanks.
[8] Not found.

9. Wed. [Hawarden]

Castle Chapel prayers. St George's service at 10.30. Saw Sir T. Biddulph—Mrs Wellesley. Off at 12.35. Reached Hawarden Rectory about 8. Read & finished Kenelm Chillingly: a book of high aims and much high workmanship: the latter part is harrowing, yet not untrue. Found Stephy & all well. Read the Tragedy of Israel.

10. Th.

Church (H.C.) at 8 AM; evg prayer & Serm. 7 PM. Wrote to Prince Leopold—Mr Hutchinson[1]—Mr Ayrton—Mr Harrison—Ld Crewe—Mr Richard MP.—and minutes. Read Pattison on Academic Organisation[2]—Panam & Duke of Coburg.[3] Saw Mr Burnett on a long series of affairs. Walk with C.

11. Good Friday

Ch 11 AM 7 PM. Wrote minutes. Conversation with Stephy. Walk with the boys, getting primroses. Read Huber on Strauss (finished)[4]—Mossman's Hist of the Church[5]—Origen (Engl.)—Tragedy of Israel (finished)—Colenso, Ten Weeks in Natal.[6]

12. Sat.

Church 8 AM. (with H.C.) and 7 P.M. Wrote to Chairman LNW.RR.—Rev Mr Harvey—Rev Mr Brodrick—Mr Morier—and minutes. Saw Mr Burnett. Cutting part of a large ash. Read Pattison on Acad. Orgn—Young Greek Lady[7]—Rennell on Antediluvian History.[8]

13. Easter Day.

Service at 8 AM—H.C.—11 AM—and 6.30 P.M. Our five present children all went to the Holy Altar. Wrote to Ld Hartington—Ld Granville—Sir G. Prevost. Walk with my sons. Wrote minutes. Read

[1] G. Hutchinson of the C.M.S., preferring his correspondence with Henry *Venn in 1849-50 should not be published; Add MS 44542, f. 110.

[2] M. *Pattison, *Suggestions on academical organisation, with especial reference to Oxford* (1868).

[3] *Memoirs of a young Greek Lady, Madame P. A. A. Panam, against his Serene Highness the reigning prince of Saxe-Cobourg* (1823).

[4] See 21 Jan. 73.

[5] T. W. *Mossman, *A history of the Catholic Church of Jesus Christ* (1873).

[6] J. W. *Colenso, *Ten weeks in Natal* (1855).

[7] See 10 Apr. 73.

[8] J. *Rennell, probably *Remarks on the topography of ancient Babylon* (1816).

Colenso's Ten Weeks—Mossman's Hist. of the Ch.—Molloy's Geology and Revelation.[1]

14. M.

Church 8¾ AM. Wrote to Duke of Argyll—Sir W. Knollys—Mr Hall—Mrs Th.—Robn G. (2)—Scotts—and minutes. I cancelled No 2 to Robn for fear it should wound.[2] The tree was brought down this forenoon: a difficult but successful fall. Read Narration of D. of Coburg—the Greek Lady: bad enough is the picture.—Pattison's Suggestions—Milton's Poems. Worked a short time on my accounts.

15. Tu.

Ch. 8¾ AM. Wrote to Archdeacon Stopford—Robn G (& Mem.)—Miss Watson—Bp of Lichfield—M. Musurus—Duchess of Sutherland—and minutes. Read Pattison (finished)—Macknight's Bolingbroke.[3] Saw Mr Burnett. Arranged my published productions: and worked on accounts.[4] Tooth or face ach in evg.

16. Wed.

Ch. 8½ AM. Wrote to Ld Granville—Mrs Bennett—Mr Stapleton—and minutes. Walk with Stephy to the Pentre to examine premises. Suffering off & on. Read Newman on Universities[5]—Macknight's Bolingbroke—Swinburne's Atalanta—The Odyssey—Colenso's Ten Weeks.

17. Th.

Ch. 8½ A.M. My bag today brought four or five hours reading. Wrote to Mr Hammond—Chancr of Exr—Mr Bright—Sir W. Knollys—Ld Granville—and minutes. Saw Mr Burnett. A pleasant conversation with Herbert on his Oxford life & work. Read Newman on Univv. Still pressed with face ach. But we began cutting an oak.

To E. HAMMOND, 17 April 1873. Add MS 44542, f. 112.

I send back your budget[6] which contains a good deal of matter for reflection. I am not much surprised that the Law Officers of 1873 should have reversed

[1] G. *Molloy, *Geology and revelation* (1870).
[2] Querying R. Gladstone's accounts *re* the Seaforth estate; Hawn P, marked 'cancelled'.
[3] See 14 Mar. 63.
[4] Of Seaforth estate; Add MS 44620, f. 150.
[5] See 20 Jan. 73.
[6] Not found.

(if they have reversed) the law of 50 or 60 years back. There was then a state of things, or the tradition of a state of things, in which we had friends & enemies & nothing else. Since then we have had an age marked by the internal divisions of countries, breaking up & re-arranging. Hence has arisen all this taking sides without making war: which I for one do not like & shall not be sorry to see reproved in any way in which we can safely & effectually get at it. As to the publication of the opinions it can hardly be a matter of wonder—it is only at the time of giving that they are confidential—the presumption of anything undue seems to me the faintest possible. I was confined to bed on the day of the Euphrates Railway Debate & did not therefore hear the speech of the Chancellor of the Exchequer.

To R. LOWE, chancellor of the exchequer, Add MS 44542, f. 113.
17 April 1873.

1. On Monday afternoon I hope to see this wonderful head called of Aphrodite, & we can speak of the collection in the evening—the sum is stiff but the purchase may be proper.
2. Do you know Pattison's book on Academical organisation? I have only now become acquainted with it, & I think it the most powerful & searching (though not free from exaggeration) that I have seen. On his practical proposals there is a great deal to be said; but it may be called a gallant scheme.
3. Might you not with advantage invite one or two of the best Railway men to offer to you suggestions as to the best mode of giving them some relief as to their low-fared passenger traffic in such a shape as to be not a mere boon but rather an inducement to them to do something more for the public? I do not know whether Excursion trains at present share in this relief: there is a good deal to be said against new inducements to run them in preference to the regular traffic. I send you a letter from the Lord Advocate on which also we can speak.

18. Fr.

Ch. 8½ AM. Wrote to Duchess of Sutherland—Mr Godley Tel. & l.—Robn G.—J. Watson & Smith—and minutes. Saw Mr Burnett. We felled the oak. Read Newman on Univv.—Macknight's Bolingbroke.

19. Sat.

Ch. 8½ AM. Wrote to Ld Provost of Glasgow—Sir T. Biddulph—Ld Chancellor—Sir R. Phillimore—Mr Godley Tel.—& minutes. Finished Newman. Read Macknight's Bolingbroke—Odyssey (the Geogr.)—Colenso's Ten Weeks. Visited Oaks Farm with Mr Burnett. Saw Mr Lyte.

20. 1 S.E.

Ch 11 AM (with H.C.) and 6½ P.M. Walk with C.G.—Saw Mrs Povah:

near death. Read Picton's Xtn Pantheism[1]—Mossman's Hist. of the Church—and [blank]. Wrote to Mr Godley—Mrs Hampton—and minutes. Saw Mr Burnett.

21. M. [London]

At 8 AM bade adieu to Stephy and his pure, active, happy home. Euston at 2.30. Saw the Hanmers: we travelled together from Crewe. To Crewe, a geological & coalmining conversation. Drove to the Museum to see the Castellani antiquities. H of C. 4½-9¼ and 10¼-1¼. Spoke on Dubl. Tests Bill.[2] Read Owen's India.[3] Wrote to The Queen —and minutes.

22. Tu.

Wrote to The Queen (2)—Ld Chancellor—C.G.—& minutes. Saw Mr Glyn—Mr Bruce—Mr Sanders (who operated freely)[4] and others. Cabinet 2-4¼. Saw Louisa G. H of C. 4½-8¼ and 9½-12¾.[5] Read Q.R. on Greek Studies & Irish Univ.[6]

Cabinet. Ap. 22/73. 2 P.M.[7]

Questions.
√ Lopez—terms of Answer.
√ Gregory—left between Ld Ch[ancellor] & A. G[eneral].[8]
√ Stapylton—terms cons[idere]d to be settled with Granville.[9]
√ Divinity School Dublin Univ. WEG stated circs.—agreed to shun the invitation.[10]
√ Brewer Licences. WEG to reply to Sir S[elwin-]Ibbetson.[11]
√ Ld Selborne's Bill. WEG informed Cabinet of Ld S's proposals acc[ording] to his note.[12]
√ Howard & Read [Agricultural Children] Bill. Support 2d reading—but take as little initiative or prominent share as possible.[13]
√ Ld Granville—preparatory cases on Suez—Zanzibar.

[1] See 30 Mar. 73.
[2] University Tests (Dublin) (No. 3) Bill: *H* ccxv. 768.
[3] See 28 Feb. 73.
[4] i.e. the dentist.
[5] Told Lopes of decision that there would be no local taxation measure this session; *H* ccxv. 798.
[6] *Quarterly Review*, cxxxiv. 457, 552 (April 1873).
[7] Add MS 44641, f. 98.
[8] On vacancy in the Rolls, answered by Gladstone on 24 April; *H* ccxv. 899.
[9] J. Stapleton, on aid to Carlists, answered by Gladstone on 24 April, ibid. 896.
[10] To receive a dpn.? Correspondence untraced.
[11] Question not put; for Ibbetson's views, see *H* ccxv. 1636.
[12] *Selborne circulated cabinet memoranda on his Land Title and Transfer Bill and his Real Property Limitation Bill; Add MS 44620, f. 154.
[13] The bill received 3°R on 8 May, but failed in the Lords; Howard was not an official sponsor; *H* ccxv. 1708.

23. Wed.

Wrote to The Speaker—Mr Dixon MP.—Mr Freshfield—C.G.—and minutes. Dined at Mr Thistlethwayte's. Breakfast with Mr C. Field to meet Mr Emerson.[1] Saw Duke of Argyll. Saw Mrs Graham—E. Terry. Saw Temple X & another. 56 GC Griffins.[2] Read Hare on Spain.[3] Saw Beresford Hope on Univv.

24. Th.

Wrote to The Queen—Ld Granville—Col. Hogg[4]—C.G.—& minutes. Thirteen to breakfast. Read Q.R. Saw Ld Granville—Lord F. Cavendish—Mr Glyn—Chancr of Exr—Att. General—Income Tax Deputation.[5] H of C. $4\frac{1}{4}$-$8\frac{1}{2}$ and $9\frac{1}{2}$-$1\frac{1}{4}$.[6]

25. Fr.

Wrote to Sir T. Brinckman—The Queen—& minutes. H of C. $4\frac{1}{2}$-$8\frac{1}{2}$ and $9\frac{1}{2}$-$12\frac{1}{4}$: leaving early from being unwell.[7] Saw Ld Hanmer—Ld F. Cavendish—Mr Glyn—Ld Granville—Mr Burnett. Read S.C. Hall's Memories.[8] Examined before the Wrexham & Birkenhead R.R. Commns at 12.[9] Sat to Mr Nottage[10] Photographer: saw some Tichborne letters.

26. Sat.

Wrote to Ld Ripon—The Queen (2)—D. of St Alban's—Ld Provost of Glasgow—Mr E. Hamilton—Mr J. Gibson[11]—& minutes. Saw Ld Kimberley—Mr Glyn—Ld Ripon—Rose in time for the Cabinet at 12 (in the diningroom) & sat till 4. Read Outlines of German Literature[12]—Q.R. on Middlemarch, and on Montalembert.[13] Saw Dr A. Clark.

[1] Ralph Waldo Emerson; see B. Perry, *The heart of Emerson's journals* (1938), 336.
[2] This phrase in pencil.
[3] A. J. C. *Hare, *Wanderings in Spain* (1873).
[4] On London bridge tolls and local taxation, printed in the *Daily Telegraph*, 26 April 1873.
[5] From the Anti-Income Tax League; *The Times*, 25 April 1873, 5f; his 'own desires were in the same direction as those of the deputation'.
[6] Made statement on Spanish situation, spoke on licences; *H* ccxv. 896, 910.
[7] Only missing three-quarters of an hour; *H* ccxv. 1023.
[8] S. C. *Hall, *A book of memories of great men and women of the age, from personal acquaintance* (1871).
[9] Unsuccessfully supporting its extension to Hawarden; *Chester Chronicle*, 3 May 1873.
[10] Not further identified.
[11] James Gibson, commissioner of Irish national education; on O'Keeffe; Add MS 44542, f. 115.
[12] J. Gostwick and R. Harrison, *Outlines of German Literature* (1873).
[13] [R. Laing, A. Hayward], *Quarterly Review*, cxxxiv. 336 (April 1873).

Cabinet. Ap. 26 (at noon) 1873. 11 Carlton H. Terrace.[1]

Week's business.

√ Smith's motion—arrange for debate. Lowe to follow [W. H. Smith].[2]

√ Irish Railways. Some are [?].[3] Ask for Lord C. Hamilton's Resolution. WEG or Ld H[artington] to follow.[4]

√ Callan Schools. Information to be had respecting O'Keeffe's position *quoad* the schools in the event of an adverse judgment.[5] Ld H[artingto]n to signify to the Comm[issione]rs the inclination of Parlt. & its probable course in the event of a judgment favourable to O'Keeffe.

√ Women's Disabilities—open.

√ Tithe Commutation Bill (Chancellor absent). Bruce to communicate with Ld Chr.[6]

√ Fawcett's Bill. Wilson Patten's sketch of amendment. No decision except to avoid initiative.[7]

√ Holms: question on Cape Contract. C. of Exchequer to ask Co. whether they wd. go back on their old contract: offering at the same time to reconsider terms of East side contract.[8]

Stansfeld's notice: as to finance, stand upon my answer to Lopez. Four parts—two Bills. a. repeal of exemptions. b. valuation of property: for uniformity of answer. c. Consolidated Rate. d. Definitions & general provisions. New rule of valuation of Govt. buildings for local taxation will apply to buildings owned by local authorities as to their valuation for Imperial taxes. Exemption of palaces to be maintained not extended. Churches, Chapels, Meeting Houses exempt. Ragged Schools & Sunday ditto. Repeal Act allowing Parish to pay. Local Govt: touches motion for a Committee.[9]

O Ld C. Hamilton: shipwreck motion. Fortescue gone.[10]

√ P. A. Taylor: Sunday opening of Museums & [blank]. Refer to state of public opinion & negative accordingly. Not a Govt. decision.[11]

√ Layard's Telegram: to shelter Topele & Serrano in the Legation. Assume that the 'armed bands' are anarchical.[12]

√ Zanzibar—Committee of Cabinet (open) on Monday 3 PM. respecting the question of further instructions to Sir B. Frere.

√ Postal Contract with Australia. Telegram agreed to. Colonies not being unanimous we cannot decide. Make known offer of P. & O. for prolongation—& offer to accept them.

√ Ld Chancellor's Bills. No objection to his introducing them.

√ Peace Preservation Act & Westmeath Act. Expire June 1—to be renewed.

[1] Add MS 44641, f. 102.

[2] Attempt by tories to link unpopularity of income tax with demands for local taxation reduction: *H* ccxv. 1041; see 1 May 73.

[3] Word unclear.

[4] Lord C. Hamilton moved the state purchase of Irish railways; see 29 Apr. 73.

[5] See 3 May 73.

[6] Referred to select cttee; *H* ccxv. 1178.

[7] He supported Patten's amndt. on professors of theology; *H* ccxv. 1532.

[8] Ibid. 1488. See 3 May 73.

[9] Stansfeld brought in two bills, and a Consolidated Rates Bill, on 5 May; ibid., 1491.

[10] Presumably, from the cabinet room.

[11] Question not put.

[12] Serrano, the ex-Regent, was already in the Legation; Layard eventually had to smuggle him in disguise to a boat for France; see G. Waterfield, *Layard of Nineveh* (1963), 336. 'Topele' is a slip for Admiral J. B. Topete, 1821–85, colleague of Serrano.

27. Sat.

Mg prayers in mg: bed: Chapel Royal aftn. Wrote minutes. Saw Mr Glyn—Mr Elliot—Ld Lyttelton. Read Angelique Arnauld[1]—Pusey's Sermons—Examnn of Liddon[2]—and Tracts. Saw Mr Glyn.

28. M.

Rose at 11, after seeing Dr Clark. Wrote to Col. Ponsonby—Cambridge Secretaries—Ld Hartington—Mr Grieve—Dr Döllinger—Mr Cardwell—The Queen—& minutes. Luncheon at 15. G.S. Saw Ld F. Cavendish—Mr Glyn—Mr Burnett—Lady E.M. Pringle—Mr Cardwell. H of C. 4½-8¼ & 9¼-1¾.[3] Read S.C. Hall's Memories—Harrison Germ. Literature. Saw Mr Forster—Mr Childers—Ld Advocate—Mr Cardwell.

29. Tu.

Wrote to Ld Hatherley—The Queen (2 Mema and l.)—M. Musurus—Mr Jacob Bright: & minutes. H of C. 4½-8¼ and 9¼-12¾. Spoke on Irish Railways.[4] Saw Mr E. Freshfield—Ld Granville—Mr Glyn—Ld F. Cavendish—Ld Hartington—Mr [Lowes] Dickinson—Mr Bruce. Visited Christie's. Spent near an hour in the gentle hands of Mr Sanders.[5] Visited Mr Dickinson's. Read German Literature—Westmr Rev. on WEG's 'Defence of the Faith'.[6]

30. Wed.

Wrote to Abp of Canterbury—Abp Manning—Fortnum & Mason—Sec.Met.Dist.Co.—& minutes. Dined at Mad. Ralli's. Sat to Mr Dickinson. Saw Ld F. Cavendish—Mr Stansfeld—Mr Glyn—
Mr Russell }
Mr Benjamin } virtù. i.e. vice—
Lord Chancellor—Count Beust—The Wortleys—Sir J. Benedict. I went to see the remains of my dear friend James Hope Scott.[7] Many sad memories: but more joyful hopes. Read German Literature—Ed. Rev. on the Ministry[8]—On German Religious Movement.

[1] F. Martin, *Angelique Arnauld* (1873).
[2] *An examination of Canon Liddon's Bampton Lectures. By a clergyman of the C. of E.* (1871).
[3] W. H. *Smith's motion on direct and indirect taxation: *H* ccxv. 1041.
[4] *H* ccxv. 1157.
[5] His dentist.
[6] *Westminster Review*, xliii. 367 (April 1873).
[7] Who d. 29 April.
[8] Vindication by [H. *Reeve] of whiggery as true conservatism, *Edinburgh Review*, cxxxvii. 581 (April 1873).

To FORTNUM and MASON, grocers, Add MS 44542, f. 116.
30 April 1873. 'Private.'

I have often heard that it is the custom of grocers & all who deal in sugar to sell that article upon rather bare profits as compared with the usual & what may be called regular profits of trade. Would you kindly give me the advantage of hearing on authority whether this is so. There would be no necessity for my naming you in any reference I might make in Parliament to the subject.[1]

Thurs May One SS.Phil. & J.

Wrote to Mr Ormsby Gore—Mr H. Reeve—The Queen—& minutes. Worked on Finance: for the Budget Debate. Saw Ld F. Cavendish—Mr Glyn. Read 'German Literature'. Arr. some ornaments for sale. H of C. 4½-8½ & 9½-1¼. Spoke 1¼ h. in closing the debate. A strange ending.[2]

Frid. May 2.73.

Saw Ld F. Cavendish—Mr Ouvry—Mr Sanders. Private view R.Acad. Exhibn twice. H of C. 4¼-8½ and 9½-12¾. Spoke on (Ld G. Hamilton's) Oregon & St Juan.[3] Wrote to The Queen—Read German Literature.

3. Sat. [*St. George's Hill, Weybridge*][4]

Wrote to The Queen—Ld Chancr—Mrs Th.—and minutes. Cabinet 12¼-3½. Breakfasted at Grillion's. Conversation with Ld Houghton on Homer. Saw Mr Glyn—Ld Granville. Off at 3.45 to St George's Hill. Walk with Adm E[gerton]. Read Hist. of Cartmel[5]—D. d'Aumale's Montalembert.[6]

Cabinet. May 3. 73. Noon.[7]

√ O'Keeffe case. Commissioners propose a Committee on their 'action'. Agree to one on the facts: not to report an opinion on conduct. A small Committee. They shd. request it.[8]

√ Univ. Tests Dublin Bill. We stand by the promoters as a body. If they split, we support Wilson Patten's amendment.[9]

[1] He dealt with this point in his speech on 1 May.

[2] After a powerful appeal by Gladstone against irresponsible taxation, W. H. *Smith's amndt. to the budget resolutions was not divided upon; *H* ccxv. 1371.

[3] *H* ccxv. 1446.

[4] F. Egerton's; see 6 Aug. 70.

[5] J. Stockdale, *Annales Caernoelenses; or Annals of Cartmel* (1872).

[6] H. E. P. L. d'Orleans, Duke d'Aumale, 'Discours [on Montalembert] . . . à l'Académie Française' (1873).

[7] Add MS 44641, f. 104.

[8] Reported evidence only, 18 June: *PP* 1873 ix.

[9] See 26 Apr. 73.

√ Young's Scotch Church Bill. May not be introduced BECAUSE there is no chance of finding time to pass it.
√ Ld Chancellor's Bill—order of business for the Session—consider hereafter.
√ Cape Packet Contract. Counsel Western—renegotiate Eastern—(or Zanzibar) giving them the first chance. Acq[uaint] parties Cabinet had not absolutely announced they wd. not propose the contract.[1]
√ Whalley: Tichborne question—referring to the Treasury.[2]
√ Dilke. oppose Abstract Resolution.[3]
√ Trevelyan. C[ardwell] to oppose passing as proposed.[4]
√ Eykyn. Motion on Police. Oppose if possible.[5]
√ Crimean Monument. C[ardwell] or Gr[anville] to ask D. of Cambridge to put it on Patriotic Fund.
√ Stansfeld. New Clause on Govt. property: considered & settled—and some other points.

4. 3 S. Trin.

Weybridge Ch (2 m. off) and H.C. Saw Mr Currie. Wrote to Ld Kimberley—Ld Granville. Read Union Review—Orations on Montalembert (finished)—Martins Angelique Arnauld.

5. M. [London]

Wrote to Mr Cardwell—The Queen—& minutes. Eight to dinner. Luncheon at 15. G.S. H of C. 4¼–9½ and 10½–1½.[6] Read Outline of German Literature. Saw Ld F. Cavendish—Mr Lambert—Mr Glyn—Ld Advocate—Returned to London by the train (nominally) at 11.1.

6. Tu.

Wrote to Dean of St Paul's—Sir T. Acland MP—The Queen—& minutes. H of C. 4¼–8¼. Spoke on redistribn of seats.[7] Dined with the Jameses. Saw the Light experiment.[8] Saw Bp of Winchester—Ly E.M. Pringle—Mr Murray—D. of Sutherland—Chancr of Exr—Mr Childers *cum* Ld Chancr—Mr Glyn—Ld Lyons. Saw Lawrence—& another X. Read Westmr Rev. on Theology.[9]

[1] 'Articles of agreement' with Union Steamship Company, giving more favourable terms to the Company, in *PP* 1873 xxxix. 487.
[2] See *H* ccxv. 1485.
[3] On distribution of electoral power; ibid. 1561.
[4] On honorary colonelcies; ibid. 1591.
[5] Motion for select cttee. on metropolitan police; ibid. 1733.
[6] Stansfeld's Rating Bills introduced; *H* ccxv. 1491.
[7] On *Dilke's motion (see 3 May 73); *H* ccxv. 1575.
[8] Experiment illuminating Big Ben by electricity; *The Times*, 7 May 1873, 7f.
[9] See 29 Apr. 73.

To Sir T. D. ACLAND, M.P., 6 May 1873. Add MS 44542, f. 117.

In answering your kind letter[1] let me first say how much we have lamented the cause of your absence from town. I am glad however to learn from yourself that you do not regard your son's case as excluding hope. I am glad to think that there seems at this moment to be no special cause for your being pressed to attend Parliament. It is a pleasure to me to have your approval of my speech on Mr Smith's motion;[2] but what a motion it was, & what an advantage it gave us. It has done more than I should have thought possible to repair that loss of *vital force* which we suffered from the affair in March, though I am far from thinking we are restored to full vigour. As to the Times, I suppose it thinks us decrepit knowing us to be old; since it whipped round in the University Bill it has virtually been Disraeli's paper; & hostility to this Government has I believe long been the breath of life to the Pall Mall Gazette, a circumstance which I can but faintly regret. Our present measures on Local Taxation are really the clearing of the ground. Stansfeld's committee will be a step in construction. The great question really is whether we can convert a scheme of plunder into one of Reform. I have not a doubt that the whole system of subvention now existing must be or should be carefully revised, & thanks to Dizzy & Mr Smith we may find ourselves strong enough to do this in the interest of self government & of economy local as well as public: for neither of which Lopez seems really to care provided he can as a leech draw blood from the Exchequer. But there remains a formidable consideration. Suppose all preliminaries settled—good local government established—all the old subsidies revised, controul reduced to its minimum, sound provisions for economy established—& then further a considerable additional transfer of Imperial Funds to local purposes proposed & effected. Let me suppose this transfer to be of $1\frac{1}{2}$ millions annually. That will in the first instance relieve the occupier. But only in the transition stage. Ultimately & infallibly it will be a gift to the owners of realty in town & country: a gift of 50 millions or thereabouts. How is this to be compensated? How, without compensation, is it to be excused, or endured? I send herewith copy of a speech on the University Bill. I think the former one was sent to you.

7. *Wed.*

Wrote to Mr Gale [*sc.* Gore] (cancelled)[3]—Mrs Th.—& minutes. Saw Ld F. Cavendish—Mr Forster *cum* Ld Lyttelton & Mr Glyn—Mr Glyn—Lady Ashburnham—Mr Sanders: he supplied me with a frame: it is a sensible step towards the putting off of this tabernacle. Visited Christie's—Donaldson's.[4] Attended Belshazzar in the evening at the Albert Hall; with much pleasure.[5] Read Jackson's Bath Archives.[6]

[1] Not in Add MS 44092.

[2] See 1 May 73.

[3] G. Gore had sent the *Westminster Review*; Gladstone complained at the title, 'Defence of the Faith', given to his Liverpool address; Add MS 44438, f. 262.

[4] George Donaldson, art dealer in New Bond Street.

[5] Part of the International Exhibition; *The Times*, 8 May 1873, 6f.

[6] Sir G. *Jackson, *The Bath Archives. A further selection from the diaries and letters . . . from 1809 to 1816*, ed. Lady Jackson, 2v. (1873).

8. Th.

Wrote to Ld Kimberley—and minutes. Saw Ld F. Cavendish—Mr Cardwell—Bp of Lichfield—Mr Webb—Mr A. Peel—Dean of Manchr—Ld Lyttelton—The Sassoons[1]—Ld Chancellor—Mr Glyn—Ld Chancr *cum* Ld Granville—Mr Forster—Mr Fortescue. Dined with M. Van de Weyer to meet the K. & Q. of the Belgians. Read Jackson—Unorthodox London[2]—Virgil. H of C. $4\frac{1}{4}$-$7\frac{1}{2}$ and 11-$12\frac{1}{2}$.[3] Saw one[R].

To LORD KIMBERLEY, colonial secretary, 8 May 1873. Add MS 44542, f. 117.

I have been much exercised in mind about Fiji & its annexation or Protectorate.[4] Individually I do not see that there are before us facts which ought to make us move at all. But I am not in possession of the same information as you, nor I think are our colleagues, & I also feel that they & the world without may be much more disposed to move on in this matter than I am. All therefore that I would now say is that I feel a great anxiety to be well informed & should be very glad if you would direct to be prepared as soon as you like a sound general account of what we really know as a Government at this time, about Fiji on these points which bear upon the question whether we ought to establish closer relations with it. There is no likelihood that the question can be raised on Monday. If we get to the choice of one or more Commissioners, that will be a very anxious matter; but clearly in my mind the man, or one of the men, ought to be a man thoroughly possessed of the principles of Colonial Statesmanship as it is understood among us.

9. Fr.

Wrote to Lady Ashburnham—The Queen (2)—Sir J. Cowell—Rev. S.E.G.—Robertson & N[icholson]—Mr Cardwell—Mr Grieve MP.—Ld Kimberley—and minutes. Went to sale at Christie's: portrait of Sir R. Peel.[5] Saw Ld F. Cavendish—Mr Bramwell—Mr Glyn—Ld Normanton. Dined with the F.C.s. H of C. $4\frac{1}{4}$-$8\frac{1}{4}$ and $9\frac{1}{2}$-$1\frac{1}{4}$.[6] Read Dubl.Rev. on Univ. Bill[7]—S. Hall's Memories.

[1] (Sir) Albert Abdullah David *Sassoon, 1818-96; merchant, m. 1858 Hannah; settled in Britain; knighted 1872; cr. bart. 1890.

[2] C. M. Davies, *Unorthodox London; or phases of religious life in the metropolis* (1873).

[3] Misc. business; *H* ccxv. 1699.

[4] Dispatches sent by Kimberley, 30 April, Add MS 44225, f. 29, amplifying telegram (see 25 Feb. 73n); Kimberley suggested sending a commissioner.

[5] He bought *Linnell's portrait of Peel for £57.

[6] Spoke on supply; *H* ccxv. 1774.

[7] *Dublin Review*, xx. 448 (April 1873).

10. Sat.

Wrote to Mr Baxter—Mr Stansfeld—Mr Grieve—Mrs Hope—Mr Bright—The Spanish Minister[1]—The Queen (l. & Tel.)—& minutes. Saw Mr Glyn—Ld F. Cavendish—Mr Lawley—Mr A. West—Ld Granville—Mr Humphrey. Dined with the Sydneys to meet the K. & Q. of the Belgians. Saw Livingstone X Lawrence & . . . . Read Outlines of Germ. Literature. Cabinet 2¼–6.

Cabinet. Sat. May 10. 73. 2.P.M.[2]

√ Gloucester Election. Conversation.[3]

O Course of Procedure—as to the greater Bills—stands over.

√ Whitsuntide Holidays—Tues. May 27—Evg. sitting & adjourn; Thur. June 5 —Reassemble.

√ Week's business—considered. Monday: Supply—Stansfeld Committee—Peace Preservation? Thursday: Hart[ingto]n Committee—Scotch Entail Bill —Peace Preservation Committee? Friday: Miall—Supply. Monday 19th. Local Taxation. Thursday 22d. Education?—Judicature?—consider next week.

√ Endowed Schools: Forster's plan[4] agreed to.

√ Zanzibar—Ld G. reported the proceedings of Committee of Cabinet respecting Zanzibar. Dispatch to Kirk approved.[5] Circular to representatives d[itt]o —answer to Ld [blank];[6] to be reserved. Cabinet Wedy. on this subject.

√ Sugar Refiners. Question to be kept open. C. of E[xchequer] will see F.O. to obviate misunderstanding.

√ Public Prosecutor Bill. Take care there shall be no vested interest. Bill may be brought in.[7]

√ Ld Gr. reported Musurus's having asked whether Holland wd. accept the mediation of Sultan with Achin.[8] We do not encourage the idea.

√ Export of Arms from Singapore and Penang [to Acheen]. Prohibition already assured may continue.[9]

√ Plimsoll's Bill on Wedy: oppose but Fortescue brings in his own Bill on Tues. —for circul[atio]n Wedy.

√ Bouverie's am[endmen]t to the H[artingto]n Committee discussed.[10] Case thought to stand up all right.

√ Dover Harbour. Principle of plan accepted: subject to agreement with the parties as to mode & amount of their contribution.[11]

[1] Accepting his thanks for his Commons' comments; Add MS 44438, f. 266.

[2] Add MS 44641, f. 106.

[3] Govt. lost Gloucester city and Bath on 7 and 8 May.

[4] Two words here deleted. The Emanuel affair; see *H* ccxv. 1950.

[5] Note passed in cabinet by Goschen reads: 'Is India to pay any portion of this Slave Trade business'; Add MS 44641, f. 108. Condemnation of *Frere's action *ultra vires* in ordering seizure of slave-bearing ships; see R. J. Gavin, 'The Bartle Frere mission to Zanzibar 1873', *Historical Journal*, v. 146.

[6] Name deleted; might possibly read 'Tenterden'.

[7] Brought in 22 May, withdrawn 7 July.

[8] Granville's note of 9 May, and dft. to Elliot 15 May, PRO FO 73/2263.

[9] See 5 Apr. 73, and dft. sent with F.O. approval, 12 May, PRO CO 273/73.

[10] The O'Keeffe affair; Bouverie's amndt. defeated by 28; *H* ccxv. 2053.

[11] See 29 Mar. 73.

√ Commission on judicial expenditure acc[ording] to desire of Committee.[1]

To John BRIGHT, M.P., 10 May 1873. Add MS 43385, f. 215.

Though not grudging you your present repose I hope as well as think that the great public interest & importance of the questions to be debated on Tuesday (Emanuel Scheme) & Thursday (Committee on Callan Schools—Irish National Education) will bring you to London. I therefore avail myself of this probable opportunity to ask you whether you would breakfast here at 10 on Thursday morning (15th) to meet the King of the Belgians whom I think you would much like?

[P.S.] I am certain the King would be very glad of an opportunity of meeting you.

11. 4 S.E.

Ch Ch Maryleb. 11 AM. to hear Mr Ll. Davies,[2] who certainly afforded matter enough for thought. Ch. at Putney in aft. Went to see the T. G[ladstone]s at Grantham House—and remained till night. It was most touching to see Ida.[3] Returned by the 10.40—Late. Read Examn of Liddon[4]—Life of Mère Angelique.

12. M.

Wrote to Mrs Hope—Duc d'Aumale—The Queen l. & 2 Mema—Mr [C. T.] Newton B.M.—Ld Granville—Ld Chancr—and minutes. Read Jackson.[5] Saw Ld F. Cavendish—Marq. of Lorne—Mr Glyn—Mr Forster. Luncheon at 15 G.S. H of C. 4¼-8½ and 9½-1¼.[6]

13. Tu.

Wrote to The Queen—Ld Lytton—& minutes. Went down to Windsor & had audience of H.M. Saw Sir T. Biddulph—Dean of Windsor—Ld F. Cavendish—Mr Glyn—Mr Barker. H of C. 4¼-7¾ and 10¾-1¼. Spoke on Emmanuel Hospital & voted in 286 : 238. A great good.[7] Dined at Stafford House to meet K. & Q. of the Belgians. Read Dubl. Rev. on M. Arnold.[8]

[1] Commission set up on request of select cttee. on civil service expenditure, reported in December 1873; *PP* 1873 vii. 400, 1874 xxiv. 557.

[2] John Llewelyn *Davies, 1843-1916, rector of Christ Church, Marylebone, 1856-89; alpinist and disciple of F. D. *Maurice; formulator of the 1870 'Cowper-Temple' clause.

[3] Ida Gladstone, already seriously ill; she d. 1874.

[4] See 27 Apr. 73.

[5] See 7 May 73.

[6] Questions; *H* ccxv. 1789.

[7] Crawford's much delayed motion; *H* ccxv. 1875; defeat was anticipated, see his audience this day.

[8] *Dublin Review*, xx. 357 (April 1873).

Windsor Audience. May 13. 73.[1]

Q. spoke as to *Dissolution* in the event of new crisis—though she cd. not again apply [*sic*]. I said it wd. be difficult to decide anything before the fact.

D. of Edinburgh's marriage—Mr Ayrton—Mr Mill's death—Tennyson.

14. Wed.

Wrote to The Queen—Mr Stansfeld—Scotts—Ld Leicester[2]—Rev Dr Miller—Chancr of Exchr—Ld Chancellor—and minutes. H of C. 12¼-3¼. Spoke agt Occl Sermons Bill and voted in 199:53.[3] Cabinet 3½-6½. Dined at Mr Glyn's. Saw Ld F. Cavendish—Mrs Hope—Mr Glyn—Sir G. Grey—Mr Arnold. Saw Russell X.

Cabinet. Wed. May 14 (3¼ P.M.) 1873.[4]

√ Zanzibar. Require Sultan to sign Treaty. No slave market in the Island: war carried from one part [? *sc.* port] to another. On his refusal blockade the island. If he signs & vessells [*sic*] are still allowed to go refer home.[5]

√ Ragged Schools exemption.[6] Cabinet willing to concede.

√ 2R Mr Stansfeld's Bills: Thursday.

√ Try 2R Judicature Bill Monday week.

√ Ld Blachford's Bishops and Clergy Bill. Bps. propose to abolish mandate. Object to this. Favour the Bill.[7]

√ O'Keeffe Committee Case. Commissioners have not acted as a whole. We are not able on that account to change.[8]

√ Oriental Bank Corporation Bill. Treasury to examine & advise.

√ Bank Act. Provision for relaxation considered—promise an[swe]r next week if question cannot be postponed.[9]

Canada Loan—Juries—Registration—Peace Preservation—Judicature—Stansfeld's Bills.

15. Th.

The King & Queen of the Belgians came to breakfast at ten: a party of twenty. They were most kind: & all went well. Saw Ld F. Cavendish—Ld Breadalbane—Mr Glyn—Mr Goschen—Dined with the Talbots. Wrote to Professor Owen—Dr Ingram—Mr Gurdon—The

[1] Add MS 44761, f. 127.

[2] Successfully offering the Garter to Thomas William Coke, 1822-1909, 2nd earl of Leicester 1842.

[3] *H* ccxv. 1973.

[4] Add MS 44641, f. 110.

[5] Reading of last two words uncertain. Note at foot of page: 'Minute embodying the decision taken by Granville'. The result of the cabinet cttee.'s recommendation; see R. J. Gavin, 'The Bartle Frere mission to Zanzibar 1873', *Historical Journal*, v. 146; the treaty was signed on 5 June; *PP* 1874 lxii. 917.

[6] i.e. from local taxation.

[7] Blachford's colonial Church Bill, dropped in cttee.

[8] Cabinet paper, printed 13 May 1873, at Add MS 44621, f. 10.

[9] Question not put. See 17 May 73.

Queen—and minutes. Read C.J. Pigott's Pamphlet[1]—Jackson's Letters &c. H of C. $4\frac{1}{4}$-$8\frac{1}{4}$ and $9\frac{1}{2}$-1.[2]

16. Fr.

Wrote to Ld Derby—Ld Sydney—Mr A. Arnold—The Queen—& minutes. Luncheon at Baroness M. Rothschild's: saw instead of hearing. Saw Ld F. Cavendish—Ld Derby—Mr Glyn—Ld Stratford de Redcliffe—Mrs G. Hope—Chancr of Exr. H of C. $4\frac{1}{4}$-$8\frac{1}{4}$ and 9-2. Spoke agt Mr Miall's motion for Disestablishment.[3] Read Jackson.

To [R.] Arthur ARNOLD, 16 May 1873. Add MS 44095, f. 412.

I felt with regret on receiving your letter of yesterday,[4] that I should be unable to agree to your request that I would preside, or even undertake to attend, at the meeting on Tuesday.

I have since seen Lord Derby and my conversation with him much confirms my impression that a meeting is not necessary for the purpose in view, while it is open to the objection that under the circumstances it might develop cross purposes and conflicting opinions.

I understand Lord Derby to be of opinion that it would be the wisest course to avoid a meeting.

He and I are I think both of opinion that the proper course would be to form a Committee and we should both be ready to serve upon it. Of such a Committee Lord Stanhope, as a representative of Literature might agree to be Chairman. If he failed, the name of Lord Russell has occurred to me as one that might be suitable. The terms of invitation to join the Committee should be carefully considered as all difficulty would I think disappear, if there were in the first instance a safe definition of the object. I have no words to suggest but in a general way I take the purpose to be this, to suggest some method of commemorating the name of Mr Mill, such as all persons might join in apart from the particular shades of any opinions they entertain, who consider it right & requisite to hand down in honour to posterity his eminent virtues, talents, attainments and services. I should not have said so much, but that, questioning the advantage of one particular method of procedure, I was desirous to do something if I could towards providing another.

17. Sat. [*Chislehurst*]

Wrote to Mr Moon—Mr Dalgleish—The Queen—Mr Burnett—Mrs Th.—and minutes. Cabinet 2-$3\frac{3}{4}$. Off to Chislehurst at 4.12: a *home*. Saw Ld F. Cavendish—Mr Forster—Mr Glyn—Mr Watson—Ld

[1] Perhaps D. R. Pigot, 'A letter on the removal of R. O'Keeffe from the office of manager of the Callan Schools' (1873).

[2] Select cttee. on Callan schools appointed; *H* ccxv. 2053.

[3] *H* ccxvi. 37.

[4] Add MS 44095, f. 410 asking diarist to preside at memorial meeting for J. S. Mill who d. 8 May 1873. See 19 May 73.

Kimberley—Ld Chancellor. Read Life of Stothard[1]—Laugel, L'Angleterre.[2]

Cabinet. Sat. May 17. 2 P.M.[3]

Minor matters mentioned before a few [Cabinet members]. Central Asian line of RR—nothing to be done.[4]

√ Ld Chancellor's Bill. 2R Monday 26 or Tues 27 (mg).

√ Bank Act proposal. Ld Overstone's letter read. Plan adopted. Goschen & Childers not satisfied. Detail & wording to be further considered.[5]

√ Shall we have an Education Bill? Yes. Govt. to bring in a Bill to be 2R imm[ediately] after Commee. on Stansfeld's Bills. A small commee. of Cabinet.[6]

√ Medical Bill; object to Headlam's provision for electing some members of Medical Council by suffraging the profession.[7]

√ Week's business. Contagious Diseases Wedy—open question.

18. 5 S.E.

Chiselhurst Ch. mg (with H.C.) and aftn. Saw the Empress [Eugènie] worn, but full of energy & conversation. Saw Bp of Winchester: on sad matters touching J. S. Neill.[8] Read Divers Tracts—Gavin Carlyle's book[9]—Bp Forbes on the Spiritual Life[10]—Old Graduate on Paley's Ev.[11] Agnes gave me the sad & grave tidings about M.H.[12]—Both she & Mary [Glynne] appear to have acted with excellent feeling & judgment.

19. M. [London]

Wrote to Mr A. Arnold—Mrs Wm Gladstone (Qu. Gate)—Lord Derby—The Queen—Mrs Hope—Mr Bruce—and minutes. Saw Mr Repington—Mr Cardwell—Ld Digby—Mr Dalgleish—Mr Glyn—Ld F. Cavendish—Col. Hogg?—Dr Woodlock. Returned to C.H.T.

[1] A. E. *Stothard, *Life of T. Stothard* (1851).

[2] A. Laugel, *L'Angleterre politique et sociale* (1873).

[3] Add MS 44641, f. 115.

[4] Proposed railway from Caspian to Teheran; see Ramm I, ii. 380.

[5] Digest of letter, not in Gladstone's hand, and not attributed on the digest to Overstone, proposing a special notes issue when bank rate reaches 10%; Add MS 44641, f. 119; Overstone's letter untraced, but see D. P. O'Brien, *Correspondence of Lord Overstone*, iii. 1250. See 31 Mar. 73.

[6] Cttee. listed: 'Ripon, Kimberley, Halifax, Forster, Stansfeld'.

[7] Headlam's Medical Act (1858) Amendment Bill was dropped.

[8] Obscure; Neill unidentified; an unsuccessful ordinand?—no record in diocesan archives.

[9] G. Carlyle, *The light of all ages* (1873).

[10] A. P. *Forbes, *The deepening of the spiritual life* (1873).

[11] 'Remarks on Paley's Evidences. By an Old Graduate' (1873).

[12] Probably decision of S. *Herbert's da. Mary (see 12 Nov. 65) to marry the Roman catholic modernist Friedrich von Hügel, which she did 27 Nov. 1873.

at 11¾. H of C. 4¼–8 and 9¼–1½.[1] Read Jackson—Æneid Book I—Mr S.C. Hall's Memories. Luncheon at 15. G.S.—Visited Jones & Bonham's.[2] Eight to dinner.

To [R.] Arthur ARNOLD, 19 May 1873. Add MS 44095, f. 418.
'Private.'

It is only within the last half hour that I have read with inexpressible pain, & with another & deeper feeling, the third Paragraph of a printed Circular dated May 12, addressed to Mr Stopford Brook, signed 'the writer of "John Stuart Mill" in the Times'.[3] I do not doubt that you like myself were in ignorance of the existence of this circular when we met on Wednesday. Loathsome as must be the office of dealing with such a circular or acting in any manner upon it, it is evident to me that it cannot be passed by, & I take the earliest opportunity of informing you that until the question has been carefully considered, & a decision arrived at as to the proper steps to be taken, I can for myself proceed no further in the matter of the testimonial to Mr Mill, & I request what you will I am sure readily grant, that in this (I hope only provisional) state of the affair, no further use may be made of my name. If you could wish to see me on this very sad subject, you will find me at the House, where I hope to be free after half past four, or I could receive you if you prefer it at this house tomorrow forenoon. I send to Ld. Derby a copy of this note.[4]

20. Tu.

Wrote to Sir T. Biddulph—Ld Hartington—The Queen l. & Mema (2)—D. of Argyll—& minutes. Read Jackson. Saw Mr Glyn—Ld Granville—Ld Lisgar—Mr Arnold—Ld F.C.—Ld Derby—Mr Fowler—Mr Cardwell—Ld Ripon—Shopping in Aftn. Saw Livingstone[R]. Saw Refiners' Deputn.[5] H of C. 4¼–7¾.[6] Dined at the Club.

21. Wed.

Wrote to D. of Argyll—Mr Hayward—Ld Rosebery—Rev S. Gobat—Mr Levy—General Schenk—Mr G. Richmond—& minutes. Saw Livingstone X. Saw Duke of Argyll—Ld F. Cavendish—Mr Glyn—Lady Duff Gordon (84th birthday). Went to hear M. Dulau at Baroness Meyer Rothschild's. Dined at Argyll House. Read 'The Want of the Age'—Castle Court.[7]

[1] Navy estimates; *H* ccxvi. 106.
[2] Auctioneers in New Oxford Street.
[3] A. *Hayward, claiming Mill had advocated birth-control.
[4] Arnold failed to gain adequate retraction from Hayward, and Gladstone withdrew his name formally on 22 May; Add MS 44095, f. 429.
[5] It was hostile to the Paris sugar conference, *Daily Telegraph*, 21 May 73, 7.
[6] Spoke on parlt. business; *H* ccxvi. 171.
[7] Both untraced.

22. Th. Ascension Day.

Wrote to Ld Granville—Mad. Novikoff—The Queen—Ld Kimberley—D. of Argyll—Ld Chancellor—Mr Graham—A. Arnold—Mrs Hope—and minutes. Saw Ld F. Cavendish—Chancr of Exr—Mr Glyn—Att. General. Whitehall Chapel 11 AM (with H.C.) Scottish P.C. Committee on Educn 2–4. H of C. 4¼–8¼ and 9¾–2. We were defeated by a very foolish Vote.[1] Dined at Ld Ripon's. Read Jackson.

23. Fr.

Wrote to The Queen—Mr Bruce—& minutes. Visited Sotheby's. H of C. 4¼–8½ (home to see Pembroke) and 9¾–2.[2] Saw Ld Rosebery[3]—Ld F. Cavendish—Mr Glyn. Read Caleb Cushing's Washington Treaty[4]—Jackson's Diary &c. Saw Chancr of Exr—Attorney General—Mr MacLaren.

24. Sat.

Wrote to Col. Hogg—The Queen—and minutes. Cabinet 2–6¾. Dinner of 32 & evg party. Saw Ld F. Cavendish—Mr Gurdon—Mr Glyn—Ld Granville—Ld Ripon—Lady Aylesbury (M.H.)[5]—Ld Chancellor—D. of Devonshire—Mr Repington. Read Jackson—Life of Stothard.[6]

Cabinet. Sat. May 24. 1873. 2 PM. prompt.[7]

√ Cont[agious] Dis[eases] Act. Pet[itio]n named.[8]

√ Ld Mayor—proposes a dinner in July. What about the Shah? Impossible to go twice more.

√ Valuation Ireland Bill. Ld Hartington stated the question of the Land Act amendments of Sir J. Gray. Limit the amt. to 20 years.[9] Numbers to be determined hereafter.

√ Royal Bank of Scotland. Branch in London. Lowe to obtain further information.

√ Writers in Public Offices. Otway: writers question. Childers stated case agt. Treasury. Lowe the reverse case. Cabt. thought Treasury entitled to be heard first: but Lowe did not wish it.[10]

[1] Harcourt's amndt. to put Playfair on the select cttee. on the Callan schools carried in 200:182, despite an appeal by Gladstone; *H* ccxvi. 327.

[2] Spoke on Alabama; *H* ccxvi. 411.

[3] See 7 Apr. 73n.

[4] C. Cushing, *The Treaty of Washington* (1873).

[5] i.e. Master of the Horse, her husband's office or, possibly, on Mary Herbert (see 18 May 73).

[6] By A. E. *Stothard (1851), sent by Lord R. Gower, Add MS 44542, f. 123, and 17 May 73n.

[7] Add MS 44641, f. 124, '*prompt*' was clearly optimistic; see 17 May, 7 June 73.

[8] Anglican petition agst. the acts; ibid., f. 127.

[9] 'subsequently decline' noted at foot of page.

[10] Select cttee. under Otway appointed: *PP* 1873 xi. 1.

○ Fiji.[1]
√ Colonel Hogg's letters. ans. *no*. WEG. writes.[2]
√ Ld Granville. Reference to Law Officers on the question of terms in wh or with wh to submit the Three Rules. Shall we give any ground[?] in construction? No. A negative ans[wer] excluding the propositions affirmed by the Arbitrators in their preamble in the lump.[3] Ld. G. & Chancellor to see Law Officers.
√ Ashantee War.[4] Export of Arms to Assinee. Enlarge the present Act (by declaration?) so as to be able to prohibit partial export.[5]
√ Alabama Query. Our only obligation was an obln. to the U.S. govt.—the question was whether by neglect or otherwise it had been infringed.
√ Judicature Bill—refer to a Select Committee?—Discourage—Chancellor to see Lawyers. many changes—judgment to be reserved.
√ Impending business generally.
√ Course of inquiry before Expenditure Committee & report. Opportunity to be given to Judges &c. to be heard on evidence already given.
√ Callan Schools Committee. Cardwell stated the view discussed between him & WEG. Case to be tried on the facts. Cabinet of the same mind.

25. S.aft Asc.

Chapel Royal Noon. Wrote to Archdn Harrison—Ld Granville—Ly Herbert—Ld Pembroke. Dined with the Heywoods. Saw Ld Aylesbury—Mr Glyn—Ld Granville—Ld Pembroke. Read Angélique Arnauld—Examn of Liddon—and many Tracts. Dined with the Heywoods.

26. M.

Wrote to Ld Chancr (2)—Musurus Pacha—The Queen—Bp of Winchester—Ld Rosebery—& minutes. H of C. 4¼-8¼ and 9½-1. Spoke on Alabama Vote.[6] Luncheon at 15 G.S. Ten to dinner. Saw Sir R. Phillimore—Mr Sanders—Ld F. Cavendish—Mr Glyn—Scotts—Atty General. Sat to Mr Dickinson. Read 'More St Liverpool'[7]—Jackson's Diary &c.

27. Tu.

Wrote to Mr Hubbard—Baroness Burdett Coutts—The Queen—Mr Ouvry—Ld Hartington—Ld Chancellor (2)—Mrs Th.—Abp of

[1] Gladstone's note to Granville: 'Shall *I* mention Fiji today or leave it alone. . . .' Granville suggested he ask Kimberley; Add MS 44641, f. 126.
[2] Metropolitan Board's Thanksgiving Day expenses; Add MS 44542, f. 123.
[3] Apparently *sic*.
[4] See W. D. McIntyre, 'British policy in West Africa', *Historical Journal*, v. 28.
[5] New proclamation to be issued: PRO CO 879/4/411.
[6] *H* ccxvi. 470.
[7] Untraced.

Canterbury—& minutes. Dined with Sir D. Marjoribanks. Duchess of Manchester's Ball afr. Saw Blake—Maclagan—& another[R]. Saw Sir R. Phillimore—Bp of Winchester—Mr Blewill[1]—Mr Ouvry (Clerk)—Col. Hogg—Ld F. Cavendish—Mr Glyn—Musurus Pacha. H of C. 2¼–6.[2] Read Jackson—Literary Fund Addresses.[3]

To J. G. HUBBARD, 27 May 1873. Add MS 44542, f. 122.

I know not whether technical reasons will require any Bill which the Chancellor of the Exchequer may introduce to be called a Bill to amend, but you may rely upon it, I am certain, that no language will be used either in the measure or by its authors which can tend to discredit the [Bank] Act of 44. Indeed among those whom the term includes are persons who perhaps of all now living have the best title to the parentage of that Act. A copy of the Bill shall be sent to you when it is printed & your letter shall be seen by the Chancellor of the Exchequer.

28. Wed.[4]

Wrote to Col. Hogg—Lady Herbert—Ld R. Gower—Ld Kimberley—and minutes. Sat to Photographers. Saw Ld F. Cavendish—Ld R. Gower. Shopping. Read Paley's Iliad[5]—Stothard's Life (finished)—Jackson Bath Archives.[6] Saw Maclagan: who with the friend is in the congrn of St Thomas's.[7]

29. Th. [*Chatsworth*]

Wrote to Ld Kimberley (2)—Ld R. Gower—Mary Gladstone—Col Ponsonby Tel.—and minutes. Off 11.15 to Chatsworth. Saw Mr Gurdon. Read Jackson—Equilibre Social en France[8]—Life of George Grote.[9]

30. Fr.

Wrote to Ld Chancellor—Dean of Westmr—Mr Gurdon—Chancr of Exr—Mr Glyn—Dean of Windsor—Mr Hammond—and minutes. Read Wall on Symbols[10]—Life of Grote—Jackson's Bath Archives. Walk with the Duke & party.

[1] Unidentified.
[2] Misc. business: *H* ccxvi. 500.
[3] Papers of the Royal Literary Fund; see next day's note.
[4] Omitted mention of his speech at Royal Literary Fund dinner; *The Times*, 29 May 1873, 12 and B. A. Booth, *Letters of Trollope* (1951), 517.
[5] F. A. *Paley, *The Iliad of Homer. Books 1–12* (1867).
[6] See 7 May 73.
[7] Presumably a rescue case.
[8] Untraced.
[9] H. *Grote, *The personal life of George Grote* (1873).
[10] C. W. Wall, probably *An examination of the ancient orthography of the Jews* (1835).

31. Sat.

Wrote to Ld Stanhope—Ld R. Gower—Mr Glyn—and minutes. Read Jackson—Grote's Life—with ever growing interest—Epicteti Enchiridion[1]—Sundries, in the Library. Ride with the Duke & F.[2]

Whits. June One 1873.

Wrote to Ld Granville—Mrs Begbie—The Queen—and minutes. Read The Fairhaven[3]—Memoir & work—Archd. Sinclair's Charge.[4] Edensor Ch. mg with H.C.—Baslow evg: Mr Stockdale preached with some eloquence.[5]

2. M.

Wrote minutes. Finished the Life of Grote, a truly remarkable record. Read Epictetus (finished)—Jackson's Bath Archives. Walk with the party.

3. Tu.

Wrote to Mr Gurdon 2 & Tel.—& minutes. Read Jackson—Döllinger's Universitäten.[6] A long drive to see Hardwicke[7] & a severe thunderstorm. It was well worth the pains. An hour with Sir J. L[acaita] in the Library.[8]

4. Wed.

Wrote to the Queen—Sec. Westmr Working Men[9]—Mr Sanders—& minutes. Two hours in the Library among the Treasures with Sir J.L. —Rode with the Duke. The party, in the main, broke up.—'All that's bright must fade'. Read Jackson—Döllinger.

5. Th. [London]

Wrote to Ld Chancellor—The Queen—Robn G.—Ld Hartington—

[1] Epictetus' main statement of his Stoicism.

[2] i.e. 7th duke of Devonshire and Lord F. Cavendish.

[3] S. *Butler, *The Fairhaven* (1873), recommended by Lord Pembroke, to whom Gladstone wrote a dismissive critique; Add MS 44439, ff. 45, 55.

[4] J. *Sinclair, 'The primitive Church' (1873).

[5] Jeremiah Stockdale, vicar of Baslow.

[6] J. J. I. von Döllinger, *Die Universitäten sonst und jetzt* (1867).

[7] i.e. Hardwicke Hall.

[8] *Lacaita catalogued the Chatsworth library.

[9] Not found; the Westminster Working Men's Liberal Association had voted to contest both Westminster seats at the next election; *The Times*, 23 May 1873, 10b.

Saw Mr Glyn—Ld Advocate—Ld Hartington—Mr Childers. H of C. 4¼-8½ & 9½-1¾.[1] Read Jackson—Stewart on Cosmical Physics.[2] Left Chatsworth 9½. Home at 3¾.

To LORD KIMBERLEY, colonial secretary, 5 June 1873. Add MS 44542, f. 124.

A propos of Fiji, I was rather struck with Consul March's first paper,[3] so far as concerned the plan proposed in it. Perhaps you could have it examined & developed for consideration. It has many recom[mendatio]ns[?] over sending a Commissioner, & as Granville has, I believe, sent out a good man as Consul, it might perhaps be found fit to refer to him for a Report if the Cabinet so think fit, & you approve.

6. Fr.

Wrote to Mr Robinson—Mr Burnett—Mr Heywood—Mr Martineau—Mr Western—The Queen—Chr of Exr—and minutes. Saw Sir D. Marjoribanks—Mr Gurdon—Mr Glyn—Mrs Robertson—Sir H. Ingilby[4]—Mr Whitbread—Ld Granville—Mr Childers. Read Jackson. Visited Christie's. H of C. 4¼-8¼ and 9¼-1¾.[5] Visited my dentist. Luncheon at 15 G.S. Read Telegr. Monies Report.[6]

7. Sat.

Wrote to Ld Carysfort—Ld Granville—Mrs Robertson—Sir W. Knollys—The Queen—& minutes. Saw. . . . Cabinet 2½-6. Saw Sir W. Knollys—Chancr of Exr—Mr Gurdon. Read Jackson—M. Arnold Lit. & Dogma.[7]

Cabinet. Sat. June 7. 73. 2 PM.[8]

√ Hospital Sunday. The Prince of Wales. No objection. *Before Cabinet was full.*
√ Circular on local charges.
√ Game Laws Committee. Legislation. Give Hunt.
√ Committee of Cabinet on Telegraph Capital misappropriation: Halifax, Cardwell, C. of E., WEG.[9]

[1] Juries Bill: *H* ccxvi. 515.
[2] B. *Stewart, *Lessons in elementary physics* (1870).
[3] E. B. March, consul in Fiji, suggesting a consul with magisterial powers over British subjects; Kimberley's mem., 10 June 1873, Add MS 44225, f. 45, disputes this plan.
[4] Sir Henry Day Ingilby, 1826–1911, 2nd bart., Marjoribanks' s.-in-law.
[5] Deb. on trade unions; *H* ccxvi. 572.
[6] Report by *Welby and others, printed for the cabinet; Add MS 44621, f. 31.
[7] M. *Arnold, *Literature and dogma* (1873).
[8] Add MS 44641, f. 128.
[9] Lowe had authorised Scudamore to balance overspending on telegraph reorganisation from Post Office revenues and 'other balances'; Scudamore had used £656,000 from the P.O. Savings Bank Deposits; a political storm had begun in March 1873; see J. Winter, *Robert Lowe* (1976), 285.

√ Judicature Bill—resist Select Committee—& the other motions on 2R.
√ Denison's question on the Shah: *No.* Navy & Army review at Windsor. No free boats trains or tickets.
√ Garter for the Shah: give, with reluctance.
√ Stansfeld's Bill: Grove's motion: oppose it—not agree to a Commee. on the mode of assessing govt. property. Resist Crawford.[1]
√ D'Harcourt's question as to [Spanish] Federal Republic. Ld G's projected answer approved.[2]
√ Fiji. Discussion. Inquiry to be made probably by Consul & by Capt. Goodenough who will be summoned to town. Recognition to stand No 1.[3]
√ Otway's motion. Resist. Discussion on policy of recent change.[4]
√ Partial prohibition of export of arms. Given up. Communicate with French Govt.[5]
√ Mundella's Bill. Mr Bruce & any other to give an opinion as he thinks best.[6]

8. Trin.S.

Chapel Royal at noon. It was touching to see Dean Hook, & hear him: now old in years & very old I fear in life: but he kindled gallantly. Saw Ld Granville—Ld Spencer—Mrs Graham X—Mr Glyn—Mr C. [A.] Gore. Wrote to Dean of Chichester—Ld Granville—Ld Russell—Mr Greswell—Mr Sanders—& minutes. Wrote Mem. on Ath. Creed.[7] Read Voysey & Th. Parker[8]—The Fair Haven—Prov. Hawkins on Ath. Creed[9]—Sermon by Dr [blank]. Dined with G. Glyn.

9. M.

Wrote to Ld Carysfort—Miss Martineau[10]—Robn G.—Sir R. Phillimore—Ld Elcho—Sir W. Knollys—C.G.[11]—Mr Hubbard—The Queen—Bss Burdett Coutts—Mrs Th.—and minutes. Read Jackson. Another visit to Mr Saunders. Saw Sir H. Ingilby—Ld F. Cavendish—Mr Glyn—Mr Gurdon—Mr Browne—Mr Moffatt—Mr Stansfeld.

[1] Mem. by diarist of 23 June 1873 apparently giving cttee.'s recommendations, Add MS 44761, f. 149. Grove had withdrawn his motion to refer the bill to a select cttee.; Stansfeld accepted E. H. J. Craufurd's proposal to extend the Bill, in part, to Scotland; *H* ccxvi. 736, 910. Gladstone's mem. of 10 June 1873 on govt. property, at Add MS 44761, f. 148.

[2] Count Bernard d'Harcourt, 1821-1912; French ambassador in London 1872-3.

[3] Edgar Leopold Layard, 1824-1900, br. of Sir A. H.*, consul (later administrator) in Fiji Feb. 1873-75 and Captain J. G. Goodenough, commodore of the Australian station, commissioner with Layard 1873; 'recognition' was Gladstone's preference, annexation Kimberley's; see Morrell, *Britain in Pacific Islands*, 162.

[4] Otway's motion for select cttee. on civil service writers accepted; *H* ccxvi. 1108.

[5] On law officers' opinion: PRO CO 879/4/419; see 24 May 73.

[6] Factory Acts Amndt. Bill 2°R withdrawn, Bruce disapproving; *H* ccxvi. 1552.

[7] Add MS 44761, f. 144.

[8] See 19 Jan. 73; see 6 Nov. 59.

[9] Earlier version of E. *Hawkins, *Considerations on the Athanasian Creed and the proposed synodical declaration* (1874).

[10] Gladstone had offered her a pension, which she declined; Add MS 44439, f. 13.

[11] See Bassett, 197.

Conclave on Currency. Luncheon in G. Square. H of C. $4\frac{1}{4}$–$8\frac{1}{4}$ and $9\frac{1}{4}$–$1\frac{3}{4}$.[1]

10. Tu.

Wrote to Ld Granville—Ld Dalhousie—The Queen—Messrs Kirch Son & Hamburg[2]—and minutes. H of C. $2\frac{1}{4}$–$6\frac{3}{4}$ & $9\frac{1}{4}$–$1\frac{1}{4}$.[3] Dined with the Jameses. Saw Capt. Goodenough—Ld F.C.—Mr Glyn. Read Jackson—Tract on Tramways. Visited Sotheby's.

11. Wed.

Wrote to Chr of Exr (2)—Sir R. Phillimore—Dft note to P[ublic] A[ccounts] Committee—and minutes. H of C. 1–2 and 3–$4\frac{1}{4}$.[4] Dined at Lady Herberts. Saw Mr Stansfeld—Ld F. Cavendish—Mr Glyn—Calls. Read Zincke on Switzerland.[5]

To R. LOWE, chancellor of the exchequer, 11 June 1873. Add MS 44542, f. 126.

[First letter:] The Parliamentary danger of which we have been warned in connection with the Zanzibar case from the miscarriage or irregular handling of papers I think deserves your consideration. It seems necessary that a department like the Treasury should have *at least one* person as a centre, who should be cognizant of every paper as it passes through the office. This person cannot be the Chancellor of the Exchequer on account of the weight & variety of his general duties. At least so I assume—certainly I never attempted it. But I think that during the whole of my tenure of that office there were two such persons, viz. the Permanent Secretary & the Financial Secretary. This seems to be the proper basis. Further, my recollection, as far as it goes, is that this was the established practice of the Department. If it has been unfixed, would it not be well to do something for the purpose of fixing it again?[6]

[Second letter:] So far as I am concerned, the Report may go forward. I have sketched out the possible form of a covering note which might with a proper heading be the vehicle for carrying the Report to the committee.
Draft. The First Lord of the Treasury & the Chancellor of the Exchequer upon receiving the report of the committee of Public Accounts relating to the &c &c &c passed the following minute of the Board. In pursuance of this minute, the accompanying Report has been drawn up by the Gentlemen to whom the task

[1] Spoke on Zanzibar contract; *H* ccxvi. 710.
[2] Problems with rescue cases; see letter on 14 June 73.
[3] Navy deb.; *H* ccxvi. 756.
[4] Spoke on Scottish Roads Bill; *H* ccxvi. 815.
[5] F. B. *Zincke, *A month in Switzerland*, 3v. (1873–5).
[6] Lowe replied that Baxter was the barrier to efficiency, 12 June 1873, Add MS 44302, f. 127.

was intrusted, & is now submitted for the information of the Committee on Public Accounts. Inasmuch as the conduct of the Treasury itself, as well as the other Departments concerned, is now under review, the First Lord & the Chancellor think it most becoming to abstain from giving, in this covering note, their opinion as to the conduct of any of those persons or departments who may or may not be thought responsible for the irregularities which have occurred. But those opinions, & likewise the views they have been able to form as to the provisions to be made for the future with a view to the prevention of like errors, are entirely at the service of the Committee, should it be their pleasure to call for them in evidence.

12. Th.

Wrote to Ld Granville—Ld Kimberley—Mrs Th.—Mr Leeman—The Queen—& minutes. 10 to breakfast. Visited Sotheby's. Saw Mr H. Freshfield[1]—Mr Knowles—Mr Glyn (2)—Ld F. Cavendish—Mr Gurdon—Ld Bessborough—Ld Kildare—Mr Holms—Mr Rathbone—Ld Houghton. Dined with the Jameses. Read S.C. Hall's Memories.[2] H of C. 4¼-8½ and 9½-2.[3]

13. Fr.

Wrote to Ld Cowper—Mr Hugessen—Mr Cardwell—The Queen l. & Mem.—Sir S.R.G.—& minutes. H of C. 2½-6¾ and 9-1¼. Spoke on Fiji: as well as I could.[4] Saw Ld F. Cavendish—Sir R. Anstruther—Mr J. Russell—Mr Glyn (2)—Mr Cardwell—Mr Gurdon. Dined with the Glyns at 7.30. Read Zincke on Switzerland.

14. Sat.

Wrote to The Lord Mayor—Mr H. Freshfield—The Queen—Chancr of Exr—and minutes. Dined at D. of Cleveland's. Walk with C. Cabinet 2¼-6½. Saw Ld F. Cavendish—Mr Cardwell *cum* Ld Granville & Mr Glyn—Mr J. Russell—Mr Elliot—Mr Bright. Read Vansittart Papers[5]—Poems by. . . .

[1] His London solicitor; he had asked to see any one of the partners 'on a personal matter'; Add MS 44439, f. 24; see 14 June 73.

[2] See 25 Apr. 73.

[3] Answered questions; *H* ccxvi. 839.

[4] Arguing against annexation; *H* ccxvi. 951.

[5] Attack in Rome on C. Arthur Vansittart: *PP* 1873 lxxv. 663.

Cabinet. Sat. June 14/73. 2 PM.[1]

√ Ld Mayor's dinner. *No.*[2]
√ Father O'Keeffe. Read mem. WEG to thank [blank]. Seeing.[3]
√ Crown. Private Estates. Yes. Bill to be introduced by Ld Chancellor in H. of L.
√ Vienna Commission. Within limit of 20m[ille], money to be given for the purposes reviewed so far as they are of a character wh parties should not bear.[4]
√ Zanzibar Contract. Agree to postponement if asked in order to a [*sic*] proposal for Committee. Agree to Committee.[5]
√ Otway's Motion. Motion to stand on a day point—not to be conceded. Resist Committee on remaining point.[6]
√ Callan Schools. Ld O'Hagan's draft read: scarcely a basis—matter to be resumed.[7]
√ Military Review—questions for Monday. Cancel charge on Land Revenues. Vote to be taken for stands in Windsor Park.
√ Naval [Review]—ask notice—[M.P.s] will be received on board ships—one lady each—no charge on Naval Officers—Tariff [for] luncheon.[8]
√ Fawcett's Bill—on Wedy—take no part as a Govt.[9]
√ Recognition of Spanish Republic—not to reject appln, but to proceed slowly.
√ Anstruther Tues. Scots Patronage.[10]
√ French Treaty may be given up. Clause for a limited term[11]
√ Shah. Language to be held by Ld Gr. on Reuter railway Concession. Affghan Arbitration.[12]

To H. N. FRESHFIELD, solicitor, 14 June 1873. Add MS 44439, f. 42.

Any communication that may reach me from Messrs. Froggart, or otherwise in the Davison & Cooper business,[13] will simply be sent to you: & *if* you should have occasion to call you will find me at 10.30 on any morning except Thursdays, & Monday the 23d. As I came back from your office, thinking over the matter, I remembered one or two things confirmatory of your opinion that this is a 'plant' as it is called. Kisch, after inviting our interview, had nothing to say, & what I told you, which was not much, I drew from him. Moreover I now remember that the same person Mrs Cooper several years back told me some story or fable about a *subpoena* which I was to have received had it not been prevented.

[1] Add MS 44641, f. 130; note summoning Cardwell to discuss Zanzibar contract at 2.00 p.m. ibid., f. 132.

[2] Letter declining invitation on grounds that 'it has not been usual for the members of the govt. to dine . . . twice in the course of the session' in Add MS 44542, f. 128.

[3] Apparently thanks conveyed orally; probably to Bouverie, see 21 June 73.

[4] Grant to the Vienna Exhibition Commissioners; see Add MS 44542, f. 128.

[5] Committee conceded on 19 June; *H* ccxvi. 1214; the contract was the result of the treaty; see R. Winter, *Robert Lowe* (1976), 288, *PP* 1873 ix. 233, xxxix. 493, Add MS 44439, f. 27.

[6] See 7 June 73.

[7] Not found.

[8] Arrangements for the reviews announced in *H* ccxvi. 997.

[9] Bruce announced this; Fawcett's Parliamentary Elections (Expenses) Bill put off; ibid. 1132.

[10] Sir R. Anstruther's resolution on Scottish church patronage, withdrawn; ibid. 1108.

[11] See PRO FO 27/2006/236.

[12] No papers found in PRO on this arbitration.

[13] Both rescue cases, see 19 Mar., 5 June 72, 27 Nov., 5 Dec. 62, 26 July 63. Freshfield's archives unfortunately bombed out.

To this I paid little attention: but it comes up in my memory, now that I find that she seems to have lied both to me & about me. When I mentioned to my wife the kindness of Davison to Mrs Cooper & the representation of its perfect innocence, she was wiser than I & said 'You are too credulous'.

15. 1 S.Trin.

Chapel Royal mg & aft. Saw Bp of Winchester—Mr Glyn—Lady Dunmore,[1] respecting Mary Herbert. Wrote to The Prince of Wales —Lord Cowper—Robn G.—and minutes. Dined with the Herberts. Read The Fair Haven (finished)—Mere Angelique—Theodore Parker.

16 M.

Wrote to E. of Pembroke—Mr H. Freshfield—Mr Hubbard—The Queen—and minutes. Luncheon in G. Square. Saw Ld F. Cavendish —Mr Glyn—Chancr of Exr—Mr Bates MP.[2]—Adm. Hamilton. Visited Christie's. H of C. 4¼-9½ and 10½-1¾.[3] Read Percival on Universities[4]—D. of Argyll's Address[5]—Maine on Prop. of Married Women.[6]

17. Tu.

Wrote to Mr M'Coll—Ld Chancellor—Robn G.—Chancr of Exr— The Queen—Provost of Oriel—& minutes. Nine to dinner. We had a long conversation with Mr Holloway[7] (of the Pills) on his philanthropic plans; wh are of great interest. Saw Lord F. Cavendish—Mr J. Russell—Mr Glyn—Mr Cardwell—Ld Advocate. H of C. 2¼-7 and 9¼-1¼. Spoke on Scots Patronage question.[8] Read London Fish Supply[9]—M'Coan on Consular Jurisdn[10]—Wilson on Euph Valley Railway[11]—and other Tracts.

[1] See list following 13 Apr. 48.
[2] (Sir) Edward Bates, 1816-96; tory M.P. Plymouth 1871-80, 1885-92; cr. bart. 1880.
[3] Spoke on Zanzibar contract; *H* ccxvi. 1001.
[4] J. Percival, *The connection of the universities and the great towns* (1873).
[5] G. D. *Campbell, duke of Argyll, 'On glaciation', *Geological Society Quarterly Journal*, xxix. 51 (1873).
[6] H. J. S. *Maine, 'The early history of the property of married women as collected from Roman and Hindoo Law' (1873).
[7] Thomas *Holloway, 1800-83, used his fortune from patent medicines for charity, including Holloway college.
[8] *H* ccxvi. 1103.
[9] Untraced.
[10] J. C. MacCoan, *Consular jurisdiction in Turkey and Egypt* (1873).
[11] Sir C. W. Wilson, *The strategical importance of the Euphrates Valley Railway* (1873).

18. Wed.

Wrote to Ld Pembroke—Miss de Crespigny[1]—The Queen—Mr [C. H.] Christie—Mr Brodie[2]—Mr Burnett—and minutes. Saw Ld F. Cavendish—Mr Glyn. Visits in the West; failed—saw Seymour, Mills, & Poole, & another X. Saw Sir J. Paget[3] & Dr A. Clark respecting S.R.G.[4]—We have much cause to be thankful. Read Plimsoll's Appeal[5]—Swinburne's Prologue to Tr. & Iseult[6]—Cobden's Mission[7] —Rinuccini's Life.[8] Dined at Baroness M. Rothschild's: music afterwards.

19. Th.

Wrote to E. of Pembroke—The Queen—& minutes. H of C. $4\frac{1}{4}$-$7\frac{1}{2}$ and $10\frac{3}{4}$-$1\frac{1}{4}$.[9] Saw Bp Moriarty—Dean of Westmr—Ld Lytton—Sir A. Gordon—Mr Strut [*sic*]—Ld F. Cavendish—Mr Glyn—Ld R. Grosvenor—Ld Granville—Sir P. Braila. Attended Court to be presented to the Shah & had an audience with Lord G.[10] Sixteen to breakfast. Dined at Marlborough Ho. and found myself converted into a big man, sitting by the G. Vizir. Also saw & was much pleased with the Czarowitch.[11] Read Owen's India.[12]

20. Fr.

Wrote to Robn G.—Mayor of Liverpool[13]—The Queen—Mrs. Th. —and minutes. H of C. $2\frac{1}{4}$-$5\frac{1}{2}$.[14] $8\frac{1}{2}$-$11\frac{1}{4}$. Splendid suffering at the Guildhall where a party was given for the Shah. Saw Archbp of Canterbury—Mr Humphry—Mr Glyn—Ld F. Cavendish. Read Owen on India.

21. Sat. [*Chislehurst*]

$9\frac{3}{4}$-12. All Saints [Margaret Street] for the funeral service of Mr

[1] Probably Emma H. D., sister of Sir C. C. de Crespigny, 1st bart.

[2] Successfully offering lord-lieutenancy of Nairn to James Campbell John Brodie of Lethen, 1848-80.

[3] Sir James *Paget, 1814-99, surgeon.

[4] Already ill; he d. 17 June 74.

[5] S. Plimsoll, *Our seamen. An appeal* (1873).

[6] A. C. *Swinburne, 'Queen Yseult' from *Undergraduate Papers* (1858).

[7] V. H. *Hobart, Baron Hobart, *The 'Mission' of Richard Cobden* (1867).

[8] Probably A. Hutton, *The embassy in Ireland of . . . G. B. Rinuccini* (1873).

[9] Spoke on Zanzibar contract; *H* ccxvi. 1214.

[10] *The Times*, 20 June 1873, 9f.

[11] Alexander (III) of Russia, 1845-94; succ. 1881 on his fa.'s assassination.

[12] See 28 Feb. 73.

[13] Presenting his portrait of W. Ewart to the city; Add MS 44542, f. 129.

[14] Misc. business; *H* ccxvi. 1230.

Richards.[1] It was very solemn & beautiful: but consecration was (as far as I saw) without any communion. Wrote to Ld Granville (2)—Mr Ayrton—The Queen—Mr Glyn—& minutes. Cabinet 2¼-6¼. Dined at Lady Cowper's. Off to Chiselhurst at night. Read Döllinger's Universitäten[2]—Read Owen's India. Saw The Ld Chancellor—Ld F. Cavendish—Mr Glyn—Mr Quaritch—Ld Sydney—Ld Granville.

[*21 June*] *1873. Cabinet.* [*2 P.M.*][3]

√ Judicature Bill Amendts—New Vice Chancellor Clause—expunge. Three new persons from among the judges. To be *any* persons. Are[?] new Law Judges then to be reduced. Harcourt's Amt.: oppose. Judges of appeal—to be at [£] 5 m[ille]. But James & Mellish to continue as now. Chief's Clause (letter of Ap 21) refused. Pensions: Chan[cello]r's pension to be on condition of accepting a seat in Court of Appeal unless he has served full term.[4]
√ Cardwell & the Review. No step to be taken.
√ Members of Govt. to make a House Monday & Tues.
√ Duke of Argyll on[5] Clause Ld Adv's Conveyancing Bill. D of A to comm[unicate] with Ld. A[dvocate].
√ Civil Expenditure Committee. Childers reported state of the evidence—wh. is sent regularly to Treasury.
√ Ld Granville. Persian relations with Turkey. P. right in offering arbitration on Treaty right—T. as to the substantial purpose in view.[6]
√ Valuation Ireland Bill—as we were.[7]
√ Endowed Schools Bill. New Bill to be introduced acc[ording] to the Report.[8]
√ Ld Redesdale's proposal to make the 4 Chiefs Life Peers. Object: but without disfavour to the principle of Life Peerages.[9]
√ Stanhope's Order of Merit—Ld Granville may oppose.[10]
√ Norwegian Coronation.[11] Squadron to attend.
Cable on Irish Coast. B. of Trade to ascertain our position.
O'Keeffe Committee. Cardwell reported Mr Bouverie's pacific comm[unic]ation and a draft of a possible rule for the Board was agreed on. Irish Govt. to write to the Board & propose a rule acc[ordingl]y.[12]
Dover Harbour. Bill may go on.

[1] The tractarian priest, see 2 Oct. 42.
[2] See 3 June 73.
[3] Add MS 44641, f. 135.
[4] Details at ibid., f. 137. Gladstone's statement on 1 July (*H* ccxvi. 1630) explained details of recruitment to the Appeal Court.
[5] Number here smudged; on 3 July, Argyll's speech discussed clause 3; *H* ccxvi. 1691.
[6] Elliot told to facilitate Shah's visit to Turkey; Shah arrived in August; PRO FO 78/2263.
[7] '*Informed*' written in the margin.
[8] Introduced 26 June, royal assent 5 August.
[9] Redesdale's proposal respecting the four principal judges, withdrawn; *H* ccxvi. 1758.
[10] He did so, successfully: *H* ccxvi. 1472.
[11] Of Oscar II, on 17 July.
[12] Bouverie withdrew his motion of censure on the commissioners after publication of the rule accepted by the commissioners; *H* ccxvii. 211.

22. 2 S.Trin.

Parish Ch mg & aft. Saw the Napoleon *Niche* in the R.C. Chapel. Saw Miss F. Robertson. Much conversation with Dr Liddon & Dr A. Clark. Read Principles of Free Kirk[1]—Angélique Arnauld (finished).

23. M. [London]

Off to town at 10¾. Wrote to Ld Chief Justice of E.—Sir W. Stephenson—Robn G.—The Queen 1 & Mem.—Ly Marjoribanks—& minutes. Saw Sir R. Blennerhassett—Ld F. Cavendish—Mr Glyn—Mr W.O. Stanley—Mr Monsell—Conclave (quasi Cabinet) on the Ayrton-Street Controversy.[2] H of C. 3¾-8 and 9¼-1¾.[3] Luncheon in G.S. Saw Mrs Th X.

To A. J. E. COCKBURN, lord chief justice, Add MS 44542, f. 129.
23 June 1873.

I received on Saturday the letter addressed to me with counterparts to the Ld. Ch. & the Ch. of Ex., by yourself together with the L. C. Baron & the L. C. Justice of the Common Pleas; inclosing a paper in which you suggest by way of amendment to the Court of Judicature Bill a clause for relieving Judges from the expenses of ordinary circuits.[4] This letter was considered by the Cabinet with the care & respect due to the high quarter from which it proceeded. I think the Cabinet are not insensible to the disadvantage arising from inequality in the manner you described. But the particular method which is recommended for the removal of this inequality appears to amount to an increase of salary; & this increase we do not find ourselves able to recommend or agree to. We must therefore reluctantly decline to accede to the suggestion.

24. Tu.

Wrote to Sir W. Knollys—The Queen—& minutes. Saw Ld F. Cavendish—Sir H. Rawlinson—Mr Glyn—Conclave on Telegr. Monies affair. Audience of the Shah with Ld Gr. & D. of A.—Came away after 1¼ hour, when it was not over. He displayed abundant acuteness: his gesticulation particularly expressive. Dined at Ld Granville's to meet him: but he did not appear. H of C. 2¼-6¾. Spoke on Canada Guarantee.[5] Read Döllinger—S. Owen on Mogul Empire[6]—Houghton's Monographs[7]—Saw two X.

[1] Untraced.
[2] See 28 June 73.
[3] Army estimates; *H* ccxvi. 1255.
[4] Letter of 21 June from Cockburn, Bovill and Fitzroy Kelly; Add MS 44439, f. 63.
[5] *H* ccxvi. 1326.
[6] See 28 Feb. 73.
[7] R. M. *Milnes, Baron Houghton, *Monographs personal and social* (1873).

25. Wed.

Wrote to Sir H. Rawlinson—Bss M. Rothschild—and minutes. Attended Queen's Ball. Saw Seymour X. Saw Ld Portman—Mr Bagwell—Mr C. Wood—Sir A. Panizzi—Ouvrys—Mr Glyn. Read Seyd's Letter on Currency[1]—Dollinger Universitäten (finished)—Outlines of German Literature[2]—The True Reformer.[3]

26. Th.

Wrote to The Queen l. & Mem.—Chancr of Exr—Mr Ayrton—Rev. S.E.G.—Robn G.—Ld Stratford de Redcliffe—and minutes. Sixteen to breakfast. Mad. Norman Neruda[4] played for us. She is *also* most pleasing in manner and character. Went to Windsor afterwards. Had an audience of H.M. who is much pleased with the Shah. Saw Count Munster—Count d'Harcourt[5]—Mr Glyn—Sir P. Braila—M. Moret—Ld Granville—Mr Childers. H of C. 4¾-8 and 9-1.[6] Read The True Reformer.

27. Frid.

Wrote to The Queen Mem—Dean of Chester—Ld Lyttelton—& minutes. Dined at Mr C. Forster's. Saw Mr Wade—Mr Sneyd—Ld F. Cavendish—Mr Glyn—Sol. General—Chancr of Exr—The Speaker—Mr Welby—Mr Monsell—Mr Stansfeld. H of C. 2¼-6¾.[7] Saw Mad. Ristori in Mary Stuart.[8] Read Blyden's Tour[9]—The True Reformer.

28. Sat.

Wrote to Ld Lyttelton—Ld Stratford de R.—Major Trench—Ld Advocate—Mr Ayrton—The Queen—H.J.G.—and minutes. Cabinet 2-6¼. Dined at Chancr of Exchrs. Saw Lee[R]. Saw Ld F. Cavendish—Ld Granville—Mr Glyn—Ld Overstone—& others. Read 'Contrasts'.[10]

[1] See 11 Feb. 73. [2] See 26 Apr. 73.

[3] [F. R. Chesney], *A true reformer*, 3v. (1873).

[4] Wilma *Neruda, 1839-1911, violinist; m. 1864 L. Norman, 1888 Sir C. *Hallé.

[5] i.e. the German and French ambassadors.

[6] Spoke on the Rating Bill: *H* ccxvi. 1441. [7] *H* ccxvi. 1496.

[8] Adelaide Ristori, 1821-1906, Italian tragedienne.

[9] E. W. Blyden, *From West Africa to Palestine* (1873).

[10] [W. *Gilbert], *Contrasts. Dedicated to the rate-payers of London* (1873).

[*28 June 1873*] *Cabinet.* [*2 P.M.*][1]

√ Parl. & Munic[ipal] Eln. Rolls Bill. Rathbone's Bill? support it.[2]

√ Law Courts. Ayrton-Street. Ayrton heard. Decision conveyed in WEG's letter wh was read to the Cabinet.[3]

√ S. Kensington. Ld Ripon. 1. Bring Educational part into closer union with [Privy] Council Office. 2. Educn. Dept. in comm[unicatio]n with C of E[xchequer] to ascertain from the Trustees of B[ritish] M[useum] whether a plan can be framed for their undertaking in a satisfactory manner the superintendence of the collections at S. K[ensington].

Ask members of Cabinet to consider respecting withdrawal of Bills.

√ Transport of the Shah—allow the French to take him & in what manner they like.

√ Fishery question as per Ld K[imberley]'s letter. Have the French the exclusive right to the fishing on the French shore? Propose a. to open negotiations. b. *status quo* for the present c. immediate instructions acc[ordingl]y—this highly urgent. d. we shall desire expedition in the proceedings for settling the point contested.[4]

√ Withdrawal of marines from Gold Coast. Agreement as to instructions to be sent. Naval officers on coast to be consulted.[5]

√ Persians. Ld Granville reported the efforts he was making to settle the difference with Turkey as to Persian subjects.

√ Bouverie's motion.[6] If Irish & Scotch sentiment appears favourable, resolved to accept—*modus operandi* to be considered on Monday at 3.45.

√ Callan Schools. New Rule: wording further amended & altered.[7]

√ Licensing Bill Ireland: & Harcourt's motion. Amending Bill to be limited to a single point: H. not accepted.[8]

To A. S. AYRTON, chief commissioner of works, 28 June 1873. Add MS 44542, f. 131.

The Cabinet have considered the present state of the question with reference to the new Law Courts. They are very sensible of the energy & ability with which you have striven to keep down expense in the important undertakings under the charge of your Department; & they would much regret any measure tending to weaken your hands. At the same time they have felt that the question

[1] Add MS 44641, f. 138.

[2] Note of 27 June to Gurdon asking for memorials; Liverpool, Rochdale, Walsall, Huddersfield had sent addresses; ibid., f. 144. Govt's bill lost in the Lords on 26 June. Rathbone's Vexatious Objections (Borough Registration) Bill was 2°R on 18 February 1873, but was withdrawn on 28 July.

[3] Drafts read to cabinet at Add MS 44641, f. 140; see also Kimberley, *Journal*, 39, and below.

[4] On 27 June 1873 the French commodore at St. André demanded 'exclusive' fishing on the French shore; instructions of cabinet's decision sent to Lyons this day; see Hertslet's *resumé*, 31 July 1873, F.O.C.P. 2276.

[5] The marines left early in August; *PP* 1874 xlvi. 177ff.

[6] On Scottish and Irish appeals under the Judicature Bill; see statement on 30 June, *H* ccxvi. 1561.

[7] See 21 June 73.

[8] *Harcourt's amndt. was intended to widen discussion to the English licensing system; he moved a quasi-resolution instead; *H* ccxvi. 1415, ccxvii. 1058.

is more than a departmental one; it has in truth from the very first been treated in the Cabinet as well as by Statute. They think it of great importance that the work should now at once be proceeded with; & they think it fatal to all reasonable hope of speedy progress if sweeping changes are now ordered to be introduced into the designs. They are also very apprehensive of an increase of charge upon the public as a consequence of further delay. An unanswered letter of yours to the Treasury has been laid before them. They regret the proposal contained in that letter, as it is through the Department of Works only that the business of that Department can be transacted. But the best mode of winding up the correspondence will probably be considered with the greatest advantage, when the course to be pursued shall in substance have been agreed upon. With reference then to the main issues, the Cabinet have arrived at the following conclusions, which they must request you to accept as definitively limiting your action in the execution of the Plans for the Law Courts. They consider that, under all the circumstances of the case as it stands, the architect cannot be required to confine himself absolutely to the limit of £710,000, or to effect a reduction of or exceeding £100,000: & further, that it ought not to be exacted of him to omit the Central Hall, or to re-design the South Front. What they desire is that the Plan, as it has been designed & approved under the Statute, should now be put in execution in the best & most effectual manner; which, as they understand, is still practicable within very nearly the limits of cost prescribed by Parliament, notwithstanding the heavy increase of prices now prevailing. Now that the Cabinet has arrived at these conclusions, we may, I am sure, rely on your cordial co-operation.[1]

29. St P. & 3 S.Trin.

Chapel Royal mg & aft. Dined with the Argylls. Wrote to Ed.D.Tel.[2]—Rev. S.E.G.—& minutes. Read Life of Simpson: 'Roots': all through, & wrote on them (not Sunday rest).[3] Finished off my It. version of Lowe's Epitaph.[4]

30. M.

Wrote to Chancr of Exr—The Queen—Ld Chancellor—Pres. Hungarian Acad. of Sciences[5]—Ld Lyttelton—& minutes. Luncheon at 15 G.S. Saw Ld F. Cavendish—Ld Granville—Mr Glyn—Mr Stansfeld—Chr of Exchr. Conclave on Bouverie's Amendt.[6] Arrangements

[1] No reply by Ayrton found.

[2] Not found; not published.

[3] Lord Pembroke had recommended *Roots, a plea for tolerance*, a defence of free-thinking; Gladstone denounced it, sending a lengthy list of questions for Pembroke to give to its author: Add MS 44439, ff. 99, 114–26, 131.

[4] Printed in A. P. Martin, *Life . . . of Sherbrooke* (1893), ii. 411.

[5] Thanking him for election as a foreign member; Add MS 44542, f. 132.

[6] To the Judicature Bill, on Scottish and Irish appeals; Gladstone anticipated the amndt., which Bouverie withdrew; *H* ccxvi. 1562.

respecting the Shah party for tomorrow. H of C. 3¾–8½ and 9¼–1.[1] Read Laveleye, Causes de Guerre.[2]

Tues. July One. 1873.

Wrote to Duke of Roxburghe—Ld Hartington—Mr Howell—The Queen (& Mem.)—Mr R. Duff[3]—Ld Chancellor—& minutes. Dined at Ld Lansdowne's. Saw Ld Granville—Ld F. Cavendish—Mr Glyn—Mr Millais—Mrs Holford[4]—Chancr of Exr—Col. Barthelot—Read The True Reformer. Saw Maclagan X. H of C. 2¼–4¼ and 5¾–7. Spoke on Judicature Bill Amendments.[5] Received the Shah of Persia in the interval. I think he has advanced greatly since his arrival here. Much arrangement in the House beforehand. The party was a notable assemblage of beauty.[6]

2. Wed.

Wrote to Ld Chancellor—Att & Sol.Gen.—Sir A. Panizzi—Mr Ayrton—& minutes. Read The True Reformer—Laveleye, Causes de Guerre. Saw Duke of Argyll—Mr Goschen—Ld F. Cavendish—Mr Glyn—Mr Gurdon—Mr Millais—Att. General—Sir E. Perry. Dined at Sir H. Rawlinson's: much conversation with the G. Vizir. Saw Cox: a case wh vividly recalled Bewick's observation.[7]

To LORD SELBORNE, lord chancellor, 2 July 1873. Add MS 44542, f. 133.

The debate of yesterday in the House of Commons threw further light on our position as to the Bill & impressed me with the belief that though there had been a very strong wish (of a minority) to support an amendment made by the House of Lords for the establishment of a new Vice Chancellorship, it was very uncertain indeed what turn matters might take if we, having already enlarged the number of judges (until after three Common Law vacancies) by a proposal of our own, were now to make the claim of Scotland to representation in the judicial body a ground for further immediate demand. We have left it open to ourselves to do this; & I am ready to concur in it if thought necessary, as I wrote to you yesterday, but I arr[ive] at the conclusion for myself that our safest course would be to take the three openings as intended & to say that we should not

[1] Questioned on Alabama; *H* ccxvi. 1556.

[2] E. L. V. de Laveleye, *Des causes actuelles de guerre en Europe et de l'arbitrage* (1873).

[3] Robert William Duff, 1835–95; liberal M.P. Banff 1861–93; minor office 1882, 1886; governed N.S. Wales 1893.

[4] Perhaps Mrs. Gwynne Holford of Grosvenor Square and Brecknock.

[5] *H* ccxvi. 1630.

[6] *The Times*, 2 July 1873, 5d.

[7] 'I often felt my self so overpowered with reverence in their [prostitutes'] presence that I have been almost unable to speak'; see T. Bewick, *A Memoir* (1862), 96–7.

hesitate to apply next Session for power to make another appointment if upon examination it was found necessary. In this conclusion I understand the Attorney General and Solicitor General to concur & I send this note through them as they will have to communicate with you today on the form of the amendments. The subject matter is altogether slippery in the present state of politics, but this appears to present the smallest amount of danger in connection with our acceptance of Bouverie's amendment.

3. Th.

Eleven to breakfast. Wrote to Ld Chancellor—The Queen (L. & Mem)—Mr Elliot—Mr Childers (2)—Mr Rathbone—Bp of Winchester—& minutes. Luncheon with the Fortescues. He is a great gentleman. Saw Mr Glyn—Sir W. Boxall—Ld F. Cavendish—Mr Aked—Prov. of Oriel—M. Laveleye—Canon Rawlinson (Hom. &c.) —Bp of Winchester—Mr Lefevre—Mr Childers. Visited Christie's. Also Nat. Gallery to see the new Picture. H of C. 4¼-8¼ and 9-1¼: spoke on Judicature Bill.[1] Read Blyden (finished)[2]—The True Reformer. Wrote Mem. on the Eccl. Jurisdiction.[3]

Mr [Gathorne] Hardy came to me in the House at midnight & said he meant, on the 18th Clause of the Judicature Bill, to raise the question of the transfer of the only branch of appellate jurisdiction now remaining outside, to the new Court of Appeal, viz. the Jurisdiction in Ecclesiastical Causes. He has now given notice of an amendment, and it will come on tomorrow at two o'clock.

I asked him how it would be received on his side of the House. He said that he had consulted Mr Disraeli & the front Bench, also the members for Cambridge Univ.[4] and various gentlemen below the gangway: all these were favourable; and he understood that Lord Sandon intended to move it.

I told him that I would consult the Cabinet; & that I did not see my way to any change on the instant in the 18th Clause, as it might be dealt with on the Report or on the intended recommitment.

Thereupon however I consulted with the six members of the Cabinet present, whose names I have struck out in double lines;[5] they all, and likewise the Law Officers, agreed that the thing should be done. I therefore have thought it right thus summarily to consult our colleagues not present: for although I think it would be best to reserve the matter to a future stage we may find the whole House or nearly to rush at it, and in that case it may be a question whether we should even tomorrow divide against it for postponement.[6]

4. Fr.

Wrote to Sir E. Perry—Mem. on Dover Harbour Case—Archbp of

[1] *H* ccxvi. 1723. [2] See 27 June 73. [3] See following mem.
[4] *Walpole and Beresford *Hope.
[5] On the printed list of the cabinet; this one not found.
[6] Hardy's amndt., supported by Harcourt, was accepted; *H* ccxvi. 1795. Initialled and dated 'July 3-4. 1873', Add MS 44761, f. 160; presumably for circulation to Cabinet colleagues.

Canterbury—Ld Hartington—Archbp of York—J. Watson & S.—Ld Pembroke—Bp of London—The Queen—Bp of Winchester—Ld Chancellor—& minutes. Saw Persian Minister—Mr Cardwell—Sir W. Heathcote—Ld F. Cavendish—Ld Granville—Mr Glyn—Ld Granville *cum* Ld Ripon—Ld Ripon—Mr Wade. Dined with the Glyns. H of C. 2¼–7. Spoke on Eccles. Appeals:[1] and 9–1½. Spoke on Civil Service Ireland.[2] Read Memoirs of J.S. Mill[3]—The True Reformer.

To R. LOWE, chancellor of the exchequer, 4 July 1873. Add MS 44542, f. 134.

Dover Harbour. I am startled at the position of this affair, on which I sent into the Treasury for information. When it was mentioned in the Cabinet nothing was said, so far as I recollect, of the Public Works Loan Commissioners, or of any departure from the usual course with respect to Public Works.

I am not *sure* as to what may have happened in each & every case; but I am under the impression that it has been our uniform rule in lending money for the construction of public works, to remit to the Public Works Loan Commission the question of the sufficiency of the security. Is this so?

If it is, a more important innovation in financial matters can hardly be conceived, than a precedent for the introduction of Bills for particular Loans, in which Parliament & Government undertake to decide this question apart from any really competent & safe Tribunal.

If there is a case for a public grant, no doubt that should be considered on its merits; but I speak exclusively of the danger, which I can hardly overstate, of departing from the system upon which one of the very best & most successful parts of our whole scheme of administration has been organised.

To LORD SELBORNE, lord chancellor, 4 July 1873. Add MS 44542, f. 135.

I send herewith copy of a letter I have addressed to the Archbishop of Canterbury. We are between dangers on the right & dangers on the left all along, but my hope is that the change which we have rather brusquely made will impede the consummation of the plot said to have been formed yesterday by Cairns & Disraeli for the strangling of your Bill on its return to the Lords.

To A. C. TAIT, archbishop of Canterbury, 4 July 1873. Tait MSS, 92, f. 176.

If you will kindly refer to the journals of tomorrow morning you will find a detailed account of an amendment adopted by the H. of C. in the 18th clause of the Judicature Bill, by which the reservation, withholding Ecclesiastical Appeals from the new Appellate court, has been struck out. And if you will take the pains to read my observations at the close of the discussion you will find what was intended to be a full & clear account of the position & views of the Govt. in

[1] See 3 July 73.
[2] Govt. defeated in 117:130 on Irish civil servants' salaries; *H* ccxvi. 1819.
[3] Perhaps G. J. Holyoake, *J. S. Mill, as some of the working classes knew him* (1873).

relation to this proposal. The whole of the speeches were however interesting; especially for a harmony so striking, that I was obliged to abandon the intention I had announced to Hardy last night when he opened the subject to me, & in lieu of asking for time to assent to the change at once. My colleagues, I had already ascertained, were favourable to the change, upon the merits of the case; & the collateral points standing to be considered do not appear to present any great difficulty. I certainly could have wished & so I am sure would the Government at large, to have communicated fully with your Grace, & also with the Archbishop of York & Bishop of London, on the adoption of this alteration. But I waited until the question was on the point of being put, for more members to speak; & there really remained no materials or points of support for even a temporary resistance.[1]

5. Sat. [Chislehurst]

Wrote to Ld Stratford de R.—Prince of Wales—Rev Mr Allon—Mr Disraeli—The Queen—and minutes. Cabinet 2-5½. Off to Chiselhurst at 5.45. Read Laugel L'Angleterre[2]—Br.Quart.Rev. on The Ministry—And on the French Reformation.[3] Saw Ld F. Cavendish —Mr Glyn.

Cabinet. Jul 5/73. [*2 P.M.*][4]

√ Vote of last night on Mr Plunkett. Official Committee to be appointed. Question to be arranged.[5]

√ Judicial Committee & Eccles. Appeals. Proceedings narrated by WEG.[6] Nil at present.

√ Ld Cairnes [*sic*] threatened discussion on Tuesday: Protest & damage. 'Notes compared'. 'Proceedings'[7] in Scotch cases; to stand over.[8]

√ Judges appointing their own vacations. Consent of Chancellor might be required. No occ[asio]n to give power to enlarge it.

√ Dropping of Bills. Numbers 15-18 and 20—as to No 7 Fortescue absent.[9]

√ Callan Schools. Harcourt's proposal of an amt. to Bouverie.

√ Irish Constabulary. Ld H[artington] to consider with C of E[xchequer] proceeding provisionally by Estimate.

√ Crown Private Estates. If left to a successor to the Crown, *might* cease to be private. Intended to give effect to the intention of the Legislation. Communicate with Disraeli.

[1] Similar letters sent to Selborne, abp. of York, and bp. of London. Tait replied he must oppose the Bill when it returned to the Lords if it made 'so serious a change in the Constitution of the Church as seems to be contemplated'; 5 July 1873, Add MS 44331, f. 105. Tait's opposition ensured compromise: bps. to be present for ecclesiastical appeals; Marsh, *Victorian church*, 130.

[2] See 17 May 73.

[3] *British Quarterly Review*, lviii. 189, 1 (July 1873).

[4] Add MS 44641, f. 145.

[5] See 4 July 73n.

[6] Notes for this at Add MS 44641, f. 153 and see 3 July 73.

[7] Word smudged.

[8] Cairns and Salisbury argued the Judicature Bill attacked Lords' privileges; *H* ccxvii. 10.

[9] i.e. Prevention of Crime, Bank of England Notes, Building Societies (N. 3), Fisheries (Ireland), Public Prosecutors; N. 7 was the Trade Marks Registration Bill, on Orders of the Day, 7 July; annotated copy at Add MS 44641, f. 154.

√ Mr White's question. No 1. Not prepared to underwrite. 2 [Lord] Chanr. will endeavour to arrange. 3. not prepared to legislate.[1]
√ Dover Harbour. C of E[xchequer] with Mr Fortescue, Mr Welby & Mr [W.] Willink[2] for going forward upon the known & understood rules, in lieu of the instructions recently given.
√ Mint. C of E[xchequer] to sug[gest] 1st Commr. that H.M. Govt's attention has been called for [blank] & that he must proceed forthwith.
√ Registry of Birth. Stansfeld: Endeavour to detach from the question of local taxation.
√ Entries of Cadets for Navy & numbers of the Ranks of Officers. Discussed—proposed ⟨Committee of a Controul.⟩
√ Royal Bank of Scotland. The privilege [of a London branch] not to be refused any longer.

Promises[3]
Locke King—Harcourt—Indian Finance—Bouverie—Mundella.

To Reverend H. ALLON, 5 July 1873. 'Private.' Add MS 44095, f. 327.

I am much obliged by your letter,[4] & by your kindness in sending me the article, which I shall at once read with care. The spirit of frankness in which you write is ever acceptable to me. I fear there may be much in your sombre anticipations. But if there is to be a great schism in the Liberal Party, I hope I shall never find it my duty to conduct the operations of either the one or the other section. The Nonconformists have shown me great kindness & indulgence: they have hitherto interpreted my acts & words in the most favourable sense, & if the time has come when my acts & words pass beyond the measure of their patience, I contemplate with repugnance, at my time of life especially, the idea of entering into conflict with them. A political severance, somewhat resembling a change of religion, should not at most occur more than once in life. At the same time I must observe, that no one has yet to my knowledge pointed out the expression or arguments in the speech on Mr Miall's motion,[5] which can justly give offence: & I am not upon a review of the facts able to think that I did more than my duty in speaking at once on behalf of the Government: or that my so speaking can be truly characterized, as I think it has been in some arguments on the question, as an attempt, or as indicating a desire, to prevent fair discussion.

To B. DISRAELI, M.P., 5 July 1873. Add MS 44542, f. 135.

A Bill respecting the Private Estates of the crown has passed the House of Lords, & is under my charge. I should be glad if you would allow me a moment

[1] On civil service; *H* ccxvi. 1855; annotations on Orders for the Day at Add MS 44641, f. 155.
[2] Sec. of public works loan board, see 5 Oct. 62.
[3] Undated holograph; private members' Bills; Add MS 44641, f. 150.
[4] Of 2 July 1872, Add MS 44095, f. 326, enclosing article on disestablishment in the *British Quarterly Review* (lvi. 195), attempting to 'allay the irritation' of nonconformists, but anticipating schism. See Morley, ii. 458.
[5] See 16 May 73.

on Monday behind the Speaker's chair to explain the purport of the Bill, which touches the Queen's personal arrangements.[1]

6. 4 S.Trin.

Chiselhurst Ch 11 AM (with HC) and 3½ P.M. A day of Sabbath. Read Union Review on Buddhism &c.[2]—The Ch of Eng. by Member of Carlton[3]—Macleod on Religion[4]—Jesus v. Xty,[5] & other T. Scott Tracts.—Br.Quart.Rev. on Catholm.[6]

7. M. [London]

Back to London 11¾. Wrote to Maj. MacMahon MP.—Ld Granville (2)—Ld Ripon—The Queen—& minutes. Luncheon at 15 G.S. H of C. 4¼-8½ and 9½-1.[7] Read Laugel, L'Angleterre—The True Reformer—Paley on Homer.[8] Saw Ld Granville—Ld F. Cavendish—Mr Glyn—Mr Goschen—Mr Disraeli.[9]

8. Tu.

Wrote to The Ld Mayor (2)—The Grand Vizir of Persia—Ld Kimberley—Mrs Th.—Sir W. Knollys—H.N.G.—Ld Hartington—Ld Sydney—The Queen—& minutes. H of C. 3-7 and 9-12½. Spoke on Mr Richard: beaten again: so much the worse for the beaters.[10] Saw Ld F. Cavendish—Sir T. Biddulph—Mr Glyn—Ld F. Cavendish—Mr Stansfeld—Ld Granville—Mr Forster. Eight to dinner. Read The True Reformer—Laveleye, Causes de Guerre.[11]

To LORD HARTINGTON, Irish secretary, 8 July 1873. Add MS 44542, f. 137.

I have seen the Ch. of Ex. & really believe there is no choice but 1. to remain as we are. 2 to abandon permanently all further intended local contribution to

[1] See 21 July 73n.
[2] 'Buddhism and Christianity', *Union Review* (1873).
[3] *The Church of England, dissent and the disestablishment policy. By a member of the Carlton* (1873).
[4] A. *Macleod, 'Christian worship' (1873).
[5] T. *Scott, free-thinker, probably *The English life of Jesus* (1872). See 23 June 72.
[6] *British Quarterly Review*, lviii. 60 (July 1873).
[7] Judicature Bill: *H* ccxvii. 1865. [8] See 28 May 73. [9] See 5 July 73.
[10] Govt. failed to move previous question to H. *Richard's motion for 'a general and permanent system of international arbitration'; Gladstone asked Richard to withdraw his motion; *H* ccxvii. 73. Thirteen members of the govt. failed to vote; *The Times*, 10 July 1873, 11a.
[11] See 30 June 73.

the Constabulary. 3. to bring in a Bill & fail with some ignominy. 4. to proceed by vote—which comes pretty much to No 4 only. But it may be a question whether you should mention the subject in the Cabinet. The vote would of course be understood not to bind the future judgment of Parliament though it would express the view of the Government so far as State contribution is concerned.[1]

9. Wed. [Windsor]

Wrote to Ld Hartington—Circular to MPs (official)[2]—The Queen Tel.—& minutes. Saw Sir T. Biddulph—The Speaker—Sir T.E. May—Ld F. Cavendish—Mr Glyn. H of C. at 2.[3] Off to Windsor at 4. Read The True Reformer—Prof. Mangeot on Persia[4]—O'Malley on Home Rule.[5]

10. Th. [London]

Back to London at 11. Wrote to The Queen (2 l.)—Mr Cartwright —Mrs Th.—and minutes. H of C. 4¼-8½ and 9½-3½. Spoke on Privilege of Lords.[6] Cabinet 2-4. Saw Mrs Tyler: (her burdens are heavy indeed)[7]—Ld Granville—Mr Gurdon—Mr Goschen—Ld Chancellor—Sir T.E. May—Mr Bouverie—Ld F. Cavendish—Mr Glyn. Read O'Malley on Home Rule—The True Reformer.

Cabinet. Thurs. Jul. 10.73. 2 PM.[8]

√ Richard's Address.[9] No necessity for action.
⟨O'Keeffe's Case⟩
√ Cairns & Privilege. May's plan & WEG's Mem. adopted.[10]
√ Alderney [Harbour] question. Keep in repair.
√ Khedive. Treaty as to Slavery. Telegram approved: but saying we will not *insist* upon an article against slavery itself.[11]
√ French Treaty. Accept the short m[ost] f[avoured] n[ation] Clause *non obstante* the German privilege—as it was a condition of the peace.[12]
√ *Order of business*
1. Judicature Bill—through the recommitment. 2. Rating Bill—Report. 3. Educn. Bill—2d R—time of 2r Educn. Bill to be consd. further on Sat.

[1] See 5 July 73.
[2] Not found; probably on party discipline.
[3] Irish drink; *H* ccxvii. 96.
[4] Probably an untraced article by Henri Mangeot.
[5] T. *O'Malley, *Home rule on the basis of federalism* (1873).
[6] Discussing *Blackstone; *H* ccxvii. 154.
[7] His cousin, see 23 Jan. 34; her da. Mary Jane was marrying a man 'without profession'; Add MS 44542, f. 139.
[8] Add MS 44641, f. 156.
[9] See 8 July 73.
[10] Mem. on privilege and Judicature Bill untraced; but see this day's statement.
[11] Proposed convention for suppressing Egyptian slave trade; PRO FO 84/1370.
[12] The treaty was signed on 23 July, valid until 30 June 1877; *PP* 1873 lxxv. 629.

11. Fr.

Wrote to Mrs Th.—The Queen. Saw Ld F. Cavendish—Chancr of Exr—Mr Glyn—Mr Childers—Mr Goschen—Mr Cardwell—Sir G. Grey—and others. Dined with Panizzi. H of C. 2-7 and 10-1.[1] Read Macaulay on Ireland.[2]

12. Sat. [Hatfield][3]

Wrote to Ld Advocate—The Queen l. & Mem.—Abp Manning—& minutes. Cabinet 2-4½. Visited Mr Noble's to see the Hope Scott & Aberdeen busts. Off to Hatfield 4½. Saw Ld F. Cavendish—Mr Gurdon—Mr West—Ld Chancellor. Large & pleasant party at H. Read Memoirs of Dean Ramsay[4]—Laugel's Angleterre.

[*Cabinet. 12 July 1873. 2 P.M.*][5]

√ Telegraphic Monies. Discussed. To wait for Monsell's Evidence.[6]

√ Privilege of Lords. Ld Advocate brought in. Extend qualification of members of Appeal Court.

√ Order of business—Govt. Bills. 1. Judicature Bill. 2. Rating Bill—report. 3. Education. Constabulary Vote.

√ Landed Estates Judge: prob[abl]y temporary Bill.

√ Red River: proclamation. Amnesty, except murderers, by H.M. Govt.

√ Ld Kimberley stated the course taken as to Atlantic Telegraphic Cable. P.O. to report.

√ Mr Ayrton's letter of the 11th. Ld Halifax to communicate with him. See mem. within.[7]

√ Mr Forster to have liberty to alter 3rd clause of Education Bill.

13. 5 S.Trin.

Chapel H.C. 9 AM. Parish Ch 11 AM. Chapel service 6 P.M. Much conversation with Mr Brewer[8]—Ld S.—Ld R. C[avendish]—& others. Read Simcox on Mill[9]—Memoirs of Dean R (finished)—Miss P.s Manzoni[10]—F. Stephen on Morality[11]—Macmillans M. on OConnell.[12]

[1] Spoke on O'Keeffe; *H* ccxvii. 210.

[2] See 7 Mar. 73.

[3] As a memento of the visit, Gladstone sent *Salisbury a 'little work on prayer'; Add MS 44439, f. 175.

[4] Probably collected funeral orations.

[5] Add MS 44641, f. 158.

[6] Papers circulated on 2 July 1873; PRO 30/29/69.

[7] Add MS 44641, f. 161.

[8] J. S. Brewer, see 7 Mar. 48; he catalogued Hatfield MSS.

[9] E. Simcox, 'On the influence of John Stuart Mill's writing', *Contemporary Review*, xxii. 297 (July 1873).

[10] C. M. Phillimore, 'Manzoni', *Macmillan's Magazine*, xxviii. 270 (July 1873).

[11] J. F. *Stephen, *Liberty, equality, fraternity* (1873), iv.

[12] *Macmillan's Magazine*, xxviii. 222 (July 1873).

14. M. [London]

Wrote to Ld Blachford—The Queen Mem. & l.—Col. Ponsonby Tel. Returned from Hatfield at 12¼. Read The True Reformer. Saw Ld F. Cavendish—Abp Manning—Mr Glyn—Mr Stansfeld—Ld Advocate—Prince of Wales—and others. H. of C. 4¼-8¼ & 9-2¼.[1] 2-4. Entertainment to the Cesarewna.[2] Pr. & Prss of Wales, D. of Cambr. & a party. The negro band sang.[3] It was all very interesting & seemed to go well. Ristori, Jenny Lind, J. Voight, & all manner of notabilities.

In conformity with what was sketched and hypothetically discussed in the Cabinet on Saturday, I propose, after the discussion of tonight in the House of Commons which was altogether in favour of such a course, to relinquish altogether the plan of recommitting the High Court of Judicature Bill. Do you agree? H of C. Jul. 14. 73.[4]

I entirely approve. S[elborne].

15. Tu.

Wrote to Ld Hartington—H. Robertson[5]—Ld Halifax—The Queen Tel. & 3 letters—Archd. Harrison—Chr of Exr—and minutes. H. of C. 2-7 and 9¾-2. A plot of Dizzy defeated by silence on Charley's motion.[6] Dined with the Wests. Read a True Reformer. Saw Ld F. Cavendish—Mr Monsell—Ld Halifax—Abp Manning—Mr Glyn—Chancr of Exr.

16. Wed.

Wrote to Mr H. Robertson—Mr Hugessen—The Lord Mayor—each of the Sheriffs[7]—H.I.H. The Cesarowich—Rev. Mr Pike[8]—Ld Granville—M. Chevalier—& minutes.[9] Radcliffe Trust 2½-4¾.[10] Saw Ld F. Cavendish—Mr Gurdon—Mr Glyn—Mr Forster. Tea &c. at Miss Talbots. Dined at Lambeth. Conversation with Abp of Canterbury (on Appeals & B. Mus.):[11] also five colleagues on Col. Ponsonby's

[1] Spoke on Judicature Bill; *H* ccxvii. 325.

[2] See *The Times*, 15 July 1873, 9f; for the Grand duchess, see 16 July 73n.

[3] i.e. The Jubilee Singers.

[4] Holograph note sent to *Selborne; Add MS 44641, f. 162.

[5] Henry Robertson, 1816-88; railway engineer; liberal M.P. Shrewsbury 1862-8, 1874-85, Merionethshire 1885-6.

[6] Charley's motion disapproving of ecclesiastical policy in Trinidad, defeated in 69:83; *H* ccxvii. 433. (Sir) William Thomas Charley, 1833-1904; tory M.P. Salford 1868-80.

[7] Honours consequent on the Shah's visit; Add MS 44542, f. 138.

[8] Thanking Rev. G. D. Pike for success of his Jubilee Singers on 14 July. Add MS 44542, f. 138.

[9] Gladstone this day forwarded to Bruce and Stansfeld a list of complaints about trade union legislation received from G. Howell; Add MS 44439, ff. 152, 163.

[10] See 25 May 55.

[11] See 4 July 73.

letter respecting 'present' to Grand Duchess.[1] Saw Maclagan X: singular & sad revelations. Read Contemp. Review.

To E. H. KNATCHBULL-HUGESSEN, colonial undersecretary, 16 July 1873. Kent Record Office.

It is I think far from improbable that we shall some day hear from Disraeli, as an impromptu, the speech about the Colonies & concurrent endowment which he could not uncork last night. Will you therefore kindly get for me in the C.O. an answer to the following question—with a selection of illustrative figures:— Was not Concurrent Endowment established before our accession to office in all (or nearly all) of the West Indian Colonies? though in such measures of quantity, as to be quite unsatisfactory in view of the principles of religious equality.

17. Th.

Wrote to Ld Granville—Mr West—Mrs Tyler—Professor King—The Queen—and minutes. Saw Dr Carpenter—Lord F. Cavendish—Mr Glyn—Mr Childers—Mr Goschen—Mr Cardwell. Read Telegr. Evidence—The True Reformer. H of C. 4¼-8¼ and 9-1.[2]

18. Fr.

Wrote to Rev. Mr Pike—The Queen l. & Mem—and minutes. Saw Cox X: with interest. Saw Ld A. Hervey—Ld Granville—Mr Gurdon—Ld F. Cavendish—Mr Glyn—Ld Halifax—Conclave on Army Purchase Commission.[3] H of C. 2-7.[4] Dined at Ld Lyttelton's. Read Q.R. on Engl. Poetry[5]—The True Reformer. Made up my *Latin* Version of the Lowe Epitaph: the Italian already finished.[6]

19. Sat. [*Holmbury*]

Wrote to Mr Murray—Mr Ayrton—Mr Salomons—Mrs Tyler—The Queen—and minutes. Cabinet 1.45-4¼. Saw Ld F. Cavendish—Mr Glyn. Visited Baron L. de Rothschild. Off at 4.25 to Holmbury.[7] We were enjoying that beautiful spot, & expecting Granville with the Bp of Winchester, when the Groom arrived with the message that the

[1] Grand duchess Marie Alexandrovna, da. of Alexander II, m. Prince Alfred, duke of Edinburgh, 1874. Ponsonby's letter untraced in Royal Archives.

[2] *Forster's bill amending third clause of 1870 Education Act; *H* ccxvii. 502.

[3] *Richmond moved on 21 July for a royal commission on the working of abolition of purchase; *H* ccxvii. 621.

[4] Spoke on pilgrimages to Canterbury; ibid., 603.

[5] *Quarterly Review*, cxxxv. 1 (July 1873).

[6] See 29 June 73.

[7] Lord E. F. Leveson-Gower's house in Surrey.

Bp had had a bad fall. An hour & a half later G. entered pale & sad: 'it is all over'. In an instant the thread of that very precious life was snapped. We were all in deep & silent grief.[1]
Read Max Müller on Darwin[2]—Zincke on Switzerland.[3]

Cabinet. Sat. Jul. 19. [1873] 1.45 P.M.[4]

√ Trevelyan's [Household Franchise (Counties)] Bill. Open question. Desirable there shd. be no division. Previous question—not approved.
√ Duke of Edinburgh's marriage. 1. 10 m[ille] Ann[ual] annuity. 2. 6 m[ille] jointure 3. Proviso of Sect. 2. to be refused.
√ Army Purchase Commission. Ld Halifax reported meeting with D. of Cambridge & D. of Richmond. Oppose commission. No objection to a committee of H. of L. on the conduct of the Govt.[5] Terms agreed on & put by Cardwell in a note to Ld Lansdowne.
√ Crown Private Estates. Notice & expl[anatio]n from the Chancellor.
√ Bourke's amendment. Resist—(small Cabinet at the beginning).[6]

20.

Ewhurst Ch 2¼ m.mg. Walk in aft. Mr Bowman[7] dined: conversation with him. Read F. Harrison on Fitzjames Stephen[8]—Bp Ld A. Hervey's Charge[9]—Hole on St Peter's visit to Rome[10]—and other Tracts. Woke with a sad sense of a great void in the world. Wrote to Dean of Westminster—Dean of Windsor—Mr Godley.

21. M. [London]

Wrote to The [blank]—Mr Fawcett (Tel.)—The Queen—& minutes. Returned to town 1.15. H of C. 4¼-8¼ and 9-1½.[11] Saw Dean of Westminster—Ld F. Cavendish—Mr Glyn—Ld R. Cavendish—Mr Harley—Ld Halifax—Capt (Harris?)—Mr Farrer. Drove in mg with Ld G. to Abinger Hall.[12] Saw *Him* for the last time in the flesh: resting from his labours. Attended the inquest. Inspected the spot: all this cannot be forgotten. Read Fortnightly Rev:[13] and M. Muller on Darwin.

[1] *Wilberforce fell from his horse riding with Granville from Leatherhead station; see *L.Q.V.* 2nd series, ii. 262. See Morley, ii. 459.
[2] F. M. *Müller in *Fraser's Magazine*, lxxxviii. 1 (July 1873).
[3] See 11 June 73.
[4] Add MS 44641, f. 164.
[5] See 18 July 73 and *L.Q.V.*, 2nd series, ii. 266.
[6] Bourke's motion for a royal commission on the Indian army, withdrawn; *H* ccxvii. 1058.
[7] Probably Henry Bowman, retired curate living in Surrey.
[8] F. *Harrison's review of J. F. *Stephen, *Fortnightly Review*, xix. 677 (June 1873).
[9] Lord A. C. *Hervey, 'Charge . . . at the general visitation' (1873).
[10] Untraced tract by C. Hole.
[11] Spoke on Crown Private Estate Bill: *H* ccxvii. 693.
[12] T. H. *Farrer's house, where Wilberforce's body reposed.
[13] *Fortnightly Review*, xx (July 1873).

22. Tu.

Wrote to the Queen (2 l.)—Dean of Windsor Tel.—& minutes. Saw Mr Goschen—Mr Harcourt—Ld Chancellor—Mr Cubitt—Ld R. Cavendish—Mr Glyn—Ld F. Cavendish—Mr Hope—Ld Hartington—Ld H. Scott—Mrs Hope. 9 to dinner. H of C. 2-7 and 9¼-2.[1]

23. Wed.

Gave way under great heat, hard work, & perhaps depression of fever. Kept my bed all day. Wrote to Mr Forster (on the Household Franchise Bill)—Sir R. Phillimore—Ld Granville—Mrs Th.—and minutes. Saw Sir R. Phillimore—Ld Granville—Dr A. Clark—Ld F. Cavendish—Mr Glyn. Wrote Mem. on Treas. business.[2] Read J. Miller's Life among the Modocs.[3]

To W. E. FORSTER, vice president, 23 July 1873. Add MS 44542, f. 141. 'Imme[diate].'

I had fully intended as you know to be in my place today for the purpose of speaking on the Household Franchise Bill: but an attack of indisposition, due probably to the hot weather, makes it improper for me to leave my bed. Will you therefore in your speech kindly say a few words on my behalf: to the effect that while the Government as a Government has not any opinion or recommendation to offer to the House on this question, & while I regret that it has only been in Mr Trevelyan's power to bring it forward at so late a period of the Session as to give the Debate too much of the character of a discussion on an abstract Resolution, I retain the opinion I have more than once indicated, & believe the extension of the Household Suffrage to counties to be one which is just & politic in itself, & which cannot long be avoided. Of course, I make no reference to the arguments on which I found my conclusions: & I hope it will not be thought an impertinence on my part under the circumstances to have asked you to say a few words on my behalf, expressive of the general purport of this note.[4] I hope I may be able to get up & out to-morrow.

24. Th.

Wrote to Lady Gladstone—The Queen 3 l. & Mem.—& minutes. Cabinet 2-4¼. H of C. 4¼-8¼ & 9¼-2.[5] Incessant interviews much of the day. Long conversation with D[ean] of Windsor.

Cabinet. July 24. 1873. 2 PM.[6]

√ Read Col. Ponsonby's l[etter] of yesty.

[1] Education Act Amndt. Bill: *H* ccxvii. 753.

[2] Not found.

[3] J. Miller, *Life among the Modocs; unwritten history* (1873).

[4] *Forster voted for *Trevelyan's Household Franchise (Counties) Bill, 'as an individual'; he briefly related Gladstone's position; *H* ccxvii. 835.

[5] Endowed Schools Bill: *H* ccxvii. 921.

[6] Add MS 44641, f. 167.

√ Also WEG's to Mr Forster.
√ Ld Chancellor read proposed Amt. respecting Eccl. Jurisdiction referring completion of arrangements to H.M.
√ Lengthened discussion on Telegr. Monies Report.[1]

25. Fr. St James.

Marriage anniversary & Tom's birthday. A golden day. Were I worthy! Wrote to Mr Monsell—The Queen 3 l[etters] & Mem.—The Duke of Wellington—Mr Glyn—Sir S. Scott & Co—and minutes. House & Cabinet 2¼–7: and House 9¼–1¾.[2] Saw Mr Glyn—Ld F. Cavendish—Mr Adam—Mr Gurdon—Mr Bruce—Mr Cardwell—Ld Ripon[3]—Att. General—Mr Grieve—Dr A. Clark—Mr Bates. Saw Lea & another[R].

Cabinet. July 25. 1873. 2 PM. Irregular andirivieni[4]
√ Large discussion on the Telegraphic accounts business. Leaning of Cabinet to an amendment on Cross's motion. WEG stated he could not pledge himself to speak but wd. do so if he shd. see an opp[ortunit]y of being useful.
√ Sandon's motion for a Committee on outpost Clerks.[5]
√ C. of E[xchequer] to act on the Resolution of Zanzibar Committee.[6]

26. Sat. [Chislehurst]

A slight relapse: I kept my bed closely & with such good effect, also aided by Dr C[lark']s medicine, that in the afternoon I got up & went at Dr C's advice to Chiselhurst. Wrote to Sir W. Farquhar—Sir W. Heathcote—Mr Bruce—The Ld Mayor—The Queen—Archdn Utterton—Mr Cardwell—Mrs Th.—& minutes. The Cabinet met below. I sent down Mema: Saw Ld G. before—Ld G. & Mr Cardwell after. Saw Dr A. Clark (2)—Ld Granville—Mr Gurdon—Ld F. Cavendish—Dean of Windsor. Read Miller & the Modocs.

[1] Probably the report of the cabinet cttee., see 6 and 7 June 73n, and see 26 July 73n.
[2] Spoke on Crown estates; *H* ccxvii. 1004.
[3] Probably the occasion on which diarist accepted verbally (and deliberately so?) Ripon's resignation on the county franchise question, offered in his letter of 24 July; Wolf, *Ripon*, i. 279.
[4] 'confused talk' or 'cross currents of people'; a further complaint at late starting; Add MS 44641, f. 171.
[5] Postponed this evening, deb. and withdrawn on 29 July; *H* ccxvii. 1058, 1242.
[6] Two notes to Granville in cabinet, (1): 'I think I shall mention my view as to the mode of meeting any hostile motion about Zanzibar?' 'Is it necessary at this stage—there is *a* chance that the subject may be used to paint Lowe in the blackest colour, but no motion made. [Granville]'; (2): 'I can find no mem. of any proceeding in the Cabinet on the £26000—but minutes on June 14 1873 about a prior stage.' 'Have you asked Cardwell what his precise recollection is' [Granville]. 'Not precise. There is really no doubt' [Gladstone].

Select cttee. on postal contracts reported 23 July, recommending the contract of 8 May be renegotiated; *PP* 1873 ix. 243.

[*Cabinet. Sat. July 26. 73. 2 PM. 11 Carlton House Terrace*][1]
Ld Granville: will you kindly note down such slight particulars of proceeding on the inclosed & any other matters as will enable me to write to the Queen? WEG. Jul. 26. 73.

I did not attend but saw Ld G. and Mr Cardwell after the Cabinet. I asked Ld G. to write for me to the Queen.[2]

27. 7 S.Trin.

Ch in aft only. Morning prayers in my bed. Wrote to Provost of Oriel—Ld Pembroke—Mr Rollo—and minutes. Read Theodore Parker—Dr Hawkins on Ath Creed MS.[3]—Trevor's Sermon[4]—Contemp. Rev. on Strauss—and on Greg respecting Luxury.[5] Much conversation with Dr Clark.

28. M.

Another slight relapse. Kept my bed until 6.30 PM. Wrote to Ld F. Cavendish (Tel.)—Mr Bruce (Tel.)—Chr of Exr—Dr Woodford—Bp of Ely[6]—D. of Wellington—Sir W. Dunbar—and minutes. Saw Ld F. Cavendish—Dr Clark. Read Miller's Modoc Indians—an absorbing book—Janet's Questions du 19[e] siecle.[7]

To R. LOWE, chancellor of the exchequer, 28 July 1873. Add MS 44542, f. 144.

I am afraid that if the Union Steamship company decline to re-open the [Zanzibar] negotiation, you are not in a condition consistently with what I understood to be the view of the Cabinet on Friday to refer the matter to arbitration as you suggest, but if you adhere (as was I think anticipated) to the path marked out by the Committee, you will have to consider the means of bringing other parties into the field & making a temporary arrangement with the U.S. company so as to prevent any offence to Parliament. Should you desire a Cabinet on the subject of course one can be called immediately.[8] I assure you that on Friday in expressing my desire to fight out the battle, as far as you were concerned, on the ground of the services which you have done for the country, I was only rendering a debt of justice, which it is always a pleasure to acknowledge:

[1] Dictated to Gurdon; Add MS 44641, f. 177.
[2] This para. holograph, added at foot of page; notes by Granville on week's business follow. Granville's report in *L.Q.V.* 2nd series, ii. 269.
[3] See 8 June 73; his letter this day on it in Lathbury, ii. 91.
[4] G. *Trevor, 'Athanasian Creed; the damnatory clauses' (1873).
[5] *Contemporary Review*, xxii. 37 (June 1873); article by Froschammer; xxi. 616 (March 1873).
[6] Successfully offering him Winchester; Add MS 44542, f. 143.
[7] P. A. R. Janet, *Les problèmes du XIXe siècle* (1872).
[8] New contract signed on 1 Aug.; *P.P.* 1873 xxxix. 501.

a pleasure certainly enhanced by your estimation of the act. I hope to be in Town to-morrow before noon.

29. Tu. [*London*]

Wrote to Mr Samuelson—The Queen 2 Tel. l. & Mem—Hon Sir A. Gordon—and minutes. H of C. 2–7. spoke on D. of Ed. & shortly on Cross & Lubbock[1]—also after dinner. Saw G.G.G. (Ld Wolverton)[2]—Ld F. Cavendish—Mr Adam. Saw Cox X. Came up from Chiselhurst at 10. Then came the Negro breakfast[3] & their very remarkable singing. Got up the D. of E.s case. Read The True Reformer.

To LORD KIMBERLEY, colonial secretary, 29 July 1873. Add MS 44542, f. 144.

You will I am sure excuse the tardiness of my reply[4] about Fiji under the circumstances of actual business & indisposition which have unfortunately impeded me. I have made one or two suggestions on the margin, applicable to the passages over against which they are written. The general strain of the dispatch seems to me very good, & it is comprehensive in its scope—but I would offer two remarks for your consideration. 1. The dispatch necessarily consists in the main of a list of suggestions in the form of query. They are woven into a continuous text. I think it would present them more clearly to the minds of the Commissioners if they were carved out into a list of queries with numbers to them. 2. Though the dispatch ought certainly to be colourless in its general tenour, yet I think that we ought to indicate clearly what we consider the natural & normal course of proceeding. To explain my meaning I inclose a paragraph for consideration.
Mem:— You will readily understand that it is the desire of H.M. Government to obtain with reference to all the points of inquiry presented to you, & to all others which may suggest themselves to your minds, the expression of your perfectly deliberate & impartial judgment. At the same time you will understand, with reference to the general principles obviously applicable to all such cases, that H.M. Government not only do not desire the acquisition of further territory, but regard it as an evil, only to be accepted if it should unhappily be found to be the indisputable & only means of escaping from greater evils, & from greater evils of a nature that they might, unless a remedy were applied be justly set down to the account of this country. It will be far better for the British Empire, & far better for the Fiji Islands that if they are capable of being ruled in a tolerable manner, or with diminishing difficulty by a government which is in any real even if qualified sense their own & indigenous, they should be so ruled, rather

[1] On Edinburgh's annuity on his marriage; answering Cross's motion on post office misappropriations, and Lubbock's amndt.; *H* ccxvii. 1227.

[2] Had just succ. his father; A. W. *Peel replaced him as chief whip during the restructuring of the govt.

[3] Pike's Jubilee Singers; see 16 July 73; lengthy description of the occasion published by C. N. *Hall in the New York *Independent*, 21 August 1873; see Add MS 44440, f. 139.

[4] Kimberley sent draft instructions on 19 July, Add MS 44225, f. 66.

than that a sovereignty should be constituted, having the seat of its power & its responsibility at the furthest extremity of the globe from the Islands.[1]

30. Wed.

Wrote to The Queen (3)—Ld Kimberley (2)—Mr Hammond—Mr Adam. House & Cabinet 12-7. Spoke on the scandals.[2] Eight to dinner. Ld Salisbury's afterwards. Saw Chr of Exr—Mr Baxter & Mr Adam—Conclave of all these with Mr Stansfeld—Ld Kimberley—Ld Ripon—Ld F. Cavendish (2)—Mr Fortescue—Ld Granville.[3]

Cabinet. Jul. 30. 73. 2 PM.[4]

Irregular andirivieni.[5] WEG & Commons Ministers arrived at 3.30

√ WEG described the scandals in the H. of C.

√ Zanzibar Contract. Arbitration not accepted. Have the Co. knowing this any terms to offer. This answer to be made today.[6]

√ Telegram from Gibraltar senior Naval Officer—reporting probable bombardment of Malaga.[7] Att. General & Sol. Gen. attended also Mr Hammond—and left. If we interfering we interfere 3.[8] on ground of general humanity with security of British subjects—& no govt. to perform the duty of protection. 2. as having no title to carry on war. 1. as pirates (rejected). If we do not it is either 1. we have no right, or 2. we have no power. Resolution of Cabinet sent to Hammond.

√ Slater [*sic*] Booth's notice for tomorrow.[9]

31. Th.

Wrote to Bp of Brechin—Mr R. Wilberforce—The Queen—The O'Donoghue—Lady Harry Kerr—Ld Pembroke—& minutes. Read Hero & Leander.[10] Nine to breakfast. Saw Ld Wolverton—Mr Cardwell—Chr of Exr—D. of Argyll—Mr Adam—Ld F. Cavendish—B. Benjamin—Sir A. Gordon. H of C. 4¼-8½ and after dinner. Spoke on D. of Ed & C of E.[11] Saw Mrs Th. X

[1] Kimberley replied, 30 July, with a 'somewhat weaker' version, which Gladstone accepted that day, ibid., ff. 68, 70.

[2] Disavowed a speech by Ayrton on ministerial responsibility; *H* ccxvii. 1265.

[3] Gladstone's holograph mem. dated by Hamilton 'July 1873' (Add MS 44761, f. 158) lists *inter alia*: Home secretary, Lowe; Ld. President, Bruce or Ripon; Admiralty, Childers; Exchequer, Goschen; Irish secretary, Forster; duchy of Lancaster, Bright.

[4] Add MS 44641, f. 187.

[5] See 25 July 73.

[6] See 28 July 73n.

[7] Bombardment of Malaga was stopped on 1 August by British and German forces; F.O.C.P. 2435, pp. 15-28.

[8] Points written in given order, later renumbered by diarist.

[9] On the Zanzibar contract; *H* ccxvii. 1358.

[10] *Hero and Leander*, tr. E. Arnold (1873).

[11] *H* ccxvii. 1352.

Frid. Aug. One 1873.

Wrote to Mr Hammond—Ld Chancellor—Mr Childers—Mr . . .—Mr Baxter—The Queen—and minutes. H of C. 2-7. (D. of Ed. Annuity Bill) and after 9.[1] Six to dinner: incl. Tom [Gladstone] whose fair & pure child Ida is I fear withering under the cold touch of the last enemy. Read The True Reformer. Wrote the Paragraphs of the Queen's Speech. Saw Ld F. Cavendish—Also Ld Granville, Ld Wolverton, Mr Cardwell, repeatedly, on the crisis.[2] Saw Mr Childers—Mr Forster.

2. Sat. [*Chislehurst*]

Wrote to The Queen (2)—Ld Hartington (2)—D. of Argyll—Mr Bright—Mr Cardwell—& minutes. Read Birch on Shakespeare.[3] H of C. 12-1½ and at 2¾.[4] Saw The Speaker—Mr Childers (3)—Mr Monsell—Ld Gr. Ld Wolvn & Mr Cardwell 12-1. Ld Gr. & Ld W. at 1.45. Cabinet 2¼-6.

An anxious day.[5] The first step was taken: Cardwell broke to Lowe the necessity of his changing his office. Also I spoke to Forster—& to Fortescue—this about the Ld Lieutcy of Essex.[6] The Speech was amended and agreed on. Dined with Adm. Hamilton at Blackheath. Then drove on to Chiselhurst. Saw Rev Dr Miller.

Cabinet. Sat. Aug. 2. 73. 2 PM.[7]

√ Protection of Italians in Spain agt. the reds who have seized the fleet. Seizure of the two red ironclads. Instructions: 1. hold the ironclads (safely landing the crews) until they can be delivered to representatives of the Spanish government able to take & hold them. If there is joint possession, arrange for separate possession. 2. As to Italians. Nothing to be done in opposition to the *de facto* Govt. of Spain.[8]

√ Queen's Speech in draft—amended[9] & approved.

[1] *H* ccxvii. 1441.

[2] Situation in Malaga, persistent radical opposition to duke of Edinburgh's annuity, climax of the scandals, and preparation for restructuring of the govt.; see Morley, ii. 462.

[3] W. J. Birch, *The philosophy and religion of Shakespere* (1848).

[4] Questions; his appearance at 2.45, during the cabinet, was presumably to see the Speaker; *H* ccxvii. 1474.

[5] The chief changes were: Gladstone took the exchequer, Bright the duchy of Lancaster, Bruce became Lord Aberdare and president of the council, Lowe home secretary; Ripon, Childers and Monsell retired. Ayrton became judge advocate-general, Playfair postmaster, Adam commissioner of works; Jessel became master of the rolls, succeeded as solicitor-general by H. James.

[6] Fortescue was gazetted as ld. lieut. of Essex on 24 Aug. as a sop for lack of promotion.

[7] Add MS 44641, f. 189.

[8] Instructions from Hammond and Granville to this effect, in *PP* 1874 lxxvi. 236-7.

[9] A para. was deleted, see Add MS 44641, f. 190.

√ Parl. to be prorogued to Oct. 22.
√ Ashantees. Flank movement under Capt. Glover decided on. Front attack may have to be cons[idere]d hereafter.[1]
√ Commission on officers. Derby, Penzance, Ld J. James.

3. 8 S Trin.

Chiselhurst Ch. mg (with H.C.) and aftn. Saw Mr Torre—Miss Robn. Wrote Tel. with various directions to Mr Godley. Conversation with F. C[avendish]—& R.C. Read Birch on Religion of Shakespeare—The Renaissance[2]—Dowden's Sermon[3]—& other Tracts.

9. [sc. *4*] *M* [*London*]

Off to London at 9.30. Wrote to Abp of Canterbury—Ld Houghton—Mr Bruce (2)—and minutes. H of C. 3-6.[4] Six to dinner. Back to C.H.T. at 11. Saw Ld F. Cavendish—Mr Forster—Mr Adam—Ld Granville—Dr Clark—Mr Cardwell—Att. General—Ld Wolverton *cum* Ld Granville—Count Strzelecki—Mr Bright[5]—Mr Welby. A very anxious day of constant conversation and reflection: ending with an evening conclave.

5. Tu.

My day began with Dr A. Clark.—Rose at 11. Saw 1. Mr Bright—2. Ld Ripon—Ld Wolverton—Mr Cardwell—Ld F. Cavendish—Ld Granville—Ld Halifax—Mr A. Peel—and most of them again in the evening.[6] Wrote to The Queen l. & Tel.—Mr Monsell—Mr Baxter—Mr Ayrton—Mr Childers—Mr Fortescue—& minutes. Most of these carried much powder and shot! Some were Jack Ketch and Calcraft letters.[7] Read The True Reformer.

[1] (Sir) John Hawley Glover, d. 1885; appt. commissioner on the Gold Coast 18 August 1873; later governed colonies. A frontal attack led by (Sir) Garnet Joseph *Wolseley, 1833-1913, was already being prepared by the War Office partly without diarist's knowledge; see W. D. McIntyre, 'British policy in West Africa: the Ashanti expedition of 1873-4', *Historical Journal*, v. 31. Glover had written on 30 July pressing his qualifications; the colonial office this day summoned him; *PP* 1874, xlvi. 271.

[2] Probably W. H. *Pater, *Studies in the history of the Renaissance* (1872).

[3] J. *Dowden, 'The Saints in the Calendar and the Irish Synod' (1873).

[4] Misc. business; *H* ccxvii. 1516; news of the restructuring not yet public; parliament prorogued next day.

[5] Offered the duchy, accepted it conditionally on 6 August, 'now or in October', i.e. on Childers' retirement; Walling, *Bright's Diaries*, 354.

[6] Dining with Bright at the Cavendishes'; Walling, *Bright's Diaries*, 355.

[7] William Calcraft, 1800-79, the London hangman 1829-74. Gladstone this day accepted Baxter's resignation, offered on 2 August; Add MS 44439, ff. 250, 256.

6. Wed.

Wrote to The Queen 3 l. Mem & 2 Tell.—Mr Fortescue—Mr Forster—Mr A. Greville[1]—Robn G. (2)—and minutes. Dined at 15. G.S. Saw Mrs Th afr X. The day as yesterday of incessant interviews. Mr Cardwell at 10—Lord Wolverton *passim*—The Speaker—Mr Dodson—Ld F. Cavendish—Passim—Ld Granville—do—Mr Adam—Mr Ouvry (Clerk)—Mr A. Peel—Ld Kimberley—Mr Childers—Ld Chancellor—Ld Ripon—Chancr of Exr—Mr Gurdon—Mr Fortescue. Cabinet 3¼–5¼. A sad escapade of Lowe's before it. Much anxiety respecting the Queen's delay in replying. Saw Ld W[olverton] late with her reply.[2]

Cabinet. Aug. 6 73. 2 PM.[3]

√ O'Keeffe. Ld Hartington to represent officially to the Commrs. the policy of proceeding at once, not delaying till Novr. Draft read, amended & approved.

√ Spanish ships. If demand is made for surrender, we will consult the Germans: but incline to think they shd. be restored. Say *we* should deal with Contreras like the other prisoners.[4]

√ Suez Canal. Agree to meet at Constantinople.[5]

√ Stated to the Cabinet the changes meditated & discussed. Read mem. framed to be the basis of any commun[icatio]ns to the Press. Discussed the case of Ayrton. My proposal to HM approved.[6]

7. Th.

Wrote to The Queen l. 2 Tell.—Mr Ayrton l. & Tel.—and minutes. Read 'The True Reformer'. Saw Ld Wolverton—Mr Cardwell—Mr Lingen—Att. General—Mr Gurdon—Dr A. Clark—Mr Palgrave—Mr Richmond. Finally corrected Mem. for communicating the changes to the papers.[7] Six to breakfast: a very interesting party.[8] Incessant communications: but some diminution of pressure. Saw Sir E. Landseer: most touching.[9] 6¾–10¾. with Dr A. Clark to the Medical

[1] Algernon William Fulke Greville, 1841–1910; liberal M.P. Westmeath 1865–74; junior whip Aug. 1873–4.

[2] Grudgingly accepted the changes, save Ayrton; Guedalla, *Q*, i. 421.

[3] Add MS 44641, f. 191.

[4] General J. Contreras, 1807–81, led the Intransigents; led abortive coup in June 1873; see C. A. M. S. Hennessy, *The federal republic in Spain* (1962), 204 and F.O.C.P. 2435, p. 19.

[5] Suez Canal Tonnage Commission; F.O.C.P. 2358.

[6] That Cardwell should deal with some of Ayrton's business with her; Guedalla, *Q*, i. 422. *The Times*, after several hints, announced the changes on 8 August.

[7] Add MS 44761, f. 172, forming basis of *The Times* announcement, 8 August 1873, 7f.

[8] Among others, George *Richmond, the artist, F. T. *Palgrave, the anthologist, and Joseph *Hooker, the botanist; see Add MS 44784.

[9] Mentally ill; he d. 1 October.

Festival where I spoke in reply to Sir A. [*sc.* J.] Paget's most undeserved eulogium: & on the position of the profession.[1]

8. Fr.

Wrote to Mr Dodson—The Queen Tel—Tel—Mem—Ida Gladstone—Ld Ripon—D. of Argyll—Mr Ouvry—Dr Woodford—Sir T. Bazley—Sir T. Biddulph Tel.—Ld Russell—Mr Ayrton. Saw Sir W. Stephenson—Sir T. Fremantle—Mr Rivers Wilson—Ld F. Cavendish—do *cum* Mr Dodson—Mr Gurdon—Ld Ripon—Sir E. Landseer—Mr Benjamin—Ld Wolverton (*passim*)—Sir A. Panizzi. Dined at Sir A. Panizzi's. Finished the day with Ld W. Read divers poems.

9. Sat.

Wrote to Mrs Thistl.—Sol. General—Ld Halifax—The Queen (Mem)—Mr Hubbard—D. of Devonshire—Att. General—and minutes. 8¾-6½. Off to Osborne. A long & satisfactory audience of HM. Attended the Council & received a third time the Seals of my old office. Saw Sir J. Cowell—Sir A. Helps—Ld Ripon—Mr Gurdon—Mr Godley—Mr Lowe—Mr Liddell—Two Secs & 2 boys dined. Conversation (various) on the difficulty started about Greenwich.[2] Read The True Reformer.

10. 9 S.Trin.

Chapel Royal mg and Westr Abbey aftn. Saw Ld Spencer—Ld Aylesbury—Mr Godley. Tea with the two Mrs Talbots. Wrote to Mr Hammond—Mr Lowe—Robn G.—and minutes. Dined at Roehampton with the Levens and saw the T.G.s—saw dear Ida[3] in her suffering purity and meekness. Read I. G. Smith Bampton Lectures[4]—Reply to Bp. of Lincoln's Past.[5]—Vaughan's Trin. Sermon.[6] Saw Cox [R].

[1] Praising the 'upward aspiration' of the British Medical Association; *The Times*, 8 August 1873, 6a.

[2] The 1867 Representation of the People Act, 30 & 31 Vict., c. 102, cl. 52 and Schedule H., altered the Queen Anne Act, so that 'the subsequent Acceptance by him from the Crown of any other Office or Offices described in such Schedule in lieu of and in immediate Succession the one to the other shall not vacate his seat'. How this clause and the Queen Anne Act affected Gladstone's acceptance of the chancellorship in addition to the first lordship was a matter of intense dispute, unresolved before the dissolution. It was probable that he would lose Greenwich at a by-election. See R. R. James, 'Gladstone and the Greenwich Seat', *History Today*, ix. 344 (1959) and 3 Oct., 1 Dec., 10 Dec., 29 Dec. 73, 21 Jan., 2 Feb. 74.

[3] His dying niece.

[4] I. G. Smith, 'Characteristics of Christian morality' (1873).

[5] Probably W. Lindley, 'A reply to the Bishop of Lincoln's pastoral to the Wesleyan Methodists' (1873).

[6] Probably C. J. *Vaughan, 'The Father of light. A sermon' (1873).

11. M. [*Hawarden*]

Wrote to Ld Houghton—Sir H. Johnstone[1]—Ld Chancellor—Rev. E. Wilberforce[2]—Mr Bruce—Dean of Chichester—Ld Devon—Ld Aylesbury—Mrs Th.—Lady Ossington—Mr B.H. Cooper—Miss Cox—& minutes. Read Q.R. on Grote.[3] Saw Sir W. Stephenson—Ld Granville—Mr Gurdon—Mr Lambert—Mr Adam—Ld R. Cavendish—Mr A. Peel—Ld Kimberley—Mr Levy—Mr Cardwell: to whom at the W.O. I told in deep secrecy my ideas of the *possible* finance of next year: based upon abolition of Income Tax & Sugar Duties with partial compensation from Spirits and Death duties. This *only* might give a chance.[4] Mr E. Hamilton.[5] Much work in arranging & packing books for departure. Off at 8.50: with a more buoyant spirit and greater sense of relief than I have experienced for many years on this which is the only pleasant act of moving to me in the circuit of the year. This gush is in proportion to the measure of the late troubles & anxieties.[6]

12. Tu.

Reached Hawarden ab. 3.30 AM. Mrs Dryden[7] gallantly appeared: keeping the rest in bed. Wrote to Sir W. Stephenson—Mr Lambert—The Speaker—Mr Gurdon (l. & Tel.)—Archbp of York—Robn G.—Ld Hartington—and minutes. Read Fielding's Peerage[8]—Lucas's Van[9]—Day on Early Use of Iron.[10] A restful day, thank God.

To H. B. W. BRAND, the Speaker, 12 August 1873. Add MS 44542, f. 151.
'Private.'

This letter does not come to notify to you that I have vacated my seat by an acceptance of office; but to state that, the point having been raised in the public journals, I am now having it got up with care for the guidance of my own judgment, as it seems to rest with me to take the first step. The whole law of 'acceptance of office' sadly I think wants clearing & defining.

[1] Unsuccessful request for a peerage from Sir Harcourt Vanden-Bemp-de-Johnstone, 1829–1916; 3rd bart. 1869; liberal M.P. Scarborough 1869–80; cr. Baron Derwent 1881; Add MS 44542, f. 149.

[2] Offering Seaforth parish, vacant on Gobat's d., to Ernest Roland Wilberforce, 1840–1907, s. of S.*; vicar of Seaforth 1873–8; bp. of Newcastle 1882–95.

[3] *Quarterly Review*, cxxxv. 98 (July 1873).

[4] These comments apparently added next day.

[5] i.e. E. W. *Hamilton (see 7 Sept. 66), who had joined the secretarial office from the treasury at the end of July; his hand appears in the letter books on 17 August.

[6] See Morley, ii. 465, 478.

[7] The housekeeper.

[8] J. Fielding, *New peerage of England, Scotland and Ireland*, 2v. (1784).

[9] S. Lucas, *The Noaic deluge* (1873).

[10] St. J. V. Day, 'On some evidence as to the very early use of iron' (1873).

To LORD HARTINGTON, Irish secretary, 12 August 1873. Chatsworth MSS 340. 537.

Spencer, who left London for Dublin on Sunday night, names Dec. 1 as the day when he would like to leave his office. I understand you not to mean to remain after him; & it would not be advisable to change both the great functionaries at once. What I have then to ask is, whether you would like to return to your old post as Post Master General about Oct. 1 when Monsell is *formally* to surrender it? Substantially he goes in a few days or a week hence when the change will be announced. And I should be very glad if you would let me have by post or telegraph your answer to my query as soon as may be, because it would be well to arrange also as to Forster who I expect will succeed you.[1]
[P.S.] Spencer was horrified at the (intended) postponement of the O'Keeffe case & very desirous to see you about it, especially as to the Workhouse branch, to determine the exact course to be taken towards the poor old man. I am extremely glad you are going to Balmoral.

To J. LAMBERT, secretary of the local government board, 12 August 1873. Add MS 44542, f. 150.

The curious points raised about my seat for Greenwich almost drive me to the conclusion that declaratory or defining legislation is required in order to bring things to a satisfactory state with regard to the vacating of seats. At least it seems to me quite clear that the present Act [of 1867] is unworkable *without the assumption of a large liberty of interpretation.* At this moment Mr Lowe & Mr Adam are still Lords of the Treasury. But they have accepted other offices, & I understand that in the case of a Secretary of State the lawyers have some time ago determined that the Secretary of State's office passes completely by delivery of Seals, & Patents are no longer taken. How then (except in common sense) are the new offices 'in lieu of & in succession to' the old ones, when both are actually in being together? The purpose & intention of the Act must here be called in to modify the merely literal construction. My contention is that my old office is (about to be) completely avoided by the re-grant under a new Patent of Treasury with a new commission, & that my commissionership is 'another office' for the purpose & in the meaning of the Act. As in the supposed case of the captain's commission, which I mentioned to you yesterday. You heard the argument made by Mr Gurdon, & also I understand by Mr Gray the Solicitor to the Treasury, about the distributive reading of the words 'other office, or offices'. On reflection I contend that this construction is not mere verbalism: but that it satisfies a purpose & gives consistency to the Act which it would not otherwise possess *supposing my previous contention to be bad.* For on that supposition my commissionership under the new Patent is not *another* office but wholly the same as before. Now if so, Mr Gray's construction enables that to be done which must be presumed to be within the intendment of the Act; but which without this construction *cannot be done.* The Act must be presumed to have contemplated all lawful & usual combinations of offices, as well as exchanges by passing

[1] Hartington wrote on 14 August, Add MS 44144, f. 111, expressing surprise at Spencer's going, not wishing to remain without him, but refusing to return to the Post Office; Gladstone's letter of 15 August, ibid., f. 112, urged him not to leave office, and he remained Irish secretary.

from one to another. And it is undisputed that the Act does provide for combinations when both the Offices taken are (in common parlance) new offices. How ridiculous to hold that a man may become First Lord & Ch. of Ex. without re-election, but that, having been First Lord, he cannot become C. of E. without re-election. In this view the Act requires re-election for the minor change, & not for the major. But under Mr Gray's reading the 'offices' to be taken, or any of them, may be other or not other, & all is straight & square. I ought to say that I have not the Act by me, & I fear that this contribution to your studies may be a very trivial one.

To Sir W. H. STEPHENSON, chairman of the board of inland revenue, 12 August 1873. Add MS 44542, f. 150.

Will you kindly send me your consanguinity table, with the amounts paid *at each rate*, for Legacy & for Succession duties separately, through any series of years which can soon & conveniently be given. It will then be easy to see the effect of any given change.

13. Wed.

Church 8½ AM. Wrote to Lord F. Cavendish—Ld Granville—Mr Lowe (2)—Ld Cowper—Mr Gurdon—Mr Craufurd—Mr Binns[1]—and minutes. Saw S.E.G. upon the School plans for the parish—Sir A. Gordon. The Gordons came. Read Freytag.[2]

To R. LOWE, home secretary, 13 August 1873. Add MS 44302, f. 144.
'Private.'

I do not know whether the word 'timid' was the right one for Liddell, but [at] any rate I will give you proof that I am not 'timid'; though a coward in many respects, I may be.

I always hold that politicians are the men whom as a rule it is most difficult to comprehend, i.e. understand completely; & for my own part, I never have thus understood or thought I understood above one or two, though here & there I may get hold of an isolated idea about others.

Such an idea comes to me about you. I think the clearness, power & promptitude of your intellect are in one respect a difficulty & a danger to you. You see everything in a burning, almost a scorching light. The case reminds me of an incident some years back. Sir D. Brewster asked me to sit for my photograph in a black frost, & a half mist, in Edinburgh. I objected about the light. He said this is the best light. It is all diffused not concentrated. Is not your light too much concentrated? Does not its intensity darken the surroundings? By the surroundings I mean the relations of the thing not only to other things, but to persons, as our profession obliges us constantly to deal with persons? In every question flesh & blood are strong & real even if extraneous elements, & we cannot safely omit them from our thoughts.

[1] Congratulating J. A. Binns of Bradford on Lord F. Cavendish's unopposed re-election in N.W. Riding; Add MS 44542, f. 151.

[2] Perhaps G. Freytag, *Pictures of German life*, 2v. (1862).

Now, after all this impudence, let me try to do you a little more justice. You have held for a long time the most important office of the State. No man can do his duty in that office, & be popular *while* he holds it. I could easily name the two worst Chrs. of the Exchr. of the last 40 years: against neither of them did I ever hear a word while they were in: (I might almost add, nor for them after they were out.) 'Blessed are ye, when men shall revile you.' You have fought for the public tooth & nail. You have been under a storm of unpopularity; but not a fiercer one than I had to stand in 1860, when hardly any one dared to say a word for me, but certainly it was one of my best years of service, even though bad be the best. Of course I do not say that this necessity of being unpopular should induce us to raise our unpopularity to the highest point. No doubt, both in policy & in Christian charity, it should make us very studious to mitigate & abate the causes as much as we can. This is easier for you than it was for me, as your temper is good, & mine not good.

While I am fault-finding, let me do a little more, & take another scrap of paper for the purpose. (I took only a scrap before, as I was determined then, not to 'afflict you above measure'.) I note then two things about you. Outstripping others in the race, you reach the goal or conclusion, before them; &, being there, you assume that they are there also. This is unpopular. You are unpopular this very day with a poor devil, whom you have apprised that he has lost his seat; & you have not told him *how*. Again & lastly, I think you do not get up all things, but allow yourself a choice, as if politics were a flower garden, & we might choose among the beds: & as Ld. Palmerston did, who read F.O. & War papers, & let the others rust & rot. This I think is partially true, I do not say of your reading, but of your mental processes.

You will, I am sure, forgive the levity & officiousness of this letter for the sake of its intention.[1]

14. Th.

Ch. 8½ AM. Wrote to Ld Kimberley—Ld Granville—Mr Lambert—Bp of Chester—Mr Gurdon l. & Tel.—Ld Houghton—Scotts—Sir T. Biddulph—Mr Bright—Duke of Devonshire—and minutes. Saw Rev. S.E.G. (Educn)—Rev. Ernest Wilberforce—Sir A. Gordon. Read Shelley's remains[2]—Weatherly's King René.[3] Walk with A.G. & Willy.

To John BRIGHT, M.P., 14 August 1873. Add MS 43385, f. 219.
'*Very Private.*'

(Let us bid farewell to *Misters*)[4] 1. I am not sure whether your going to Balmoral will be necessary but I presume you will be in Scotland and therefore able to do it without inconvenience or with little. Through some muddle of somebody, I have not yet kissed hands on taking the office of C. of E.

[1] In Morley, ii. 464.
[2] Probably D. F. *MacCarthy, *Shelley's early life* (1873).
[3] By F. E. Weatherly.
[4] Begun 'Dear Bright' for the first time.

I will find out for you exactly what is *indispensable.*
2. As you will have no trouble at Birmingham, I am glad your acceptance[1] is as to its execution postponed: for I hope in the interval to arrange the further changes which affect the Secretaryship for Ireland and the V.P. Ship of Education. This will I hope smooth your path.
3. As to the Parliamentary future of the question of Education, we had better talk when we meet. I remember your saying well and wisely how we should look to the average opinion of the party. What we want at present is a *positive* force to carry us onward as a body. I do not see that this can be got out of Local Taxation—or out of the Suffrage (whether we *act* in that matter or not, and individually I am more yes than no)—or out of Education. It may possibly, I think, be had out of *Finance*. Of course I cannot as yet see my way on that subject: but until it is cleared, nothing else will to me be clear. If it can be worked into certain shapes, it may greatly help to mould the rest, at least for the time.
4. I think the effect of the reconstruction may be described as follows. First, we have you. Secondly, we have emerged from the discredit & disgrace of the exposures by our administration of mild penal justice, which will be complete all round when Monsell has been disposed of. Thirdly we have now before us a clear stage for the consideration of measures in the Autumn. We must, I think, have a good bill of fare or none. If we differ on the things to be done, this may end us in a way at least not dishonourable. If we agree on a good plan, it must come to good, *whether* we succeed or fail with it. Such are my crude reflections, & such my outlook for the future.

Let me again say how sensible I am of the kindness, friendship, and public spirit with which you have acted in the whole of this matter.[2]

To LORD KIMBERLEY, colonial secretary, Add MS 44542, f. 153.
14 August 1873.

Of the policy to be pursued towards the Ashantees I do not consider myself a good judge, & it would not seem self-evident to me why if the Ashantees are likely to remain where they are they should necessarily remain as enemies. But assuming this, which indeed I am not able to dispute, I quite agree that what is quickest done is best done, & I can perfectly understand that you may be right in giving a special allowance to Sir G. Wolseley.[3] As to the Glover plan I think it is a good one, but it seems to me that a man like Capt. G. cannot properly be invested with the power of the purse beyond very narrow limits, & that a *responsible* person with him, carefully chosen, should not only keep the accounts, but report constantly upon & controul the expenditure. I trust no separate expedition to Coomassie may be found necessary.

15. Fr.

Church 8½ AM. Wrote to Ld Hartington (2)—Ld Granville L. & tel. —Mr Gurdon Tel.—The Queen—Mr Thomas Tel.—Mr Bruce—

[1] Bright formally became chancellor of the duchy of Lancaster on 30 September.
[2] Part in Morley, ii. 478.
[3] Kimberley, 13 August, Add MS 44225, f. 73, reported he, Cardwell, and Cambridge, had offered 'the whole civil and military power' to Wolseley, who accepted, and that Glover was to raise a flanking force of 10,000 'natives'.

Mr Hubbard—Mr Lowe (2)—Ld Kimberley—Mr Lingen—Mr Childers—Dean Hook—Mr Pope Hennessy—Ld Hatherley—Robn G.—Mr Wingfield Baker—and minutes. Read Freytag's Sketches—Shelley's Remains. Walk with Sir A.G. 5-6¾. Attended & spoke at the Parish Meeting for supplying deficiency of Education by voluntary schools.[1]

To R. R. W. LINGEN, secretary to the treasury, 15 August 1873. Add MS 44542, f. 154.

Please to observe that no Treasury papers are to be sent to me without having been seen by Mr Dodson (or Ld. F. C[avendish]) except: 1. Such as would come to me direct were we all in town, & in full Session. 2. Such as are of an urgency not admitting of any delay by reference to them.

16. Sat.

Ch. 8½ AM. Wrote to Mr Cardwell—Mr Gurdon (2)—Mrs Hampton—The Speaker[2]—Mr Lowe—Atty General—Mr Morgan—Sir R. Phillimore—Mr Bright—& minutes. H. & I cut a tree: walk afterwards. Read Zincke's Egypt[3]—Edgeworth's Lame Jervas.[4]

17. 10 S.Trin.

Ch. 11 AM with H.C. and 6½ P.M. Wrote to Mr Gurdon 2 l. & tel.—Ld Granville 2 l. and 2 tel.—The Queen Mem.—Mr Lambert—Mr Tupper—Dean of Windsor—Mr Hammond—Sol. General—& minutes. Read Irish R.C. Bps Letter—Funeral Sermons on Bp of W.[5]—Address for Old Catholics—Lightfoot & Westcott Addr. & S.[6]

18. M.

Church 8½ AM. Wrote to Rev. Dr Lightfoot—Ld Granville Tel.—Ld Kinnaird—Robn G.—Mr Wilberforce—Mr Newton—Sir W. Stephenson—Mr Gurdon Tel.—Mrs Jacobson—Mr C. Howard—and minutes. Cutting trees with W. Conversation with Mr Wickham:[7]

[1] The meeting raised half the required sum to allow Hawarden schools to continue voluntarily, without a School Board; *The Times*, 18 August 1873, 9f; after widespread public comment, especially from J. *Chamberlain, Godley wrote to stress the local circumstances; ibid., 25 August 1873, 3e. See 27 Aug. 73.

[2] On Greenwich, in Morley, ii. 467.

[3] See 11 June 73.

[4] M. *Edgeworth, *Lame Jervas* (1861 ed.).

[5] Probably those by Liddon, Woodford, and Claughton.

[6] By B. F. *Westcott and J. B. *Lightfoot (1872).

[7] E. C. *Wickham, who m. Agnes Gladstone 27 Dec. 73; see 18 Oct. 42n, 26 Aug. 73.

a superior man: perhaps his appearance does not do him full justice. Saw S.E.G. Read Zincke on Egypt.

19. Tu. [*On train*]

Worked post in the morning & on the rail. Wrote to Ld Hartington (2)—Ld Granville—Mr Godley Tel.—Mr Gurdon—Mr Fremantle —Mr Hammond—& minutes. To Mold at 9.45 for the Eisteddfod: addressed the meeting ab. 35 m.[1] Then to Chester special.[2] Saw W.H.G. on Ch preferments. Went to Liverpool & saw Robn G: then by 2.20 PM to the N. Read Etoniana.[3]

20. Wed. [*Balmoral*]

Reached Aberdeen at 4. Travelled with Alamayu[4] up to Ballater: a gentle & pleasing boy in manner. Reached Balmoral at 6.30 and took a supplemental sleep in my bed & the old & rather loved 'Ministers room'. Saw Col. Ponsonby. Wrote to Ld Granville 2 l. & tel.—Ld Wolverton—C.G.[5]—Mr Gurdon—S. Lyttelton[6]—Ld F. Cavendish —Mr Hammond Tel.—and minutes. Saw Col. Ponsonby. Drove to Mr Mackenzie's[7] & walked back over the Lochs. Read Khomiakoff Eglise Latine[8]—Etoniana.

21. Th.

Wrote to Rev. Mr Mayow—Mr Gurdon Tel. Tel Tel.—Mr Rivers Wilson—Mr Forster—Mr Bright—Ld Kimberley—Attorney General —Ld Granville Tel.—Ld F. Cavendish—C.G.—Mr Godley Tel.— & minutes. Lastly to H.M. to excuse myself from dining. I went out to drive tea & walk with Prince Leopold: had a very private conversation with him & was sharply seized in the midst. Took to bed on return. Read Etoniana—Khomiakoff—Geography of the Highland Clans.[9]

[1] Recalling his appt. of J. *Hughes as bp., and reporting he had 'modified his opinion' on the Welsh language; *The Times*, 20 August 1873, 4d.

[2] i.e. by special train.

[3] Perhaps *Ancient and modern Etoniana* (1865).

[4] See 22 Jan. 72.

[5] Letters during this visit in Bassett, 198–9.

[6] Who joined the private secretaries' office.

[7] Perhaps J. Mackenzie of Daldownie, Ballater.

[8] A. S. Khomyakov, *L'Église Latine et le Protestantisme* (1872).

[9] Untraced.

To C. RIVERS WILSON, treasury clerk, 21 August 1873. Add MS 44542, f. 160.

I have received your letter of the 19th & the accompanying papers.[1]

The question on which I cannot move till I see my way clearly is that relating to the India Stock which you propose to take by arrangement with the broker—now I do not see that this proceeding is covered by the precedents in the useful table you have sent me (but I telegraph for an explanation of the entry about paying off 5 per cents. I do not know whether this relates to a small quantity created I think some twenty years back). There is no doubt about its legality, I believe: there can be more about its economy. The only question is whether it is such a departure from usage as the 'City' would be entitled to complain of. It is not nearly so querulous on these matters now as it used to be; & I am extremely glad that the Governor of the Bank approves. Still I cannot throw on him any responsibility. We have hitherto it is plain gone thus far, that when the C. of E. has himself been both a seller & a buyer we have made a book transaction of it & kept out of the open market. This is economical & rational, & is also established. It is another thing to say that when some other public body is a seller & the C. of E. is a buyer, or *vice versa*, a private arrangement (at the price of the day) shall be made. For I think (1) it cannot, if done, be confined to the Indian Government—why should it not be done with a colonial Governor, the Bank of England, the Metropolitan Board & many other bodies? (2) If good to be done when we buy & they sell, it is also good when they buy & we sell. I quite agree that we cannot go through the form of a public proceeding with the substance of a private one, & the question really seems to be whether there shall be a considerable extension of the established practice. And the argument is not all on our side; for I do not doubt that in time of prosperous revenues the purchases in the open market & the knowledge that they would take place, materially helps to sustain the price of the funds. In short I cannot regard the transaction as an isolated one but must consider well the principle on which it is based. I should be glad to know what Sir A. Spearman thinks of it. Indeed I do not much like disposing of it by correspondence & should be glad, unless there is any great urgency, to keep to the established course until I can in October consult fully the financial authorities both in & out of the Cabinet. If it is done, it should be done on a minute dealing with the subject & showing how far we mean to go. If however Sir A. Spearman with his long experience & conservative instincts saw no objection after considering the case, I should regard this as an important element in the matter to be decided.

22. Fr.

Up to luncheon. Wrote to The Queen l & Mem.—and copies of each.—Mr Monsell—Mrs Th.—Dean of Windsor—Mr Delane[2]—Ld Lyttelton—Robn G.—Ld Granville—Ld Chancellor—Mr Godley 2 Tel.—Mr Hammond—C.G.—and minutes. Read Khomiakoff—Etoniana (finished)—Lauth's Homer u. Ægyptos.[3] A gentle walk. Long conversation with The Queen.

[1] See Add MS 44439, f. 242.

[2] Details of govt. changes; Add MS 44542, f. 161.

[3] F. J. Lauth, *Homer und Aegypten. Programm* (1867).

23. Sat.

Wrote to Ld Granville—Mr Jas Watson[1]—Mr Welby—Mr Gr. Vernon—Mr A. Peel[2]—Sir Geo. Jessel—Lord Ebury—Mr Lowe—C.G. —Mr R. Wilson—Mr Caird—Mr Hamilton 2 Tel.—Dean of Winchester—Mr Kitchin—Bp of Ely—and minutes. Calls. Saw Dr Taylor—Dr Watson.[3] Read Houghton's Keats[4]—Khomiakoff Eglise Latine—Kitchin's Report.[5] Studying hill geography. Dined with H.M.

To James CAIRD, agriculturist, 23 August 1873. Add MS 44542, f. 165.

I have to thank you much for a very interesting letter:[6] & though I feel the force of your argument about French demand in its influence upon price, I would hope that the unusually long notice which importers have had may have enabled them to provide better in point of time & of quantity for the wants of the country than would otherwise have been practicable. The facts about the reaping machine are curious & satisfactory. I myself noticed them a fortnight back when I had never seen them before. This is the one legitimate & wholesome check on a rising market for wages.

24. 11 S.Trin.

Attended Crathie Ch at 12.[7] Wrote to Ld Granville—Dean of Windsor—C.G.—Ld Pembroke—and minutes. Conversation with Dr Watson—Prince Christian. Walk with the two Princes to Abergeldie mains. Read Khomiakoff—Kalisch on Leviticus.[8]

25. M.

Wrote to Ld Lyttelton—Marq. of Huntley—C.G.—Sir R. Phillimore—and minutes. Dined with HM. Read Buxton on Language[9] —Quousque[10]—Khomiakoff—Houghton's Keats. Drove to Corndavon for luncheon. Walk over the hills to Invercauld & part of the way home: ab. 13 m—quite fresh. The Queen spoke about Railway Accidents wh as usual impress her much.

[1] Instructing his broker to sell £11,500 Metropolitan District Railway stock, and buy Pennsylvania Bonds; Add MS 44542, f. 162.

[2] Asking for his forecast of election losses 'upon the return enclosed'; ibid., f. 162.

[3] Perhaps James Jonathan Watson of Great Ormond St.

[4] R. M. *Milnes, Baron Houghton, *Life, letters and literary remains of John Keats*, 2v. (1848).

[5] By G. W. Kitchin, probably on eastern churches.

[6] Untraced.

[7] The presbyterian church; this was the first visit to Balmoral on which he did not organise anglican prayers in the house; but see 31 Aug. 73.

[8] M. M. *Kalisch, *A historical and critical commentary on the Old Testament* (1858).

[9] Or Baxter; perhaps article by W. E. Baxter.

[10] [W. E. *Jelf], *Quousque? How far? How long?* (1873).

26. Tu.

Wrote to Bp of Ely—The Queen Mem. & Copy—Mr Godley Tel. Tel Tel—Rev. E. Wilberforce—Robn G.—C.G.—Agnes—& minutes. Read Houghton's Keats—Khomiakoff's Eglise Latine. We went out at noon, to gather round the Prince's obelisk Memorial, & drink (whisky) to his memory. In aft drove to Altnagussach[1] and walked back 8½ miles, 2 h. 10 m. Received the stirring news of Agnes's marriage as settled. It is indeed a great event in our settled household. It has I believe every promise of the blessing of God. Saw Sir T. Biddulph on Army Commn.[2]

27. Wed.

Wrote to D of Argyll tel.—Mr Rivers Wilson Tel. & l.—The Queen Mem.—l. & copy—Mr Mundella—Sir H. Verney—Mr Bright (2)—C.G.—Mr Godley Tel.—Helen—Mr Wickham l. & copy—Mr T. Bayley Potter—Bp of Peterborough and minutes. Saw Sir T. Biddulph —Prince Christian. Dined with H.M. Read Khomiakoff—Houghton's Keats. Drove to Invercauld to see the hills: walk in Glen Beg.

To John BRIGHT, M.P., 27 August 1873. Add MS 43385, f. 227.
'In haste. Private and confidential.'

I have just received your kind & considerate letter.[3] The Manchester Examr. had been sent to me and I sent it to Granville as containing a true account of my little speech. There is no time to read your inclosures for the messenger goes in ten minutes and I think that in that limited time I can say what is necessary.
1. First I expect to be at Hawarden in the course of the 4th instant & you will be very welcome then if you like to come. Or I could meet you in Liverpool on that day if it be more convenient.
2. You completely understand me as to my speech. It was meant to leave in the *status quo* not the Bill but the *question*. I do not think the present state of mind in the party, or its external fortunes are such as to allow of any movement whatever on the part of the Government with advantage.

It may or may not be possible hereafter to agree on some movement. I dare not give an opinion on this head for some of the differences seem to cut deep.

But for the moment I think it must be to a limited extent an open question in the Government itself. It is impossible fairly to expect for example that you & Forster should hold in public identical language.

My view about finance is this. It is in finance *only* that I see a possibility—I will not yet say more—of our being able to do something that may raise us to a higher and firmer level.

[1] The queen's house in the forest, also known as 'The Hut'.
[2] See Add MS 44542, f. 168.
[3] Of 25 Aug., Add MS 44113, f. 64: 'I see the note [from Godley] to Mr Chamberlain & think it sufficient.' See 15 Aug. 73.

If we can once thus raised, if we feel that we are breathing a more healthy and 'nimble' air, then I think will be the time when there will be the best hope, the best likelihood, of an improved understanding among ourselves about the question Education. At a time like this of comparative depression men are disposed to view all things in dark colours, but *then* they would have more disposition to abate severally what they could honourably part with in their schemes of their opinions, as they would feel there would be a real value in agreement if once obtained, and that it was worthwhile to make some effort to obtain it.

I hope that this note may convey to you at least in part my view of what is called 'the situation'.

28. Th.

Wrote to Ld Granville (2)—Ld Kimberley—Mr Dodson—Sir W. Stephenson—Ld Provost of Aberdeen[1]—Sir C. Locock—Sir Thos G.—The Queen 2 l. and copy—M.F. Tupper[2]—Ld Cowper—Mr Godley Tel. Attended the Braemar Games a very pretty sight 2½-6¼. Wrote Notes on the Russian Counter Project.[3] Saw Mr West (Buckhurst Title)[4]—Prince Christian (Cumbd St)—The Queen (on the m[arriage])—Col. Farquharson—Mr Pease—Ld Fife. Dined with the Queen. Read Khomiakoff—Houghton's Keats.

29. Frid.

Wrote to C.G.—L. & tel.—Post master Aberdeen Tel.—Rev Mr Mayow—Mr Godley—Attorney General—Mr C. Howard—Dr Liddon—Landlord, Kingussie—Ld F. Cavendish—Mr Cardwell—Ld Granville—Sir T. Biddulph—Dean of Windsor—Rev. S.E.G.—& minutes. Long conversation with the Queen on the [royal] marriage —P. Leopold—& the Army Commission: with some other matters. Also with P. Leopold. Also with D. of Edinburgh. Also saw Mr West. Dined with H.M. Read Houghton's Keats.

To E. CARDWELL, war secretary, 29 August 1873. Add MS 44542, f. 168.

Two days ago Sir T. Biddulph opened fire upon me in the Queen's name about the composition of the army complaints commission. We had a good deal of argument with little impression either way, certainly on my side none. Today the Queen entered upon the subject. She said that if we were to grant a Commission we had better do it in a way that would make it acceptable: described the

[1] Informing him the Queen could not stop in Aberdeen for an Address; Add MS 44542, f. 167.

[2] Giving him a civil list pension of £120 p.a.; see Add MS 44542, f. 167 and D. Hudson, *M. Tupper* (1949), 262.

[3] Of a marriage treaty; see Ramm I, ii. 404 and Add MS 44761, f. 176.

[4] Its succession; *Complete Peerage*, ii. 385.

discontent in the army as very formidable: lamented the absence of names like Lord Grey & Sir G. Grey: suggested the adding [of] two military officers. I gave no way upon any of these points: but seeing that neither was she disposed to yield I said probably it would be well to make known H.M's sentiments to the Cabinet which would meet in no very long time. Of course I held out no expectation that the Cabinet would alter its course: but I felt that she was not likely to yield to any other authority. I hope no great inconvenience will arise from the delay. It is needless for me to mention the arguments I used: they will readily occur to you. When however she mentioned, too truly, the defection of our Peers on the occasion of the Debate, I referred to the very different sentiment that would be aroused in the H. of Commons.

To LORD F. CAVENDISH, 29 August 1873. 'Private.' Add MS 44542, f. 168.

Many thanks for your report.[1] I heartily congratulate you on your reelection. But the attitude of the Nonconformists means mischief in the future. I do not see what can be done at this moment but to avoid sharp issues. They have power to throw us into a minority, & they probably will use it: but they have not power to do more. You will see a letter of mine to Bright explaining my view rather more fully. I have no doubt that you did all that could be done with your people.

30. Sat. [Invercauld]

Wrote to Mr Cardwell—Postmistress Ballater Tel.—Ld Chancellor—Mr Childers—Stationmaster Carlisle—Ld Kimberley—Mr Hammond—& minutes. Finished Houghton's Keats. Saw Master of the Rolls—The Queen (audiences 2)—Prince Leopold—Sir Arthur Helps—Duke of Edinburgh. Drive & walk with Gen. Ponsonby to Invercauld where I was most kindly received. But a heavy post followed me.

To LORD KIMBERLEY, colonial secretary, 30 August 1873. Add MS 44542, f. 169.

Your drafts[2] have been sent to me unfortunately at the moment when I was to leave Balmoral & through some miscarriage of the post they have only reached me at 8 this evening, sent up by special messenger from Balmoral. I will make upon them in haste such general remarks as occur to me, to save the post. 1. Speaking generally I think they do not leave a clear impression on the mind as

[1] On his answer to the Liberation Society, but not in Add MS 44124; see Cavendish to Gladstone, 31 August 1873, ibid., f. 30.

[2] Of instructions to Wolseley from colonial and war offices; Add MS 44225, f. 81; Kimberley added, 29 August, ibid., 'You will see that we have left open the decision as to what steps Wolseley is to take and whether a force is to be sent out from this country.' Final drafts sent on 8 and 10 September 1873, appointed Wolseley Administrator to the Gold Coast, and mentioned instructions to the governor-in-chief of the West African settlements not to interfere; Kimberley's supplementary dispatch of 10 September enclosed the 1831 Convention: it 'seems to form a reasonable basis for any fresh Convention'; *PP* 1874 xlvi. 407.

to the limits of the discretion of the new Governor; what he may undertake on his own responsibility & for what he must refer home. This remark I think applies especially to the War Office Draft. 2. It is the more important that this line should be clearly drawn because I think the Cabinet has never yet considered how far it can itself go without calling Parliament together. I consider it to be very doubtful, & at the least to require to be very carefully weighed, whether we can of ourselves venture to authorize an Expedition to Koomassie without obtaining Parliamentary sanction. But I understand your Draft A. to Sir Garnet Wolseley to proceed on the principle that he is to report home before any great operation, apart from that of Capt. Glover, is undertaken. And this is confirmed by your letter, from which I gather clearly that we may expect to be called upon to consider this matter by the end of November. It is evidently most desirable that this opportunity should be afforded us; & the state in which the marines have returned will naturally bring the public mind into a sensitive condition. So that I am glad to learn that the limits of the healthy season will give time for the reference you propose. 3. I do not understand why you have not, as your first offer to Sir G.W., desired him to make a fair offer to the Ashantees, stating what we require, giving them no more than a sufficient time to consider it, & letting them know that if they refuse or delay we cannot be trifled with. This I think we did to the Chinese in 1859; & is it not evidently reasonable. 4. It seems to me the more important that we should thus endeavour to avoid the last extremity, because the impression left by the statement in your Dispatch A is not comfortable. I know hardly anything of the history of the transactions: but much misgiving is excited by the dispatch as to the recent exchange with the Dutch. This dispatch will be published, & will be taken as the full statement of our case. Has it been composed with that idea sufficiently in view? I do not say it has not, for I am not master of the facts. But if our case is not a very perfect one, it becomes the more material that we should exhaust the means of accommodation before we make the direct attack.

31. 12 S. Trin.

Episc. service at Mar Lodge—8 miles off. Luncheon with Ld Fife. Walk & drive. Saw Mr Pease to sign & seal for tomorrow.[1] Read Quousque (finished)—Stop the Leak[2]—Birch's Sermon—Courtenay's Sermon—Temple on the Catholic Faith.[3]

Invercauld Monday Sept. One. [*Kingussie, Inverness-shire*]

(Wrote to Ld Granville Tel.—Col. Farquharson Tel.) Off at 9.15 to Castleton & Derry Lodge, driving. From the Lodge at 11.15. 33 miles to Kingussie on foot: arrived 9.30.[4] Half an hour for luncheon: ¼

[1] i.e. to agree to the walk; Pease unidentified.

[2] Perhaps [Mrs H. N. Baker], *Stopping the Leak* (1865).

[3] T. *Birch, 'The unreasonableness of revenge, and the great duty of Christian charity considered' (1720); C. L. Courtenay, 'God's work and God's glory' (1873); H. Temple, *The Catholic faith; or what the Church believes and why* (1873).

[4] i.e. they walked W. and then N. through Glen Feshie, then by Drumguish to the Duke of Gordon hotel at Kingussie on the Spey.

hour waiting for the ponies (road so rough on the hill): touched a carriageable road at 5: the top at 3. Very grand hill views: floods of rain on Speyside. After dark I walked barelegged from the knee. Good hotel at Kingussie but sorely disturbed with rats. The Pease party very friendly company. Saluted by an odious Telegram on arriving.[1]

2. [Naworth Castle]

Wrote to Gen Ponsonby—Robn G.—C.G. Bid farewell to my companions and left K[ingussie] at 9.30. Met Sir G. Grey in the train and had much conversation on recent events. Carlisle at 7.40 and Naworth Castle[2] (by road) at nine. Most kindly received. Discussion with Mr Colvin on the 'Aphrodite'.[3] Read Homer u. Ægypten[4]—Middy on Irish Churches &c.[5]

3. Wed.

Wrote to Mr Lowe (2)—Ld Granville—Mr Cardwell—Sir W. Stephenson—Mr Childers—M. of the Rolls—Robn G. (l. & Tel)—The ODonoghue—C.G. (l. & Tel)—Ld F. Cavendish—Mr Godley (Tel) —Mr Hammond—Att. General—Mr Rivers Wilson—Mr Godley— & minutes. Read acc. of Lanercost Abbey. Drove to the Carlisle Statue—Lanercost—and the beautiful banks of the Irthing. Conversation with Mr Motley on Joachim Miller[6]—and on Canada. With Mr Bell,[7] & Mr Howard jun.[8] on the state of Art.

To E. CARDWELL, war secretary, 3 September 1873. 'Private.' Add MS 44542, f. 171.

Granville reminds me that the D. of Cambridge was against putting soldiers on the Commission[9] & this being so I think I ought to be able to manage the matter with the Queen by letter & so escape the delay. There is more backstairs pressure in these matters than is altogether agreeable or right.

[1] Untraced.

[2] Seat near Brampton with a fine picture collection, of William George Howard, 1808–89, rector of Londesborough 1832–77, 8th earl of Carlisle 1864.

[3] (Sir) Sidney *Colvin, 1845–1927; art and literary historian, directed the Fitzwilliam 1876, keeper of prints at British Museum 1883. They discussed a photograph of a bust of Aphrodite offered to the Museum by Castellani; see Colvin's *Memories and Notes* (1921), 191ff.

[4] See 22 Aug. 73.

[5] *Sic*; untraced.

[6] Cincinnatus Heine Miller, 1841?–1913, known as Joaquin, 'the Oregon Byron'; in London 1873.

[7] Unidentified.

[8] Perhaps Gerald Richard Howard, b. 1853, the earl's cousin.

[9] Commission on soldiers' grievances on purchase abolition payments; papers in PRO 30/48/10.

To R. LOWE, home secretary, 3 September 1873. Add MS 44542, f. 170.

[1]I have not seen the speeches at the Edinburgh meeting,[2] but I have read the resolutions & I make due note of your remarks upon them. It is quite out of my power to meet the points you raise. I hope you will look thoroughly into the question. What I have heard said upon it in Parliament does not satisfy my mind. No one would be better qualified than you, hardly anyone so well qualified to get a firm grasp of the questions of law & the questions of principle involved in what may become a very serious controversy. For my part I have no fear of the labouring classes, were it only because the *adamantini clavi*[3] are driven so hard into them, except the fear of being embarked against them in a bad cause.

4. Th.

Wrote to The Queen—Dean of Windsor—C.G.—Mr Hammond—Agnes G.—Ld Halifax—Mary G.—Mr Stirling—Lord Ln—Mr Morier—Ld Kimberley—& minutes. Today we underwent photographing in a group. Drove to Corby:[4] saw much that is of interest, in nature, & some in Art too. Read Frohschammer Das neue Wissen u. der neue glaube.[5]

To E. HAMMOND, 4 September 1873. PRO FO 391/24.

1. The instruction to [H. C.] Rothery[6] seems to stand perfectly well. The printed paper with the claims for 60 million dollars (to be 28 million in all) is, I now hope & suppose, only a draft, & I also trust that no claim will be made by *us* except in perfect good faith and according to our estimate of the value which can be justly attached to the concession. If the Canadians differ from us, may they not make their own agreement, & let us find some middle course between disavowing them & taking upon ourselves what would amount to an identification with what we may think an unjust demand.

I am not surprised at your slipping in *for once* the wrong paper.

2. A perusal of the draft of August 30 brings back to my mind the subject of the promise to protect the Italians.[7] I presume it must hold good for the present. Nor do I see any objection to it in principle as far as moral & diplomatic protection, in the absence of their own representatives, may be concerned. Beyond this, I think it open to the strongest objections on all the principles which lie at the

[1] Passage on grocers' licences omitted.

[2] Trade union demonstration against the Criminal Law Amnt. Act and Masters and Servants Act; M.P.s not pledged to their repeal not to be supported; *The Scotsman*, 23 August 1873.

[3] Horace, *Odes* 3. 24. 5: 'However rich you are, you cannot escape your fate once stern Necessity drives into your head her nails of steel.'

[4] Seat near Carlisle, with fine picture collection, of P.H. Howard, 1801–83, quondam whig M.P.; see 16 Mar. 42.

[5] J. Frohschammer, *Das neue Wissen und der neue Glaube* (1873); sent by R. *Morier; comments sent on 29 September 1873; Add MS 44542, ff. 173, 190.

[6] Probably H. Cadogan Rothery, registrar of the Admiralty; on the payment of the Alabama claim's arbitrated sum.

[7] See 2 Aug. 73.

root of law & order. Protection, that is protection backed by *voies de fait*, & obedience are reciprocal: we have no business to protect those over whom we have no control. It becomes a complete substitution of the arbitrary for the legal. Possibly indeed cases may occur when on the spur of the moment it may become a duty on grounds of absolute humanity: but then what is done should, it seems to me, be done *pro hâc vice*, & not under an engagement covering all cases, which engagement we have no right to make. I do not know whether in giving this opinion I am liable to be overturned by precedent or authorities; but I speak of the case as it presents itself to me.

3. It strikes me that Macdonnell's reception of the reproof is particularly modest sensible & pleasing.

4. As regards the ships manifestly we have no option but to wait for Yelverton's[1] letters. It is perhaps fortunate that we are compelled to wait. But I must say that I agree with Ld. Granville's letter & not with Mr Goschen's. We have unfortunately departed from 'neutrality' by the seizure of the ships which has essentially compromised our position: & I cannot agree that when once we have interfered we are as matter of course to view the two parties as exactly on a level though I do not say there is any other *absolute* rule of action which can be laid down without regard to the circumstances of each case.

It may be a very nice question indeed, whether we are to hold ourselves bound by Admiral Yelverton's promise to recommend.

Please let Ld. Granville see this. My address is at no 10.

I had not read Tenterden's Mem. till just now—I think his basis safe, but I hope great care will be observed.

To LORD KIMBERLEY, colonial secretary, 4 September 1873. Add MS 44542, f. 172.

I am extremely glad that the general tenour of my remarks of last Sat. commended them to your judgment.[2] I now send back your drafts with a few suggestions in pencil which I do not think will raise objection. viz. Draft A. in one sentence only—as I think the text without alteration corresponds too little to the conclusion of the dispatch, in which you reserve to H.M. Govt. the final decision. Draft B. (p. 3) explains itself. (p. 5) we assume, & I should think properly, the innocence of these prisoners. I think the assumption may well appear on the face of the dispatch (pp 7.8.). You will be amused at my pleading, so to speak, on behalf of human sacrifices. I am of course all for getting rid of them. But:— 1. They are not crimes under the moral law as recognised in Africa. 2. They were not crimes under the moral law as recognised by the most civilized nations of antiquity, though the Greeks in early days had a strong & laudable repugnance to them. 3. They were only put down by the influence of Christianity, & that slowly. 4. Within no great number of years we had a British officer at Dahomey on the occasion of the sacrifices—which I think, at least in part, he saw. With all this I have only softened you a very little.[3]

[1] Sir Hastings Reginald Yelverton (1808-78; commanded the Mediterranean 1870-4) had seized two Spanish ships and on 1 Sept. sent them to Gibraltar; *PP* 1874 lxxvi. 225.

[2] See 30 Aug. 73; Kimberley sent amended drafts, Add MS 44225, f. 87.

[3] Kimberley 'accepted all your alterations in both drafts except the words "in themselves excusable" as regards the human sacrifices'; ibid., f. 93.

5. Frid. [Courthey, near Liverpool]

Wrote to Mr Cardwell—The Speaker—D. of Argyll—Ld Kimberley—Miss Marsh—Bp of Ely—& minutes. Went about the place with my host (what a host, too) and afterwards witnessed the very interesting games of Cumbrian wrestling and pole-leaping: a capital specimen of true local hospitality. Off at 4.30 to Courthey 10.30. Read Bohn on Printing.[1] Conversation with Mr G. Howard—Mr Colvin—Robn G.

To E. CARDWELL, war secretary, 5 September 1873. Add MS 44542, f. 174.

My criticisms on the African drafts were founded on the assumption (this again I think resting on Kimberley's explanatory letter) that you & he were agreed unequivocally in the opinion that Sir G. Wolseley was to report to the Cabinet before undertaking any expedition inland. It seemed to me & I think rightly that his position in this respect ought to be defined with the utmost precision, in justice alike to him & to Parliament & to both more even than to ourselves. At the same time I can make no objection to what you say in your letter[2] that if Sir G.W. should find it possible soon after his arrival to deal a decisive blow with only the force then at his disposal, we ought not to prevent it: too happy indeed if this should be the case. But would not the proper form of instruction be first to impress clearly & decisively the limitation we intend to impose (& which really has reference to the contingency of a need for further military means): & then to acquaint him that the limitation has no reference at all to the case you have supposed, in which a decisive advantage or some very great advantage, may appear attainable with the force actually at his command. I feel so confident that this will meet your view, as to think I had better send a copy to Kimberley—who has little time to spare & ask him—& ask him [*sic*] to provide, in the best way he can, for thus giving him the sense of the instruction on which we all seem to be agreed. I have written without having your draft at hand.

I have written to H.M. about the Army Commission.

6. Sat. [Hawarden]

Wrote to Dean of ChCh—Archdeacon Jones—Mr Hammond—Ld Granville (Tel.)—& minutes. Further conversation with Robn G. on divers matters of business. Off at 10 to Hn.—Saw Mr Barker in Chester on marriage arrangements: these I afterwards discussed with C. Settled down again at Hn where a happy family party gathered today: dearest Agnes is the centre bow. Read Frohschammer—Newman's Disc. on J.R. Hope Scott.[3] Conversation with Harry who is to be a Trustee.

[1] H. G. *Bohn, *The origin and progress of printing* (1854).

[2] Of 3 September 1873, Add MS 44120, f. 119, on charge that Cardwell had given Wolseley too great discretion.

[3] J. H. *Newman, 'Sermon preached at the requiem mass for . . . J. R. Hope Scott'(1873).

7. 13 S.Trin.

Church 11 A.M. with H.C: and 6½ evg. Saw W.H.G. on eccl. arrangements. Wrote to Rev E. Wilberforce (with presentation)—Gen. Ponsonby—Ld Granville—Abp of York—Mr Ouvry—and minutes. Read Philojudaeus[1]—Frohschammer—M'Caul.[2] We were all nine at the Altar today—and I think eight were worthy.

8. M.

Ch. 8½ A.M. Wrote to Ld Hartington—Mr Godley—& minutes. Saw Mr Wickham: & settled with him the marriage arrangements. Also conversation on Oxford—he is excellent. Saw J.S. Wortley—respecting legal matters (public)—W.H.G. respecting the settlements. Attended the Agricultural Machinery Exhibition, at work on Roberts's Farm. Read Romayne's Pamphlet—Frohschammer—Ld Lytton Duch. de la Vallière.[3]

9. Tues.

Wrote to Ld Granville (2)—Ld Chancellor—Mr Bellairs[4]—Ida Gladstone—Mr C. Gore—Mr Hammond Tel. Tel. Tel.—Bp of Brechin Tel.—Prince Christian—Mr Bright—Prince Leopold—Mr Gurdon —Ld Hartington—& minutes. Read Frohschammer—Lytton's La Valliere. Treecutting. Then went to the Implement show: & saw Roberts's stock. Conversation with Wortley on the law applicable to the Spanish case.[5] Saw Sir T. Frost on Chester seat.[6] Ch. 8½ A.M.

10. Wed.

Ch. 8½ AM. Wrote to Mr Hammond Tel.—Bp of Ripon—Ld Acton —Mr Welby—Ld Granville—and minutes. Saw Mr Courtenay Boyle.[7] Conversation with Herbert on Homer. Messenger in evg. from Granville. Woodcutting. Read Frohschammer—Lytton's La Vallière.

[1] Untraced.

[2] J. B. MacCaul, *Dark sayings of old* (1873).

[3] E. G. E. L. Bulwer *Lytton, *The Duchess de la Vallière* (1836); verse drama.

[4] Henry Walford Bellairs, 1812-1900; vicar of Nuneaton 1872-91; educationalist. Should replace H. Bellairs at 22 May 40n, see Add MS 44357, f. 157.

[5] See letter to Hammond on 4 Sept. 73.

[6] Sir Thomas Frost of Chester suggested Gladstone should stand for Chester; declined after consultation with Wolverton; in 1874 Frost stood and lost; Add MS 44542, f. 178.

[7] (Sir) Courtenay Edmund *Boyle, 1845-1901; sportsman and Spencer's secretary 1868-73, 1882-5; local govt. inspector 1873.

To LORD ACTON, 10 September 1873. Cambridge University Library.

Only lately I saw & read a tract with which you are certain to be familiar: Döllinger's 'Universitäten sonst u. jetzt'.[1] Independently of the admirable outlining of the immediate subject, it contains the simplest & best popular description that I have seen of the position & work of the German mind at the present epoch of the world's history. I cannot but wish it were translated for the benefit of the people of this country, who waste on so curious a scale their mental resources and import so much that they ought to grow. I thought that perhaps if you agree in this view you might have easy means of suggestion to some one who might not dislike the undertaking.
[P.S.] A tenant of mine has just had a young German with him for 15 months to learn farming. I am glad we are exporters of at least one kind of knowledge.

11. Th.

Ch. 8½ AM. Wrote to Ld Kimberley—Ld Granville Tel.—Mr Goschen—Mr Hammond—Miss Hope Scott—Mr Fremantle—& minutes. Woodcutting. Saw Mr C. A. Wood (Railways &c.). Read Frohschammer—Lytton's La Vallière—it is lofty, and has much poetry. Read through my Letters from James Hope: over one hundred.

12. Fr.

Ch. 8½ AM. Wrote to Lord Wolverton—Mr Hammond Tel.—Mr Gurdon 2 Tel.—Miss Doyle—Lady Westminster—Mr Sherratt—Ld Chancellor—Ld Halifax—Dean of Windsor—Miss Hope Scott—& minutes. Also began a lengthened letter to Miss Hope Scott about her father.[2] Read Frohschammer—Viollet le Duc's Lecture.[3] 2¼–6¼. Drive into Chester to the Agricultural Show: put myself under my friend [J.] Roberts's[4] guidance. Then to Sherratts and Hollands.[5] A little cutting followed.

13. Sat.

Ch. 8½ AM. Finished the long & sad but profoundly interesting task of my letter to Miss Hope Scott. Also sent her fathers (105) letters to her.[6] Wrote also to Jas Watson & Smith—Dean of Chichester—

[1] See 3 June 73; already tr. as 'Universities past and present' by C. E. B. Appleton (1867).

[2] A long and remarkable appraisal, printed as Appendix III in Ornsby, ii. 273, copy in Add MS 44440, f. 44.

[3] E. E. Viollet-Le-Duc, perhaps *Histoire d'une maison* (1873).

[4] i.e. John Roberts, diarist's tenant, of Wellhouse Farm, Bretton; see 7 Aug. 58.

[5] James Holland, a Grosvenor tenant.

[6] Ornsby's biography was published 1884; the letters were returned to become Add MS 44214.

Scotts—Ld Kenmare—and minutes. Wrote minute of instruction for the marriage settlement. It will be a simple one. We finished cutting down a great beech. Our politicians arrived—conversations with Bright—with Wolverton—with Granville; and with all three until long after 12 when I prayed to leave off for the sake of the brain. Read Orations on General Church.[1]

14. 13 S.Trin.

Ch. mg & evg. Wrote to Earl of Pembroke—The Queen (Mem)—Sir T. Frost—Sir R. Cunliffe[2]—Mr Jolly[3]—Earl of Granard—and minutes. The first of these, a stiff task for a half exhausted brain.[4] But I cannot desist from a sacred task. Oh that *He* would give the increase. Conversation with Ld G.—Ld W.—Mr Bright. Read Bray on Pantheism: outrageous.[5]

15. M.

Ch. 8½ A.M. Spent the forenoon in conclave, till two: after a preliminary conversation with Bright. Wrote to Ld Chancellor—Ld Spencer—Ld Morley—Mr Cardwell—Ld Wenlock—Mr Forster—Mr H. James[6]—and minutes. Spent the evening also in conclave: we have covered a good deal of ground. Also conversation with Granville. Read Frohschammer. Cut down the half cut alder.

To E. CARDWELL, war secretary, 15 September 1873. Add MS 44542, f. 178.

I congratulate you upon the success of the Autumn manoeuvres, which from your account seems even to have exceeded that of former years. It would I think be very difficult to recede from our recommendation about the Army Commission: & even if it were possible for us to take this step I doubt whether Gen. Peel would be the proper man.[7] About the African expedition I of course am ill able to separate true from false among the newspaper accounts of preparations. It is said that over 40 officers have gone with Sir G. Wolseley. Doubtless if it is so

[1] Orations on Sir R. *Church by P. Chalkiopulos and P. Gennadius.

[2] Sir Robert Alfred Cunliffe, 1839-1905, 5th bart.; liberal M.P. Flint 1872-4, Denbigh 1880-5.

[3] John Robert Jolly, liberal organiser in Greenwich, declining to commit himself to speaking there; Add MS 44542, f. 178.

[4] Letter to S. Herbert's s., 13th earl of Pembroke, becoming a sceptic despite his mother's ultramontane influence; see Add MS 44542, f. 178.

[5] C. *Bray, *Illusion and delusion; or modern pantheism versus spiritualism* (1873).

[6] Offering solicitor-generalship to (Sir) Henry *James, 1828-1911, liberal (unionist) M.P. Taunton 1868-85, Bury 1886-95; solicitor-general Sept.-Nov. 1873, attorney-general Nov. 1873-4, 1880-5; cr. baron 1895, chancellor of duchy 1895-1902.

[7] Cardwell reported suggestions that Peel be on it, disapproving of them personally, PRO 30/48/10 f. 19.

you have good reason but they are I presume much beyond the limits of a staff, & are intended I suppose to make him to act at once, with the other materials he possesses, should he find it needful. The story of the railway & of two regiments I put down as fiction. About the hospital ship I do not understand particulars but I told Goschen I thought the Cabinet should be consulted upon any preparations novel in character or object or serious in amount. It is very fair that expenditure distinctively incurred from a local war should be charged under a corresponding head, but it ought not I apprehend to become in any way civil expenditure. I have settled with Granville the last week in Oct. for a Cabinet, but if your Commission or any other matter require it we ought to meet sooner. It gives me pleasure to find Sir G. Wolseley (whom I only know by reputation) has had such good advice. I hope to hear of your coming hither.

To W. E. FORSTER, vice president, 15 September 1873. 'Private.' Add MS 44542, f. 179.

Having still before me one or two matters of official arr[angemen]t[?] I wish to ascertain whether my impressions as to the state of your mind are correct. When it was arranged that a successor would take Ripon's place, I said it would probably be in my power to place the Irish Secretaryship at your disposal, & this I did under the impression that on the dissolution [*sic*], from circumstances of your very close connection with Ripon, it would be less agreeable to you to renew them with any other Ld. President. If however I understood you right I found you willing but not desirous to go, & on this point it is that I am anxious to be corrected if I am wrong. Gratuitous changes are not to be desired: & especially this applies after a series of difficult alterations have been effected for cause, which on the whole seems to be app[rove]d. And if you are willing at present to continue where you are, I think there is the less difficulty in your way because it seems unlikely that any question of Education can be formidably aired among us at this juncture, or until after some of the critical months of the coming Session shall have passed.[1]

16. Tu.

Laid up for my foot with a little poultice. Final conversation with Granville: with Wolverton: & with Bright, who went last. Read Frohschammer—Jean Paul's Life.[2] Dined at the Rectory. Saw S.E.G. respecting Sealand. Wrote to Watson & Smith—Mr Hammond (Tel.)—Mrs Norton—Gen. [A.] Gordon—D. of Argyll—Abp of York—Mr K. Hodgson—Mr Morley—Dr Schaff[3]—Scotts—and minutes.

[1] Forster replied, 17 September, Add MS 44157, f. 84, that he did not '*wish* to go to Ireland' and was '*quite* willing' to stay.

[2] Perhaps *Life of J. P. F. Richter*, tr. C. B. Lee, 2v. (1845).

[3] Philipp Schaff, German theologian, on proposed mission in New York; Add MS 44542, f. 181.

17. Wed.

Wrote to Watsons—Dean of Westmr—Mr Christie—Miss Hope Scott —Mr Cardwell—Mr Gurdon Tel.—& minutes. Woodcutting with Herbert. Wrote additions to my Recollections of Hope Scott.[1] Read Jean Paul—Frohschammer.

To E. CARDWELL, war secretary, 17 September 1873. Add MS 44542, f. 181.

I am not very well pleased, I own, with the Queen's tenacity about the Military Grievances Commission. I have g[rea]t fear as I told her that her plan would end in a *divided* report: & then almost irreparable mischief might have been done. She admitted that if officers were there, some advocate of the Government should also be there. Granville will look to this matter. Many thanks for your explanation about the Cape Coast. Do you not think it would be well if a Mem. were prepared in Kimberley's office yours or both, to put the Cabinet in possession of information which at present is I think almost confined to you two as to the circumstances of the quarrel & the local features of the country with the chances they afford? You see the *quivering* state of the public mind. Some of our colleagues are I think uneasy even about what we have done, chiefly perhaps because it was done upon narrow information. Bright believes that the Ashantees are the only people on that coast who are worth a rap, & that they have made war in order to get free access to the Coast. I own myself very ignorant. I quite understand the propriety of your answering the question of railway, but I do not presume on even an inkling[?] of a judgment without some knowledge of particulars. I had understood that when you get a little distance inland there is jungle & danger to health commences or recommences. (unsigned).[2]

18. Th.

Wrote to Ld Hartington—Mr Hammond Tel.—Mr Cardwell—Mr Forster—Ld Granville—Mr Bright—& minutes. Wrote a little Hom. Mythol. Ch. 8½ AM. Woodcutting with Herbert. Then went up to Stephy's School Feast: an animated and happy scene.[3] Read Frohschammer—Jean Paul—De Beauvoir on Australia.[4]

To E. CARDWELL, war secretary, 18 September 1873. Add MS 44542, f. 182.

I inclose for your perusal a letter about Abyssinia[5] which Bright has sent me & appears to me to deserve examination: especially as to the Fantees & as to

[1] Add MS 44440, f. 56, Gladstone had his letter returned for emendation; ibid., f. 80.

[2] Note by copyist. Cardwell replied, 19 September 1873, PRO 30/48/10, f. 24, that he thought the C.O. had explained, but that he could not 'for the history of the Dutch transactions & of Gov. Hennessy's proceeding is very partially known to me . . . my office is an executive one'.

[3] At the Hawarden village school.

[4] L. de Beauvoir, *Australie . . . voyage autour du monde*, 3v. (1869-72).

[5] *Sic*; presumably a slip by the copyist for Ashantee.

their conduct. But my prejudices are all in favour of a strong native state: & I write as an ignoramus. Will you kindly return it to Bright. I had an intention of speaking, very privately to you about my own (very crude) financial views for next year; & I cannot recollect whether I carried it into effect before leaving town or not. Can you help my memory?[1]

19. Frid.

Ch. 8½ AM. Wrote to Lord Chancellor—Mr Cardwell l. & Tel.—Ld Granville l. & Tel.—The Queen (Mem)—Mr Gurdon—Mr C. Howard—Robn G.—Mr Ellis Eyton—Mr Hammond—Bp of Chester—O'Donoghue—and minutes. Woodcutting with Herbert. Read Frohschammer—Jean Paul's Life—Horne on Australia.[2] Conversation with S.E.G. & S.R.G. on the Saltney separation.[3]

20. Sat.

Ch. 8½ AM. Wrote to Sir W. Stephenson (2)[4]—Ld Kimberley—Mrs Th.—Mr Childers—The Speaker—Rev Mr Kennion[5]—The Queen—Mr Hammond—and minutes. Woodcutting. Read Frohschammer—De Beauvoir on Australia.

21. 14 S.Trin. & St Matt.

Ch. 11 AM & H.C.—6½ PM. Wrote to Viceroy of Ireland—Mr Hammond 2 Tel.—Mr Goschen—Sir C. Locock—Ld Granville—Mr Quaritch—Mr Cardwell—and minutes. Much plague of Telegrams today & messenger at night. Read Frohschammer—Stanley's Serm. on Bp Wilberforce[6]—Dykes on the Beatitudes[7]—Manning's Letter to Abp of Armagh.[8] There is in it to me a sad air of unreality: it is on stilts all through.

[1] Cardwell replied, 19 September 1873, Add MS 44120, f. 139: 'You did tell me what an important object you have in view. I hope this Ashantee expenditure may be chiefly provided for in the current year.'

[2] *Parting legacy of R. H. Horne to Australia* (1868).

[3] A restructuring of the Hawarden estate.

[4] Asking for details about the produce of House Tax 'if all exemptions were abolished & the Tax made a House & Building Tax, embracing everything wh. is embraced by the Income Tax, under these heads, but retaining the two rates and the limit of £20'; Add MS 44542, f. 185. Reply by C. J. Herries on 22 November stressed the 'very unsatisfactory state' of the duty; Add MS 44441, f. 81.

[5] George Wyndham Kennion, 1845-1922, vicar of St. Paul's, Hull 1873-6; bp. of Adelaide 1882, Bath & Wells 1884; Add MS 44441, f. 187.

[6] A. P. *Stanley, 'How are the mighty fallen' (1873).

[7] J. O. Dykes, *The beatitudes of the Kingdom* (1872).

[8] H. E. *Manning, 'A letter to the . . . Archbishop of Armagh' (1873); see also *The Guardian*, 17 Sept. 1873, 1200.

To G. J. GOSCHEN, first lord of the Admiralty, 21 September 1873. Add MS 44161, f. 245.

Your meeting with Kimberley & Cardwell tomorrow in London will be very convenient & in this letter I will try to put my view of the position as clearly as I can before you & them. First I am glad to think that, so far as I can know, there is not actual difference of view in the Cabinet (& when I speak of the Cabinet I include Bright whose foot is on the threshold) as to the policy to be pursued on the Gold Coast.—it is fairly described by Bright's correspondent: the invasion must be repelled, & (so far as is necessary for security) punished. Into the question of our permanent policy on that coast it is not necessary now to enter, but there too we should probably agree. We all I do not doubt also think that what is to be done ought to be done promptly, & within the limit offered by the coming 'healthy' season. But now comes the question of the authority which is to act. Remember that when the Cabinet separated in August, they had given their sanction to the river expedition & to nothing else. The assents that have been given by me on the part of the Treasury (which touch a very much smaller amount than the one you name) have been given, I think, under the belief that we were assenting to what was required for carrying into effect the River expedition as it had been authorised by the Cabinet.[1] You will also bear in mind that the Cabinet parted in the expectation of being summoned about the first week in October for the further consideration of the subject. The question of an expedition to Coomassie, to be carried on with the aid of an European force now stands over till the end of November. I think the Cabinet would be surprised & ill satisfied, if, coming up for the 1st time some weeks hence, they found that extensive & costly preparations had been made in anticipation of an affirmative decision as to that expedition; & this without their having been even supplied with the particulars of what was being done, or with any information local military or political, to give them any clear comprehension of the state & prospects of a question on which they are necessarily ignorant. Both you & Cardwell have spoken of the hospital ship & railway respectively as urgent in point of time: but I am not informed of the date when they can be wanted, or the actual time necessary for the execution of the orders that may have to be given; while on the face of the case it wd. rather have appeared to me as if there was ample time to allow the Cabinet to meet & deliberate. There is another question behind that of the Cabinet, which the Cabinet only can decide but which appears to me not so entirely speculative as I had hoped it might be —the question how far we can proceed in this matter without taking Parliament into our councils. It was exceedingly unfortunate that circumstance brought about, without any blame to anyone, our deciding on the River or Glover expedition without the privity of Parliament, & this at a moment when the H. of Commons had just missed through unhappy accidents the discussion which had been desired & anticipated on the whole question. Thus viewing the case it seems to me to deserve consideration whether we might not with advantage fall back on the original plan & summon the Cabinet say in the earlier days of Oct. I should be quite ready sooner but Granville will hardly be in the South till Sept. has expired & it will take time to complete the arrangements necessary for Bright's attendance. All might be done, I should think within a fortnight: & I wrote to prepare G. for the possibility of a Council earlier than we expected some time back. If you arrive at my conclusion, you can either

[1] See 2 Aug. 73.

telegraph to me or write to him direct, & when we know how soon the affair of the Council can be dispatched we can fix about the Cabinet. Childers & Bright must I believe meet at the Council. There is very quaky ground under our feet & I cannot but think we shall do well to have the aid of all our colleagues.

22. M.

Ch. 8.30 AM. Wrote to Ld Granville tel. & l.—Mr Gurdon Tel.—Ld Wolverton—& minutes. Worked on arranging library. Finished Frohschammer—Began life of Schleiermacher.[1] Read De Beauvoir. Dined at the Rectory: where we had much interesting conversation.

23. Tues.

Ch. $8\frac{1}{2}$ AM. Wrote to Mr Gurdon Tel.—Ld Hartington l. & Tel.—Sir W. Stephenson—Mr Hammond—Ld F. Cavendish—Mr Woodall—Mr Cardwell—Mr Goschen—Mr Hugessen—Mr De Lisle—Mr Fairbrother—& minutes. Read De Beauvoir—Schleiermacher's Life. Sixteen to dinner. Saw Mr R. Frost—Mr Leveson—Dr Munro.

To E. CARDWELL, war secretary, 23 September 1873. Add MS 44542, f. 185.

Your letter of yesterday[2] requires I think no direct reply but I send you herewith a copy of a letter I have written to Goschen. Please let it go on to Kimberley. The Dover Election, unless it can be explained, appears the most significant event we have yet had to confront. You will have observed the obliging list with which the Times article concludes.[3] But the general state of affairs makes our early meeting convenient.

24.

Ch. $8\frac{1}{2}$ A.M. Wrote to Ld Granville l. & Tel.—Mr Gurdon Tel.—Bp of Ely—Ld Hartington—Mrs Norton—The O'Donoghue—Mr C. Gore—Mr Reverdy Johnson—Mr Hammond—Sir T. Biddulph—& minutes. Worked on Library. Walk with Mr Leveson.[4] Conversation with Ld Hanmer.[5] Read De Beauvoir—Schleiermacher's Corresp. Large party in evg.

[1] *The life of Schleiermacher*, 2v. (1860).

[2] Report on consultations about Wolseley; Add MS 44120, f. 144.

[3] Leader on liberal losses and divisions; *The Times*, 23 September 1873, 7. The liberals were this day heavily defeated in a by-election at Dover.

[4] i.e. F. Leveson Gower, Granville's br.; see 3 Apr. 62 and Hawn. Visitors' Book.

[5] See 9 Mar. 26.

25. Th.

Ch. 8½ AM. Wrote to Mr Gurdon Tel.—The O Donoghue—Ld Delawarre—Miss Hope Scott—Mr Austin—Mr Hammond—Sir W. Stephenson—& minutes. Worked on arranging my Library. Forenoon went chiefly in conversations with Mr Leveson on politics: with him & Ld Hanmer on rural economy. Woodcutting with Herbert. Conversation with S.R.G. & C.G. respecting West Rendlesham vacancy.[1]

26. Fr.

Ch. 8½ AM. Wrote to Bp of Ripon—Mr Cardwell—Mr Bright—Sir S. Scott & Co—and minutes. Walk with Sir S. & Mr Hearne. Conversation with Ld Hanmer: Homeric, & political. Also with Mr [F.T.] Palgrave.[2] Dinner party. Read Memoir of Morrison[3]—Holyoake's Tract on Mill[4]—Dubl.Univ.Mag. on Socrates[5]—De Beauvoir's Australia—Schleiermacher's Life & Corr.—Journey to Scotland 1704.[6]

To John BRIGHT, M.P., 26 September 1873. Add MS 43385, f. 236.

I am very sorry to have to call upon you so soon to go to London. But I think you will yourself approve the measure when we meet. Not only because it may be well that we should all be enabled to compare notes on the general situation of the Government. But also & chiefly because the pressure of the three Departments with a view to military preparations has gone beyond what I feel competent to deal with & beyond the mere execution of the orders of the Cabinet. I think our concern[?] will be materially cleared by meeting. I quite agree with the Ministers of the Colonies War & Admiralty that all which it is right for us to do should be done quickly.

We can then talk over the last of our many local defeats. I have heard as yet no explanation of a nature to sweeten the pill.

The Speaker is only at Wiesbaden.

27. Sat.

Ch. 8½ AM. Wrote to Viceroy of Ireland—Ld Granville—Mrs Th.—Bp of Norwich—Mr Lowe—Mr Childers—and minutes. Conversation

[1] F. W. B. Thellusson, 3rd Baron Rendlesham, had made unacceptable requests about filling the crown living; Gladstone asked the bp. of Norwich to report; Add MS 44542, f. 189.

[2] Compiler of *The Golden Treasury* and other anthologies; see 30 Mar. 60.

[3] E. Morrison, *Memoirs of . . . R. Morrison* (1839).

[4] See 4 July 73.

[5] *Dublin University Magazine*, lxxxii. 300 (September 1873).

[6] Perhaps *An account of Scotland in 1702*; see Boswell, *Johnson* (1900 ed.), ii. 423.

with Mr Palgrave chiefly on Symonds & the Greek Mythology. Wrote Mem. upon it.[1] Read Schleiermacher—Lady Lyttelton's letters—Finished Journey of 1704. Conversation with C. Lyttelton on her mother's book. Cut a tree with Herbert.

To R. LOWE, home secretary, 27 September 1873. Add MS 44542, f. 189.

Bright is very anxious about the laws affecting the condition of labouring men. Some ideas which he expressed to me appeared to run in the same channel as yours: & I encouraged him to place his views before you. It occurred to me however as possible that they might require the institution of some rather careful inquiry with a view to any practical measure or measures. I therefore suggest for your consideration whether you could avail yourself of the opportunity to be afforded by our meeting next week to mention the subject if your preparations in regard to it require the aid or authority of the Cabinet.[2] In any case you would I think do well to communicate with Bright & with Aberdare. Do not take the trouble to reply.

28. S.16 Trin.

Ch 11 AM and Wrote to Duke of Argyll—Ld Granville—Dr Lowe—and minutes. Also read Pembroke's last letter: and began a reply. Read Schleiermacher—Galloway Gill's Tract[3]—Mivart's paper in Contemp. Review.[4] Conversation with Mr Palgrave—He is tremendous: but in other respects good, & full of mental energy and activity: only the vent is rather large.

To the DUKE OF ARGYLL, Indian secretary, 28 September 1873. Add MS 44542, f. 189.

Being at such a distance you will wish for information as to the Cabinet. S. Africa is the immediate and sole actual cause of the summons. At the same time, though I think the ministers will disperse again after a day or two, the general situation may be considered and also some questions of next year's legislation may come up. You know very well that all information of this kind is only to be taken at *valeat quantum.*

I have read Mivart's paper which is a very remarkable one. I have not yet read Newman's Grammar of Assent and this paper of Mivart's is the only contribution known to me from a Roman Catholic source in this country towards dealing with the difficulties of the day. It will be hard to form a complete opinion until the sequel appears. This paper as it stands is not quite fair to the non-Roman forms of Christianity: and I think it *monstrously* overstates the case of the

[1] Untraced.

[2] See 3 Oct., 26 Nov. 73.

[3] H. G. Gill, *The pretensions of Ultramontanism* (1873).

[4] St. G. *Mivart, 'Contemporary evolution', *Contemporary Review*, xxii. 595 (September 1873).

Christian Church in regard to liberty of conscience. In other aspects I agree with him generally, and in some very emphatically.

29. M. St Michael

Ch. 8¾ AM. Wrote to Miss Hope Scott—Mr Morier—Ld W. Hay—Mr Austin—Mr Goschen—and minutes. Also finished my letter to Pembroke.[1] And finished revision of my letter of Sept. 13 respecting James Hope Scott. Conversations with Mr Palgrave: pretty stiff. Woodcutting with Herbert. Read Symonds on the Greek Poets.[2] Wrote a rough Mem. & computation for the Budget of next year.[3] I want 8 m to handle!

30. Tu.

(Deluded as to Church). Wrote to The O Donoghue—Mr W. Williams—Mr Gurdon—Mr A. de Lisle[4]—Mr Dodson—Ld Chancellor—Mrs Hampton—Col. Farquharson—and minutes. Conversation with C. respecting Herbert's future. With C. Lyttelton on our Glynne nieces. Wrote Mem. on Greenwich seat.[5] Read Symonds Greek Poets—Mitchell Introd. to Aristoph.[6]—Began the Acharnenses: with M.s & Frere's translations.[7]

Wed. Oct. One 1873.

Ch. 8½ AM. Wrote to Bp of Ripon—Mr Gurdon—J. Watson & S.—Mr Barker—Mr Cardwell—and minutes. Saw Mr Clark of Dowlas[8]—Mr J.H. Parker. Read Mitchell Introd.—Panizzi's Additions: beautiful language and argument—Aristoph.Acharn. Kibbling: saw Potter: walk with C. Preparation for departure.

2. Th. [*London*]

Off at 8: London (Eust) at 3. Wrote to Messrs Watson—Mr Palgrave—Dean Hook—Mr C. Landseer[9]—& minutes. Saw Mr Gurdon—Ld Wolverton—Dined at Mrs Th's to meet Mrs Anderson. Gave to one mending: & one mended. Read Symonds 'Greek Poets'.

[1] See 14 Sept. 73n, Lathbury ii. 92; Add MS 44440, f. 122.
[2] J. A. *Symonds, *Studies of the Greek poets*, 2v. (1873-6).
[3] Not found.
[4] A. L. M. Phillipps de Lisle; see 20 July 71.
[5] On distinctions between the various treasury commissionerships; Add MS 44761, f. 179.
[6] T. *Mitchell, *Aristophanis Comœdiæ* (1794).
[7] See 8 Jan. 73.
[8] George Thomas Clark of Dowlais, 1809-98; engineer and antiquarian.
[9] On his brother's d.; Add MS 44542, f. 192.

3. Fr.

Wrote to Count Strzelecki—Mr Hankey—The Speaker—Duke of Bedford—The Queen—C.G.—& minutes. Read on the Pen Folk.[1] Saw Mr Gurdon—Mr Welby—Ld Granville (2)—Ld Granville *cum* Ld Wolverton—Mr Cardwell—Ct Strzelecki—Ld Kimberley—Ly Westbury. Dined with Panizzi: much interesting & some solemn talk. Cabinet 3–6½. Read Gold Coast Memm.

Cabinet. Oct. 3. 73. 3 PM.[2]

√ Ashantee measures. Explanations & Discussion. Ld K[imberley]'s Mem.[3] not having been read, no question was decided by the Cabinet.
O Greenwich Seat.
√ Newfoundland Fisheries. Rough language of Col. to be reproved[?] & France exhorted to moderation.[4]
O Law of Conspiracy.[5]
√ Indian Guage [*sic*]. D. of Argyll's opinion confirmed.
√ Telegraph: Cape Verd to Sierra Leone. Proposal for a Subsidy. Decline.
√ Conduct of Aden—Gibraltar. Dft. to be prepared.

To H. B. W. BRAND, the Speaker, 3 October 1873. Add MS 44542, f. 192.

In conformity with the announcement conveyed in your letter of Sept. 19th, your secretary has forwarded to me a copy of the certificate received by you from Mr Lowther[6] & Mr Winn with the accompanying letter.

As these are documents of a formal character & as in the letter of these gentlemen it is recited that they are advised by high legal authority that my seat for Greenwich is vacant, it appears proper that I should place you formally in possession of the fact that I am advised by high legal authority to a contrary effect. At the period when I had just received the seals of the Chancellorship of the Exchequer, the question was submitted with all such information as was at hand, first to the Solicitor General now Master of the Rolls, who happened to be personally accessible and then to the Attorney General. The opinion of both the Law Officers was that I have not vacated my seat.

4. Sat.

Wrote to J. Murray—The Queen (2)—Ld Lyttelton—C.G. Saw Mrs Booth—Mr Peel—Ld Chancellor—The Wortleys—Mr Gurdon—Mr Kinnaird. Cabinet 12–5. Dined at Ld Wolverton's: conclave on

[1] Untraced.
[2] Add MS 44641, f. 193; no report on this cabinet found in R.A.
[3] In PRO CO 879/5/465.
[4] Row with French about a weir; PRO CO 194/188.
[5] See letter to Lowe on 27 Sept. 73.
[6] James Lowther, 1840–1904, tory M.P. York 1865–80, Thanet 1888–1904 and Roland Winn, 1820–93, tory M.P. Lincolnshire 1868–85, cr. Baron St. Oswald 1885, had sent in a certificate of vacancy at Greenwich, asking the Speaker to issue an election writ; writs issued in the recess required the vacating member's assent under 21 & 22 Vict. c. 110. See Add MS 44194, ff. 165–7.

official appts and Peerages. Saw Vane—Heaphy—and [blank]; two strange cases of human experience[R].

[Cabinet] Sat. Oct. 4. 73. Noon.[1]
Ashantee. Instructions & Dispatch to Wolseley framed.[2] Railway—letter of O[ctober] 2 withdrawn. Hospital Ship. Minimum amount of depot accom[modatio]n for sick with a view to carrying them off as quickly as possible.
Read H M's letter on Railway accidents.
Letter on Adm. Yelverton's[3] conduct.
Next Cabinet (barring an African necessity) for about Ld Mayor's Day.
Language to Ameer of Affghanistan. No comm[unicatio]n to be made to Russia.

Cabinet. 4 Oct. 73. 3 PM.[4]
Conversation with Ld Granville. Household offices—Cambridgeshire Lieut[enanc]y, 1. D. of Bedford 2. Ld Dacre.
√ Peers: Maharajah? (stand over),[5] James, Monsell, Moncrieff, Howard, Odonoghue [*sic*]. Ld Wolverton points on W.E.G.'s mem.[6]
√ P.O. 1 Whitehead 2. Baxter.
√ Groom [in Waiting] Ask Qu[een].

[*Cabinet minute*][7] There is no adequate reason for maintaining exclusive military controul of the whole of the Gold Coast; provided our Forts & settlements while they are held be efficiently protected.

The object of our military measures should be effectually to clear the neighbourhood of E[fflatu] & C[ape] C[oast] C[astle] of the Ashantees: the same wd. apply to any other Forts. And the security of the Forts & their neighbourhoods as connected with them is the object of our policy. But this presumes a previous failure to arrange upon fair terms with the Ashantees for their retirement.

It is not expedient as far as our knowledge goes to entertain the project of a warlike expedn. inland to Coomassie.[8]

Inform protected tribes, *after* the above has been done, that any future aid will depend on their satisfying us of the justice of their cause & their ability to uphold it.

5. 17 S.Trin.

St Peter's Vauxhall 11 AM: a notable combination. St James's evg:

[1] Add MS 44641, f. 195.

[2] PRO CO 96/108; late attempt by Gladstone to contain Wolseley, warning him against desultory operations and expectation of English battalions; *Historical Journal*, v. 37. Several despatches from Kimberley of 6 October in *PP* 1874 xlvi. 546.

[3] See 4 Sept. 73.

[4] Headed thus, but apparently the conclave at Wolverton's, Add MS 44641, f. 199.

[5] Duleep Singh, Maharajah of Lahore, 1838-93; lived in Norfolk on pension after deposition on annexation of Punjab; proposed for peerage by Biddulph; see Ramm I, ii. 404; undated note at Add MS 44641, f. 202 reads: 'Maharajah—Granville will speak to H.M.'

[6] In Gurdon's hand, G. G. Glyn, now 2nd Lord Wolverton, recommending Lord Kensington as assistant whip; ibid., f. 200. Further jottings on honours etc. ibid., f. 201ff.

[7] Undated holograph, Add MS 44641, f. 197.

[8] Wolseley from his arrival was clearly intent on an inland march; see McIntyre, 'British policy', *Historical Journal*, v. 38.

an onward movement there also. Dined at Ld F. Cavendish's. Wrote to Mr T. Scott. 1¼-6. Went down to Roehampton to see Ida and the T.G.s: the prospect is a sad one. T.G. explained his son's case. Read The Pen Folk, finished—Methodism in Halifax—Suffield on Conversion to R.C. Church[1]—and other Scott Tracts. Much conversation at the F.C. house.

6. M.

Wrote to Mr C. Landseer—The Queen 2 l. & Mem.—C.G.—Messrs Bickers—and minutes. Saw Mr Lambert—Duke of Argyll—Mr Gurdon—Mr Dodson cum Ld F.C.—Ld Granville (2)—Do *cum* Ld Wolverton & Mr Peel—Ld Hartington—Mr Thomson Hankey—Mr Kinnaird. Shopping: & sent books to Mrs Heaphy[R]. Dined at Mrs Th.s. Saw Mrs Graham: Vane: Maitland: Hill[R]. Saw Stokes Count S[trzelecki']s trusted servant: and was admitted by him to view the dead as he lay in deep calm.

7. Tu. [Garendon Park, Leicestershire]

Wrote to The O Donoghue—Mr Goschen—Dr Ogle—Ld Clanwilliam—The Queen (Mem)—& minutes. Saw Mr Gurdon—Ld Wolverton—Mr Godley. Packed. Off at 2.30 to Garendon Park.[2] Much conversation with Mr De Lisle. Read Bagehot's Lombard Street.[3]

8. Wed.

Wrote to C.G.—Panizzi—& minutes. 12-6. A long drive over the Charnwood hills to the points of view buildings & places of interest especially the Monastery.[4] We went over the whole and I had some conversation with the monks & with an Italian Benedictine. Mr Ottley[5] dined: he said the graces as did Archdn Fearon[6] yesterday. Read Fairbairn on Religion and Race.[7] My conversations in the day with Mr De Lisle were wound up with one at night wh only terminated at 2.15 PM [*sic*].

[1] M. O. Suffield, *Five letters on a conversion to Roman Catholicism* (1873).

[2] Seat near Loughborough of Ambrose Lisle March Phillipps *de Lisle, 1809-78; convert to Roman catholicism 1824; encouraged Roman-anglican ecumenism; played important role in preparation of Gladstone's *Vatican Decrees* 1874.

[3] *Bagehot's classic, just published, sent by the author; see 16 Oct. 73.

[4] Founded by *de Lisle.

[5] John Bridge Ottley, vicar of Thorp Acre, Leicestershire.

[6] Henry Fearon, archdeacon of Leicester.

[7] A. M. Fairburn, 'Race and religion', *Contemporary Review*, xxii. 782 (October 1873).

9. Th. [Hawarden]

Went over the garden &c. and at Loughborough after further conversation bid farewell to my kind, devout, and liberal-minded host: a very interesting person. Saw Archdeacon Fearon—Bp of Chester. Reached Broughton at 6 PM. Read Bagehot's Lomb. Street. Broughton Ch. Harvest Home service. Mr Johnson entertained us aft. Tea at Mr Haynes.

10. Frid.

Ch. 8½ A.M. Wrote to Ld Hartington—Mr Whitbread[1]—Mr Bright—Sir A. Panizzi—Mr De Lisle—Mr Newton[2]—Mr Hine—Ld Dacre—Mr Godley—Mr A. J. Macdonald (U.S.)[3] Saw Mr Roberts—Sir G. Prevost (2)—Canon Wood—C.G. (on family matters). Woodcutting with W. & H. Read Bagehot—Aristoph. Acharn.[4]

To J. BRIGHT, chancellor of the duchy, Add MS 43385, f. 238.
10 October 1873.

About sub-legislation for Ireland I entirely concur with you:[5] indeed I am not certain that I would not go a *step* further than you do. I will send your correspondent's very calm & notable letter to Hartington—who wishes, I think, to produce something in this sense.

In the African matter, I incline to think that though the decision about Glover was right it was taken in extreme weariness in a moment of haste & with scanty information. I believe that what we have now done is the right thing, for the circumstances & the time.

[P.S.] The matter by far the most important, now in the offing, is (I think) finance.

11. Sat.

Ch. 8½ AM, Wrote to The Ld Advocate—Capt. Hayter MP.[6]—Mr A. Peel—Herbert J.G.—Ld Spencer—Gen. Ponsonby—Ld Chancellor

[1] Unsuccessfully offering him the postmastergeneralship, adding 'Perhaps I ought to mention, though it can hardly be necessary in writing to you, that the recent rumours of dissolution and *crisis* have been weak interventions from the opposite camp'; Add MS 44542, f. 193.

[2] Asking C. T. *Newton to bring to Hawarden Schliemann's photographs of Troy, sent by Schliemann to Newton 'expressly for your [Gladstone's] inspection'; Add MS 44440, f. 176; see 13 Oct. 73.

[3] American journalist, had asked Gladstone to write on the British constitution at 'five hundred dollars in gold for each article' for '3 or 4 [articles] a week'; he declined, suggesting Bagehot; Add MSS 44542, f. 195, 44440, f. 113.

[4] See 30 Sept. 73.

[5] Bright's letter of 7 October 1873, Add MS 44113, f. 76, enclosing unknown correspondent's letter, and suggesting provision for private Bills to be obtained in Dublin, and on Kimberley's 'rather wild' dispatches.

[6] See 27 June 67: had gained Bath for the liberals on 9 October.

—The Ld Justice Clerk—Adm. Howard—and minutes. Conversation with Sir G. P[revost] & walk. Read Aristoph. Acharn.—Bagehot Lombard Street.

To A. W. PEEL, chief whip, 11 October 1873. Add MS 44542, f. 196.

I would advise your consulting Wolverton about the answer to Baxter Langley.[1] For my own part I am very sensible how much may be said about inconvenience which Greenwich sustains from having me for its representative: though I do not know precisely how far he is the man to say it. But, however that may be, I do not know any remedy unless it be thought that the time is come for stating that I shall not stand for it at the general election. As long as I continue in Parliament, I consider that the question where I am to stand must be determined, not by my private judgment but by the joint consultation & for the general interest of the party. In truth, no one has had so little to do with my now being member for Greenwich as I have myself. As far as my personal opinion goes, I suppose it to be little likely that I should ask the suffrages of that constituency at the general election.

12. 18 S.Trin.

Ch 11 AM & 6½ PM. Wrote minutes only. Read Schleiermacher[2]—Union Rev. of Septr—Tracts by Ingle[3]—Houldey[4]—Harrison[5]—Irish Protestant Assocn Address.

13. M.

Ch. 8½ AM. Wrote to Ld Rendlesham—Mr Austin—Mr Bate—Mr Hugessen—Mr Hurst[6]—The Queen—Robn G.—Lady Ashburnham[7]—and minutes. Evening with Mr Newton on the Schliemann[8] Discoveries & Photographs: also on University Reforms. Conversation with Sir G. P[revost] & Sir C. Anderson[9] on Bp Wilberforce. Saw Mr Burnett 3-4¼ on Estate matters & his health.[10] Read Aristoph. Finished Acharn. and began Hippes. Read Bagehot.

14. Tu.

Ch. 8½ AM. Wrote to the O'Donoghue—Mr Stanhope—and minutes.

[1] The Greenwich 'advanced liberal'.
[2] See 22 Sept. 73.
[3] J. Ingle, 'The Roman meeting house in the Mint' (1873).
[4] W. E. Houldey, 'Auricular confession and the Church of England' (1873).
[5] J. Harrison, 'The last days of Irvingism' (1873).
[6] The game-keeper? See 28 Oct. 73.
[7] Catherine Charlotte, *née* Baillie, wife of 4th earl of Ashburnham; she d. 1894.
[8] Heinrich Schliemann, 1822-90, excavator of Troy; these discussions led to his friendship with the diarist, later broken by quarrel over home rule.
[9] See 19 Oct. 54.
[10] He d. January 1874.

Spent the morning with Mr Newton, in continuation, on the Photographs. These discoveries much confirm me.[1] Partially unwell: lay up. Finished Bagehot. Read Schleiermacher's Letters.

15. Wed.

Rose at 11. Wrote to Ld Advocate—Ld Granville—Mr Bate—Mr Cardwell—Mr . . .[2]—and minutes. Read Schleiermacher—Bp Forbes Charge & Letter[3]—Aristoph. Hippes. Further long conversation with Mr Burnett chiefly respecting Mr Wade.[4]

To E. CARDWELL, war secretary, 15 October 1873. Add MS 44542, f. 198.

The moderation of next year's estimates is a matter of very special interest; & independently of this I apprehend that on general grounds the charge of all necessary replacement of stores should fall on the present year for the service of which you have given them out. I thought from some correspondence I have seen that this had already been arranged with the Treasury; but I will make known your note & my reply to prevent any miscarriage.

On Saturday last I bid goodbye to a Lyttelton nephew[5] who is an officer of the Rifles, & is a singularly fine fellow—just going to India—sorely vexed & grieved at the pretended grievances petition, & exulting in the fact that only one man of his battalion had signed it. I said 'who did it'. He replied 'the half pay officers & the military newspapers.'

16. Th.

Ch. 8½ AM. Wrote to Mr Norwood l. & Tel.—Ld Wolverton Tel.Tel.—Miss Cartwright—Mr Pethick—Mr Bagehot—Dr Mozley—Dowager Duchess of Somerset—Gen. Ponsonby—and minutes. Read Aristoph. Hipp.—Schleiermacher—Highton on Socrates.[6] Saw Mr Gurdon—Mr Wadc. Woodcutting.

To W. BAGEHOT, 16 October 1873. Add MS 44542, f. 198.

I hope that I sent you at the proper time an acknowledgment of your kindness in presenting to me a copy of your work happily named 'Lombard Street'. But in my new capacity of Chancellor of the Exchequer I must not be content

[1] In his belief of the historical accuracy of parts of Homer.

[2] C. Norwood, offering unqualified support to Reed at Hull by-election, but warning him of responding to 'the absurd letter of Mr Disraeli'; Add MS 44440, f. 221.

[3] A. P. *Forbes, 'Charge, the claims of the laity' (1873) and 'Pastoral letter on foreign missions' (1873).

[4] The Mold floods case (see 27 Nov. 73); Gladstone this day asked the chairman of the L.N.W.R. for information; Add MS 44440, f. 195.

[5] N. G. Lyttelton, later C.I.G.S.; see 27 Nov. 45.

[6] H. Highton, 'Dean Stanley and Socrates' (1873); see Lathbury, ii. 96.

with that bare acknowledgment. I have now read it through attentively, & know not whether more to admire its cleverness or its force. I should be disposed were it worth your while to fight a little side battle with you about Savings Bank Balances. I do not admit the doctrine of Bank Reserves to be applicable to them without qualification. But I made a step, nay a stride, towards you in the larger conversion of Savings Bank Stocks into Annuities which brings at short intervals a very heavy roll of money into the coffers. But this is a mere parenthesis, & not meant as any qualification of the thanks which I tender to you for this new & important contribution to the comprehension by the public of the great money question. I expect to spend most of November in town, & hope you will some day look in upon me.[1]

17. Fr.

Ch. 8½ AM. Wrote to Attorney General—Ld Granville—Mr Herries—Ld Houghton—Mr Newton—Mr T.M. Gibson—and minutes. We brought down a great beech in the Rookery. Saw Mr West. Read Hippes—Ld Houghton's Address[2]—Mitchell's Proleg. (finished)[3]—Schleiermacher.

18. St Luke. Sat.

Ch 8¾ AM. Wrote to Ld Granville 2 L. & Tel.—Mr Fortescue—Mr Godley Tel.—Ld Wolverton Tel. Tel.—Sir R. Hill—Mr Chidlaw—Mr Scott—Bp of Ripon—Ld Lisgar—Mr Bright—Mr Sneyd[4]—and minutes. Conversation with Gurdon & W.H.G. on vacant preferments. Read Hippès—Schleiermacher. Walk with G. & W.

19. 19 S.Trin.

Ch 11 AM (with H.S.) and 6½ PM. Long conversation with Mr Wickham respecting Herbert.[5] Also we spoke of his investment: and instructed Harry about it. Wrote to Ld Pembroke—Mrs Th.—& minutes. Read Manchr Friend[6]—Barclay's Apology[7]—Schleiermacher—&c.

[1] Bagehot replied on 21 October: 'I wish I could think that the main thesis of my book was not now almost alarmingly confirmed. . . . The state of the City is certainly worse than I have seen it since 1866; and especially in the foreign stock market there is much apprehension. The collapse of Spain & the impending collapse of Egypt and Turkey are very serious events in that world'; Add MS 44440, f. 230; circulated by diarist to Lowe, Goschen, etc.

[2] R. M. *Milnes, Baron Houghton, 'Address . . . on social economy' (1862).

[3] See 30 Sept. 73.

[4] W. Sneyd of Keele, see 17 Oct. 28, 5 Nov. 73.

[5] As a result, Gladstone wrote to the Master of University college, Oxford, suggesting that Herbert Gladstone change from classics to history; Add MS 44543, f. 2.

[6] Untraced.

[7] R. *Barclay, *An apology for the true Christian divinity* (1678).

20. M.

Church 8½ AM. Wrote to Ld Granville (Tel.)—The Speaker—Ld Sydney—Ld Wolverton—Watson & S.—Herbert J. Gladstone—and minutes. Saw Mr West on India Office—& other matters. Read Aristoph—Finished Hippes, began Nephelai—Q.R. on Holland House[1]—&c.

21. Tu.

Ch. 8½ AM. Wrote to Mr Cardwell—Ld Granville Tel. & l.—Mr Wickham—Mr Dodson—Mr Smythe of Methven—and minutes. Walk with Mr [Benjamin] Webb & Sir James Lacaita. Wrote Mem. on 'Three Rules'.[2] Read Nephelai—Life of Mary Jennison[3]—Mendham & Watson.[4]

22. Wed.

Ch. 8½ AM. Wrote to Ld Chancellor—Rev Dr Mozley[5]—Mr W. Thorn—Rev Dr Lowe—Mr Gurdon Tel.—Messrs Watson & Smith—Mr Smythe of Methven—and minutes. Treecutting with Willy. Saw Mr Burnett—Mr Webb. Read Hugessen's Speech[6]—Aristoph. Neph.—Life of Mrs Jennison.

23. Th.

Ch. 8½ AM. Wrote to Ld Hartington (2)—Master of Univ. Coll.—Dr Woodford—Bp of Ripon—Mr Cardwell—Mr Thorn—Mr Burnett—& minutes. Dined at the Rectory. Saw Mr Johnson—S.E.G. on Sealand Cure. Tree cutting with W. Read Q.R. Polit. Article[7]—Aristoph. Neph. & Sphekes.

24. Fr.

Ch. 8½ A.M. Wrote to The Queen Mem.—Ld Granville l. & Tel.—Ld Wolverton l. & Tel.—Mr Gurdon Tel.—Mr Sneyd—Mr F.L. Gower

[1] [A. *Hayward], *Quarterly Review*, cxxxv. 405 (October 1873).

[2] In Ramm I, ii. 419.

[3] Untraced life of Mary Jenison, da. of *Beauclerk, S. *Johnson's friend.

[4] W. Watson, *Important considerations*, ed. J. Mendham (1831).

[5] Lathbury, ii. 96.

[6] Perhaps E. H. K. *Hugessen, 'Speech upon education, January 26, 1872' (1872).

[7] [*Salisbury], 'The programme of the radicals', *Quarterly Review*, cxxxv. 539; Gladstone told Wolverton on 20 October: 'I have just looked into Lord Salisbury in the Q.R. He seems much more civil towards the Govt.'; Add MS 44542, f. 202.

—Robn G.—Sir D. Corrigan—Sir T. Frost—Mr G. Trevelyan—Ld Chancr—& minutes. A large tree finished by W. & me today. Arranging books. Read Sphekes—Johnsons (not S.) Poems[1]—Watson's Important Considerations (1601).[2]

25. Sat.

Ch. 8½ A.M. Wrote to Ld Kimberley—Ld Granville—Att. General—Mr Gurdon (Tel)—The Ld Mayor—Dean of Elphin—The Queen Mem—Gen. Ponsonby—& minutes. Read Sphekes—Watson—finished. Treecutting with W. Much company continuing.

26. 20 S.Trin.

Ch. 11 AM and 6½ PM. Wrote to Lord Chancellor—Mr Chidlaw—Mrs Norton—Mr Forster—Dr Burr[3]—and minutes. Saw Mr MacColl—Mr Granville Vernon. Read Q.R. on Preaching—Schleiermacher Vol. II—Barclay's Apology—Burr's Lectures.

27. M.

Ch. 8½ AM. Wrote to Bp of Chester—Mr Hugessen—Adm. Howard—Mrs Burnett—Mr Barker—Ld Justice Clerk Tel.—Ld Granville Tel.—Mr Gurdon Tel.—Mr Baxter[4]—& minutes. Tree cutting with W. Read Sphekes finished—Mr Bright's Speech[5]—Schleiermacher's Life & Letters Vol. II.

28. Tu. SS.Simon & Jude.

Church 8.45 AM. Wrote to The Queen (Mem)—Mr De Lisle—Mrs Th.—Ld Hatherley—Rev Mr Gott[6]—Sir W. Knollys—Mr Sawer[7]—Mr Macmillan—and minutes. Saw Hurst about encountering expected poachers. Tree-dressing with W. Read Aristoph. Ornithes &

[1] G. B. Johnson, *Poems and sonnets* (1874); presumably an advance copy sent by the publishers.

[2] See 21 Oct. 73.

[3] Enoch Fitch Burr, 1818-1907, American congregationalist, wrote *The doctrine of evolution* (1873).

[4] Unsuccessfully offering him the postmastergeneralship; Add MS 44543, f. 3; see Ramm I, ii. 420.

[5] In Birmingham on 22 October Bright attacked the 1870 Act and Forster, producing sundry recriminations; Reid, *F*, i. 556, *The Times*, 23 October 1873, 5d.

[6] Appointing to Leeds John Gott, 1830-1906, vicar of Leeds from 1873.

[7] J. L. Sawer, executor of *Strzelecki, who left diarist a watch; Add MS 44440, f. 286.

Lacy's Pref.—Lady C. Davies, Recollections:[1] M'Mechen on Ch & State.[2]

29. Wed.

Ch. 8½ AM. Wrote to Ld F. Cavendish—Ld Granville—Mr Holland—Dowager Lady Westbury—Mr Laing—& minutes. Saw Canon Blomfield—Mr Wade. Attended conference on the Sealand severance & endowment at Queensferry. Read Ornithes—Schleiermacher—Ultramontane Action.[3]

30. Th.

Ch. 8½ AM. Wrote to J. Watson & Smith—The Speaker—Mr Bright—Mr Forster—Robn G.—Mr Newman Hall—and minutes. Tree-cutting with W. Read Ornithes—Schleiermacher—Mrs Jennison's Life. Saw Bp of Chester.

To H. B. W. BRAND, the Speaker, 30 October 1873. Brand MSS.

Bright has spoken very well and I have little fear of his health if he will take care: but the medical department has not been, ordinarily, well managed in his case.

I wish he had left it more clearly to be seen from his speech, that further change in the Education Act does not immediately impend.

The Financial question looms large & probably will be the hinge of the Session—possibly of the Election too.

To J. BRIGHT, chancellor of the duchy, 30 October 1873. Add MS 43385, f. 241.

I am really concerned to find that the offer which I made to Dr. Tate was such a shabby one.[4] I will bear his name in mind, in case it should be in my power, & not in yours, to do any thing better for him.

I know from our conversations the moderation of your views about the Education Act. Still I am not sure that if I had not been actually informed about them I should have estimated them quite accurately from your speech.[5] What I find after forty years of practise is that words have all measure of bearings besides that known to and intended by the utterer of them. And when the public mind, through being constantly whipped up on both sides, has become sensitive, it is almost impossible to guard against unforeseen constructions. Were I to criticise I should say that you said nothing as to our future policy but what you were in

[1] Lady L. C. *Davies, *Recollections of society in France and England*, 2v. (1872).

[2] W. MacMechan, *To disestablish the Church is to discrown the Queen* (1868).

[3] *Sketches of Ultramontane Action during the autumn* (1873).

[4] Low salary for Tate at Buckland Brewer; Add MS 44113, f. 78.

[5] See 27 Oct. 73.

every sense entitled to say: but it was perhaps open to people to infer from what you did not say that some proposals on the Education Act would enter into the opening programme of the Session; which, I think, under the actual circumstances, neither you nor I desire.

If it is your opinion that the Bill was injured by the main changes made in it as it went through, so it certainly is and always has been mine. I yielded reluctantly to what appeared to be the general, almost the universal wish, until they had been adopted, when on both sides there were signs of misgiving and dissent.

Like you I feel much anxiety as to the African Coast: we have had I think no real news of importance since the Cabinet nearly four weeks ago.

I am very glad you have been able to get through the great effort at Birmingham without our hearing of any evil consequences.

To W. E. FORSTER, vice president, 30 October 1873. Add MS 44543, f. 7.

It is pleasant to see the spirit of concord in which both you & Bright write to one another[1] even on points on which you have not the same view. I (as you will recollect) was not promoter of the changes made in the Education Bill during its passage, that is to say the main changes. But they are balanced changes, & I cannot but agree with you that as between Church & Dissent they were on the whole more favourable to the latter than the former. Bright touches the political world in a special sense at the meridian of Birmingham, & hearing incessantly the voice of the League must operate a good deal even on a strong mind when favourably predisposed. I return the letters with thanks.

31. Fr.

Ch. 8½ AM. Wrote to Ld Chancellor—Ld Granville—Mr Woodard—& minutes. Finished Ornithes—Began Lusistratè—Read Schleiermacher—White on Gradation in Man.[2]

Sat. Nov. One 1873. All Saints

Ch. 8¾ AM. Wrote to The Queen Mem.—Ld Granville (2) Also Telegram—Mr C. Hall—Ld Wolverton—Mr Wickham—Mr Kinnaird—Mr Godley—Mr [W. O.] Stanley MP.—Duke of Argyll—Mr Kinnaird—& minutes. Read as yesterday. Walk & conversation with Dr Clark, also with C.G.

To DUKE OF ARGYLL, Indian secretary, 1 November 1873. Add MS 44543, f. 8.

I return Sir B. Frere's letter, & think you have hardly observed the nature of the point taken by me as to parallel with the Gold Coast.[3] Treaties of protection

[1] Copies of letters on education in Add MS 44157, f. 87.
[2] Perhaps E. White, 'The mystery of growth' (1863).
[3] Argyll's comments not in Add MS 44102.

with particular Arab chiefs bind our hands as against other Arab chiefs, & this is the parallel to which I referred. Against our remonstrating with Turkey I have said nothing & have nothing to say.

A storm is already rising about the break of gauge.[1] I send another letter from Kinnaird.

2. 21 S.Trin.

Ch 11 AM with H.C.—and 6½ P.M. Wrote to Lady Ashburnham—Ld Kensington—Mr Godley—D. of Argyll—Sir F. Doyle—and minutes. Much conversation with Dr Clark on most interesting matters. Also on Mr Burnett's case. Also with W. on Church preferments. Read Burr's Lectures—Hancock's Sermons[2]—Noel's Poems[3]—Suffield's Sermon.[4]

3. M.

Ch. 8½ AM. Resumed conversation with Dr Clark. Wrote to Mr Godley Tel.—Ld F. Cavendish Tel.—Ld Granville—Robn G.—Attorney General[5]—Miss Scott—Mr Knowles[6]—and minutes. Finished the Lusistratè. Began [Aristophanes'] Eirenè. Read Life of Mrs Jennison—Quatrefages on Prussian Ethnology.[7] Walk with C.G: speculating on little possible improvements.

4. Tu.

Ch. 8½ AM. Wrote to Ld Tenterden (Tel)—Ld Granville—Mr Sneyd—Messrs Watson—Mr Barker—Mr De Lisle—Mr Ayrton—Mr Furnival—Mr Goschen—& minutes. Read the Eirenè of Aristophanes—Also ....

Nov.5.1873. [*Keele Hall*][8]

Ch. 8½ AM. Wrote to Ld Tenterden Tel.—Mr Godley Tel.—& minutes.

[1] Broad *vs.* narrow gauge in India; the Indian govt. had decided on the latter; see Add MS 44542, f. 180.
[2] T. Hancock, *The return to the father* (1873).
[3] See 24 Dec. 72.
[4] M. O. Suffield, 'Is Jesus God' (1873).
[5] Offering J. D. *Coleridge the chief justiceship on d. of *Bovill.
[6] Published in Knowles' *Contemporary Review*, xxiii. 162 (December 1873), and *The Times*, 1 December 1873, 5b, replying to H. *Spencer's criticisms of his Liverpool address in 'Study of Sociology', serialised in the *Contemporary*. See 13 Nov. 73.
[7] J. L. A. de Quatrefages de Bréau, *The Prussian race ethnologically considered* (1872).
[8] Gladstone left his journal at Hawarden; 5–9 November are written on a sheet of Althorp letter paper, tipped into the journal. On 8 November Gladstone asked his daughter Mary to forward it: 'In my table drawer, probably the right hand division, & forward part of the drawer, you will find my little Journal Book, purple in colour, which I rather stupidly left behind'; Add MS 46221, f. 76.

Saw Mr Burnett—Mr Barker. Preparations for departure. Finished (under pressure) the Eirenè of Aristoph. Thus far I should certainly have given the prizes as the Athenians gave them. Read Guadagnoli's Poems.[1]—The Sale of Souls.[2] 3¼-6¼. Journey to Keele,[3] where we found a large & pleasant party: & saw in the evening some of the various & beautiful objects.

6. Th.

Wrote to Mr Cardwell—Mr Godley (Tel)—& minutes. Saw the Ivories—Church—gardens—grounds—Farm: & so divided my day with work. Saw Mr Hollis, the very able agent. Read [Aristophanes'] the Ploutos (began)—La Monacologia.[4]

7. Fr. [Althorp Park]

Wrote to Gen. Ponsonby Tel.—Ld Granville—& minutes. Saw the Porcelain: wh is not equal to the remarkable collection of Plate—also some Book treasures. Drove to see the Silverdale works. Off at 2¼. Reached Althorp[5] at 6½: again a full house, & a most kind reception. Long conversation with Ld Spencer—Saw Granville. Read the Ploutos.

Nov. 8. Sat.

Wrote to The Lord Chancellor. l. & Tel.—The Attorney General—Mr Moffatt—Archdeacon Jones—Mr Adam—Lady Waldegrave—Ld Advocate—Mary Gladstone—& minutes. Conversation with Ld Granville—Mr Beesley[6]—Rev. Mr Alderson.[7] Introduced to some of the vast treasures of the Library: it was only a taste; & yet a surfeit. We went to Holmby.

Nov. 9. 22 S. Trin.

Parish Ch. mg and aft—Mr Ponsonby[8] preached; & very well. A little

[1] A. Guadagnoli, *Poesie Giocose* (1872). [2] Untraced.

[3] Seat of Rev. W. Sneyd, his Christ Church friend; see 17 Oct. 28.

[4] Apparently *sic* but the ink has faded.

[5] *Spencer's great house near Northampton; see 11 Oct. 52.

[6] Hardly likely to be the socialist E. S. *Beesley; most probably John Beasley of Chapel Brampton by Althorp.

[7] Frederick Cecil Alderson, 1836–1907, rector of Holdenby, Northamptonshire 1865–93; royal chaplain 1899.

[8] Frederick John Ponsonby, rector of Brington, Northamptonshire 1868–77, vicar of Mary Magdalen, London 1877.

more looking at the House. A fair day's reading. Wrote to Sir R. Phillimore—Mr Lowe—& minutes.

10. M. [London]

Wrote to The Queen—Sir J. Coleridge—Mr Knollys—Ly M. Alford —Govr of Bank—Sir F. Knollys—Sol. General (for consn)—and minutes. Saw Ld Spencer—Ld Kimberley—Mr Cardwell—Ld Granville—Mr Bright—Mr Forster—Ld Chancellor. Cabinet 3¼-6¼. Attended Guildhall Feast & spoke for the toast of Ministers.[1] Read Ploutos. 10-1½. Althorp to C.H.T.

Cabinet. Nov. 10. 73. 3 PM.[2]
O Greenwich seat.
√ Succession of Law Officers. Agreed that claims to particular judgeships shall drop.[3]
√ Reuter Telegrams. announ[cemen]t to be made to I[ndia] O[ffice].[4]
O Dufferin's inquiry.[5]
√ Dispatch from Sir G. Wolseley. Cardwell may ship *stores* for 1500 men (European) in preparation, for the mail of Sat[urda]y shd. we find it necessary to send them.[6]
√ French offer of forts[?] in exchange[?] on coast of Africa. Through the Naval Attaché! Refer him to F.O.
√ Ld Kimberley (person singular[)] will approve [?apprise] Sir G. Wolseley. (WO & CO being committed already[)].

11. Tu.

Wrote to Ld Chancellor (2)—Mr Cardwell—Ld Lyttelton—D. of Cambridge—& minutes. Luncheon at 15 G.S. Saw Ld Wolverton—Ld Granville—Mr Peel—All these in conclave—Ld F. Cavendish—D. of Argyll (2)—Sol. General[7]—Mr Adam. Saw Hill. X. Dined at Panizzi's: we had an interesting discussion on Dante Par. IV. the *dubbio* lines.[8] Struggle with Chaos in my room.

[1] *The Times*, 11 Nov. 1873, 7d.

[2] Add MS 44641, f. 209; the dates on the cabinet minutes of 10 and 15 November are indistinct, but are clarified by Gladstone's reports to the Queen, CAB 41/5/36.

[3] Note to Selborne at Add MS 44641, f. 210, reads: 'Do you agree with me that claims of succession to particular Judgeships on the part of the Attorney General or the Law Officers naturally drop with your reconstruction of the Judicature by the recent Act? WEG.' 'Affirmative'; in diarist's hand.

[4] Julius de Reuter had gained concession from the Shah of monopoly of railway etc. construction in Persia; *PP* 1873 lxxv. 681.

[5] On nomination of Roman catholic bps. in Canada; see Ramm I, ii. 425.

[6] See 17 Nov. 73.

[7] i.e. *James, offering him the attorney-generalship, but without inevitable promotion to judge (see 10 Nov. 73n); Add MS 44441, f. 38.

[8] Dante's exposition to Beatrice in *Par.* IV, 1-9.

12. Wed.

Wrote to Sol. General—Mrs Norton—Att. General—The Queen l. & 2 Mema—Mr Harcourt[1]—Mr Adam—Gen. Ponsonby—Ld Advocate (Tel)—Mary G. (Tel)—& minutes. Saw Dr L. Playfair—Mr Bagehot—Mr Ouvry—Mr Fremantle—Mr Gurdon—Ld Granville—Mr Bright—Ld Wolverton. Saw Lady James. Saw Bennett X. Dined with the F. Cavendishes. Breakfasted with Sir J. Lacaita to meet Prince Lucian Buonaparte[2] with whom I was greatly pleased. The conversation (1½ h) was on Dante, philology, & Belief. [3]Cabinet 3-6. C. of Exchequer (Sheriffs) 2-2¾.

Cabinet. Nov. 12. 73. 3 PM.[4]

√ Plan of Metrop. Board for road southward from Hamilton Place. We do not adopt.[5]
√ Narrative respecting the Greenwich seat given by W.E.G. & discussion thereupon. No meeting of legal authorities on Sat. Case to stand over for the new A.G. & S.G. Chanc[ello]r will inform Coleridge.
√ O'Keeffe. Ld Hartington's narrative—papers to be printed.[6]
√ Queen's letter respecting Railway accidents & legislation.[7]
Next Cabinet Saty.

13. Th.

Threatening of an attack: kept my bed till one. Wrote to Gen. Ponsonby—J. Watson & S.—Mr Grieve MP.—Dowager Lady Spencer—Mr Monsell—Mr Gurdon—Mr Herbert Spencer[8]—and minutes. Saw Ld Wolverton—Ld Advocate—I went to 5 P.M. Tea with Lady Ashburnham & we spoke much on grounds & measures of belief. Dined at Lady Herbert's: a painful occasion; but we were few & the company good i.e. interesting. C. had fought the battle well. Read Bismarck v. Christ[9]—Voltaire aux Delices[10]—Mill's Autobiography[11]—Memoir of Sara Coleridge.[12]

[1] Successfully offering him the solicitor-generalship; Add MS 44543, f. 12, Gardiner, *Harcourt*, i. 258.

[2] Louis-Lucien Bonaparte, 1813-91, scientist and senator; lived in London, given royal pension 1883.

[3] Rest of entry written at foot of page.

[4] Add MS 44641, f. 216.

[5] To improve traffic at Hyde Park Corner; letter of rejection in Add MS 44543, f. 12.

[6] *PP* 1874 li. 617.

[7] Guedalla, *Q*, i. 429.

[8] Thanking Herbert *Spencer, 1820-1903, sociologist, for *The Study of Sociology* (1873), and informing him of his letter to be published (see 3 Nov. 73); Spencer recalled (*An Autobiography* (1904), ii. 255): the correspondence 'ended quite amicably, and established between us social relations of a pleasant kind'.

[9] *Bismarck versus Christ. By a convert* (1872).

[10] G. Desnoitesterres, 'Voltaire aux délices', in *Voltaire et la société au XVIIIme Siècle* (1871-3), v.

[11] J. S. Mill, *Autobiography*, ed. H. Taylor, just published.

[12] *Memoir and letters of Sara Coleridge*, ed. E. Coleridge, 2v. (1873).

14. Fr.

Wrote to Gen. Ponsonby—Lady Ashburnham—Sir T. Biddulph—Ld Dalhousie—Mr Fortescue—Robn G.—Ld Granville—& minutes. Dined with the Goschens. Luncheon 15 G.S. & saw Mrs Th. Saw Mr Gurdon—Mr Moffatt—Sir W. James—Col. Hogg—Ld A. Hervey—Ld Wolverton. We had much anxiety today about Ld R. Cavendish.[1] Read Memoir of S. Coleridge—Autobiogr. of J. Stuart Mill.

15. Sat.

Robns birthday: God bless him in all things. We remain very anxious about R. C[avendish]. Wrote to Messrs Bickers—The Queen—Mr Dodson—and minutes. Cabinet 2¼-6. Dined at Ld Granville's. Saw Mr Harcourt (S.G.)—Ld Wolverton—Mr Fortescue—Ld Granville—Mr Lowe—The Ld Chancellor—Ld Kimberley—Duke of Edinburgh—Count Münster (the Ch controversy)[2]—Dr Carpenter (physiology)—Ly Aylesbury (family). Saw Cox X. Read J. Stuart Mill.

Cabinet. Sat. Nov. 15/73 2 PM.[3]

√ Prorogation of Parliament. Arr[angemen]t may be postponed.
√ Case of Ld Midleton mentioned[4]—*quoad* Greenwich seat.
√ War Office & Admiralty. The embankment land may be laid out.
√ Ld Advocate & Scotch Bills. See over & my letter.[5]
√ Aden aggression. Wait answer from Elliot to Tel. already sent.[6]
√ Railway circular: proposed by Mr F[ortescue] in an amended form. Further amended & agreed to.[7]
√ Virginius.[8] Telegraph to say that reserving the question at present of executions wh have already taken place, we shall hold the Spanish Govt. & all concerned responsible for any further executions of British subjects under the circs. as they have been stated to Madrid[9] and Havana.
√ Alderley Harbour. Follow Lords Committee.
√ E. [African] Coast Slave Trade. Ld Granville, Mr Goschen, Mr Dodson: to consider scale of expenditure.
√ House[10] Government for Private Bills. Migratory Tribunals without appeal—discussed. Circulate copies of old Bill.

[1] See 19 Nov. 73.
[2] Clerical oath of obedience imminent in Prussia.
[3] Add MS 44641, f. 211. See 10 Nov. 73, for dating.
[4] 1st Lord Middleton became Commissioner of Public Accounts in 1725 without re-election.
[5] Jottings on Bill, and note from Gurdon[?]: 'The Lord Advocate is waiting all this time'. G. Young had sent a list of five proposed Bills on 5 November 1873; Add MS 44441, f. 18.
[6] Turkish aggression at Aden, F.O.C.P. 2420, 2431.
[7] See 12 Nov. 73.
[8] Cabinet learnt from newspapers, consul I. V. Crawford having neglected to telegraph, that most of the Cuban, American and British crew of the 'Virginius', an American ship, were executed in Cuba on 1 November for running guns to assist Cuban insurgents; American protests forced Castelar to surrender surviving prisoners; authorities in Havana refused until 12 December; see *Annual Register 1873*, 253 and *PP* 1874 lxxvi. 299 for these telegrams to Crawford and Layard.
[9] Two words here illegibly overwritten.
[10] May read 'Home'.

16. 23 S. Trin.

Chapel Royal mg & aft. Wrote to Mr Scott (Norwood)[1]—Abp Manning—Ld Kimberley—Dr A. Clark—& minutes. Saw the Heywoods (Luncheon)—The Farquhars (dinner)—Evelyn Ashley—Ld Wolverton—Mad. Novikoff—Dr Eustace Smith[2]—D. of Devonshire. Increased anxiety about R.C. at night. Read (over) Abp M. on Dr Nicholson—with much pain[3]—Dr Ryder on Baptism[4]—'Foreign Chaplain' on Eternal Punishment.[5]

17. M.

Much improvement in R. C[avendish]—thank God. Saw Ld G.C. —Ld F.C.—Ld Wolverton—Mr Godley—Sir C. Anderson—Mr Cardwell—Ld Halifax. Read Mill's Autobiogr.—C.M.P.s Marie Antoinette.[6] Cabinet 3¾–7¼. Wrote to Bp Browne—Ld Advocate—The Queen—& minutes. The discussion in C[abinet] bore I thought rather hard upon Bright: but ended well. Dined with the Godleys: much interesting conversation.

Cabinet. Nov. 17. 73. 3.30 PM.[7]

√ Prorogation of Parlt. to 5 of February for dispatch of business.

√ Virginius. Telegrams read. Tell newspapers the names—*general* nature of our proceeding—and assurances given by Spain.[8]

√ Gold Coast. Dispatches to 26th read.[9] Action of 14th: Between Elmina & Ampenne. Oct. 21: Amonquatta's letter & reply.[10] Operation (March) of the 14th to Essarman & the Coast. No dependence on native Units.[11] Dispatch of 26th Oct: marching on. Dispatch of 13th Oct. for European force. 24th Oct.—No native levies: apathy if not cowardice. Coomassie more distant than supposed.

Agreed to send the battalions 2 + 1. Dispatch on policy of the war & the peace to be prepared for Cabinet on Friday. No need to call Parlt. on account of the inconvenience of losing time.

√ D. of Argyll proposed a broad guage [*sic*] & a light rail by way of compromise—agreed. to. Cost 600m[ille].

Virginius.[12] Telegram arrived at 6 asking us 1) to unite our claims with that

[1] i. e. T. *Scott; see 16 May 55; on Mill and eternal punishment, in Lathbury, ii. 97.

[2] Cavendish's doctor; see 19 Nov. 73.

[3] J. J. Guiron, *The Sacred Heart* (1873); exchange of letters between Guiron, Manning's secretary and A. Nicholson.

[4] A. G. Ryder, *The baptismal regeneration of infants* (1873).

[5] 'Everlasting punishment. A letter to T. Scott. By a foreign chaplain' (1873).

[6] Untraced. [7] Add MS 44641, f. 218. [8] See 10 Nov. 73.

[9] Printed in *PP* 1874 xlvi. 691; Wolseley thus asked for British troops before he had confirmed the insufficiency of local levies; three British battalions left on 19th–21st November; see McIntyre, 'British policy', *Historical Journal*, v. 38. For these actions, see G. A. Henty, *The march to Coomassie* (1874), ch. 4.

[10] King Kofi's local commander; Henty, op. cit., 125.

[11] Wolseley had persuaded Fremantle of the marines to disregard orders and assist him.

[12] See 10 Nov. 73.

[*sic*] of the U.S. or 2) to arbitrate ourselves. Ans: 1) we do not know the US would agree 2) think ourselves disqualified &c.

Nov. 17.[1]

Send English troops as requested. Sufficient instructions to Glover to be amenable & obedient. Make peace if he can. If not strike a blow. At a point as far short of the Prah, or Coomassie, as he can. Endeavour to establish *friendship* with the Ashantees—give them free & secure access to the coast. The allied nations, leaving it to us to fight their war, have no claims upon us ulterior to the present operations.

18. Tu.

Wrote to Mr Adam—Ld Acton—Mr Bright—Ld Granville—& minutes. Bp of Winchr Memorial Comm. Meeting 2-3. Saw Mr Wilberforce—Mr Locke King—Mr Gurdon—Mr Macmillan—Mr Gregory—Ly Ashburnham—Bp of Winchester. A sad retrogression in R.C. today: yet we hope—less. Dined with the Wortleys. Read Mill's Autobiogr.

19. Wed.

Wrote to Col. Hogg—Gen. Ponsonby—J. Watson & S.—Mr Cardwell—Ld Kimberley—& minutes. Read J.S. Mill—Holland House by Princess M.L.[2]—Sara Coleridge. Saw Mr Rivers Wilson—Ld Granville—Mr Forster—D of Argyll—Rev Mr Lowe—Mr Godley—Scotts—Ld F. Cavendish—Dr Eustace Smith: at 4 P.M. They were then looking forward to Galvanism, within an hour. But a change came on soon after which cut off all hope. At 7.30 I was summoned *rapidly* to the bedside. With difficulty he said 'God bless you'. At ¼ past 8 we saw him die: amidst the prayers offered by Mr Murray.[3] The world is now a shade darker. But he is gone to peace. We spent the evg sorrowfully with the F.C.s.

20. Th.

Wrote to Ld Hartington—Lyon Playfair—Mr Bouverie—Sir R. Phillimore (2)—Mr Newton—Earl of Kimberley—Sir T. Biddulph—& minutes. Read Mill's Autobiogr. (finished)—Sara Coleridge.

[1] Notes for dispatch, Add MS 44641, f. 220; see 21 Nov. 73. The printed version (see 21 Nov. 73) added that if Wolseley crushed the Ashanti he might reach Kumasi and find no-one to negotiate with, as indeed happened; see W. D. McIntyre, *The imperial frontier* (1967), 149.

[2] Princess Marie Liechtenstein, *Holland House*, 2v. (1873).

[3] For Lord R. Cavendish by Francis Henry Murray, d. 1902; Christ Church; rector of Chislehurst from 1846.

Saw Dean of Westminster—Sir W. Boxall—Mr Gurdon—Mr Stansfeld—D of Argyll—Mr J.S. Wortley—Mr Bright. Six dined. Long conversation with Mr B. on Ashantee &c. Saw Sir W. James.

To LORD KIMBERLEY, colonial secretary, 20 November 1873. Add MS 44543, f. 16.

I think your Draft dispatch[1] includes all the points which are material to the Ashantee case & to the present juncture & handles them in the proper spirit; so far as my individual recollections go. I have offered a few suggestions chiefly of single words in pencil on the margin for your consideration. I think they are in harmony with the spirit of the draft. I hope to have some conversation with Bright this evening, in which the subject of Ashantee can be concluded.

21. *Fr.*

Wrote to The Queen—Mr F. Leveson—Mrs Th.—Ld Robartes—& minutes. Saw Ld Granville—Mr F. Leveson—D of Argyll—Ld Chancellor—Mr Gurdon—Sir R. Phillimore—Mr A. Peel—Mr Knowles. Read Delaware Water Gap[2]—Fifine at the Fair.[3] Dined with the Argylls. Cabinet 2½-6¼. Not over well.

[*Cabinet. 21 November 1873. 2.30 P.M.*][4]

√ Virginius case. Recital.
√ Ashantee. Ld Kimberley's draft read & approved.[5]
√ Subjects of legislation summarily gone over. *Not* to take Co. Suffrage, *not* to take Land Laws—nor include Ireland in the financial part of Local Taxation.
√ R.C. Univ. Degrees. Inform[atio]n from Irish L[aw] O[fficers] & as to Church

England:[6] Mr Stansfeld's Bills on Exemptions, Consolidated Rate and [blank].
W.E.G. Bill on Friendly Societies Deficit, Savings Bank Interest.
H[ousehold] Suffrage—Budget—Labour contracts—Conspiracy.
Scotland: Patronage committee—Ld Advocate's Bills on Judicature, Entails, Church payments.
Ireland: Committee on Constabulary, Bill on Judicature.

22. [*Chatsworth*]

Kept my bed till noon. Wrote to Sir R. Phillimore—The Queen (Mem)—Mr Lowe—Messrs J. Watson & Smith—Mary G.—& minutes. Read Lytton's Parisians[7]—Macmeadow on Turf question.[8]

[1] See next day; sent by Kimberley on 19 November, Add MS 44225, f. 111.
[2] Untraced. [3] By R. *Browning (1872). [4] Add MS 44641, f. 222.
[5] Expansion of Gladstone's notes of 17 November; printed, with holograph alterations, ibid., f. 223; final version, sent by Kimberley on 24 November, in *PP* 1874 xlvi. 735. See 17 Nov. 73.
[6] Notes on proposed legislation, Add MS 44641, f. 226.
[7] E. G. E. L. Bulwer *Lytton, *The Parisians*, 4v. (1873). [8] Untraced.

Saw Mr Gurdon—Lord F. Cavendish. 2½-8. Journey to Chatsworth. Found many: all, except Lacaita, relatives, and chiefly here without reference to the sad loss.

To R. LOWE, home secretary, 22 November 1873. Add MS 44543, f. 16.

I send you, with previous papers, a communication I have had from the Limerick Amnesty Association. Cardwell some time ago informed me that he was examining the cases of the soldiers. I wish you would kindly look into those of the civilians, who are I believe only four, in two twos. My impression is that the Brett murder men have had punishment enough, but I do not give this as a final conclusion in my own mind. The other case I know still less in detail. The probability is that pressure upon us would much increase, when we come near the Dissolution. It is desirable, if allowable, to anticipate that pressure; which I think would very probably be yielded to, with some discredit.[1]

23. Preadv.Sunday.

Ch mg & Chapel in the House aftn. Wrote to Sir S. Northcote—Mr Wilberforce—C.G.—Mr Burnett—Mr Gurdon—and minutes. Read Union Review—Life of Montalembert[2]—Frohschammer Fels Petri[3]—Greg. Enigmas of Life.[4] Walk with the Duke.

24. M.

Wrote to Mr Goschen—Lady M. Herbert—Mr Gurdon—Read Ploutos (finished)—Greg's Enigmas of Life—Bulwer's Parisians (finished I). Saw Ld F.C. (treasury).[5] In the afternoon came the Greys and others for the funeral. The coffin was deposited in the Chapel.

To G. J. GOSCHEN, first lord of the admiralty, Add MS 44543, f. 17.
24 November 1873.

I do not doubt you have in the Admiralty figures which will show for a course of past years down to the present time say since 1840 the cost of Ship-building in the Navy. I should much like to see the figures, both for Estimate & outlay year by year, & it would increase their interest & value if the paper showed the kind of ship built as wooden sailing—Paddle Steamers—Screw Steamers—Iron coated & true Iron, though this I believe is called Iron clad.[6] I am to return to town tomorrow.

[1] Lowe regretted 'I can find nothing on which to found a recommendation' and opposed release, 25 November 1873, Add MS 44302, f. 153.
[2] M. O. *Oliphant, *Memoir of Count de Montalembert* (1872); see 17 Dec. 73.
[3] J. Frohschammer, *Der Fels Petri in Rom* (1873).
[4] W. R. *Greg, *Enigmas of life* (1872).
[5] Lord F. Cavendish was a junior whip.
[6] Goschen took his time, see 1 Jan. 74.

To BARON ROBARTES,[1] 24 November 1873. Add MS 44543, f. 17.

I am afraid that when you open this note from me, & find that its subject is the representation of East Cornwall, your first sentiment may be one of displeasure or surprise. I am given to believe, on what should be good authority, that the seat for that division is at the command of your son, probably without contest—that he is disinclined—that his hesitation does not rest on the ground of differences of political principle—& that you have been reluctant to press him; from considerations which, as myself a parent, I heartily appreciate. Nevertheless I would venture with all respect to express the hope that you may feel this to be a case of public duty, while I am sure that, if you so feel it, you will use every means of fair persuasion to induce your son to stand. The Liberal Party is now suffering, not for its sins but for its virtues, & from the reaction consequent upon the strain of public spirited effort to which it had worked up the country. For my own part, after more than forty years of toil, I can say with truth that if I am a candidate for a seat at the next general election it will be entirely from a sense of my obligation to the liberal party & in the teeth of all my desires. I do not mean to say that obligations in all cases are the same, but may it not be fairly urged that there is a substantial obligation, wherever ability to render public service, and a position consistently & peculiarly favourable for rendering it, plainly appear to exist? I thoroughly respect the modesty which may be placed in the opposite scale; but even that most estimable & not now very common quality ought sometimes to be contended against & overcome. I own it appears to me that the country, & that the political party also with which men may respectively be in cooperation, has very strong claims on those who find ready-made for them in the world positions of great power & advantage, resulting from the labours of those who have preceded them. I hope you will think I have not exceeded due bounds in offering these remarks for your consideration.[2]

25. Tu. [*London*]

It was a walking funeral: the day lovely, the scene perfect in calm and beauty. I follow R.C.[3] much into the other world, where he is in the hands of the same Father as here, but nearer Him. Though he walk through the valley of the shadow of death, let him fear no evil. I find from the Duke that in a letter he has remembered both me & his godson Harry. After an early luncheon I started for town & arrived at 7¼ PM. John Grey[4] gave me an interesting account of the beginning of *their* religious life at Cambridge.

Saw Mr Gurdon. Wrote to General Ponsonby—Mr Hugessen—Mr A. Peel—Mrs Grote—& minutes. Read Life of Montalembert—The Parisians. Dined at Dean Stanleys. Saw Dean Church—D. of Argyll.

[1] Thomas James Agar-Robartes, 1808–82; liberal M.P. E. Cornwall 1847–68; cr. Baron Robartes 1869. His son Thomas Charles (1844–1930, 2d Baron Robartes 1882, 6th Viscount Clifden 1899) did not stand in 1874, but won the seat 1880.

[2] No reply found.

[3] Lord Richard Cavendish; see 23 June 27.

[4] John Grey, 1829–95, s. of 2nd Earl Grey; rector of Houghton-le-Spring from 1836.

26. Wed.

Wrote to Mr Morley—Ld Portsmouth—Mr Barker—Sir T.D. Acland—Robn G. (2)—Duke of Argyll—Mr Barker—The Att. General—The Queen—& minutes. Saw Mr Gurdon—Mr Godley—Mr A. Peel—Duke of Argyll—Ld Granville. Cabinet 2¾-6¾. Dined at Panizzi's. Read The Parisians.

[*Cabinet*] *Nov. 26. 73.* [*2 PM.*][1]

√ Greenwich seat. Ask[?] for speedy opinion.[2]

√ O. Morgan. Burials Bill. Regret inability.[3]

√ Conspiracies not to be punishable where the act is not punishable—with exceptions: plan to be prepared for cons[ideratio]n. Also where when the act is only punishable summarily[4] whether the magistrates may have jurisdiction over conspiracy within the same limits of punishment—plan to be prepared in like manner. Clauses to be prepared in accordance with Lowe's proposal to make breach of contract no longer an offence: qualified as far as he thinks it may be by the Chancellor's proviso for future cons[ideratio]n. Criminal Law Am. Act to be made general.[5]

√ Indian Distress. D. of Argyll made a statement. Leave the matter in the hands of the Viceroy, while tendering any inform[atio]n or suggestion.[6]

√ Virginius. Tel. to Layard agreed to (MS of WEG given to Ld Gr.)[7]

27. Th.

Wrote to Mr Burnett—Mr Forster—Mr Riv. Wilson—Mr Welby—Rev Mr Williams—Lady Egerton—Prince L. Bonaparte—Mr Ward Hunt—& minutes. Saw Mr Boydell & Mr Roberts—Mr Childers—Mr Peel—Sir T. Fremantle—Mr Gurdon—Conclave on Mold Drainage Floods 12-1½.[8]—Mr Moon—Mr Agnew—Mr Holman Hunt—

[1] Add MS 44641, f. 229. Cabinet also refused to subsidise *Frere's Arctic expedition, see Add MS 44441, f. 137.

[2] Letter to *James requesting a quick opinion, in Add MS 44543, f. 18.

[3] Morgan requested a govt. Burials Bill; Add MS 44441, f. 104.

[4] 'conspiracy to be ditto no offence' deleted; this Cabinet decision rejected original proposal in favour of limitation not abolition of punishment.

[5] Lowe proposed 'to abolish all conspiracies, to commit offences punishable by summary jurisdiction before a magistrate', to abolish 'conspiracies to commit acts not in themselves criminal', to acknowledge that in the working classes' hostility to the 1867 Master and Servants' Act 'they appear to be so entirely in the right', but defending the 1871 Criminal Law Amndt. Act. These proposals anticipate the 1875 Conspiracy and Protection of Property Act, clause 3. Selborne wanted 1. magistrates' power continued, 2. recognition that some actions became criminal through conspiracy, 3. some punishments under the 1867 Act retained. Their mem. printed for the cabinet on 7 November 1873, Add MS 44621, f. 130. Lowe was instructed to draft a bill 'for further consideration'; CAB 41/5/41.

[6] Letter from viceroy printed for cabinet 27 November 1873, Add MS 44621, f. 160.

[7] Demanding release of British subjects; F.O.C.P. 2541, p. 31.

[8] Law suit between Gladstone's tenants, Roberts and Sheen, and the L.N.W.R., resulting from flood damage at Mold; Add MS 44440, f. 195.

Mr Agnew. 3-4. Mr Holman Hunt's remarkable picture.[1] At 5 attended meeting of Portrait Gallery Trustees. Saw Russell—Maclagan—Legh (Smith)[R]. Read The Parisians—Montalembert's Life.

28. Fr.

Wrote to Att. General—The Queen 2 l. & 2 Mema—Mr Forster—Sir F. Doyle—Sir T. Fremantle—Attorney General—Gen Ponsonby—Ld Chancellor—& minutes. Saw Mr Gurdon—Mr Bright—Mr Peel—Ld F. Cavendish—Mr Lowe—Mr Goschen *cum* Mr Lowe—Ld Granville—Mr West. Cabinet 2¾-6½. Dined with the West's. Read Life of Montalembert. Saw Lewis—Wade—Ramsay[R].

Cabinet. Friday Nov. 28. 73. 2.30 P.M.[2]

√ Amalgamation of the Customs & Inland Revenue. WEG. mentioned the question of amalgamation—proposed to appoint Goulburn subject to any future arrangements in the public interest—& to start a cons[ideratio]n of plan of continuation when practicable.[3]

√ Thornton's Tel. of yesty. respecting Virginius read. No step thought necessary. Make known Tel. to Layard.

√ Khiva. Queen inquires whether Russia has violated an *engagement* to G. Britain. No: but there is an inconsistency. Discussion whether subj. shd. be noticed. Ld G. will consider whether to prepare draft.[4]

√ Anything to be said about Merv? No call today; Ld G. to reopen if he shd. see cause.[5]

√ Mr Stansfeld's Mem. on Local Govt. discussed. Question ans[were]d & Committee of Cabinet appointed as within.[6]

Virginius. Dispatch from Jamaica read, with account of the transactions.[7]

29. Sat.

Wrote to Sir B. Frere—Miss Hope Scott—Agnes G.—and minutes. Went with C. to Holman Hunt's picture[8]—& Watercolour, Suffolk St. & French Exhibns. Saw Mr Goulburn—D. of Argyll—Mr Dodson—Mr O. Morgan—Mr Gurdon—Mr Grote (noteworthy)[9]—Mrs Th.—Sir R. Phillimore. Read Fraser on Mill's Autob.[10] Six to dinner.

[1] 'The shadow of death', exhibited at 39B Bond Street.

[2] Add MS 44641, f. 232.

[3] F. Goulburn (see 21 June 59) succeeded Fremantle at the Customs; amalgamation planned but never executed, see Add MS 44441, f. 142.

[4] i.e. Shuvalov's assurance in January on no Khiva expedition; Ramm I, ii. 371, 374.

[5] See Ramm I, ii. 430.

[6] Stansfeld's mem. of 26 Nov. and answers to questions circulated to cabinet in PRO T 168/82. Cttee. of Kimberley, Halifax, Stansfeld, Goschen, Aberdare, Lowe, Forster, Fortescue; Hartington's name deleted; Add MS 44641, f. 234.

[7] Report of 8 Nov., from J. P. Grant, governor of Jamaica, in *PP* 1874 lxxvi. 239.

[8] See 27 Nov. 73.

[9] Probably Arthur *Grote, 1814-86, br. of G.;* retired from Indian service.

[10] *Fraser's Magazine*, viii. 663 (December 1873).

30. Adv.S.

Chapel Royal mg & aft. Wrote to Gen. Ponsonby (2)—Ld F. Cavendish—Mr Peel—Ld Granville (2)—Mr Trevelyan—Ld Clarendon[1]—& minutes. Dined with the Enfields. Read Biley on Joshua X[2]—Tom & his Grandfather[3]—Dusautoy on the Apostasy[4]—Manning on the S. Heart[5]—Notices of the Speaker's Commentary.[6]

Dec. One 1873. London.

Wrote to Bp of Norwich—Mr Granville Berkeley—Sir W. Stephenson—Attorney General—Mr Cardwell—The Queen—and minutes. Saw Dr Woodford—Mr Hayward—Ld Aberdare—Mr Gurdon—Mr Lambert—Mr Knowles—Sir W. Stephenson—Sir R. Phillimore. Dined at Mr Forsters & went to Drury Lane to see in Antony & Cleopatra how low our stage has fallen.[7] Miss K. Vaughan[8] in the ballet, dressed in black & gold, danced marvellously. Read The Parisians.

[*Cabinet*] *D.1. 73.*[9]

√ Greenwich Seat. A.G. & S.G. attended. They & Ld. Chr.[10]
√ Order of Bills. Arranged—see mem.[11]
√ Ashantee Dispatches read. A toning[?] or harmonising dispatch or dispatches; retrospective, to be written—no new instructions required.[12]
√ Legal Education. Chancellor will frame his personal plan & send to Inns of Court without committing us.
√ Women Doctors. A short enabling act to remove an unintended doubt.
√ Lowe's Conspiracy Bill. Hartington Local Govt. Bill. √ Ayrton Army Discipline. √ Young Scotch Church pay[men]ts, Conveyancing, Scotch Jurisdiction. Ld Chancr. Transfer of Land. √ Stansfeld's Bills—all to be ready for the opening of the session. √ = to be ready at opening of Session.[13]

[1] Unsuccessfully offering court office to Edward Hyde Villiers, 1846-1915; whig M.P. Brecon 1869-70; 5th earl of Clarendon 1870.

[2] E. Biley, *On the miracle recorded in the 10th chapter of the Book of Joshua* (1873).

[3] Untraced.

[4] F. Dusautoy, 'The great apostacy of the last sixteen centuries [a sermon]' (1873).

[5] H. E. *Manning, *The divine glory of the Sacred Heart* (1873).

[6] A. Kuenen, *Three notices of the 'Speaker's Commentary'* (1873).

[7] This and extracts through December, in Morley, ii. 476.

[8] Kate *Vaughan, 1852?-1903, dancer and comedienne.

[9] Add MS 44641, f. 235. A note by Gladstone to Fortescue, ibid., f. 241, reads: 'Mr F. Let us speak on your letter W.E.G. D.1.' 'When Fortescue'.

[10] Note by Cardwell, ibid., f. 238, reads: 'The Law Officers think G. has a good Parliamentary Case: & do not wish to be pressed in Cabinet on technical points. They think he ought to leave the Case to the House of Commons & not to decide it himself either way.' Gladstone wrote to Coleridge next day (Add MS 44543, f. 21): 'No definite decision of any kind is likely to be taken before the 2d. week in January when the Cabt. will probably reassemble.'

[11] Not found; or perhaps the concluding item.

[12] Kimberley's despatch of 3 December, *PP* 1874 xlvi. 751, refers back to those of 6 October and 24 November.

[13] List of bills at Add MS 44641, f. 236.

To E. CARDWELL, war secretary, 1 December 1873. Add MS 44543, f. 20.

There are several reasons which incline me to think that if your ass[istan]ts will permit, the question of the Estimates had better stand over until we meet say about the 2d week in Jan. 1. I hope & believe we are now upon *falling* not rising markets. 2. It is desirable to know more clearly than we now know even after today's news whether we are likely to be clear of Ashantee. 3. Plenty of Bills ought to be ready at the beginning of the Session, so that we shall not be in so great a hurry as usual for the Estimates. Perhaps you may be able to let me know at the Cabinet whether this is right.

2. Tu. [Windsor]

Wrote to Ld Kimberley—The Queen Mem.—Lady Russell—Mr Richard—Ld Hartington—Mr Bohn—Dean of Windsor—Mr Godley—and minutes. Saw Mr Gurdon—Mr Heald—Ld Kimberley—Gen. Ponsonby (at Windsor)—To Windsor at 4, & had a long audience of the Queen. Dined with H.M. Whist (at Court) in evg. Read the Parisians—Antony & Cleopatra.

3. Wed. [London]

Castle Prayers at 9. St George's at 10.30.—Off to Twickenham at 11.25. Visited Mr Bohn & saw his collection: enormous, & of very great interest.[1] Then to Pembroke Lodge: luncheon, & long conversation with Ld Russell. Went to Twickenham (Ly Waldegrave's) at 4. Wrote to Sir A. Panizzi—Chief Justice Coleridge—Ld Granville. Saw Sir T. Western—Mr Fortescue—Mr Hayward—Mr Harcourt—Mr. . . . Read The Parisians (finished II).

4. Th.

Wrote to Ld Kimberley—Col. Romilly—Mr Lowe—and minutes. Saw Mr Trevelyan—Lady Scott (Newc. family)—Mr Welby *cum* Mr R. Wilson—Ld Kensington—Ld Granville (2)—Mr Godley—Mr Arch cum Messrs Taylor[2]—Cox. 11-12[R]—Scotts. Luncheon at 15 G.S. The Balfours dined: much conversation. Read Knight's Discourse &c.[3]

[1] Publisher and antiquarian bibliomaniac; see 14 July 55.

[2] Joseph *Arch, 1826-1919, founder of the Agricultural Labourers' Union 1872, and Henry Taylor, on its cttee. The Union had instructed Arch to lead a dpn. on the county franchise; Godley's letter arranging a meeting in January is in *The Times*, 3 December 1873, 9f.

[3] W. Knight, 'Prayer; the two spheres', *Contemporary Review*, xxiii. 20 (December 1873).

To R. LOWE, home secretary, 4 December 1873. Add MS 44543, f. 21.

Though our correspondence, protracted as it is, about the Brett case cannot be said to be a sea without a shore, yet its Melody is certainly rather unmelodious. The case of the first of the two worthies however I am prepared to dismiss, for the use of fire-arms in the rescue is a great fact & brings the man[?] very near the murder. If you think me pertinacious in this matter, it is perhaps because the people outside have from the first insisted on making it mine at every step. Would it be a bad plan to refer to the Judge again about Melody? As to identity, I am not well able to judge whether the draft on that subject is such as to call for any further proceeding. But assuming his identity to be proved it seems that he took part in the riot & rescue, which should be considered as if it were of an ordinary criminal—but not in prior proceedings, nor in any act directly tending to threaten life. I cannot but feel doubtful whether in such a case as this, which has only a technical relation to murder, there is not room for the mercy of the Crown.[1]

5. Fr.

Wrote to J. Watson & S.—Ld Advocate—The Queen—Col. Romilly—Sir H. Thring—and minutes. Dined with Sir D. Marjoribanks. Packing books. Saw Ld Granville—Mr Godley—Mr Peel—Sir A. Panizzi—Mr Delane—Mr Murray. Saw Sheppard—& 2 more X.

6. Sat. [Hawarden]

Wrote to The Queen Mem.—Mr Lowe—Lady Enfield—Abp of Canterbury—Sir R. Phillimore—Ld Granville—and minutes. Saw Mr Godley—Mr M'Coll—Mr Billson. Packing &c. Off to Hn at 2.15 arrived at 8.15. Read Biley on Joshua X.—Montalembert's Life (finished I.)—The Parisians (III)—Results of Census of U.S.[2]

7. 2 S.Adv.

Ch mg (with H.C.) and 6.30. Wrote to Mr Godley—C.G.—& minutes. Read the curious Pro-Mahomn antiXtn MS[3]—Szyrma on Science & Relign[4]—The Disciples, by Miss King.[5]

8. M.

Early breakfast & Ch. at 8.30. Wrote to Earl Russell—Mr Goschen—

[1] Lowe continued to oppose the release of the Fenian, Melody; Add MS 44302, f. 167ff.
[2] F. A. Walker, *Ninth census [Reports]*, 3v. (1872).
[3] Untraced.
[4] W. S. Lach-Szyrma, 'True relations of science to religion' in *Pleas for the Faith* (1873).
[5] H. E. H. King, *The disciples* (1873).

Mr Dodson. Read Etrurian Researches[1]—Aristoph. Ploutos (re-exam), Thesmoph (began)—Lytton's Parisians. Walk & call with SRG.

To G. J. GOSCHEN, first lord of the admiralty, 8 December 1873. Add MS 44543, f. 23.

My reference to Estimates in the last Cabinet must have appeared to you rather abrupt. I now send you a copy of a letter I had written to Cardwell, which will explain it so far as he is concerned.[2] I had not (from some delay) received his answer as I expected before the Cabinet or I should [have] had a prior communication with you also.

To EARL RUSSELL, 8 December 1873. Add MS 44543, f. 23.

I feel rather concerned at the Pope's undertaking to grant civil degrees in these realms, but I am afraid your view is a wise one.[3] Possibly in the development of the plan of this Roman Catholic University this question may take a new direction which might give occasion for a new step. The election of the next Pope, come when it may, will prove an epoch of immense importance to the politics of Europe, & for the religion of the world. It will probably be the last chance for the friends of reason & moderation within the Roman Church. As to the present Pontiff, I am, & for many years have been sorrowfully of the opinion, that with good intentions & many virtues, he has done wider & deeper mischief than any other living man. I was heartily glad to see you in such health & spirits, & I trust your daughter is making satisfactory progress towards recovery.
I had great pleasure in offering Col. Romilly the Vice Chancellorship of the Board of Customs. No offer ever had stricter regard to capacity & service.

9. Tu.

Ch. at 8.30 as yesterday. Wrote to Ld Chancr of Ireland—Ld Granville—Mr Wickham—Mr P. Dundas—Mr Woodard—D. of Argyll—Mr Townley[4]—Mr Knowles—Mr Lowe—C.G.—Walter—& minutes. Saw Mr Vickers. Read The Parisians—Macaulay on Mitford[5]—Thesmophoriuzousai—Etruscan Researches (finished). Walk with H.—& call.

[1] Perhaps Lord Crawford and Balcarres, *Etruscan inscriptions* (1872).
[2] See, presumably, 1 Dec. 73.
[3] That the Pope's authority in this case be not opposed, 6 December 1873, Add MS 44294, f. 264.
[4] Successfully offering him—a last resort—the Cambridgeshire lord-lieutenancy; Add MS 44543, f. 24.
[5] T. B. *Macaulay, review of Mitford; *Works*, xi. 365.

To BARON O'HAGAN, Irish lord chancellor, Add MS 44543, f. 23.
9 December 1873.

I thank you very much for your letter & its inclosure.[1] The report amply suffices to show that the comments on your speech about the Land Act offered in the Times were unjust & unwarrantable. So far as I know we are justified in holding language of confidence about the Land Act, as a law that neither requires nor admits of great amendment, & this is a great cause of thankfulness. I look back with pain & regret on the rejection of the University Bill, tho [*sc.* through] the action of the Bishops adroitly turned to account by Mr Disraeli & Col. Taylor his whipper-in: but with the general state of Ireland I am by no means disappointed.

10. Wed.

Church 8.30 (after early breakfast) and 7 P.M. Wrote to Mr Macmillan—Ld Granville—Mr West—Ld Halifax—& minutes. Saw Archdn Ffoulkes. Walk with S. and call. Read Macaulay on Mill—The Parisians—Thesmophoriuzousai. C.G. came in evg.

To LORD HALIFAX, lord privy seal, Add MS 44543, f. 25.
10 December 1873.

Many thanks for your note[2] & outline of proceeding to which I have little to object. The Law officers have not however as yet reached their conclusion, & as I understand while they hesitate to affirm that the seat is full they would yet more distinctly decline to affirm the opposite. I do not wish to meddle further with the argument, but my opinion [is] that Mr Canning did the very thing that I have done. It is most improbable that when he accepted the First Lordship of the Treasury he intended to take the Exchequer 1. because this would surely have been mentioned in moving his writ. 2. & yet more because as we all know at the time when he became First Lord he desired & sought to keep the old Government together. Moreover it appears from Hatsell writing in 1812[3] that the modern doctrine of acceptance anyhow effected was then only known as acceptance testified by an overt act such as kissing hands or the receipt of seals. My own opinion is that the matter has not yet been properly examined & I cannot give myself to the examination: but I think Harcourt is disposed to go further into it, & especially into this case of Canning.
I think the Greenwich seat is safe in all likelihood, but this can only be determined in January. Your suggestion would be very deferential to the House; but we could not afford it if it is to cause the loss of a seat.

[1] Of 7 December, with report of meeting of Dublin law students' debating soc. on Irish land; Add MS 44441, f. 191.
[2] Of 9 December, on the Greenwich seat, suggesting the Commons would appt. a cttee.; in Morley ii. 471.
[3] J. *Hatsell, *Precedents of Proceedings*, 4v., various eds.

To A. WEST, commissioner of inland revenue, 10 December 1873. 'Private.' Add MS 44543, f. 24.

You gave me a kind of promise to supply me with materials for the purpose of showing that the India Office is less economical in administration (perhaps also in its composition) than our Government generally i.e.[?] as these Treasury principles, so to call them, would require.[1] I have at present only a strong, a very strong, suspicion, but no particulars. If you could supply them I think it would be of great use, in a not improbable contingency. In my opinion it would be of great advantage that one place at the Council should be filled on the nomination of the Board of Treasury: & that the person so appointed should be invested with the title to record his reasons officially against any proposed expenditure where he conceives it to be contrary to any rule established for Imperial administration.

11. Th.

Ch. 8½ AM. Wrote to Sig Massari—Bp of Lincoln—Mr Cardwell—Ld Advocate—Ld Lyttelton—Sir R. Phillimore—and minutes. Walked with Stephy to Sealand to see Mr Broadbent's[2] drawings: they seem to show much talent. Also saw Mr Maddock.[3] Read the Parisians—Macaulay, Essays—Finished Thesmophor. Began [Aristophanes'] Batrachoi.

12. Fr.

Ch. 8½ AM (early breakfast no more!). Wrote to The Queen (Mem)—Ld F. Cavendish—Mr Lowe—Ld Spencer—and minutes. Read Batrachoi—The Parisians (finished 3)—O'Daunt's Fin. Report[4]—Massari's Ricordi di Cavour.[5] Walk to Buckley with Herbert: also saw Mr Ward of Aston Hall Works.

13. Sat.

Ch. 8½ AM. Wrote to Sir A. Buchanan[6]—Mr Pitt Dundas—Mr Dodson—The Queen—Mr Godley—Mr Goulburn—Ld Cowper—& minutes. Walk with SRG. I opened to him that I must give up my house at or about the expiry of the present Government. Read Batrachoi—Cavour, Ricordi—Morland's Life.[7] Unpacking books &c.

[1] West's figures sent on 15 December 1873, Add MS 44341, f. 134.

[2] J. H. Broadbent, farmer at Sealand.

[3] Henry Maddock, farmer at Sealand.

[4] On Irish finance; see Add MS 44543, f. 26.

[5] G. Massari sent his *Il Conte di Cavour* (1873); Add MS 44441, ff. 146, 205.

[6] Sir Andrew *Buchanan, 1807-82, ambassador to Russia 1864, to Austria 1871-8; cr. bart. 1878.

[7] J. O. *Halliwell, *A brief account of the life, writings and inventions of Sir S. Morland* (1838).

14. 3 S.Adv.

Ch 11 AM & 7. Wrote to Duchess of Buccleuch—Bp of Ripon—Mr Lowe—Ld Granville—Sir Thos G.—Sir S. Scott & Co—Robn G. —& minutes. Mr Chamberlain preached in the evening a very good manly earnest farewell.[1] Read Gresley's Philosophers & Priests[2]—Life of Montalembert Vol. II.

15. M.

Confined to bed till 1½. Wrote to D. of Argyll Tel.—Mr Godley Tel. —Duke of Devonshire—Mr Shuttleworth—Mrs Th.—Marquis of Huntly—Jas Watson & S.—& minutes. Sat to Mr Herbert.[3] Read Montalembert's Life. Also my article of 1852 on him.[4] Mr Herbert (R.A.) came & I sat to him for a short time.

16. Tu.

Ch 8½ AM. Wrote to Mr Gurdon Tel.—Ld Kimberley—Mr C. Innes[5] —Sir J. Lawrence—Mr Lowe—Duke of Argyll—Mr Brassey[6]—Mr Salkeld[7]—Mr Vickers[8]—and minutes. Walk with Mr Herbert. Read Batrachoi—Montalembert's Life—Brassey on the State of Wages.

To T. BRASSEY, M.P., 16 December 1873. Add MS 44543, f. 28.

I have read the whole of your very interesting pamphlet, & I may add I strongly sympathize with the spirit in which it has been conceived & written. The subject to which you have specially referred me undoubtedly seems to deserve attention when interference with the labour of women is in principle admitted. I would advise your calling Mr Lowe's attention & I will do so if you prefer it. It is with some dismay that I read your statement that the price of Coal at the pit's mouth is not likely to go below 15/- per ton. I venture to be more hopeful. The figures of the Swiss export of textile fabrics amaze me.

[1] See 4 Jan. 69.

[2] W. *Gresley, *Priests and philosophers* (1873).

[3] His pre-Raphaelite friend, J. R. *Herbert, see 17 June 53; portrait untraced.

[4] In the *Quarterly*; see 10 Nov. 52n and Matthew, 'Vaticanism', 424.

[5] Giving permission for his letters to be used in a biography of E. B. *Ramsay, never published.

[6] Thomas *Brassey, 1836-1918; liberal M.P. Hastings 1868-86; admiralty lord 1880-4; parlt. sec. to admiralty 1884-5; cr. baron 1886; statistician and naval authority; had sent his 'Wages in 1873', Social Science Assoc. Address.

[7] Perhaps Joseph Salkeld of Upper Woburn Place.

[8] J. S. Vickers of Townsend and Barker; became Hawarden agent, see 5 June 74.

To LORD KIMBERLEY, 16 December 1873. Add MS 44543, f. 28.

Like you[1] I have felt the great difficulty of the question raised by Glover's £5 purchases of slaves to make them recruits. On the whole however I arrive at the conclusion that we should not authorise the continuance of these payments,[2] while as to those which have been already effected we should do no more than enforce what would have been reasonable conditions in a contract of enlistment had the parties been free. There is but one reason the other way, so far as I can see; namely the danger of interfering with military operations. But 1. Glover's position is a secondary one. 2. So far as the military operations of the present year are concerned they will pretty well have been settled, at least the preparations must be near completeness, when your reply to the present dispatches reaches its destination. On the other hand I think the reproach is great, & I think not endurable. For us, or for the country. It is a real *reductio ad absurdum* to go to a country for a philanthropic errand, & then to undertake the protection of people by military means who will not give you the loan of their time without being paid for it now but their slaves serve you without receiving first what appears to be their value in full. On the serious side, this operation might, it is quite possible, in the mouth of hostile criticism ring through the world, & the damage to the fame of England & to her authority as the advocate-general of freedom, might be great out of all proportion to the advantages in view. As for ourselves, I should expect in Parliament not comments but a motion, & I doubt not only whether the H. of C. would sustain but whether the Cabinet would undertake the defence.

To R. LOWE, home secretary, 16 December 1873. Add MS 44543, f. 28.

Please to look at the Article from the Examiner of Dec. 13[3] herewith inclosed, on common lands inclosed by Act for the public good, & then suffered to lie waste. This is a subject very keenly dwelt upon by Mr Arch. Indeed it is desirable to obtain a report upon the *facts* from the Inclosure Commnr. I hope that they would crumble away upon inquiry. If they do not there might be proposals more unreasonable than that contained in the article.[4]

17. Wed.

Ch. 8.30 AM and 7 PM, when Mr Walsham How[5] preached, very well. Wrote to Mr Gurdon 2 Tell.—Mr Fortescue—Mr Moon[6]—Sir W. Boxall—Mr Monk—Mr Cardwell—Mr P. Dundas—Canon Woodard—and minutes. Read Batrachoi—Life of Montalembert (finished). It was a pure & noble career personally: in a public view unsatisfactory: the Pope was a worm in the gourd all through. His oratory is

[1] Draft dispatch sent by Kimberley, 15 December, Add MS 44225, f. 129.

[2] Kimberley telegraphed Wolseley to this effect; ibid., f. 133.

[3] On landlords' abuse of common lands; *The Examiner*, 13 December 1873, 1231.

[4] Lowe replied it was impolitic to take action, 19 December 1873, Add MS 44302, f. 173.

[5] William Walsham *How, 1823-97; canon of St Asaph; bp. of Wakefield 1888.

[6] R. Moon, on railway safety; Add MS 44543, f. 29.

great. Read also Kenrick on Johnson's Shakespeare.[1] Walk with S.R.G. and Mr Herbert.

18. Th.

Ch. 8½ AM. Wrote to Sir T. Fremantle—Ld Granville—Mr Cardwell—Ld F. Cavendish—Mr Moffatt—Mr Hignett—Mr Ayrton—Ld Spencer—Mr Dodson—Mr Lowe (2)—Mr Lingen—Lady A. Russell[2]—Mr Gurdon (Tel.). Saw Mr Burnett—Mrs Burnett respecting him—S.R.G. (on Estate)—S.E.G. (on Schools). Sat to Mr Herbert. Read (no time for Aristoph) Cambridge Reform Papers[3] (of no great value) and Dangerous Classes of New York.[4]

To E. CARDWELL, war secretary, 18 December 1873. Add MS 44543, f. 31.
'Private.'

Though I have spent some time in examining the papers you have kindly sent me,[5] I have been unable to gather from them with certainty what is intended to be done with regard to Short Service & other than Infantry Reserve. I am afraid it is only what appears in the first page; & if so I need hardly say it is to me extremely disappointing. At the same time, I am sensible of the inadequacy of my own means of judgment. I am therefore quite open to correction but my impression is 1. that the present state of the labour market supplies a special argument for three years enlistments. 2. That without such enlistment you will never get your infantry reserve. 3. That the time is come for an effective prosecution of a scheme for Cavalry Reserve (I am not quite sure how you stand as to Artillery). My first desire would be to know whether you are satisfied with the present arrangements: & to have some conversation when we meet again in town, either to find means for satisfying myself if possible supposing you to be satisfied, or to consider whether we can exercise any further pressure upon the 'military authorities'. What I fear inwardly is that, in this & many other matters, we have indirect but significant & certainly multiplying indications that the authority necessary for carrying on with credit & efficiency the government of this country, is now in our hands seriously impaired & that if we cannot *soon* sound our position it had better be abandoned. This is rather a dark view, but we must all wish to know truth whatever it may be.

19. Fr.

Ch. 8½ AM. Wrote to Mr Tennyson—Duke of Argyll—H.N.G.—Ld Chancellor (2)—Ld Hartington—Mr Ouvry—and minutes. Saw Mr Barker. Sat to Mr Herbert. With Herbert G., set about making a walk

[1] W. *Kenrick, *A review of Dr. Johnson's new edition of Shakespeare* (1765).
[2] Declining to be godfather to Caroline Diana Rosalind, da. of Laura and Arthur Russell; Add MS 44543, f. 32.
[3] Perhaps *A few brief remarks on Cambridge University and College reform* (1870).
[4] C. L. Brace, *The dangerous classes of New York* (1872).
[5] On recruiting; Add MS 44120, f. 190.

from Glynne Cottage to the WEG door. Read Batrachoi (finished)—Lucas[1]—Gavarniano[?].[2]

To DUKE OF ARGYLL, Indian secretary, Add MS 44543, f. 32.
19 December 1873.

I have received your letter of the 17th,[3] & I am sorry we are not altogether agreed about the line of conduct proper to be taken with respect to the Lesseps envoys. The letter sent from the India Office was really a declaration of hostility outright: & so far I am glad that this was not intended. But now with respect to the Mission of these people. You say there is alarm in Affghanistan, but we are not going to authorise their doing anything in Affghanistan. I had supposed this line of Railway ran further to the East. If it is intended to go through Affghanistan, I think it would be very fair to say on account of circumstances at this moment exciting some interest or apprehension in that country we should prefer that no examination of our contiguous territory should take place at this time; but without anything binding us to object hereafter. I cannot enter into your arguments about the unprofitableness of this Railway; any more than I can envy those who may have to raise the money to make it. All the force of those arguments, whatever it may be, will be felt by those people where they ought to be felt, viz. in the money market. But I think the act, I may say the churlish act, of refusing to individuals, the name of one of whom immediately suggests the unhappy business of the Suez Canal, common personal & permissive civilities upon a journey when their object is to form some estimate of the possibility of carrying a railway (not through Affghanistan) out of the British territories into the Russian, would place us in a deplorable position before the world; a position which would by no means be mended if, making ourselves judges of the commercial question, we were to found our refusal upon commercial grounds. I am sure Granville would not wish to say anything in haste upon this matter: but it is more than a Departmental one, although it specially touches a Department.

20. Sat.

Ch. 8½ AM. Wrote to Ld Chancellor—Mr Cardwell—Mr Lowe—Mr Chadwick—Mrs Nimmo—& minutes. Sat to Mr Herbert. Worked on version of the Shield [of Achilles]. Worked on new path with H.J.G. Read Aristoph Ecclesiaz.—'Recent work at Chaucer'.[4]

21. St Thos & 4 S.Adv.

Ch 11 AM (with H.C.) & 6½ P.M. Wrote to Ld Granville—Mr Lowe—& minutes. Read Bp of Rochester's Charge[5]—Reform, or Dis-

[1] See 12 Aug. 73.
[2] Perhaps Gavarni [G. S. Chevallier], *L'homme et l'oeuvre* (1873).
[3] Not in Add MS 44102.
[4] F. J. Furnivall, *Macmillan's Magazine*, xxvii. 383 (March 1873).
[5] By T. L. *Claughton (1873).

endowment[1]—Talbot on Assyrian Religion[2]—A. de Lisle on Mahometanism.[3]

22. M.

Ch. 8½ A.M. Wrote to Mr M'Clure—Ld Granville—The Queen—Mr Goschen—Robn G.—Ld Huntley—Mrs Hampton—Minute on Sir T. F[remantle']s retirement[4] and minutes. Sat to Mr Herbert. 2¼ hours. Worked on Version of the Shield. Worked with H.J.G. on path. Read Aristoph. Ecclesiaz.—Thoms on Hannah Lightfoot.[5]—Dang. classes of New York.

23. Tu.

Ch. 8½ A.M. Wrote to Mr L. Winterbotham[6]—Sir G.G. Scott—Mr C.A. Wood, & minutes. Sat 1¾ hours to Mr Herbert. Worked on correcting Version of the Shield: and finished writing it out. Read Aristoph. Ecclesiaz.—'Ireland Ur of the Chaldees'[7]—Finished Mr Thoms.

24. Wed.

Ch. 8½ AM. Wrote to Gen. Ponsonby—Captain [G. H.] Wildes—Scotts—Sir W. G. Craig—& minutes. Sat to Mr Herbert as yesterday. He explained to me a plan which he has kindly made for a house I am to build.[8] Worked with Herbert [Gladstone] on the Cottage path. Finished the Ecclesiazousai the last of the plays of Aristophanes—Ireland = Ur: and Thoms Notelets on Shakespeare.[9] Conversation with Lucy Cavendish on Hartington's prospects & F.C.s.

25. Th. Xmas Day.

Ch. 8 A.M. for H.C.—11 A.M.—7 P.M. Wrote to Ld Granville—Mr Dodson—Ld Spencer—D. of Sutherland—and minutes. Read Lach

[1] Perhaps *The Church of England. Reform or disestablishment, which? By one of her Presbyters* (1873).

[2] W. E. F. *Talbot, *Records of the past* (1873).

[3] A. L. M. Phillipps [de Lisle], *Mahometanism in its relation to prophecy* (1857).

[4] Untraced; on proposed peerage, see 31 Dec. 73.

[5] W. J. *Thoms, *Hannah Lightfoot—Queen Charlotte and the Chevalier d'Eon* (1867).

[6] On sudden d. of his br., H. S. P. Winterbotham; Add MS 44543, f. 35; see 29 Dec. 73.

[7] A. Wilkes, *Ireland: Ur of the Chaldees* (1873).

[8] Never done to Herbert's design.

[9] W. J. *Thoms, *Three notelets on Shakespeare* (1865).

Szyrma's Pleas (finished)[1]—Ld Hatherley on Conty of Scripture[2]—and [blank]

26. Fr. St Stephen

Ch. 8¾ AM. Wrote to Mrs Wm Gladstone—Ld Granville—D. of Argyll—Ld Ilchester[3]—The Queen—Mr Gurdon (Tel)—Scotts—& minutes. Read Aristoph. Fragm.—Shooter on the Kafirs.[4] Worked on the walk with Harry and Herbert. 24 to dinner: a large party gathered for the marriage. We executed the settlements (Willy & Harry Trustees for their sister): and the directions needful for the Banker. Saw F.C. on Treasury matters.

27. Sat. St John.

Ch. 8.45 AM. Wrote to Gen. Ponsonby l. & tel.—Mr Gurdon l. & Tel.—The Queen—Ld Chancellor—Ld Monson—Sir T. Biddulph—Mr Playfair—Serj. Sherlock[5]—Ld Granville—Sir E. Watkin—and minutes.

The House continued full. At 10.30 the weather broke into violent hail and rain. It was the only speck upon the brightness of the marriage.[6] Two hymns were added to the service: large numbers inside the Church and out. Agnes's demeanour was perfect. Stephy read, with immense emotion strongly and repeatedly suppressed. The first part was under the Chancel Arch: where with good heart but yet oppressed I gave her away. Before the altar rails the bridesmaids knelt in a semicircle. The little interval of space was singularly becoming. *He* led her away: now first more his than ours. Her mother had been at H.C. with her at eight.

All manner of entertainments followed. I had to speak at 5 to what I thought was a private company.[7] On all sides overflowing kindness & love. God be thanked & praised for all.

To LORD SELBORNE, lord chancellor, 27 December 1873. Lambeth MS 1866, f. 86.

The question of the release of the Fenian prisoners has been more than a Depart-

[1] See 7 Dec. 73.
[2] W. P. *Wood, Baron Hatherley, *The continuity of Scripture* (1867).
[3] Successfully offering him court office; Add MS 44543, f. 37.
[4] J. Shooter, *The Kafirs of Natal and the Zulu country* (1857).
[5] David Sherlock, 1814–84; law serjeant and liberal M.P. King's Co. 1868–80.
[6] Of his oldest daughter, Agnes, to E. C. Wickham; see 18 Oct. 42.
[7] His comments on Victoria's kindness to Agnes were published without authorization; see Guedalla, *Q*, i. 433.

mental one: indeed I think the whole pressure of the correspondence & demands for their release has been on me for a long time past.

There are sixteen soldiers still confined, with respect to whom I am hardly able to form an opinion: the 'military authorities' silence one.

There are four others in two pairs. One of the pairs consists of two men still imprisoned for the Brett murder at Manchester (for which three men were hanged, very properly I imagine). One of the two men carried fire-arms & is sworn to have used them once. The other man Melody did not but assisted in the riot & rescue. On *his* case Lowe and I differ. I suggested communication with the judge but this he says is unusual. It seems to me that if it had been a murder in an attempt to release an ordinary criminal Melody would by this time after 5 or 5½ years of imprisonment have been released: and the political aim, I think it is admitted, ought not to aggravate the punishment. I wish you would kindly look into the matter. I inclose Lowe's last letter.[1]

28. Holy Innocents & S. after Xmas.

Ch. 11 AM & Walk with the party in aftn. Wrote to Ld Westminster—Ld Poltimore[2]—Ld Houghton—Sir G. Bowyer—Mr L. Playfair—Prince L. Bonaparte—and minutes. Read Sara Coleridge Vol. II[3]—Hancock's Prodigal Son[4]—Bickersteth's Parables.[5]

29.

Ch. 8½ AM. Wrote to Mr C. Edmonds[6]—The Speaker—Robn G.—Ld Granville—Scotts—Mr Gurdon—Mrs Th.—Mr Burnett—& my dearest Agnes: also minutes. Read divers Tracts—Cornish on Darwinism.[7]

Sixty four years complete today, what have they brought me? A weaker heart, stiffened muscles, thin hairs: other strength still remains in my frame. But what inwardly? Continued strain & tossing of the spirit: I dare not say any solid improvement: but a hope of release, recollection, and penitence, growing more eager as the time gets nearer.[8]

To H. B. W. BRAND, the Speaker, 29 December 1873. Add MS 44543, f. 40.

The death of Winterbotham happening so suddenly was a shock & grief to us all. Parliament, the Liberal party, & especially the nonconforming part of the

[1] Selborne docketed the letter: 'I agree with Gladstone as to Melody's case' and wrote thus to Gladstone, 30 December 1873, Add MS 44296, f. 348.

[2] Accepting resignation as treasurer of royal household of Augustus Frederick George Warwick Bampfylde, 1837-1908; 2nd Baron Poltimore 1858; became active tory. Add MS 44543, f. 39.

[3] See 13 Nov. 73.

[4] See 2 Nov. 73.

[5] E. H. *Bickersteth, *The reef and other parables* (1873).

[6] Unidentified.

[7] Actually by Stebbing, see next day's n.

[8] See Morley, ii. 476.

Liberal party, suffer a serious loss in his removal, & one that could not be well afforded. He leaves behind him high character & repute, & the best hopes of his future in the unseen world. I am extremely glad you have enjoyed your run of the Continent. Some new light has been cast on the Greenwich question, serious doubt having arisen whether the Act of Anne ever was intended to apply to cumulation of office. There are precedents both ways. It seems likely that Mr Canning cumulated without vacating. The counter-precedents (as far as known to me) are all where non-political office was assumed i.e. the Cinque ports. The lawyers are at work now, & are to be ready with their advice on the course to be taken when we meet again about the 19 January. We shall then I hope have the power of communicating with you as far as it may be desirable. All are agreed that I cannot put you in motion[?] by declaring my seat vacant. I think it is plain that we never could have had the present absurd confusion had it not been that the absolute power of the House in the matter of writs prevented any question as to the course of practice pursued & took away the necessity for being consistent. Cambridgeshire has been offered to Mr Townley, but I have not yet got his answer.

30. Tu.

Ch. 8½ AM. Wrote to Rev. Isaac Taylor[1]—Mr Robinson—Mrs Burnett—Viceroy of Ireland—Mr Gurdon Tel.—Ld Wolverton—& minutes. 1-5½. Went to Chester with S.R.G. & attended meeting of Governors of King's School. 2-3¾. Walked home. Saw the Dean. Ball in evening. Dined at Rectory. Worked on accounts and papers. Read Spedding [*sic*] on Darwinism.[2]

To LORD WOLVERTON, 30 December 1873. Add MS 44543, f. 41.

I cannot say half what I should like to say upon your letter,[3] which is too kind & too warm even from you: & that is saying much! Rely upon it that I am truly & deeply grateful to you for all you have been to me & done for me: & I should not have been able to bear the severance even as I have borne it, but for the double feelings first that my sand is very nearly run out, & second that we shall still I hope at least in London see much of one another and now shall I seem to draw upon you unduly if I mention that I expect to be there about the 15th & if you chanced to be in Town about that time, I should prize your presence highly. It is a critical moment. The next Cabinet will be about the 19th or 20th. Pray recollect that whenever you are in town, Downing St & all my letters are open to you exactly as of old; & that this may be well understood I will send it through No 10, which I had not meant to do. Our marriage on Saturday was most difficult to bear, for excess & overflow of kindness from every quarter *are* hard to bear. Only I am vexed that that so-called speech has got into the papers —it was delivered only to labouring & cottage folk, to none others could I have

[1] Isaac *Taylor, 1829-1901, archaeologist and priest; on Homer, Add MS 44441, f. 253.

[2] J. Stebbing, *Essays on Darwinism* (1871); 'Cornish' deleted, 'Spedding' written over.

[3] Of 28 December, Add MS 44348, f. 316: how much he enjoyed serving Gladstone as chief whip.

spoken in that manner. I have not an idea how any reporter got in or report got out. I am waiting for Adam's report about Dshire[1] & will send him your inclosure. Post time is come & I am the less discontented at leaving off because I *hope* to see you soon.

31. Wed.

Ch. 8½ A.M. Wrote to Sir J. Shuttleworth—Lord Chancellor—Gen. Schenk—Dr Kynaston—Mr A. Peel—Mr Wilberforce—Scotts—Mr Fairbrother—The Queen—and minutes. Again worked on accounts. Cut a tree with W.H.G. Read Cornish on Darwinism—Shooter on Natal Caffres. Still a full house.

The year ends as it were in tumult. My constant tumult of business makes other tumult more sensible. Upon me still continued blessings rain: but in return I seem to render nothing except a hope that a time may come when my spirit instead of grovelling may become erect, and look at God. For I cannot, as I now am, get sufficiently out of myself to judge myself, and unravel the knots of being and doing, of which my life seems to be full. Meanwhile my children continue to be blessed & a blessing: & Catherine to grow nobler & more heroic, as well as stronger, from year to year.

·

To A. W. PEEL, chief whip, 31 December 1873. Add MS 44543, f. 42.

1. Have you any opinion on the subject of Ld. Westminster's note inclosed?[2] If I stand again—& *if* I leave Greenwich, & *if* S.W. Lancashire cannot be had (as I expect) my own leaning is to Newark; but I should among seats wish to try for that which the general interests, & general advisers, of the party recommended.[3] 2. [Blank] has heard a rumour of a Fremantle Peerage (on which nothing has been decided) & is a little uneasy about the son. 3. I expect to be in Town on or about the 15th. I have mentioned this to W[olverton] in case there should be any chance of his coming up then. There are one or two matters depending, in which he might be useful. 4. I hope, rather than expect, you have fair news of the electioneering prospects.

[1] i.e. W. P. Adam, probably Dumbartonshire.

[2] On the Chester seat; see 3 Jan. 74n.

[3] Peel replied, 2 January 1874, Add MS 44270, f. 291, deprecating Greenwich, advising a borough, Chester rather than Newark; also advising only a G.C.B. for Fremantle, in view of his son's toryism.

Hawarden Th. Jan 1. 74. The Circumcision.

Ch. 8¾ AM. Wrote to Mr M'Clure—Mr Lambert—Mr Ruffles—Mr Goschen—Mr Lowe—Mr J.L. Ross—Mrs Th.—Sir Thos G.—Mr Welby—and minutes. Saw Mr Vickers. Wrote on 'The Shield'.[1] Read Shooter[2]—A.S. Murray on Homer[3]—Pope on The Shield[4]—A little Iliad & Odyssey. Servants Ball in evg.

To G. J. GOSCHEN, first lord of the admiralty, 1 January 1874. Add MS 44543, f. 42.

I am very sorry to hear that the return for which I asked has been the occasion of so much labour [since] approximate average would, I think, be quite enough for me.[5] I am not surprised at your difficulty as to ships. It has always been so, when I can recollect. The F.O. is pressed from every quarter, by people whom it costs nothing to ask, & it not unnaturally transmits the progress[ion] [?]. When the Duke of Somerset was First Lord, he had at first over 80m[ille] men, & always, I think, over 70m; but I remember his making a formal appeal to the Cabinet, declaring he was at his wits' end, & could now [*sc.* not] satisfy the F.O. demands. Now Granville is the most reasonable of men: why should you not send him a list of all the points at which you are now keeping ships and ask him to retrench, suggesting the best places. This was brought to my mind, before reading your letter, when I was perusing despatches from Bilbao.

2. Fr.

Ch. 8½ AM. Wrote to Bp of Lincoln—Earl Stanhope—Mr De Lisle—Mr A.S. Murray—H.J.G.—Mr Hubbard—Mr Dodson—Mr A. Arnold—Mr Gurdon Tel.—D. of Argyll Tel.—and minutes. Conversation with Mr R. Burnett respecting measures to be taken in his Father's critical state. Tree cutting. Sat a while to Mr Herbert. Read Shooter on Kafirs—Fitzjames Stephen on Parl. Government: not wizardlike—(No. II).[6]

[1] See 9 Jan. 74n.

[2] See 26 Dec. 73.

[3] An article on Homer and art in *Contemporary Review*, xxiii. 218 (January 1874), sent by A. S. Murray; reply in Add MS 44442, f. 1.

[4] See 26 Dec. 64.

[5] Goschen reported in an undated letter that the return (untraced) was almost ready; Add MS 44161, f. 253. See 24 Nov. 73.

[6] J. F. *Stephen, *Contemporary Review*, xxiii. 165 (January 1874).

To J. LAMBERT, secretary of the local government board, 2 January 1874.[1] Add MS 44543, f. 43.

1. Page 8 of your mem:[2] The principal paragraph does not represent my idea which is this, & which I desire to have tested. Let Lancashire for example be found to pay House Duty £60m[ille] Licenses £60m. It will then have a *credit* standing in the State Bank of £120m. Against this credit would be charged the State grants it now receives. So that it might have some interest in economising grants to be met out of a purse of its own. And this *might* be done without any change[3] in the Local Authorities, however desirable that may be.

2. I am anxious to know whether the fund can be further subdivided, as between the different towns, & the rest of the county: as between the different Local Authorities: or in any other way. We must have more figures, I think, before deciding this.

3. As regards the overlapping of areas between different counties, I think, it seemed there would be no difficulty in making an adjustment.

4. I have no doubt it is *desirable* for us to deal, as far as possible, with one Local Authority only, & if we proceed on this basis, it will give us a strong case for making it a good one.

5. I do not regard it as in any way necessary to conform to the Terms or particulars of the Lopez Resolution:[4] & I doubt very much whether he himself expects it.

6. To continue the Union grants from the C[onsolidated] F[und] would, I fear, destroy the whole basis of the measure. You will see that the difficulty does not exist which alone (I think) could recommend this mode of proceeding: for a *Central* Fund will be retained.

7. I suppose we could use the Boons we are to give as inducements to the Small Boroughs (up to what figure?) to give up their separate Police. Can a strong case of inconvenience from the present System be shown?

8. Will it not be necessary to obtain at once an account showing a. the House Duty and the Licenses (as far as may be) obtained from each county; b. the Grants now made to each county; c. the approximate distribution of any further grants, say e.g. those proposed by Sir M. Lopez.

And to this if possible should be added a rough Estimate of the effect of rating Government property in the Metropolis, & places where it principally exists. (You say the Metropolis would raise much less than at present—that means, I suppose, if only Licenses were transferred).

9. I think I can answer your two closing paragraphs effectually, but we must not argue this on paper. The figures I have asked for are, I think, the main condition of progress in the question for me: but your paper contains much valuable matter.

I thank you alike for it, & for the kind words & wishes of your note.

3. Sat.

Ch. 8½ AM. Wrote to Ld Spencer Tel.—Mr Gurdon Tel.—Ld Granville—Dean of Windsor—Robn G.—The Queen Mem.—Marquis of Westminster—& minutes. Walk with W. & Mr Herbert. Dinner party.

[1] Dated thus on the secretary's copy; probably drafted by diarist on 1 January and sent this day.

[2] Not found.

[3] Appears to read 'charge', but 'change' surely intended.

[4] See 16 Apr. 72.

Sat a short time to Mr H[erbert]. Luncheon at the Rectory to meet Mr Hallam the Wesleyan Minister. Read Shooter on Kafirs—Pistash Parney[1]—The Parisians Vol. IV.[2]

To the MARQUIS OF WESTMINSTER, 3 January 1874. Add MS 44543, f. 44.

I could not take upon me to answer your letter,[3] without referring to what I may term headquarters for all electioneering purposes. And now before replying let me say how much I am obliged for the great kindness of that letter. I am afraid it will seem an ungrateful return when I express my fear that I both am now, & must remain until n[ea]r[?] the crisis, myself unfixed: for the simple reason that while I may remain in public life, I must go where the interests of the party are supposed most to call me, & moreover must allow others rather than myself to be the judges of that question. It has certainly, for example, been by no act of my own that I am now member for Greenwich. Under these circumstances, I can only express the hope that you will, without reference to me, proceed as you may think best on independent grounds. I cannot even pretend to give any information on the probable course of politics which could be of material use: but I should say about next May is the time when it is most likely, or least unlikely, that we may see our way rather better than at present.

4. 2 S.Xmas.

Ch. 11 AM and H.C.—6½ PM. Wrote to Mr Fortescue—Mr Bickersteth—Miss Marsh—Mr Cardwell—Mr Lambert—& minutes. Read Sara Coleridge[4]—A new world of Being—Cornish on Darwinism—and [blank].

To E. CARDWELL, war secretary, 4 January 1874. PRO 30/48/10, f. 68.

I return with pleasure this excellent letter.[5] It tends to confirm that feeling of confidence which Sir G. Wolseley's proceedings from their outset have more & more produced in our minds.

To J. LAMBERT, secretary of the local government board, 4 January 1874. Add MS 44543, f. 44.

When the figures are ready & when we meet in town, I will explain my view about the Balance. Meantime I will say it is doubtless vital to the plan that the local authorities should have an interest in the fund from which they draw. And I by no means say *in limine*[6] that there can be *no* handing over of *funds*, as

[1] Title indistinct; untraced. [2] By *Lytton; see 22 Nov. 73.

[3] Of 30 December 1873, Add MS 44337, f. 308, offering to attempt 'to secure yr. election for *Chester* . . . you would be supported by the whole strength of the Liberal party, & without a contest. I write this without having suggested it to *anyone* else.'

[4] S. *Coleridge, *Memoir and letters*, 2v. (1873).

[5] Dispatches and letter from Wolseley; see PRO 30/48/40, f. 69. See 22 Feb. 74.

[6] 'At the outset.'

distinguished from the cash to meet this or that ascertained charge. What I wish to exclude[1] is merely the maintenance of the system of payment from the Consolidated Fund: through this hole I think all the benefit of the scheme might, & much more,[2] leak out.

5. M.

Ch. 8½ AM. Wrote to Viceroy of Ireland—Mr Gurdon Tel.—Ld Chancellor—Agnes—Dean of Windsor—Mr Barker—Sir T. Biddulph—The Queen—& minutes. Saw Mr Burnett—a sad interview with an excellent man & friend. Saw B. Potter. Sat to Mr Herbert. Worked (after Post) on finishing up Preface for the 'Shield'. Read Fitz James Stephen No 1—Cornish on Darwinism—Finished Shooter. Added some testamentary provisions to my 'Paper of Directions'.

6. Epiph.

Ch. 8¾ AM. Dearest C.s birthday: God be ever with her noble soul. Wrote to Duke of Bedford—Ld Granville—Mr Newton—Mr Lambert—Mr Childers—Mr A. Strahan—Mrs Th.—Ld Lyttelton—& minutes. Cut trees, with Herbert. Sat to Mr Herbert. Read The Parisians—Munro's beautiful version of Gray's Elegy[3]—Witherow's Derry and Enniskillen[4]—and the Dizzy Pamphlet on the crisis.[5]

7. Wed.

Ch. 8½ A.M. Wrote to M. Reitlinger—M. Turnorelli[6]—Mr Godley Tel.—Dean of Westmr—Ld Granville (2)—Sir W. Stephenson—Ld De Tabley—C. Lyttelton—and minutes. Sat to Mr Herbert. Arranged some literary & personal papers. Read Schliemann's remarkable account of his own youth[7]—Witherow's Derry &c.[8] Saw Mr Husson. God bless Herbert on his birthday.

8. Th.

Ch. 8½ AM. Wrote to Ld Spencer l. & tel.—Mr Godley Tel.—Robn G.

[1] Secretary wrote 'include', but this was clearly an error of transcription.

[2] Barely legible; written over another word.

[3] Earlier version of H. A. J. *Munro (1880).

[4] T. *Witherow, *Derry and Enniskillen . . . in 1689* (1873).

[5] Perhaps Disraeli's speech of 22 November 1873, reprinted, or 'The Crisis Examined' (1834) or 'The Present Crisis' (1853); see also Ramm I, ii. 437.

[6] Untraced.

[7] H. Schliemann, *Ithaka, der Peloponnes und Troja* (1869); see 9 Jan. 74.

[8] See 6 Jan. 74.

—PMaster Chester (cancelled)—Rev. B. Browne—Mr Peel—Ld Granville—Mr Vickers—(Also revised & sent off the long letter to Ld G. on the political situation, wh I wrote yesterday)[1]—and minutes. Went to Chester to see Messrs Townsend & Barker,[2] & to arrange provisionally for the care of these Estates. Saw Mr Barker, alone & with them—Mr Vickers, alone & with them. Mr Burnett sinks, & suffers grievously. Half walk from Chester, and axe work. Read The Parisians—Derry & Enniskillen.

9. Fr.

Ch. 8½ AM. Wrote to Mr Parker MP.—Mrs Hampton—Mr Strahan—Rev Mr Munro—Mr Godley—Lord Chancellor—Dr Schliemann—& minutes. Tree cutting with Herbert. Sent off with some final touches my Version of the Shield [of Achilles][3] and Preface. Saw Mr Wade. Sat to Mr Herbert 12½-2. Read The Parisians—Derry & Enniskillen. Arranged some papers.

To H. SCHLIEMANN, archaeologist, 9 January 1874. Add MS 44543, f. 47.

I have to offer my best thanks for your letter[4] & a copy of your work published in 1869. That this had not previously come to my knowledge will not appear surprising to anyone who knows how nearly public business claims & possesses a monopoly of my time while I hold my present office. I have read the preface to your book with an extraordinary interest. After reading it I comprehend better your energetic exertions & I the less wonder at, while still more admire, your success. As yet I have got little further, but the work only reached me yesterday & it is now in the hands of one of my daughters. Notwithstanding the great degree of disability under which I labour I shall await with extreme interest the arrival of your work on your discoveries in the Levant with the Photos. The facts which you appear to have established are of the highest importance to primitive history; & I may take even a selfish pleasure in them when I contemplate their bearing on my own interpretations of the Homeric Text. I hope that during the course of this year you may be led to visit London, & that I may be favoured with some opportunity of making your acquaintance.

[1] Dissolution undesirable, finance the only, and uncertain, way of lasting the session; Ramm I, ii. 440. This letter also sent to Wolverton who replied, 12 January 1874, Add MS 44349, f. 1: 'I share all your feeling and your apprehensions, if "circumstances" interfere with the financial programme.'

[2] On Burnett's d., Townshend and Barker, Chester Solicitors (see 9 Mar. 40) became interim, then permanent, agents.

[3] His tr. of 'The Shield of Achilles' from the *Iliad* was published in the *Contemporary Review* (February 1874).

[4] Of 28 December 1873, from Athens, sending his book and supporting diarist's view that the Trojans spoke Greek; Add MS 44441, f. 243.

10. Sat.

Ch. 8½ AM. Mr [Gregory] Burnett[1] died at one A.M. *Requiescat*! I grieve over this good & able man sincerely apart from the heavy care and responsibility of replacing him, which must fall on me of necessity. Wrote to The Queen Mem.—Lord Tenterden l. & Tel.—Mr Godley l. and 2 Tell.—Rev Mr Wray Tel.—Ld Chancellor (2)—Ld Advocate (2)—Mrs Th.—Mr Bright—Ld Wolverton—Mr Dodson—Ld Spencer—Robn G.—Mr R. Burnett—Sec. Bp of London's Fund[2]—and minutes. Saw Mr R. Burnett—bis. Cutting & kibbling with the two H.s. Sat to Mr Herbert ¾ hour. Finished Siege of Derry—Finished Parisians.

To J. BRIGHT, chancellor of the duchy, Add MS 43385, f. 245.
10 January 1874.

I have received your letter.[3] The vacancy on the Scotch Bench will I think not be filled up at present. Your Candidate seems good.

I am engaged in a polemical correspondence (I regret to say) with the Irish Government about the vacancy on that Bench—which it seems to me ought also to await the Bill.

The political pulse is low and the spirit of action and (especially) of economy feeble, as it seems to me, in all ranks and classes. 'Rest and be thankful' seems to rule the constituencies.

I am very anxious to see you in London before Monday week's Cabinet. Could you make it convenient to give me an interview on Saturday the 17th at your own hour?

I do not expect the Cabinet work to be very severe. It is not by a multitude of small details, however well handled they may be, that we can mend the position of affairs. It wants some one issue, clear, broad & straight.

I hope you keep in the course of improving health: what the men of the last century quaintly but conveniently called 'on the mending hand'.

11. 1 S.Epiph.

Ch. 11 AM and 6.30 P.M. Wrote to Bp of St Asaph—Ld Granville—Dr Hervey—Mr Godley—& minutes. Read Stebbing on Darwin[4]—Bartle on Interm. State[5]—Hancock on Prod. Son[6]—Divers Sermons. Conversation with Mr [A. J.] Balfour[7]—Dr Acland.

[1] i.e. the agent of the Hawarden estates.
[2] Philip Wright.
[3] Of 9 January, Add MS 44113, f. 85, asking diarist to consider John McLaren, son of D. *McLaren, for a Scottish judgeship. See 9 Feb. 74.
[4] See 30 Dec. 73.
[5] G. W. Bartle, *The Scriptural doctrine of Hades* (1869).
[6] See 2 Nov. 73.
[7] Identified from Hawarden Visitors' Book.

12. M.

Ch. 8.30 AM. Wrote to Mr Herbert Spencer[1]—Mr Beesley[2]—Mr Ouvry—Ld Tenterden—Mr Welby—Messrs Williams & Co.—and minutes. Saw Mr Wade—Mr Townshend & Mr Barker (2)—Dr Acland—Mr Balfour—Ld Aberdeen—Sir S.R.G. Sat to Mr Herbert 12¼-2. Worked on the path with Herbert. Some threatenings in afternoon caused me to lie up. Read Stebbing (finished)—Siege of Enniskillen.

13. Tu.

Rose at nine. Wrote to Gen. Ponsonby Tel.—Gen. Schenk—Ld Granville—Sir J. Murray—Mr Vickers—Ld Selborne—Ld Spencer—Mr Strahan—Dean of Windsor—Mr Godley Tel.—& minutes. Conversation with Sir SRG on vacant Agency. Walk with him. Read the Derry & Enniskillen Narrative—Dang. Classes of New York.[3] Corrected proofs of the Shield. Saw Mr Herbert—Lady Aberdeen.

14. Wed.

Ch. 8½ AM. Wrote to Mr Gurdon Tel.—Rev. F. Barker[4]—Mr Milbank—Mr P. Pickering[5]—Ld Tenterden—Townshend & Barker—Mr Jas Wright—Col. Neville—Col. Ackroyd—Mr Salkeld[6]—& minutes. Saw Mr Wade—Sir S.R.G. respecting Agency. Read Derry & Enniskillen finished—Dang. Classes of New York. Worked with Herbert.

15. Th.

Ch. 8½ AM. At 10¼ we went to Mr Burnett's. A slow & solemn march to the Church, then the funeral service. Wrote a long letter to Mrs Burnett with my recollections of him.[7]

Saw Mr R. Burnett—Dr Moffatt—Mr Barker—E. Griffiths. Worked with H.—we finished gravelling the path. It rather strains my chest. Wrote also to Mr Goulburn—Mr Herbert Spencer—Dr Acland—& minutes. Preparations for going.

[1] Accusing him of misrepresentation in the *Contemporary* wrangle (see 13 Nov. 73n): Add MS 44442, f. 35.

[2] *Sc.* Beasley; considered for the agency, but too ill; Hawn P.

[3] See 18 Dec. 73.

[4] Offering living of Middleham to Frederick Barker, curate in Chester; Add MS 44543, f. 52.

[5] P. A. Pickering, serjeant of county palatine of Lancaster.

[6] Joseph Salkeld of London.

[7] Add MS 44442, f. 49.

16. Fr. [*London*]

Off to town after an early breakfast. Reached C.H.T. about 3 PM. Saw Ld Granville—And others. Dined with Mrs Th. who behaved bravely and well. D.G. Wrote to Duchess of Montrose[1]—Sir W. Stephenson—Ld Spencer—Messrs Williams—Baron Dowse—Ld Hartington—Mr Welby—Sir A. Panizzi—Gen. Ponsonby—Mr A. Peel—and minutes. Read. . . .

To A. W. PEEL, chief whip, 16 January 1874. Add MS 44543, f. 53.

Some time ago, when in search of topics of consolation, I obtained them from you in the shape of figures. I again repair to the same source. It is *alleged* that, as a rule, the Liberal party fares ill, even in good political times, at single elections as compared with general Elections. Have you records which will enable you to show the number of seats won & lost by the Liberal party in 1831, & again the number won & lost during the existence of the Parliament then chosen? Together with like figures for each following Parliament, down to the present & including it to this date. This would fairly test the allegation—I am afraid our last remaining allegation. There may be *something* in it.[2]

17. Sat.

Wrote to Mr Goschen—Gen. Ponsonby—D. of Argyll—Mr Cardwell—The Queen—Ld Granville—and minutes. Saw Dean of Windsor—Ld Wolverton—Mr Bright—Ld W. *cum* Ld Granville—M. Gavard—Mr A. Peel—Mr Wickham—Mr Crowe[3]—Mr Gurdon. Dined with Sir A. Panizzi: alone: so we had some conversation on high matters. Read. . . .

The prospects of agreement with the two Depts on Estimates are for the present bad.[4]

To the DUKE OF ARGYLL, Indian secretary, 17 January 1874. Add MS 44543, f. 53.

I have received your letters[5] & a Telegram which had its wording spoilt about the famine in India. Your detention is a matter of much regret, but you will be well represented by Halifax. I do not well understand the attitude of the [India]

[1] Caroline Agnes, wife of James, 4th duke of Montrose, on vacant Dumbartonshire lord-lieutenancy; she d. 1894, marrying 2nd W. S. Stirling-Crawfurd, 3rd M. H. Milner; Add MS 44543, f. 52.

[2] No reply found.

[3] Eyre Crowe of the cttee. on art and design.

[4] Selections 17-23 January in Morley, ii. 484.

[5] Especially of 15 January, Add MS 44103, f. 101; 'I am annoyed to hear today that Frere who happens to be Vice President this year of the Council & therefore presides in my absence [from gout], is opposed to passing any Despatch expressive of Confidence in Northbrook—because Frere has always supported the refusal to prohibit exports [of food].'

Council, but no doubt we shall hear what they allege in favour of a course which appears to be a strange one. I am very far indeed from sanguine about the position of the party & the Government generally, & I see no chance anywhere but in finance of mending the position, while in that department there are great difficulties for we are not I think so economical as we were at the outset of our ministerial career. I sincerely hope you will soon be able to report yourself well off the list of invalids.

To G. J. GOSCHEN, first lord of the admiralty, Add MS 44543, f. 54.
17 January 1874. 'Secret.'

The season for treating Estimates is now so close & the subject is one of such great importance generally, so much enhanced by the circumstances of the time, that I should like very much to see you upon them, at least in a preliminary way, with two or three of our colleagues—Granville, Cardwell, Bright—whom I have invited to come to my house at 11.30 on Monday.[1]

18. 2 S.Epiph.

Chapel Royal & St James's. Wrote to Mr Goschen—C.G.—Mrs Th.—and minutes. Read Henslow:[2] other Sunday reading.

This day I thought of dissolution. Told Bright of it. In evening at dinner told Granville & Wolverton. All seemed to approve. My first thought of it was as escape from a difficulty. I soon saw on reflection that it was the best thing in itself.

19. M.

Confined to bed all day with tightness on the chest. Wrote to Williams & Co—Ld Granville—C.G.—Townshend & Barker—& minutes. Saw Dr Clark (mg & evg)—Ld Granville—Mr Bright—Mr Cardwell—Mr Godley. Read Q.R. on Sacerdotalism—on Liberal Party—on Mrs Somerville—on Mill's Autobiography[3]—Henslow on Evolution. Much physicking.

Secret *Memorandum*[4]

I have now obtained the most accurate information available,[5] & am able to state more particularly, & slightly to modify, the computations which I put down at Hawarden in my letter to Lord Granville.[6]

1. The statements presented by the revenue authorities show a surplus of 4½m.

[1] An almost similar summons went to Cardwell; Add MS 44543, f. 54.
[2] G. Henslow, *The theory of evolution* (1873).
[3] *Quarterly Review*, cxxxvi. 103-50 (January 1874).
[4] Initialled and dated 19 January 1874, Add MS 44762, f. 4.
[5] From Welby's mem. of 18 January 1874 on army and navy estimates; Add MS 44338, f. 27.
[6] See 8 Jan. 74; also calculations of 17 Jan. in Ramm I, ii. 444.

2. As they state that these figures are on the whole moderately taken I venture with their acquiescence to add $\frac{1}{2}$m making the surplus 5m.

3. I think that with a Budget of great boons we might venture upon opening new sources of revenue to the extent of 2m. making 7m.

4. But I require (for the losses to be met during the financial year)

I[ncome] T[ax]	4775 m.
S[ugar] D[uties]	1960 m.
L[ocal] T[axation] approx.	800 m.
	7,535 m[ille].

5. If on the one hand it is possible that, all circumstances continuing favourable, the surplus of 7m may by the end of the financial year have slightly grown, it is clear on the other hand that some further sums will be required to supply a small surplus on the Budget Account, & to provide a margin for any small remissions or unforeseen items of charge. (Something might be fairly anticipated from the effect of remission of I.T. in strengthening general revenue)

6. The result is as follows:

In order to lay a fairly probable ground for an effectual budget, there is wanting a sum of (say) 600m., as a minimum.

On reduction of A[rmy] & N[avy] Estimates

1. Have the pledges of 68/ been sufficiently redeemed by these estimates as they now stand?
2. Are the principles of Economy sufficiently applied by them? (even admitting as is fair that any *larger* question of reduction should stand over to a new Parliament).
3. Have the Govt. & party any other mode of giving their friends fair play at the Elections than by such a Budget as has been sketched?
4. I must add that in my opinion the larger part should be furnished (as far as I can judge) by the Admiralty, and a good deal from the Building Vote.

My own mind is swayed by the three first of these considerations; and as regards the two first of the three I feel that I have a very special responsibility.

1. Write with my most sincere regrets to Mr Hankey that I am absolutely forbidden to leave my bed to day—& excuse me.
2. See Mr Villiers & tell him I shd. hope to be ready to see him on Thursday forenoon or wd. receive his comm[unicatio]n in any other way.
3. Acquaint Lord Granville—give him this Memorandum—beg that those who meet at 11.30 will carry the question in my absence as far as they think useful.
4. Cabinet. See over [the page].

Memorandum

I. Foreign Office—Information.

II. Gold Coast—Information.

III. Domestic. a. The Melody case—Papers are in my table—If the Cabinet has doubts, I should like to be heard before they decide against my views—or the Chancellor's. b. The Lancashire proposal for a great dinner. c. The Indian Famine dispatch.[1] d. British Museum & S. K[ensington]—Mr Lowe will state what has been done. e. It has been proposed, partly for the sake of the

[1] See 23 Jan. 74.

party in prospect of a Dissolution to issue a Commission on the Liquor question[1]—the Cabinet might like to talk this over.[2]

20. Tu.

Bed all day: rather more obstinacy than usual. Read Henslow. Wrote to C.G.—and minutes. Saw Dr Clark (bis)—Ld Wolverton mg & evg —Mr Gurdon—Mr Godley. Spent the chief part of the day & evening in reflection on our 'crisis': and then in preparing a letter to go to the Queen for her information at once, & a long Address[3] to an unnamed constituency—almost a pamphlet—setting out the case of the Govt on an immediate appeal to the country.

Secret[4]

1. We gain time, & avoid for the moment a ministerial crisis.
2. This gain of time will put us in possession of better & closer information before we finally settle the Estimates & the Budget.
3. We arrest the certain drain of the single Elections, in which every succeeding reverse additionally impairs our credit, and diminishes our power of carrying measures, and of preserving the integrity of their form.
4. This series of defeats now a long series takes the heart out of the party & damages it more & more for the final struggle.
5. What we look to if the Parlt. continue[s] is founding our appeal on a good & successful Budget; but then:
a. it is necessary to secure the conditions of such a Budget
b. if this cannot be done, any schism happening now will materially aggravate all the chances against us.
c. The essential particulars of such a Budget may be stated in an Address to a Constituency as was done in 1834-5 by Sir R. Peel. Thus the party may have its programme. Of course it may be said a programme is a promise. But we may reply by pointing to promises fulfilled.
6. The formidable divisions in the party would be aborted[?] or held in suspense if we have an *immediate* Dissolution upon a question of universal & commanding interest.
7. If the internal difficulty be only *adjourned* till after this Dissolution, still we should be in a stronger & fresher condition to face it. But it *might* have disappeared.
8. I think our victory is as likely in an immediate as in a postponed Dissolution. While we run fewer chances of a crushing defeat.
9. It must not be forgotten that every *week* of a Session has its dangers during our present weakness: with a triumphant enemy without the walls, and a majority far from being thoroughly compact within them.

[1] Not done.
[2] Undated; Add MS 44762, f. 3.
[3] Add MS 44762, f. 14; see 23 Jan. 74.
[4] Initialled and dated 20 January 1874, Add MS 44762, f. 6.

21. Wed.

Saw Mr Peel—Mr Gurdon—Dr Clark—Ld Wolverton—Mr Cardwell *cum* Mr Goschen—Ld Granville—Deputation on the County Suffrage.[1] Wrote to W.H.G.—C.G.—Sir T.E. May—& minutes. Altered & modified letter to the Queen—wh went off.[2] Came down at two: much conversation today on the question of my own seat. Dined with the Wortleys: music really rich & rare, though unpretending. Read Henslow on Evolution—Sharpe's Man a Special Creation.[3]

To Sir T. E. MAY, clerk of the Commons, Add MS 44543, f. 54.
21 January 1874.

It is indeed refreshing, even to a bed-ridden and too much occupied man, to read a luminous paper such as that which you have written on the very anxious question of the Greenwich Seat:[4] in which the spirit and qualifications of the historic student appear side by side with those of the constitutional lawyer.

Though not yet quite out of my bed, I am about to quit it, and I will venture to ask you if you can favour me by dining with me to meet a very few friends on Saturday at eight.

22. Th.

Wrote to Ld Granville—Mrs Th.—J. Watson & S.—Mr Leeman—Messrs Townshend & Barker—Mr Ogilvie—The Queen (Mem). Tel. —Mem. for Mr C. & Mr G.—Abp Manning—Ld Acton—Dean of Windsor—C.G. Saw Ld Granville—Mr Villiers—Mr Leeman—Mr Gurdon—Mr Lowe—Dr Clark—Ld Wolverton & Mr Peel—Ld Halifax—Mr Bright—and others. Wrote also fully to the Queen on the Church letter.[5] Dined with the Lowes. Finished Mr Henslow's work. Saw an Italian[R?].

Mr Cardwell, Mr Goschen:[6] We arrived yesterday at the conclusion that, apart from this or that shade of view as to exact figure of the Estimates, the measure now proposed stood well on its own general grounds.

This being so, after consulting Ld Granville, & indeed at his suggestion, I have in a preparatory letter to the Queen founded myself entirely on general grounds.

[1] Mostly of trade unionists; 'my opinion is that this question has not come before the general public'; *The Times*, 22 January 1874, 8a and leader. Gladstone's manifesto hoped for the franchise 'at no distant day' for 'our loyal, patient, and (as I hold) intelligent peasantry'.

[2] Guedalla, *Q*, i. 436.

[3] W. Sharpe, *Man a special creation* (1873).

[4] Planned between Cardwell and May on 13 January, supporting the view that the Greenwich seat was not vacant, but not sent until the 19th, too late to affect the decision to dissolve; see R. R. James, 'Gladstone and the Greenwich Seat', *History Today*, ix. 350 (1959). May was unable to dine; Add MS 44154, f. 52.

[5] Guedalla, *Q*, i. 438.

[6] Initialled and dated 22 January 1874; Add MS 44762, f. 8. In Morley, ii. 484.

This being so I would propose to consider the point raised between us as one adjourned though with a perfect knowledge in each of our minds as to the views of the others.

My statement to the Cabinet must be on the same basis as my statement to the Queen.

The actual decision of the Estimates would stand over from tomorrow's Cabinet until we saw our way as to their position & as to the time for their production. I am sure I might reckon on your keeping the future as far as possible open, & unprejudiced by contracts for works or for building or construction.

Any reference to economy which I make tomorrow will be in general terms such as I propose to use in an address.

If I have made myself clear & you approve please to signify it on this paper[1] —or to speak to me, as you may prefer.

I am reluctant to go out, with my chest still tender, in the fog.

To ARCHBISHOP H. E. MANNING, 22 January 1874.[2] Add MS 44250, f. 145.

It is very kind of you to send me your tract on Ultramontanism & Caesarism,[3] for I fear you can hardly regard me as an apt disciple.

I have at once begun to read it, with interest: I limp after you as well as I can! If Caesarism be the same thing (in effect) as Erastianism I can look on with comfort or equanimity while you pummel it, for I think that Erastianism is a debased offspring of the human mind and one which debases in its turn. But when you get to your heights I am deaf and blind: my rudimentary perceptions seem to differ from yours: Nature has made a mistake in one or other of us. My only comfort is this, that a time will come when if I am a tenth part as good as you are we shall know how a Higher Power solves all these problems for us.

I shall reply upon you by sending you a composition of mine on which, as to principles, I think we cannot quarrel, a translation of the Shield of Achilles.

23. Fr.

Wrote to Ld Halifax—The Queen—various Tell. Mem and long letter —C.G.—Mr Peel—W.H.G. Tel. and two letters. Revised & corrected my Address. Cabinet 12¼-4: Address further amended there, on partial perusal. Saw Ld Granville—Ld Wolverton *cum* Mr Peel—Count Münster—Mr Delane (cum Lord G.)—Mr Levy (*cum* Ld W[olverton])[4]—Sir A. Buchanan (malgrè moi)—Mr Goschen. In evg corrected proofs of Address: wh runs pretty well. A very busy, stirring day, of incessant action. Dined at Ld Granville's. Read Sullivan's Irish Records.[5]

[1] Neither did so.

[2] Holograph, marked for copying in Letter Book (see Add MS 44543, f. 54); thus perhaps not sent.

[3] See Add MS 44250, f. 144.

[4] i.e. editor of *The Times* and owner-editor of the *Daily Telegraph*.

[5] W. K. Sullivan, *On the manners and customs of the ancient Irish* (1873).

Cabinet. Friday Jan. 23. 74. Noon.[1]

√ Statement by WEG of motives for Dissolution—& recomm[endatio]n to Dissolve: on the grounds of general advantage. Granville concurred. All agreed.[2]

√ WEG's address described—all the most material parts read. 'Ultramontane' Par[agraph] cut out[3]—also 'Reformed Religion'. Par[agraph] respecting personal service of W.E.G. rather softened.

D. of Argyll—amended dispatch of confidence to Northbrook to be sent.[4] Absolute secrecy this evg. except by post.[5]

W.E.G. might give up the Cship of Exr. G[oschen] take it. WEG take the Budget in redemption of Election pledges. C[hilders] succeed G[oschen].[6]

24. Sat.

Read the six morning papers: well satisfied on the whole. Wrote to Mr Rock (Greenwich)—Col. Neville—Sir W. Knollys—Mr Goschen—Mr Richmond—Ld Granville—Robn G.—Ld Kimberley—and minutes. Luncheon at 15 G.S. Saw Birley X. Saw Ld Hartington—Ld Wolverton—Mr Bright—Ld Granville—Mr Dodson—Mr Gurdon—Mr Trench—Mr Lambert—Ld Acton—Mr Trench—WHG. Lengthened walk. Continued in evg.

To LORD KIMBERLEY, colonial secretary, 24 January 1874. Add MS 44543, f. 55.

1. Quaere whether to add to your Par[agraph] of [*sc.* on] Fiji: 'And I have to observe with reference to a passage near the commencement of the Mem. that H.M.'s Govt. have given no authority to anyone to intimate on their behalf any intimation to annex these islands.' I am afraid this passage, if not noticed [*sic*] may hereafter be quoted against us.[7]

2. These papers are without doubt extremely crude. There is however one piece of sound doctrine in the Mem. where the New Zealand Ministers say 'Local

[1] Add MS 44641, f. 245.

[2] Note, for private secretary, ibid., f. 243: '*Tel. to Queen in cipher immediately: Cabinet concurs.*'

[3] Para. attacking dangers of Ultramontanism to British institutions, Add MS 44762, f. 10, printed in Matthew, 'Vaticanism', 433. Note at Add MS 44641, f. 246, lists as 'against Ultramontane Clause': Granville, Argyll, Kimberley, Bright, Halifax, Selborne. Final version in *The Times*, 24 January 1874, 8a.

[4] On the Indian famine; Add MS 44622, f. 1.

[5] But the news escaped this day; see secretary's notes, Add MS 44641, f. 251.

[6] Undated note, ibid., f. 248.

[7] Draft despatch to New Zealand on South Sea islands sent this day by Kimberley, who observed: 'The views of the N. Zealand Govt. are most extravagant. . . . Perhaps the draft ought to be seen by the Cabinet but this you will decide'; Add MS 44225, f. 138. New Zealand argued Fiji 'imperatively requires the control of Her Majesty's Government'; see W. P. Morrell, *Britain in the Pacific Islands* (1960), 164.

efforts to maintain peaceful relations with an uncivilized race are far more successful than those directed by a distant Power.' And, singular to state, the Mem. seems to partake of the nature of a retractation [*sic*] as to New Zealand of the contemptuous answer received from (I think) New South Wales to our observation that *they* might if they pleased frame for consideration a plan for annexing or governing Fiji. I suggest for your consideration whether it might not be politic to advert with some degree of assent to the words I have quoted & to say, at the end of the Paragraph before the Fiji Paragraph that you are, nevertheless, quite ready to consider any plan which may be framed in New Zealand for the purpose of directing such local efforts to the establishment of closer friendly relations with the uncivilized races of Polynesia beyond the limits of the Colony.
3. I should think the Cabinet ought to approve the draft—it might not be necessary to read to them the papers with which it deals.

25. S. Conv.St P. 3 Epiph.

Chapel Royal mg & aftn. Wrote to Ld Hartington—Mr Tallents (2)—Mr Ouvry—General Ponsonby Tel.—Lady Egerton—Ld Spencer—The Queen—Mr Crum Ewing—Sir H. Verney—Duke of Argyll—& minutes. Dined with the Phillimores. Saw Mr Peel—Mr West—Sir R. Phillimore—Ld Wolverton—Mr Wortley—and [wrote] minutes. Dined with the Phillimores. Read Contemp.Rev. Decr on Prayer & on J.S. Mill[1]—Shadows of a Sick Room[2]—Manning on Ultramontanism.[3]

To LORD HARTINGTON, Irish secretary, 25 January 1874. Add MS 44543, f. 56.

With the whole substance of your note[4] I agree. I have no addition or qualification to suggest except this: it is not necessary perhaps for them to use the word Union, & they may I think safely express a desire to facilitate & extend local self-government (a) in all parts of the country (of course for them in Ireland specially) (b) under the supremacy & controul of the Imperial Parliament. These two restrictions or specifications I think make all safe.

To G. TALLENTS,[5] 25 January 1874. Add MS 44543, f. 56.
'Private & confidential.'

[First letter:] My great desire, I may say ambition, had been to avail myself on this occasion of the most kind feeling which subsists with you, & I believe with many, at Newark, & to offer myself there. But I consider it my first duty to place myself, as to any such purpose, in the hands of those who generally advise

[1] *Contemporary Review*, xxiii. 20, 53 (December 1873).
[2] Published anon. (1873).
[3] H. E. *Manning, *Caesarism and ultramontanism* (1874).
[4] Not in Add MS 44144. See 28 Jan. 74n.
[5] Son of his agent at Newark in the 1830s and 1840s; see 31 July 32, 14 Sept. 40. No letter found from Tallents on the Newark seat.

for the Party in Election matters. They point out to me that after the difficulty which was thought to have arisen about my seat it was my duty to do nothing which could seem like running away, & in consequence I have issued my Address to the Electors of Greenwich. But I wished you to know what, with all deference (& much gratitude) to them, had been my desire.

[Second letter:] I have been asked to make provision at Newark for preventing any intervention of the agents of the Newcastle estate in the coming election in a sense adverse to the Liberal party.[1] Any title of mine in this respect is of course limited to the Trust property. And I place upon you, to the extent which I have stated, an entire reliance. I will send a copy of this note to the gentleman who asked me.

26. M.

Wrote to Mr Harvey—and minutes. 8¾-5¾. To Osborne. Audience of H.M. who quite comprehends the provisional character of the position. Saw Ld Wolverton & others—Ld Aberdare—Ld Granville—Mr Gurdon. Dined with Lady James. Boundless newspaper reading.[2] Read Markham on Voyage of the Arctic[3]—Walpole's Spencer Perceval.[4]

27. Tu.

Wrote to Mr Lowe—The Queen—Mr Barker—Mr Beales—and minutes. Cabinet 2½-5¼. Dined with Panizzi. Saw Mr [W. F.] Rock *cum* Mr Bell from Greenwich (Wolverton & Gurdon present)—Ld Wolverton—Mr Lowe—Sir T. Fremantle—Mr Lingen. Read Markham—S. Walpole's Perceval.

To J. BRIGHT, chancellor of the duchy, Add MS 43385, f. 247.
27 January 1874.

I cannot repay you for your letter[5] by much news: but according to all intelligence that reaches here, the feeling of our friends is excellent.

Your statement of a specific difficulty is the only incident in the nature of an exception.

The Dissenters will in my opinion greatly damage their own cause, not generally alone but in connection with the specific matter of the Education Act, if

[1] i.e. in his capacity as a trustee of the Newcastle estate.
[2] Selections 26 January-3 February, in Morley, ii. 490.
[3] Sir C. R. *Markham, *The threshold of the unknown region* (1873).
[4] Sir S. *Walpole, *The life of . . . S. Perceval*, 2v. (1874).
[5] Of 26 January, Add MS 44113, f. 89: 'I am afraid the Education question will throw many of the Catholic voters in the Northern Towns into the ranks of our opponents—for they vote as the Priests tell them, & the Priests are for public money for Catholic schools—& they have no politics apart from their Church.'

they ask from our Candidates a positive pledge to go against the present denominational grants to the R.C.s.

The fact is, it seems to me, that the Noncons have not yet as a body made up their minds whether they want unsectarian religion, or whether they want simple secular teaching, so far as the application of the rate is concerned.

I have never been strong against the latter of these two which seems to me impartial, & not, if fairly worked, of necessity in any degree unfriendly to religion.

The former is in my opinion glaringly partial & I shall never be a party to it. But there is a good deal of leaning to it in the Liberal party.

Any attempt to obtain definitive pledges now will give power to the enemies of both plans of proceeding. We have no rational course as a party but one which [is] to adjourn for a while the solution of the graver parts of the Education Problem. And this I know to be in substance your opinion.

You have not lost much by not attending the Cabinet.

To [E. BEALES], 27 January 1874. *The Times*, 31 January 1874, 7d.[1]

I have always been very anxious that some representatives of the working men should find their way into the House of Commons; and I have never heard of any worthier representative they could have than Mr. Howell, of whom you speak, I believe with justice, in such high terms, and who, I understand, is opposing a Conservative candidate. It cannot but be agreeable to me if it is of the slightest advantage to Mr. Howell, that this opinion should be made known, but I must beware of the imprudence, signally exhibited, not long ago, in a memorable example, of obtruding my sentiments on any constituency or any persons in such a way as to show anything like a pretension to influence their vote. Of course I should add that I am in no way a judge of the expediency of Mr. Howell's becoming a candidate for any constituency in particular. With these cautions, which I am sure you will have anticipated and will approve, I leave the matter in your and Mr. Howell's hands, with my earnest good wishes for his success, not only on personal grounds, but as a matter of real public importance.

28. Wed.

Wrote to Ld Fermoy—Ld Hartington—& minutes. Got up the Malacca case[2] for Greenwich. Saw Sir W. Boxall—Ld Wolverton (3)—Mr Gurdon—Ld Granville—Bp of Winchr. 2-5. To Greenwich. Spoke an hour to 5000.[3] An enthusiastic meeting. But the general prospects are far from clear. Read Disraeli's Glasgow Speeches[4]—Markham's 'Arctic'. Dined with the Farquhars.

[1] Letter not recorded in Add MS 44543; printed in *The Times* as being written to 'an old and staunch friend of the Liberal cause'; clearly *Beales, of the correspondents listed by the diarist this day. *Howell stood in Aylesbury with N. M. de Rothschild, but finished third, though with more votes than in 1868. See 31 Jan. 74.

[2] Disraeli's Address described the govt.'s 1871 relinquishment of a treaty on the Malacca Straits as 'an act of folly or of ignorance rarely equalled'; *The Times*, 26 January 1874, 8a.

[3] In rain; *The Times*, 29 January 1874, 5c.

[4] B. *Disraeli, 'Inaugural Address . . . to the University of Glasgow, including the occasional speeches' (2nd ed., 1873).

To LORD FERMOY, 28 January 1874. Add MS 44543, f. 57.

I thank you for your letter & good wishes.[1] In my address[2] I have endeavoured to state clearly the principle on which I should endeavour to deal with all questions relating to the increase of local or sectional powers in the U.K.[3] With respect to Home Rule I have not yet heard an authoritative or binding definition of the phrase which appears to be used by different persons in different senses. Until this phrase comes to have a definite & certain meaning, I have not thought myself justified in referring to it, but have indicated plainly in another form the test which I should apply to its interpretation.

29. Th.

Wrote to Ld Granville—Ld O. Fitzgerald—Scotts—Ld Tenterden—J. Watson & S.—Adm. Hamilton—W.H.G.—Editor of Echo[4]—Mr Forster—Mr W.H. Smith—and minutes. Dined with the Wests. Read Mivart[5]—Markham. Saw Deptford Deputation[6]—Sir W. Drake—Ld Wolverton—Mr Godley—Ld Granville—Dowager Duchess of Somerset—Sir W. Stephenson. Saw Fitzroy[R].

30. Frid.

Wrote to Bp of Winchester—W.H.G. (Tel)—Mr Milbank—Rev M. O'Halloran[7]—Dean of Windsor—& minutes. Dined with Ld President (Sheriffs).[8] Saw Ld Wolverton—Mr Gurdon—Mr Wortley—Ld Kimberley—Ld Aylesbury. Saw Holmes X—Cooper. Read Burnouf on Schliemann[9]—Anderson on Acheen & Gold Coast.[10]

To F. A. MILBANK, 30 January 1874. Add MS 44543, f. 58.

I will not fail to make known your recommendation with my own attestation of it to the Lord Chancellor, who appoints to County Court Judgeships.

I cordially reciprocate your good wishes and humbly advise you to work well and often the question of the gross extravagance of the late Government; the constant efforts of the [tory] party while in opposition to increase expenditure, and the utter indefiniteness of their present financial views and expectations.

[1] Not found.
[2] See 23 and 25 Jan. 74.
[3] 'Permanent and solid as is the Union of the three kingdoms, they present varieties of circumstance, of organisation, and even of law. . . . I think we ought not only to admit, but to welcome, every improvement in the organisation of local and subordinate authority, which, under the unquestioned control of Parliament, would tend to lighten its labours. . . .'; *The Times*, 24 January 1874, 8b.
[4] Correcting inaccuracy of reporting of Blackheath meeting in *The Echo*, 30 January 1874, 5.
[5] S.-G. J. *Mivart, *Man and apes* (1873).
[6] See *The Times*, 30 January 1874, 5e.
[7] Non-anglican.
[8] Preparing for 'pricking the sheriffs' on 3 February.
[9] See 7 Jan. 74.
[10] J. *Anderson, *Acheen and the ports of the North and East coasts of Sumatra* (1840).

31. Sat.

Wrote to Mr Lambert[1]—Prof. Fawcett—Ld Dudley—Ld Provost of Glasgow—Mr Jolly (Tel.)—& minutes. 1¼–6½. Woolwich Meeting & journies. The meeting disturbed by design was strangely brought round again by doggerel.[2] Saw French Ambassador—Ld Wolverton—Sir W. Drake—Mr Godley—Adm. Hamilton. Eleven to dinner. Read Markham.

To N. G. LAMBERT, 31 January 1874. Add MS 44543, f. 59.

I have received your letter of 30th[3] suggesting that I ought to request Baron Rothschild[4] to support Mr Howell. I apprehend that I must leave the relations between the Candidates to be settled locally. But a letter of mine published in the papers of this morning (I read it in the Times)[5] will show that (as I think you will agree) I have already done for Mr H. all that is in my power.

Septa S. Feb One. 1874.

Chapel Royal Noon (with H.C.) and 5.30 PM. Wrote to Dowager Lady Westbury—The Queen—Ld Spencer[6]—and minutes. Saw Ld Tenterden—Ld Wolverton—Mr Gale—Ld Lyttelton—Ld Aberdare. Dined with the Wolvertons. Read Benty's Sermon[7]—Shadows of a Sick Room[8]—Hunt in Contemp. Review[9]—Max Müller's Lecture with Stanley's introduction.[10]

To LORD SPENCER, Irish lord lieutenant, 1 February 1874. Add MS 44543, f. 59.

I thank you for your letter & inclosures. I have not seen Hartington's address, but he & I have been in correspondence & in entire accord about Home Rule. The paragraph in my address to which you find that objection is taken by some rather weak-kneed brethren was read to & unanimously approved by the Cabinet.[11]

[1] Nathaniel Grace Lambert, 1811–82; whig M.P. Buckinghamshire 1868–80.

[2] Crowd of at least 15,000; tories were involved in scuffles; Gladstone defused the tension by rhyming 'Malacca' with 'bacca'; *The Times*, 2 February 1874, 5.

[3] Not found.

[4] i.e. the liberal candidate, with Howell, at Aylesbury.

[5] See 27 Jan. 74.

[6] Rest of entry placed at foot of next page.

[7] Probably from S. Bentley, *Sermons on prayer* (1871 ed.).

[8] See 25 Jan. 74.

[9] *Contemporary Review*, xxiii. 437 (February 1874).

[10] F. M. *Müller, 'On missions . . . with an introductory sermon by A. P. Stanley' (1873).

[11] Spencer's letter of 30 January, Add MS 44307, f. 221, reported: 'Touching "Home Rule" I think it right to tell you that in certain quarters a sentence of your Address has been interpreted into encouragement of "Home Rule".' See 25, 28 Jan. 74n.

2. M.

Wrote to D. of Argyll—Ld Kimberley (Tel.)—Mr Hirst—Ld Granville (Tel.)—and minutes. Dined with the Wortleys. Saw Ld Wolverton (2)—Mr Wortley—Sir W. Drake—Duke of Argyll—Mr Godley. 2¼-5. Third great meeting & speech of an hour at New Cross for Deptford.[1] Much enthusiasm & fair order. Read Markham.

To A. S. AYRTON, chief commissioner of works, 2 February 1874. Add MS 44543, f. 59.

I thank you for your note:[2] but for once I think you have not been perfectly informed. Two conservative members *did* certify that my seat was vacant. But the Speaker, by the Act, could not move, unless he likewise received a notification from me, which I did not send. Privately I may mention that Sir E. May has given a strong opinion that my seat was full.[3]

3. Tu.

Wrote to Ld Kimberley—Ld Robartes—C.S. Parker—Mr Crawfurd—and minutes. Dined with Granville. Read Markham. Long walk. Saw Lee[R]. Saw Ld Wolverton—Ld Granville *cum* Ld W.—Mr Milner Gibson—Mr Godley—Ld Granville.

Many Telegrams & much conversation with Granville & Wolverton in the evening. The general prospect was first indifferent, then bad. My own election for Greenwich, after Boord the distiller,[4] is more like a defeat than a victory, though it places me in Parliament again.[5] A wakeful night; but I believe more from a little strong coffee drunk incautiously than from the polls: which I cannot help, & have done all in my power to mend.

To LORD KIMBERLEY, colonial secretary, 3 February 1874. Add MS 44543, f. 59.

For myself I see no reason for doubting the wisdom of Wolseley's proceedings with the King of Ashantee;[6] but it would not be possible at this moment to assemble the Cabinet to consider them. Might it not be well if you were to postpone any official reply & to state to W. privately the reason to which I have just

[1] *The Times*, 3 January 1874, 5d.
[2] Not found.
[3] See 21 Jan. 74.
[4] (Sir) Thomas White Boord, 1838-1912, tory M.P. Greenwich 1873 (by-election on d. of Salomons)—1895; cr. bart. 1896; partner in Boord & Son, distillers.
[5] T. W. Boord, tory, 6193; Gladstone, 5968; J. E. Liardet, tory, 5561; J. B. Langley, liberal/radical, 5255.
[6] Kimberley reported arrival of despatches from Wolseley, wished to approve his answer to the King, and suggested Cabinet approval also before Friday's mail; Add MS 44225, f. 140.

referred, telling him what you think & if you deem it proper referring also to what I have said. I should not like to put a pressure on Bright at this moment & we could hardly call upon Forster or Cardwell, or upon Stansfeld & Fortescue, or even well upon Goschen & perhaps one or two more to come & consider the question; which I hope in God will be virtually settled long before any reply from you can reach Wolseley. Of whom I must say that the more I see of him, the more I like him.

[P.S.] Granville happened to come in & wishes me to say he agrees.

4. Wed.

Wrote to Mr Waddy MP.[1]—Ld Granville—Mr Delane—Mr C. Reed[2]—Mr Otway—Sir A. Panizzi—Mr Welby—and minutes. Seven to dinner. Read Perceval's Memoirs—finished Markham. Saw Ld Wolverton—Ld Granville—Mr Godley—Ld Lyttelton—Mr S. Lyttelton—Ld Gr. *cum* D. of Argyll—D. of Argyll. Saw [blank].

5. Th.

Wrote to The Electors of Greenwich my Address of 'Thanks'.[3] Wrote also to C. Lyttelton—Mr Bright—Mr Delane—Mr Morris—Mr Parker (Tel.)—and minutes. Dined with Panizzi; a better conversation on religion. Saw Sir W. Stephenson—Ld Wolverton—Mr Godley—D. of Argyll—Mr Cardwell. Long conversation with C. & afterward with Wolverton on the early future 6–7¾. The issue of the Elections is now irrevocably bad. Saw three[R]. Read Rogers on Cobden.[4]

To J. BRIGHT, chancellor of the duchy of Lancaster, 5 February 1874. Add MS 43385, f. 249.

I have a good deal to say to you when occasion offers on the course of the Elections, our probable prospects, and proper line of conduct, so that if your footsteps turn this way I reckon on your kindly coming to see me.

But my present object is to call your attention to the enclosed letter from Charles Lyttelton.

Under present circumstances it appears most probable that if the scale be turned against us it will be by the cases in which undue multiplication of Liberal Candidates, or their egotistical or crotchety obtrusion, will have been the means of introducing a Conservative.

I am *sure* you will do what you can to relieve Charles Lyttelton from his difficulty. I do not believe him to be an Advocate of the [Contagious Diseases]

[1] Samuel Danks Waddy, 1830–1902; liberal M.P. Barnstaple 1874–9, Edinburgh 1882–5, Lincolnshire 1886–94.

[2] (Sir) Charles Reed, 1819–81; chaired London School Board 1873; liberal M.P. Hackney 1868–74; kt. 1874.

[3] Very brief; *The Times*, 6 February 1874, 6a.

[4] J. E. T. *Rogers, 'Cobden and modern political opinion' (1873).

Acts: but the party opposed to them refused our Bill of 1871 (or 2) which gave them nearly all they asked but which withheld a little *modicum*. It was a most signal example of bigotry on their part: but it would be an outrage if Mr Allbright now insists upon destroying the chances of one of the best & most promising young men of the day.

As there is no time to lose I send this by a Messenger who will obey your orders.[1]

[P.S.] See the inclosed from Wolseley. Thank God.

To J. T. DELANE, 5 February 1874. Add MS 44543, f. 61.

I was really ashamed to give you trouble yesterday,[2] but I am thankful for the notice of today. The reports of my speeches, so far as I have examined them, appear to me to be *excellent*. It is fair to say that I find the reading of my own speeches to be a highly penal operation; & it is accordingly one which I restrict within the bounds of a strict necessity.

6. Fr.

Wrote to Ld Granville—Mr Cardwell—Robn G.[3]—The Queen—Mr Peel—Ld Spencer. Saw Duke of Argyll—Mr Kinnaird—Mr Godley —Ld Wolverton—Mr Peel—Mr Lambert—Mr West—Mr Morris (binder)—Sir R. Phillimore. A round of calls. Each day grows blacker. Ten to dinner: & conversation. Read Spencer Perceval—Major on Zeno's Narrative.[4]

To A. W. PEEL, chief whip, 6 February 1874. Add MS 44543, f. 61.

First let me say do not let this letter interfere in any way with your own occupations for the moment. But I am very desirous that as soon as convenient there should be obtained confidentially from the local agents of towns & counties where the Elections have gone wrong or less favourably than had been hoped ⟨for⟩ a brief statement of the cause—to make it short this might be in reply to some such questions as was it Conservative reaction? Licensed Victuallers? Liberal dissension on the side of Nonconformists? On the side of the Irish vote? or any other special causes? Further I am very desirous to have before the *end of next week* an account of those Conservative *members* who have pledged themselves in their Addresses (I do not say Speeches because this might be more

[1] Bright replied on 6 February, Add MS 44113, f. 91: 'I have written urgently to Mr Albright . . . but I am not sanguine of success.' See 13 Feb. 74.

[2] Denying accusation in *The Times*' leader this day that he found time to write his 'Shield of Achilles' article while in office; rather, he had revised the 1867 draft.

[3] The famous 'gin and beer' explanation of the election, as also used in this day's letter to Spencer; Morley, ii. 495.

[4] R. H. *Major, *The voyages of the Venetian brothers, N. and A. Zeno, to the North Seas* (1873).

difficult to obtain) to the repeal of the Income Tax & the terms in which they have done it so as to show whether it is absolute or conditional?[1]

To LORD SPENCER, Irish lord lieutenant, 6 February 1874. Add MS 44543, f. 62.

I am very much obliged by your letter.[2] If the prospect of gains in Ireland is realized, they will be of great value, in keeping down the adverse majority: that is the point to which we are now reduced. We have been swept away, literally, by a torrent of beer & gin. Next to this comes Education: that has denuded us on both sides for reasons dramatically opposite; with the Nonconformists, & with the Irish voters. This is an unstable foundation to build power upon. It is a most singular, & perhaps a premonitory, fact that in most of the cases where we have recently suffered some losses at single elections the verdict has again turned in our favour; for example at Stroud,[3] Hull, in Renfrewshire & elsewhere. Grave questions will probably arise as to our course when the Elections are actually or substantially at end. I hope Charles Lyttelton is safe, but do not feel quite sure as he is persecuted by a Quaker about the C[ontagious] D[iseases] Acts. I must say that, looking not to the quantity but the quality of gains, none can be more acceptable than any which may come spontaneously from Ireland on account of the Land Bill & its fruits. Your principal elections are I suppose due to the Ballot[;] this is so far very good.

7. Sat.

Wrote to Ld Granville—Sir A. Panizzi—Mr Godley—my sister Helen—Mr Cardwell—& minutes. All Saints Ch. 5. P.M. Seven to dinner. Saw the Speaker—Mr Stansfeld—Mr West—D. of Argyll—Mr Goschen—Ld Kimberley—Sir S.R.G.—Sir T.E. May—S.E.G.—Sir W. James—Mr Peel. Also Sir S.R.G. on Estate. Also conversation with C.G. on the probable changes in our position & consequent measures: at first she was startled. Also saw E. Reed: some good[R]. Read Sp. Perceval—Major on the Zeno Voyage.

8. Sexa S.

Chapel Royal mg. Wells St aftn. Wrote to Sir A. Panizzi—and minutes. Dined with the Phillimores. Much & satisfactory conversation with C. & with S.R.G. on the future. Saw Mr Stanley. Read T. A Kempis—

[1] Lists of figures, but not of causes or details on income tax, dated 26 February 1874, in Add MS 44270, f. 297.

[2] Of 2 February, Add MS 44307, f. 225, with election news: tenant farmer gratitude 'will redeem other Irish misfortunes'.

[3] The liberals won both Stroud seats (having lost one as recently as 8 January 1874), but after a petition lost one again.

Cowpers Devotional Poetry[1]—Jenkins on Justification[2]—Gresley's Priests & Philosophers.[3]

9. M.

Wrote to Ld Granville—The Queen l. & Mem.—Ld Advocate—Sir H. Verney—Mr E. Ashley (Tel)—Mr Locke King—Mr T. Hughes—Mr Forster—Mr Bright—Mr [G. W.] Kitchin—& minutes. Dined at Argyll Lodge. Luncheon in G. Square. Read Perceval's Memoirs—Major on Zeno's Voyage. Saw Mr Cardwell—Mr Repington—Mr Kinnaird—Mr Godley. Long conversation in evg with D. of A[rgyll]. Saw Mrs Th.—Lady E.M. Pringle. Packed two boxes of books for Oxford (unattached) Library.[4]

To J. BRIGHT, chancellor of the duchy, 9 February 1874. Add MS 43385, f. 251.

Many thanks for your letter.[5] It would certainly be a comfort and satisfaction to me to see you *before* Monday, for we have many ideas and views in common with reference to the present state of politics and I should like to talk over the situation with you freely and at large.

I am doubtful how far we suffered through any want of organisation which time would have repaired; and I am not aware that either Wolverton or Peel ever saw in this point an objection to the Dissolution. It may be that you are right; but I have no knowledge tending to confirm you. To me it would have been pleasant to go on and fight the Budget—but remember we looked much to the platform on which our friends were to fight the general Election and we thought this moment & a prospective plan of finance would give them a much better one than we could have secured for them in any other way.

I return the note about Mr Maclaren. The question is a very nice one but I have reason to believe that if the Judgeship is filled the Ld Advocate might claim it for himself.[6]

To G. YOUNG, lord advocate, 9 February 1874. Add MS 44543, f. 64.

I am rejoiced to hear of your good prospects & trust you will give the adversary a thorough beating. There is no truth whatever in the statement that the Government either have adopted or contemplate *any* particular course as to resignation. The leaning of my own mind is in favour of the old constitutional

[1] See 13 Feb. 74n.

[2] Probably R. C. Jenkins, *A few words on the Creed of Pius IV as justifying separation from the Roman Church* (1842).

[3] See 14 Dec. 73.

[4] Sending books to G. W. *Kitchin as censor for non-collegiate students at Oxford; they form basis of St. Catherine's college library, where this day's letter to Kitchin is.

[5] Of 8 February, Add MS 44113, f. 93: 'It would have been wiser to have secured the budget . . . the organisation has been almost wholly wanting.'

[6] See 10 Jan. 74n; G. Young became a judge June 1874.

course of meeting Parliament. But the Cabinet must decide. This *can* hardly meet before next week in all likelihood. It is refreshing to see that old Scotland stands to her colours. The question of your Judgeship beyond the Tweed, with the sister question in Ireland, may become serious & rather delicate matter for the consultation of the Cabinet.[1] I will do all in my power to secure it. I have little doubt that the party will profit by its present sore adversity: & I am confident the Conservative party will never arrive at a stable superiority while Disraeli is at their head.

10. Tu.

Wrote to Mr Milbank—W.H.G.—and minutes. Dined with Sir A. P[anizzi] alone. We had much conversation on the character & authority of religion: some on Thomas a Kempis. Saw Mr Goldwin Smith—Mr Godley—Mr A. West[2]—Sir E. Perry—Mr Goschen—Mr Herbert RA—Ld Granville. Worked on books: sent more to Oxford. Saw Mrs Th. X. The last thus? Saw Dowager Lady Stanley. Read Spencer Perceval—Major on Greenland.

11. Wed.

Wrote to Lord Spencer—The Queen Mem.—Rev Mr Kitchin—D. of Argyll—Ld Chancellor—Ld Houghton—Sir H. Johnstone—Mr Fortescue—Mr Danby Seymour—Ld Aberdare—Ld Hartington—& minutes. Saw Ld Granville—Mr Godley—Ld Monck—Mr Forster—Mr Gurdon—Ld Advocate—Mr Peel—Mr Cardwell—Dr Clark—Mr Ayrton—Mr Levy. Twelve to dinner. Finished Major on Zeno—Read Sp. Perceval.

12. Th.

Wrote to D. of Argyll—Sir J. Esmonde—Mr Barnes—Mr Childers—and minutes. Read Merchant of Venice. Saw Mr Gurdon—Mr Dodson—Ld Wolverton—Conclave on Patronage 12-2¾: Ld G., Ld W., A. Peel; Gurdon Sec.—Count Münster (position of R.C.s—entente of Engl. & France from 1830)—Mr Lowe. Dined with Count Münster.[3]

[1] Dispute about the reconstruction of the judicial establishment in Scotland and Ireland and its costs; Add MS 44442, ff. 27, 71.

[2] Who reported *May's views on constitutional implications of not resigning; Add MS 44341, f. 138.

[3] The inside back cover has some indistinct pencilled writing which follows this entry.

To H. C. E. CHILDERS, 12 February 1874. Add MS 44543, f. 66.

I thank you much for your note[1] & I shall be very glad to see you again in Town. Our course will be determined next week, probably on an early day of it, upon the point, nearly the only one that now remains, of meeting Parliament for a formal decapitation, or anticipating the event by resignation in order to save time. This is a great change for many; to some greater than to me, not in what it looks but in what it is in what I must make it [*sic*]. You & I have done much work together. It has ever been to me most satisfactory, cheerfully prosecuted, sadly intermitted & joyfully resumed.

[1] Of 9 February, Add MS 44128, f. 256, from Nice, regretting the defeat, 'although I confess I throughout expected it'.

[VOLUME XXX][1]

Private. No 30.

FEB. 13. 74–JUL. 20. 75.

My ventures are not in one bottom trusted
Nor to one place: nor is my whole estate
Upon the fortune of this present year:
Therefore, my merchandise makes me not sad.
Merch. of Venice I.1.

Confess Him righteous in his just decrees:
Love what He loves, and let His pleasure please.
(Cowper, from Mad. Guyon).[2]

[in pencil:—]

NB Mr L. Stanley's letter. Seymour £5
Aldrich—Wilmot—Tollemache Watch 1 1
Monday Sept. 7–11 C.H.T. Ouvry 3½ PM.

London Feb. 1874.

13. Fr.

Wrote to Archdn Utterton—Sir D. Marjoribanks—W.H.G.—Lady Herbert—Mrs Th.—Sir W. James—Mr Monk—Sir J. Shuttleworth—Mr Adair—Mr Tennyson—Mr Bright—The Queen l. & Mem.—Ld Chancellor—Robn G.—and minutes. We had a personal grief today in C. Lyttelton's defeat:[3] to balance the pleasure of yesterday (F. Cavendish.) Dined with the Wests. Walk with C. Saw Ld Hartington

[1] Lambeth MS 1444.
[2] Final stanza of 'Glory to God alone' in *Poems of Madame de la Mothe Guion*, tr. W. *Cowper (1801).
[3] For E. Worcestershire. See 5, 6 Feb. 74.

—Ld Wolverton—Mr Knowles—Mr Gurdon—Mr Welby—Ld Hartington. Read Rae's Memoir of Wilkes.[1]

14. Sat.

Wrote to Col. Tomline—Pres. American Acad. A. & S.[2]—Ld O. Fitzgerald—Mr Villiers—Ld Crawford—Ld Huntley—Viceroy of I. (Tel.)—Ld Halifax—Ld Advocate—The Queen (Mem.)—& minutes. Dined at Mad. Ralli's. At Lady Ashburnham's 5 P.M. Saw Ld Wolverton—Sir W. Boxall—Mr Gurdon—Sir S.R.G. (Hn Agency)—Mr T.M. Gibson—Granville, Cardwell, & Wolverton in Conclaves on the arrangements which are to follow the resignation. Saw Mr Hayward. Read Rae's Wilkes—Merchant of Venice. I had a letter from the Queen which seemed to me to be of scant kindness.[3] Saw Cowan—poverina[R].

15. Sexa S.

Chapel Royal mg and 5.30 P.M. Saw Ld Wolverton—Mr Cardwell. Walk & conversation with C. Wrote to The Queen—Ld Lyttelton—& minutes. Read Cowper—Thomas a Kempis—Gresley's Priests & Philosophers—Anglocont. Society's Report—Mr Capes's Oxford to Rome & back.[4]

16. M.

Wrote to Ld Chancellor—Sir S. Scott & Co.—Mrs Th.—Mr Chadwick—Mr Strahan—Mr Tennyson—Mr Pease—Earl of Crawford—Sir R. Levinge—Sir D. Marjoribanks—Mr Lambert—Gen. Ponsonby (2 Tell.)—Mr Greville—Duke of Devonshire—Viceroy of I. (Tel.)—Dean of Windsor—The Queen—Letter and four Memoranda. A long hard day. Saw Ld Wolverton—Sir S.R.G. (O.F. & Estates)—Mr Stansfeld—Mr Gurdon—Mr Bright—Mr Fortescue—Conclave on Honours 3-6.

Cabinet Dinner 8-12. See Mem. It went well. I did something toward snapping the ties, and winding out of the coil.[5]

[1] W. F. *Rae, *Wilkes, Sheridan, Fox; the opposition under George the Third* (1874).

[2] C. F. Adams; he was elected foreign honorary member in room of J. S. Mill; Add MS 44442, f. 117.

[3] Complaining at personal inconvenience of Gladstone's wish to meet Parliament; Guedalla, *Q*, i. 446.

[4] J. M. Capes, *To Rome and back* (1873).

[5] His 'startling announcement' that 'he would no longer retain the leadership of the liberal party, nor resume it, unless the party had settled its difficulties'; see *Letters of Lord Aberdare*, i. 360 and Morley, ii. 497. The separate memoranda here mentioned are untraced.

Conversation afterwards with Granville: on the flags, up and down. Then with Wolverton. To bed at 1¾: but lay 3 hours awake (rare for me) with an overwrought brain. But such hours are not wasted, or need not be. In them we are alone with God: and no medicine can at this time be better: the blessed words of Thomas a Kempis are good for me. But indeed all is good. That which is now come is the old aim of my wishes & my most unworthy prayers.

17. Tu.

Wrote to D. of Argyll—Sir J. Lefevre—Ld Sydney—Sir W. Stephenson—Mr Wood—H.M. 2 Mema—Mr Welby—Dean of Windsor—Dr Burrows—Sir C. Trevelyan—Ld Enfield—Marq. of Westminster—Mr Forster—Sir Thos Fremantle—Mr Law—Ld Hartington (Tel.)—Mr M'Clure—Ld Chichester. Saw Ld Wolverton (3)—Ld Granville (2)—Mr Gurdon—Sir W. Boxall—Mr Hayward—Mr Cardwell—Gen. Schenk—Count Münster—Mr Hayward—Dean of Windsor. Twelve to dinner. 12½-6. Went to Windsor and on behalf of the Cabinet resigned. See Mema. Circulated a short Mem. to give account of it. Took with me Merchant of Venice & T. a Kempis: each how admirable in its way!

I was with the Queen today at Windsor for three quarters of an hour, and nothing could be more frank, natural, and kind, than her manner throughout.

In conversation at the audience, I of course followed the line on which we agreed last night. She assented freely to all the honours I had proposed. There was therefore no impediment whatever to the immediate & plenary execution of my Commission from the Cabinet: and I at once tendered our resignations, which I understand to have been graciously accepted.

She left me, I have no doubt, to set about making other arrangements.

We shall be duly informed of the day of final farewell.[1]

18. Ash Wed.

Chapel Royal 12-1¾. Wrote to the Duke of Bedford—Ld Prov. Glasgow[2]—Mr Reed MP.—Mr M. Wilson MP.[3]—Mr Grove—Mr H.S. Thompson—Mr Miller—The Queen (2 Mema)—Ld Sydney—Mr Amory MP.[4]—Gen. Ponsonby—and minutes. Saw Rev Mr Freshfield[5]—Ld Bessborough—Mr Gurdon—Ld Wolverton—Mr Goschen

[1] Dated 7 P.M., 17 February 1874, Add MS 44762, f. 28, circulated to the cabinet.

[2] Diarist's stockbroker, James Watson, offering a knighthood; Add MS 44442, f. 308.

[3] (Sir) Mathew Wilson, 1802-91; liberal M.P. Clitheroe 1847-53, W. Riding 1874-86; cr. bart. 1874.

[4] (Sir) John Heathcoat Heathcoat-Amory, 1829-1914; liberal M.P. Tiverton 1868-85; cr. bart. 1874.

[5] John Minet Freshfield, rector of Stanton Abbey 1862.

—Conclave on disposing of Estimates for 1874-5.—Ld Granville—Sir T. Fremantle. Read Mem. of Wilkes—Merch. of Venice (finished). Saw Ly Lyttelton 5 P.M. tea.

19. Th.

Wrote to Sir W. Hayter—Mr [R.] Green Price—Mr Vickers—Mr Forster—Ld Spencer—Ld Methuen—Mr Gurdon—Draft of (supposed) letter to Mr A. Peel on my intentions—Mr Burton—The Queen (Mem.)—and minutes. Read Rae's Sheridan[1]—As You Like it. Saw Ld Wolverton (2)—Ld Lyttelton—Mr Gurdon—Mr Grogan—Gen. Ponsonby—Lady Waldegrave—Bp of London. Working & clearing in D.St. Luncheon at 15 G. Square—Saw Lady E.M. P[ringle] & Mrs Th. Dined at Panizzi's: much conversation with him & Lord Acton.

To [A. W. PEEL, chief whip], 19 February 1874. Add MS 44762, f. 29.

It is not my intention to assume the functions of Leader of a Parliamentary Opposition in the House of Commons to the new Government. I could even give my opinion if it were generally desired upon the question whether it is expedient that those functions should be at present assumed by anyone else.

Reserving the second point for consideration hereafter if need be, I am desirous not to be misapprehended upon the first. In adopting this resolution I do not found myself (as might possibly be surmised) upon the supposition that I have cause of complaint in any form against any person or body of persons. Such a supposition is untrue in fact, and would even if it were true be insufficient to justify my intention.

In my judgment, public men who have given their best years to the service of the country, are not bound, in the absence of any strong and special cause, to spend that old age, of which I have already crossed or at the least touched the threshold, in the career of stress and contention which the House of Commons offers to me as the leader of a great political party. And I do not recognise any such strong and special cause, in the discharge of the ordinary duties even of Government and certainly still less of Opposition.

I might go further, and observe that after my labours since 1868, I have need of rest; that I have almost entirely neglected the reasonable care of my private affairs: that in my opinion the country has suffered occasionally from undue prolongation of active public life, never from its undue curtailment by voluntary action: that I made an endeavour, the best I could, in 1866-8, to lead the Liberal party in the ordinary sense and for the ordinary purposes of Opposition, and that the result was unsatisfactory. But I do not now seek to open these and other important matters, which are matters of opinion and might be the subject of much discussion. The statement with which I began regarding the prolongation into old age of a contentious life is one upon which it will be felt that each man must of necessity decide for himself.

[1] See 13 Feb. 74.

And the present epoch is like a break in a lease: except indeed that no one can know when it would occur.

Perhaps you will kindly make these sentiments known to anyone who may speak to you or who you may think would be interested in hearing them.[1]

20. Fr.

Wrote to Gen. Schenk—Sec. S.Kensington Museum—Ld Fitzwilliam —Mr Ouvry—Ld Saye & Sele—Mr Welby—Duchess of Sutherland —Helen (sister)—Ld Kimberley—and minutes. Read Rae's Sheridan. Saw Mr Strahan—Ld Chancellor—Mr Gurdon—Ld De Tabley —Mr Grogan—Ld Granville—Mr A. Wood—Ld Bessborough—Ld Sydney—Ld F. Cavendish—C.A. Wood—Dean of Windsor. Went by 5.10 to Windsor: final audience, & kissed hands. H.M. very kind: the topics of conversation were of course rather limited. Dined with the F. Cavendishes.

To LORD KIMBERLEY, colonial secretary, Add MS 44543, f. 73.
20 February 1874.

I had hoped to offer you informal but sincere thanks for your most kind note[2] by word of mouth tomorrow. But I am summoned by anticipation to an audience at Windsor this evening & I suppose I shall not accompany the party tomorrow which I regret. Immolation in good company is better than alone. I must however return my thanks in this way if not in the other. I feel that my colleagues have had much to bear with and from me and therefore I also feel and especially the weight and kindness of your words. I must say that it would have been strange if I had found difficulty in the transaction of official business with one who in all his correspondence sees his way to the point so clearly and finds it so directly and with such a rejection of irrelevant matters, as yourself. In truth I must say in this hour of outward discomforture that there never has been a time in the whole course of our career since 1868 when I felt better pleased either with the acts and attempted acts of the Government or with its members. I trust your official holiday may be accompanied with an effectual relief from domestic anxieties on your own behalf & on that of Lady Kimberley.

21. Sat.

Wrote to Ld Selborne—Mr J.S. Vickers—Ld E. Clinton—Robn G. —W.H.G.—Ld Tenterden—Mr Villiers—and minutes. Read Rae's Sheridan—Metrop.Distr.R. Rs Meeting Report. I cleared my room in D. Street and bad it farewell, giving up my keys, except the Cabinet

[1] Not published; presumably not sent; attributed as intended for Peel from today's diary entry.

[2] Of 18 February, Add MS 44225, f. 148: 'The great and lasting benefits which you have conferred on this country will be remembered long after this passing gale of adverse feeling has been forgotten.'

Key. Saw Sir W. Stephenson—Mr Goulburn—Mr Herries—Mr Rivers Wilson—Mr Welby—Mr Fremantle—Mr Law—Mr Lingen—Sir W. Boxall—Ld Granville—Mr Buxton. Dined with the Jameses. Saw Terry [R]. Five o'clock Tea with Lady Lothian: a noble creature, as ever.[1]

To LORD SELBORNE, lord chancellor, 11 P.M., 21 February 1874. Lambeth MS 1866, f. 113.

Would it not be well that you should hand over to the incoming Lord Chancellor 1. a note of the case and claim of Sir R. Phillimore, for which he of course can supply any materials which you do not possess 2. an intimation of the judgement of the Cabinet respecting the suppostitious [*sic*] claim of Law Officers as such to Judgeships viz. that whether it has been anything or nothing, & whatever it has been, no such claim should exist or be recognised under your Judicature Act? & the full concurrence of our Law Officers with this judgement. I shall take your silence as implying that you agree, & proceed accordingly.[2]

22. 1 S.Lent.

Chapel Royal mg and aft. Dined with the Farquhars. Wrote to Sir Garnet Wolseley—Mr Godley—& minutes. Saw Count Münster. Read To Rome & Back—Greg's Creed of Christendom[3]—First Principles of Religion[4]—Wilkinson on Education[5]—Bennett's Defence of Faith.[6]

To Sir Garnet WOLSELEY, 22 February 1874. Add MS 44543, f. 75.

In quitting an office which has made me cognisant of your military proceedings and in some degree of your character, I call to mind at all events one agreeable duty, as yet unperformed. At least I think it a duty, and I have certainly a desire, in a few brief words to express [to] you my sense of the services which you have been rendering and what is still more of the qualities you have exhibited while engaged in the discharge of your arduous work. This is not the first time when it has been [my] duty in an official capacity to watch closely the course of your military proceedings abroad; and perhaps the force of contrast at least with one memorable case, may have contributed to deepen my impressions. I commenced my observation without prepossession, knowing only in a general way the reputation you have acquired by the skilful conduct of an operation in British North America where you had difficulties to face. In this case of the Gold Coast, it appears to me you were placed under severe and testing trial. You had to deal with enemies savage but intelligent, with [a] pestilential climate,

[1] See 2 Sept. 46; a Roman catholic.
[2] No reply found.
[3] By W. R. *Greg (1851).
[4] Perhaps [T. Downe], *The first principles of the oracles of God explained* (1677).
[5] J. Wilkinson, 'School boards in country parishes' (1874).
[6] By W. J. E. *Bennett (1873).

a country practically (and to a degree I cannot yet comprehend) unknown; and all you had to do was to be done under the closest limitations of time, a circumstance of the greatest embarrassment. It was much to cope with all these difficulties—but it was more that you encountered them in a spirit of humane wisdom and with enlightened and truly Christian views of policy. My congratulations are now those only of a private individual, and of one who, having[1] lived long in the turmoil of business, hopes henceforward to be freed from it. But I cannot help offering them, and offering them most warmly. We owe you gratitude for the bold, intelligent and guarded management of a business, in which even small mistakes might have produced enormous mischiefs. I must not wish, that future difficulties may spring up in order to afford you opportunities of meeting them, but, if they should spring up, I cannot help hoping that it will be found that our country possesses in you one in whose mind and hand may be of value to her in the time of need.[2] Nor will you think it mere prejudice on my part if, in conclusion, I wish on your behalf that, in the contingencies of the venture, you may never be worse supported than you have been on this occasion by the local department and the Admiralty and especially of course by Mr Cardwell.[3]

23. M.

Wrote to Mr A. Peel—The Speaker—Sir S.R.G.—Sir Thos G.—Mrs Grote—and minutes. Read 'To Rome & back'. Saw Sir Chas Reed—Mr Thompson (S. Kensington)[4]—Mr Hayward—Mr Gurdon—Ld Halifax. Saw Fitzroy, X going to BNA. Dined with the Halifaxes.

To H. B. W. BRAND, the Speaker, 23 February 1874. 'Private.' Add MS 44543, f. 75.

I am truly sorry that I did not notice your having called upon me sooner than Saturday evening when I learned you had left town. Your re-election will, I am afraid, be rather tame, in the absence of the Ministers. I will take [it] that nothing that depends upon me is wanting; if I find upon inquiry or rather reference that there ought to be someone to offer you congratulations from the non-Ministerial side. There should certainly I think be an amendment of the language of the Act relative to a voidance of seat on acceptance of office. But this will be a matter proper for the Government to look to. For myself I can do nothing, at my age, to compromise that gift of freedom which the nation has forced upon me, but I do not mean, as at present minded, to quit the House of Commons or to renounce any opportunity of effecting any great national good which time may bring about and in which it may be open to me to take a share. I have thought much during the last seven or eight years on the working and discipline of the Liberal Party, and I suspect it will have to pass through a period of trial and of reflection, before it can again be in a position for regular and thorough service.

[1] Secretary's copy reads 'has'; presumably a slip of the pen.
[2] Wolseley commanded the expedition to Egypt in 1882.
[3] The Gladstones presented Wolseley with china on his return.
[4] Probably E. M. Thompson, assistant keeper of oriental MSS.

To Sir T. GLADSTONE, 23 February 1874. Hawarden MSS.
'Private.'

Accept my best thanks for your kind note of yesterday.[1] My reply to the Queen was first made twelve months ago when we proposed to resign simply from the failure of a great measure in the House of Commons. I repeated it this year with similar expressions of gratitude but with the remark that even if my mind had been open on the question I did not think I could have accepted anything while under that national condemnation which has been emphatically enough pronounced at the elections. I may be wrong in my view of the matter generally but I can only judge for the best. I do not see that I am wanted or should be of use in the House of Lords: and there would be some discrepancy between rank and fortune, which is a thing rather to be deprecated. On the other hand I know that the line I have marked out for myself in the House of Commons is one not altogether easy to hold: but I have every disposition to remain quiet there, and shall be very glad if I can do so.

I cannot tell you with how much pleasure I heard the accounts of Saturday and yesterday from your home of suffering and anxiety. God grant they may be continued, and yet further improved. I take care not to overvalue them, or hastily assume that they secure the future, but at least they are a step towards it. I shall be very glad if in a few days there is relief enough to let me call without the fear of being in the way. What a time of trial you have all had.

24. Tu.

Wrote to Mr Rathbone—Mr Gavin Turriffs[2]—Ld F. Cavendish—and minutes. Visited Christie's. Dined with the Malcolms. Read Rae's Mem. of Fox—As You Like it—Saw Sir D. Marjoribanks—Mr Childers—Mr Gurdon—Agent from S. K[ensington] Museum (respecting objects, wh I value at £2700, sent there.)[3] Street conversations with Mr G. Bentinck—Lord G. Lennox—Ld Bessborough—Mr Franks. Set seriously to work upon my books & papers wh will find me much to do before I establish Cosmos & get rid of superfluities.

25. Wed.

Saw Mrs F[itzroy] on the occasion of her departure to her friends & a good life beyond the Ocean. Wrote to Mr Rugg—Lady Strangford —Mr Goulburn—& minutes. Worked much on books & papers. Saw Dr Clark—Mr Bowman—Scotts—Mr Gurdon. Ten to dinner. Read = yesterday. Conversation with C. on W. & the Agency, S. & the Mission Manifesto.[4]

[1] From Wimbledon, expressing regret at news from Catherine Gladstone that the diarist had declined a peerage; Hawn P.

[2] Had sent work on Aberdeen.

[3] Start of dismantling of his porcelain collection, later sold; see 25 July 74n.

[4] Rescue work.

1. A minister dismissed from office by the nation is in a considerable degree entitled to take counsel with himself.
2. A minister who has lived over 40 years of very laborious life in Parliament is not bound to spend his old age in leading a party.
3. A minister who on his dismissal, in his 65th year, sets about constructing and conducting an Opposition virtually enters into a re-engagement (supposing strength to continue) for the term of that opposition and from the term of Power which may probably succeed it: in short for a time which may very well extend over seven or ten years & to carry him, if he lives, far into old age.
4. If these general propositions are liable to be constrained[?] and restricted[?] in cases where there is some great public cause for which to contend, they are eminently applicable to the present juncture, as there is no such cause which the Liberal party are unitedly prepared to prosecute.[1]

26. Th.

Wrote to Mr Brassey MP.—Mr Bentley—Mr Feilden[2]—and minutes. Read To Rome & back—As You Like it finished—Turriff on Aberdeen[3]—Mines and Miners.[4] Saw Mr Kinnaird—Mr C. Howard—Mr Gurdon—Sir H. Thring—Mr A. Peel—Sir A. Panizzi—Mrs Th.—Mr Cardwell. Arranging prints & papers.

27. Fr.

Wrote to Lady E.M. Pringle—Messrs Freshfield—Miss Faithful—Mr Salusbury—Mr Townley—Mr H.B. Samuelson—Lady Gladstone—Sir T.D. Acland—& minutes. Dined with the Wortleys. Saw Mr Morris (Binder)—Ld R. Grosvenor—Mr Gurdon—Mr Ouvry—Baroness L. de Rothschild. Wrote farewell minutes for the Priv. Secretaries,[5] & the Office Keeper. King's Coll.Hosp. Meeting 2–4. The Duke of Cambridge who has tact & talent used them in the Chair today for a good end & with much effect. Read Vivian Grey[6]—Rae's Memoir of Fox.[7]

28. Sat.

Wrote to Sir R. Phillimore—Dean of Windsor—Sir H. Taylor—& minutes. Saw Ld Prov. of Glasgow—Mr Brand (Ex Speaker)—Mr

[1] Dated by diarist, but apparently at a later time, 25 February 1874; Add MS 44762, f. 34.
[2] Montague Joseph Feilden, 1816–98; liberal M.P. Blackburn 1853–7; cotton spinner.
[3] Untraced work of G. Turiffs; see 24 Feb. 74.
[4] Perhaps *Mines. Reports of Inspectors of Mines . . . for the year 1872* (1873); or an untraced piece by Brassey; letter to him this day also untraced.
[5] Add MS 44762, f. 36.
[6] By *Disraeli (1826); see 20 Mar. 74.
[7] See 13 Feb. 74.

Bowman—Mr Godley—Mr Gurdon. Dined with the T.G.s, happy in their reviving hopes. Read Vivian Grey—Hayward on Parliament.[1] Set aside ab. 300 vols of pamphlets for the shambles!

2 S.Lent March 1.1874.

Chapel Royal mg (H.C.) and aftn 1. Luncheon with the Jameses. Saw R. Neville—Read To Rome & Back (finished)—Manning's Sermons on Sin[2]—and a number of Sermons and Tracts. Wrote to Mrs Th.

2. M.

Wrote to Rev. Mr Christie—Daughter Helen—The Queen—Rev. Sir G. Lewis—Max Müller—Bp of Lincoln—Sir B. Frere—Ld Provost of Glasgow—Mr Saunders—Mr Brand—and minutes. 5 P.M. Tea at Lady Ashburnham's. Saw Mr Hamilton—Col. Taylor—Mr Gurdon—Sir H. Elliot—Mr King. Saw one X. Continued to prosecute the work of order. Dined with the Wortleys. Read Rae's Fox—Vivian Grey.

3. Tu.

Wrote to Ld Odo Russell—Mr Childers—Mr Allen—Mr Ouvry—Robn G.—and minutes. Worked on books papers &c. 5 P.M. Tea at Lady Stanley's. Read Perceval's Memoirs—Vivian Grey. Saw Mr A. Peel—Mr Hamilton—Mr Westell—Mr Knowles. Sir T. Acland *cum* Mr C. Howard, on the Leadership & the Liberal party. I have given up all my keys: quitted D. St a week ago: not an official box remains: bid goodbye to the Ld Steward's Put [*sic*] on Sunday. But I have still the daily visit of a kind Private Secretary: when that drops all is over.

To LORD ODO RUSSELL, ambassador to Germany, Add MS 44443, f. 58.
3 March 1874.

It would pass my ingenuity to misconstrue your letter of Feb. 23.[3] unless indeed I were to charge you with an excess of kindness in writing it. Among the real losses & privations of quitting office will I must say be that I shall no longer read your contributions to the correspondence of the Foreign Secretary from which I have at all times so much both of profit & of pleasure. Granville has probably told you all respecting the recent past which I might less expressively

[1] A. *Hayward, 'The British Parliament' in *Biographical and critical essays*, 5v. (1858-74).
[2] H. E. *Manning, *Sin and its consequences* (1874).
[3] Add MS 44443, f. 22.

repeat: our points of view are I believe exactly the same. The people of this country have condemned us: we naturally think them wrong, & think it odd that they should condemn us for doing what we were charged, & what we engaged, to do. Such is the situation. But I have not time to wait the process of reconversion, which some think will be slow & others quick. For they have give[n] me an opportunity, more *clear* than could have been hoped of fulfilling for myself the great desire of my life, to be delivered from the prospect of passing my old age in the excessive contention & high strain of politics. I am afraid that in the future our ministers & diplomatists are to have no easy time of it. Not least I augur cares for him of Berlin: France & Germany—Church & State: you are hit both ways.

Bismarck's ideas & methods are not ours: they spring out of other traditions, but my sympathies though they do not go with him (& they are not worth a straw) are more with him than against him. I cannot but say that the present doctrines of the Roman Church destroy the title of her obedient members to the enjoyment of civil rights. In this country, I should object to any infringement of them, but out of reverence for the general principle, not because in the particular case there is an unimpeachable claim. I should hate to say this publicly, for I want no more storms; but it may become necessary.

I hope you will fulfil your kind promise of again trying to see us when next you are on leave; & that if you are at my brother in law's in Flintshire you will manage with Lady Odo to come to that quiet retreat. I am so glad there was that GCB available at the last moment.

4. Wed.

Wrote to Lady M. Alford—Rev Mr Kitchin—Mrs Grote—Ld Granville—and minutes. 5 P.M. Tea at Ld Aberdare's. Dined at Sir A. P[anizzi']s: much conversation. Saw Mr Childers—Mr A. Peel—Mr Franks—Mr Hamilton—Ld Acton—Mr Hubbard. Worked on papers books &c. Read Rae's Fox (finished)—Mackay on Popular delusions[1]—Crookes on Psychic Force Phenomena[2]—Vivian Grey.

5. Th.

Wrote to Mr Ouvry—Mr E. Bruce—Mr Highton—Mr Reverdy Johnson—Sir W. Stephenson—Rev. R. Crelly[3]—Ld Spencer—Mr Hamilton—Ld Cottesloe—& minutes.

Conversation with C. on the situation: she is sadly reluctant to my receding into the shade.

Bid goodbye to Turner: who is to come no more.—[E.] Hamilton paid me his last visit: tomorrow I encounter my own correspondence single-handed.

[1] C. *Mackay, *Memoirs of extraordinary popular delusions*, 3v. (1841).
[2] Sir W. *Crookes, *Researches in the phenomena of spiritualism* (1874).
[3] Or Cully; unidentified.

Saw A. Peel (2)—C. Howard—Mr Hamilton—D. of Argyll—Ld Granville; who, after contesting manfully my intentions outright, proceeded to suggest & consider the terms in which they are to be made known. Peel aided. G. takes them tonight to Cardwell & Selborne for digestion.

Dined at Argyll Lodge: conversation with the Duke—who is of my mind on the situation. Read Bp Lincoln on Simony[1]—Calvert on Inns of Court[2]—Vivian Grey. 5 P.M. Tea & music at home. 2-3—attended the House and offered my congratulations to the Speaker after his Election.[3]

For a variety of reasons personal to myself I am not able to enter into any engagement. It is unnecessary to enter into those reasons farther than by observing first that my assumption of the leadership of the Liberal party at this juncture would constitute an engagement of honour reaching in all likelihood over a considerable term of years: and secondly that I am convinced it is beyond my power, in the present state of circumstances and of opinions, to promote the union of the party as its leader and to maintain its credit & efficiency.[4] Under these circumstances it is of course not for me to prejudge or indicate in any manner the course which the Liberal party may take. If they shall deem it their duty to arrange in the usual manner with some other person to discharge the functions hitherto entrusted to me, such person within the limits of action which circumstances at present impose upon me, will have all the support which in an independent position I can give him[5] and I shall be desirous, subject to his consent and approval, to consult for the benefit of the party, confining myself in other respects to individual action.[6]

6. Fr.

Wrote to Mr Goulburn—D. of Roxburghe—Mr Shaw—Mr Plumptre—Mr Highton—Marq. of Ripon—Ld Granville—Mr Granville Vernon. Saw Ld F. Cavendish—Ld Spencer—Ld Ripon—Mr Merritt—Mr Murray—Mrs Th (& luncheon)—The Speaker—Ld Halifax—Duchess of Roxburghe—Duke of R.—Mr Murray. Saw Stanley = Cox: and Laidlaw. X. A little further progress in the work of order. Read Vivian Grey—Deas on the River Clyde.

7. Sat.

Wrote to Mr Millar—Mr Salomons[7]—Ld Sydney—Mr J. Eaton—

[1] C. *Wordsworth, 'On the sale of church patronage and simony' (1874).
[2] F. Calvert, *Remarks upon the jurisdiction of the Inns of Court* (1874).
[3] Brand re-elected; *H* ccxviii. 12.
[4] This sentence added in by diarist on 7 March.
[5] Rest of sentence added in by diarist on 7 March.
[6] Unsigned holograph dated 5 March 1874, Add MS 44762, f. 37.
[7] Unidentified relative of his now deceased colleague at Greenwich.

Ld Wolverton—Mr T.G. Adams—Mr Pulling—Mr Bosanquet[1]—Mr Hamilton—Ld Carlingford. Dined at Ld Cottesloe's (Sir T. Fremantle). They are so pleased.[2] Saw Mr G. Richmond—Sir Turner Paget—Ld Granville (2)—The Speaker—Mr Cowper Temple—Sir A. Panizzi—Lady Lothian—Ld Lisgar: with most of whom I discussed the question of the Leadership. In my view clear & easy enough: but much otherwise by the wishes of others. Read Vivian Grey—The Strauss commemoration Service.[3] Breakfasted at Grillions.

1. To engage now, is to engage for the term of Opposition, & the succeeding term of a Liberal Government. These two cannot probably embrace less than a considerable term of years. (1830-41. 1841-52. 1866-74.)
This is not consistent with my views for the close of my life.
2. Failure of 1866-8.
3. My views on the question of Education in particular are I fear irreconcileable with those of a considerable portion of it. Into any interim contract I cannot enter.
4. In no case has the head of a Govt. considerable in character & duration, on receiving what may be called an emphatic dismissal, become Leader of Opposition.
5. The condition of the Liberal party requires consideration.
   a. It has no present public *cause*[4] upon which it is agreed.
   b. It has serious & conscientious divisions of opinion, which are also pressing, e.g. on Education.
   c. The habit of making a career by & upon constant active opposition to the bulk of the party, & its leaders, has acquired a dangerous predominance among a portion of its members. This habit is not checked by the action of the great majority, who do not indulge or approve it: & it has become dangerous to the credit & efficiency of the party.[5]

8. 3.S.Lent

Vere St Chapel at 11 to hear Dr Coghlan[6] who seemed to me a very notable & very good preacher. St James's (prayers) evg. Much conversation on my future course with Ld Halifax—do *cum* Ld Selborne —Ld Granville—Duke of Argyll. Read Hope on Ch. Congr.[7]— Bartholmess on Huet[8]—Plumptre on Confn & Absolution.[9]

[1] Probably C. B. P. Bosanquet, sec. to the Charity Organization Society.
[2] Fremantle's peerage.
[3] See 21 Apr. 74.
[4] Written over original word, probably 'course'.
[5] Holograph dated 7 March [1874], Add MS 44762, f. 37.
[6] Probably J. C. Coghlan, rector of Mourne Abbey, Mallow, and Irish viceroy's chaplain.
[7] A. J. B. *Hope, *The place and influence in the Church movement of Church Congresses* (1874).
[8] C. J. G. Bartholmess, *Huet, Évêque d'Avranches, ou le scepticisme théologique* (1850).
[9] E. H. *Plumptre, 'Confession and absolution. A sermon' (1874).

9. M. [*Windsor*]

Wrote to Earl Sydney—Dr Haig Brown—Mr Reeve—Mr Shaw Stewart—F. Helbert—Mr Spottiswoode—Mr Ouvry—Dr Carpenter—Sig. Cesare—Rev Mr Chesshyre[1]—Mrs Th.—Archbp Manning. Worked further on the Leadership: & held a meeting with all my old colleagues on it.[2] Saw Mr E. Hamilton—Duke of Edinburgh—Ld Wolverton (2)—Mr A. Peel—do cum Mr Levy—Mr Wellesley—Ld Derby—Ld Cardwell—Mr Walpole—Dean of Windsor—Pr. Leopold. Off at 4.45 to Windsor for the fête, admirably given. We dined in St George's Hall. I was presented to the Duchess of E[dinburgh][3] by the Queen & had a few kind words from H.M. Began Schliemann's Book on Trojan Excavations.[4]

10. Tu. [*London*]

Back to C.H.T. at 11.30. We travelled with the Germans & the Belgians. Wrote to Mr [R.] Dudley Baxter—L.A. Tadema[5]—P. Sayle—J. Ames Stark[6]—C. Thomas. Dined at Ld Essex's. Read Schliemann—Holyoake on Political Gambling.[7] Saw Ld Wolverton 1 + 1 + 1[8]—Mr Cartwright—Rev Mr White—Duchess of Sutherland (respecting HM)—Ld Granville *cum* Ld Wolverton—Mr S. Gladstone—Mr A. Peel. Saw one[R].

11. Wed.

Wrote to Ld Cardwell—Mr Hamilton—Mr Goschen—Mr Vincent—Mr Beal—Sig. Mancini—Mr Belford—Dean of Rochester—Lady Green Price[9]—Mr Edw. Jones[10]—Mr F. Ouvry—Mr T.S. Cooper—Suicidal Circular[11]—Two copies of letters.

11-2—Spent in a discussion raised by Granville on the subject of the leadership, and on the terms of the draft letter which was prepared and provisionally accepted yesterday. With pain & difficulty,

[1] Probably Humphrey Pountney Chesshire, d. 1900?, vicar of Stratton St. Margaret 1864-79.

[2] A. W. Peel wrote on 6 March 1874, Add MS 44270, that the ex-Cabinet 'will call on you tomorrow after a meeting which they propose to hold on the subject of your leadership'.

[3] Marie Alexandrovna, da. of Alexander II, m. duke of Edinburgh Jan. 1874.

[4] H. Schliemann, *Trojanische Alterthümer* (1874).

[5] (Sir) Lawrence *Alma-Tadema, 1836-1912, painter, esp. of archaeological subjects; kt. 1899.

[6] Name scribbled.

[7] G. J. *Holyoake, *Contemporary Review*, xxiii. 638 (March 1874).

[8] See Wolverton's report of talk with 'our friend' (unnamed, ? Hartington) on the leadership; Add MS 44349, f. 5.

[9] Frances Milborough, *née* Dansey, wife of Sir R. Green-Price, see 12 Jan. 66.

[10] Edward Jones of Liverpool, spelling reformer; Add MS 44443, f. 78.

[11] Untraced.

& the aid also of Wolverton & A. Peel, the draft was at last readjusted *tant bien que mal.*

Saw Rev. Mr Macleod—Col. Wilson Patten—W.H.G.—Count Cadorna—Sir W. Gull—Mr Harrison (Lond. Libr.)—Abp Manning 9-11. It is kind in him to come: but most of it is rather hollow work, limited as we are. Read Life of Chorley[1]—Vivian Grey—Baxter on Local Taxation. Attended the Levee. 5 P.M. Tea at Lady Ripons.

12. Th.

Wrote to Dean of St Paul's—Mr Shaw Stewart—Dr Smith—Mr Herbert R.A.—Mr Peake—T. Sidney Cooper (P.S. note)—J.E. Simons—H. Merritt—Ld Granville 2 (*the* letters in final form)[2]—Miss Williams—Sec. Tower Hamlets Meeting[3]—Mr A. Peel. Ten to breakfast. Saw Mr Lyon Playfair—Mr Agnew—Mr C. Parker—Mr Sellar—Sir Thos G.—Mr M. Bernard. Dined with the Wortleys. Saw the Procession: we were recognised at the well known corner.[4] Luncheon at 15 G.S.—X. Read Chorley's Biography—Vivian Grey—Wright on Dublin Univ.[5] Worked on Pictures.

13. Fr.

Wrote to Prof. Blackie—Duke of Westminster—Mr Morton—Rev J. Gommack[6]—Mr Bishop—Rev W. Butler—Mr Matson[7]—Mr Macknight—Mr Ouvry—Mr F. Knollys. Dined at Lady Waldegrave (Carlingford)s. Saw Dean of St Paul's—Ld Granville—Mr Mundella—Count Beust—Count Münster—The Speaker—Sir C. Forster—Mr Eykyn—Lady W[aldegrave] (C.)—Lord Blachford. Attended the Court. Fourteen to breakfast: Herr Joachim (with Miss Stephenson) afterwards: & Mr Wilson. It was very charming music. Read Vivian Grey—Chorley's Biogr. & Autobiogr.

14. Sat. [Worksop]

Wrote to Ld Wolverton—Mr M. Moir[8]—A. J. Marsden[9]—J. Ander-

[1] H. F. *Chorley, *Autobiography, memoir and letters*, 2v. (1873).

[2] See Ramm I, ii. 449 also in *The Times*, 13 March 1874, 8a, with circular to liberal M.P.s on meeting of Commons.

[3] No account found.

[4] Queen and duke of Edinburgh's return from Windsor; *The Times*, 13 March 1874, 10.

[5] C. H. H. *Wright, *The university of Dublin* (1873).

[6] James Gommack or Gomall, nonconformist minister in Oldham; Hawn P.

[7] Thanking William Tidd Matson, 1833-90, Congregational minister, for verses; *The Times*, 21 March 1874, 7f.

[8] Macrae Moir, barrister, on the leadership; Hawn P.

[9] Unidentified.

son—W.J. Durell[1]—D. of Argyll—Mr France[2]—Mr A. Peel—L.N.W. Manager—Mr E. Hamilton. Saw Mr Ouvry—Scotts—Mr Hignett—Dr Liddon. Off at 2.15 for Worksop. Evening conversation with Mr Ouvry and Mr Williams.[3] Also visited the market. Good quarters at the Lion.

15. S 4.Lent. [*Nottingham*]

Shire-oaks Ch. mg & aft. Examined the state of the structure, with regret. Mr O. Brown[4] whom we liked much entertained us. Walked to see the beautiful Steetley Chapel: & the site of the new workings. Drove to Mansfield, seeing some of the Duke of P[ortland']s eccentricities on the way.[5] Reached Nottingham 7.30. Wrote to C.G. Read Scots Congr. Mag.—Hebert Duperron on St Clement.[6] Saw Mr Hine—Mr Williams—Mr T. Wright—Mr Ouvry—Mr O. Brown.

16. M. [*London*]

Wrote to J.W. Conger—Mr A. Strahan. Circuit of business in Nottingham. Saw Church Deputn—Vicar thereon—Mr Ward[7] & others on the Museum. Luncheon at Mr Ward's. Off at 3.15.—C.H.T. at 7. Saw Mr Hignett. Read Vivian Grey—Hebert Dup. on S. Clement—We dined at Marlborough H. Divers Royalty conversations, nothing very notable. A civil talk with Disraeli.[8]

17. Tu.

Wrote to Speaker's Secretary—Mr E. Edwards—P. Wylde—Elijah Oakes—W. Dale[9]—Thos Ensor[10]—W.H.G., MP.—G. Cameron[11]—W.T. Mowbray—Robn G.—Sir W. Drake[12]—Sec. Science & Art Dept—Rev. Dr Haig Brown—Sir T.F. Grove.[13] Dined at Mrs Th's.

[1] Unidentified.
[2] John F. France had sent a book; Hawn P.
[3] Newcastle estate affairs; he was still a trustee.
[4] George Osborne-Browne, d. 1892; vicar of Shireoaks from 1870, advowson held by Newcastle trustees.
[5] At Welbeck, with 'vast and crazy' constructions; see N. Pevsner, *Nottinghamshire* (1951), 197.
[6] V. Hébert-Duperron, *Essai sur la polémique et la philosophie de St Clément d'Alexandrie* (1855).
[7] William George Ward of the Nottingham school of art.
[8] See Morley, ii. 499.
[9] William Dale of Gloucester sent verses; Hawn P.
[10] Thomas Ensor of Exeter; see Add MS 44437, f. 140.
[11] Col. George Poulett Cameron, 1805-82; later a correspondent, Hawn P.
[12] Sir William Richard Drake, 1817-90, solicitor and art historian; kt. 1869.
[13] Sir Thomas Fraser Grove, 1823-97; liberal M.P. S. Wilts 1865-74, 1885-92; cr. bart 1894.

Music at home in evg. Saw Maitland X. Saw Ld Granville—Harry—Mr Merritt—Mr T. Palgrave. Worked on *Chaos* for Kosmos. Read V. Grey—Bray's Anthropology[1]—Van Praet.[2]

18. Wed.

Wrote to Robn G.—Belgian Minr—Mr Ouvry—Mr Broadbent—Dr Barry—Syed Abdoollah—Mr Legge—Mr Pierce[3]—Mr Macdermott.[4] Dined with the Lytteltons. Worked on my papers &c. Saw HNG. (Seaforth)—Agnes (arranging for some gifts).—Lord E. Bruce—Sir R. Phillimore—Ld Granville. Read The Norman People.[5] Saw Graham = Scott. 2-4, Shopping.

19. Th.

Wrote to J. Watson & S.—Sec. Science & Art Dept—Mr G.H. Stanton[6]—Mr F. Hine—Mr F. Ouvry—Mr A. Peel. Dined with Sir W. James. Read The Norman People—Vivian Grey. Twelve to breakfast. Saw Mr Sidney Cooper—Mr Merritt—Mr Bryce—Ld Wolverton—Ld Emly—Mr Newdigate—The Speaker—Mr Leeman—Mr W. Williams—Conclave on Q.s Speech. H of C. 4½-8. Spoke in reply to Sir W.S. Maxwell. I am tempted to say, I would it were the last.[7] Visited Christie's.

20. Fr.

Wrote to Ld Lyttelton—Mr Cowley—H.R. Taylor[8]—R.T. Burnaby—Col. Ackroyd—Mr Hare—G. Spencer—G.J. Walker[9]—Ouvry. Saw Ld Carlingford—Ld Granville—Ld Hartington—Ld Wolverton—Mr Ouvry—Mr Crum Ewing—Mr Wade—Dr Hayman—D. of Argyll. Dined at Panizzi's—much interesting conversation. H of C. 4½-7¾ & after dinner. Spoke on report of Address.[10] Finished Vivian Grey. The first quarter (*me jud.*) extremely clever, the rest trash.[11]

[1] C. *Bray, *A manual of anthropology* (1871).

[2] See 12 Aug. 70.

[3] J. T. Pierce, barrister, sent verses; Hawn P.

[4] C. Macdermott of Portadown sent respects; Hawn P.

[5] *The Norman people and their existing descendants* (1874).

[6] George H. Stanton, of Holy Trinity, Holborn.

[7] *H* ccxviii. 73.

[8] Henry Ryder-Taylor of Ardwick had written to Gladstone on party organization, and published his reply; Ryder-Taylor was denounced as a fraud in the *Manchester Examiner*, 7 April 1874. Add MS 44443, f. 128; see 24 Mar. 74n.

[9] George J. Walker of Teignmouth, sent writings; Hawn P.

[10] *H* ccxviii. 127.

[11] See Morley, ii. 499.

21. Sat.

Wrote to Syed Abdoollah—F.J. Levy—Editor of Echo. Dined with the Balfours. Music afterwards. Worked on arranging the ivories: also papers. 10-12¼. In V.C.s Court to hear the Hayman Judgment: a sad case.[1] Visited Sotheby's. Saw Ld Lyttelton. Read The Norman People—Fonblanque's Memoirs[2] and [blank].

22. 5 S.Lent.

Chapel Royal 10 A.M. & 5½ PM. Luncheon with the Salisburys: dined with the Lytteltons. Saw Russell[R]. Saw Ld Granville. Read Spurgeon's Sermons.[3] J.F. Stephen on Abp Manning[4]—Duperron on St Clement—and many Tracts.

23. M.

Wrote to Ld Wolverton—Mr Rathbone—Robn G.—Mr Simpson—Mr J. Watt.[5] Worked on arr. books & papers. Dined with the Beauchamps. Conversation with Stanhope on Homeric & Aristophanic morals. Saw Mr Morris (binder)—W.H.G. & H.N.G. (on H.s matters) Saw Mrs Russell and her daughter. Read Hayward's Essays[6]—Memoir of Fonblanque. Saw Scotts—Luncheon at 15 G.Sq.

24. Tu.

Wrote to Mr Ouvry—Sec. Science & Art Dept—Mr J.W. Barry[7]—Mrs Willis[R]—Mr J.W. Tonks[8]—Sir W. Drake—Registrar Col.O.—Mr H.R. Taylor.[9] Dined with Mr Murray—much conversation with Dr Smith—Mr Fergusson—Lady R on Weigall—Mr Dickinson—Mr Weigall[10]—also Saw Denison—Warner. Examined Newcastle Papers. Worked on my books. Read Fonblanque—Forsters Dickens[11]—Inscr. Assyriennes.[12]

[1] *Hayman (see 4 Feb. 52) failed in suit to prevent his dismissal as headmaster of Rugby, despite many scholars' sympathy.

[2] E. B. de Fonblanque, ed. *The life and labours of Albany Fonblanque* (1874).

[3] See 29 Dec. 61.

[4] J. F. *Stephen, 'Caesarism and ultramontanism', *Contemporary Review*, xxiii. 497 (March 1874).

[5] John Watt, a well-wisher; Hawn P.

[6] See 28 Feb. 74.

[7] Perhaps John Wolfe Barry, engineer.

[8] Of Birmingham, sent verses; Hawn P.

[9] 'There is little doubt that superior organization . . . has been the main cause of the [tory] victory', but declining to preside at meetings to improve liberal organization; in *The Times*, 1 April 1874, 11d. See 20 Mar. 74n.

[10] Henry Weigall, a sponsor of the Newport refuge; see next day.

[11] J. *Forster, *The life of C. Dickens*, 3v. (1872-4).

[12] J. Menant, *Rapport . . . sur les Inscriptions Assyriennes du British Museum* (1862).

25. Wed. Annunciation.

Saw Mr A. Peel—Mr Dodson—Sir C. Pressly—Dr Smith—J. Wortley. Read Fonblanque—Forster's Dickens. Wrote to Mr Bryce—Author of The Norman People[1]—Rev. J.G. Smith—Mr D.J. Hutt—Rev. C.J. Brown.[2] Saw Temple. Worked on books. Visited Christie's. Presided & spoke at Newport Market Meeting.[3] Eleven to dinner: Sir G. & Lady Wolseley[4] included. Pleased with both: he seemed all he ought to be, & nothing else.

26. Th.

Wrote to Mr W. Pridde—Adm. S. Osborne[5]—Mr Watherley. Saw Mr Aked—Duke of Argyll—Ld F. Cavendish. Worked much on arranging books &c. Went with the F.C.s to see W. Richmond's fine picture of Prometheus. Then to Argyll Lodge—tea. Pleasant dinner at Lady M. Alfords. Read Fonblanque—Osborne on Impressment.[6] Examined for the first time the P. Consort's Memorial. It seems to have much good sculptural work.

27. Fr.

Wrote to Mr E.E. Thomas—Rev. Mr Kitchin—Mr F. Thum—Bp of Brechin—Dr Birch—Messrs Townshend & Barker. Luncheon at 15 G.S. Visited Christie's. Saw Dr Acland—Ld Halifax—Ld Bathurst. Dined at Ld Halifax's to meet the Wolseleys. H of C. 4½-6½.[7] Saw two[R]. Read Fonblanque—De Praet[8]—Florestan of Monaco.[9] 4 hours packing & arranging in the *early*. Visited Suffolk St Gallery.

28. Sat.

Wrote to Mr Ouvry—Lady Wolseley—Mr Main—Ld Cardwell—Mr J. Davis—Rev Mr Jenkins—Dr Orton[10]—Ld Carnarvon—Mr Nicholson—Mr Taylor Innes—Mr H.R. Taylor. Saw Sir A. Wood—Mr Westell—Mr Goschen—Duke of Bedford—Ld Cardwell—Col.

[1] Sent anon., see 18 Mar. 74.

[2] Charles John Brown, Scottish Free-Churchman.

[3] *The Times*, 26 March 1874, 10e.

[4] Louisa, wife of Sir G. *Wolseley (see 2 Aug. 73), whom Gladstone had commended in the Commons on 20 March.

[5] *Sc.* *Osborn; see 2 Dec. 62.

[6] S. *Osborn, *On the impressment of British seamen* (1874).

[7] Ballot: *H* ccxviii. 361.

[8] See 17 Mar. 74.

[9] *Dilke's anon. satire, just published.

[10] Dr Frederick Orton of Hornsey had written on tree-felling; Hawn P.

[C.] N. Sturt. Dined at D. of Bedford's. Worked on House arranging. 12-8½. To the B[ethnal] Green Museum with Col. N. Sturt. An astonishing display of the wealth of one; & in many respects a surfeit of beauty.[1] Visited the French Exhibn.

29. Palm S.

Chapel Royal 10 AM. St Jameses evg. We went to Wimbledon for luncheon & I was delighted to see Ida [Gladstone] who has a reprieve, & a hope at least of more. She seems so ready & fit for *all.* Tea & conversation with Lady Lothian. Dined with the F.C.s. Conversation with him. Conversation with T.G. on Leith Anglesea The House of G & Co &c. Read Duperron on St Clement of Alex.—and many tracts.

30. M.

Wrote to Dr Butler—E.W. Hamilton—Robn G.—J. Watson & S.—Mr Blyth—Rev. Mr Goalen—Mr Saunders—Mayor of Carnarvon[2] —Sec. N. Portrait Gallery—Mr J. Harvey.[3] Worked on books &c. Saw Ld Granville—B. Benjamin—Mr Merritt—Dr Birch (on Achaioi) —Mr Peel—Mr Taylor Innes. My work on arranging my Library closed today. I have here some 3500 volumes. St James's (H.C.) at 8 AM. Read Owen's Autobiogr.—Fonblanque—Milton Areopagit. & Decrees: wh are somewhat horrible.[4]

31. Tu.

St Martin's 8 AM. Wrote to E.W. Hamilton—Mr Thos Machin[5]—W. Greig[6]—N.E. Clery[7]—A. Sargent[8]—Mr Cyrus Field—Ld C.J. Coleridge—Mr Cookesley—Mr Vickers. 6¾-9½: To St Paul's for the Passion music & service. The music was fine, the organisation was admirable. Saw Mr Falck[9]—Mr Peel—Lady Salisbury—Mr Smollett. Arranging maps—Court Uniforms &c. Also Newc. papers. H of C. 4½-5½.[10] Saw Mr Macmillan—Messrs Wms & Norgate (on Homeric matters). Read Milton Areop. (finished).

[1] The Wallace collection was deposited in the Bethnal Green Museum for a year.
[2] James Rees; business unmentioned in city's records.
[3] Joseph Harvey, organiser of liberals in Leicester; Hawn P.
[4] First published in 1644.
[5] Bookseller in Old Kent Road.
[6] Possibly Walter Greig, Soho merchant.
[7] On Irish land; Add MS 44543, f. 80.
[8] Ambrose Sargent, oil supplier.
[9] Perhaps Ernest Falck, stationer.
[10] Misc. business: *H* clxviii. 480.

Wed. April One. 1874.

St Martin's 8 AM. Wrote to J. Watson & S. (Tel.)—Sir G. Wolseley—Harry—Sir W. Harcourt—Robn G.—Mr Dickinson—Sir Thos G.—Wms & Norgate—Mr Ouvry—Mr Ballard—Mrs Ralli—Editor of Daily News[1]—Mr E. Hamilton—and minutes. Saw Sir Harc. Johnstone—Mr B. Benjamin—Ld Granville—Mr Playfair—Sir A. Panizzi—Dr Birch—Mr Hamilton—who showed me his very singular and interesting musical invention.[2] At the Museum 4-6 read & made notes from De Rougé.[3] Read also Forster's Dickens—Fonblanque.

2. Th.

St Martin's 8 AM. Wrote to Mr S. Bannister—Mr Linell—Mrs Th.—Mr Pryer[4]—Mr . . .—Mr J. Russell—Sir A. Panizzi—Mr Ambrose de Lisle. Luncheon at 15 G.S. & Goodbye. Sat to Mr Dickinson. Saw Dr Clarke—Mr Hamilton. Calls, business, much packing & arranging papers. Read Fonblanque.

3. Good Friday [Hawarden]

St James (with H.C.) mg—and St Anne's aft. (Bach's Passion). Wrote to Mrs Russell & delivered the letter myself with books for her daughter. God speed them. Wrote to Williams & Norgate—Dr Buchanan—Ed. Echo—Edmn & Douglas—Mr J. Chambers. Wound up with a good deal of labour: & closed my door, perhaps hardly now mine, behind me. Off at 8¾. Reached Hawarden at 3.30 AM. and so to bed. Read Renan's *Apôtres.*[5]

4. S.Easter Eve.

Ch 7 PM. Rose only for breakfast. Wrote to Townshend & Barker—Mr R. Barker—C.G.—Mr D. Geddes.[6] Long conversation with Mr Vickers. Another with S.R.G. to whom I spoke not only of the Agency, but of the general state of my affairs. Also in part with Willy. Read Ramsay's Reminiscences[7]—Wickham's Horace[8]—*Touched* Homer.

[1] Sending correction to report of his letter to H. Taylor (see 24 Mar. 74); *Daily News*, 2 April 1874.

[2] Obscure; E. W. *Hamilton was a keen opera-goer.

[3] Viscount O. C. C. E. de Rougé, probably *Mémoire sur l'origine égyptienne de l'Alphabet Phénicien* (1874).

[4] Charles Pryer, cabinet maker.

[5] J. E. Renan, *Les Apôtres* (1866).

[6] (Sir) William Duguid *Geddes, 1828-1900, professor of Greek at London 1860-85, principal of Aberdeen University 1885.

[7] See 10 Sept. 59.

[8] E. C. *Wickham, *Works of Horace with a commentary* (1874).

5. Easter Day.

H.C. at 8.—Morning Prayer at 11. Evening 6½. All my family save only A[gnes]. Read Memoir of Ramsay—Newman's Sermons[1]—Stoughton's Hist. of the Ch.[2] Wrote to C.G.—Rev Mr Bullock—Sec. G.P.O.

6. Easter M.

Ch. 8¾ AM. Wrote to Mr H.J. Whitling—Mr Dobbie[3]—C.G.[4]—Mr Beresford Hope. Saw Mrs Burnett (and spoke of Mr V[ickers].) Set hard at work on a translation of the great Reply.[5] It is a work that enchains when once begun. Read [blank's] Homerische Frage.[6]

7. Tu.

Ch 8 AM. Holy Communion. Wrote to C.G.—Mr Cassidy[7]—and Mr Macdona.[8] Saw Mr Vickers—Mr Wickham on the admn of Jews. Worked well at the Version. Also began a Preface. Read Richardson on the Simplicity of Life[9]—Homerische Frage. Treecutting with my sons. This Rectory interior is truly notable, truly holy, and truly priestly.

8. Wed.

Ch. 8½ A.M. The party went off. Wrote to Sec. Royal Acad.—Mr R. Stanton[10]—Mrs G.—Sir S. Scott & Co. Cut four trees with Herbert. Conclave on the Cross Tree Farm. Saw Mr Vickers. Finished in the rough my Translation of the Reply of Achilles, & wrote it out. Read Stanton's Pamphlet.

[1] J. H. *Newman, *Tracts, theological and ecclesiastical* (1874).

[2] J. *Stoughton, *Ecclesiastical history of England* (1874).

[3] James J. Dobbie, sec. of Glasgow University Liberal Association, invited diarist to stand as rector of Glasgow University; reply untraced; Gladstone defeated Northcote for the post 15 Nov. 1877. Hawn P.

[4] Bassett, 201.

[5] His tr. of 'The reply of Achilles to the envoys of Agamemnon' in *Contemporary Review*, xxx (May 1874); Add MS 44693, f. 282.

[6] H. Duentzer, *Die Homerischen Fragen* (1874); see 12 May 74.

[7] B. J. Cassidy, otherwise unidentified.

[8] John Cumming MacDona, rector of Cheadle, formerly of Sefton, had sent china; Hawn P.

[9] R. Richardson, *The simplicity of life* (1873).

[10] *Sic*; not further identified; his pamphlet not found.

9. Th. [*Courthey, Liverpool*]

Ch. 8½ AM. Wrote to W.S.V. Northy(?) Esq.[1]—Mr Edwards—Mr Agnew[2]—Canon Woodard—Mr Rathbone—Mrs Th.—C.G.—Mr A. Wilson—Mr Bullock. Reviewed my Translation of the Reply of Achilles. Worked on accounts and (private) affairs. Off at 2.15 to Chester. Courthey at 6. Saw Mr R. Barker (Agency &c.)—Messrs Townshend & Barker—Robn G. respecting Seaforth in evg. A hearty welcome here as ever: dinner of 10, all *men* alas. Read Hayley's Cowper.[3] Wrote some Preface to the Reply of Achilles.

10. Fr.

Wrote to Mr Knowles—C.G.—Mr Wilberforce. Finished Preface to the Reply & dispatched it. 12-2½ Conclave on Seaforth matters. They are very bad, but I hope we laid the ground of some improvement.[4] Saw the Pictures at Mr Agnew's. Larger party: music in evg. Read Hayley's Cowper.

11. Sat. [*Hawarden*]

Left Lpool at 1.40. Wrote to Mr W.T. Pears[5]—Messrs Townshend & Barker. Attended Chester School Meeting. Saw Town Clerk of Lpool —Robn G. further on Seaforth—Mr Harris on do. Wrote *Preface* to the Thesauros Homerikos[6] (which does not yet exist). Read Cowper's Letters—Amos on Internat. Law.[7] Hawarden Ch. 7 PM.

12. 1 S.E.

Church 8 AM (H. Commn) 11 A.M. and 6.30 P.M. Wrote to Sec. P.M. General—Keeper of the Vote Office—Mr A. Clayden[8]—W.H. Pearce—R.H.I. Palgrave[9]—H. Bowie (Ed.Philos.Ind): Mr J.E. Hughes —A.W. Peel. Read G. Words (Livingstone—Butler)[10]—Guettée's Pape Schismatique[11]—Cowper's Letters—Littledale Tract on Ch. of

[1] Possibly W. H. Northy, later a correspondent on Cornish liberalism.

[2] (Sir) William *Agnew, 1825-1910; art dealer; liberal M.P. S.E. Lancs. 1880-85, Stretford 1885-6; cr. bart. 1895.

[3] W. *Hayley, *A tribute to the memory of William Cowper* (1808).

[4] The family estate; see 18 Apr. 74.

[5] William T. Pears, of Pears, Logan and Eden, Liverpool solicitors.

[6] See Add MS 44762.

[7] S. *Amos, *Lectures in international law* (1874).

[8] Arthur Clayden, agricultural trade unionist; wrote *The Revolt of the Field* (1874), see next day.

[9] (Sir) Robert Harry Inglis Palgrave, 1827-1919, ed. *The Economist* 1877-83.

[10] *Good Words*, 279, 233 (1874).

[11] F. R. Guettée, *La Papauté schismatique* (1863).

E.[1]—and other Tracts. Conversation with C. on home matters, Vickers, Wade and the rest.

13. M.

Ch. 8½ AM. Wrote to Messrs Watson & Smith—Rev Mr Bullock—Mr S. Amos—Messrs Cassell[2]—Mr Vickers—Dr Russell (Maynooth). Worked on Homeric writing: began my Thesauros Homerikos. Cut three trees with Herbert. Conversation with him on Homer. Unpacked 3 cases of books. Read Amos's Lectures—The Revolt of the Field.

14. Tu.

Ch. 8½ AM. Wrote to M. Michel Chevalier—Sir W. Farquhar—Mrs Begbie—Messrs Cassell. Cut two trees with H. Worked on Homer. Read Garibaldi, a Play[3]—Hayley's Cowper.

15.

Ch. 8½ AM. Wrote to Mr B.J. Cassidy—Mr Jas Knowles—Mr Peel—Abp Manning—Dr Liddon—Mr Panter[4]—Rev Mr Wilberforce. Revised my 'Reply of Achilles', corrected Proofs and enlarged Preface. Also other work on Homer. Cut a tree with W., another alone. Read Cowper's Letters—Revolt of the Field—Pope's Homer.

16. Th.

Ch. 8½ AM. Wrote to Ld F. Cavendish—Mr Newton—Mrs Hamilton—Mr G. Weeks[5]—Messrs Watson & S.—Mr F. Maskelyne[6]—Mr J. Barnard[7]—Mr E. Greenep[8]—Mr W.H. Hitchin. Cut up an Oak bough for firewood. Conversation with S.R.G. on Homer. Worked on Thesauros. Read Revolt of the Field—Hayley's Cowper.

17. Fr.

Ch. 8½ A.M. Wrote to W.H.G. (2)—Mr Tilley (Tel.)—Went with C. to the Silver Well Wood to inspect. Worked on Thesauros: did κήρυξ.

[1] R. F. *Littledale, 'The relation of the clergy to politics', *Contemporary Review*, xxiii. 92 (December 1873).
[2] London publishers.
[3] Perhaps *Garibaldi; or the rival patriots; a dramatic operetta in two acts* [by R. Davis] (1860).
[4] John Panter of London.
[5] Perhaps G. W. Weeks, wrote on India.
[6] Untraced.
[7] James Barnard of Erith, on religious reform; Hawn P.
[8] *Sic*; untraced.

Read Br.Q.Rev. on Gladstone Govt.[1]—Hayley's Cowper Finished I. Saw J. Bailey:[2] & much busy measurements & arrangements for more stowage of papers & for an addition of 1100 volumes.

18. Sat.

Ch. 8½ A.M. Wrote to Duke of Norfolk—Mr Childers—Mr Godley —Mrs Begbie—Mr Picton—Speaker's Sec.—Sir A. Panizzi. We went to Queensferry in the morning to see the Bore which was very striking & requires much precaution at the Ferry. Soon after passed a market boat at 12 m an hour: then a raft which first broke a chain & then was broken by one. Worked on Homer. Read Cowper's Letters. Conversation with C. on Agency—with Harry on Seaforth & the incomprehensible though doubtless kindly meant proceedings of Robn there, which now appear to have lost i.e. destroyed for me £6000.

19. 2 S.E.

Holy Communion 8 A.M. Ch. 11 AM & [blank]. I am ashamed to have been wakened between 4 & 5 by the Seaforth trouble which I thought I had dismissed from my mind there being no doubt as to what ought next to be done. Wrote to Mr Stanley Lucas[3]—Rev. Mr Jenkins—Mr Tuck—Dean of St Asaph—Mrs Th.—Mrs Hamilton —W.H.G.—Lady F. Cavendish—Mr Ambrose de Lisle. Conversation with Harry on the Seaforth Business: lest he should be worried. Read Mr Jenkins's Tract[4]—Br.Qu.Rev. on Ultramontm—Cowper's Letters.

20. M.

Ch. 8½ AM. Wrote to Mr Knowles—Mr Vickers. Saw Mr Vickers—Mr Wade (2). Began felling a large ash with Stephy. Worked a good deal on Thesauros Homerikos. We moved to the Castle: where C. & I keep house till August, & S. is at once host & guest.

21. Tu.

Ch. 8½ AM. Wrote to Ld Lyttelton—Mr Bass M.P.—Mr Morier—Dr Döllinger—Robn G.—Mr Kinsman. Worked on Thes. Hom. Also

[1] *British Quarterly Review*, lix. 470 (April 1874).
[2] John Bailey, Hawarden joiner. [3] Untraced.
[4] Probably E. Jenkins, 'Glances at inner England' (1874).

on partially arranging pamphlets. Also examined Mr Moncure Conway's charge agt me respecting Strauss.[1] Pursued the cutting job with Stephy. Read Q.R. on Schliemann.[2]

To J. J. I. von DÖLLINGER, 21 April 1874. Add MS 44140, f. 293.

It was in the Autumn of 1845[3] that I had the honour and pleasure of making your acquaintance; and, as your words and acts ever since have shown, acquiring your friendship. Even that period appeared to me critical; but through what, and into what, a time have we since lived! and what may or may not the next term of thirty years produce? At that time, I as little dreamt of the great movements and agitations of States, Churches, nations, which have since occurred, as I did of the actual course of my own life, and the responsibilities to which, without my own seeking, I have been called.

It is most true, with respect to this country, as you state more generally, that there is a strong process of dogmatic and of religious decomposition at work among us. In 1845, this had not begun. My public life began in 1832, and so did my social life in connection with the capital. For the first half of it, for over 20 years, everything was tending to the extension and consolidation of belief. During its latter half, has set in a strong reaction, adverse to religious dogma in whatever shape. And the seat of the first spring of the earlier movement has also been the centre and base of the recoil, namely Oxford. It is the fashion to ascribe the change to science, i.e. physical science, and to criticism and research. Such is not my view. There were some traditional superstitions among us, dating in some degree from the sixteenth century, which could not bear the light, and which in their fall have damaged or destroyed the ill-grounded faith of some. But I consider that other influences have acted with greater force in the same direction; on which I will not now enter. For I must not be too long: and I wish to say that all along, by the side of this counter-movement, and in despite of it, the original religious and dogmatic movement has continued, both in Oxford and out of it. And though for the last ten or fifteen years it has been divested of its Romeward aspect, it has constantly assumed a more Catholic character. That insularity, with which you most justly reproach the English form or forms of religion, is in progressive diminution; and our Churchmen have a wider outlook than formerly. I do not speak here of those called Ritualists, who have given great offence, but have perhaps had a considerable influence in stopping the secessions, which were a greater and more ruinous mischief than any that indiscretion on their part can bring in. I will explain my meaning by an anecdote of Archbishop Manning. In 1847 he was very ill, and thought himself dying, all but dead. Perhaps wrongly, for the habit of his mind is exaggerative; but truly. In 1848 he had got well; and spoke to me of his mental experience during his illness. He said that his nearness to the other world had permitted him to see more, and more clearly, than is given to others who have not gone so near. That he had tried and tested his own spirit on the subject of his religious position in the Church of England. That no words could sufficiently convey to me the strength of his conviction on two

[1] M. D. Conway, *David Friedrich Strauss* (1874) accused Gladstone of having 'falsely interpreted' Strauss's *The Old Faith and the New.*

[2] *Quarterly Review*, cxxxvi. 526 (April 1874).

[3] See 30 Sept. 45.

points: first that the Church of England remained what it had ever been, a part of the Catholic Church: secondly that his security of position depended on her character in this respect, and that he wholly renounced all claims in respect of her political establishment or national authority. This frame of mind, in which he then dwelt with all the appearance of certainty and solemnity, and I am sure with all the sincerity, that he has since shown in a different direction, though renounced by him, has become more and more the prevailing frame among Churchmen of thought and knowledge. But I turn from this great subject, though I should have much more to say on it.

My sheet fortunately leaves me but little room for egotism. Of that little, I will use at least one portion well, by expressing the delight with which I learn from Mr. Morier that you are in great health and vigour. May these long be continued to you, for the work which you have to do.

In all that relates to myself personally, your letter is singularly congenial to me. The liberty, which has long been the object of my desire, has in a manner been forced upon me by the emphatic dismissal I have received through the vote of the English constituencies. I have not recorded any vow on the subject of return to office; but I think it very unlikely that any adequate cause should arise to bring me back to my recent position. I have already recommenced my former labours. The main immediate purpose I have before me is to prepare and publish a work which is to be termed 'Thesauros Homerikos; an Index or Account of things noted from the text of the Iliad and the Odyssey.' I know of no book—certainly Friedrich's *Realien*[1] is not one—which gives a full and easily accessible account of the *contents* of the Poems: and such a work I am convinced will be of great value: of much more probably, than my speculations upon them.

22. Wed. [*London*]

Off at 8.15. Reached 21 C.H.T. at 3. Wrote to Mr H. Lawrence—Mr Phillips—M. Botting—Hankin[2]—J.A. Smith—T. Bruce[3]—Ash—Dyler. Saw Ld Granville—Ld F. Cavendish—Mr Morier—The Speaker—Mr Lowe—Sir W. Harcourt—Mr Stansfeld—W.H.G. Read The Revolt of the Field. Book shopping. Dined with the Speaker.

23. Th.

Wrote to Dr Collins—Mr Woosnam[4]—H. Reich[5]—A. Bourne—W.T. Deverell[6]—Mr J. Barry—G.E. Jones—S.J. Wright—Adm. Collier. Conclave on finance at Ld Granville's. Saw Mr Goschen—Mr Knowles—Mr Peel—Mr Bass—Mrs Grote—Mr Hankey—Mr Childers. Luncheon at No 15 G.S. H of C 4½-7. Spoke on Budget.[7] Dined at Sir A. Panizzi's.

[1] See 10 June 57.

[2] H. A. T. Hankin of Canonbury; see Add MS 44443, f. 151.

[3] Of Gibson Square, London.

[4] Perhaps Richard Woosnam, wrote on tithes.

[5] Perhaps Henry Reich, London marquetry cutter.

[6] Possibly William Henry Deverell, London barrister.

[7] Supporting Northcote's first budget: *H* ccxviii. 991.

24. Fr.

Wrote to Earl of Devon—Rev M. M'Coll—Mr Draper—Mrs Tyler—Mr Ouvry—Treasurer of Guy's—and minutes (for W.H.G.). Dined with the Lytteltons: a most pleasant family party. Saw Mr Fayerman—Ld Lyttelton—Mr Strahan—D. of Norfolk—Mr Bright—Messrs Sotheby—Mr Peel—Ld Granville. H. of C. 4¾–7. Spoke in ansr to Mr Smollett's attack.[1] Read Q.R. on Schliemann—on the Liberal Party.[2] Revised and further corrected my Translation, with the aid of Lyttelton's criticisms.

25. Sat. St Mark. [*Hawarden*]

Wrote to Editor of the Echo[3]—Rev. Mr Molesworth—Mr Strahan—Mr Hubbard—Ld Lurgan—Bp of St Andrew's—Robn G.—Mr Maclehose. Left 21 C.H.T. 4.40. Hawarden at 11. Saw Mr Ouvry—Lord F.C. (on finances). Visited Christie's. Saw Ld Cardwell. Had a long interesting conversation with Mrs Grote, & made some inspection of Jeremy Bentham's theological MS. Finished Revolt of the Field. Luncheon at 15 G.S.

26. 3 S.E.

Ch. 11 AM & 6½ P.M. Wrote to Mr Ambrose de Lisle—Rev. Mr Rowley[4]—C.G.—Editor of the Rock[5]—S.H. King. Read Lpool Poem on W.E.G.—Jones on Spiritualism[6]—Remarks on Spiritual Phenomena[7]—Q.R. on Bp Wilberforce.[8]

27 M.

Ch. 8½ AM. Up at 6.15 when Harry & I finished the large ash before breakfast. Wrote to Ld Wolverton—Mr Kinsman—Mr Picton—C.G. Worked on Ἵππος. Read Chabas[9]—Buchholz Realien[10]—Nathalie.[11] Rummaging and arranging Pamphlets. Saw Mr Vickers.

[1] P. B. Smollett moved to censure the 'precipitate' dissolution; rejected without division: *H* ccxviii. 1113.

[2] See 21 Apr. 74; *Quarterly Review*, cxxxvi. 566 (April 1874).

[3] Not published.

[4] Adam Clarke Rowley, ultramontanist and vicar of St Matthias, Bristol.

[5] In *The Rock*, 1 May 1874, denying truth of its article on 24 April.

[6] J. Jones, *Spiritualism the work of demons* (1871).

[7] Perhaps *Spiritual phenomena or invisibles* (1867).

[8] *Quarterly Review*, cxxxvi. 332 (April 1874).

[9] F. J. Chabas, probably *Études sur l'antiquité historique* (1872).

[10] E. Buchholz, *Die Homerischen Realien*, 3v. (1871–85).

[11] J. *Kavanagh, *Nathalie; a tale*, 3v. (1850).

28. Tu.

Ch. 8½ AM. Wrote to J. Watson & Smith—Dr Smith—Mr Murray—Robn G.—C.G. Felled a small oak. Worked on Thes.Hom. 'Hippos'. Arranging pamphlets. Tea party at five. Read Nathalie—Eastmead on Juventus Mundi.[1]

29. Wed.

Ch 8½ AM. Wrote to Sec.Soc. Antiquaries[2]—Rev. H. Allon—Mrs Grote—Ld Provost of Glasgow—Ld Selborne—Mr A. Jennings.[3] Worked much on Hippos, and began Metals. Felled an Oak. Saw Mr Wade—C.G. came—Read Nathalie—Q.R. on German Ch. battle.[4]

30. Th.

Ch. 8½ AM. Wrote to Rev. E. Wilberforce—Mr Smollett—Mr Tallents—Mr Randle—Mr Macleod—Mr Jevons[5]—Prof. Rawlinson. Worked on the Place of Homer in History and Chronology. Read Nathalie. Part felled an Oak. Walk with C.

Frid. May 1.74. SS.Philip & James.

Church 8¾ A.M. Wrote to Canon Rawlinson—Mr Coleman MP[6]—Mr Hanson—Bp of Manchester—Mr A. Peel—Rev. Dr Flemyng.[7] Brought the oak down: & walk with C. Also worked on arranging pamphlets. Worked on Thes.Hom. Article Metals. Read Nathalie—Chabas, Etudes sur l'Histoire Ancienne.

2. Sat.

Ch. 8½ A.M. Worked on the Place of Homer in Hist & Chronol. Arranging pamphlets. Felled (with Harry) two oaks. Read F. Lenormant[8]—Lauth, Homer u. Ægypten[9]—the King's Coll. Hospital

[1] Untraced review.
[2] C. Knight Watson.
[3] Angus Jennings of London, on publication of speeches; Hawn P.
[4] *Quarterly Review*, cxxxvi. 289 (April 1874).
[5] W. S. *Jevons had sent his *Principles of Science*, 2v. (1874) the last chapter of which discussed Gladstone's Liverpool address; Add MS 44443, f. 184; diarist's views in Lathbury, ii. 100.
[6] Thanking Norwich Liberals for their address, in *The Times*, 7 May 1874, 8a.
[7] Francis Patrick Flemyng, 1823-95; in South Africa; from 1870, priest in Scotland.
[8] F. Lenormant, *Les premières civilisations*, 2v. (1874).
[9] See 22 Aug. 73. Sometimes rendered as 'Lauch' by diarist.

Pamphlets—Kortright's A little lower than the Angels.[1] C. kept her bed for a heavy cold.

3. 4 S.E.

Ch. 11 AM with H.C. and 6½ P.M. Wrote to Ld Wolverton—Bp of Brechin—Mr King—Ld F. Cavendish—Robn G.—Lady F.C.—Ld R. Montagu—Herbert J.G. Read Via Cathol. Part III[2]—Miss Noel, Name of Jesus[3]—Thompson on Ultramontanism[4]—Germs of Romanism in the Prayerbook[5]—Irons on New Legislation[6]—Colenso's Argument.[7]

4. M.

Ch. 8½ A.M. Wrote to Mr C.T. Newton—Mr Meacock—Rev S.E.G. —Mr T. Ogilvy (Packet Cont.Rev.).[8] Saw Mr Wade—Rev. S.E.G. Walk over the Park with S. & Mr Wade to consider 'improvements'. Worked on Thes.Hom. and on Homer in History.[9] Read Morris's Poems[10]—Lenormant Hist. & Premières Civilisations.

5. Tu.

Ch. 8½ AM. Wrote to Mr C.T. Newton—Ld Wolverton—Mr Vickers —Herbert J.G. Worked on Thes.Homer. and on Place in History. Saw Mrs Catherall. Read Manchr Cathedral letters—Lenormant Prem. Civilisations. Felled an oak.

6. Wed.

Ch. 8½ AM. Wrote to Watsons. 10½–11½. Conclave with Mr Hanson on Schools, &c. Worked on Thes.Hom. and (principally) on Place in Hist. & Chronol. Felled an oak. Made a money-plan for [J.] Ellen Griffiths, & saw her.[11] Read Cowper's Letters—Kemble on Macbeth.[12]

[1] F. A. Kortright, *A little lower than the angels* (1874).

[2] See 9 Feb. 73.

[3] C. M. Noel, *The name of Jesus and other poems* (1873).

[4] J. P. Thompson, 'The contest with Ultramontanism in Germany' (1874).

[5] Untraced.

[6] W. J. *Irons, 'New legislation for the Church' (1874).

[7] J. W. *Colenso, probably *The argument . . . before the Supreme Court of the colony of Natal* (1867).

[8] On Knowles' staff?

[9] 'The place of Homer in history and in Egyptian chronology', *Contemporary Review*, xxiv. 1, 175 (June, July 1874); Add MS 44693, f. 306; Schliemann's annotations on it at Add MS 44443, f. 249ff.

[10] W. *Morris, probably *The Earthly Paradise*, 3v. (1868–70).

[11] A further instalment; see 13 Aug. 65 fl.

[12] J. P. *Kemble, *Macbeth and King Richard the Third* (1817).

7. Th.

Ch. 8½ AM. Wrote to Ld Granville—Messrs Knowles—Mr Dodson—Worked on Thes.Hom. and Place in History. Read Cowper's Letters. Finished Kemble's Macbeth: it is not very high criticism. Read Chabas. Walk with S.R.G. Tea party in afternoon.

8. Fr.

Ch. 8½ AM. Wrote to G.K. Matthews[1]—Ld Stanhope—Rev P. Frost[2]—Mr Hankey MP. Worked on Thes.Hom. & (chiefly) on Place in History which makes progress. Walk with C. & in the wood. Read Cowper—Lauch's Homer und Ægypten.

9. Sat.

Ch. 8½ AM. Wrote to Rev. Mr Molesworth—Bp of Brechin—Dr Gregory — M.Gen. Bowie — Mr Bradley[3] — Miss Kortright —W. Campbell and worked through a good deal of trash. Tree cutting with H. Read Cowper's Letters—Anti-Civil Service Co-op. Report[4]—Archd. Denison's Speeches.[5] We were actually *nine* to dinner.

10. 5 S.E.

Ch. 11 A.M. & 6½ PM. Wrote to Ld Wolverton—Prof. Jevons—Mrs Th.—Robn G. Walk with C. Read The Nonconformist—Jevons, Concluding Chapter[6]—Mrs Butler's remarkable Pamphlet[7]—Dr . . . on the 'Acts': very smashing—And divers other tracts.

11. M.

Ch. 8½ AM. Wrote to Bp of London—
Mr Jolly
—A. Reed
—J.C. Grey } Greenwich matters
Mr S.G.F. Perry—Mr R. Rowe. Worked on Homer, Place in History

[1] Unidentified.

[2] Percival Frost, vicar in Halesworth, sent mistake in Gladstone's 'Shield of Achilles' tr; Add MS 44443, f. 218.

[3] G. M. Bradley of the United Universities Club, on a resolution; Hawn P.

[4] Report of inquiry into retailers' accusations that London civil service members ran their co-operative stores in official time; an important issue in certain constituencies in the 1874 election.

[5] G. A. *Denison, *The Archbishop's Bill. Speeches* (1874).

[6] See 30 Apr. 74n.

[7] J. E. *Butler, *Some thoughts on the present aspect of the crusade against the state regulation of vice* (1874).

and Thes.Hom. Felled an oak with Willy. Read Lauch—Thirlwall—Grote—And G. Onslow on the claimant.[1]

12. Tu.

Ch. 8½ AM. Wrote to Prince Leopold—Mr Jos. Dunn[2]—Miss E. Ward. Worked on Thes.Hom. and Place in History. Preparing to get my new crop of books into order. Read Lauth's Homer und Ægypten—Duentzer Hom. Frage—Buchholz Realien—Greg on Rocks ahead[3]—He deals chiefly with phantoms & does not seem to see at all the great & threatening shoal if not rock, that of plousiocracy.

Today I said a few words of joy and encouragement to our dear daughter Helen:[4] they are well deserved. It is the steady force of religion that works upon her.

13. Wed. [London]

Ch. 8½ AM. Wrote to Sir C. Foster Bt.[5]—Mr Jas Knowles—Mr J.C. Grey—Mr W. White.[6] Left at Hawarden at 11 AM.—Euston at 5¾. Worked on a mass of papers. Saw Ld Selborne—Mr Godley. Read Bosworth Smith on Mahometanism.[7]

14. Th. Ascension Day.

St Anne's (& H.C.) 11-1¼. Wrote to Mr Bosworth Smith[8]—Rev. T. Shore[9]—Mr Hayden—Mr N.T. Cox[10]—Mrs Grote—Mr Hodgson Pratt. Luncheon at 15 G.S. H. of C. 4½-5¼.[11] What a moderate allowance! Off to Windsor at 6. Back at twelve. Saw Lord Nelson—The Dean of Windsor—Ld Granville—Prof. Blackie—General Ponsonby—and had much interesting conversation with Mrs P. at the dinner. Canning Memorial Comm. Meeting at 3.30.

15. Fr.

Wrote to Mr J. Curtis—Rev. Dr Booth—W.P. Adam—Mr Carswell[12]

[1] G. Onslow, *'Tichborne'. Reasons why he should have the benefit of the doubt* (1874).
[2] London oyster-merchant?
[3] W. R. *Greg, 'Rocks ahead', *Contemporary Review*, xxiii. 856 (May 1874); follows diarist's 'Achilles' article.
[4] Now aged 24.
[5] *Sc.* Forster; see 18 Mar. 58.
[6] William White, 1806-93, doorkeeper of the Commons 1854-75, and author.
[7] R. B. *Smith, *Mohammed and Mohammedanism* (1874).
[8] Reginald Bosworth Smith, author and schoolmaster at Harrow.
[9] Thomas Teignmouth Shore, anglican minister of Berkeley Chapel, Mayfair.
[10] London picture dealer, see 21 May 74.
[11] Misc. business: *H* ccxix. 288.
[12] Wine merchants.

—Stokes—Barlow—O'Connor—E. Reed—Rev. F.B. Zincke. Saw Mr Knowles—Mr Sturt—Rev Mr Molesworth—Ld Derby—on Porcelain—Ld Granville—Sir J. Lubbock—Dean of Westminster—Mr Macmillan—Sir A. Panizzi—Sir R. Phillimore. Charterhouse Meeting at 2 PM.

Emperor of Russia's[1] reception at 3.15. He thanked me for my conduct to Russia while I was minister. I assured HM I had watched with profound interest the transactions of his reign & the great benefits wh he had conferred upon his people. He hoped the relations of the two countries would always be good—I expressed my conviction that that was the desire of his heart.

H of C. at 4.30.[2] Read Rawlinson, Poole, & others at Lond[on] Lib[rary] on Egyptology.[3] Read Osorio[4] also. Dined at Marlborough House. Stafford House Ball afterwards. The Emperor complained of the burden & late hours of evening entertainments with an ardent sincerity. Princess of W[ales] so nice about her picture. D[israeli] complained of my absence: said they cd not get on without me.[5]

16. Sat.

Wrote to Agnes—Mr Rawlinson—Mr Grey—Rev. A. Church[6]—Mr Dickinson—Mr Macmillan—Mr Cookfoye.[7] Dined at Sir C. Forster's[8] & went with him to the Play. Between the Marriage [*sc.* Married] for Money & the Critic, we went behind the scenes and made acquaintance with Mr C. Matthews & Miss Farrer.[9] Saw Ld Lyttelton—Mr Gurdon—Sir C.A. Wood—Mr Theodore Martin—Baroness Burdett Coutts. Read 'Supernatural Religion'.[10] Saw Kennedy—Scott[R].

17. S.aft Asc.

Vere St Ch. 11 AM.—St Thomas Regent St. 4 PM (Mr Knox Little).[11] Saw Mrs Tyler—Mr Heywood—Ld Acton. Dined with Panizzi. 5 PM

[1] Alexander II; emperor 1855, assassinated 1881; see B. F. Sumner, *Russia and the Balkans* (1937), 85.

[2] Irish railways: *H* ccxix. 315.

[3] Works by G. *Rawlinson and R. S. *Poole.

[4] Probably S. T. *Coleridge, *Osorio, a tragedy; as originally printed in 1797* (ed. of 1873).

[5] See Morley, ii. 499.

[6] Alfred John Church, priest and Homerist.

[7] Henry Cookfoye, kept private school in London.

[8] Baronetted by diarist in March; see 18 Mar. 58.

[9] Charles Mathews and Nellie Farren at the Gaiety Theatre.

[10] *Supernatural religion, an enquiry* [anon.], 2v. (1874).

[11] William John *Knox Little, 1839–1918, curate of St Thomas, Regent St., 1874–5, rector of Cheetwood, 1875–85; noted preacher, later militarist.

Tea at Devonshire House. Worked on Proofs.[1] Read Studies of Character[2]—Dr Laing's What is Xtianity?[3]—Wilson's Letters to Abp of Cant.[4] Saw Scott late: who is I hope going into a good way[R].

18. M.

Wrote to Sec.Trin. House—Rev Mr Bayne[5]—Mr Ouvry—Dr Cowie—Mr Hayden—Miss E. Irving. Read Osorio. Breakfast at Granvilles. Sat to Mr Dickinson 2½-4.[6] H. of C. 4½-5½.[7] Saw Mr Macmillan—Ld Wolverton—Ld Acton—Sir W. Harcourt. Worked on proofsheets. Dinner party at No 21. Saw Belmore[R].

19. Tu.

Wrote to Mr Strahan—Worked five hours on Proof sheets. Sat to Mr Watts 3-4.40.[8] Luncheon at 15 G.S. Saw Mrs Th. Saw Mr Knowles—Ld Wolverton—Mr Newton—Ld J. Manners—Sir T. Chambers—Mr Hubbard—Mr Kinnaird—Mr Adam. Queen's Ball in evg. Dined at Ld Wolverton's. H. of C. 5¾-7½. Voted agt Sunday [museum] openings.[9]

20. Wed.

Wrote to Ld Spencer—Canon Rawlinson—Mr Ouvry—Lord Wolverton—Rev W. Graham—G. Mulchinoak.[10] Saw Mr Wilberforce—Mr W. Grogan—Deptford Deputn 12-1.[11]—Ld Stratford de Redcliffe—Lady Duff Gordon[12]—Admiral (unnameable, at the F.O. dinner)[13]—Sir Jos Whitworth. At Christie's Sale. Worked on proofs. Dined at the F.O. to meet the Emperor. This was very kind of the D[erby]s. Conversation with Mrs Stonor. Read Osorio.[14]

[1] See 4 May 74.

[2] T. *Guthrie, *Studies of character from the Old Testament*, 2v. (1867-70).

[3] In D. Laing, *Sermons* (1847).

[4] E. Wilson, 'Prayer for the dead, and the "Mater Dei". A letter addressed to . . . the Archbishop of Canterbury' (1870).

[5] Thomas Vere Bayne, 1829-1908; student of Christ Church 1849; proctor 1867.

[6] See 14 June 71.

[7] Questions: *H* ccxix. 391.

[8] The third of Watts' portraits of him (see 14 June 59); Watts destroyed the picture, unable to capture Gladstone's complexion; see A. M. W. Stirling, *The Richmond Papers* (1926), 236.

[9] *H* ccxix. 528.

[10] Unidentified.

[11] On the Creek Bridge; *Kentish Mercury*, 23 May 1874, 4.

[12] Fanny, wife of Sir Maurice Duff-Gordon, 4th bart.

[13] Admiral Popoff, accompanying the Czar; for the dinner, see *The Times*, 21 May 1874, 7b.

[14] See Morley, ii. 499.

21. Th.

Wrote to Mary G.—Sir W. Harcourt—Mr S. Smith—Messrs Bickers —Mr Forsyth—Mr Chichester—Rev F. Davis—Attended Mr Cox's Gallery. Saw Mr Ouvry—Mr Stansfeld. Attended Ld Redesdale at H. of L. Saw Mad. Ralli—Ld Harrowby—Mr Adam. Saw Kennedy. H. of C. 4½–5½.[1] Read divers pamphlets. Dined with Lady Herbert. Devonshire House afterwards.

22. Fr. [Hawarden]

Wrote to Mr Arnott—Crown Estate Commn—Mr Jas Knowles—Mrs Kennedy. Saw Ld Granville. Preparations for going: off at 11.30. —reached Hn at 6.30. Read Bosworth Smith on Mahometanism.[2] Early to bed, a cold having settled on my chest. Worked on proofs.

23.

In bed all day with strong perspirations to fight against the tightness. Read Gurney's Translation of Goethe's Faust Part II.[3] Saw Harry on his matters. Worked on proofs (a necessity). Wrote to Mr Strahan—Robn G.

24. Whits.

Rose in afternoon having in the main mended. But no Church today. Read Harris on Priesthood and on Chapel v. Church[4]—Bosworth Smith (finished)—Arnold on Literature and Dogma[5]—Dupanloup on Miraculous Manifestations.[6]

25. Whitm.

Rose after breakfast. Walk in afternoon. Saw S.R.G. on O[ak] F[arm] matters. Wrote to Mr Macmillan—Mr Strahan—Mr Ouvry—Rev. J. Harris—Mr J. Russell—Ld Kimberley. Worked on Homer Transln & Thes. Homer.[7] Read Faust II—Russell on J. Mill's Autobiogr.[8]

[1] Army: *H* ccxix. 623.
[2] See 13 May 74.
[3] By A. T. *Gurney (1842).
[4] H. Harris, *The church and the priesthood* (1869).
[5] See 7 June 73.
[6] F. A. P. Dupanloup, 'Lettre . . . sur les prophéties contemporaines, avec l'opinion de plusieurs Conciles' (1874).
[7] Gladstone's Thesaurus to Homer, begun long before, now apparently prepared for publication with a preface, but never published; Add MS 44762, ff. 45–128.
[8] E. R. Russell, *On the autobiography of John Stuart Mill* (1874).

26. Whitt.

Ch. 8.45 AM. Wrote to Mr A. Kinnaird—Mr Planché[1]—Mr. . . . Walk with S.R.G. & W.H.G. Worked on Thes. Hom: with reading Friedreich —Buchholz &c.[2] Read Brandis Sieben Thore Thebens[3]—Faust Part II.

27. Wed.

Ch. 8½ AM. Wrote to Mr Vickers—Rev. Mr Davidson—Mr Milne—Mr Jos. Edkins[4]—Mr Evelyn Ashley. Worked long on Thes.Hom. Woodcutting with W.H.G. Read Brandis.

28. Th.

Ch. 8½ AM. Wrote to Mr A. M'Cowan[5]—Mr A. Reed—Mr S. Langley. Attended the Concert in evg: excellent Chorus singing. Saw Mr Vickers—Mr R. Frost. Worked on Thes.Hom. Woodcutting with WHG. Read Friedreich—Buchholz—&c.

29. Fr.

Ch. 8½ AM. Wrote to Prince Leopold—Messrs Ouvry—Mr Jervis.[6] Spent much of the morning in hunting up the case of Aidoneus! My Juv. Mundi was I really think the best.[7] Worked on Thes.Hom. Read Brandis (finished). Woodcutting with W.

30 Sat.

Ch. 8½ AM. Wrote to Mr Macmillan—Mr Bowers—Mr Evans—Worked much on Thes.Hom. Read Gurney's Faust II. Went with W & H. to see the embankment works—5 or 6 m. off. Reckoned up the state of my affairs & income: there apparently being no present resource in Seaforth.[8]—I am afraid it will startle C. It is the more necessary to proceed at once lest if it please God to remove me there should be confusion or embarrassment.

31. Trinity.

Hawarden Ch. & H.C. 11 AM. Wrote to Townshend & Barker—Mr

[1] James Robinson *Planché, 1796-1880, herald, antiquary and dramatist.
[2] See 27 Apr. 74.
[3] See 1 Feb. 68.
[4] Joseph Edkins of Partick, wrote on Greek, Hawn P.
[5] Untraced.
[6] G. W. Jervis of Sheffield grammar school had written opposing the Public Worship Bill; Hawn P.
[7] *Juventus Mundi*, ch. viii, sect. iv.
[8] Mismanaged by Robertson Gladstone, see 18 Apr. 74.

A. Strahan—Mr Cassidy. Read Cont.Rev. on Maurice,[1] & Manning on Xty & Antixtn[2]—Also Arnold Liter. & Dogma and examined Annual Register with Mr [A. J.] Balfour on some of Abp M.s assertions. Conversation with Mr B.: who charms me. Considered at night the state of my affairs: a subject bearing much on the purposes of this day.

Hawarden June One 74.

Ch. 8½ AM. Wrote to Townshend & Barker—Mr A. De Lisle—Rev. Dr Rainy[3]—Conversations with S.R.G.—with C.G.—with W.H.G.—on the Agency matter. Framed a Mem. & saw Mr Barker in Chester on it.[4] Worked on Thes. Homerikos. Saw Bp of Chester—Meeting of Govrs K[ing's] School 2½-4¾ at the Deanery. Wrote Mem. respecting my present Income. Read Faust (Finished Part II.)—Blackie on Hom. Mythology.[5]

Expulsion from office has given me time to examine the state of my affairs, and the withdrawal of my official income, which supplied the greater part of my expenditure, has made it necessary.

The result is in general terms that although my property is very considerable, & might be called large, so that if *sold up* we should be rich, from a variety of causes my income is exceedingly reduced: neither am I prepared as I ought to be to find capital sums which may [be] required on behalf of some of our children within perhaps a very short time; and were I to die, as I am the only person who holds the threads of very various matters connected with my circumstances at command, some perplexities would be encountered.

I consider this half year as winding up the past state of things and reckon as from July 1. 1874.

At that date, my payments on Hawarden Estate Reversion account, with interest, will have turned £70,000: which is of course so much abstracted from *present* funds. A further sum of £13,700 remains payable and bears interest in the meantime at 5 per Cent.

The Seaforth property, with from 35 to 40 m[ille] cannot yield me over £700 per ann.; my investment in the Metropolitan District Railway, of a present value, under extreme depression, of somewhat less than 20 m[ille], at this time yields no dividend: the house in Carlton H. Terrace, and my various collections, represent a value, which might be readily realised, of between 50 and 60 m[ille].

I have used every effort to sell the whole, and also parts, of the Seaforth property: but without avail: probably nothing can be done in this quarter.

[1] *Contemporary Review*, xxiv. 23 (June 1874).

[2] H. E. *Manning, 'Christ and AntiChrist, a sermon' (1867).

[3] Replying to Robert *Rainy, 1826-1906, principal of Free Church College, Edinburgh 1874-1901, on the Scottish Patronage Bill; in P. C. Simpson, *Life of Rainy* (1909), i. 271.

[4] See 8 Jan. 74.

[5] J. S. *Blackie, 'On the scientific interpretation of popular myths, with special reference to Greek mythology', in *Horae Hellenicae* (1874); he dedicated the book to Gladstone.

Examining carefully my present sources of Income I find them as follows.

Flintshire Estates, nett, not exceeding	£4 900	
Seaforth	700	
Trinity College [Glenalmond] Mortgage } American Railway Bonds }	450	
	£6,050	
Interest on outstanding payt. for Hawarden	£685	
On Scott's advance of £5500	275	
On other debts about	1 290	2,250
Leaving		£3,800
The necessary allowances for C.G. and (five of) our children are	£1,530	
I cannot put less for Charity and Religion than	£670	£2,200
Leaving		£1,600
The positive charges on the House and Stables one year with another at least		600
Leaving for all general expenditure whatsoever, in which is included everything relating to myself		£1,000

This speaks for itself.

It has been practicable under the very peculiar circumstances of this year to obtain an addition of fifteen hundred pounds to my income by letting the House for the season. But it would not be useful or perhaps creditable to go on with this from year to year: it would be like publicly advertising need: nor *could* it possibly be so let, as that the nett return should represent any reasonable interest upon the capital which the House & its contents represent.

£1000 per ann. in round numbers might be had by realising the investments in the M[etropolitan and] D[istrict] Railway: but it would be improvident to do much now in this way, especially with reference to the probable provision of capital to which I alluded near the outset of this paper: nor would this addition to income be sufficient to meet our necessary expenditure and that which our children might require.

From the House & furniture, part of my collections, and other sources might be obtained over £50,000,[1] which would raise my income to over £6000 per ann., though without any provision for a house.[2]

2. Tu.

Ch. 8½ A.M. Wrote to Mr Kinnaird—M. Reynald[3]—Mr Littler—Sir W. Harcourt. Felling trees with W. Conversation with him on the

[1] In fact realised £48,000 from the various sales 1874–5.

[2] Initialled and dated 1 June 1874; Hawn P.

[3] Hermile Reynald, 1828–83; French historian and biographer.

Agency. With C.G. on Mr Balfour & M.[1] Worked on Thesauros Homericos. Read Stokes's Poems[2]—Account of Shetland.[3]

3. Wed.

Ch. 8½ AM. W.s birthday: God be with him. Wrote to Mr Townshend—Sir A. Panizzi—Mr Scurr—Louey Gladstone—Mr Ouvry. Saw Mr Hanson & Mr Ward[4]—Worked on Thes.Hom. Cut a large oak with W: diam. full 3 f. on the ground: by way of closing the season. Read Barthelemy St Hilaire Introduction to Homer.[5]

4. Th.

Ch. 8½ AM. Wrote to Mr A. Kinnaird—Lord Selborne—Dr Acland. Saw Mr Vickers. Attended Mr Bowers's majority celebration and spoke.[6] Worked on Thes.Hom. Read Account of Shetland. Finished B. St H. Introduction, & read some of his Translation.

5. Fr.

Ch. 8½ AM. Wrote to Ld Tenterden—Dr Schliemann—Mr J.R. Herbert—Mr Knowles—Mrs Th.—Messrs Townshend & Barker. Worked on Thes.Hom. Read Freeman's Comparative Politics.[7] Saw Mr Vickers & settled that he should be my Agent. Visited Mr Roberts's Farm and saw his stock.

6. Sat.

Wrote to Mr Scurr—Rev Mr Gray—Mr Cook—Robn G. Aftn party to tea. Saw Mr Vickers—Mr Roberts—H.N.G. on Seaforth & the House. Read Freeman—Account of Shetland. Worked on Thes. Homerikos.

7. 1 S.Trin.

Ch. 11 AM (with H.C.) and 6½ P.M. Wrote to Rev Mr Hutton—Rev

[1] Unclear whether Mary Gladstone or Mary Lyttelton; Balfour was friendly with the first, in love with the second.
[2] H. P. Stokes, *Poems of later years* (1873).
[3] Probably R. Cowie, *Shetland: descriptive and historical* (1871).
[4] Evan Hanson, manager of the Aston Hall colliery; see 8–9 June 74.
[5] J. Barthélemy-Saint-Hilaire, introduction to his *Iliad*, 2v. (1868).
[6] No account found.
[7] E. A. *Freeman, *Comparative politics. Six lectures* (1874).

Mr Medd—Mr Montagu Bernard—Principal of Magd. Hall—Mayor of Blackburn.[1] Saw S.E.G. Read Literature & Dogma[2]—Martineau on God in Nature[3]—Divers Tracts—Carpenter's new Vol.[4] Expedition after Poachers at night: who had decamped.[5]

8. M.

Ch. 8½ AM. Wrote to Baron de Bunsen[6]—Aston Miner-Tenants[7]—Hon. C.L. Wood—W.H.G.—Robn G. Saw Mr Vickers—Do *cum* Mr Ward. Drove to Chester & attended Yeomanry Luncheon. Spoke afterwards. Saw Ed. Chester Chronicle.[8] Worked on Thes.Hom. Also preparing papers for a great move. Read Godwin on Man.[9]

9. Tu.

Ch. 8½ AM. Wrote to Sir W. Harcourt—Mr Stansfeld—Scotts—Mr Playfair—Robn G.—Mr Goldwin Smith—Mr Ouvry—Mr A. Reed. Attended at 3 the meeting of Miners and addressed them on their demand for the dismissal of the minority. Many were there besides my own tenants.[10] Accommodation for 1200 more volumes came in today: busy directing, and did a little in arranging books, wh must now go on gently from day to day until completed. Worked on Thes. Hom. Read Simms's Iliad, and Preface.[11]

10. Wed.

Ch. 8½ AM. Wrote to Townshend & Barker—Mr H. Taylor—Rev. C. Simms—Mr W.T. Pears—H.N.G.—Mr W. Ellison—Mr Ward—Messrs Button & Co.[12] 3-4. Went with Stephy to the three schools:

[1] Not found.
[2] See 7 June 73.
[3] J. *Martineau, probably 'A word for scientific theology . . . an address' (1868).
[4] W. B. *Carpenter, *Principles of mental physiology* (1874).
[5] See I. Thomas, *Gladstone of Hawarden* (1936), 55.
[6] See 3 Apr. 55.
[7] Summoning next day's meeting, printed in E. Rogers and R. O. Roberts, 'History of trade unionism in the coal mining industry of north Wales', *Denbighshire Hist. Soc. Trans.* xix. 201.
[8] Giving details of the Aston dispute; *Chester Chronicle*, 13 June 1874, 7.
[9] W. *Godwin, *Thoughts on man* (1831).
[10] Aston Hall miners, save four non-unionists, struck against 15% wage reduction, and declined compromise until the four were dismissed; Hanson, the colliery manager, asked diarist to evict the many miners in Hawarden estate cottages. Gladstone defended the right of the four to accept lower wages, adding 'it is my duty to give every reasonable support that is in my power to Mr Hanson . . .'; under the implied threat of eviction, the miners accepted a 10% wage reduction; Rogers and Roberts, art. cit., *Chester Chronicle*, 13 June 1874, 7.
[11] C. S. Simms, *The first book of the Iliad* (1866).
[12] Duignan, Button & Smiles, London solicitors.

all looked well. 4–5. Further conversation with eight tenant-miners. They were very reasonable. We wound up with tea. Worked on Thes. Hom. Worked on rearranging books. Read Turriff on Aberdeen[1]—Freeman's Comp. Politics.

11. Th. St Barnabas

Ch. 8¾ AM. Wrote to Sec.Coll. Physicians[2]—Rumney & Lowe[3]—H.N.G.—Thomson Hankey. Worked much on arranging letters and books. and on Thes.Hom. but it suffers. Saw Mr Vickers. Went into Chester: saw Mr Townshend—Mr Pears cum Robn G.—Robn G.—Miss Jacobson. Read Chinese Fragment.[4]

12. Fr.

Ch. 8½ AM. Wrote to Mr MacColl—Dean of Chichester (Abp's Bill)[5]—Mr F. Morrison[6]—Mr J.B. Bayly.[7] Saw Mr Ward & the miners who have happily withdrawn their demand. Worked much on books & letters. Worked on Thes.Hom. but am much limited in this dept. Read Chinese Fragment. Mr Torre[8] dined. Cut down a yew-tree.

13. Sat.

Ch. 8½ AM. Saw Mr Torre—Mrs Jacobson (Abp's Bill): & H.N.G. on his position & the House at Lp. & in Ln. Conversation with C.G. on the state of our affairs. Wrote to Rev Mr Heygate—Ld Hartington—Mr Myers—Mr Marshall—Mr Davis—Mr Redmond[9]—Mr Craddock. Again revised Part II of my historic paper. Read Chinese Fragment. Cutting with H. at the Rectory. Worked on Thes.Hom. Also on arranging books & papers.

14. 2 S.Trin.

Ch. 11 AM and 6½ PM. Wrote to Ld Wolverton—Mrs Th.—Sir R. Phillimore—W.H.G.—Ld Granville—Mr Stokes[10]—Robn G. Conversation with C.G. on the House question & our future. Read Chinese Fragment—Literature & Dogma.

[1] See 26 Feb. 74.
[2] William Gurner.
[3] Perhaps Peter Rumney, London solicitor.
[4] By [E. Bates] (1786).
[5] i.e. the Public Worship Regulation Bill.
[6] Frederick Morrison, secretary to National Chamber of Trade.
[7] John Bethune Bayly, lawyer.
[8] William Fox Whitbread Torre, 1829–1912; vicar of Buckley, 1873–85.
[9] Perhaps Francis Redmond of Dublin, later a correspondent.
[10] Probably the poet, see 2 June 74.

15. M.

Ch. 8½ A.M. Wrote to Mr Carvel Williams—Rev Mr Collins—Mr Hanson—Mrs Nimmo—Mr de Vere. Conversation with C. and payment of accounts. She went to London. Worked much on shifting & ordering books. Cut some small trees. Worked on Thes. Hom. Read Chinese Fragm. (finished)—De Vere's Alexander the Great.[1]

16. Tu.

Ch. 8½ AM. Wrote to Dowager Duchess of Somerset—Ld Hartington—Mr Tilley—Mr J.F.A. Lynch[2]—Mr Grogan—W.B. Gurdon—Mr A. Reed—Mr R. Cowtan—Mr W. Bowles[3]—Mrs Ryder—W.H.G.—C.G. Worked on Thes.Hom. and 2 h. (only) on arranging books. Explored Tinkersdale & near parts. Read Lefevre on Game Laws[4]—De Vere's Alfred [*sc.* Alexander] the Great—Brunn on Art in Homer.[5]

17. Wed.[6]

Ch. 8½ AM. Wrote to Mr Goschen—Mr Leake (Tildesley)—W.H.G. Tel.—C.G. Tel. & 2 l.[7]—Mr Vickers.

Arranged books & worked on Thes.Hom. Then Mary and I went to water some burnt up grass in the flower garden. Walter came out about half past four with a Telegram, which I always dread. It was the sad intimation all but sure of dear Stephen's having suddenly died yesterday in Shoreditch,[8] from the Coroner. I answered instantly by Tel. to Willy: saw the Postmaster & with a heavy heart kept all quiet until near six when there came the undisguised certainty. Saw Mary—Stephen: who with Albert [Lyttelton] came down to dine. Saw the Sec. to the Hawarden Institute, on postponement of the festival from tomorrow. This is a heavy and bewildering blow. It alters the whole frame of life:[9] and I make a great stride towards its close. He is gone: that singularly refined and pure spirit, most upright in all his intentions before God and ever firm in the Catholic Faith of Christ. In that land of light whither he has been carried by the storm

[1] A. T. *de Vere, *Alexander the Great. A dramatic poem* (1874).
[2] Perhaps of Lynch Bros., city merchants.
[3] London bookseller.
[4] G. J. S. *Lefevre, *The game laws* (1874).
[5] H. von Brunn, *Die Kunst bei Homer* (1868).
[6] This and next nine days have thick black ink borders ruled around.
[7] Bassett, 202.
[8] Sir Stephen Glynne died while searching for antiquities in Shoreditch High Street.
[9] His brother-in-law's death made the diarist very briefly owner in possession of the Hawarden estate.

of a moment, may he have rest and joy until the day of his full consummation.

18.

A sad night and waking. Our post showed us that our knowledge here was the first. I went to Church: & there read prayers, with some difficulty. S[tephen Gladstone] came down: & Harry arrived soon from Liverpool. I gave last night to S. & A. as well as I could a sketch of the romance, for such it is, of the financial history: and this morning to S. & H. I explained fully, also to Mary, the arrangement of 1865 with regard to my purchase of the reversion of this Estate. We found on reference that it seems to go at once to Willy.[1] I had always a strong repugnance to becoming either the actual or the virtual master. On this account I doubted last night about appearing on the Inquest. This morning, under an erroneous belief that the first devolution was on C. & much desiring to be with her I decided to go up in the evening. But on learning the true state of the case, & being also in some fear of my old enemy, I changed & determined to remain, S., H., and M., all agreeing.

Tel. to C.G. 9½ and 2½: and 1. Letter to Mr Barker: & tel. To the Coroner for Middx—Mr T.C. Leslie—Mr Ouvry—Ld F. Cavendish—W.H.G.—Sir R. Phillimore—Mr W. Ellison. Read Lefevre on Game Laws—Alfred the Great.

Worked a little on books: and we made some of the arrangements: but most of the day I was in fear of an attack. Worked a little on my books: as my room must be got into order. We dined at the Rectory with S. and Albert [Lyttelton].

19. Fr.

Ch. 8½ AM. Saw Mr Vickers—do with J. Bailey (for the funeral arrangements)—Col. Cook.[2] Wrote to C.G. l. & Tel.—The Chester Stationmaster—Mr R. Barker—Mrs Th.—Rev. Mr Henderson—Mr Planché—Mr Stibbs—Mr A. Reed—Ed. Echo—Mr H.S. Syre[3]—Sec. Coll of Physicians. Finished Alfred the Great. Worked on books. The drawing room was got ready. Harry went with Stephy to meet him in Chester. The arrival here was before midnight. Mary had made

[1] See 25 Aug. 65, 16 Dec. 67; the 1865 agreement and the 1867 settlement meant that the estate was conveyed in trust to W. H. Gladstone, a process completed in April 1875; Morley, i. 344.

[2] Of Royal Engineers; worked on Russian advances in Asia; PRO F.O.C.P. 1687.

[3] Unidentified.

the place of his rest beautiful. There we placed him for his last tenure of this the house of his fathers. We all went singly into the room at last.

20. Sat.

Ch. 8½ AM. Wrote to Ld R. Grosvenor (Tel.)—Mr Barker—Duke of Argyll—Mr De Lisle—Capt. Allen.[1] Saw Dr Moffatt on the causes of the death. We arranged that the people of Hawarden might visit the Drawingroom in the afternoon. At 6.30 Catherine came to the saddened house of her fathers in deep but resisted grief. We had much conversation. Worked on my books, & at length got my room into order. Saw S. on the arrangements. Walk with Harry. Read Memoir of Panizzi[2]—Wallace on Numbers of Mankind.[3]

21. 3 S.Trin.

Ch. 11 A.M. with H.C. after an admirable expository Sermon from S. Wrote to Duke of Westminster—Ld Wolverton—Mr Winsall[4]—Mr J.J. Ffoulkes—Mr Parker—Ld Lyttelton—Miss Gilby—Capt. Gilmore. Conversations with C. on what seems to grow between W. & his Cousin G.G.[5]—Under the circumstances I should be thankful: it would soothe and please me. Read Duncan Forbes Thoughts on Religion[6]—Dr Routh on overwork[7]—Literature and Dogma.[8]

22. M.

Ch. 8½ A.M. Wrote to Rev Dr Monsell—Mr R. Barker—Sir Thos G. —Mr J. Russell—Col. Cook—Mr C. Townshend—Mr Evan Hanson. In the afternoon, the two H.s having managed the beech tree, we worked at the roadway and the Bridge Arch for *him*. In concert with C.G., Harry, John Bailey, and Mr Vickers, we made all the arrangements for the funeral movement on Wednesday and embodied them in a Memorandum sending the needful extracts out in different quarters. Willy & Gertrude arrived. By arrangement with John Bailey the lid of the Oak was removed today and a beautifully designed cross in oak placed upon it. Read Wallace on Numbers—Maud on Endless Torments.[9] Worked a little on making out the figures.

[1] Of Trinity House, Hawn P.
[2] By R. Cowtan (1873).
[3] A. R. Wallace, *Contributions to the theory of natural selection* (1870).
[4] London hatter.
[5] Gertrude Glynne; she m. Lord Penrhyn 1875; see 24 Sept. 50.
[6] D. Forbes, *Some thoughts concerning religion* (1750).
[7] C. H. F. Routh, *On overwork and premature mental decay* (1873).
[8] See 7 June 73.
[9] J. Maud, *The doctrine of endless torments* (1755).

23. Tu.

Ch. 8½ A.M. Wrote to Mr Beresford Hope—T.M. Gladstone—Sir Thos G.—Ld Prov. Glasgow—Mr W. Wynne—Mrs Havill—Mr Lucas. Lyttelton came: much conversation on the deceased, & on the puzzle as to affairs. Saw further on the arrangements Rev. S.E.G.—Mr Vickers—Mrs Hampton—Mr Wade—Harry, Herbert & I looked further to the way: to see that all is as befits *him*. Read Lucas on horizontal Wells[1]—Maud on Future Punishment. Wrote out, for explanation to those most nearly concerned a Mem. on the Reversion, the Will, and the state of Stephen's affairs. Also reflected on the proper mode of proceeding: & conversation with C.

24. Wedn. St John Baptist.

Holy Communion at 8 AM. All our children were at the Altar with us (as well as others) and Agnes was in the same holy office at Wellington College. Rest and light and peace to those departed in the faith: and specially, for today to dear Stephen, and dear Ida.[2] In a conversation with C. we both came I think to a pretty clear & an united view of what is to be desired for the future, and of what is to be done accordingly.

Immediately after the Funeral I saw Mr W. Hignett of Chester and from him first obtained a clear view of the state of the succession. By Providence rather than by plan the intestacy which will prevail as to most of the Estate remaining to Sir Stephen will work equitably & well. After him I saw Sir G. Prevost on the Archbishop's [Public Worship] Bill: F. Cavendish on affairs in London & bade farewell generally to the guests. Also I explained the state of the questions about the property more or less fully to Ld Lyttelton; to W.H.G.; to Gertrude; to Harry.

The arrangements for the funeral were pretty well matured before this morning, and all did their part with heart and will. Notwithstanding a short hailstorm in the forenoon the day was on the whole mildly bright with a few very slight showers. There was a great gathering, with perfect order, and deep feeling and silence. Stepping the distance yesterday we had found it 1150 yards. The coffin was passed through the drawing room window to the bier outside: with 25 to 30 bearers and others. The Magistrates & Guardians then passed out of the anteroom window: & the procession moved at one.

At the Library window the relatives and friends joined, as it passed

[1] J. Lucas, *Horizontal wells* (1874).

[2] Ida Gladstone, his niece, who d. 22 June 1874; see 30 June 74.

on, round the house, towards the North, the light rail of the flower garden having been removed. The Volunteers & Militia, followed by the Constabulary, here took the head of the column, & struck diagonally across the Lawn, upon a line pegged out, round the limes, & to a point between the iron gate into the Wynt Lane, and the great rooty beech within it. Here we fell upon the line of the marriage procession of July 25 1839.

From outside the iron gate the tenantry fell in, four abreast. Not a sound was heard but the stepping of the drilled men. My wife, Helen, Gertrude, fell in at the opening of the Rectory Lane. We reached the Church Yard Gate in 28 or 29 minutes. Here there was a short delay before the Clergy appeared. The opening sentences were read & chanted as we passed into the Church, which was crowded to excess, but most reverently silent. As we moved out from the North door, the wide view over land and sea seemed to lift up the soul. Both the chanting at the grave side, and our son Stephen's reading were perfect. Catherine knelt all that time but bore up in spirit.

When we got back to the Church it was a quarter past two.

Taken for all in all it was a most soothing, most Christian funeral, such as *he* deserved, such as *he* would have loved.

Then came the interviews and explanations. And I spent an hour or two with C. in examining the monokleid[1] & papers so far as to see that there was no sign of any paper bearing upon present duties. All went except George [Lyttelton]—we were only 10 at dinner: and all I think as one. Willy expressed his perfect readiness to act as I recommended under the new arrangements.

Read Maud. Wrote to Wrexham Advertiser[2]—Mr L. Playfair—Mr Strahan (sending up last revise).

25. Th.

Ch. 8½ A.M. Wrote to Sir R. Phillimore—Ld Delamere—Mr Watson—Ld Denbigh—Dr Clark—Mr Martin—Agnes W.—Rev. Mr Meagher[3]—Mr Barker—Lord F. Cavendish—Mr Vickers. Saw J. Bailey (to thank)—Mr Lamont (valuation)—C.G.—Harry—further on arrangements. George went off. I cannot but be glad something out of the not large inheritance will go in that direction. Cutting holly for S. in the Rectory Garden. Read Maud on Fut.Pun.—Miss Edgeworth, Patronage[4]—Brunn, Kunst bei Homer.[5]

[1] *Sic*. Presumably a brand name for a strong box.
[2] Sent details of Glynne's funeral, *Wrexham Advertiser*, 27 June 1874.
[3] Apparently a nonconformist.
[4] By M. *Edgeworth, 4v. (1814).
[5] See 16 June 74.

26. Fr.

Ch. 8½ A.M. Wrote to Mr Knowles (Tel.)—Messrs Cocks & Biddulph—Messrs Williams (Chester)—Ld Granville—Mr Grogan—Ld Brougham—Messrs Parry & Gamon[1]—Dean of Chichester—Lady Gladstone. Worked for 3 hours in dear Stephen's room. The labour there will be great. Much conversation with C.—The future seemed to clear a little before her. But how greedy I am—not satisfied with the last 22 years, or the last 35! Cutting holly for S. Read Pope—& his Editor—Maud on Future Punishment.

27. Sat.

Ch. 8½ A.M. Wrote to Sir R. Anstruther—Mr Barker (2)—Mr Vickers—W. White—E. Jones—J. Heaton—Supt Deptford School—Rev. B. Webb—W. Selwyn—Sir W. James—Chief Constable—Col. Cooke. Framed Mem. respecting our future arrangements for the Residence & Estate. Saw Mr Vickers: & much conversation with C. Read Maud on Future Punisht.

28. 4 S.Trin.

Ch 11 A.M. where Bp of Chester preached the Funeral Sermon. Saw Bp on the Public Worship Bill, & other matters. Wrote to Ld F. Cavendish—Ld Lyttelton—Mrs Th.—Mrs Helen G.—Mr J. Rigby—Mr W.T. Pears—Robn G.—Mr A. Scott—Mr V. Smith. Renewed conversations with dearest C. on the future. Read Vance Smith on the Word of Christ[2]—Maud on Future Punt. My sister Helen's birthday. God send all blessings on her: then may even come unity in communion: surely where she is, she is estranged.

29. M. (St Peter). [*Fasque*][3]

Preparations for journey. Wrote to Messrs Williams & Co. Saw Mr Vickers (Hn)—Mr Barker—Mr Biddulph—Chester; Robn G. respecting Harry, Mr Harris respecting Seaforth Sale—Liverpool. Off at 3.10. Worked on reckoning Speech v. narrative in Iliad. Read Vaughan's Life and Poems. At midnight reaching Perth I fell in with Tom & his party grieving but resigned as Christians should be. We reached Fasque about 3.30. Got a good rather short night: up at 9.

[1] Perhaps Parry and Garnham, London chemists.
[2] G. V. *Smith, *The spirit and word of Christ, and their permanent lessons* (1874).
[3] His brother Tom's seat in Kincardineshire.

30. Tu.[1]

Wrote to C.G. Read Vaughan's Poems[2]—Scott's Ballads.
In the forenoon I went with Tom to the Chapel and Vault about the arrangements.[3] Saw my dearest Jessy's Coffin lying there in peace. He wished me to let fall the earth at the proper place in the service.

The funeral was at one. It was calm, simple, & becoming. No music as the daughters naturally could not undertake it. Mr Winslow's[4] officiating is perfect. All knelt on the grass. At the close she was taken down. We all took the wreaths of flowers off, and replaced them when she was placed below, with the crosses. Annie most kindly gave me a wreath for Jessy, and they placed another. Then Mr W. most solemnly but quietly read the commendatory words of the Service for the sick: all fervently said Amen.

In the afternoon I walked with Tom. We had conversation about Robertson's matters.

Wed. Jul. One. 1874.

Prayers in the Chapel at 11. (Family prayers mg & evg.). Wrote to Ld F. Cavendish—Mr Parkins (Gresford)[5]—C.G. Read Scott—Vaughan —Buchholz Realien.[6] Worked a little on Thes.Hom: after this sad last fortnight, which ought indeed to have brought me nearer to Christ. Walked with Louisa and my nieces up the hill.

2. Th.

Wrote to Duke of Argyll—Mr G. Bramwell—C.G. Read Buchholz —Life of Bp Patteson.[7] Worked on Thes.Hom. Called at the houses of the two ministers: & had a further survey of the place in its old and still dear details. Much in Tom's society.

3. Fr.

Wrote to C.G.—Lady F. Cavendish—Sir A. Panizzi. Conversation at & after breakfast on Prayer and Religious belief. Also with Tom on

[1] This day surrounded by a thick black line.
[2] See 9 Nov. 72.
[3] For his niece Ida's funeral—the coffin placed in the vault with that of his da. Jessy, see 10-13 Apr. 50.
[4] Apparently Charles de Blois Winslow, incumbent in Liverpool; Andrew H. Belcher was the incumbent at Fasque.
[5] William T. Parkins.
[6] See 27 Apr. 74.
[7] C. M. *Yonge, *Life of John Coleridge Patteson*, 2v. (1872), reviewed by diarist in *Quarterly Review*, cxxxvii. 458 (October 1874); Add MS 44693, f. 172; *Gleanings*, ii. 213; see 20 Oct. 72.

Scotch Patr. Bill. And I explained to him the position of matters at Hawarden. We measured the principal trees: and took a hill walk between the showers. Worked on Thes.Hom. Read Life of Bp Patteson.

4. Sat. [*London*]

Wrote to W.H.G.—Sec.Gen. Post Office—Editor of Echo—Sir Chas A. Murray. Worked on Thes.Hom. Read Buchholz—Life of Bp Patteson. Walk to F[ettercairn] House. Farewell at 4.20 and off to London.

5. 5 S.Trin.

St Anne's Soho mg. St James's evg. Reached Euston at 10. Read on Scotch Patr. Bill. Wrote to Townshend & Barker—Mr Burnett—Mr Grogan—Lady Mayoress—Mr Fifes[1]—Dr Plimsoll. Dined with Ld Wolverton, & much intimate conversation. Saw Ld W. *cum* Ld Granville—Sir J. St Aubyn[2]—Ld Mostyn—Mr Murray Gladstone—Ld Bessborough. Explained much to the F.C.s whom I invaded this morning.

6. M.

Wrote to Mr Kingsley—Rev. Mr Forsyth[3]—C.G.—Rev. J.R. Crewe[4]—Mr Hanbury—Mr Falshaw—Mr A. Sinclair. Saw Dr Rainy—Mr Baxter—W.H.G.—Ld Wolverton. Worked on letters & papers, mountain high. Also on Scotch Patr. Bill. Dined at Sir C. Forsters. H of C. 4¼-8 and 10½-1½. Spoke (long) on Scotch Patronage Bill.[5]

7. Tu.

Wrote to Ld Brownlow—Mr Barker—Mr Vickers—Mr McKeane[6]—Mr J. Freeman—Mr S. Keen—Dr Collins—M. Rabbinowicz.[7] Dined with Sir A. Panizzi.[8] Saw Mr Grogan on sale of House and contents—Mr Peel—W.H.G. on Hn arrangements, & on letters—Ld

[1] Perhaps Frederick Fysh, priest; corr. this year on Homer; Hawn P.

[2] Sir John St. Aubyn, 1829-1908; liberal (unionist) M.P. W. Cornwall 1858-87; 2nd bart. 1872; cr. Baron St. Levan 1887.

[3] W. Forsyth, presbyterian minister in Abernethy, wrote on the Patronage Bill: Hawn P.

[4] Non-anglican.

[5] *H* ccxx. 1113, and see 1 June 74n.

[6] Edward McKeane of Holloway had sent a portrait; Hawn P.

[7] Israel Michel Rabbinowicz, 1818-93; French Jewish scholar and grammarian.

[8] See *DLFC*, ii. 172.

Selborne on Abp's Bill—Ld Hatherley on do—Sir R. Phillimore on do. Saw Manchr Cathedral Plans.

8. Wed.

Wrote to Mr Healey[1]—Mr Bennett—Wingate—Snow[2]—Sir R. Phillimore—Ld Wolverton—Mr Corkran—Batley—Hawkins. Breakfast with Mr C. Field. Saw Judge Daly (Hom.)[3]—Mr Andrews (Hom. &c.)—Dr Hayes—Mr Grogan—Mr Merritt—Sir M. Wilson—Mr Herbert—Sir R. Phillimore—Lady W[illiam] Russell—Chief Baron. Dined at Mr Thistlethwaytes. Framed Resolutions on the Archbishop's Bill.

9. Th.

Wrote to Mr Reed—Mr W.T. Pears—Mr Bailey—Town Clerk. Attended Peel Memorial Meeting.[4] Saw Sir Augustus Paget—Ld Wolverton—Mr Merritt—Ld Granville—Ld Cardwell—Ld Lyttelton—Mr Hugessen—Mr F. Lawley—Ld Wilmarleigh[5]—W.H.G.—Mr Forster—Mr Hubbard—and others. Further considered and wrote out fair my Resolutions. In melting heat went to H. of C. and delivered a rather difficult Speech on the Archbishop's Bill. The Resolutions seemed to obtain a good reception on both sides. I was there 4¼-8 and 11-1.[6] Dined at Sir C. Forster's. It was almost impossible to get sleep.

10. Fr.

Wrote to Mr Whitehead—M. St Hilaire—Mr Bennett—Rev Mr Hutton—M. Le Normant—Mr A. Balfour—Dr J. Brown—Mr Hubbard—Ld Tenterden—Pres.Acad. Sciences Mor. et Pol.[7]—Professor Lauth.[8] Saw Mr Palgrave—Sir R. Anstruther—Farrer and Ouvry (Clerk)—Mr Agnew—Mrs Th.—Mr Goschen. Read Poems by V.[9] Dined with the Goschens.

[1] Perhaps Patrick Healy, a constituent; Hawn P.
[2] Albert Snow, spiritualist; see Add MS 44444, f. 38, 40.
[3] Probably Charles Patrick Daly, 1816-99, American judge and scholar; Field's guest?
[4] No account found.
[5] Apparently *sic*, but none of this name.
[6] Announcing six resolutions to be moved modifying the Bill; *H* ccxx. 1391; Harcourt followed with a speech of unremitting erastianism. See Marsh, *Victorian Church*, ch. 7 and Add MS 44622, f. 167.
[7] Barthélemy-Saint-Hilaire was its *doyen*; see 3 June 74.
[8] Franz Joseph Lauth, 1822-92; German classicist.
[9] *Poems by V* [Mrs A. Clive] (1840).

11. Sat. [Wellington College]

Wrote to Mr Hignett—Rev. Mr Malet—Rev. Mr Gott—Rev. Mr Stevens—Mr Agnew—Mr Rigdon—Mr Pugin—Mr H. Danby Seymour—Mr Dickinson—Mr De Witt[1]—Mr Josey—Mr Hopps.[2] Saw U.P. Scotch Deputn—Woolwich B. of Health Deputn[3]—Ld Granville—Mr Winans[4]—Mr Lawley—Ld Wolverton—[5]E. Hamilton. Read Philol. Journal. Off 4¼ for Wellington College.[6] Agnes met me at Bracknell & drove me over. Service at 8.20. Agnes & I surreptitiously heard the Debate of the Society's window.

12. 6 S.Trin.

Chapel at 9½ AM. noon & 8½ P.M. The HM preached, & of course very well. Long walk in evg: the heat being just bearable. Read Patteson—Robn on Ritual[7]—Tracts.

13. M. [London]

Wrote to Mr Corkran—Mr Brittain. . . . Chapel 8½ AM. Off at 10.10. In C.H.T. 12.45. Saw Sir H. Thring—Mr Baxter—Ld Hartington—Mr Agnew—Mr Playfair—Mr Adam—Mr Forster—Duchess of Marlborough. 2-4 Radcliffe [Trustees]. 4¼-6 Mr Dickinson. 6¼-7½ and 11¼-12¼ Ld F. Cavendish.

14. Tu.

Wrote to Mr Grogan—Ld A. Russell—Mrs Th.—Mrs Grote—Miss Bekker[8]—Mr Agnew. Saw Sir A. Panizzi—Bp of Winchester—Mr Childers—Mr Agnew—Mr Forster—W.H.G. 10-12 To Old Bailey to give evidence in Herbert v. Pugin.[9] H. of C. 4½-8¼ and 10¼-1¼. Spoke on Endowed Schools Bill, & voted in 209 : 291.[10]

[1] Cornélis Henri de Witt, 1828-92; French historian and Jefferson's biographer.

[2] John Page Hopps, 1834-1911; unitarian minister and journalist; ed. *The Truthseeker* 1863-87; from 1876 a frequent correspondent.

[3] On land rating; *Kentish Mercury*, 18 July 1874, 8.

[4] William Louis Winans of Grosvenor Square.

[5] Entry from here to end of 13 July in faint pencil.

[6] At Wokingham, Berkshire, where diarist's son-in-law, E. C. Wickham, was headmaster.

[7] J. C. Robertson, *How shall we 'conform to the liturgy of the Church of England'?* (3rd ed., with two articles on ritualism added, 1869).

[8] Lydia Ernestine Becker of the Manchester National Society for Women's Suffrage sent a memorial signed by 18,000 women, requesting Gladstone's support; Add MS 44444, f. 3; his noncommittal reply, in *The Times*, 18 July 1874, 8b.

[9] As witness for Herbert in his unsuccessful action against E. W. *Pugin; *The Guardian*, 15 July 1874, 878.

[10] Against the Bill; *H* ccxx. 1699.

15. Wed.

Wrote to Bp of Winchester—Dean of Chester—Mr Havill—Mr Disraeli—Mr Fawcett. Luncheon at 15 G.S. Dined with the German Ambassr. Saw Ld Wolverton (2)—Do cum Ld Granville—Sir R. Phillimore & Mr Phillimore—Mr Woolner—Mr Cowper—Mr Cyrus Field and HNG—Mr Macmillan—Mr J.R. Herbert—Miss Talbot—Lady Ossington—Mr Rainsford.[1] A little conversation with Crown Princess [Victoria]—Duchess of Manchester—Mr Hayward—More with Musurus on Greek pronunciation. H. of C. 4-6½. P.W. Bill.[2]

16. Th.

Wrote to Count Cadorna—Sec. Liverpool Museum—Mr H. J. Baself[3]—Mr Hignett—Mr W. Robertson. Conclave on Amendments to Abp's Bill 11-1½. Therefore withdrew my Resolutions.[4] Royal Acad. 8½-9½ with Mr Herbert. Saw Ld Granville—Mr Herbert—Ld Acton—Mr Ouvry—W.H.G.—Ld Wolverton—Mr Joseph—Ld Hartington. Explained Hawarden affairs at some length to J.S. Wortley—Also to Sir R. Phillimore.[5] Dined with the R.P.s: conversation on Abp's Bill. Saw Herbert & another. Read Robertson on Rubrics.[6]

17. Fr.

Wrote to Ld Granville—Mrs Lewis—Rev. R. Yonge—Robn G.—Wms & Norgate—Rev N. Hall—Mr Engelbach[7]—Mr Farnfield[8]—Mr Saunders—Mr Creswick. Wrote Mem. on Valuations. Arranged papers &c. H of C. 2.15-7 and 10.15-1.45: working on the strange Public Worship Bill; which will in H of C. more or less improve.[9] Dined at Sir C. Forster's. Read Robertson.

18. Sat.

Wrote to Mr Watts R.A.—Ld Pembroke—Mr Dickinson—Mr Gott—Sir R. Phillimore—Rev Mr Wilberforce—Ld Blantyre—Mr C.A. Davis—Mr Westell—Bp Medley—Mrs Tyler—Mr Sellers—Ld Coleridge—Bp of Winchester—Mr Dana—Bp of Brechin—Mr Herbert—Sir D. Marjoribanks—and minutes (W.H.G.) Saw Mr Knowles

[1] Unidentified, could read 'Bainsford'.
[2] *H* ccxxi. 13.
[3] *Sic*; untraced.
[4] *H* ccxxi. 118; at the conclave: Hartington, Goschen, Forster, W. Cowper, Childers, Hugessen, Add MS 44762, f. 129 (dated there 15 July).
[5] A trustee of the estate.
[6] See 12 July 74.
[7] Lewis J. Engelbach of W. Bromwich, on books; Hawn P.
[8] John Albert Farnfield, London solicitor.
[9] *H* ccxxi. 247.

—Mr M'Coll—W.H.G.—Mrs Malcolm—Mr Balfour—Ld Granville—Saw Helen—calls. Read Wheatley.[1] Dined at Mr Balfour's.

19. 7 S.Trin.

St Peter's V. St mg & St Anne's evg. Saw Ld Granville
Gertrude }
H.N.G. } on my niece's affairs.
Wrote to Mr J.D. Chambers—Mrs Lewis—Scotts—Mr Grogan. Read Letter to Two Friends—Mr Falkner's Tract—Mr Gover's Tract[2]—Divers Tracts—Mr Taylor Innes in Cont.Rev.[3]

20. M.

Wrote to Bp of Winchester—Prof. Milligan—Mr Noel[4]—Dr Allon—Mr Sedgwick—Mr Gattie—Mr W. Brown—Dr Hayman—Mr Knowles—Sir A. Panizzi—Lord Lisgar. Saw Mr E. Joseph[5]—Scotts—Depn on Manchester School—Mr Grogan—Lord F.C.—Mr C. Howard—Mr Forster—Luncheon at 15 G.S.—Mr Goschen. Saw Ld Bathurst—Mr Lowe. Sat to Mr Watts in a Studio over 90°. H of C. 5¾-8 and 10½-1: on Endowed Sch. Bill.[6]

21. Tu.

Wrote to Bp of Winchester—Sec. L.N.W. Company—Mr E.W. Blyden—Helen G.—Mr Hodson—Sir R. Phillimore—Mr Cowper Temple (2) on his Amendment.[7] Saw Ld Granville—Mr Forster—Mr Herbert—Mr Granville Berkeley—Mrs Bickers—Messrs Wms & Norgate. Sat to Mr Dickinson. Saw Mr Childers (who went to Mr R. Gurney)[8]—Mr Adam—Mr Merritt. H. of Commons 5½-8 and 10-1. Spoke on Endowed Schools Bill.[9]

22. Wed.

Wrote to Mr Westell—Mr M. Barry—Mr Agnew—Messrs Townshend & Barker—Mr H. Cox—Mr Caldwell.[10] Saw Ld F. Cavendish—Mr

[1] Probably J. H. Wheatley, *The legend of Ravensholm* (1874?).

[2] W. Gover, *The Church of England or disestablishment, which?* (1874).

[3] On Ultramontanism and the Free Kirk, *Contemporary Review*, xxiv. 254 (July 1874).

[4] Roden Berkeley Wriothesley Noel, 1834-94, poet.

[5] Edward Joseph, art dealer.

[6] *H* ccxxi. 303.

[7] Probably to the Endowed Schools Bill, but not moved.

[8] Russell Gurney, 1804-78, tory M.P. Southampton 1865-78, sponsor of the Public Worship Regulation Bill.

[9] *H* ccxxi. 464.

[10] Indian merchant.

W. Cowper—Mr Knowles—Mr Grogan—Dr A. Clark. H of C. 12½-2 and 3-6.[1] Read Q.R.—Sympathy with Germany.[2]

23. Th.

Wrote to Mr Brodrick—Sec. L.N.W. Company—Mr E. Joseph—Dean of Chester. Luncheon at 15 G.S. Saw Mr Forster—Mr Bancroft—Sir T.D. Acland—Mr Quaritch—Scotts—Mr Russell Gurney. H of C. 4¼-7¾ and 11¼-12½. Spoke on P. Leopold & on Schools Bill.[3] Read Brodrick's Pamphlet[4] and other Tracts.

24. Fr.

Wrote to Ed. Daily News[5]—Mr C.C. Mowbray—Mr Barnes—Mr J.Y. Calyer—Robn G.—Madame Rio—Mrs Scott—Rev. M. Walcott—Mr Grogan. Dined with the Wortleys. Saw Rev. Mr Molesworth—Mr Knowles—Ld Granville—Ld Lyttelton—Mr Gurney—Mr Talbot—Ld H. Scott—Scotts. Read [blank]. H of C. 2-5. Spoke on withdrawal of Endowed Schools Clauses.[6] Packing & preparing for departure. Luncheon at 15 G.S.

25. Sat. [*Courthey, Liverpool*]

After a night nearly sleepless off at 5.45 for Liverpool. Arr. 12.30.—Saw Robn G.—Mr Pears's partner. Visited the Museum & went over my Porcelain[7] for a kind of valuation. Evg at Courthey. Matters do not brighten there: & the welcome seemed not quite so warm. Wrote to Helen G.—Barker & Hignett. Read Shairp's Introdn[8]—Miss Wordsworth's Journal—Reynald on Mirabeau.[9]

26. 8 S.Trin.

Drove into Liverpool: then by Rail to Seaforth. Walked round Litherland, then over the property. The desolation of Seaforth House is mournful: what mania can have possessed my brother in reducing it to this condition I know not. Church at 11: here things are improved & improving.

[1] *H* ccxxi. 490.
[2] Perhaps the article on the *Kulturkampf, Quarterly Review*, cxxxvi. 289 (April 1874).
[3] *H* ccxxi. 558, 560.
[4] G. C. *Brodrick, *The Irish land question* (1874).
[5] Not published.
[6] *H* ccxxi. 628.
[7] On exhibition and deposit there; the collection was sold at Christie's, 23 June 1875.
[8] D. *Wordsworth, *Recollections of a tour made in Scotland A.D. 1803*, ed. J. C. Shairp (1874).
[9] H. Reynald, *Mirabeau et la Constituante* (1872).

Saw Dr Smith—Mr Lloyd & Mr Swinney[1]—Back to Courthey in aft. Wrote to Mr Dixon—Read Dixon's Tracts[2]—Legge's Confucius[3]—Life of Bp Patteson. What a noble simple heroic saintly character. Conversation with Robn—And with Mr Thorneywill.

27. M. [Hawarden]

Off at 10.10 to Edgehill and Chester. There saw Mr Hignett. Home at 1.30. Wrote to Ld Granville—Mr G. Harris—W. England[4]—Ld F. Cavendish—T. Edwards—C.G. Unpacking; went through a heap of letters & papers. Read Br.Qu.Rev.Pol. Article[5]—Miss Wordsworth's Journal[6]—Bp of Lincoln's Speeches[7]—Richardson on Superstition.[8] Saw Mrs Burnett, & others.

28. Tu.

Wrote to Williams & Co—J. Watson & Smith—Mr Rodwell—Bp of St Asaph—Mr T.B. Woodward.[9] Ch. 8½ AM. Saw Mr Vickers. Worked a little on Homer. Read Records of the Past[10]—Wordsworth's Journal—Br.Qu.R. on Parker's Rome—Manning on the Dignity of Labour.[11]

29. Wed.

Ch. 8½ AM. C.G. returned: but avows this dear place is too *sore* for her to stay. Wrote to Ld F. Cavendish—Count Jarnac—Ed. Echo—Ld Lyttelton—M.D. Davis—Dean of Chester—J.G. Gilbert—Jos. Thompson—Mr Grogan. Saw Mr Spencer. Read Miss Wordsworth's Diary—Count Jarnac's Sir R. Peel.[12]

30. Th. [London]

Ch. 8½ AM. Wrote to Miss Kortright—W.H.G. Tel.—Mr G. Harris

[1] Of Seaforth.

[2] Perhaps R. W. Dixon, *Second essay on the maintenance of the Church of England as an established church* (1874).

[3] J. *Legge, *The life and teachings of Confucius* (1867).

[4] Perhaps William Holmes England, Liverpool grocer.

[5] *British Quarterly Review*, lx. 171 (July 1874).

[6] See 25 July 74.

[7] C. *Wordsworth, *Twelve Addresses delivered at his visitation* (1873).

[8] A. S. Richardson, *The revival of superstition: and how shall we meet it?* (1874).

[9] Thomas Best Woodward, author.

[10] *Records of the past . . . vol 1. Assyrian texts* (1874).

[11] H. E. *Manning, 'The dignity and rights of labour' (1874).

[12] P. F. A. de Rohan-Chabot, Count de Jarnac, 'Sir Robert Peel', *Revue des Deux Mondes*, 284 (July–August 1874).

—Ed. Echo Tel.—Hon H. Parker[1]—Chairman Met.Dist.RR.—Sir A. Panizzi—Mrs Th.—Mr Grogan. Read Miss Wordsworth's Journal —Adderley on Education[2]—and other Tracts. Preparations for departure & off at 3.30. Reached Suffolk St at 10.30.[3]

31. Fr.

Wrote to C.G.—Mrs Th. Saw Ld F. Cavendish—Mr Dyke—Bp of Winchester—WHG—Archbp of York—Mr Grogan—Sir W. Harcourt—Mr Gurney—Mr Forster—Ld J. Manners—Mr Hardy. H of C. 2½-7 and 9½-12 on the Church Bill.[4] Some good was done. Dined with Mrs Th. & there afterwards X. Read Tracts.

Sat. Aug. One. 1874.

Wrote to Mr G.F. Watts—Bp of Chichester—Ld Selborne—Ld Lyttelton—C.G.—Bp of Oxford—Mr Grogan. Saw Mr [A. J.] Balfour (who came to breakfast)—Sir A. Panizzi—Dowager Duchess of Somerset—Bps of Winchester & Ely. Dined at 15 G.S. Read Cockburn's Journal.[5] St Andrew Wells St 5 P.M.

2. 9 S.Trin.

Chapel Royal mg. St Paul's afternoon: a noble service. H.C. at C. Royal. Luncheon at 15 G.S.: & Mrs T. went with me. Saw Ld Beauchamp—Ld Lyttelton—Sir F. Doyle. Dined with the Wortleys. Wrote to Bp of Winchester—Bp of Lichfield—Mr Rodwell—Mr J. Carvell Williams. Wrote a little on Ritualism.[6] Read Rimius on the Unitas Fratrum.[7]

3. M.

Wrote to Messrs Field—Ld R. Gower—Sir W. Harcourt (& copy)—Messrs Pears Logan & Eden—Ld Shaftesbury—C.G. Dined at 15 G.S.—met Mr [J. R.] Herbert—& much conversation. H. of C.

[1] Probably Henry Parker, London solicitor.

[2] C. B. *Adderley, *A few thoughts on national education and punishments* (1874).

[3] Probably one of its private hotels; he subsequently stayed with Lord F. Cavendish at 21 Carlton House Terrace; Bassett, 203.

[4] *H* ccxxi. 1066.

[5] H. Cockburn, Lord Cockburn, *Journal*, 2v. (1874).

[6] Start of 'Ritualism and Ritual', *Contemporary Review*, xxiv. 663 (October 1874) and of literature of the Vaticanism controversy; see J. L. Altholz, 'Gladstone and the Vatican decrees', *The Historian* (May 1963) and Matthew, 'Vaticanism', 434.

[7] H. Rimius, *A candid narrative of the rise and progress of the Herrhuters . . . or Unitas Fratrum* (1753).

4¼-7½. Spoke on 3d R.Publ. Worship Bill.[1] Saw Temple. No good prospect there. X. Saw divers persons. 10½-1¼. Sat to Watts; with very much interesting conversation.

4. Tu.

Wrote to C.G.—Abp Manning—Dr Clark—and others. Saw Ld Granville—Bp of Winchester—Mr Kinnaird—Mr Seeley—Mr Herbert—Mr Knowles—and others. Read Contemp.Rev. Mr Greg—Mr Mivart.[2] H. of C. 4½-7½. Spoke on Fiji.[3] A day of very great anxiety about Mr Holt's amendment.[4] The issues involved almost unhinge me. Dined at 15 G.S. and remained late. Singular experiences.

5. Wed.

Wrote to W.H.G. Tel.—Mr Adam—Mr Binger—Ld Lyttelton—C.G. —Mrs Th. H. of C. 12-3½. Spoke in reply to Harcourt: it had become needful.[5] Saw Bp of Winchester—Ld Prov. Glasgow—Mr Forbes—Scotts—Sir Thos G.—Mr Bass—Sir W. Harcourt—Mr Potter. Dined with Kate and her sister. Then to bed tired in body but intensely relieved and with my heart back[6] as it is full of hymns. Saw Mr Balfour —Rev. Mr M'Coll—Mr Benjamin jun.

6. Th. [Penmaenmawr]

Wrote to Mr G. Gilbert[7]—Editor of Echo—Mr T.B. Potter—Mr Agnew—Sir S. Northcote. Packed & arranged my things. Saw Mr F. Lawley—Mr Joseph—Mr Havill—H. Gabbitas—Sir J. Lacaita—Sir A. Panizzi. Shopping. Saw Duke somebody's collection, in George Street. Luncheon at 15 G. Square: and Mrs Th. drove me to the 5.10 train at Willesden Junction. Reached Penmaenmawr[8] before midnight. Read Account of Libraries 1739.[9]

[1] *H* ccxxi. 1172.

[2] *Contemporary Review*, xxiv. 339, 360 (August 1874).

[3] Opposing McArthur's motion for annexation: *H* ccxxi. 1282.

[4] Holt's amndt. to the Public Worship Regulation Bill which Gladstone severely criticised next day; *H* ccxxi. 1363.

[5] Harcourt made further erastian denunciations, on the Lord amndts. to the Public Worship Regulation Bill: *H* ccxxi. 1337.

[6] Reading uncertain; could read 'bad'.

[7] Perhaps George Hine Gilbert, spirit dealer.

[8] The Gladstones' first holiday there since 10 Sept. 68.

[9] *A critical and historical account of all the celebrated libraries in foreign countries* (1739).

7. Fr.

Wrote to D. of Sutherland—Ld Granville—Scotts—Professor Blackie—Mrs Th.—Mr Foxton—Mr Stibbs—H.N. Gladstone—Chairman of M[etropolitan] D[istrict] Railway.[1] Bathed 1°. Walk with C. & call on the M[urray] Gladstones.[2] All seem to know and greet us. Arranged my traps: our house, Ty Mawr, is only middling, but air & view delightful: the outline of the hills I think seems even more beautiful than it used. Read Life of Patteson—Mathews on the Great Conversers.[3]

8. Sat.

Bathed 2°. Wrote to Mrs Hampton—F.R. Lawley—Mr Vickers. Read Mathews—Life of Colenso[4]—Account of Libraries. Walk over Pen Maen Bach, and five o'clock tea with Mrs Darbishire. But the day went I scarce know how.

9. 10 S.Trin.

Penmr Ch. 11¼ AM and 6½ PM. Bathed 3°. But I am troubled with some giddiness. Wrote to Ed. Guardian[5]—Mr Salkeld—Mr Dutton—Scotts. Corrected Speech of Aug. 5. Read Patteson's Life—Renan's Antichrist[6]—Wilkinson, Sermon on Confession[7]—Lundie, Sermon on Mr Allan.[8]

10. M.

Bathed 4°. Wrote to Mr A. Rowlands—Mr Balfour MP—Mr Agnew—Mr Rostron[9]—Dr Döllinger. Wrote a little on Ritualism: but my head will hardly allow it. Read Mathews's Vol.—Life of Bp Patteson. We walked up the Duchess's pass, then down Gwdwglas: and had tea at Mrs M. Gladstone's.

[1] Urging lower fares and two classes only, read to shareholders' meeting on 11 August, printed in *The Guardian*, 12 August 1874, 1025.
[2] See 12 Aug. 74n.
[3] Sir W. Mathews, *The great conversers and other essays* (1874).
[4] No *Life* found this early; probably one of the many pamphlets on the *Colenso row.
[5] Probably forwarding his letter; see 7 Aug. 74n.
[6] J. E. Renan, *L'Antichrist* (1873).
[7] G. H. *Wilkinson, 'Confession, a sermon' (1874).
[8] R. H. Lundie, *The late Mr Bryce Allan. In memoriam* (1874).
[9] Samuel Rostron, barrister.

11. Tu.

Ch. 8½ A.M. We moved our effects over to Mr Kneeshaw's.[1] Luncheon at the Victoria. Visit to Mrs Macdonald, who is wonderful at 83. Wrote to Sir S. Northcote—Watsons—Scotts—Mr Strahan—Mr Westell—Editor of the Guardian. Suspended bathing on sanitary grounds. Saw Mr Lamport.[2] Read Mathews—Life of Patteson: with ever growing admiration.[3]

12. Wed.

Under physic. Wrote to Bp of Lichfield—Dr Pankhurst[4]—Rev T.E. Jones—Rev Mr Henderson—Mr Corkran. Tea with Miss Wynn, the Bride.[5] Shore walk with C. Round game in evening: as we had yesterday evening. Read Bp Patteson's Life—Mathews's Essays—Dublin Univ. Magazine on Machiavelli—Music Halls—Irish Presb. Church.[6]

13. Th.

Breakfast in bed. Wrote to J. Watson & Smith—Mr W. Grogan—Scotts—Mr Cowtan—Mr Walford—Baroness Burdett Coutts—Rev J. Gornall[7]—Mr Goodier—Sir A. Panizzi—Mr Adams—Farrer Ouvry & Co—Mr Vickers. Read Bp Patteson (finished Vol I.)—Account of Libraries. Round game in evg. We went up Moel Ynion: were wet to the skin: forded the stream knee deep: excellent tea in the cottage above Aber 9d a head.

14. Fr.

Forenoon in bed, & more physic. Wrote to Lady E. M. Pringle—Mr C.T. Newton—B. Quaritch—D. Clarkson[8]—Rev. J. Pryce[9]—A. Bathe[10]—Mrs Th. Read Bp Patteson—Finished Account of Libraries—Congregational Magazine, three Articles on Church matters. Round game.

[1] Richard Kneeshaw, 1797–1878, of Plas Celyn, Penmaenmawr, quarry owner.
[2] Charles Lamport of Dwygyfylchi.
[3] See 2 July 74n.
[4] Richard Marsden Pankhurst, 1836–98; Manchester merchant and radical; husband of the suffragist.
[5] Emily Anina Wynn, da. of Lord Newborough, m. Sept. 1874 Murray Gladstone.
[6] *Dublin University Magazine*, lxxxiv. 129, 108, 205 (1874).
[7] Probably John Gornall, vicar of Calder Vale.
[8] London merchant.
[9] John Pryce, rural dean and vicar of Bangor.
[10] Anthony Bathe, anglican priest without benefice.

15. Sat.

Wrote to Sister Helen—Mrs Winans—Mr Cyrus Field. Harry returned from Iceland. Saw Mr Risk—Rev Mr Rogers. Read Life of Patteson—Contemp Rev. on Ld Ellenborough—& on Protestant Pulpit in Germany.[1] Backgammon with W.H.G.

16. 11 S.Trin.

Wrote to Robn G.—Rev E. Marston[2]—G.W. Muir—Rev D. Jones—Mr Grogan—Scotts—Bp of Carlisle. C. & I. arranged a letter to Willy about G.G. to be given after her departure.[3] Penmaenmawr Ch and H.C. mg. Llanfairfechan evg: returned by the sands. Read Renan's Antichrist—Life of Bp Patteson—Hennell on Dogmas[4]—Newman's Two Theisms[5]—Cranbrook on Responsibility.[6]

17. M.

Ch. 8½ A.M. Resumed bathing (5°). Saw Mr Davis—Dr A. Clark—Mr Duncan. Wrote to Editor of the Guardian[7]—Mrs Bennett—Mr J. Murray. Read Mathews—Life of Bp Patteson. Tea with Mrs M. Gladstone. Round game.

18. Tu.

Ch. 8½ A.M. Wrote to Chairman M D RR.—Mr Kneeshaw—Dr Lowe—Capt. Moresby[8]—Mr Snowie—Rev Mr Stuart Menteith.[9] Bathed 6°. Walk over the shoulder of P. to the Aber cottage: tea & back by Rail. Read Mathews—Life of Bp Patteson. Saw Dr Clark. Backgammon with W.H.G. Conversation with Harry on his matters & the journey to India.[10]

[1] *Contemporary Review*, xxiv. 374, 397 (August 1874).

[2] Edward Marston, 1818-95; *Derby's chaplain 1847-62; rector of Chester from 1862.

[3] i.e. Gertrude Glynne; see 21 June 74.

[4] S. S. Hennell, 'On the need of dogmas' (1874).

[5] F. W. *Newman, *The two Theisms* (1874).

[6] J. Cranbrook, *On responsibility* (1874).

[7] Denying he was ungrateful to the clergy in the debs. on ritualism; in *The Guardian*, 19 August 1874, 1074.

[8] John *Moresby, 1830-1922; explored New Guinea 1872-4; rear admiral 1881; see Add MS 44443, f. 308.

[9] Granville Wheler Stuart Menteath, rector of Morcott 1868.

[10] H. N. Gladstone spent December 1874-December 1875 working for Gladstone, Wyllie & Co. in Calcutta.

19. Wed.

Wrote to Ivall & Large[1]—Bp of Lichfield—Sir Thos G.—Robn G. (2). Saw Mr Grogan—Mr Branston—Dr Clark—Mr M. Gladstone—Mr Lamport. Bathed 7°. Recommenced writing on Ritualism: also began on Bp Patteson.[2] Read Mathews—Bp Patteson's Life—Woodward on Human Nature.[3] Tea party at 5. Round game & backgammon in evg.

20. Th.

Ch. 8½ AM. Bathed 8°. Wrote to Bp of Lichfield. Wrote on Bp P. & on Ritm. Read Bp Patteson's Life. Tea at Cottage on Penmr. Backgammon with Dr C[lark] in evg.

21. Fr.

Wrote to Ld Wolverton—Lady Ripon: on the very startling intelligence from her that R. can no longer honestly continue a member of the Church of England.[4] Wrote on Bp Patteson. Walk over the hills to Pendyffryn.—Bathed 9°. Read Patteson (finished)—Chambers. Backgammon with Dr C.

22. Sat.

Ch. 8½ AM. Bathed 10°. Wrote to Sec. General P.O.—Mr Faulkner—Mr Bramwell—Messrs Farrer & Ouvry—Mr Hayward. Wrote on Bp Patteson. Walk to the top of Drim (2500 f.) and down on Aber. Wrote on Bp Patteson. Read Blackwood Tales.[5] Backgammon with W.

23. 12 S.Trin.

Ch mg & evg. Bathed 11°. Wrote to Rev. B. Wilberforce[6]—Scotts. Conversation with Dr Clark. Read Rimius on Moravians (finished)[7]—Lavington on the same[8]—Cranz's Hist. Unitas Fratrum[9]—A Barrister on Prayer[10]—Signs of the Times.[11]

[1] London carriage builders.

[2] See 2 July, 2 Aug. 74.

[3] T. B. Woodward, *A treatise on the nature of man regarded as triune* (1874).

[4] News of *Ripon's conversion to Rome became public in early September 1874.

[5] *Blackwood's Edinburgh Magazine*, cxvi (August 1874).

[6] Albert Basil Orme Wilberforce, 3rd s. and chaplain of the bp.; rector of St Mary's, Southampton, 1871.

[7] See 2 Aug. 74.

[8] G. Lavington, *The Moravians compared and detected* (1755).

[9] D. Cranz, *Alte und Neue Brüder-Historie* (1771).

[10] *Orthodox theories of prayer. By a barrister* (1874).

[11] C. C. J. von Bunsen, *Signs of the times* (1856).

24. M. St Barth.

Wrote to Barker & Hignett—Mrs Th.—Mr Morier—Mr M. Moir. Bathed 12°. Wrote on Bp Patteson. Tea at Miss Duncan's. Backgammon with Dr Clark. Saw Mr Chidlaw.[1] Read Hist. Wesleyan Hymn Book.[2]

25. Tu.

Bathed 13°. Wrote to Sir A. Panizzi—Ld Coleridge—Scotts—Mr Macmillan—Ld Granville—Col. Neville. Tea at 5 with the Duckworths at Llanfairf. Went by the sands, back over the hill: 62 minutes. Wrote on Bp Patteson. The Jameses came. Read Renan's Antichrist and [blank]

26. Wed.

Bathed 14°. Wrote to Marchioness of Ripon (Eheu)[3]—Mr Craven—Mr S. Carter—Farrer & Ouvry—C. Brooks—Rev. Mr Dykes. Finished draft of Article on Bishop Patteson. Saw Dr Risk.[4] Conversation with Sir W. James. Walk with Mary by trams & over hill to Aber Cottage & tea. Backgammon with Mrs Clark. Read Sir R. Phillimore's Judgmt.[5]

27. Thur.

Ch. 8½ AM. Bathed 15°. Wrote to Barker & Hignett Tel.—Townshend & Barker—Vicar of Mold—Miss Helen G.—Mrs Maxwell Scott—Mr Bass. Saw Dr Clark—W.H.G.—Vicar (Mr D. Jones)—Mr Lamport. Sat to[6] Photographer. Wrote on Ritualism. Tea at Mr Lamport's: & long conversation with Monsig. Nardi[7] who is visiting there. Backgammon with Dr Clark. Read Theodore Hook.[8]

28. Fr. [Hawarden]

Wrote to Mr Tilley—Rev H.G. Henderson—Mr W.D. Henderson[9]—Mr T.G. Shaw—Mr Bromley—Mr T.B. Potter M.P. Bathed 16°. Saw

[1] Charles Chidlow, vicar of Cayo.
[2] W. P. Burgess, *Wesleyan hymnology* (1845).
[3] See 21 Aug. 74.
[4] James George Risk, naval staff surgeon stationed at Penmaenmawr.
[5] R. J. Phillimore, perhaps *Judgment ... in the case of the office of the judge promoted by Sheppard v. Bennett* (1871).
[6] Illegible word in brackets.
[7] Of Rome; see 3 Nov. 66.
[8] T. E. *Hook, *Humorous works* (1873).
[9] Perhaps of Belfast; published on Irish land.

Dean of Chester—Mr Hignett (when we arranged for C.s administering)—Mr L. Barker. We returned to Hawarden by Chester where C. took the Oath as Administratrix. Conversation with Sir W. James. Read Miss Wordsworth's Journal.[1] Began to stow & arrange papers in my new table. We left P[enmaenmawr] with very many kind tokens of good will.

29. Sat.

Ch. 8½ AM. Wrote to Mr Thornewill—Mr Macmillan—Robn G.—Mrs Burnett—C.C. Smith—J. Watson & Smith—Mr Courroux—Mr Ribbans—Sec.S.Kens. Museum—Rev. R. Coleridge[2]—Mr Forrest—Mr Darton—Captain Matthews—Prof. Blackie. Wrote on Ritual. Worked on arranging papers and new table. Read Miss Wordsworth. Backgammon with M. Glynne.

30. 13 S.Trin.

Ch. mg & evg. Saw Miss Burnett—Rev. S.E.G. Wrote on Ritual. Read W. Lyttelton's Sermon[3]—Herbert Spencer's Essay[4]—Döllinger on Reunion.[5] But searched in vain for my MS of conversations with him in 1845.[6]

31. M.

Ch. 8½ AM. Wrote to Sir R. Phillimore—Messrs Brown & Lamont—Williams & Co.—Mr Hughes—D. of Argyll—Mr Knowles—Sir M. Coomara Swarmey [*sc.* Swamy]. Finished & revised paper on Ritual: sent it off. Read Wallace on the Numbers of Mankind[7]—Wordsworth's Tour (finished). Cut into a large Spanish chesnut. Saw Mr Vickers.

Tues. Sept. One. 1874.

Ch. 8½ A.M. Revised my Patteson MS. Began work on the Hymn to Apollo. Wrote to Messrs Hoare—Ld Granville—Mrs Th.—Mr English. Saw Messrs Townshend & Barker. Conversation with W.H.G. The Wolvertons came: conversation in evg. W. & I felled the Chestnut. Read Wallace—Dixon's Tract.

[1] See 25 July 74.
[2] *Sic*; but none with this initial found.
[3] W. H. *Lyttelton, 'Sins of trade and business. A sermon' (1874).
[4] H. *Spencer, *The morals of trade* (1874).
[5] See 27 Mar. 72.
[6] Found later, printed in Lathbury, ii. 383.
[7] See 20 June 74.

2. Wed.

Ch. 8½ A.M. I read the lessons, as on & since Monday: but was put out by the sore intelligence from Robn that he has lost his son Hugh by scarlet fever. Wrote to Robn G. l. & Tel.—Dr H. Jackson[1]—Watsons—Mr A.P. Dexter—Mr Tilley—Mr F.A. Bailey. Spent the forenoon chiefly in conversation political & personal with Wolverton. In the afternoon we walked by the Oaks to the Colliery. Saw Hurst jun. —W.H.G. on Estate matters.

3. Th.

Ch. 8½ AM. Wrote to Sir E. Watkin—Mr Newton—Rev E. Simms—Dr Rabbinowicz—Mr J.G. Robson—Sir J. Lacaita—Mr T.W. Marchant[2]—Mr T. Davison—Mr G. Peffaius[3]—Rev C.S. Upperton.[4] Attended the flowershow: a creditable first effort. Tree-walk with Lord W. and Mr C. F[ield]. We felled an oak. Read Wallace.

4. Fr.

Wrote to Mr Vickers—Messrs J. Watson & Smith (2)—Ld Lyttelton—Scotts—Mr English—Mrs Th.—Wms & Norgate—Mr Knowles—Housemaid C.H.T.—Farrer & Ouvry—Mrs Hope—Mr B. Quaritch—Barker & Hignett—Sir R. Phillimore—Marchioness of Ripon. Ch. 8½ A.M. Took Ld W. & Mr Field to the Old Castle. Kibbling. Walk with Ld W. in evg. We have had a good deal of harmonious conversation. Corrected proofs of Article on Ritualism.

5. Sat. [*London*]

Up at 6.30 and after looking to the Post off by the first train to Edge Hill for the very sad funeral at Knotty Ash. I saw poor Robertson after, but only for a moment. Saw Mr Townshend—Mr Thornewill—Mr Hardman Earle—Sir Thos G. Off at 1 to London. Dined with Mrs Th. Arranging papers &c. afterwards, *again* in No 11 [Carlton House Terrace] but only as a bird of passage. Read Contemp.Rev. on Heat and Living Matter—Ethics of Christ—&c.[5]

[1] Perhaps not H. but Edward Jackson, physician in Lancashire.
[2] Possibly W. T. Marchant, song collector.
[3] Probably George Peffani of Rotherhithe.
[4] Charles Stuart Upperton, 1829-1916; vicar of Ince, Cheshire, 1867-86.
[5] *Contemporary Review*, xxiv. 516, 503 (September 1874).

6. 14 S.Trin.

St James's mg with H.C. and St Paul's evg. Wrote to Messrs Longman—Author of Supernatural Religion[1]—Mr F.M. Adams[2]—Mrs Th.—Barker & Hignett—Mr Michie—Sec. S.K. Museum—Mr J. Knowles—Mr Murray. Luncheon at 15 G.S. Dined with Sir A. Panizzi: retd to 15 G.S. & saw Mrs Th. X. Much preparation for departure: in consequence of going to Liverpool for the funeral yesterday. Saw Sir Jas Hudson in B.Sq. Read Meditations on the Song of Solomon.[3]

7. M. [Cologne]

Up at 6¼. Off at 7.40 to Cologne. A good passage. Arrived at midnight. Read little but newspapers on the way. A few hours at the Hotel Disch: one of them in conversation with my sister Helen whom I had not seen for over 6 years; and in indirect preparation as I hope for her departure. Also conversation with Mr Parker.

8. Tu. [Munich]

Off at 6 PM: reached Munich at 9½. Conversation with Mr Parker—Mr Morier—Read Dante I.II.—Bädäker &c. We were met by Mr Morier[4] & most kindly received at his house.

9. Wed.

Wrote to C.G. Much conversation with Mr Morier. With Dr Döllinger 10½-1 and 3-6. Also 1-3 he dined with us. Read Dante—III.IV. *No* sights or acts of business: except the Univ.

10. Th.

We went to see the Pinakothek which exceeded my recollections.[5] Also Saw Dr D. 11½-1, 3-6: again in the evg 8-10. with Professor Helferich.[6] Read Dante V.VI.—Sybel, Clerikale Politik.[7] Corrected revise of Art. on Ritualism. Visited the Arcaden with Dr D.

[1] Unidentified.
[2] Frank Mantell Adams, wrote on trade marks.
[3] [N. Cole], *Meditations on the Song of Songs*, ed. G. C. White (n.d.).
[4] R. B. D. *Morier (see 23 June 52), then chargé d'affaires for Bavaria; for diarist's visit, see R. Wemyss, *Memoirs and letters of Sir R. Morier* (1911), ii. 301.
[5] See 1 Oct. 45.
[6] Perhaps Johann Alfons Renatus von Helferich, 1817-92; German economist and professor at Freiberg.
[7] H. C. L. von Sybel, *Klerikale Politik in neunzehnten Jahrhundert* (1874).

11. Fr.

Wrote to my sister Helen. W. & H. went off to the mountains. Saw the Glypothek with the M[orier]s & Dr D.—The Antiquarium with Dr D. & Professor of Archaeology. Spent the afternoon as usual in walking with Dr D: after the drive to Palace of Schliessheim. Saw Professor Brunn[1] in evg to discuss my Cameo: He dined here. Visited Mr Lainbach's[2] Studio. A portrait was agreed on at Mr M's instigation: I am purely passive. Read Sybel.

12. Sat.

Wrote to C.G.[3]—Barker & Hignett. Photographed for Leinbach [*sic*]. Saw the Schutzkammer & the Reiche Kapelle: both of them wonderful: many new lights. A last afternoon spent with Dr D.—We met the Abp of Munich![4] At 5.45 an affectionate farewell. God be with him. Read Sybel—Dante VII.VIII.

13. S.15 Trin.

Gastkirch 9½. Cathedral 4½. What a contrast! (Katzenmaier & Canon [blank]). Engl. service at 3. Visited various Churches. Conversation on Religion with my kind host. Wrote to Mr Knowles. Further corr. & addn to Art on Ritualism.[5] Read Sybel—Friedr. Wilh. Briefwechsel.[6] Saw Madame Minghetti.

14. M.

Wrote to C.G.—Mr J. Patrick—Mr Graser. 10-12 Sat to Mr Leinbach. 12-2½. National Museum: interesting, in some things even wonderful: e.g. the ivories. Hans Hemmling books—12th Century Crucifixion—H.H. Madonna & Saviour. Visited the Basilica. Much conversation with Mr M[orier]. Read Briefwechsel—Schwartz on Dies Irae[7]—Mr M. on Cooperation Banking.[8] Preparations for expedition tomorrow to the Bavarian Alps.

[1] Heinrich von Brunn, 1822-94; art historian.

[2] *Sic.* Franz Lenbach, reproduced in Bassett, 78.

[3] Bassett, 205.

[4] Gregor von Scherr, d. 1877; abp. from 1856; excommunicated Döllinger 1871.

[5] The insertion of the notorious passage in para. 35: 'Rome has substituted for the proud boast of *semper eadem* a policy of violence and change of faith . . . she has refurbished and paraded every rusty tool . . . no one can become her convert without renouncing his moral and mental freedom, and placing his civil loyalty and duty at the mercy of another. . . .'

[6] L. von Ranke, *Aus dem Briefwechsel Friedrich Wilhelms IV mit Bunsen* (1873).

[7] A. Schwartz, 'On the sequence "Dies Irae" ', *Macmillan's Magazine*, xxx. 455 (September 1874).

[8] Untraced article by *Morier.

15. Tu. [*Unkel*]

We set out at 9. 9.35 to 12:30 train to Traunstein. Carriage by Inzell to the Reichenhall junction. Then we walked 7 m to Unkel,[1] carrying our baggage. The scenery *to* Inzell was beautiful & *riant*: from Inzell grand, without a break. Inn good. All manner of interesting objects on the way. Read Dante.

16. Wed. [*Ramsau*]

Wrote to Mr Morier. We set out at 7.30 & walked to Lofer. No horses available: on foot to Frobenwies: together 14 miles. We dined: & on again by the mountain top to Ramsau:[2] seeing the wonderful *Klamm* [gorge] of Saisenberg on the way. Helen's walking was wonderful: not less than 29 miles or thereabouts. We took the first Inn at Ramsau—a mistake. Read Dante. Examined Churches Chapels by the way as occasion offered. Beauty & grandeur accompanied us at every step. Bad beds: fair food: much appetite.

17. Th.

Tel. to Mr Morier. Walked to the Konigsee Lake Inn[3] & took up our quarters; which were comfortable. Went on the lake to the upper end. Saw the Obersee—Bartholomäus Haus (& the singularly beautiful waitress) with the Church, & then an exp. to the Eiskapelle,[4] curious, & placed in a scene of unequalled grandeur within the rock walls of the Wachzmann 9000 feet high. The echo of pistols[5] on the lake was astonishing: its whole character wonderful: we saw in the clear water 30 or 40 feet of shadow of the nearly perpendicular sides. Read Dante.

18. Fr. [*Munich*]

Saw the Relief Plan. Off after breakfast to Berchtesgaden by the beautiful river walk with a Führer und Träger who was a charming specimen of these bold hardy active South Bavarians. At B. saw the fine old Church with a good modern W. end & the very singular Salt mine. Then drove to Salzburg. At Grödingen bid farewell to a line of glorious scenery unbroken for some 70 miles. Salzburg has a most

[1] On the Austrian border, about 20 miles SW. of Salzburg.
[2] 5 miles WSW. of Berchtesgaden.
[3] At the N. end of the spectacular lake, s. of Berchtesgaden.
[4] A collapsed glacier on the Walzmann.
[5] A regular feature of the row on the lake.

interesting site and incidents but we were spoiled children. Saw the Cathedral (Font pictures of Archbishops notable in some ways, the Eternal Father (so at Lofer) in the Altar Reredos—) the Franciscane Kirche, *recoil* interesting—the Burial ground—St Peters with its fine gateway and apse: the strange leaden monument: the Drauerei zur Hölle!![1] Dined on an open gallery by the River & off at 6.20 to Munich, parting from my company at Rosenheim. Tea & conversation with Mr Morier. Also a letter from sister Helen which gave me much material of thought, very mixed. Read Dante.

19.

Wrote to Helen—To W.H.G.—To C.G. Accounts of the Bonn Conference:[2] for which & its results God be praised. Also picked up arrears in papers Germ. & Engl. Shopping. Visited Cathedral again, & Churches. Sat 2 hours to Lehnbach. Mr Tachard[3] (of Alsace) dined in evg & we had much conversation on the future of Europe & on its public men. Saw Professor Brunn. Ascertained Dr D's return.

20. 16 S.Trin. [*Nuremberg*]

Off at 9 to the Gasteich where Catzenmeier[4] preached an interesting Sermon on the One fold, one shepherd: in a spirit liberal, firm, and orthodox. The small Church was overcrowded.—Then to the Cathedral where the sermon was over and the Tratiner: & so to the English Ch. where Mr Jones[5] preached earnestly & we had the H.C.

Dr D. came to dinner at one and I passed the time with him from dinner to five when I put up my things and went to Lehnbach's (to sit for some 20 m) and the Station. Here Dr D. said remarkable parting words. Mr Morier & I had much conversation & reached the Bauerischer Hof, Nuremberg, a good Inn, before midnight. Read Juvenal, ein Sittenrichter &c.[6] Pichler, Kirkliche Trennung.[7]

21. M.

We spent the hours 9-1 and 3-6 in the town with extreme interest. It

[1] *Sc.* Brauerei; i.e. a small brewery, 'the Hell Inn'.

[2] Döllinger's conference of anti-ultramontanists, 14-16 September, including Anglican observers.

[3] Pierre-Albert Tachard, b. 1826, represented Haut-Rhin 1869-71.

[4] Anton Gatzenmeier, prominent member of the Old Catholic movement.

[5] Peter Jones, the embassy chaplain.

[6] P. Doetsch, *Juvenal ein Sittenrichter seiner Zeit* (1874).

[7] A. Pichler, *Geschichte der kirchlichen Trennung zwischen dem Orient und Occident*, 2v. (1864-5).

is above all notable for the development of strong individuality, especially in its houses. We saw The Schloss—The Rathhaus—S. Sebaldus—S. Lorenz—Frauenkirche—The Gallery—The Museum—Rare gems of architecture: 7 & 10 Altars in two great Protestant Churches: The Sacramentshaus—Krafts marvellous relief of the Entombment: & Vischer's most remarkable Apollo:[1] A. Durer's truly grand Charlemagne (compare his Sigismund)[2] and much that I cannot now name. Off at 8.55. read my Juvenal ein Sittenrichter.

22. Tu. [*Cologne*]

Reached the Disch Hotel Cologne about midday. Saw the Cathedral twice and formed my general impressions: also some other architectural points. But I spent 9 hours (3 and 6) in conversation with Helen. She has reached a point where we can largely sympathise and my earnest desire is to aid her both as to her religious position, on which she shows me much confidence, & by bringing about if possible her removal from this hotel to a more natural and available position. I told her as well as I could what had passed between Dr Döllinger and me. To bed at two A.M. Tried bookbuying but with indifferent success.

23. Wed.

Rose late: & resumed conversations with Helen. Wrote to C.G.—Housekeeper at C.H.T.—Dr Döllinger (began). Dinner & entertainment at No 14 Hölle. About six hours with Helen today. Read Fugger Glott 'Warum sind wir Römisch Catholisch?'[3] Visited the Cathedral and other Churches. Some survey of the town wh has much interest.

24. Th. [*Travelling*]

Wrote to Dr Döllinger (finished)—Sir A. Panizzi—Bishop Reinkens (for HJG)[4] reading the first and third to Helen. Many hours of conversation with her: I think seven. (See inf.) Rested in the forenoon from fear of diarrhoea. Read Fugger Glött—Juvenal, ein Sittenrichter &c—Häckel Anthropogenie.[5] About ten I quitted Helen. She is deeply to be felt for: her mind and soul are in a great strait, but she is striving to battle for the truth and may she be blest. Travelled all night.

[1] Both in St. Sebaldus.
[2] Both in the Germanic Museum.
[3] Fugger-Gloett, 'Warum sind wir Römisch-Katholisch?' (1874).
[4] Joseph Hubert Reinkens, 1821-96; Old Catholic bp. of Cologne 1873.
[5] E. H. P. A. Haeckel, *Anthropogenie* (1874).

25. Fr. [*London*]

Wrote to C.G. Reached London after a fine passage at 6. The cliffs of Dover in the slanting sun were truly grand—even after the scenery of the Bavarian Alps. Read Rossetti's Spirit of Dante[1]—Juvenal ein Sittenrichter—Strauss's Ulrich Hutten.[2] Dined at No 15. G.S. and met Americans: they were interesting in divers ways.

26. Sat. [*Hawarden*]

Wrote to Mr G. Tallents—Mr Hine—Farrer & Ouvry—Dr Molony[3]—M. Henri Dumont[4]—Mrs R. Lawley—Ed. of Echo—Mr J. Parker and others—Mr Thos Bell—Mr Fenton—Sec. Mayor of Liverpool.[5] Saw Sir A. Panizzi—Mr Craik (Macmillan)[6]—Mr Westell—Scotts—Mr Quaritch (assistant). Luncheon at 15 G.S. Packed—and off with C. to Hn at 4.40: arrived soon after eleven. Sat *opening* letters until 1.30.

27. 17 S.Trin.

Hn Ch mg & evg. Corrected proofs of the Patteson Article.[7] Wrote to Lord Coleridge—Messrs Clowes—Robn G.—Mr C.T. Newton. Read Church Parties[8]—Möhler Symbolik[9]—Life of De Dominis—Works of Do[10]—Life of Bp Gardiner.[11]

28. M.

Ch. 8½ AM. Wrote to Mr Guildford Onslow—Dr von Döllinger—Thos Scott—Bp of Argyll—H.J.G.—Watson & Smith—W.H.G.—Ld Cottesloe[12]—Sir A. Gordon—Mr Swinfen Brown[13]—Mr H. Cox—Rev Mr Halcombe[14]—Mr Meyrick—Mr Vaughan Williams[15]—Rev Mr Molesworth—Mr Strahan—Mr R. Turnbull[16]—Senington—

[1] Probably D. G. Rossetti, 'On the Vita Nuova of Dante', published 1870, reprinted in W. M. Rossetti, *The Works of D. G. Rossetti* (1911).

[2] D. F. Strauss, *Ulrich von Hutten*, 2v. (1858).

[3] Perhaps Patrick John Molony, physician in Cambridgeshire.

[4] Perhaps of Murray & Dumont, scholastic agents.

[5] Business untraced.

[6] (Sir) Henry *Craik, 1846-1927, in education dept. from 1870; his poems published by Macmillan.

[7] See 2 July 74.

[8] Perhaps W. J. *Conybeare's famous article, *Edinburgh Review*, xcviii. 273 (October 1853).

[9] See 18 Oct. 45.

[10] See 22 May 59.

[11] Untraced life of Stephen Gardiner, bp. of Winchester.

[12] See 22 Dec. 34.

[13] C. W. Swinfen Brown of Mirfield had sent a print of Hawarden.

[14] John Joseph Halcombe, 1832-1910; rector of Balsham from 1874.

[15] Had been given a pension on retiring as judge: *The Guardian*, 30 September 1874, 1243.

[16] Robert Carr Turnbull, London solicitor.

T.B. Vernon—Treslove Cox[1]—Rev. Bullesley[2]—Stanier[3]—D. Robertson—Mr Joseph—Mr Tupper—J. Hill—Cowtan—E. Buller[4]—Librarian London Libr. Cutting a beech with Herbert. Read Taylor's Autobiogr.[5]—Erasmus on Pilgrimages.[6]

29. St Mich. Tu.

Ch. 8¾ A.M. Wrote to M. Coomara Swamey—Mr W. Williams—Sir Thos G.—Mr F.T. Palgrave—Dr Burgess—Sir R. Phillimore—Mr M'Coll—Mr M. Whitwell—Sir H. Taylor. Arranging papers. Prolongued conversation in evg with Dr King, who dined. Cutting a beech with H. Read Taylors Autobiogr.—Wallace on Numbers of Mankind[7]—Plutarch de Is[is] et Os[iris].

30. Wed.

Ch. 8½ A.M. Wrote to Sec.Metr.Distr.Co.—Mr Homersham Cox—Mr F.J. Davis—Mrs Th.—Major Cameron[8]—Mr Derry—Messrs Hoare—W.D. [*sc.* P?] Adams—Rev. Mr Perry. Conversation with Dr King and Archdeacon Ffoulkes. Corrected revises of Patteson Article. Read H. Cox on 'Protestant'[9]—Friedrich's Gebetbuch.[10] Wrote Notes on the Old Catholic position v. Rome. Read Wallace (finished)—Taylor's Autobiogr.

I. 1. The adoption of an erroneous proposition touching Christian belief, or *circà fidêm*, by a Christian Church is a very serious matter at best.

2. Its adoption as *de fide*, as a thing to be believed for necessity of salvation, is a thing far more serious.

3. But this act becomes tremendous in its consequences, when the particular Church, or Churches, however extended, claim the entire authority of the Church Universal.

4. And lastly when they teach as a matter of faith that the authority so claimed embraces infallibility *in such a manner* that the seal of infallibility is set to the proposition in question by the act of its adoption. This is a repudiation and breach of duty, in vital matter, to be repaired only by repentance. And this is the truth, in every word, with the dogma of Papal infallibility recently adopted by the Vatican Council.

While however the decree of Papal infallibility considered with a view to

[1] Alfred Treslove Cox, London surveyor.
[2] A nonconformist.
[3] Perhaps William Stanyer, sec. of the National Education Union.
[4] Or Bullen; perhaps Edward Bullen, rector of Eastwell.
[5] G. L. Taylor, *The autobiography of an octogenarian architect*, 2v. (1870–72).
[6] D. *Erasmus, *Peregrinatio* (1540?).
[7] See 20 June 74.
[8] Col. George Poulett Cameron, wrote on Vaticanism; Hawn P.
[9] H. Cox, *père, Is the Church of England Protestant?* (n.d.).
[10] J. F. Friedrich, *Gott meine einzige Hoffnung; Christkatholisches Andachtsbuch* (1873).

practical effects, leaves a door open to much equivocal argument by the condition that in each case the utterance of the Pope shall be *ex Cathedrâ*, the Council has provided another more ready and effectual arm against the private conscience, in another of its decrees, which has not received the attention it well merits.

It has decreed that the acts of the Pope may not be questioned, and that his orders must be obeyed. This is without qualification or exception.

There is no *Ex Cathedrâ* here: and by this decree the consciences and actions of the faithful are effectually bound, in all cases where they might have escaped from the reach of the other, in so far as it shall at any time please the Pope or those who from behind move the Pope, to bind them.

It is easy to perceive how the power hereby given might be used in reference for instance to the Temporal Power of the Pope.

Prayer might be ordered for its restoration.

It might be declared vital to the independence of the Church and thus mediately to Christianity itself.

To impugn its necessity, or its legitimacy, might be prohibited under pain of mortal sin.

In what manner could the meshes of *this* net be escaped?

II. The Old Catholics, if I understand them aright, are by no means Protestants, nor are they Rationalists in disguise, but they are men who believe as the moderate, Cisalpine, or Gallican divines and members of the Western Church generally, always believe, and as the Council of Constance in effect decreed; and who will not be bound to an article of the Christian Faith which they know to be novel, and therefore to be false as an article of Faith; even if it were true, which they hold it not to be, as a proposition.

Reformers doubtless they are, but within the limits compatible with the maintenance of their ancient Faith: that is to say within the province of discipline, which however encircling to high Roman authorities is a very wide one: and if of doctrine also, only of such doctrine as has been truly accepted by the Church.

It seems to me, however, probable that they are in one sense too good for the age in which they live; an age for the taste and apprehension of which not only things abstract, but things remote, are as if they were not.

At the same time, in Germany, the roots of intellectual life are vigorous, and the legitimate authority of human reason, as a factor of life and conduct, is thoroughly naturalised in idea and practice.

These men are, eminently, if not exclusively, the professors of historical Christianity; and the desire, disposition, and capacity, to maintain the basis thus defined will not easily die out among them.

It seems highly probable that they will seek strength in a quarter where they may legitimately obtain it, namely by union with the Eastern Church, immediately represented by the See of Constantinople. Of the two more serious points of distinction between East and West, one, the Papal Supremacy, is already virtually disposed of: and there seems no reason why the other should not be adjusted provisionally on the footing marked out at Bonn or one resembling it. The services, usages, and local privileges & powers generally, would remain intact.

III. It appears to be indubitable in principle that the great duty of Christian Communion, when it calls us to consider between conflicting claims, likewise provides us with the rule, by which those claims are to be decided. We are not to consider—if we act on Catholic principles—what communion best suits our tastes. Nor even what Communion is, by the usages it follows, or the promise it holds out, most likeably furnished for the supply of our personal religious needs. It is, what Communion holds the title of the Apostolic Church? For this end it must produce to us the original Charter of the day of the Ascension: and it must teach the Christian Faith—perhaps we should say most specifically the Faith of the undivided Church—without diminution, and without addition. For where these marks are, God has set his hand: and where He has set his hand, our souls will be best trained and moulded: and we have no more right to go elsewhere, than the Child to leave the house of his Parents, because he happens to know some other house where the Father is richer, or the Mother fairer.

Neither must it be an intrusive Church. But this does not touch the case as between the Old Catholics and the Church of Rome; to which alone these remarks apply.[1]

Thurs. Oct. One 1874.

Church 8½ A.M. The 30 Retreat Clergy present. Wrote to J. Watson & Smith—Ld Harrowby (for consideration)—Messrs Dawson—Dr King—Mr Henly—Mr Hine. The new Lyttelton party came with l & Mr [Montague] Bernard. 12 to dinner. Read Taylor Autobiogr.—Wren & Sanderson on the Prayerbook.[2] Cutting with Herbert.

2. Fr.

Ch 8½ AM. Wrote to LNW Goods Manager—Mr Mackingly—F. Lawley—Rev G.V. Smith—Mr Picton—Mrs Schwabe—Mr Strahan—Mr Scrivener—Mr F. Oakeley. Walk with Mr Bernard & Ld Lyttelton. Much conversation with Mr B. respecting the sad case of Lord Ripon.[3] Read F. Lawley on Sir B. Tarleton[4]—Disestablishment from *Broad* Ch. point of view(!).[5] Bp of Brechin came: conversation with him on Döllinger & O[ld] C[atholic] movement.[6]

3. Sat.

Ch. 8½ AM. Wrote to Mr E. Yarnall—Miss King—Mr Dalton—Mr

[1] Holograph dated 30 September 1874, Add MS 44762, f. 134; in Lathbury, ii. 400.

[2] R. Sanderson, *Fragmentary illustrations of the history of the book of Common Prayer from . . . Bishop Wren* (1874).

[3] See 21 Aug. 74.

[4] F. C. *Lawley, 'Sir Banastre Tarleton', *Blackwood's Edinburgh Magazine*, cxvi. 432 (October 1874).

[5] Perhaps J. Hopgood, 'A scheme for gradual disestablishment', *Contemporary Review*, xxiii. 966 (May 1874).

[6] A. P. *Forbes, much involved with Old Catholics; see W. Perry, *A. P. Forbes* (1939), 150.

E. Joseph—Mr Ouvry—Dr Macleod—Mr Cowtan—Mrs H.J.G.—Sir G. Bowyer M.P. Read Löher, Deutschlands Weltstellung[1]—Taylor's Autobiogr. Saw Professor King. Walk & long conversation with Bp of Brechin. Cutting with Willy. 14 to dinner: as yesterday.

4. 18 S.Trin.

Ch. 11 AM with H.C. Wrote to Ld Ripon: a stiff letter in answer to one from him[2]—Rev. R. O'Keeffe—Mr Brough—Rev Mr Greathead[3]—Mr Lynch—J. Watson & S.—Dr Sinthall—Dr Schidrowitz[4]—Mr J. Murray—Ed. Guardian.[5] Corrected revise of Patteson Article. Conversation with Bp of Brechin. Read Sermons on Ritual & on Secession: and other Tracts.

5. M.

Ch. 8½ AM. Wrote to Mrs Th.—Sir Thos G. Saw Bp of Brechin (who went)—Mr Vickers—Mr Griffiths. Conversation with W.H.G. and worked on my Memorandum respecting the Succession: which will for the future fix his position, C.s, and mine.[6] Cut a tree with W. Read Löher (finished)—Taylor's Autobiogr.

6. Tu.

Ch. 8½ AM. Wrote to A. Kinnaird—Ld Emly—Mr Vickers—Mr Farish[7]—S.E.G.—F.J. Seard—Mr Ouvry—Messrs Barker—Mr M. Cooke. Further corrected and completed my Memorandum respecting the place and Estate. Conclave at 2½ respecting the Memorial to dear Stephen [Glynne] and the arrangements as to movable personalty. We were very harmonious. Read Taylor Autobiogr.—v. Döllinger, Vergangenheit u. Gegenwart der Kath. Theologie.[8] We cut a lime down.

[1] F. von Loeher, *Über Deutschlands Weltstellung* (1874).

[2] *Ripon had written to protest at Gladstone's anti-Roman comments in his 'Ritualism' article; letters in Wolf, *Ripon*, i. 297.

[3] Probably John Greatheed, curate in Oxford.

[4] Samuel Schidrowitz of London had written on 'Ritualism'; Hawn P.

[5] Public thanks for flood of letters on 'Ritualism'; *The Guardian*, 7 October 1874, 1265.

[6] Hawn P.

[7] James Farish of St. John's Wood.

[8] J. J. I. von Döllinger, *Die Vergangenheit und Gegenwart der katholischen Theologie* (1864).

7. Wed.

Ch. 8¾ A.M. and 7 P.M. (Harvesthome). Wrote to Ld Coleridge—Sir A. Gordon—Rev Mr Owen—Broughton Hall Stationmaster—Mr P. Keith. Read Adderley's Pamphlet[1]—Law of Husband & Wife[2]—Bayley on The Deluge[3]—Von Döllinger's very remarkable Address (finished). Consulted Harry on the letter to Mr Keith[4] after it was written. Walk with Lyttelton. The harvest service (near 2 h.) and congregation were really remarkable.

8. Th.

Ch. 8½ AM. Wrote to *Rev.* W. Maskell—Ld Ripon—Mr W. Hughes—Mr W. Brough—D.D. Sheldon[5]—F. Lawley. Walk with Lyttelton. Conversation with C.G. and W. on the Agency matter. Conversation with Miss Burnett—W.H. Lyttelton. Read Taylor Autobiogr.—M'Ghee on the Papish question.[6]

9. Fr.

Ch. 8½ AM. Wrote to Mr A. Kinnaird—Mr B. Quaritch—Dr Lowe. Read Maynooth Evidence of 1855[7]—Taylor Autobiogr. (finished)—Macmillan on Prussia & the Vatican[8]—Walker on Ritualism.[9] Woodcutting in afternoon.

10. Sat.

Ch. 8½ AM. Wrote to Mr Beal. Saw Fuller Preston. Wood cutting. Conversation on Harry's matter. Read Lee on Validity of Anglican Orders & made Notes[10]—Walker on Ritualism—Erasmus on Pilgrimages.[11]

[1] See 30 July 74.
[2] Perhaps E. J. Worboise, *Husbands and wives* (1873).
[3] Untraced.
[4] Patrick Keith of Liverpool, arranging H. N. Gladstone's departure for India; Hawn P.
[5] Untraced.
[6] R. J. MacGhee, probably *Rome and England; the two Churches, the two Reformations and the two Creeds* (1852).
[7] Report on its management; *PP* 1854–5 xxii.
[8] *Macmillan's Magazine*, xxx. 559 (October 1874); article by R. Morier.
[9] S. A. Walker, 'How long will the laity bear it?' (1864).
[10] F. G. *Lee, *The validity of the Holy Orders of the Church of England maintained and vindicated* (1869).
[11] See 28 Sept. 74.

11. 19 S.Trin.

Ch mg & evg. Wrote to Ld Emly—Mr P. Keith—and [blank]. Read Barrister on Commn[1]—Audin's Life of Luther[2]—Bp of Worcester's Charge—AngloContinental Corresp. on O.C. Movement.[3] Conversation on Harry's matters.

12. M.

Ch. 8½ AM. Wrote to Bp of St Andrew's—Mr E. Leicester—Sir H. Verney—Robn G. Treecutting at the Rake. Worked a little on the Hymn to Apollo. Read Pichler, Theologie des Leibniz[4]—Morley's Rousseau.[5] Conversation with C. on my reply to Robn.

13. Tu.

Ch. 8½ AM. Wrote to HJG (on her position)—Mr Quaritch—Mr Joseph—Gen. Ponsonby. Read Morley's Rousseau—Pichler Theol. des Leibniz—Matthiae, Ilgen, Hermann on the Hymns.[6] Tea with Mr Griffiths of the Rake. Wood cutting there.

14. Wed.

Ch. 8½ AM. Visited John Bailey who is dying. Wrote to Mr A. Kinnaird—Rev. Mr Jenkins—Rev. Mr J. Pulling[7]—Mr P. Keith. Woodcutting at the Rake. Read Pichler's Leibniz—Morley's Rousseau—England's Sympathy with Germany (documents).[8]

15. Th.

Ch. 8½ AM. Reply at Bailey's he was but just alive. Wrote to Mr T.B. Potter—Mr J. Severn—Mr Buchan—Mr Jos. Botting[9]—Mr Monro—Mr T. Bailey. Wood cutting with W. We spent the forenoon in discussing the difficult question of the Agency which has become so complicated thro' unforeseen occurrences that it seems now almost impossible to do justice to every one affected. W. writes to make

[1] See 23 Aug. 74?

[2] J. M. V. Audin, *Histoire de la vie . . . de Martin Luther*, 3v. (1839-46).

[3] F. Meyrick, ed., *Correspondence between members of the Anglo-Continental Society and 1. Old Catholics 2. Oriental Churchmen* (1874), with app. on the Bonn conference.

[4] A. Pichler, *Die Theologie des Leibnitz*, 2v. (1869-70).

[5] J. *Morley, *Rousseau*, 2v. (1873).

[6] A. H. Matthiae, *Animadversiones in Hymnos Homericos* (1800).

[7] James Pulling, 1814-79; Master of Corpus, Cambridge, from 1850.

[8] See, perhaps, 22 July 74.

[9] Untraced; could read 'Bolting'.

further inquiry about Mr Shrosbery. Read Pichler—Morley's Rousseau. Worked a little on the Homeric Hymns.

16. Fr.

Wrote to Mr L. Barker—Messrs Watson—Mr Ouvry—Mr Childers—Robn G.—Messrs Cassell. Worked a little on Homer. Read Pichler's Leibniz—Morley's Rousseau. Woodcutting. Conversation with C. on Harry's matters.

17. Sat.

Ch. 8½ AM. Wrote to Marquis of Ripon—Sir T.D. Acland—Capt. Hastings—Sir H. Verney—Rev Mr Howard. To Chester with C. Saw there Mr R. Barker—Mr Hignett—Mr C. Townshend. King's Sch. meeting 2-3½. Herbert went, & leaves a blank. He is meditating about his profession.[1] I shall be glad when this is more advanced. Read Morley's Rousseau—Q.R. on Ritual—Q.R. on Jesuits.[2]

18. St Luke. 20 S.Trin.

Ch 11 AM & H.C.—6½ P.M. Agnes's birthday: God be ever with her. Wrote to Gen. Ponsonby—Mr J. Roberts—T. Hadden[3]—Mr D. Saunders—H. Brittain[4]—Rev. R.C. Jenkins. Read Pichler's Leibniz—Winterbotham's Sermon[5]—Maud on Et. Torment & the Origin of Evil (finished)[6]—Miss Besant on Et. Torment[7]—Dr Reichel on Xtn Evidences.[8]

19. M.

Ch. 8½ A.M. 11-12. Attended John Bailey's Funeral. Wrote to Rev. R. Winterbotham—Messrs King & Co.—Lord Acton[9]—Mrs Malcolm—J. & H. Jones—Rev. Dr Reichel[10]—Mr Morier. Cut a large

[1] He had taken a third in Mods at University college, and had to retake divinity.

[2] *Quarterly Review*, cxxxvii. 542, 283 (October 1874).

[3] Denying he had said he was 'not in favour of Establishments'; *The Times*, 23 October, 9c.

[4] Of Birmingham; had sent a pamphlet, Hawn P.

[5] R. Winterbotham, *Sermons and expositions* (1874).

[6] See 22 June 74.

[7] A. Besant, *On eternal torture* (1874).

[8] C. P. Reichel, 'The necessary limits of christian evidences. A sermon' (4th ed. 1874).

[9] Proposing to expand his anti-papal comments in 'Ritualism' into a pamphlet; Acton encouraged him; Matthew, 'Vaticanism', 434.

[10] Charles Parsons Reichel, 1816-94, professor at Queen's 1850, archdeacon of Meath 1875.

ash with W. by Wellhouse Farm: we had tea there. Sir H. Verney came.[1] Read Pichler's Leibniz—Howard's Legend of St Pauls.[2]

20. Tu.

Ch. 8½ A.M. An attack of diarrhoea came on: but not violent. Conversation with Sir H. Verney. Arranged with Willy a letter which will cause the Agency to be offered to Mr T[ownshend]. Wrote on the Papal question.[3] Lay up a good deal & went early to bed. Wrote to Dr Smith—Mr Salkeld.

21. Wed.

Kept my bed until dusk. Read Morley's Rousseau—Greenwood Cath. Petri.[4] Wrote on R.C. matter. Wrote to Mr Newton—Rev Mr Morton —Scotts—Mr A. Dawson—Mr Soden.

22. Th.

Up at noon. Wrote to Rev. N. Walker—Sir A. Gordon—Ld Halifax —Mr T.H. Birmear[5]—A. Dowling—Mr Jas Knowles—W. Soleman[6] —Mrs Th. Read Greenwood. Worked on my papal argument.

23. Fr.

Ch. 8½ A.M. Wrote to Townshend & Barker—Ld Lyttelton—Mr Ouvry—Ld Wenlock—Mr Coplestone—Rev Mr Soden—Robn G. Conversation on Agency. And on Harry's matters. Attended Churchwarden meeting on Bells. Woodcutting with W. Worked on my Roman argument. Read Greenwood.

24. Sat.

Ch. 8½ AM. Wrote to Sir L.T. Stamer[7]—Mr A. de Lisle[8]—The Primus

[1] See 5 Dec. 33; Florence *Nightingale's brother-in-law.

[2] G. B. Howard, *An old legend of St Paul's* (1874).

[3] Published as 'The Vatican Decrees in their bearing on civil allegiance: a political expostulation' (1874), reprinted in *Rome: newest fashions in religion* (1875); Add MS 44693, f. 197; see above, introduction to vol. vii, section X.

[4] See 25 Sept. 58; quoted in appendix D. of 'the Vatican Decrees'.

[5] Unidentified.

[6] William Soleman of Granpound, wished to dedicate to diarist; Hawn P.

[7] Sir Lovelace Tomlinson Stamer, 1829-1908; rector of Stoke 1858, archdeacon there 1877; 3rd bart. 1860.

[8] Summoning him to discuss Vaticanism; Purcell, *De Lisle*, ii. 89.

—Mr Leigh Williams. Wrote on Papal Arg. Read Greenwood. Wood-cutting. Tea with Miss Scott.

25. 21 S.Trin.

Ch mg & evg. Albert [Lyttelton] alone. Read the Lessons mg. Wrote to Townshend & Barker—Rev. Mr Churton—Mr Dowling—Mr Yates—Mr Francis. Read Bericht über die Bonn-Conferenzen[1]—Collette's ans. to Baring-Gould[2]—Wilkinson on Absolution[3]—Dykes on Eucharistic Truth.[4]

26. M.

Ch. 8½ A.M. Wrote to Mr E.W. Brightman—Messrs T. & B.—Sir A. Gordon—Ld Wolverton—Mrs Th.—Mrs Helen G.—P.T. King—Warden of Trin Coll. NB. Saw WHG & C.G. on the Agency—Messrs Townshend & Barker 11-1.—Mr Vickers at 2.30. Drew Mem. of the Agency arrangements.[5] Conversation with C. & Harry on Lpool and R.s letter.[6] Read Greenwood.

27. Tu.

Ch. 8½ AM. Wrote to Sir J. Lacaita—Mr Bramwell—Lord Acton—Gen. Bowie—Ld Halifax—Mr Dowling—Robn G.—Sir R. Phillimore—Agnes W. Large arrival of papers & letters from London. Conversation with Mrs Malcolm—Mr de Lisle, who has come on a visit, & to whom I explain the whole position.—Mr Wade—on the plan for him. Walk with Mr De Lisle. Cutting with W.

28. Wed. SS.Simon and Jude.

Ch. 8¾ AM. Wrote to Mr Bosworth Smith—Mr C.L. Eastlake—Ch. Abbot—Ad. Scott[7]—T. Baskham—J.D. Brand—Professor Ornsby[8]—Mr Laird—H.N.G.—Watsons—Rev Mr Bull. Cutting with W. & walk with Mr De Lisle. I gave him my MS. to read, & we had a great

[1] Untraced pamphlet.

[2] C. H. Collette, 'S. Baring-Gould on "Luther and justification". A reply' (1873).

[3] G. H. *Wilkinson, 'Absolution. A sermon' (1874).

[4] J. B. *Dykes, 'Eucharistic truth and ritual. A letter' (1874).

[5] Hawn P. Townshend and Barker, the Chester solicitors, became permanent agents.

[6] On his leaving Liverpool for India.

[7] Adam Scott, London engineer.

[8] Robert Ornsby, 1820-89; convert to Rome; professor of classics, Catholic university, Dublin, 1854-82; biographer of *Hope-Scott.

deal of conversation on it & on kindred topics. Read Suetonius (Calig.)—Greenwood.

29. Th.

Ch. 8½ AM. Wrote to Lord Acton (Tel)—Sir Geo. Prevost—Rev Mr Leeke—Lady Burrell—H.N.G.—Rev Dr Burgess.

Sir A. Gordon came last night; he read my MS this day. Also Ld Acton came in evg. With each of these & with Mr De Lisle I had a great deal more of conversation on the MS and kindred topics. Afternoon walk. Mr de Lisle's decl[aration] on finishing it was 'There are things in it wh I could wish altered, but as a whole I think it will do great good['].

Read Ld R. Montagu's fanatical Lecture[1]—Greenwood—Dalling's Sir R. Peel.[2] Showed the Churches to Mr De Lisle.

30. Fr.

Ch. 8½ AM. Wrote to Mr G. Bentley—Mr Mugford[3]—Mr Vickers. Read Milman's Inn.III.[4]

A. Gordon & Ld Acton have now read my article. I had varied conversations with all the three guests for much of the day. They all show me that I must act mainly for myself.[5]

31. Sat.

Ch. 8½ AM. Wrote to J. Watson & Smith—Mr Mullen—Rev Mr Holland[6]—Warden Trin Coll. Glenalm. Read The Month on WEG[7]—Mivart on Evolution (last)[8]—Milman's Innocent III—Doyle on Cath. Claims.[9] A.G. went early. With Ld A. I had some six hours of conversation: told him as well as I could Dr D[öllinger']s mind.

[1] Lord R. Montagu, 'Civilization and the See of Rome' (1874), discussed in 'The Vatican Decrees'.

[2] W. H. L. E. *Bulwer, Lord Dalling, *Sir Robert Peel. An historical sketch* (1874).

[3] Perhaps Herne Mugford, another engineer.

[4] See 27 Aug. 54.

[5] 'Objections in detail were attended to, but to all political, spiritual, and other obvious arguments against publication he was deaf'; Acton to Simpson, 4 November 1874, in J. L. Altholz, D. McElrath, J. C. Holland, *The correspondence of Lord Acton and Richard Simpson* (1975), iii. 319.

[6] Perhaps Henry Scott *Holland, 1847-1918; student of Christ Church 1870, canon of St. Paul's 1884; 'christian socialist' and liberal.

[7] *The Month*, iii. 257 (November 1874); Roman catholic journal, with article on 'Mr. Gladstone's "Durham Letter" '.

[8] See 29 Jan. 74.

[9] See 20 Dec. 70.

All Saints & 22 S.Trin. Nov. 1. 74.

Ch. 11 AM & H.C. 6½ PM. Wrote to Dr Döllinger—Ld Cardwell—Mrs Th.—Sir J. Lacaita—Sir A. Panizzi—Mr Murray.[1] Conversation with C. on family matters. Ditto with Harry on his. Read Mrs Laird's Address[2]—Scott Tracts[3]—Dyke on the H. Eucharist.

2. M.

Ch. 8½ AM. Wrote to Madame Minghetti—Ld Granville—Lord Acton—Dean of Windsor—Mr de Lisle—Bp of Ontario[4]—Mr Knowles—Ld Wolverton—Mr Murray—Gen. Ponsonby—Sir C. Wood—Bp of Lichfield—Mr Ouvry—Mr W. Williams—Ed. of Echo—Miss Lyttelton—Messrs Sotheran. Read Lytton's Memoir of his Father[5]—Milman's Innocent III. Our guests May Lyttelton, Mrs Malcolm, Miss Simmons,[6] went off. Cutting with W. & H.

3. Tu.

Ch. 8½ AM. Wrote to Robn G.—Ld Prov. Glasgow—Ld Cardwell—Mr Adam—Mr Murray—Scotts—Mrs Th.—Rev Mr Harris. Again revised & amended the Mem. of Family arrangements. Drew another Mem. for Mr Townshend. Saw Mr T.—W.H.G.—C.G.—each on family matters. Read Carlisle Dioc. Conference, & divers Tracts. Corrected report of my Speech on Scotch Patronage Bill.[7]

4. Wed. [*London*]

Off at 8. Left Harry's route at Chester. Corrected the four Proof sheets on the Rail where I now write. Wrote to Ld Tenterden—Mr Morier—Mrs Th.—Dr Döllinger (pr. sheet)—Messrs G. and Co.—Mr G. Howard—Mr Murray. Dined with Sir A. Panizzi. Saw Ed. Guardian—Sec. Metrop.Distr.RR—Sir James Lacaita—Sir A. Panizzi—respecting Italy and my Tract. Saw two Sinclairs—Herbert—& another[R]. Read Mr de Lisle.

5. Th.

Wrote to Rev C.G. Lane—Mr F. de Preston—C.G.—Sec.Metr.Board

[1] Dispatching 'The Vatican Decrees' for printing.

[2] Perhaps early version of Mrs E. Laird, 'The true solution of the present religious difficulties' (1875).

[3] More tracts by T. *Scott of Ramsgate.

[4] John Travers Lewis; bp. there from 1862.

[5] E. R. B. *Lytton, *Speeches of Edward, Lord Lytton . . . with a prefatory memoir* (1874).

[6] Emily Simmons.

[7] See 6 July 74.

—Mr Gowing[1]—Treas. of Guy's—Mr W. Macdonald. Saw Mr G. Howard—Sir J. Lacaita—Mr Ouvry—Messrs Clowes—Mr Knowles—Ld Cardwell—Mr Murray—Count Münster—chiefly on my Tract. Made references & further corr. of Proofs and Revises. Saw Sinclair[R]. Dined at Mr Th's. Saw the Jacobite Patriarch[2]—Mrs Finn—Mr Kinnaird.

6. Fr.

Wrote to Mr Murray—Mr Cashel Hoey—Sir W. Stephenson—C.G. (2)—Rev Mr Husband—Mrs Sinclair—Mr Cooke—Mr Ouvry—Warden of Keble—Helen—Prince Bonaparte[3]—Mr Ashton—Sir A.H. Gordon—H.N.G. Again at H. of C. Library for references: rather anxious. Saw Sir J. Lacaita—Ld Lyttelton—Mr Grogan—Mr M'Coll—Mr Levy—Mr Kinnaird—Mr Joseph—Mr Guiness[4]—Mr Kinnaird—Sir A. Panizzi—Mr Guiness—Sir W. Stephenson *cum* Mr Hanson—Count Münster. Breakfast with Lacaita. Luncheon in G. Square. Dined with Count Münster.[5] Broke down from over work & hurry in afternoon with diarrhoea. In the night I rose & took castor oil.

7. Sat.[6] [*Keble College, Oxford*]

Dr Clark came between 8 & 9. Again at 1.30. Authorised my going to Oxford. Windsor was given up. Luncheon in G. Square. Reached Keble Coll., a real home, at 5½ P.M. Saw Dr Mozley in evg about the Eirenic writers.[7] Much conversation and most favourable. Read Mr De Lisle.[8] Wrote to Dean of Windsor (Tel.)—C.G.—W.H.G.—Harry—Mr Murray—Mr Levy.

[1] Richard Gowing, 1831-99, ed. *The Gentleman's Magazine* 1873-7, sec. of Cobden Club from 1877.

[2] Obscure; a nickname? Possibly a play or picture, but not found advertised.

[3] Prince Napoleon Eugene Louis Jean Joseph Bonaparte, 1856-79; cadet at Woolwich 1871-4, killed in S. Africa.

[4] Arthur H. Guiness, secretary to the Protestant Alliance, sent its *Monthly Letter* (1 Sept. 1874) abusing Catholics; Hawn P.

[5] Pre-publication copy sent to Germany this day; Bassett, 205.

[6] 'The Vatican Decrees' published this day.

[7] See L. Talbot to C. S. Talbot, 9 November 1874 (Hagley MSS): 'You ought to hear of the success of Uncle William's visit—he is just gone off with every sort of hearty good wishes to us & the College. He arrived on Saturday afternoon not very well, but quite up to any amount of talk, & we had a capital Munich, Dollinger & Bonn talk, Edward & all, & then at 9 came Dr Mozley for the first of many consultations over a scheme of Uncle W's own promoting the editorship of a series of books on eirenic writers from before the Reformation'; the scheme came to nothing.

[8] A. L. M. Phillipps de Lisle, probably *On the future unity of Christendom* (1857).

8. 23 S. Trin.

ChCh. 10 AM. Keble 4½ and 10.15. Heard remarkable Sermons from Dr Pusey and Mr Milne.[1] Wrote to Mad. Novikoff—Mr Gurdon—Mrs Th.—Mr De Lisle—C.G.—Mrs Helen G. Read Malleus Ritualistarum[2] —Mr De Lisle's Pamphlet—and other Tracts. Dean of ChCh took me over the Cathedral. Saw & introduced the subject of the Eirenic writers to Dean of ChCh—Dr Pusey—Dr Liddon—Mr Talbot—The Keble Common Room: all approved. Saw P. Leopold: he has suffered much.

9. M. [Aldenham Park, Shropshire]

Wrote to Lord Crewe—Sir A. Gordon—Mr De Lisle. Read Girard, Sentiments Religieux en Grèce[3]—Brouwer Civilisation des Grecs.[4] Keble Chapel 8 AM. Mr [W.] Palmer, Mr Crichton,[5] & others, to breakfast. Saw Herbert. Mr Geflowski:[6] & saw the All Souls Reredos: very remarkable. Travelled with Ld Acton & Sir R. Blennerhassett to Aldenham:[7] much conversation on the way and there.

10. Tu.

Wrote to C.G.—Mr J. Watson—Sir G. Bowyer—Dean of Windsor—Hon B. Lawley (& draft).[8] Saw Mr Leeman—Mr Cary. Read Hoffmann's Introdn to Baader[9]—Revolutionskirchen Englands.[10] Visited Bridgnorth. Walk & much conversation in this interesting house where Time flies at double speed.

11. Wed. [Crewe Hall, Cheshire]

And I reluctantly fly also. 9½-1½. Journey to Crewe. On the way saw Bridgnorth Carpet factory: met the Lawley partisans at Ironbridge: and had much conversation with Mr Cary. Wrote to Dr Hooker—Mrs Wm Gladstone—Helen G. Read C. Greville.[11] Some examn of

[1] Louis George Mylne, 1843–1921; tutor at Keble 1870–6, bp. of Bombay 1876–97.

[2] Anon. (1872).

[3] By J. A. Girard (1869).

[4] By P. van Limburg Brouwer, 8v. (1833–42).

[5] Unidentified.

[6] Emanuel Edward Geflowski, 1834–98; Polish sculptor, settled in England; restored All Souls reredos 1873–5.

[7] *Acton's seat near Bridgnorth. Acton's letter of 8 November on the 'expostulation' ('Your indictment would be more just if it were more complete') in *The Guardian*, 11 November 1874, 1456; *The Times*, 9 November 1874, 9f.

[8] Letter of support for by-election at Wenlock, to Beilby Lawley, 1849–1912; 3rd Baron Wenlock 1880; governed Madras 1891–6; in *The Times*, 13 November 1874, 3f.

[9] F. Hoffman, *Franz von Baader* (1856).

[10] Untraced.

[11] First v. of C. Greville's *Memoirs*, ed. H. Reeve.

Mohnike[1]—before starting. Conversation with Mr Hamilton. Went over the sumptuous restorations at Crewe[2]—and saw Ld Houghton there.

12. Th. [*Hawarden*]

Packed and went off, with Ld C. at 10.45. Wrote to Mr Murray—Mr E. Levy—C.G.—Rev W.E. Buller—Mr R. Smith—Lord R. Gower—Mr Kruse[3]—Very Rev. F. Oakeley—Mr Colborne—Sir H. Peek—Mr Chintamon[4]—Ld Coleridge—Mr Hutchison—Mr Axton. Reached Hawarden at one and found several hours of reading in letters & papers for me: very many on the Pamphlet. Read Dr Carpenter on the Ocean[5]—Chintamon on Bhagavad Ghita.

13. Fr.

Ch. 8½ A.M. Wrote to Sir A. Panizzi—Mr Bedford—Mr Murray—Mr Goldwin Smith—Mrs Th.—Mr Heinemann—Dr Ward—Rev Mr Jenkins—Mr V. Oger[6]—Mr Crompton—[C. M.] Cranwick[7]—Callcott—W.C. Brooks[8]—Jos Cowan—Ed. of Echo—Mr M'Coll—Dr M'Corry[9]—Ld Tenterden—Ld Aberdare—Ld Kimberley—Mr Barry—Mr J.R. Godley—Mr Stonor. Saw Mr Townshend. Walk with Helen. Read Tracts.

14. Sat. [*Whittinghame House, East Lothian*]

Wrote to J. Watson & Smith—Dean of Chester. Read Introduction and Discorsi of Pius IX.[10] Left Hawarden at 9.15 and reached Whittinghame[11] through Edinb. at 8. Found a *reader* in the Train.

[1] Word smudged.
[2] Lord Crewe's reproduction of the Jacobean house, burned down 1866.
[3] Perhaps Frederick Kruse, cabinet maker.
[4] H. Chintaman, sent Indian poem; Hawn P.
[5] W. B. *Carpenter, probably 'The temperature and life of the deep sea' (1866).
[6] Victor Oger, tr. 'The Vatican Decrees' into French; Hawn P.
[7] Of Stalybridge; Hawn P.
[8] (Sir) William Cunliffe Brooks, 1819-1900; banker and tory M.P. E. Cheshire 1869-88; cr. bart. 1886.
[9] Dr. J. Stewart MacCorry, nonconformist minister in Regent's Park, sent his pamphlet on ritualism dedicated to diarist; Hawn P.
[10] *Discorsi del Sommo Pontefice Pio IX*, 2v. 1872-3, reviewed stringently by diarist in *Quarterly Review*, cxxxviii. 266 (January 1875), reprinted in *Rome and the newest fashions in religion* (1875).
[11] A. J. *Balfour's house near Haddington.

15. 24 S.Trin.

Walk with Stephy to Haddington, 6 miles off, for Church. Wrote to Rev W.W. Malet—Mr J. Murray—Robn G.—Mr Hugh Mason—Mr Dyer—Mrs Benson[1]—Walter Higham.[2] Read Discorsi of the Pope—Bp of Gloucester's Addresses[3]—Nelson on High Ch. party[4]—M'Corry's Ritualism.[5]

16. M.

Read up arrear of letters and papers on the Vatican Controversy, which swells and swells. Finished Bp of Gloucester. Read Papal Discorsi—Dannreuther on Wagner.[6]

17. Tu.

Wrote to Scotts—Agnes Wickham. Off at 11.45 to Edinburgh. Attended Trin.Coll. Council Meeting. Saw Bp of Brechin, Mr Ranken, Bp of Glasgow, & others. Shopping: return to W. at 5.30. Read Dannreuther—The Pope—Middlemarch.[7]

18. Wed.

Wrote to Mr Levy—Mr Murray—Mr Collins—Bp of Gloucester—Mr R. Galloway—Mrs H.G.—Mr Ouvry—Sir S. Waterlow. Walk with Mr B[alfour] and Mary. Saw Rev. Mr Robertson.[8] Read as yesterday.

19. Th.

Wrote to Watsons—Ld Lyttelton—Mr Ouvry—Bp of Manchester—Sec.Metrop.Distr.Co.—President of Sion College—Mr M'Coll—Ld Camoys[9]—Mr H. [*sc.* Joseph] Benjamin—Scotts—Ld Hartington—Provost of Haddington.[10] Walk with Mr B & two of the Ladies. Saw Mr Smith the Factor. Read as yesterday.

[1] Mary, *née* Sidgwick, m. 1859 E. W. *Benson.

[2] Unidentified.

[3] C. J. *Ellicott, 'Church prospects' (1872).

[4] H. Nelson, 3rd Earl Nelson, *Present position of the High Church party* (1874).

[5] See 13 Nov. 74n.

[6] E. G. Dannreuther, *Richard Wagner; his tendencies and theories* (1873).

[7] By George *Eliot (1871-2).

[8] James Robertson, 1837-90; Church of Scotland minister at Whittinghame from 1865; later a prominent moral theologian.

[9] Letter of support for the 'Expostulation' from Camoys, a Roman catholic, in *The Guardian*, 18 November 1874, 1491.

[10] Unable to receive burgh's freedom, as returning home; *The Times*, 28 November 1874, 5e.

20. Frid.

Wrote to Ld Halifax—Sir A. Panizzi—Mr Murray—Sir R. Phillimore—Dr Mozley—Mr Morier. Walk with Mr B. who went off in evg. How eminently he is *del miglior luto*:[1] & how glad should we be to be nearer to him. Read Middlemarch—Wagner's Letter to Villot[2] —D. of Argyll on Taylor Innes[3]—Discorsi di Pio IX.

21. Sat. [*Mount Teviot, Jedburgh*]

Wrote to Mrs Th.—Sir A. Gordon—Ld Acton—Rev. Mr Aislabie[4] —Sir W. James—Mr Bradford[5]—Mr Cottell. Saw Bp of Edinburgh. Off at 2.15 to Monteviot:[6] arrived after six. Most kindly received. Read Discorsi di Pio IX.

22. 25 S.Trin.

Drove to Jedburgh Ch. at 11 AM. H.C. acc. to the venerable Scotch Office. A good service & Sermon. We visited the Abbey afterwards & our friend's grave:[7] also the new Presb. Ch., the best I ever saw. Walk with Ld L[othian] in evg. Wrote to Robn G. Read Ed.Rev. on Speaker's Bible[8]—Discorsi di Pio IX.

23. M. [*Hawarden*]

Mary's birthday: all blessings on her. 10½-6½ Journey to Courthey: where we dined: it was a great object to break the ice. Then 8¾-11¼ to Hn. Read Discorsi—Bp Ullathorne's Reply[9]—& worked on papers.

24. Tu.

Wrote to Dr Badenoch[10]—Mr Pattison—Mr. Stansfeld—Miss Doyle

[1] 'Of more than common clay'; probably an allusion to Prometheus' 'meliore luto' in Juvenal 14. 35.

[2] R. Wagner, tr. E. Dannreuther, 'The music of the future: a letter to F. Villot' (1873).

[3] G. D. *Campbell, duke of Argyll, *The Patronage Act of 1874 . . . a reply to Mr Taylor Innes* (1874).

[4] William John Aislabie, 1804-76, rector of Alpheton from 1848.

[5] J. G. Bradford of Dalton Rise, London, wrote for book references; Hawn P.

[6] Seat near Jedburgh of 8th marquis of Lothian; see 31 Oct. 63.

[7] Probably of *Campbell, the lord chancellor, who d. 1861.

[8] *Edinburgh Review*, cxl. 32 (July 1874).

[9] W. B. *Ullathorne, 'The Döllingerites, Mr Gladstone and apostates from the Faith' (1874).

[10] George Roy Badenoch, 1830-1912, free churchman, joined Church of Scotland 1874; tory candidate 1880; had sent, probably, *Ultramontanism, England's sympathy with Germany* (1874); Hawn P.

—Mr Hurley—Mr Eiggert[1]—Rev Mr Davies—Dean of Winchester. Read Slater's Letters[2]—Discorsi—Middlemarch. Felled a tree with W. & H. Worked on papers, Vatican & other, wh require careful arrangement.

25. Wed.

Ch. 8½ AM. Wrote to Ld Granville—Ld Lyttelton—Mr Herbert R.A. —Mr Westell—Wms & Norgate—Scotts—F. Knollys—Mr Jenkins —Mr Murray—Mr Holt—Mr Kitts[3]—Mr Perron[4]—Mr Clark. Wrote on Ch. of E. matters. Read Appendix to Discorsi di Pio IX—Middlemarch—Q.R. on Venice.[5] Walk to Aston H[all] Colliery.

26. Th.

Ch. 8½ AM. Wrote to Ld Salisbury—D. of Argyll—Mr Kinnaird—Mr Balfour—Mr Greer—Mr Salmon—Mr Ouvry—Mr Montgomery —Professor Price—Mr Johnstone—Mr Stonor—Sir A. Gordon. Read Appendix, and Discorsi—Butler's English Catholics[6]—Middlemarch. A day of caution, fearing an attack.

27. Fr.

Kept the house until four. Wrote to Professor Blackie—Mr Murray —Mr T. Young—Mr Herbert—Sir R. Phillimore—Rev Mr Dawson[7] —Rev Mr Lefroy[8]—Mr A. Arnold.

Today Mr Murray reports 52,000 sold: 20,500 more printed. Every post brings me a mass of general reading, writing or both: forty covers, of one kind & another, today: and all my time is absorbed. But the subject is well worth the pains. Today I wrote out & sent off Translations of the Latin passages. Read Ld R. Montagu's Reply[9]—Discorsi di Pio IX.—Friedrich's Acten[10]—Middlemarch.

[1] A. H. Eiggerty, on Vaticanism; Hawn P.

[2] E. Slater, *Letters on Roman Catholic tenets* (1813).

[3] John Kitts of Sunderland, correspondent on Vaticanism; Hawn P.

[4] William Perrin of Newcastle wrote in admiration; Hawn P.

[5] *Quarterly Review*, cxxxvii. 416 (October 1874).

[6] C. *Butler, *Historical memoirs respecting the English, Irish and Scottish Catholics*, 4v. (1819–21).

[7] William Dawson, rector of St. John's, Clerkenwell, 1870.

[8] Anthony Cottrell Lefroy, vicar of Longdon, 1868.

[9] Lord R. Montagu, 'Expostulation in extremis' (1874); on Gladstone.

[10] Probably J. F. Friedrich, *Documenta ad illustrandum Concilium Vaticanum anni 1870*, 2v. (1871).

28. Sat.

Ch. 8½ AM. Wrote to Emperor of Brazil—Ld Tenterden—Edr of Month[1]—Mr Buckmaster—Mr J.G. Bradford—Mr T. Greenfield[2] —Mr J. Clark—Mr J.W. Weaden[3]—Mr F. Ouvry—Mr G. Ogilvie—Dr Badenoch. W., H, & I felled the large leaning alder. Read Pio IX Discorsi—The 'Month's' Articles on WEG[4]—Middlemarch. We framed the epitaph for Mr Burnett. Conversation with W. on his charities.

29. Adv. S.

Kept my bed till evg. Read mg & evg prayer. Read Discorsi di Pio IX —Woolmer's Sermon[5]—Paus on Preaching[6]—Redesdale's strange but well meant Tract[7]—and several other Tracts & Sermons.

30. M.

Rose at 12. (St Andr.) Wrote to Sir R. Phillimore—Mr Murray—Mr J. Wilson—Mr J. Paus—Mr Jas Watson—Sir A. Panizzi—Sir J. Lacaita—Rev. Mr Dickson—Rev. Mr Woolmer—Rev. Mr M'Coll—Rev Mr R. O'Keeffe—Sir A. Grant—Sec. Distr.R.R. Co—Monsignor Patterson[8]—Mrs Morse Stewart—Ed. Glasgow News. Read Discorsi di Pio IX—Whittle on the Vatican (finished)[9]—Tracts.

Tues. Dec. One 1874.

Wrote to Ld Napier of Magd.—Messrs Bickers—Messrs Clowes—Mr Ouvry—Mr R. Bulgin[10]—Mr J. Ashley—Mr J. Tilley CB—Rev. S.E.G.—Mr Kinnaird. Rose at 11. Read Discorsi di Pio IX—Middlemarch—Sermons. Harry's last evening here before India.

2. Wed.

Ch. 8½ AM. We all rose early to breakfast with Harry who went at

[1] Answering its charges, see below, printed in *The Month*, iv. 121 (January 1875) and in *The Times*, 30 December 1874, 4c.

[2] Of Croydon, had written on Vaticanism; Hawn P.

[3] Apparently a correspondent on Vaticanism.

[4] *The Month*, iii. 478 (December 1874), attack by T. B. P., 'Mr Gladstone's "Expostulation" '.

[5] C. E. S. Woolmer, 'The shadow and the very image . . . A sermon' (1874).

[6] Untraced; see next d.

[7] J. T. F. *Mitford, Lord Redesdale, *Reasonings on some disputed points of doctrine* (1874).

[8] James Laird Patterson, 1822-1902; bp. of Emmaus 1880; a convert.

[9] See 9 June 72.

[10] Of Pimlico; sent sermon; Hawn P.

8¼.[1] May the angels of the good God go with him. Wrote to Mr T.B. Potter—Wms & Norgate—Mr Brittain—Rev Mr M'Kay—Rev Mr Coleridge—Rev Mr S. Naish[2]—Rev Mr W. Jackson[3]—Mr R. Wilberforce—Gordon Milne[4]—Edr of Month—Ld Lothian—Ld Lyttelton. Corrected new Revise of 79th thousand: with the Translations. Read Discorsi—Coleridge's Sermon[5]—T. Aquinas & Deus. Castor oil at night: to lie up tomorrow.

3. Th.

Rose at 4 P.M. Wrote to Mr Hitchman—Sir J. Watson—Messrs Bickers—Mr Whitworth—Mr E.V. Neale[6]—Mr Webster—Mr Wiesenlangen[7]—Mr Grogan—Mr Knowles—C.G.—Ld Acton. Read Discorsi—Butler's Historic Memoirs[8]—Middlemarch.

4. Fr.

Rose at 1½. Wrote to Mr E.R. Spearman—Ld Lytton—Sir A. Paget—Helen J.G.—Ld Lyttelton—Sir A. Panizzi—Bp of St Asaph—Professor Thomatis[9]—A.S. Murray[10]—J. Rowan—W. Grogan—G. Bradley—E. Colwall.[11] Read Discorsi di Pio IX—Butler's Hist. Memoirs—Middlemarch.

5. Sat.

Ch. 8½ A.M. Wrote to Dr Littledale—G.W. Tickle[12]—C.G.—Rev W.M. Goalen—S.E.G.—W.G. Smith[13]—W.S. Pratten—W.S. Malcom. Read Discorsi di Pio IX—C. Butler, Hist. Memoirs—Page Roberts, 2 first Sermm.[14] Cut down a wych Elm.

[1] To work in India; soon back; see I. Thomas, *Gladstone of Hawarden* (1936), 62.

[2] Thanking nonconformists of Launceston for their confidence; *The Times*, 7 December 1874, 10b.

[3] William Jackson, 1792–1878; provost of Queen's, Oxford, from 1861; sent a book; Hawn P.

[4] Of Portobello, Edinburgh, wrote on the League of St. Sebastian; Hawn P.

[5] H. J. *Coleridge, 'Giving glory to God. A sermon' (1873) or see 11 Dec. 74n.

[6] Edward Vansittart *Neale, 1810–92; barrister and Christian Socialist; promoted cooperatives.

[7] T. Wiesenlanger of London, wrote on Vaticanism; Hawn P.

[8] See 26 Nov. 74.

[9] David Thomatis, professor in Berlin, on Vaticanism; Hawn P.

[10] Archibald Murray, on religion; Hawn P.

[11] Perhaps Charles Colwell of Yarmouth, who sent a book on 12 Nov.; Hawn P.

[12] Perhaps George Tickell, Roman catholic translator.

[13] Untraced.

[14] W. P. Roberts, *Law and God* (1874).

6. 2 S.Adv.

Ch. 11 AM and H.C.—6½ P.M. Read the Lessons in Church. Wrote to Lady C. Kerrison—Sir A. Gordon—Mr Parkinson—Mr W.P. Adam—Mr Simpson—Mr Hopkinson—Mr Lowry Whittle[1]—Bp of St Asaph—Mr R. Wilberforce. Read Bp Clifford's Reply[2]—Page Roberts's remarkable Sermons (finished)—Dowden's Sermon[3]—Martineau's Lecture.[4]

7. M.

Ch. 8½ AM. Wrote to Postmaster Hn—Ld Wolverton—J. Murray—Ld Granville—Mr Lauch[5]—Mr Grogan—J.T. Maine—W.H.G.—G. Redford—Messrs Bickers—Rev. E.H. Bickersteth.[6] Saw Mr Townshend. Cut down a wych Elm. Read Butler Hist. Memoirs—Discorsi (finished)—Newman on Endowments[7]—Stanley's Introduction to Hyacinthe.[8]

8. Tues.

Ch. 8½ AM. Wrote to Dr von Döllinger—Mr Murray—Mrs Th.—Canon Ashwell—C.G.—Mr Hine. Saw Mr Hayes. Tidying room: which tonight officiates as drawing-room. Read Dharawansa[9]—Butler, Memoirs—Sturmayer's Speech.[10]

9. Wed.

Ch. 8½ AM. Wrote to Mr A. Blackwood—Mr Barker—Rev. S.E.G.—Prof. Mayer[11]—Mr Keogh—Editor of Echo—Mr Benson—Mr Harrison—Messrs Townshend & B. Wrote on Discorsi di Pio IX: after some scraps and efforts, an Article is now started.[12] Read Butler, Hist. Memoirs—Morier's (crushing) letter[13]—Middlemarch.

[1] J. Lowry Whittle, on Vaticanism; Hawn P.

[2] W. J. H. Clifford, 'Catholic Allegiance' (1874).

[3] See 3 Aug. 73.

[4] J. *Martineau, 'Religion as affected by modern materialism: an address' (1874).

[5] See 10 July 74.

[6] Edward Henry *Bickersteth, 1825–1906; hymnist and vicar of Christ Church, Hampstead, 1855–85; bp. of Exeter 1885.

[7] Probably F. W. *Newman; perhaps his 'A State Church not defensible' (1845).

[8] A. P. *Stanley's intr. to C. J. M. Loyson [Père Hyacinthe], *Catholic reform* (1874).

[9] Not found.

[10] Ibid.

[11] Unidentified.

[12] 'Speeches of Pope Pius IX', first intended for the *Contemporary Review*, whose articles were usually signed, but published anon. in *Quarterly Review*, cxxxviii. 266 (January 1875) reprinted in *Rome and the newest fashions in religion* (1875). Add MS 44694, f. 1.

[13] Not found.

10. Th.

Ch. 8½ AM. Wrote to Minister of U. States—Mr Hitchman—C.G.—Rev. E.G.S. Browne[1]—Mr Hibbert MP—Mr Petrie[2]—Mr Bettany[3]—Mr Birnam—Sir J. Hudson (Dft. Telegr.) Worked on Article for Contemp. Review. Read Butler (finished Vol.II)—Middlemarch—Bp Vaughan's Reply[4] Great arrivals of books & papers from London by W.

11. Fr.

Ch. 8½ AM. Wrote to Mr Macmillan—Mr Murray—Mr Tallents—Rev H.J. Coleridge[5]—Hugh Owen—Mr R.C. Waters[6]—Rev. J.S. Bright[7]—Ed. Debrett—Ld J. Manners—Mr Tovey—Mr H. Lumby[8]—Mr Delane. Worked on Article. Read Mr M. Marum's Reply[9]—Ramsgate Monk's Reply[10]—Religion of Rome—Perverter in High Life.[11]

12. Sat.

Ch. 8½ AM. Wrote to Mr Jas O'donoghue—Mr Turner—Ld Lyttelton—Rev. A. Wood—Rev. S.E.G.—Mr Arbuthnot—Mr Thompson—Mrs Webb—Mr Knowles—Mr Ouvry—Mr Croft—Mr Girard—Mr Major. Worked on rudiments of a second Vatican Tract.[12] Also on article: but determined not to send it to the Contemp. Review of January. C.G. returned. Read Two more replies—Perverter in High Life. Felling two trees with W.

13. 3 S.Adv.

Ch 11 AM & 6½ PM. Wrote to Ed. Halifax Courier—Mr Stores Smith—Mr Murray—Sir R. Phillimore—Mr Bramwell—Rev. H. Coleridge.

[1] Edward George Stanley Browne, curate in Bury St. Edmunds.

[2] F. Petrie of the Victoria Institute in the Strand, corresponded on philosophy; Hawn P.

[3] George Thomas Bettany, 1850-91, free-lance tutor in Cambridge, wrote on Vaticanism; Hawn P.

[4] H. A. *Vaughan, 'Pastoral Letters' (1874).

[5] [Henry] James *Coleridge, jesuit; corr. on his 'The abomination of desolation' (23 November 1874) in Add MS 44445.

[6] Richard George Waters of Dublin; letters on *Vaticanism* in Hawn P.

[7] Sent compliments of the Dorking Congregational Union; Hawn P.

[8] Or Lumley; sent American newspaper clippings; Hawn P.

[9] M. Marum, 'A vindication of the Pope and the Catholic religion' (1874).

[10] 'Reply to Mr Gladstone' by a monk of St Augustine's, Ramsgate (1874).

[11] *The perverter in high life: a true story of Jesuit duplicity* (1851).

[12] 'Vaticanism: an answer to *Replies and Reproofs*', published as a pamphlet February 1875, reprinted in *Rome and the newest fashions in religion* (1875); Add MS 44694, f. 213.

Read Von Schulte[1]—Thirlwall[2]—Schneemann[3]—N. Hall, Conflict & Victory.[4] Conversation with Mr Temple.

14. M.

Ch. 8½ A.M. Wrote to Dr Döllinger—Ld Blantyre—The Queen—Mr Tallents—Mrs Th.—Sir P. Braila—Mr Morier—Ld Tenterden—Mr de Lisle—Mrs Davidson. Conversation with Willy on his position, present & future, at Hawarden, & on the duties it entails. Read Perverter in High Life—Von Schulte on Papal Power.

15. Tu.

Ch. 8½ AM. Wrote to Rev. H.J. Coleridge—Ld Wolverton—Hn P. master—Lady Burrell—Wms & Norgate—Lord Acton—Rev M. M'Coll—? A. Snow[5]—A. Brickel[6]—Dr Smith. Worked on M.S. Felled a tree with Herbert. Saw Mr Nunne. Read Middlemarch. Finished Perverter in High Life.

16. Th. [sc. *Wed.*]

Ch. 8½ A.M. Wrote to Hon. H.A. Hill—Mr J.S. Phillpotts[7]—A. Rosenberg[8]—Prendergast—Messrs Barkers—Mr Hine—H.J.G.—Rev. Mr Drew. Worked on both MS: but chiefly the Reply, into which I was carried with an impetus. Worked on the snow heap. Read Baxter on Free Italy[9]—Suffield on the Vatican Decrees.[10]

17. Th.

Ch. 8½ AM. Wrote to Sir R. Phillimore—Wms & Norgate—Mrs Th. —Col. D. [*sc.* G] Cameron—Mr Salomon—Mr Murray (2)—Rev Mr Boyd—Mr MacColl—Rev Jeffrey Hill—Mr Pope Hennessy—Ld Halifax. Worked on MS for Q.R. Read 'The Liberal Party and the Catholics'[11]—Middlemarch. Drove a walk through the snow round

[1] J. F. von Schulte, *Die Macht der römischen Päpste über Fürsten* (1871).
[2] Probably C. *Thirlwall, *John Yonge Akerman, F.S.A.* (1874).
[3] G. Schneemann, *Der Papst das Oberhaupt der Gesammtkirche* (1865).
[4] C. N. *Hall, perhaps *Christian victory* (? 1874).
[5] Arthur L. P. Snow, priest in Harrow.
[6] Perhaps Robert Brickel, rector of Hoole, Preston.
[7] Of Rugby; sent a book; Hawn P.
[8] Probably Liverpool picture dealer.
[9] W. E. *Baxter, 'Free Italy. A lecture' (1874).
[10] R. R. *Suffield, *The Vatican decrees and the 'Expostulation'* (1874).
[11] *The Liberal party and the Catholics [with reference to 'The Vatican Decrees']* (1874).

the F. garden. Dined at the Rectory: read some of Oxenham on the Atonement.[1]

18. Fr.

Ch. 8½ A.M. Wrote to Sir John Lubbock—Mr Ouvry—Mr P. Healy —Mr M'Coll—Sir J. Watson—Capt. Stark—Dr Smith—Mr Gurdon—Mr Craven—Ld Acton—Mr Glyn Evans—Sir W. Stephenson. Finished the rough of my MS. My letter *reading* & preliminaries are now never under 2 hours. Read Middlemarch—Legge's Life of Pius IX.[2]

19. Sat.

Ch. 8½ AM. Wrote to Mr J. Carvell Williams—D. of Argyll—Rev. Langhorn[3]—Gen. Ponsonby—Sec.Lond.Miss. Socy—Mr W.P. Price[4] —Mr Freeland—Mr Pope Hennessy. Examined German Translator's reproduction of the Vatican Pamphlet. Worked much on revising and arranging Article for Q.R.[5] Willy & I cut two hollies. Read Legge's Life of Pius IX.

20. 4 S.Adv.

Kept on my back all day. Read the prayers. Finished the revision & sent my MS to Messrs Clowes. Wrote a lengthened letter to Helen on her case. Read Brinckman's Sermon[6]—Bp of St Asaph's Charge[7]— Dean Elliot's very clever Letter[8]—Ehrnich, Unfehlbar Papst.[9]

21. M.

Rose at 11 AM. Wrote to Dr von Döllinger—Ld Granville—Robn G. —Ld Aberdare—Mr G. Harris—Sir Jas Hudson—Mr Leeman—Sir A. Panizzi—Rev. Mr Lundy. Read Mr Th. Martin, Life of Prince

[1] See 14 May 71.
[2] By A. O. Legge, 2v. (1850).
[3] William Henry Langhorne; d. 1916; curate and vicar in Stepney 1872-83; rector in Oxon. 1883-1909.
[4] William Philip Price, 1817-91; liberal M.P. Gloucester 1852-9, 1865-73; railway commissioner 1873.
[5] See 9 Dec. 74.
[6] By A. Brinckmann (1874?).
[7] J. Hughes, 'A charge . . . 1874' (1874).
[8] G. Elliot, 'Ornaments, rubrics . . . A letter' (1874).
[9] *Sic*; perhaps a work by J. N. Ehrlich.

Consort[1]—Domenico Bomba on Primitive Christianity[2]—Blakesley, Reprinted Reviews.[3] Walk with Lord F. C[avendish].

22. Tu.

Ch. 8½ AM. Wrote to Mr Theod. Martin—Mrs Chermside—Mr Nugent—Dr Maitland Smith—Mr Dowding[4]—Mr Glyn Evans. Saw Mr L. Barker. Wrote an opening for the meditated Answer. Read Blakesley's Rev (finished)—Martin's Prince Consort—Middlemarch—Thorntons of Thornbury.[5]

23. Wed.

Ch. 8½ AM. Wrote to Miss Campbell—Mr J.D. Francis—Lord Acton—Mr Geo. Harris—Rev W. Tozer[6]—Messrs Elliot & Stock. Felling trees. Read Middlemarch—Tozer on Ch & Dissent—Th. Martin's L. of Pr. Consort—Hubbard on Ritualism.[7]

24. Th. Xm. Eve.

Ch. 8½ AM. Wrote to Mr G.F. Williams, N. York[8]—Mr H. Williams—Scotts—Hon. F. Lawley—Mr Ouvry—Mr Stewart—Mr Truman—Mr J. Johnstone—Mr Stark (Autogr.)—Mr Powell (do). Walk with F.C. & Conversation on Party. Read Middlemarch—Life of P. Consort—M'Coll on Infallibility.[9]

Fr. Xm D. 1874.

Church 11 A.M. with H.C. and 7 P.M. Walk with F.C.—Conversation on Vaticanism. Wrote to Mr de Lisle—and. . . . Read T. A'Kempis—Von Schulte on Papal Power—Draper on Relig. & Science[10]—Monsignor Capel's Reply.[11]

[1] (Sir) T. *Martin, *Life of the Prince Consort*, 5v. (1875-80), first vol. reviewed by diarist as 'Etonensis' in *Contemporary Review*, xxvi. 1 (June 1875).
[2] D. Bomba, *La Chiesa cristiana nella sua origine* (1874).
[3] J. W. *Blakesley, *English Catholics and English Ultramontanism* (1874).
[4] William Charles Dowding, vicar of Scarborough 1870; anti-catholic author.
[5] Mrs H. L. Chermside, *The Thorntons of Thornbury. A novel*, 3v. (1874).
[6] William George Tozer, d. 1899; bp. of Zanzibar 1863-73; bp. in W. Indies from 1879.
[7] J. G. *Hubbard, Baron Addington, 'Ritual revision' (1874).
[8] Of New York; had written on Vaticanism; Hawn P.
[9] M. *MacColl, *Papal infallibility and its limitations* (1873).
[10] J. W. *Draper, *History of the conflict between religion and science* (1872).
[11] T. J. Capel, 'A reply to . . . Gladstone's "Political expostulation"' (1874).

26. Sat. St Steph.

Ch. 8¾ AM. Wrote to Sec.Hosp. Nottm—Mr G. Redford[1]—Mr MacPhail—Prof. Draper—Mr R. Smith—Mr Murray—Mr R. Simpson—Dean of Bristol. Went to see the Potters after their fire. Walk with E.W. and conversation on Vaticanism. Read Life of Pr. Consort—1st Article in Month[2]—Middlemarch. Began correcting Proofs for Q.R.

27. S. aft Xmas.

In the forenoon I staid at home, read the Service for C. and saw Dr Moffat who came & found 'Erythema'. Ch. 6½ PM. Wrote to Sir A. Panizzi—Lord Acton—Mr Lake—Sir L. Mallet. And wrote the *frusta*[3] of projected letters to Granville to fix my position.[4] Read Draper, Conflict of Religion and Science—Hislop, Two Babylons—could not make head or tail of it[5]—Myers,[6] Catholic Thoughts—Butler—Sermons—Thompson, Ch. & St. in U.S.[7] Corrected a little of proofs.

28. M. Innocents.

Ch. 8¾ A.M. Wrote to Messrs Clowes (Proofs)—Old Bank Chester—Rev Mr Deacle[8]—Mr J. Wood—Mr Vincent—Ld Sydney—Mr E. Hamilton. Saw Dr Moffat (C. going on well—temperature 99)—Ld F. C[avendish] on letters to G[ranville]—(The F.C.s went off)—Mr L. Barker at much length on arrangement of accounts & other matters, with W.H.G.—Mr B. Potter—Mr Brown—Mr C. Barker. Further corr. proofs for QR. Read Middlemarch—Life of P. Consort (finished Vol I.)

29. Tu.

Ch. 8½ A.M. Wrote to Messrs Clowes—Gen. Ponsonby—Robn G.—Rev. E. Deacle—Mr C. Davis—Chairman of Meeting at Wakefield.[9] Saw Rev. S.E.G.—Dr Moffat: C.G. thank God beginning to mend.

[1] Rev. R. A. Redford in correspondence on Vaticanism; Hawn P.

[2] *The Month*, xxii. 393 (December 1874); H. J. Coleridge on Abbé de St. Cyran.

[3] 'to no purpose'.

[4] Draft of letters to Granville resigning as leader of the liberal party, Add MS 44762, ff. 147–59; final version, dated 13 January 1875, in Ramm I, ii. 464, published on 15 January; see 13–15 Jan. 75.

[5] A. Hislop, *The two Babylons* (1853).

[6] See 22 Aug. 69.

[7] By J. P. Thompson (1873).

[8] Edward Leathes Young Deacle, 1828–1915, precentor at Chester 1866–77.

[9] No account found.

Finished my additions to the Article for the Q.R. and the correction of the proof. Read Von Schulte—Middlemarch.

On this my 65th birthday I find myself in lieu of the mental repose I had hoped engaged in a controversy, which cannot be mild, & which presses upon both mind & body. But I do not regret anything except my insufficiency: and my unworthiness in this & in all things: yet I would wish that the rest of my life were as worthy as my public life, in its nature & intent, to be made an offering to the Lord Most High.

30. Wed.

Ch. 8½ AM. Wrote to Dean of Bristol—Sir Aug. Paget—Mr Morier —Mr Simpson—Mr M'Coll—Rev Mr Fysh—Grey—Hildyard— Raynes.[1] Finished Von Schulte. Read Anglocontinental Society's Report.[2] Finished Middlemarch. It is an extraordinary, to me a very jarring, book. Studies on Dr Döllinger's papers from Munich. Saw Dr. Moffatt. Cut down a couple of trees.

31. Thursday.

Kept the house for a cold: rose at 11. Wrote to William Tuck—Ld Granville—Sir A. Gordon—Sir J. Lacaita—Mr Pears—Mr Goschen —Mr Yates—Sir M.C. Swamey—Mr Laslett—Rev. R. O'Keeffe— Rev. R.R. Suffield[3]—Major Blomfield—Messrs Townshend & B. Revised the *Ebauches* of my two letters to Ld Granville and made them ready for transmission.[4] Read the Month No 2 on my Pamphlet[5]—Memorial agt the Pretender[6]—Butler's Memoirs of Engl. Cath.[7] Preparing materials for my next (I hope last) pamphlet.[8]

The dying year, with the one before it have terribly swept the threshing floor of life for me. The ranks are so fast thinning here, and filling there. Especially our dear Stephen's death has made a void never to be filled, and has advanced us greatly towards the 'last great change'. May we then be ready, and may the time between be fruitful.

Amen in nomine J.C.D.N.

[1] William Raynes, 1829-94; fellow of Clare, Cambridge, 1852-94.

[2] Its *Annual Report* (1874).

[3] Robert Rodolph Suffield, 1821-91; Dominican priest, became unitarian 1870; see Add MS 44318.

[4] See 27 Dec. 74; only one letter is extant.

[5] 'External aspects of the Gladstone controversy', *The Month*, iv. 1 (January 1875).

[6] [S. Chandler], *Great Britain's memorial against the Pretender and Popery* (1745).

[7] See 26 Nov. 74.

[8] See 12 Dec. 74.

APPENDIX

A selection of letters to Laura Thistlethwayte
1869-1870

Comments on Laura Thistlethwayte, on Gladstone's relationship to her, and on the Autobiography which the letters printed below discuss, will be found in the Introductions to Volume V, pp. lxi-lxv and Volume VII, section ix. Movements and events mentioned in the letters can be clarified by reference to the diary text. The letters printed below are all holographs, preserved by Laura Thistlethwayte and recovered after her death.

Walmer Castle.
25 August 1869

My dear Mrs Thistlethwayte

Your letter conveys an unexpected compliment, in your having looked at my book [*Juventus Mundi*]—an unexpected pleasure, in your not having been repelled by it, and an unexpected imputation in your charging me with not having sent it you. A work so *farouche* in its character I only could or did send to my bookworm friends. If you will accept a copy from me we will wait now until the 2nd Edition as that is to be out soon, so Mr. Macmillan tells me.

Do not find fault with Menelaus, or with Homer in his name. Surely all excess is ignoble. The question what is excess is quite another thing.

If you will send me your work, in anticipation of mine, I shall read it with great interest; only I pray that, if it relate to yourself, you will send it all at once, or as much of it as you can, for I shall be impatient if it come in morsels only.

Your spirit I daresay needs in the solitudes of Scotland that you should do your best to curb it. If you are as strict with yourself as you are charitable and indulgent to me, you will succeed. I wish I felt as hopeful of my own success in that great and awful work of self-government which God has assigned to us all as our first and principal task, however we may seem to be forced by daily duty into an exterior arena. But I trust He may grant me an special grace, a period of repose, and all the better if it begin soon, to call myself home before I am called to the long home.

Only today can I identify your gift of grouse. They arrived without a name, or the thanks would not have lagged so grievously—pray accept them as they are.

I expect to leave Walmer on Saturday week: and to be at Balmoral in a week thereafter.

Believe me
dear Mrs Thistlethwayte
Sincerely yours
W E Gladstone

Hawarden Castle.
1 October 1869.

My dear Mrs Thistlethwayte

I think *you* must decide the question between morsels and the whole. I told you the morsels would tantalise, and they do: but now I am not so willing to *wait* for the whole; though I mean to read all in sequence, when it is complete, and this at the risk of being put a little past my sleep as I found last night. This may help you either way.

You said you had not told me this was a memoir; yet I see I am to rely on your historic faithfulness; and, doing so, I am, as you will readily believe, struck in no ordinary degree with the incidents, passing strange of such a childhood and (where I am now) girlhood. Under the conditions of mind, and person, with which life was given to you, you were indeed sorely tried with storms commonly reserved for later life, and then for the most part arriving more rarely and with less violence. It is possible I may use the liberty you give and ask even to know more, but the general view is as lucid as the circumstances are singular, and the interest of the prose is well sustained by the thought and movement of the verse (in one or two places I think not quite accurately copied). But I am sure that when you wrote 'don't laugh' you did not inwardly think I should laugh. The tale is in a higher and sadder strain; unless you were laughing when you wrote some beautiful lines. Do not however be too liberal; you have given me much friendship and kindness: if you are generous, be not lavish on the unworthy.

I do not see that your ardour 'for the Protestant faith' was not a true loving faith in Christ as He was represented to you. The picture might be accurate or not: but 'the kingdom of Heaven' is that in which men are sand. The Church is or ought to be the continued manifestation of the Incarnation of Christ: and of this idea 'Christendom', and all that it imports, is a noble, though a most imperfect expression.

But all this is by the bye. My address is here until the morning of the 25th when I am bound for London: when there at my *house* 11 C.H. Terrace. And now much prizing your confidence I remain ever yours,

W E Gladstone

The Major and the Surgeon, near the Donegal Arms were right in trying to take you home, but not in leaving you. I do not think I should have parted company, till you were at Mrs D.s door.

Have you not some fear of disturbing the mind of your copyist by your tale and its accompaniments.

Lochleven is indeed beautiful Mrs Th.

Hawarden Castle.
5 October 1869.

My dear Mrs Thistlethwayte

I have this morning received 11-13, which were sent off by you while my thanks for 8-10 were yet on their way to you. When I read, on Thursday, the account of the Major and his companion, I little suspected how they were divided between light and darkness; and that already the hour was hanging over you. But could you really think the perusal of this last dreadful sketch, outlined especially as it is with tender hand, could arouse in anyone, had some stranger accidentally found it by the roadside, any other sentiments than these two, first a strong affectionate sympathy, and secondly a sickening indignation. I am glad the sword was hurled—it was right—there are times when on the instant the evildoer should be smitten with something he will feel, and flesh I suppose was the only thing that in him could feel.

I think that proceeding to the stage, under the circumstances, was an honourable and good action: an impulse of duty and independence led to it, perhaps combined with a sense of isolation. So at least I interpret.

There are now several things I could ask, as matters of detail, in order to fix the narrative clearly in my mind; but I will wait to ask them hereafter or not at all as may be best. I am sensible that you have shown me a *great* confidence: and little as I can trust myself, yet I do trust it will not be abused. I will make, however, one general observation, which is I suppose applicable to most autobiographies. While you are surmising that what you have written will produce a recoil, (and here I may say there are but few cases of moral descent from which except through Phariseeism I ought to recoil in reading of them) I am inclined to charge upon your *deeply* interesting tale quite another fault. I think you most unconsciously have painted yourself, thus far, as too good. All your childhood, deprived as it was of natural care and protection as well as of training and regular discipline, presents, in your pages, a picture of no other fault than that sort of wildness with which a plant of the forest is wild—They leave room only to suspect a self-consciousness, at least with respect to form which in one of these last numbers you depreciate (I must however *interject* my pleasure in reading that on the night of the appearance of Miss Dearlove there was no paint); but happy indeed was your mental and moral form also, if you had not in you much more naughtiness, I mean every day prosaic naughtiness, than your narrative discloses. Tell me how this is. I know well that human beings, even after the havock their nature has undergone, are born in conditions infinitely varying; some bear light scars, some as I am well aware deep and heavy gashes, some are such that a silken thread will lead them back to God, others can scarcely be bound with the 'cart-rope' of Scripture from following or returning to their iniquity. But yet consider my surmise for a moment: if it is wrong it can do no harm. Consider, and probe yourself, whether there is anything you could say against yourself that you have not said: anything particular, not general. That great master Saint Paul divides us into body, soul, and spirit. I speak of soul and spirit. Here it is after all that the great battle is to be fought: it is in and through these that the Evil One obtains his most signal triumphs.

I could go on writing: but other duties forbid. You will see at least that your labour is not slighted. While I recollect, I will make one remark. What you describe as a great and heavy sin of the child in the impulse of self-destruction did not, in my view, merit such a description. It was a natural recoil from unnatural evil in a creature too young to comprehend definitely the responsibility of this treasure and burden of life. Am I not right? I could tell you several things on the subject of self-destruction. But I return. Please to address here, while I remain, viz. to the 25th. And do not fail to tell me when you are going to be in London? Where I hope to be from the 25th to 9th of November.

And now I will not longer delay saying accept my thanks for your trust in me. I am glad it was my illness and weakness, that attracted it. It is on that *side* that I feel sympathy to be best for me, and safest. Perhaps I have already shown in this letter that your trust makes me intrusive. I hope however that I shall not sin against knowledge. Yours ever

W E Gladstone

Thanks for the little book: which I fear I cannot read before post-time.

Hawarden Castle.
7 October 1869.

My dear Mrs Thistlethwayte

Your letter just received (of Tuesday?) lays me under a debt of honour. Whether I am interested in your narrative I need not say: but if you grow weary, if your hand shirks from the fulfilment of the task, you must not suppose yourself bound to me, nor continue it to please me. The best of my disposition, I believe in excess, has always been to know the marvels of human nature and history. It has seemed to me part of my vocation. This has even been a delusion and a snare to me, as well as a great exercise and instruction. But clearly I must not let my selfishness act upon your kindness: There you consult yourself only and what you feel to be good and right for you. In any case, I am sure you will let me see the *omitted* verses as they belong to the past.

I remember Lord Dudley's showing me the picture with which I was greatly struck—it is even now before me: you will find it hard I think to get it back from him: you told me about it before: but not I think the *feud* with the Duke [of Newcastle].

Let me lastly say that XI–XIII about which you were timid could I am sure do no harm to *any* one. You blame yourself about going to the room: *undeservedly*, if you were at the age I suppose. For a woman it would have been blameable.

And now let me be *your* humble friend (it is at least what I ought to be)

W E Gladstone

Hawarden Castle.
11 October 1869.

My dear Mrs Thistlethwayte

I have long believed that I was for many purposes the stupidest of men and I am confirmed in it by your last letter which represents you as unhappy and me as angry.

Now the truth is this. When I read your papers, which I will not again *call* a confidence, I feel myself a spoilt child: and therefore, when you spoke of a weariness coming on you I could not in honour but absolve you from continuing to minister to me matter of so much interest.

I shall not raise that question again without cause.

So I hope that now the cloud of anger has dispersed and that in its place only remains a very different sentiment.

You have given me advice or command, whichever it be, that is good, namely to refrain from comment until I know more. You will find me absolutely conformable.

This does not forbid my denying two or three things.

1. I find your unrhymed verses to be notwithstanding alive with the Spirit on which all good rhyme itself depends. Perhaps I ought to send you back your copy?

2. I have a right to call myself unworthy which I cannot surrender and which I hope you will permit. Do not judge me by yourself. The inner world, over which my soul has to reign, is one of fiercer storms, and of more deceitful skies.

3. You say that I once covered my face with my hands. If I did it was unconsciously and spontaneously: and the act was more just and natural than if it had been designed. I neither wonder, nor regret.

Lastly I am much interested in your promise[1] about the D. of N[ewcastle]—and I must repair an omission by saying that I was not unthankful for your invitation, but firstly time put it beyond my power and secondly I scarce dare spend my very short time of freedom in a not bracing climate which commonly tends to unman me.

Ever yours
W E Gladstone

Received and read XIV-XVII. A. Kinnaird who is here gives me a charming account of your abode: and an excellent report too of Mr. Thistlethwayte's health. Your recollection of the D. of N's words has surely strayed a little.

Hawarden Castle.
18 October 1869.

My dear Mrs Thistlethwayte

As I (prudentially) rose late today, I should have postponed writing till tomorrow, had it not been your birthday. But *that* I cannot pass by without saying heartily God bless you. May you have many; and may the sun rise brightly and set serenely upon them all.

But neither today, nor tomorrow could I have written any but a

[1] Could read 'premise'.

very small part of what your letter and your narrative have prompted, and today even less than tomorrow: so be very indulgent indeed.

I reply to your question 'for what purposes I am the stupidest'? 'For observing the finer bearings of words and acts, and the finer shades of character.'

Do not be afraid of egotism in what you write. An autobiography, according to my observation, is never egotistical, and is invariably interesting. Yours is more. It is like a story from the Arabian Nights, with much added to it. And yet we have only counted the tale of fourteen years! The poor dear child had suffered how sharp a winter within doors, before she was driven out upon the wide and wild expanse of life.

But now I *am* going to be egotistical, in clearing up the part-reply I have given to your question. The slow instinct, the want of perception, that I so often deplore, are partly to be explained by reference to the master-pursuit of my life. It is a life of mental and moral excess. In me you see a weak man bearing a load under which strong men might totter. Do not take this for complaint. I may tremble indeed, but not complain, when I think that God has been pleased to lay upon me no small part of the peace, happiness, true well-being, of many of the creatures whom He so much loves. In the thought of this, in the study to do as well as I can for them by His help, I am and ought to be absorbed. Not in the sense of its shutting out all beside, but in the sense that the daily labours it entails, and its constant solicitation of my mind exhaust the powers of nature, and leave little available for other purposes except the dregs, and the dregs of dregs.

This is my excuse if I do not see what I ought to see, if I do not feel as I ought the kindness that is lavished upon me—your kindness not the least.

And now I make a leap in this fragmentary letter, like a child among the rocks. There is no time for me to describe what I ought to describe in answer to your letter: especially as I must ask you, *why* are you sad? and with a friend's privilege to ask also can I remove any of your sadness? I have given you nothing. Glad should I be if I could. You will give me only that which can be given while Faith and Honour can look on, and all that I may surely accept, and I do: confiding, let me add, much more in you than in myself.

I will not pay you any of the trivial compliments you eschew, but if you wish to know my first impressions (poor as they might be) I was struck with what seemed to me a free and forthcoming, a kindly and generous nature: and a large and most catholic spirit in a form of religion which (forgive me) is apt to be too much individualised. I will tell if you like what defect seemed to strike me too, if you will be honest and fair and tell me a *lot* of mine.

But, the Post! Make this bargain I pray you: keep my letters, and someday let me see them: I doing the same?

And now again, and again, and again, God bless you with every good and precious gift. In haste ever yours

W E Gladstone

Hawarden Castle.
19 October 1869.[1]

My dear Mrs Thistlethwayte

In my ragged letter of yesterday, I did not get *through* my answer to your question 'had you knowledge of all this when you came to see me'? Yet it may be short—No!

I told you *some* things I did perceive; and I proceed. The modesty (so to call it) struck me, with which, when I rather thrust open your door (I fear) after our friend's death, you did not hasten to call me in; it struck and pleased me. With regard to myself afterwards, I thought you interpreted me too favourably, and in all things seemed to dress me (so to speak) in colours agreeable to yourself. But I did not dream that, as among your *friends*, I was drawn into any inner circle. I have not a good opinion of myself! and if I see kindness from anyone gushing out upon me, it mainly strikes me what a fund of it they must have, to spend so liberally. Again you ask did kindness (in, not to, me) draw me to see you? There was enough in what all know of you, to draw me, without kindness: a sheep or a lamb rather, that had been astray; (I omit what you do not wish to be mentioned but what, I do not deny, enhances interest), and that had come back to the Shepherd's Fold, and to the Father's arms. Then, I had *heard* of Bishop Armstrong who knew you as a most holy man. I fretted, as oftentimes I have done, at my want of time and free mind for the cultivation of friendship; but there was no period at which I should not have been very sorry to think I was seeing you for the last time. Yet I did not then know you as I know you now through your tale, and what accompanies the tale. Now this is all, I believe, unless I were to add one or two small criticisms, and one greater word of praise.

Oct. 20.

Dear 'Broken Reed', and Wounded Spirit: from what precedes, if you have read it, you will see how unconscious I was of my offence,

[1] Dated at the top '(also Oct. 20. 21. 22.)'; these letters apparently despatched together, those of 20 and 21 October being written on the same sheet of paper.

when I received that letter of the 18th, in which you are so severe as not even to give me your address.

I *had* had misgivings about my letter of the 15th:[1] for I remembered that in it I had written, at the beginning, what seemed like a proposal to mangle your fine old Norse-English name.

I hope that the letter I wrote on Monday will have shown you this very morning that, at the very moment when your note was penned, I was writing what will show that I feel, as really as my nature will allow, the deep earnestness of purpose with which your narrative has been written throughout. I could say more of it. But this is not the time.

For you invite and wish me to speak freely, and if I did not I am sure that in after years, when I am gone, you could not remember me for good. So I will say, and I think far too highly of you to believe I shall offend, that there is exaggeration in your letter just received; exaggeration not *of* what you feel, but *in* what you feel.

However, I have wounded you: and though I hope my after writing may already have healed the wound, I will tell you what I hope you will find clear, that my unfortunate word of 'laughing' had not the slightest reference to your picture of your profoundly touching childhood and life, but to your account of the Duke of Newcastle's words (spoken as you justly say in fun) about me.

But believe this; in wounding, I am myself wounded. I *hate* myself, when any word of mine carelessly or causelessly used gives pain; I cannot be at ease until I know the pain is gone; though I could have been better if I had known where to address you; but now this must wait until I hear again. Yet I do think, whether right or wrong, that my letter of Monday, which I thought a very serious letter indeed, will have acquitted me as to intention, and that this very day you will write to me and say so, for I really am not capable of offering to anyone, and much less to you, a reproach, that would be cruel and unjust and mean; and would indeed make me unworthy to be greeted by your letter received on Monday [18 October], and dated Saturday 9th.

Do send me the naughty letter back that I may see *how* bad it was. It was written in that tumult at Chester: and you would excuse anything if you could only see the daily mass of my duty-letter business, which exhausts the brain, and makes me often hardly know what I write.

But *this* must wait undirected. So you have bidden one who, if he

[1] Not in the ancillary MSS at Lambeth; if Mrs. Thistlethwayte returned it to Gladstone as he suggests later in this letter, it would have been separated from the series she preserved.

has pride, is proud of this that as before God, he has always struggled in life to keep his words below his feelings. But if he is proud of it, he is very wrong.

Hawarden Castle.
21 October 1869.

Dear wounded Spirit

For twenty four hours I have suffered the pain of parting; and very sharp it is. For I think the inner feelings of a woman most sacred; most of all in a case such as that between us. This morning, whether it were faith or folly, I was too sanguine. I said to myself there would be a letter, and it would at least let me know where you were and so give me the means of relieving both you and myself. There is none: I looked eagerly for the well-known shape of which provokingly there were several. I must be patient till tomorrow: but I should have much prized the power of setting on its way to you yesterday the earlier contents of this envelope. And it was on your birthday that you were troubled: and by me. Suppose I am disappointed again tomorrow? But I think you will have written on receiving my letter of Monday.

Before this ill-starred episode began for me, I had (as I found) much more to say about my recollections and impressions of you, and about myself in regard to you. But I fear I must not now continue. To find fault I have (though I think only for a moment) lost my title: something I wanted to say strongly in the other sense, but not beyond the truths, would now seem officious, and fulsome. And as to myself in regard to you, I do not think that, with your letter of Monday before me as the last expression of your mind, that I have any warrant. I wait then until you see yourself, or infer from what I write, when I have the means of sending it to you, the insignificant *aim* of the words that have pierced you, and, as I may truly add, me through you—in truth that you have mistaken their sense. Then the ice will melt, the wound will close, and you will be very patient with me while I try to give you further peeps into my unintelligent self. Ever yours

W.E.G.

Hawarden Castle.
22 October 1869.

Thanks, dear spirit, wounded no longer. There the letter was, nay the letters were; and the sight before opening took a real weight off

...nat pain of paining, which I hope when it comes, ...p to me, for there can be no sadder proof of dead-...ness of nature, than insensibility to the pain we have ...cted. I did in truth *echo* it all back; but now, no more ... God, to whom we must ever carry all our troubles.

...ily sorry now about the 29th. After I had supposed you ...eady moving to the South. I grieve that you were suffering ...a cold: and I, like you, much wish we could now have met. ...cially after the experience there has been that words in letters ...ay mislead.

And now give heed a moment to the words you quote from my Chester letter. 'This' you supposed to mean the letter I was writing. It meant no such thing! I meant 'My dear Mrs. Thistlethwayte' and it was '*this*' long introduction to my letter which (silly joke!) I said made me impatient.

I had not then at all in my mind what is also true namely that from morning to night, all my life is pressure, pressure to get on, to despatch the thing I have in hand, that I may go on to the next, urgently waiting for me. Not for years past have I written except in haste a letter to my wife. As for my children, they rarely get any. In honesty, can you *conceive* such a state of life?

And how is it? I have much not only that I could say but that I ought to say, but it would take me too long; and what a *lump* of reading I am now sending you, in this small hand too, to disguise it a little. In a correspondence like this, every letter makes new occasion for more.

For instance, you justly comment on my saying I had *given* you nothing. Well, I feel my words are very poor: particularly as I keep them down by a stern self-repression. I call *them* nothing, and so to call them is a relief to me. You have given me words, and *acts*.

Writing yesterday, I named the two subjects on which I had more to say. It all grows out of the letter which *you* wrote to me on Saturday the 16th; that letter one of the shortest, but so full. It binds me to tell you all that I have seen and thought of you in London. It binds me too, I think, to speak about your gift; there are words in your letter which relate to others, and which I will not on paper try to probe. When face to face, I am sure we shall never misapprehend.

But now, have you well considered what and to whom you give? Do you think you *know* me? I do not think you do, or can as yet. There has been little opportunity, you have generously (as in your old riding) overleapt all obstacles, and have always read me in the favourable sense. Alas I think you do not know me: and you ought. If I were to send you the *counterpart* of what you have sent me,

I should certainly repel you. But to do it would be beyond my po
I must in honesty say to you, probe me deeper; I will conceal no
ing, falsify nothing consciously; but I return to my point, *make s*
that you know me. Do not take me upon trust. I have not sought
deceive you, but I am a strange mixture of art and nature. All this i
egotism, but it is also duty. You should know me deeply, while there
is time: according to the sense of your own notable words, which
laid a hold upon me:

'Thou knowest all my weakness
Thou knowest all my power'.

You must also learn to know the circumstances of my life; how my country is my first wife, and the exacting one, and how unequal I am in all things to doing what I ought to do, and being what I ought to be. You do not know the ill consequences of the exhaustion following on mental strain: how it disturbs the balance, to what dangers it opens the door, how sometimes it seems to leave religion itself a name, a sound, a shadow. The 'storms' of your life have been far beyond mine (I *hope* you are not hurt at what I said of the dear thing of fortitude?): but the storms of your mind, of your nature, are infinitely less formidable, because your mind is less entangled (though you are susceptible and imaginative,) your nature less complicated, because you are better than I am, because you love God more. Nor is that saying much for you! I could almost end with 'beware of me.'

Now I suppose that, after all this, there is no need for my answering your question whether I wish you to confine yourself to the tale? Therefore I will not answer you. But to conclude. You have, with an unflinching courage, a tender delicacy, and an unquestioning reliance, chosen to withdraw for me the curtain from your life and history. No stronger appeal can be made by a woman to the feelings of a man, if man he be. It moves me. This act requires to be spoken of, and I would also ask, why you are sad, if it is a sadness I can help.

The conclusion, God bless you. On Tuesday afternoon I am to be in London. I am afraid you will not, for days thereafter. But at least I know your *address* now; and I am certain you will be patient with my 'stupid' ways, and not again leave me in the dark. Ever yours

W E G

What a task of reading I have set you to me, *about yourself*, you cannot tell too much.

Hawarden Castle.
23rd October 1869.

Dear Spirit

Yesterday, although I wrote much, I did not touch the *core*. It is difficult. Let me try to do it now, and gently. The word you have (on paper) spoken is a great, deep, weighty word. Are you sure that it is a safe word—on the one side, and on the other. To my side, much of what I wrote yesterday referred. But as to yours. I know and am certain that your guarding epithets are true. It is pure, it is holy. Still the *word* is a great, deep, weighty word. Are you sure you are disposing of nothing, but what is yours? You will remember what you wrote, well and worthily, to me: 'Let not . . . interfere or mar thy daily duties, and love to her your wife.' These expressions are just and true; and they have not one edge but two. You will understand: you will ponder: you will pray. All blessings to you. May I never do you harm. Ever yours

W E G

As to keeping, and burning. The story, and the letters of the same period, are locked up alone, and together. I think burning dangerous. It removes a bridle: it encourages levity in thought. Why should not human beings retain the means of calling themselves to account? When I reach town on Tuesday I mean to deposit, what already I have put aside, in a separate leather case, which shall be marked as *for you*.

Towards completing my reply to your query 'did I know?' the first twinkling of light came when I read the beautiful verses

'And if within my nature'.

but when you pleaded the liberty of poets you shut it off.

Sunday. I kept this to read over, more than once.

Tomorrow I think I may hear from you here. Then in London, where I am likely to be till Nov. 11—a few evenings free after Nov. 1 and before Nov. 9. Again in London, and more free, in early weeks of December. All good be yours.

Hawarden Castle.
25 October 1869.

Dear Spirit

I have your short notes of Friday and Saturday, with XXI-III of the tale; and though I must write a little, and could write a good deal,

I feel as if it were impossible to make way by writing towards the heart of that which lies between us. I am certain I could speak to you gently of all the points stirred and not settled in my mind by a correspondence and a narrative alike strange to my experience, though it has been longer than that of most men and as wide. With the help of the eye and proceeding word by word, I could acquit myself towards you of the obligations you have laid upon me; but writing, at least in my hands, is a rude instrument, and I am afraid of seeming cold or harsh or on the other hand unreal and fulsome by words not so intended. Indeed, I cannot feel easy about even my late letters, sent off on Friday (22d) and yesterday (24th) till I have your acknowledgement of them.

I cannot describe to you how, while the interest of your story continues in full, and I am impatient when at some points you speak of hastening on and omitting in order not to be tedious, it has in XXI–III become astonishment, bewilderment! But I shall keep your injunctions, and my own word, and make no comment (except that poor Captain P's farewell verses are *not* good). At present I think what presses on me is the query—*is this then the story of her London life*? And further: you did not then 'know your own feelings'. I am quite certain that, if you had known them you would not have inflicted the pain, of which you were evidently and often the instrument: *you* would not hurt a fly or worm. You were self-deceived. Perhaps you *are*. Again: you did not know the meaning, or the full meaning, of much of the admiration. Perhaps you still have the same fault of looking at things in one of their aspects, without others.

You were never to me simply a common acquaintance. Friendships with women have constituted no small portion of my existence. I know the meaning of the words 'weakness is power': apparent weakness is real power. Quite apart from your letters, by the *covenant* with which you began your tale (or which you made soon after) you (I must use a man's fencing phrase) got within my guard—In addition to that, came the letters. I think perhaps too much about all this. But *no* creature could read any parts of your narrative without sympathy, nor some parts without, as I said, affectionate sympathy. That must be guided by faith, and honour: wherein and whereby comes the 'Daily Light' upon conduct. All this I think—with me at least—must wait for adjustment till we meet. But you see I have suggested to *you* some introspective queries. When we speak, the greatest of all advantages will be, that you can *stop* me.

What I *saw* of you soon, you have told me since: you loved admiration; you also loved *power*? Your ideas ran in their own course with almost an incapacity of diverting from it. Not very terrible. What I saw on the other, the good side, calls for what I think the highest epithet. It was *noble*. For the explication, wait. Tell me of your movements when you know them. I am determined not to go to another sheet of paper. God bless you. W E G.

P.S. *Do* take my compromise. In the gross, i.e. the money sense of value, perhaps you know that I have accepted more by a great deal from you in the M.S. Were it to fall into the hands of some rogue! Therefore, with the letters, I hold it in sacred trust, and I did last night what I told you I should do on coming to London. I shall be anxious to hear of your probable movements. Meantime here is a riddle for you. *Why have you never asked me any question, except one*?

Prepare plenty.

Be not angry about the photographs. I thought they would have a good repelling effect.

25 October [1869].[1]

I am so glad to hear that the shyness is gone; and the fear. It may interest you to note the contrast between your year 1850, and mine. It was my saddest. The great Church controversies of that year well nigh tore me to pieces, for in them as in other things I lived intensely. In March and April I saw a most beloved little daughter droop and die of brain disease—(would YOU tell me, that her name should not ever be in my prayers?)—and in September when you left London for Paris I was making ready to go off to Italy in much alarm about the health and even life of another yet younger one, spared to us, and now among very many blessings.

Thus your egotism insidious as it ever is makes me break my rule. Goodbye to Kinloch Lodge with which I feel a bond. Oct. 25

11, Carlton House Terrace.
27 October 1869.

Dear Spirit

You do not know what to call me, and I do not feel sure about the name by which I have now called you. Here is one of our dilemmas, which must wait to be cleared when we meet.

Were you not tired out with that accumulation of letters which I sent off on the Friday upon learning your address? There are many

[1] Holograph, but not dated by year, addressed, or signed.

things in your letters which I have not noticed, and many, perhaps more, in mine which you have not. It is speech to which we must look. Probably from the habits of my life I weigh words more strictly than you do, and am more fully aware that it is often necessary to consider not only the sense in which we use them, but the sense which others will put upon them. Now consider in this light the force of two of the words which you have used 'love', a great, deep, strong, weighty word, and 'sadness'. Also, the force of words is so different according to the persons between whom they are used.

In my own mind I now entirely feel the necessity of suspending not comment only but thought until the tale is complete or more advanced. The phase of character in XXI–III (the latest) pleased me less than those that had gone before while it was even more like the Arabian Nights (a book now less read, a brilliant series of Eastern romance full of magic and wonderment). *Why* I shall tell you—and everything else—or not, just as you think proper. You will say, and say properly, be patient.

Your letter of Monday received today entirely soothes me. Especially when you say 'your country is Heaven'. For in a note written on Saturday last you wrote 'when you *first* saw me, I *lived* for Heaven and Heavenly things': and then I asked myself can I have been so unhappy as to be a weight drawing her down to earth? For though I do not think I look at all sins with the horror with which a holy soul contemplates them, of one I have a perfect horror and that is of being the means through force or guile of drawing a fellow creature further from God.

The 'exaggeration' that I meant was this: that you seemed to me to feel and suffer more sharply than a reasonable construction of my words about 'laughing' (which never referred to your tale and picture of yourself, the main thread), would warrant. I meant then that it was an exaggerated construction: that was all. You now I hope understand the purely verbal mistake about the 'this'. My remark there would have been a heartless one indeed had it been as it first seemed to you.

That you in writing should use one word stronger than your belief about your feelings, when you were really speaking of them, seems to me impossible: but I will not now pursue this subject. All had better stand over.

One *other* matter. You remember I never accepted the beautiful 'gifts' which you sent me in June or July, and which you refused to allow me to send back. I propose now a compromise. I will take and keep the ring, if you will let me return the other? A ring is a bond: and in it I will have engraved 'L.T. to W.E.G.' and have the round (it is now strictly round) made the least touch more oval to fit a finger. Is not this a fair proposal.

What a singular accumulation within the last seven weeks the post between us has supplied! I can understand that conversations upon it may begin: but how will they ever end? Are you not amused at my resort to this small way of writing: it is for self-deception: it prevents my seeing how much I write. You on the other hand are all ingenuous and cover the sheets freely, but no you are not, you make me think I have got more of quantity than you have really given. Ever yours

W E G.

11, Carlton House Terrace.
28 October 1869

Dear Spirit

I did not send my letter yesterday, because you gave me Friday 29th as the day when you would be at Douglas's. I observe that any letter written on Saturday should go to P.O.—this will be a full cover: but I think it better to send one than two.

You may rely now upon my *waiting with patience*. I have foolishly made one or two remarks of a general kind on the tale from time to time instead of waiting as you bid me. Pray forgive this. It shall not be done again. This does not forbid my being also impatient for more of the narrative.

I did receive by one and the same post your letter of Monday night 18th, and that of Wednesday: and *much* did I regret the accidental delay.

Let me remove another fear from your breast. Every day, as a rule, when my wife and I are parted, which is rare, do I write to her. Only that, and almost every act, is done in haste. This is the misfortune of an overweighted man.

My 'two edges' are one towards myself, the other touching you. What you send to me, had also an application to yourself.

Do I beseech you tell me more about 'the children'. Not only have I never seen, but never did you let fall the word: until the letter which I unhappily caused you to write on the 18th.

It would not be well that I should say much more about myself without guidance from you. It all would degenerate into egotism, vanity, and subtle forms of selfishness. But if you by questions guide me you shall know the innermost that is in me as far as words can tell it, only be patient and very indulgent in the construction of them. Much do I need that.

But one thing I said, which you quoted from me, that life was wonderful, and 'truth stranger than fiction' as has been often observed. I will add another—marvellous as is this creation in the midst of which God hath planted us to live and grow, marvellous as is the experience of life which we encounter, more marvellous than either is that nature which the human being leads by the ordinance of his Maker, and which without its taint His Redeemer bore for his sake. Well it may be 'a spectacle to men and angels.' But what melancholy marvels it 'oftener' discloses: like that touching verse upon your country

'Oh once the harp of Innisfail
Was tuned to notes of gladness
But yet it often told a tale
Of more prevailing sadness.'

Very sacred, something awful too, are the words you have uttered to me. I wish to feel their weight—and to do in regard to them as I would be done by; to treat of them if God guide me, with a single eye to your honour, weal, and peace. I have not marked, and need not mark, letters as 'private'—the subject in that respect tells its own story. But I can hardly tell how we are to get through all that is to be said when we meet, or (if you prefer it) when your tale is done. Again I write 'in no mean sense yours'

W E G.

Will you, then, let me plead *his* cause? not farther, than as it shall seem to me to be yours. God ever bless you.

10, Downing Street.
30 October 1869.

Dear Spirit

I trust you were not snowed up and that you were really 'laughing' when you anticipated it. But having no letters from Edinburgh today I fear lest your movement southward should be retarded.

Do not think the weighty word pained me. Its dangers, if there are any, do not lie on that side. But I wonder what is the one you would substitute for it. This is not easy, for I doubt whether it has a synonym.

Your directions about the Chair I am most ready to obey, and about the sleep too as far as I can, but this is harder to answer for[.]

What I said about your getting within my guard may be best explained then. As to that shyness (of which I became aware last spring on one or two occasions,) surely after all these letters it will not return.

For fear a letter should have miscarried, I shall probably ask at your house when you are expected.

I feel sure another packet will arrive, notwithstanding the disturbance which you must have suffered from breaking up at Kinloch Lodge, and from your journey, which I trust has prospered.

I want your sanction to my arrangement about the ring.

All good attend you of all sorts and sizes. Ever yours

W E G.

11, Carlton House Terrace.
1 November 1869

Dear Spirit

I am concerned at the delay and concerned at the annoying and strange uncertainty. Perhaps you are equally uncertain about the duration of your stay when you have come? On Saturday I go out of town for Sunday. On Tuesday we have the Lord Mayor's feast at Guildhall. Altogether I want a great deal of time for speech, and I begin to fear about getting it, but perhaps you will be here in December and if so I must not complain now.

I adhere to my word susceptible, and I adhere also to what you say of it: your narrative proves you to be correct. My use of the word had no reference to that deep sense of it: it was in the sense sometimes now expressed by the word 'emotional' a somewhat barbarous phrase. You are a person of ready and free emotions: this is my meaning.

Can you not understand my being troubled by the weighty word? There could be no trouble were it received with *indifference*. But considering what you are, and that I cannot be indifferent about it, I ought to be troubled: full of anxiety, care, and hope. Do not dream I meant to blame you. If ever I presume to do that it will be as is in plain words. Why do you fear my answer to your questions? I do beseech you be not afraid of me—the time for it has gone by—you came 'within my guard' by placing me within your own. You brought me, with a generous confidence, into the interior of a human life, and a human heart. You laid a heavy debt upon me, and though I may be unable to pay it, believe that I do not think lightly of it, and that I earnestly desire to discern my duty in it. If I am curious and impatient it is just as one who is admitted to the inside of a great fabric, and thus sees much that he did not see before, finds in that much the occasion of desire and need to know more. What passes between us now is too fragmentary. We are accumulating matters for those conversations which I hope will be long and unreserved—they will enable me to know whether I can in the slightest degree be worthy of any boon you offer me, and whether I can in any degree requite it by soothing sadness or abating its cause. To be rational or intelligent I should perhaps be rash in promising: but I think you will find me not terrible[?] nor touched with levity. To avoid the deep things would be difficult for me, since all nearly that has passed is deep. Strange you may well say it is—strange when I remember that I was in Parliament and in Office, before you were born, that I have only known you at all in an inner sense within the last two months, for before that time I had no scales in which to weigh your words—and that I sorely doubt at this moment whether you know me, and whether you have not strewn your seed on barren ground. Until you have seen as far into me, as I have into you, you cannot be in a position to do yourself justice, and this is what above all things I wish. Very sorry am I about your chill and trembling hand; and this too comes in self-reproach, or fear that there is cause for it.

I must fight it out with you about the ring. Let it be 'L' only if you like, but it cannot be at all unless you promise to let me return the other beautiful object, and you really have no excuse for declining *now* when I have accepted from you what is indeed of value far surpassing. Do not press yourself overmuch about the Tale deeply as I am interested in it. You will I know give me the best information you can about your arrivals, and movements. Thanks for the little episode of Sir J. Simpson and the account of the children. There has been little conversation between us about the young but certainly I have always believed you would be fond of them.

Ever yours

W E G.

I cannot forgive your photograph for not showing the eyes.

Postscript and apology for the hard sayings of today.

10 Nov. 1869

It is not in my nature to give half belief.

Explicit words carry implicit, irrevocable faith.

Do thou too believe firmly that no rumour, no supposed notoriety, would have made me dream you are capable of what was bad and base.

Between bad and base on one side, and the inheritance of infirmity on the other, there is a wide interval: between things abhorred of nature, honour, truth, and things which only the Incarnate Saviour enables us poor creatures healthily to overcome.

It is the weak and helpless—can you believe this—who almost covet to find weakness and helplessness in others that that, with which they hold communion, may not be too far above their low level.

Do you understand also that when such an one supposes that in one he beholds there has been defeat, and defeat has been converted into victory, he follows it with a great reverence.

All this relates to what *was* felt. What *is*, gather from the two first sentences of this paper.

I shall grudge seeing you tomorrow evening, without quiet words? Perhaps I may call at four or thereabouts, on the way from Paddington, where I hope to be at 3.30. But I may be prevented.

Midnight. Nov. 10.

Th. morning. I am off to Windsor. Your letter just came—so glad to see one. This I send off in haste, without first reading yours.

WEG. Nov. 11.

11, Carlton House Terrace.
13 November 1869.

Dear Spirit,

So sorry, so vexed. But royal commands admit of no escape, except for necessity: not pleasure, nor rest.

It will never do that months should lapse, after the end of your tale, and before we meet upon it. But I ask you suppose I went to B[overidge] in the company you propose, which I might very well do, how much time do you think would be ours for quiet conversation? No: if I go, it must be alone, without a servant, and then there would be a little time: but very little!

I cannot, I am afraid come back before Monday when I dine with you. But I shall hope to call at ¼ before 5.

Meantime I give an answer to your question 'what' or 'how much' is to be taken back.

'As much as is needful for your peace and wellbeing: not a grain more'. And hide none.

Turning to a lighter matter, I must make you understand about my *house* which is too good for me.

Inclosed are these lines of a Latin epitaph; written upon one of the most remarkable women of the middle ages, I believe by herself. I have tried to make two versions: and shall ask for your criticism.

I shall not tell you whether I longed for the time: because you know already. Ever yours

W E G.

Twice *smartly* questioned about the ring already (not by my wife, who knows). I shall wear Precursion with it.

The words of your own which you quote against yourself, could not have been quoted by me, without belying all I think of you.

Windsor Castle.
14 November 1869.

Dear Spirit

As my wife and daughter come back, unexpectedly, to London to-morrow, I think that if you will be so good as to permit it, I ought to dine when they do, but I should come up in the evening by ten: and perhaps this would be better as I need not go away quite so early. But I intend also to call at your door at almost half past eleven in the morning and ask if you are visible. On Tuesday I come to the Castle here for one night. Ever yours

W E G.

Hawarden Castle.
2 December 1869.

Dear Spirit

Thanks for your letter received this morning: so true, considerate, and gentle. I was glad, too, to see the old L at the close.

My country-wife, i.e. the country as my wife is really very trouble-some at present. In seriousness, you, who are accustomed to feel and act for the poor, can well believe that I am oppressed day and night with the condition of Ireland, with the sad and painful spectacle it exhibits to the world, and with the painful consciousness that this springs out of past and present faults in our government of the coun-try, not out of *special* obliquity and vice in the people. I almost feel as if, until this great subject of the condition of the Irish in connec-tion with the holding of their land is disposed of, I ought to think of nothing else, pray for nothing else. You will I am sure know my meaning.

Monday night is not now very far off. Before then I look for another packet. At the point where you stand now in the tale you are before me as that almost *saddest* and *most* touching of all characters the wife-widow. I wait, as you bid me.

The last packet had a postmark from which I guessed it might have been posted in London late. God bless you

Ever yours
W E G.

11, Carlton House Terrace.
16 December 1869.

Dear Spirit

A tightness of the chest, I am sure not due to Boveridge, seized me yesterday, and has obliged me to keep my bed today, but need not prevent me from thanking you for your letters, especially that which came this morning. On the journey to London I thought of you all the way while [I] *made up* for sleep: and if I promised to think of you afterwards, the engagement has been well redeemed.

It is true we did not make so much progress in our conversations at Boveridge as might have been expected. But assuredly if you were to blame for this, I was yet more to blame. Why was it? The opportunities were perhaps not long enough: and for my part I was I think too well pleased with your trust in me to leave much disposition to disturb the silent compact.

But I have another reason to plead. I feel that I cannot yet fully take in the whole effect of your disclosures of character history and the state of your mind. I sometimes feel spell bound by them; and I should like to have days and days to think them over, in all their meaning, before I could fully comprehend them or know what calls upon me grow out of them. To some of these, I am already alive. For instance I became increasingly impatient of that misconception of you by the world, under which *you* have been and continue so nobly patient. Then I feel deeply the terrible heart privation[?] under which you have lived and I anxiously ask myself how can it best and most safely be mitigated. It may be long before I can resolve and satisfy my own mind on the question how I ought to have replied to you when you inquired of me whether I wished you to recall the weighty word. I *dared* not have asked you to speak it: I *could* not ask you to unsay it, when I saw how high and generous and uncorrupt a meaning it bore in your conception (and this of course I saw at once) and felt that the only doubt was whether the reception of it by me could be in any manner worthy of its utterance by you. It was however and is to me a mystery and marvel, out of which I have not found my way, and from which I am perhaps selfishly unwilling to be extricated, come what may of it, whether in this tumult of my life I may be or may not be able to arrive at a clearer comprehension of relations and duties in the intimacy which now prevails between us, it will never be a subject of less than pleasurable care to me as long as you, in all the warm and essential truthfulness of your nature, can tell me that I *have not done* and *am not doing* you harm. And this I know you will tell me, while you can and ought.

I have been much with you in thought at Boveridge since coming away, and your full details of these last days are yet not full enough. I wonder whether again, and when, I shall be in those rooms which were my home. The time coming on is a time when I shall cease to be able to give you signs of recollection, and can only ask you to believe, and I know you will believe, in its unfailing permanence. Bear with me one moment in reminding you of that on which we were agreed: that it is not wise to expose to the observation of others that which we know beforehand it would not be possible for them upon such observation to understand aright.

I should have greatly liked to go with you to Saint Giles's to see Lord Shaftesbury for whom I have a cordial regard and admiration, and I should have liked to see him in your company. It was very kind of him to destine a card for me: I say *a* card because the two you sent could not both have been for me: if as is probable there were three one would be for you and one for Mr Th. I hope you will struggle against the shyness you mention and will see your neighbours. You are *there* in contact with a better world, than here.

Your letter showed no marks of the confusion you describe. I wish that mine, written or scratched from my pillow (in the dining-room) may be as presentable. I am so well doctored and nursed: and please God I hope tomorrow to be moving about again. Meantime my work in a Chaos surrounds me in my bed.

I have forgotten twenty things: but I will say in one word there is nothing new in your letters that I do not seem to understand. All you have told me is as wide of the common road[1] as ever: but there are no riddles any more. I remain here till *over* Monday. After Tuesday evening my address will be Hawarden. Remember me kindly to Mr Th. and may I remember him as faithfully and honourably as you remembered another, though the spheres are not the same. I am thankful to you for praying not only in general terms on my behalf but especially about the poor Irish and their Land. God ever bless, console, defend and cherish you. Ever yours

W E G.

[1] May read 'weed'.

11 Carlton House Terrace.
18 December 1869.

Dear trustful Spirit

Many things please me, selfishly and unselfishly, today. After a stiff battle my cough is as I hope yours is, nearly gone so that I have been able to get some real hard work done and I have now rather a clearer prospect. Now, thank God, the Duchess of Argyll is really somewhat better and more hope is entertained. And among these pleasant things are your letters received today and yesterday for it is impossible not to love the character they disclose rather than display. They are really fragrant, like those extraordinarily fragrant flowers you sent me—does Boveridge always yield such. But again, & again, I come back to my old difficulty: they suggest so much that paper and time will not suffice for but only speech; and when we come to word of mouth nothing is said! What is to be done? When will there be word of mouth again?

On Tuesday 21st I hope to go with my wife, who comes up to look after her sick people, to Hawarden: to remain there until about the 14th, and to be back in London for good on the 19th or 20th. The Session to begin probably on the 8th February. During it no Sunday visit to B[overidge] will be possible. The time is too short. This is all I know now as to my own plans: and as to yours I am sadly in the dark.

There are things I may ask of you to *round* the information in your most remarkable narrative, but NOTHING I think that can tend to give you pain, dear trustful Spirit. For instance I am a little curious to know whether, at the great crisis when you gave your hand away, anyone on your behalf made any stipulations as to maintenance and settlements, or whether you wholly & only *trusted*. Such stipulation I may add would have been perfectly right and only due to you.

The dream! If you recollect you had mentioned to me the effect of red in your dress. But I have never disliked any one colour in which I have seen you. Yet though not a judge in these things I always have my ideas. Your good taste in dress has always struck me. And now I am pleased with a little group of images that dwell in my memory: L. driving, L. riding, L. in red, L. in red & black as she walked on Sunday. All these pictures are pleasant. I could expand them in detail.

One word about the world. I do not mean to speak of you to others except with your approval and permission. Weeks ago, I could not help saying to my wife that from what I had lately heard I was certain you had been misconceived. Without entering into details, I should like your *leave* to say this more definitely to her: because I do not like that any such misconception respecting *you* should linger however faintly in such a pure and generous mind as hers. Will you let me, trustful Spirit?

One word more, as post hour draws close. I well and thoroughly understood your question about the withdrawal of the weighty word and took it for what it was a distinct proof of an unsparingly high unselfish feeling, and nothing else. On my own reply I did not reason, I did not choose. To say 'recall it' was beyond my power. But if I found it was working against your health and peace, and driving the sunshine of God's presence from your soul, then indeed I ought to ask and strive for power to say 'recall it'. Till then, or till I find in my poor self some equally strong reason, I cannot, shall not.

Tell me about your cough. Be assured the ride did not cause mine: but a little trumpery cause which I told my doctors and then obstinate work & talking with an irritable chest. And now Goodnight: God bless you. How much I shall be interested in Miss Kennedy's handiwork. By the bye I have some really fine photographs from nature among which I should like to give you your choice. Believe me ever yours.

W E G.

Hawarden Castle.
2 January 1870.

Dear Spirit

I received your letter of *Sunday*: and answered it on *Tuesday* from my bedroom: so it was not *sealed*, and as I had no stamp I sent it through Downing Street. I am sorely vexed at your not having had it for it would have removed from your mind—I think—the idea that I either complained or repented about having gone to Boveridge, or that there was a change of tone. Be assured there is no change—the 'dregs of dregs', if they are no better than they were when I was at B. are assuredly no worse; and I blame nobody, and do not repent at all for though I am sorry a word should be said by anyone that draws you in for my deeds I am confident it will all work for good. Write & tell me you are at ease. I shall inquire about the letter and write again—a thousand thanks for the 'tale': I send you the pretty verses: if you do not mind, send me them back, *or* a copy of them. And God bless you at all seasons especially at this happy one. I am reading the tale but may not have time to finish. All goes well here, my wife improving fast. Ever yours

W E G.

Who told you I 'only cared for' the Tale? But it is wonderful.

Hawarden Castle.
3 January 1870.

Dear Spirit

I am pleased, and relieved: but what could have kept my letter back three days?

I will try to explain how it is that people have been led to talk. I was known to have been for some years, your acquaintance. It is now surmised that the cords are drawn closer, and are those of friendship. This I can never deny, conceal, or shrink from avowing, unless I descended to the depth of folly as well as meanness. But then, not to mere gossips, but to those amicably interested it is quite right that I should be able to hold up high your name and fame. Now the date of your marriage and your age at that date afford by far the simplest and easiest method of touching this question, for dates are facts, and these dates go near to the point of exploding the popular misconception. If you knew either the Parish, or the *Street* of your Father's house in Dublin, I could find the rest. Now I have told you my mind and meaning, and I shall be perfectly satisfied whether you know or do not know, and whether you stop me or let me go on.

I am one of those who think a great respect ought to be paid to general opinion, but not a servile obedience. I would hold up the right, the just, the true, but at the same time try to find means of convincing the *convincible*, that reason is the rule followed and not caprice.

I am sorry you suffer: my cough is in sympathy with you & will not go. My dear wife thank God improves steadily. The illness was near being bad.

The pity of your Tale grows and grows. My wish to have it all before me comes from this that I wish to appreciate fully its extraordinary character, and to see what lessons or suggestions grow out of it for me. You think I do not know your nature, and I have no great opinion of my own discernment of the finer shades of character: to a woman notably endowed with a woman's gifts its edge must I know seem very blunt and rough. Yet I think I know some things which your frank & open turn [*sic*] could not hide, and I wish if not to turn them to positive account yet to avoid harming you or any one connected with you. I suppose that human genius never concentrated on any character ideal or historical so much pity as Shakespeare has concentrated on Desdemona, and it is of Desdemona that I think when I read the Tale.

It seems as if God had called you to a destiny which in the reckonings of Heaven should be a very high one and if you have strength to meet your vocation a woe would fall on him that with or without your concurrence should stand in your way.

All this is free effusion, but I cheerfully obey and 'wait'—Remember the 20th is my time for London. Ever yours

W E G.

Hawarden Castle.
6 January 1870.

[1]You asked me whether I desired that you should recall the weighty word. I answered, *that* (perhaps because I am too, too covetous) was beyond my power to ask. But *you* would yourself be the first to say that you would limit it, keep it within the bounds prescribed by honour and pre-existing duty, and you could even teach me this, were I not sensible of it. Read then and weigh the plea I now make, and consider what can or cannot be. My relations to you, defined as you have generously defined them, must be those of unreserve, or they would be 'as sounding brass or a tinkling cymbal'. I make no more preface lest it should seem to imply what I do not mean—whereas my endeavour is to give you all my mind.

Cast one continuous retrospect over that extraordinary career which in the Providence of God you have been permitted, or enabled, or called to run: and especially look on the life-covenant which was its climax and which with all its incidents is the main bond of human, especially of Christian, society. It cannot be painful, it must be soothing, to you to remember that in that history you carry a key which must unlock, in any breast, the forces both (not to name other sentiments) of pity and of affection.

How strange, how passing strange, it is: and how special a Divine meaning it must convey! I seem to see it all as it lies, on the one side, and on the other. On the one side a compact extorted by violence; followed by caprice and outrage almost to the death: reduced to a character essentially negative; in that character loyally observed.

There are secrets of your own heart with which 'the stranger intermeddieth [*sic*] not': you know what is beyond its power, but in the marvellous history of your life you have known, & have shown, that much is within it.

On the other side, then, there seem to lie in view the great and formidable change in the sort of character which it was given you to promote, and which you have so thankfully recorded: the corresponding change in conduct which has substituted honour, confidence, affection towards you for their 'loathsome opposites'; the high & ennobling nature of the dispensation of union itself; the strength of

[1] No opening greeting.

maternal yearning. Is it *hopeless* that all these should act upon the bitter wintry frosts which originally cast your wifehood in a mould of ice, and could not but so cast it? Does your vocation include this possibility? Has the recoil, born of the horrors of the case, been once for all?

Forgive me, dear Spirit, if I have gone too far: I wish to be in all that relates to you a transparent soul before you, and to see your nature thrive vigorously and soar high. Probably all that I have said has, with a great deal nearly passed often through your mind. But sometimes to the eye looking from without, simply because it is without, aspects of things present themselves, which are not to be had within for exactly the same effect and purpose. Bear patiently with this my rude handling, and if you have anything to tell me, tell: & either in speech or letter as you think best, if at all.

What I have now written has grown in my mind out of all I have seen, & all I have read, taken together. I shall not send it to you at once: but shall keep it for days to review it, after I have re-read all, before presuming to send you these thoughts which I hardly dare to utter to myself in whispers. But considering the place of honour, & knowledge, and more, which you have given me, even my whispers ought to be at your command.

Ever yours in sympathy & 'care'.

W E G.

Hawarden Castle.
22 April 1870.

Dear Spirit

'I will believe thee to the syllable in all thou dost deliver.'[1]

This, or nearly this, says Shakespeare. Let it shut up the chapter of your fears. As you like me to praise myself, I will say I am not suspicious by nature, but trustful. About the 'vow' I am sure you will tell me nothing that will alter the sentiments with which I read your narrative. But this is to be a letter about self. First then I take from your letter the text you put into my mouth 'I am dead to you'. As far as there is truth in the words, it is in the three first only. Now, by an effort of the mind place yourself in my position: become, for a moment, me. What would you think and feel? Would it not be something like this.

'It is difficult to repel, nay to check or to dissuade, the attachment of a remarkable, a signal, soul, clad in a beautiful body. It is a call for

[1] Version of *Pericles*, v. l. 169.

recollection as in the sight of the Most High, and for self-command. No matter, that the attachment is upright. Whatever be the intention that it shall ever remain so, and if that intention be nobly fulfilled, still the hold taken is deep. Should I not beseech her to have a care? It may be that so doing will look to her like indifference. But then, like much else in this world, it will seem the very reverse of what it is; as did Cordelia's love. If I feel for her, with her, in her, must I not desire that her life may be free, long, happy, holy, finished & accomplished in all womanly and noble gifts?'

These, remember, are your thoughts, under your momentary transformation, estimated and conjectured by me. I now go back to the first person direct. Who & what am I? A man who in December last made up his tale of three score years: and, though the fire burns in me yet, forty of those years at least have been so laborious, that a deep mark is made upon me, & at no time could I be surprised if a sudden summons came. But suppose it be the will of God to leave me here yet a good while. Still, I cannot well 'continue in one stay', abide where I am. My profession involves me in a life of constant mental and moral excess. I must before long endeavour to escape from it, and I seem to myself to 'see the day approaching'. And what must be my destiny and duty, when that day arrives? Surely to try to recover & retain the balance of my mind: to awaken & cherish in myself the life of faith, of 'the substance of things hoped for and the evidence of things not seen': to unwind and detach that multitude of ties and interests which now bind me to the world I live in: to do something, if it be permitted me, for the glory of God & for my fellow creatures in a sphere very different from that turbid though stirring and not ignoble one, in which my lot is now cast. But all this is a descending course, so far as the present world and life are concerned. It is so written by the law of Nature, by the finger of God, for descending, declining years; even should they be years of the happy mellow light of sunset. But your sun is yet mounting the sky. Even in the body, your youth is not yet ended: and the quarter of a century, that separates your years from mine, is for the mind a lifetime. True, by your intensity of feeling, you can overleap it all. But with that intensity you have, and I am very thankful that you have, an elasticity of mind & character that I hope will never be exhausted, but will always keep you equal to the calls that the Almighty may have to make upon you.

Certainly we neither of us are of every day composition: and our coming into contact affords matter for musing. But the mark, which that contact has made, cannot be washed out like the wave-print on the shore. Remain it will: may it remain for good.

I think that when you have read this letter you will feel that the subject of it lies in the inner circle of my being.

God bless you. Ever yours

W E G.[1]

[P.S.] I am due in London Monday. My youngest son (whose Photograph I sent you) has been ill in a remote corner of Wales. My wife I hope brings him back today: & will probably come with or after me to town. You will all go up soon?

[1] This letter is docketed by Mrs. Thistlethwayte: 'This letter gave me new[?] Life[,] more feeling in it[.] oh! my Life!'

WHERE WAS HE?

July 1871-1874

The following list shows where the diarist was each night; he continued at each place named until he moved to the next one.

1 July 1871	Chislehurst (Cavendish)	8 April	London
3 July	London	13 April	Windsor
8 July	Windsor	15 April	London
10 July	London	27 April	St. George's, Weybridge (Capt. Egerton)
15 July	Hatfield (Salisbury)	29 April	London
17 July	London	17 May	Hawarden
22 July	Aldworth, Haslemere (Tennyson)	27 May	London
24 July	London	8 June	Chislehurst
29 July	Chislehurst	10 June	London
31 July	London	22 June	Windsor
5 August	Stanmore Park (Wolverton)	24 June	London
7 August	London	6 July	Chislehurst
12 August	Cassiobury (Ebury)	8 July	London
14 August	London	13 July	Cassiobury Park
22 August	Whitby	15 July	London
4 September	Thornes House, Wakefield (Milnes Gaskell)	20 July	Hatfield
6 September	Hawarden	21 July	London
25 September	On train	27 July	Ashridge (Brownlow)
26 September	Balmoral	29 July	London
4 October	Aboyne Castle (Huntly)	3 August	Hawarden
6 October	Glen Clova	5 August	London
7 October	Edinburgh	10 August	Hawarden
11 October	Hawarden	18 September	Courthey, Liverpool (R. Gladstone)
20 October	London	19 September	Hillfoot House, Glasgow (Sir J. Watson)
11 November	Hawarden	20 September	Banavie, Inverness-shire
9 December	London	21 September	Invergarry House, Inverness-shire (E. Ellice)
21 December	Hagley (Lyttelton)	27 September	Guisachan, Inverness-shire (Sir D. Marjoribanks)
23 December	Hawarden	3 October	Strathconan (A. J. Balfour)
15 January 1872	London	9 October	On train
17 January	Osborne	10 October	London
19 January	London		
28 March	Latimer (Chesham)		
3 April	London		
6 April	Brighton		

16 October	Chorley
18 October	Hawarden
13 November	Keble College, Oxford
14 November	London
30 November	Sandringham
2 December	London
7 December	Hatfield
9 December	Windsor
10 December	London
14 December	Hawarden
21 December	Courthey, Liverpool
23 December	Hawarden
21 January 1873	London
15 March	Cliveden (Sutherland)
17 March	London
8 April	Windsor
9 April	Hawarden
21 April	London
3 May	St. George's, Weybridge
5 May	London
17 May	Chislehurst
19 May	London
29 May	Chatsworth
5 June	London
21 June	Chislehurst
23 June	London
5 July	Chislehurst
7 July	London
9 July	Windsor
10 July	London
12 July	Hatfield
14 July	London
19 July	Holmbury (E. F. Leveson-Gower)
21 July	London
26 July	Chislehurst
29 July	London
2 August	Chislehurst
4 August	London
11 August	Hawarden
19 August	On train
20 August	Balmoral
30 August	Invercauld
1 September	Kingussie
2 September	Naworth Castle, Brampton (Lord Carlisle)
5 September	Courthey, Liverpool
6 September	Hawarden
2 October	London
7 October	Garendon Park, Leicestershire (Phillips de Lisle)
9 October	Hawarden
5 November	Keele Hall, Staffordshire (W. Sneyd)
7 November	Althorp Park, Northampton (Earl Spencer)
10 November	London
22 November	Chatsworth
25 November	London
2 December	Windsor
3 December	London
6 December	Hawarden
16 January 1874	London
9 March	Windsor
10 March	London
14 March	Worksop
15 March	Nottingham
16 March	London
3 April	Hawarden
9 April	Courthey, Liverpool
11 April	Hawarden
22 April	London
25 April	Hawarden
13 May	London
22 May	Hawarden
29 June	Fasque (Sir T. Gladstone)
4 July	London
11 July	Wellington College
13 July	London
25 July	Courthey, Liverpool
27 July	Hawarden
30 July	London
6 August	Penmaenmawr
28 August	Hawarden
5 September	London
7 September	Cologne
8 September	Munich
15 September	Unkel
16 September	Ramsau
18 September	Munich
20 September	Nuremberg
22 September	Cologne
25 September	London

26 September	Hawarden
4 November	London
7 November	Keble College, Oxford
9 November	Aldenham Park, Shropshire (Acton)
10 November	Crewe Hall, Cheshire (Lord Crewe)
12 November	Hawarden
14 November	Whittinghame, East Lothian (A. J. Balfour)
21 November	Mount Teviot (Marquis of Lothian)
23 November	Hawarden

LIST OF LETTERS BY CORRESPONDENT, PUBLISHED IN VOLUME VIII

A note on the editing of these letters will be found with the equivalent list in Volume VII

DRAMATIS PERSONAE, 1869-1874

An index to the whole work will appear in the concluding volume, together with a bibliography of Gladstone's reading as recorded in the diary. Meanwhile readers may be helped by this list of biographical notes, most of which refer to the first occasion of mention in the diary. A plain date indicates a first mention in the diary text, usually with a footnote at that date; a date with 'n' (e.g. 27 Oct. 69n) indicates a mention in a footnote to a person or event noticed by the diarist on that day.

This list covers the years 1869-1874 and must be read together with the lists at the end of volumes two, four, and six. People mentioned in those lists are not repeated here. Readers who wish to identify a person mentioned in the diary, but who is not in this list below, should refer to the three previous lists. The exceptions are names that occur in the first six volumes but are more fully identified by a footnote in volume seven or eight; these are marked † following their date, in the list below. A few cross-references from this list are to names in previous lists. Names mentioned on the fly leaf of an MS volume of the diary are marked (f.l.) with the nearest date. To increase the list's usefulness as a guide to identification, priests, the largest occupational group in these volumes, have their initials prefixed by *Rev.*, *bp.* etc., and some other occupations have been briefly indicated.

People with double-barrelled, or particuled, surnames appear under the last part of the name, except that names in M' and Mc are under Mac, Irish names in O' are under O, and D'Arcy, D'Arsonval, D'Orsey, and D'Urban are under D.

Rulers and royal dukes are given under their regal or Christian names. Other peers, and married women, are listed under their surname, with cross-references from their titles and maiden names.

Titles, given in italics in this list, are ignored in its alphabetical order, which is that of surnames, followed by full forenames, of which only the initials appear. Names of firms follow other similar surnames.

Abbott, C. S. A., *3rd Baron Tenterden*, 14 Jan. 71
Abdy, *Prof.* J. T., 31 Dec. 72
Abel, *Sir* F., 1 Aug. 72.
Aberdeen, Provost of, see 1869-73 W. Leslie
Aberdeen, *Earl and Marquis of, see* Gordon
Ackroyd, *Col.*, 20 Mar. 74
Adam, W. P., 9 Mar. 70
Adams, *Rev.* C. C., 6 May 71
Adams, F. M., 6 Sept. 74
Adair, *Sir* R. A. Shafto, *2nd bart., 1st Baron Waveney*, 21 Sept. 69
Ady, *Ven.* W. B., 30 June 71
Agar, *Mrs.* H. M., 13 Feb. 73 (?)
Agnew, *Sir* W., *1st bart.*, 9 Apr. 74
Ailsa, *Marquis of, see* Kennedy
Aislabie, *Rev.* W. J., 21 Nov. 74
Alamayu, *Prince*, 22 Jan. 72
Alderson, *Rev.* F. C., 8 Nov. 73
Alexander II *of Russia*, 15 Apr. 74
Alexander III, *of Russia*, 19 June 73
Alexander, W., *ed. Abn. Free Press*, 4 Mar. 72
Alexander, *Sir* W. J., 15 Feb. 73
Ali Murad Khan *of Khypoor*, 27 Apr. 69
d'Alice, *Madame, rescue*, 24 June 72
Alington, *Baron, see* Sturt
Allen, *Capt.* R., 20 June 74
Allfrey, *Dr.* C. H., 28 July 69
Allfrey, H. W., 15 Feb. 73
Ambassador, French 1869-Sept. 1870 Lavalette
Amcotts, *Col.* W. C., 13 June 72
Amory, *Sir* J. H. Heathcoat-, *1st bart.*, 18 Feb. 74
Amos, S., 1 Jan. 73
Anderson, *rescue*, 6 Sept. 70
Ange, St., *rescue*, 2 Feb. 72
Anson, *Sir* A. E. H., 5 Apr. 73n